A QUESTION
OF CHARACTER

A QUESTION OF CHARACTER

A Life of John F. Kennedy

Thomas C. Reeves

BLOOMSBURY

First published in Great Britain 1991
Bloomsbury Publishing Limited, 2 Soho Square, London W1V 5DE

Published in the US by The Free Press, a division of Macmillan, Inc.

A CIP catalogue record for this book
is available from the British Library

ISBN 0-7475-1029-6

10 9 8 7 6 5 4 3 2 1

Printed and bound in Great Britain by
Butler and Tanner Limited, Frome and London

For Elizabeth and Margaret

The historian is not trying the men and women of the past; he is contemplating them; he has to see them as in truth they were and to present them as such to others, and a man, as a man, cannot be seen truly unless his moral worth, his loveworthiness, is seen.

—David Knowles, *The Historian and Character, and Other Essays*

Contents

❯❯❯ ❮❮❮

Preface

IT SEEMS THAT I have always liked John F. Kennedy. I first saw him on television in 1956 when I was an undergraduate. The young senator was courageously struggling at his party's national convention to win the vice presidential nomination, and I was taken with his good looks, energy, inspiring language, and grace in defeat. A look at Kennedy's credentials as a war hero, intellectual, and liberal convinced me that he had a splendid future.

In 1960 my wife and I were all for Kennedy. We saw him at a rally in Seattle, we thrilled to his televised debates with Richard Nixon, and we told friends that the specter of "Tricky Dick" in the White House gave us thoughts about living in Canada. We greeted the election returns with loud celebration. It was a time for greatness in Washington.

We were not disappointed by the Thousand Days. The president's oratory was consistently moving, summoning all Americans to greater moral and intellectual heights. The Peace Corps, the firm stand in Berlin, the struggle against Big Steel, the push for civil rights legislation, the much-publicized devotion to good taste and high culture—we applauded it all. True, the Cuban Missile Crisis was troubling: we favored negotiations rather than nuclear war. But the event concluded peacefully, and JFK again appeared triumphant.

Along with millions the world over, we were shattered by his assassination in Dallas. Camelot had come to an abrupt, senseless halt. While Lyndon Johnson seemed in every way to be an able successor, it was clear from the start that he could not compete with the fallen chief executive's style, wit, charm, and commitment to higher truths. In a short time, as Vietnam began to absorb the world's attention, and defiance and violence started to overwhelm this nation's cities and college campuses, JFK seemed to us greater than ever.

I had no reason to doubt the early Kennedy literature. Though it was extremely adulatory, that approach seemed to fit the facts. The authors were often those closest to Kennedy; they based their accounts on personal recollections as well as documents. The credentials of, say, historian Arthur Schlesinger, Jr., and Kennedy speech writer Theodore Sorensen were unassailable; their writings were moving and brilliant. The books came from leading publishers, and the reviews were glowing. The standard college textbooks soon made Kennedy one of our great or near-great presidents.

In the mid-1970s, while working on a book about the life and times of Senator Joe McCarthy, I began to notice reviews of a few books that challenged both the facts and the interpretations of the major Kennedy studies. In 1975 a congressional investigation cast doubt on Kennedy's character and raised an assortment of disturbing questions. At the same time, books lavishing praise on Kennedy continued to appear. What was one to believe? The media and many American history textbooks clung to the traditional story. A handful of historians and journalists, on the other hand, seemed to take for granted that almost everything we knew and thought about Kennedy was bogus.

The more I read, the more I became fascinated by what appeared to be a gap between JFK's image and the historical reality. But how wide was the gap? And what were the forces behind it? My attention soon focused on the issue of character. Was there, for example, substance to the numerous allegations concerning Kennedy's personal life? If so, what were the facts? And how did one evaluate character anyway? Did anyone seriously expect politicians to be angels?

Several years ago I decided to examine the Kennedy history for myself, reading deeply in the primary as well as secondary sources. The journey was exhilarating, frustrating, and informative. The result was this book. Sadly, many of my youthful observations from the 1950s and 1960s had to be revised.

As my research progressed, in talking to people about Kennedy I observed a strong reluctance by some to acknowledge anything negative about the man. It was as though his memory was sacred, and all who would defile it—even with facts—were engaged in a somewhat scurrilous activity. For many JFK was a beloved and heroic figure whose memory should always be cherished.

As a nation have we now, almost thirty years after the assassination, become sufficiently mature to look at Kennedy and the Thousand Days without the emotional pain we felt after his death? On the whole I think so. We need never fear an objective appraisal of our heroes. Truth is ultimately more enlightening and satisfying than myth. The Kennedy story, moreover, shed of its illusions, *remains* exciting and illuminating. Like almost all true stories, it consists mostly of grays rather than of blacks and whites. In flesh and blood, rather than as King Arthur in Camelot, Jack Kennedy deserves our sympathy and praise as well as our critical judgments.

Acknowledgments

I AM AGAIN indebted to Dorothy Crowell, my longtime research assistant. Her replacement late in the project, Cathy Bothe, was equally efficient and helpful. Special thanks go to Prof. Justus Doenecke of New College, University of South Florida, for his rewarding commentary on the manuscript, and to my excellent editor, Joyce Seltzer. I wish also to thank Prof. Louis Geiger of Iowa State University for his encouragement and wise counsel over the years.

CHAPTER 1

The Vital Framework

➤➤➤ ⫷⫷⫷

ON JANUARY 21, 1961, forty-three-year-old John F. Kennedy was sworn in as president of the United States. Millions of Americans, weary of what they perceived to be an era of intellectual, cultural, and moral stagnation, eagerly anticipated the new administration. During the campaign, the young senator from Massachusetts had presented stirring visions of a bold new America, eager and able to solve virtually every national and international problem. In his brilliant inaugural address, Kennedy called for support in "a struggle against the common enemies of man: tyranny, poverty, disease and war itself." And he asked for self-sacrifice in unforgettable words: "And so, my fellow Americans, ask not what your country can do for you; ask what you can do for your country."[1]

It was not only the rhetoric that made the occasion unforgettable; there was the image. Here, in freezing weather, coatless, was a handsome, tanned, vigorous leader expressing a message of strength and hope. Nearby sat seventy-year-old Dwight Eisenhower, heavily clad and obviously suffering from the cold. He seemed to many to represent the dismal, placid, and witless 1950s. Historian Allen Matusow later observed: "So luminous was the image created by Kennedy that day that for countless of his countrymen no disaster of policy, no paucity of achievement, would ever dim it."[2]

During the Thousand Days Kennedy's popularity, at home and abroad, remained at extraordinarily high levels. He reached a high of 83 percent approval in the Gallup polls after the Bay of Pigs and stayed within the sixtieth and seventieth percentiles until the fall of 1963.[3]

There were several good reasons for this popularity. The Kennedy administration achieved the largest peacetime expansion of the economy to that time; economic growth averaged 5.6 percent annually, unemployment dropped to 5 percent, and inflation held at 1.3 percent. The administration also started the Peace Corps, backed economic development and domestic reform in Latin America, promoted financial aid for higher education, and laid the foundations for the space race, the War on Poverty, and comprehensive civil rights legislation. The president honored America's postwar commitment to halt the spread of communism but also backed the Nuclear Test Ban Treaty and made a significant overture, in June 1963, for détente with the Soviet Union. Kennedy's eloquent addresses stimulated idealism in millions all over the world. The White House, during JFK's brief residence, set high standards of style and culture.

And then there were the images of the president and his family, which had an enormous and lasting impact on a nation preoccupied with raising children and upward mobility. The Kennedys seemed young, vital, happy, warm, and caring. Their physical attractiveness was surely a powerful factor in the polls; numerous studies have shown that Americans tend to equate good looks with intelligence, sensitivity, sincerity, self-confidence, independence, poise, competence, and good character. The Kennedys belonged in the pantheon of movie and television stars.[4]

Throughout the Thousand Days a stream of articles and books celebrated the character, intellect, and political skill of the chief executive. Theodore H. White's best-selling and influential *The Making of the President 1960*, for example, praised Kennedy for high-minded ambition, energy, and intelligence. Washington journalist Robert J. Donovan lionized the president, a longtime friend, in *PT 109: John F. Kennedy in World War II*, a book excerpted in the popular *Saturday Evening Post* and made into a movie. Hugh Sidey's much-praised *John F. Kennedy, President*, written with the president's assistance, was highly flattering.

Reporters in the major media, who had overwhelmingly favored Kennedy during the presidential election, lavished attention on the handsome young couple in the White House, noting especially their devotion to good taste and learning. Many stories focused on the Kennedy family's happy domestic life. While the president's political policies sometimes drew sharp rebukes in the press, few leading writers chose to attack Kennedy personally. In an article tantalizingly titled "What You Don't Know About Kennedy," *Look* magazine reporter Fletcher Knebel revealed nothing bolder than the fact that "Kennedy uses profanity with the unconcern of a sailor, which he was and is."[5]

Not everyone, of course, embraced Kennedy. Eleanor Roosevelt and Harry Truman, for example, had long suspected that he lacked convictions and was little more than an extension of his father's ego. Voices on the Far Left and Right were often extremely critical, and there were many personal attacks, some involving Kennedy's religion. Conservatives increased the volume as the 1964 campaign came into view.

In September 1963, conservative journalist Victor Lasky published what *Newsweek* called "the first thoroughly and unmercifully anti-Kennedy book." *JFK: The Man and the Myth* was an imposing 582 pages in length (883 pages in a revised paperback edition) and heavily documented by secondary sources and newspaper research. Lasky's central thrust was aimed directly at what polls indicated was central to the Kennedy image: personal character. However charming, sincere, and brilliant JFK appeared to be in public, he was in fact, according to Lasky, cold, calculating, vain, superficial, and morally obtuse.

Although the book quickly became a best-seller, it had little impact on the media. "Mr. Lasky knows how to use the knee." sniffed *New York Herald Tribune* critic John K. Hutchens. An editorial in the liberal *St. Louis Post-Dispatch* suggested that the volume should never have been published. Kennedy's assassination three months later made Lasky's charges seem somehow murderous themselves, and the book was withdrawn from print.[6]

Kennedy's death in Dallas on November 22, 1963, devastated Americans, and all over the world people wept and mourned. The U.S. embassy in Guinea reported, "People expressed their grief without restraint, and just about everybody in Guinea seemed to have fallen under the spell of the courageous young hero of far away, the slayer of the dragons of discrimination, poverty, ignorance and war."[7] Journalists employed extravagant language, one tribute calling Kennedy "the pride of western civilization" and "a bright, racing star who lighted men's thoughts and their dreams."[8]

The media made most Americans eyewitnesses of Kennedy's dreadful death. Watching as the horror at Dallas unfolded, and then partaking of the deeply sorrowful and painful funeral service at Arlington National Cemetery, the nation participated fully in the morbid drama. As one writer observed:

> The people of America responded to the news of Kennedy's assassination and the continuing televised reports of every subsequent happening with a state of shock that went beyond mourning to something approaching melancholia, a serious collapse of self-esteem. With the assassination, something more than a man had been lost, something more abstract and more compelling—a part of America's faith in itself as a good society.[9]

Touched by the intimacy of death and mourning, most Americans forged a special bond to the dead leader. By mid-January 1964, Jacqueline Kennedy had received some eight hundred thousand messages of sympathy.

A literature of adulation, the likes of which the nation had not experienced since the death of Lincoln, soon burst into print. JFK became a sort of superman, a legendary figure who presided over Camelot (a term suggested to Theodore H. White by Mrs. Kennedy), his administration one of unmatched wisdom, virtue, and style.

American Heritage and United Press International (UPI), for example, published the popular *Four Days: The Historical Record of the Death of President Kennedy* (reprinted in 1983). In 1964 Kennedy press secretary Pierre Salinger and television newsman Sander Vanocur produced *A Tribute to John F. Kennedy*, which sold 125,000 hardback copies and almost 500,000 paperbacks. In 1965 Kennedy's personal secretary, Evelyn Lincoln, brought out *My Twelve Years with John F. Kennedy*. The book was romantic, worshipful, and dedicated "with love" to Kennedy's children. Of the president she wrote: "He was a promise that all of us might lead a better life in peace. He was a promise that excitement and courage must be kept central in our lives. He was a promise that we could expect more from ourselves, and that we were better than we knew."[10]

Of far more substance were large volumes published that same year by Theodore C. Sorensen and Arthur Schlesinger, Jr. Sorensen, JFK's longtime speechwriter and confidant, admitted that his view of the late president was "unobjective" and that his beautifully written *Kennedy* was a work of total devotion. Kennedy was "the brightest light of our time," a man whose "cool, analytical mind was stimulated by a warm, compassionate heart." Kind friend, ardent husband and father, wit, war hero, author, idealist, statesman—JFK was all of these and more. Sorensen was convinced that historians would rank his former employer among the greatest chief executives.[11]

Schlesinger's *A Thousand Days: John F. Kennedy in the White House*, for which the historian received the Pulitzer Prize, cast Camelot in concrete. For more than a thousand pages, in learned, moving, and often brilliant pose, Schlesinger lauded Kennedy's intelligence, moral courage, self-awareness, learning, style, empathy, vitality, humor, detachment, discipline, and compassion. The author used the word *character* several times, defining it once as "that combination of toughness of fiber and courage." Indeed, to Schlesinger the president and his entire family were virtually beyond reproach; the administration, so abruptly and cruelly ended, was one of history's brightest moments.[12]

Such volumes as the treacly *"Johnny, We Hardly Knew Ye,"* by Kennedy intimates Kenneth P. O'Donnell and David F. Powers; Walt Rostow's *The Diffusion of Power*; and Rose Kennedy's autobiographical *Times to Remember* were among numerous books that eulogized the late president. Collectively such works may be said to be part of the Camelot School.

Behind the scenes the late president's widow and other family members actively supported much of this literature. They cooperated, for example, with the production of a lugubrious volume of photographs and quotations, edited by Joan Meyers, entitled *John Fitzgerald Kennedy . . . As We Remember Him*. Both Sorensen and Schlesinger received assistance and won family approval of their publications.

Long extremely sensitive about their public image, the Kennedy's also took steps to suppress unflattering information about the late chief executive. In 1966 Jacqueline Kennedy pressured JFK's pal Paul B. ("Red") Fay, Jr., into cutting some two thousand words from his memoir *The Pleasure of His Company*. Later that year Mrs. Kennedy went to court to demand major deletions in William Manchester's family-authorized *Death of a President*. With the aid of Senator Robert Kennedy, the president's widow forced *Look* magazine to drop portions of a serialization of Manchester's book. In an article published in *Look* in April 1967, Manchester likened his persecution by the Kennedys and their attorneys and private detectives to an encounter with Nazis.

The Kennedys also attempted to stop publication of *White House Nannie* by Maude Shaw, nurse for the Kennedy children. They tried to delete materials from Evelyn Lincoln's *My Twelve Years with John F. Kennedy*. And Jacqueline Kennedy urged Random House not to publish Jim Bishop's *The Day Kennedy Was Shot*. (To this day, the Kennedys continue to grant interviews only to "approved" historians and journalists. Younger family members who fail to adhere to this principle are condemned for "treason.")[13]

From the start Kennedy documents were zealously guarded by the family in an effort to ensure that the president's image remains untarnished in public memory. Numerous collections at the Kennedy Library, just outside Boston, have been sealed. In the oral histories and tape recordings now available, many key paragraphs and pages are censored (some allegedly for national security reasons). Some oral histories are blatantly partisan, such as the interview of Cardinal Cushing by Teddy Kennedy, and the lengthy exchange between Kennedy loyalists Walt Rostow and Richard Neustadt. At one point Neustadt said of JFK, "He was everybody's dreamboat." Rostow agreed. In the stunningly beautiful building at Columbia Point, constructed with private funds and given to the federal government in 1979, one can find little with which to challenge or even question the imagery of Camelot. Historian Stephen E. Ambrose has called the Kennedy Library "a scandal."[14]

Still, cracks in the carefully constructed Kennedy facade began to appear as early as 1964. Richard J. Whalen's carefully researched biography of Joseph P. Kennedy, *The Founding Father*, revealed an unscrupulous manipulator, shamelessly willing to plot and spend in order to propel a son into the White House. All the Kennedys, including JFK, were seen to be wholly under the influence of the elder Kennedy. "Miraculously, he instilled in his children his belief in the innate distinction of the Kennedys, and imposed on them the responsibility for fulfilling the design that he believed had been foreordained."[15]

The Pentagon Papers, published in 1971, provided ammunition for Kennedy's critics on the Left, documenting, among other things, the president's fascination with clandestine warfare in Vietnam. (In 1983 historian Richard Walton labeled Kennedy "the most dangerous cold warrior that we have had since the end of World War II.")[16]

In 1975 liberal journalist Benjamin C. Bradlee, a close friend of the late president and his wife, revealed perhaps more than he intended in *Conversations with Kennedy*. This JFK barely resembled the almost sacred figure described by the Camelot School. He was exceedingly vain, incredibly foul mouthed, petty, penurious, insensitive, spiteful, eager for salacious gossip, and extremely manipulative. He slipped secret government documents to journalists in return for favors, got drunk, favored abortion, and denigrated liberals. Even the alleged brilliance was challenged: the president took "the better part of an hour" with a foreign service officer and his son to master "Ich bin ein Berliner." Bradlee also included several somewhat veiled references to a Kennedy interest in women other than his wife.[17]

That same year the Senate Select Committee to Study Government Operations with Respect to Intelligence Activities, headed by Frank Church, revealed Kennedy's often shocking use of the Central Intelligence Agency in Southeast Asia and Cuba. Moreover, a leak from a staff member led to the revelation that a beautiful young California woman, Judith Campbell Exner, had been secretly admitted to the White House on many occasions for more than a year to carry on a romance with the president. Exner was also close to Mafia figures Sam Giancana and John Roselli, involved in newly disclosed CIA plots to assassinate Fidel Castro. It was indicated that when FBI Director J. Edgar Hoover (who was aware of the plots) learned of the Kennedy-Exner trysts, he confronted the president directly, and the clandestine visits stopped. Giancana was murdered just before he was to testify before the Church Committee. Roselli was murdered shortly afterward. The crimes remained unsolved.

Exner reluctantly admitted the facts of her affair with the president, noting that Kennedy secretary Evelyn Lincoln had arranged her visits to the White House with the assistance of top Kennedy aide Dave Powers. Another leading aide, Kenny O'Donnell, was also said to be in on the affair. Lincoln, Powers, and O'Donnell, all involved with Kennedy's daily appointment schedule, made brief denials.[18]

Exner's 1977 book, *My Story*, written, she said, after the FBI attempted to drive her to suicide, was filled with compelling evidence, including information that could only have come from high levels of the White House. Her frank, detailed, and generally sympathetic descriptions of Frank Sinatra (closely tied to both Kennedy and Giancana), the "Rat Pack," her Mafia lovers, White House staff members, and the president himself—attentive, aggressive, strongly contemplating divorce—caused a storm in the press.[19]

Soon after the initial revelations concerning Exner, numerous articles and books began adding weight to the mounting evidence that Kennedy was not the man we had thought he was. *Time* and *Newsweek*, for example, ran lengthy and obviously well-researched articles linking the late president romantically with several well-known actresses and scores of young women, including two youthful staff members codenamed "Fiddle" and "Faddle" by the Secret Service. One former New Frontiersman was quoted as saying of the Kennedy White House, "It was a revolving door over there. A woman had to fight to get in that line."[20]

A book written by veteran White House staff member Traphes Bryant gave eyewitness accounts of a stream of young women involved with the president when his wife was away. An item from Bryant's diary:

"Dave Powers once asked the President what he would like to have for his birthday. He named a TV actress from California. His wish was granted."[21]

In early 1976 a tabloid told of a two-year affair between the president and Washington socialite Mary Pinchot Meyer, a beautiful and wealthy divorcée in her early forties. Mrs. Meyer was said to have visited the White House between two and three times a week during Mrs. Kennedy's absences. Presidential assistant Dave Powers was again linked to the visits. At one point, it was reported, the president and his guest smoked marijuana, and JFK promised to obtain cocaine later. "We're having a White House Conference on Narcotics here in two weeks," he said. The source of this story was former *Washington Post* Vice President James M. Truitt, a close friend of Mrs. Meyer. Truitt also reported the destruction of a telltale diary by a mutual friend, CIA official James Angleton.

Subsequent research confirmed at least the outline of the story. Toni Bradlee, Ben Bradlee's ex-wife and Mrs. Meyer's sister, acknowledged most of the details in an unpublished interview with the tabloid: "It was a fling, another of Jack's flings." Mrs. Bradlee and Angleton issued evasive denials and refused further comment. (Years later Angleton acknowledged the Kennedy-Meyer affair and admitted destroying Meyer's diary. According to Meyer, Angleton said, JFK at least experimented with marijuana, cocaine, hashish, and acid while in the White House.) Mrs. Meyer herself had been murdered in October 1964.[22]

Objective scholarship entered the picture in 1976 with *The Search for J.F.K.*, by Joan and Clay Blair, Jr. This exhaustively researched study was based on thousands of recently opened documents from the Kennedy Library and more than 150 oral interviews. The authors focused their attention on the years 1935 to 1947, but their research shed light on the entire history of the Kennedys.

Among other things, the Blairs revealed a Kennedy family coverup of JFK's often precarious health, from early childhood through the diagnosis of Addison's disease in 1947. They corrected traditional accounts of Kennedy's education and early literary prowess. They documented JFK's almost mechanical pursuit of women, from age seventeen on. Moreover, the Blairs completely revised Kennedy's service record, charging, "He was, in effect, a 'manufactured' war hero."[23]

In 1980 historian Herbert S. Parmet published *Jack: The Struggles of John F. Kennedy*. A sympathetic study, it was nevertheless the most reliable biography to date, making use of recent scholarship and adding valuable information and analysis. The author was especially strong on

Kennedy's heavy reliance on his father in all his political campaigns, his marital difficulties ("Politics and promiscuity were all part of being married to John Kennedy"), and his studied evasion of the censure of Senator Joe McCarthy. Parmet's account of Theodore Sorensen's dominant role in the creation of the Kennedy book *Profiles in Courage*, and of his authorship of many other "Kennedy" publications, raised new questions. (Kennedy claimed sole authorship of the book even more vigorously than he denied being a victim of Addison's disease.) His examination of the Pulitzer Prize award bestowed on *Profiles in Courage* strongly suggested the presence of Joseph P. Kennedy.[24]

In *JFK: The Presidency of John F. Kennedy*, published in 1983, Parmet made other significant contributions. He used FBI papers, for example, to explore the subject of Judith Campbell Exner and the "Rat Pack." Interviews with physicians shed light on the President's Addison's disease and severe back problems. The author tied the president and his attorney general brother directly to the CIA's efforts to destroy Fidel Castro, efforts that were secretly accelerated after the Cuban Missile Crisis.

Parmet's accounts of major administration policies and actions often contained allusions to Kennedy's questionable judgment. In the Bay of Pigs fiasco, the Cuban Missile Crisis, and the president's serious consideration of an American "first strike" over Berlin, Parmet saw evidence of Kennedy panic, macho recklessness, and lack of moral principle. JFK's approach to civil rights, Parmet thought, was basically political and pragmatic. The president's relations with Congress, he contended, faltered in part because of his preoccupation with personal enjoyment.[25]

In 1984 two popular volumes on the Kennedy family attracted the attention of scholars. *The Kennedys: An American Drama*, by Peter Collier and David Horowitz, featured, among other things, revealing interviews with K. Lemoyne ("Lem") Billings, a longtime JFK intimate, and many unpublished letters from Kennedy to Billings. *The Kennedys: Dynasty and Disaster, 1848–1983*, by John H. Davis, was especially important because of its piercing and unsentimental appraisal of Jackie Kennedy, a Davis relative. The book also caused a stir because of its charge that JFK was aware of Judith Campbell Exner's simultaneous affair with Mafia chief Sam Giancana and was using her to monitor the CIA's "dirty business" against Castro. This was "reckless in the extreme," Davis concluded. "But as we know, John Kennedy thrived on danger, risk, and intrigue."[26]

And yet for all the new evidence describing Kennedy as far less than a King Arthur, the traditional portrait of Camelot remained firmly entrenched in the media, many textbooks, and in the public mind. In celebrations marking the twentieth anniversary of the assassination, the Kennedys were widely revered. They have been called this nation's "first and only true royal family," while JFK has been named "our fallen king." A poll published by *Newsweek* revealed Kennedy to have been the country's most popular president. Three-quarters of those polled rated his presidency as good to great, and 30 percent wished he were still president.[27]

Evidence critical of Kennedy was often either ignored or dismissed as irrelevant. In 1983, for example, Arthur Schlesinger, Jr., sneered at what he called "the *National Enquirer* school of biographers," who questioned Kennedy's character. He did not deny the allegations of White House infidelities but chose instead to contend that "if anything untoward happened at all, it did not interfere with Kennedy's conduct of the Presidency."[28]

By the mid-1980s JFK seemed more popular than ever. Books with such titles as *A Hero for Our Time* and *The Torch Is Passed* were in step with the fashion. American history textbooks, with several exceptions, continued their glowing and, at times, uncritical accounts of the Thousand Days.[29]

In 1985 Roone Arledge, president of ABC Television and a personal friend of Robert Kennedy's widow, cancelled a television program on the widely discussed and much-researched relationship between John and Robert Kennedy and actress Marilyn Monroe. Hugh Downs, the show's coanchor, told reporters bitterly that he thought the story had "air-tight documentation." Private detective Milo Speriglio, a program consultant who worked part-time on the case for thirteen years, wrote of the program, "I've never seen anything comparable in shock value. I believe it would not just change our way of looking at a notorious real-life Hollywood drama, but our thinking about the Camelot years." (That same year CBS Television ran a Kennedy-family-approved three-night docudrama on Robert F. Kennedy, based on the biography by Arthur Schlesinger, Jr. *Newsweek* critic Harry Waters commented, "This adaptation exudes the adulatory reverence of a seven-hour rite of canonization. . . . Actually this Kennedy is all saint.")[30]

In 1988 the power of the Camelot imagery again became evident as Americans commemorated the twenty-fifth anniversary of JFK's death. In a highly emotional outburst of near worship, the nation's mass media lavished praise on the late president, his family, and his administration. A cover story in *U.S. News & World Report* contained such headlines as

"Beyond the Generations" and "Idealism's Rebirth" and featured glowing tributes from numerous New Frontiersmen. Arthur Schlesinger, Jr., said, "Lifting us beyond our capacities, he gave his country back to its best self, wiping away the world's impression of an old nation of old men, weary, played out, fearful of the future; he taught mankind that the process of rediscovering America was not over. He transformed the American spirit."[31]

The popular Sunday newspaper magazine *Parade* contained a reverent piece by Senator Edward Kennedy entitled "Our Brother, John Fitzgerald Kennedy." A typical sentence: "In the brief time Jack had, he touched our hearts with fire, and the glow from that fire still lights the world." At the same time, however, *American Heritage* published a poll of seventy-five prominent historians and journalists ranking John F. Kennedy the most overrated public figure in American history.[32]

The sharp contrast between the glowing imagery propounded by the Kennedys and the Camelot School and the iconoclastic view posited by others in recent years called for further exploration. Since many of the critics' questions revolved around the issue of character, Kennedy's convictions and conduct warranted scrupulous investigation. John F. Kennedy claimed consistently to be a moral leader, but was he, in fact, an exemplar of high personal character? And if not, was it not possible to be an effective president of the United States without necessarily being personally virtuous? The question of character seemed to be the pivotal issue in arriving at a clear understanding of the life and legacy of our 35th president.

Psychohistory did not seem to be a fruitful approach to the issue. That dubious art has been performed on Woodrow Wilson, Richard Nixon, Joseph R. McCarthy, and Kennedy, among others, with little success.[33] Rather than try to probe JFK's subconscious in a clinical way and become entangled with speculations concerning orality and anality, this study applies the methods of the historian to the documents, oral histories, publications, tape recordings, and photographs scholars and journalists have been unearthing for years.

→>> <<<

But first one must confront the concept of character itself. What exactly is it? And how have people thought about it over the centuries in relation to statesmanship?

The issue of character and political leadership is intertwined with the history of moral philosophy. As formidable thinkers of the ancient world grappled with the good and evil of human existence, they began to ponder the requirements of a just and effective political leader who could ensure the general good of the community.

Plato's cardinal virtues, enumerated in the *Republic*, were wisdom, courage, temperance, and justice. Only a small group of highly educated, highly rational, and morally incorruptible philosophers, Plato argued, were qualified to know what was best for the public, and they should rule. These philosopher-kings could be depended on to devote their full time and energy to the common good and be without private property or families to divert them. In the *Republic,* character formation was as important as intellectual preparation.

Aristotle divided the virtues into two closely connected moral and intellectual categories. The moral virtues were justice, courage, and temperance; they were dependent on prudence, an intellectual virtue. To Aristotle a virtuous person, a person of high character, was above all a rational, temperate person who could keep his nonrational desires under control and who was concerned about the welfare of others. In his *Politics* Aristotle argued that a prince or royal family should be chosen because of the preeminence of their personal virtue. The best state, he declared, is the one that is morally best.

While thinkers disagreed at times about how the virtues were acquired and absorbed, there was considerable accord about their nature and necessity in the hearts and minds of great leaders. Plutarch, for example, said of the Roman leader Marcus Cato that his life revealed temperance, generosity, courage, humility, and honesty. "Hence his solidity and depth of character showed itself more and more to those with whom he was concerned, and claimed, as it were, employment in great affairs and places of public command."[34] Tacitus described the Roman governor Agricola as brave, wise, just, honest, energetic, prudent, tactful, modest, dignified, and austere. "To mention incorruptibility and self-denial in a man of his calibre would be to insult his virtues."[35]

Christianity added the gifts of God to the classical virtues, and for many centuries thinkers praised leaders for possessing faith, hope, and charity as well as prudence, justice, courage, and temperance. The Venerable Bede, for example, celebrated England's King Oswald for his humility, affability, courage, generosity, discretion, and faith; indeed, the king was "a man beloved by God."[36] Einhard, a ninth century Frankish historian who was the Emperor Charlemagne's biographer, said that Charlemagne was generous, patient, loyal, temperate, articulate, and studious, adding that he "cherished with the greatest fervor and devotion the principles of the Christian religion, which had been instilled into him from infancy."[37] In the thirteenth century Jean, Sire de Joinville, said of Louis IX of France that he was brave, wise, upright, loving, generous, truthful, temperate, prudent, and devout; "no layman in our time lived so holily all his days, even from the beginning of his reign to the end of his life."[38]

While Renaissance humanists rejected much medieval thought, they continued to revere leaders who embodied those traditional moral and intellectual virtues. Vespasiano da Bisticci's *Lives of Illustrious Men* lauded statesman Cosimo de Medici for his wisdom, learning, humility, generosity, and prudence. Of Agnolo Pandolfini, we read, "His character was upright and severe, his advice well-considered, his speech candid, and he was the foe of all deceit."[39] Desiderius Erasmus's *The Education of a Christian Prince* contained a history of the ancient and medieval theories of statecraft and concluded that no one can be a good prince unless he is also a good man. "If you want to show yourself an excellent prince, see that no one outshines you in the qualities befitting your position—I mean wisdom, magnanimity, temperance, integrity."[40] Even Niccolò Machiavelli, best known for his cynical advice to rulers in *The Prince*, acknowledged that traditional virtue was good and vice evil. (*The Prince*, which assumed a separation between statecraft and morality, was widely criticized throughout Europe and condemned by the Inquisition.)[41]

During the tumultuous moral, intellectual, religious, and political changes of the sixteenth and seventeenth centuries, the ancient standards desired of leaders remained firm. Indeed, the scientific revolution reinforced the philosophy of natural law, which contended that there is a fundamental moral order, reflecting the physical order of the cosmos and knowable by reason, which applies to all people. A good king, then, would be one whose actions adhered to this objective and universal morality.

By 1700 many leading European intellectuals and popularizers had absorbed the concept of natural law and believed in reason, progress, and inalienable human rights. During the Age of Enlightenment, secularism became a powerful force, the demand for political representation increased, and the state came to be seen as the instrument of progress. But whether people favored the limited monarchy admired by Montesquieu, the enlightened despotism favored by Voltaire, or the republican commonwealth proposed by Rousseau, the qualities they sought in political leaders remained the same traits of human character extolled in moral and political theory for centuries. Kings, officials, or elected representatives—all should possess integrity in their concern for and service to others and be just, wise, courageous, prudent, and temperate in their rule.

The dominant theme of America's Declaration of Independence was the "long train of abuses and usurpations" perpetrated by King George III. "A Prince, whose character is thus marked by every act which may define a Tyrant, is unfit to be the ruler of a free people." When the Constitution of the United States was being drafted, many understood that the model for the chief executive was George Washington. The general's character gave credibility to the new document and contributed significantly to the success of his presidency. Thomas Jefferson later paid tribute to Washington's "perfect" character, noting especially his integrity, prudence, dignity, and sense of justice.[42]

Thus, from the beginning, Americans have sought presidents with good character; that is, those qualities specified by Jefferson, those same virtues agreed on throughout history. Ideally the occupant of the White House should exemplify those virtues that have seemed to ensure wise and just leadership. And thus, the issue of character has arisen in virtually every presidential campaign. The awesome power of the office has for two centuries prompted Americans to seek presidents who are morally as well as intellectually excellent to lead them.

In the post-1945 world of American politics, as demands on the chief executive for political savvy, managerial expertise, and communication skills loomed ever-larger, the traditional virtues, though still acknowledged, were often slighted. The relationship between the skills now required of an effective president and the qualities of character long seen to be vital to the office has often been obscured. However, the issue of character has never ceased to be of critical significance in the execution of presidential power, and observers have continued to probe its parameters.

In 1972 political scientist James David Barber made a systematic attempt to interpret character and the presidency. In *The Presidential Character: Predicting Performance in the White House*, Barber defined character in an indiosyncratic way: Character was a person's inner self—" . . . the way the President orients himself toward life—not for the moment, but enduringly. Character is the person's stance as he confronts experience. And at the core of character a man confronts himself." Barber believed that character was largely formed in childhood and was grounded in a sense of self-esteem. Still, he eschewed psychohistory and argued that environment played a large role in determining a president's overall outlook, including his worldview (developed largely during adolescence) and style (a product of early adulthood).

Barber thought it possible to predict presidential performance by studying the personal history of a president or presidential candidate. Above all, he wanted to know about the person's sense of self-worth, "how active he is," and "whether or not he gives the impression he enjoys his political life." Barber was not arguing that to know about character was to know about everything; presidential character was "only one element in success or failure." But it seemed clear to him that character had a direct and necessary impact on performance. "Every story of Presidential decision-making is really two stories: an outer one in which a rational man calculates and an inner one in which an emotional man feels. The two are forever connected. Any real President is one whole man and his deeds reflect his wholeness." The study of character was thus "a matter of tendencies."[43]

Although Barber was correct to call attention to the importance of presidential character as the inner core of the individual, his definition of character lacked moral content. When he ranked presidents on the basis of his criteria, all those chief executives in the highest category were liberals, betraying a personal political bias.[44] John F. Kennedy was ranked along with Franklin D. Roosevelt and Harry S. Truman in the "active-positive," or highest, category. Barber based his account of JFK's life and times almost exclusively on books highly favorable to the late president.[45]

→>> <<←

In this study character recalls its moral content, its relation to virtue as the essential root of the good person and the great leader. David Knowles has written of "the centre of the personality, the finest and most precious thing in man, his goodness of will, achieved by conscious and tenacious choice."[46]

The qualities of good character would begin with integrity, defined in one dictionary as "an unimpaired condition; soundness; firm adherence to a code of especially moral . . . values." A popular consensus of other components would be likely to include compassion, generosity, prudence, courage, loyalty, responsibility, temperance, humility, and perseverance.

Psychologists today may prefer the term *personality* to *character* because the latter has traditionally implied the existence of an objective moral standard such as the Judeo-Christian ethic. But personality can be a superficial and even misleading manifestation of character. A villain may be exceedingly charming and jovial. A saint can appear to be eccentric and misanthropic. Personality generally describes the bearing and behavior of a person, while character describes the deeper level of will and motive, of values and beliefs.

Certain basic assumptions about character are made here. They are that a strong moral sense of right and wrong is derived from our Western heritage and deeply embedded in our culture. Despite shifting lines of tolerance and permissiveness in recent decades, the vast majority of Americans hold fast to certain basic moral imperatives and can and do tell right from wrong.

Good character is formed in large part at an early age. It is neither inherent nor reflexive, and it must be cultivated by concerned parents who afford moral guidance from infancy onward. Educational consultant James Stenson has observed:

> Children learn these inner strengths through word, example and repeated practice. That is, they grow in strength from what they *hear*, from what they *witness* and from what they are *led repeatedly* to do. They grow principally by imitating the strengths they witness in their parents and other adults whom they respect.

If children do not receive the guidance essential to the development of conscience and good character, they will retain the immature character of children and remain self-centered, pleasure-driven, insecure, and irresponsible.[47]

Still, character can continue to develop and be shaped throughout life. The wise historian Jacques Barzun has written, "An explanation by childhood determinants leaves no room for one of the most easily observed facts, the *development* of character."[48] This point is especially important in the life of John F. Kennedy, for one of the most persistent claims by partisans is that he grew in wisdom and character as he grew older.[49]

Thus, to truly understand Kennedy, we will examine the full story of his life, seeking to learn the origins and development of his character and to assess the influence of that character on presidential decision making. Decision making in the White House clearly involves a president's intelligence, experience, political skill, ideology, and the circumstances of the moment, including advice received and political expediency. Still, character is the vital framework in which these elements are arranged. A knowledge of what the president sees as right and wrong, good and bad, will give us a fuller and more accurate picture of the stature of the man and the nature of his leadership.

In the case of JFK, where the image of the man has so overwhelmed the reality of his life, it is necessary to go back to his beginnings and trace his development through youth and adulthood in order to grasp the shape of his character. Only then will we be able to fully understand how and why he made his decisions and whether, indeed, they served this nation well.

CHAPTER 2

The Founding Family

➜≫ ≪←

THE FIRST KENNEDY left Ireland in the mid-nineteenth century determined to grasp the unlimited opportunities said to exist in the United States. While he failed to achieve prosperity himself, his family quickly discovered what it took to succeed, and the foundation was laid for one of the most remarkable success stories in American history. The story is not just about the accumulation of wealth. Indeed, its most interesting feature concerns the family's burning desire for respectability and power.

John F. Kennedy's paternal great-grandfather, Patrick Kennedy, emigrated to Boston in 1848 from the small Irish village of Dunganstown, in the southeast part of the country. A twenty-five-year-old farm laborer, Kennedy faced a bleak future in his native land, then plagued by the Great Famine and oppressed by rapacious absentee landlords. He was part of a flood of 64,000 Irish immigrants, seeking prosperity and freedom, who arrived in Boston between 1846 and 1851.

Patrick settled at Noddle's Island in Boston Harbor, found work as a cooper, and in September, 1849 married Bridget Murphy, a twenty-eight-year-old from County Wexford who had been a fellow steerage passenger during the forty-day voyage to America. The couple found housing in a tenement near the cooperage and a Roman Catholic church. By 1858 there were five children. Late that same year Patrick died in a cholera epidemic, leaving his wife the burden of raising her children on the profits of a small store she owned and operated and her income as a hairdresser.

It was difficult for the Irish to climb up the socioeconomic ladder in nineteenth-century Boston. For the most part the immigrants were up-rooted peasants, kept illiterate by the cruel Penal Laws of the British. Despised by the Anglo-Saxons who ruled the city for their ignorance, their rural customs, their poverty, and their Roman Catholicism, they were thought fit only for manual labor. "Even the Negro," wrote Richard J. Whalen, "with an accepted place as a skilled laborer, faced less dis-crimination than the Irishman."[1] They avoided the public schools—and assimilation—because of the curriculum's Protestant bias.

Bridget's youngest child, Patrick Joseph, dropped out of grammar school in his early teens to work on the docks in East Boston. Personable, aggressive, frugal, and hardworking, by the age of twenty-five, against all odds, he was the owner of a popular East Boston saloon and ran a profitable wholesale and retail liquor business. P. J., as he was called, would later expand his liquor interests and become involved in banking, real estate, and mining.

In 1887 P. J. married Mary Augusta Hickey, a large, handsome, strong-willed young woman, the daughter of another prosperous saloon-keeper and the sister of the mayor of Boston. Thus the Kennedys began their married life in the middle class, not quite forty years after P. J.'s father had arrived penniless in America. The first of four children born to the young couple, Joseph Patrick Kennedy, was to be the father of a president of the United States.[2]

During the Gilded Age, politics was a leading avenue for Irish ascendance in Boston. The Irish eagerly joined the Democratic party, and their rapidly increasing numbers (by 1886 their children outnumbered those of the native born) and loyalty to each other enabled them to dominate Boston politics by the turn of the century. P. J. Kennedy played a prominent role in the rise of the Irish in politics. He was a ward boss, known for his quiet fairness and willingness to listen to others' problems. He was also a shrewd insider who knew how to dispense favors effec-tively and win elections. In 1886, at twenty-eight, he began the first of five consecutive terms in the Massachusetts House of Representatives. He ran for the state senate in 1892 and 1893 and was elected both times. Kennedy would hold three important patronage positions and be a dele-gate to three of his party's national conventions.

Sometimes, of course, the road to victory required bribery and ballot-box stuffing. One of Joe Kennedy's earliest memories was the visit of two ward heelers who proudly told his election-commissioner father, "Pat, we voted 128 times today."[3] "Win at all cost" was the iron law of P. J.'s world, a dictum that would be passed on to generations of Kennedys.

But no matter how powerful or wealthy the Irish became, they were always rejected by the Yankees who reigned over "proper" Boston society. Politically and financially, P. J. Kennedy was a man to be reckoned with in the 1890s. Still, the Cabots and the Lodges wanted little to do with him and his ilk. P. J. and his wife rankled at the condescension. It would become an obsession with their son, born on September 6, 1888.[4]

Mary Kennedy especially had lofty ambitions for her son, wanting him to move beyond the liquor business and Irish politics. She named her firstborn Joseph Patrick rather than Patrick Joseph Kennedy III, P. J.'s choice, because it sounded "less Irish." She fussed over the boy and nurtured in him a fierce desire to succeed. From his earliest years Joe responded eagerly, showing a keen interest in money, an instinct for leadership, and extraordinary energy. The tall, red-haired, freckle-faced youngster, with strikingly blue eyes and a winning smile, organized backyard plays, a military drill team, and a profitable neighborhood baseball team. When some of the baseball players complained about his self-appointed role as first baseman, coach, and business manager, Joe replied, "If you can't be captain, don't play."[5]

Joe's parents had him do odd jobs, not out of necessity (the Kennedys had an expensive home on Noddle Island's "best" street and a sixty-foot yacht by this time) but for the competition against his less-prosperous peers. He sold newspapers, for example; ran errands for one of his father's banks; lit stoves for Orthodox Jews on their Sabbath and religious holidays; and delivered fine hats to Boston Brahmin women. Joe's cousin Joe Kane remembered that whenever he met his childhood friend on the street, Kennedy would invariably ask, "How can we make some money?"[6]

Joe first attended two Catholic schools. In 1901, however, his mother enrolled him in the Boston Latin School, where he would rub elbows with the sons of New England's most respected families. Joe was not much of a scholar; he would graduate one year behind his class. But he was highly popular, played baseball for four years, managed the football team, and, among other things, was colonel on an award-winning drill team. Years later classmates particularly remembered his outstanding baseball prowess (he batted .667 in his senior year) and his whole-hearted competitive spirit. One recalled a game in Salem in which Boston Latin was losing: "The game was almost spoiled by Joe's constant bickering with the umpire. I can still see him, glaring at the umpire and slamming his fist in his glove."[7] Joe Kennedy hated to lose.

The few Boston Irish who went on to college usually attended Boston College or Holy Cross, considered "safe" by the Catholic hierarchy. Joe was sent to Harvard, the cradle of Yankee elitism. Rather than commute by trolley, as did other Irish "untouchables," Joe chose to live on campus. He earned passable grades, but studying was not his chief interest. He sought to make good socially.

Joe cultivated important students on campus, and in his senior year he roomed with an All-American football player from a distinguished Philadelphia family. The "best" undergraduate clubs were closed to him, but he was elected to the Hasty Pudding Dramatic Club and Delta Upsilon, genuine accomplishments for an Irish saloonkeeper's son. He earned his letter in baseball his senior year (and pocketed the game ball) because he had gotten to know the team captain and pitcher Charles ("Chick") McLaughlin, who asked the coach to put him in for the final play of the last game. The request, it turned out, resulted more from Joe's craftiness than friendliness. Before the game, a couple of P. J.'s ward heelers had dropped in on McLaughlin to inform him that a desired movie house business permit could be his if Joe got his athletic letter. McLaughlin later recalled, "Joe was the kind of guy who, if he wanted something bad enough, would get it, and he didn't much care how he got it. He'd run right over anybody."[8]

Kennedy reacted to the Harvard Brahmins, then and later, with a mixture of envy and scorn. He knew that they would never truly accept him. In retaliation, he angrily turned his back on them. As his biographer, David E. Koskoff, put it:

> Much of Kennedy's demeanor—his aggressiveness, his proverbial indelicacy and often vulgar diction, his scorn for aristocratic blandishments and refinements, and his frequent, almost designed manifestations of just plain bad taste—can be attributed to *his* rejection of the way of life that Brahmins symbolized. . . . He remained to his death, in taste, demeanor, and even political orientation, a rather thoroughgoing Boston Irishman.

Much of Kennedy's zealous pursuit of wealth would result from a desire to "show" the proper Bostonians that he could do as much or more than the best of them.[9]

Joe emerged from Harvard in 1912 with little more than a prestigious diploma to show for his expensive liberal arts education. He had practically no interest in books or ideas. A superficial attachment to classical music was his only link with high culture. Although he attended mass regularly, and would for the rest of his life, his commitment to basic Christian principles of faith and conduct was at best perfunctory.

Though Kennedy's principal skill was with numbers, he had nonetheless had to drop an accounting course rather than fail it. He realized that there was little actual relationship between higher education and the wealth and power he sought. His classmates had not earned their status in life laboring in libraries.

Joe went into banking after graduation. He did not start at the bottom. Using his father's influence, and after passing an examination, he became a state bank examiner. This position enabled him to travel throughout eastern Massachusetts studying bank ledgers and high finance. Within a year he put $1,000 into a fledgling real estate investment company that then elected him treasurer. By the time the company dissolved during WWI, Joe could claim one-third of its $75,000 assets.

In 1913 Joe worked feverishly to raise money from friends and acquaintances to prevent the stockholders of the neighborhood Columbia Trust Company, in which P. J. held a major interest, from merging with the larger First Ward National Bank. He sought and was awarded the institution's top position for his successful effort. Joe claimed that at twenty-five he was the youngest bank president in the United States, an assertion found in newspapers of the period and in almost all the Kennedy literature. (His wife, in her memoirs, would call him "probably the youngest one in the world.") The claim was false—historian John H. Davis labels it "pure Kennedy hype"—but it left many in awe. Joe told a reporter bluntly, "I want to be a millionaire by the age of 35."[10]

Joe was soon mentioned in the press again, for another reason. The society column of the *Boston Post* announced his engagement to Rose Fitzgerald, the daughter of Boston's mayor John Francis Fitzgerald, a small, dapper, rollicking, gabby, perpetually smiling, indefatigable whirlwind of a politician widely known as "Honey Fitz."

≫≫≫ ≪≪≪

The Fitzgeralds could trace their family to a mighty Italian clan that had helped William the Conqueror become ruler of England. They had been in Ireland for eight centuries when the potato famine drove Honey Fitz's father, Thomas Fitzgerald, from County Wexford to Boston. Thomas worked as a farmhand and street peddler, and in 1857 he married Rosanna Cox, the daughter of Irish immigrants. Eventually he prospered and became a grocer and tenement owner. Rosanna bore him a dozen children and was pregnant with her thirteenth when she died at forty-eight.

John, born in 1863, graduated from the Boston Latin School and attended Harvard Medical School for almost a year before his father's death required him to end his formal education and support his eight surviving brothers. "Little Fitzie," as he was then called, worked for a time for a local ward boss, was promoted to a clerkship in the Boston Custom House, and later started a prosperous insurance business. In 1889 he married a second cousin, twenty-three-year-old Mary Josephine Hannon, an attractive, shy, strongwilled, religious, thoroughly domestic daughter of Irish immigrants who had settled in a small town northwest of Boston. The first of their six children, Rose Elizabeth, was born July 22, 1890.

Fitzgerald's totally extroverted personality and considerable ambition caused him to gravitate almost naturally toward ward politics. He got elected to the Common Council, the lowest branch of the city government, became boss of the North End at twenty-nine, and then allied himself with Martin Lomasney, the powerful chieftain of the West End. In 1892 Honey Fitz went to the state senate, where he sat near P. J. Kennedy, and then served six years in Congress. Retiring from office in 1900, he settled down in a Boston mansion, made a sizable profit from a small Catholic weekly, and continued to be active in local politics.

In 1905 Honey Fitz defied Lomasney, Kennedy, and other leading Democrats and ran for mayor. In a dizzying campaign in which he averaged more than ten speeches a night, Fitzgerald declared repeatedly, "Down with the bosses! The people, not the bosses, must rule! I want a Bigger, Better, Busier Boston!" He won the primary and was elected. He quickly made up with Kennedy.

Honey Fitz was one of the most active and popular mayors in Boston history. He handled patronage deftly (Boston soon employed almost fourteen thousand people and spent one hundred thousand dollars a day), kept himself constantly on the front pages, and was on the go up to eighteen hours a day. In his first two years in office he gave an average of six speeches a day (*Fitzblarney* was the term used to describe his rapid monologues on virtually any topic) and attended as many as two dinners and three dances each night. In his successful 1910 campaign he adopted "Sweet Adeline" as his campaign song and would bellow it at the slightest provocation for the rest of his long life. Charges of graft and vote fraud would haunt Fitzgerald over the years, and he had a notorious affair with a blond cigarette girl name "Toodles" Ryan. But the public loved him, and though he lost more often than he won, he was still running for office as late as 1942.[11]

Rose was an intelligent and attractive young woman. Petite, dark, and popular, she graduated from high school with honors at fifteen. She wanted to go to Protestant Wellesley College, but her father, after consulting the archbishop of Boston, thought better of the idea. Rose attended the Convent of the Sacred Heart in downtown Boston for a year and studied piano at the New England Conservatory of Music. In 1908 she traveled to Europe with her parents and a sister, and the two girls were placed in a convent boarding school in Holland. For a year they endured the grueling routine of the nuns, mingled with the daughters of European aristocrats, learned "domestic science" and music, and expanded their knowledge of French and German. Back in the United States, Rose was sent to the Sacred Heart Convent in Manhattanville, New York, where she completed her formal education a month before her twentieth birthday.[12]

The mayor's daughter soon made her debut, a gala event staged by Honey Fitz, which attracted the governor, two congressmen, and the entire Boston City Council. The "proper Bostonians" were not in attendance, however, and in her memoirs Rose echoed the resentments of her parents, the Kennedys, and the many other upwardly mobile lace-curtain (middle-class) Irish about the vast gulf between themselves and the Back Bay Brahmins. "Between the groups feelings were, at best, suspicious, and in general amounted to a state of chronic, mutual antagonism." Newspapers, reflecting the chasm, contained separate society columns, "one about them," Rose wrote, and "one about us."[13]

As Rose readily stated, her mother played the dominant role in the formation of her character. Honey Fitz was rarely at home, and his wife had the responsibility of seeing to the children's behavior. Mrs. Fitzgerald stressed neatness, punctuality, good manners, attention to schoolwork, and extreme frugality. "I grew up," Rose wrote, "with the idea that one should be careful with money, that none should be spent without good and sufficient reason, and there should be something—tangible or intangible—to justify each expense." Mrs. Fitzgerald was also a disciplinarian who spanked when the rules were broken.[14]

At the heart of Mary Fitzgerald's life was the Roman Catholic church, and she instilled an intense devotion in her children. Every night during Lent, for example, she would gather them in one room, turn off the lights, and lead them in reciting the rosary. During May a family shrine was decorated with flowers, and prayer to the Blessed Virgin was offered nightly. She drilled the children in their religious lessons. "I'm sure my knees ached and that sometimes I wondered why I should be doing all the kneeling and studying and memorizing and contemplating and praying," Rose wrote. "But I became understanding and grateful."[15]

Mrs. Fitzgerald may also have taught Rose, if only by example, how to look the other way and turn inward in the presence of a husband's shenanigans and infidelities. Shy and reserved, Mary chose not to accompany Honey Fitz on his raucous rounds; Rose became the mayor's hostess, aide, piano player, and translator until her marriage.[16] But Mary knew about at least some of her husband's less-than-honorable deals and relationships. Honey Fitz pulled out of the mayor's race in 1912 when his opponent, James M. Curley, threatened to deliver public lectures entitled "Graft, Ancient and Modern," "Great Lovers: From Cleopatra to Toodles," and "Libertines: From Henry VIII to the Present Day." Four years later he was removed from a House seat after instances of illegal registration and voting fraud were discovered.[17] If her mother said or revealed nothing of her heartbreak, Rose would have to learn the bitter lesson for herself. And rather soon.

➤➤➤ ❰❰❰

Rose first met Joe Kennedy when the two were children. They got to know each other in their late teens, and a quiet romance blossomed. Rose later described her suitor:

> His face was open and expressive, yet with youthful dignity, conveying qualities of self-reliance, self-respect, and self-discipline. He neither drank nor smoked, nor did I. He was a serious young man, but he had a quick wit and a responsive sense of humor. He smiled and laughed easily and had a big, spontaneous, and infectious grin that made everybody in sight want to smile, too. Even then, he had an aura of command, an attitude of being competent to take charge of any situation.[18]

Honey Fitz discouraged the relationship. He and P. J. were never on good terms for long, and the mayor did not feel that the Kennedys were quite up to the social status the Fitzgeralds enjoyed. (Joe would never forget this snub and would later be rude and disdainful on occasion toward the Fitzgeralds.) It was not until Joe became a bank president that Honey Fitz consented. Rose later admitted that she could not quite remember a proposal. "It was less a matter of 'Will you marry me?' than of 'When we get married.' "[19] Cardinal O'Connell married the couple on October 7, 1914, in his private chapel. "I'd always wanted to be married by a Cardinal and I was," Joe later boasted.[20]

After a two-week honeymoon in White Sulphur Springs, West Virginia, the Kennedys moved into a gray frame house at 83 Beals Street (now a public museum) in the Protestant, middle-class suburb of Brookline. The first four of the Kennedy children, including John Fitzgerald, would be born here—in a space of less than five years.[21]

➤➤➤ ⫷⫷⫷

The new bank president plunged into the business of making money with fierce determination. At times during his life Joe Kennedy would reveal a genuine compassion toward others, and several Bostonians later gave him high marks as a youthful banker. Usually, however, Joe was unsentimental and coldly calculating, especially when a relationship involved money. At the Columbia Trust Company, according to one biographer, "He was as quick to call a loan and foreclose a mortgage as the next moneylender."[22]

Joe continued to strive for recognition by the Brahmins. In 1917, at the age of twenty-eight, he campaigned successfully for a seat on the board of trustees of the Massachusetts Electric Company. He made it on the third try, having been earlier defeated, as the company's president admitted, because of hostility toward Irish Catholics. When asked why he had made such an intense effort to be a trustee of the powerful utility, Joe replied, "Do you know a better way to meet people like the Saltonstalls?"[23]

When America entered World War I, Joe chose not to volunteer for military service, as many of his Harvard classmates did. Instead, he accepted an offer from a wealthy Bethlehem Steel lobbyist he had impressed to manage the rapidly expanding Fore River Shipyard in nearby Quincy. Joe developed an ulcer organizing and directing the yard, which at one point had a work force of 22,000 people. Fore River soon broke one production record after another and contributed significantly to the nation's war effort. For his services Kennedy received a handsome annual salary of twenty thousand dollars plus bonuses. He made money on the side by opening a cafeteria for the workers, which fed thousands daily. A powerful friend's political connections kept him out of the Army after he was drafted. (Perhaps feeling guilty about this, he would later alter the date of his shipyard employment to the prewar period.)

Joe became acquainted with a number of important people at this time, including Bethlehem Steel chairman Charles M. Schwab and Assistant Secretary of the Navy Franklin D. Roosevelt. A friend later recalled, "Joe was born mature. He would meet powerful, socially prominent men in passing, and later they would say to each other, 'That fellow has something.' "[24]

In the spring of 1919, Joe pursued and greatly impressed Galen Stone, a wealthy broker who sat on the boards of twenty-two companies. In June, Joe accepted Stone's offer to manage the stock department in the Boston office of Hayden, Stone and Company, an investment banking firm. The salary was only half what he earned at the shipyard, but he now had the opportunity to study the stock market under the tutelage of Stone and other professionals.

Joe learned quickly and was soon making profitable private investments. He became interested in the motion picture industry, for example, and headed a group that bought a chain of New England theaters just as movies became the rage. In 1922, at thirty-four, he struck out on his own, putting "Joseph P. Kennedy, Banker" on his office door. He would never again work for anyone else in the private sector.

The stock market in the Roaring Twenties was, as one historian has described it, "the closed preserve of tipsters, insiders, and manipulators." Kennedy was a clever, tireless, tight-lipped, and at times ruthless manipulator, known for his participation in stock pools. He and a few fellow traders in a pool would take options on an idle stock and cause market activity. They would then watch the gullible drive up its price and, at a certain point, sell, pocketing the profits and sticking the suckers with overvalued stock. "It's easy to make money in this market," Joe told a friend. "We'd better get in before they pass a law against it."[25]

In early 1924 Joe worked for seven weeks straight handling a stock struggle involving the Yellow Cab Company. He lost nearly thirty pounds and did not see his new daughter Patricia until she was almost a month old. He saved the stock from bears but then may have switched sides for his own financial benefit. John D. Hertz, founder of Yellow Cab, threatened to punch Kennedy in the nose the next time they met. Joe would only say later, "Several of us emerged wealthy men."[26]

By 1924, at thirty-five, Joe was a millionaire several times over. He drove a Rolls-Royce, hired a corps of servants, and sent his family to New York two years later in a private railroad car that completed its trip at a special siding near the Kennedys' new home. The stock market and real estate speculations provided a lucrative income, but Joe was probably also involved in the illegal liquor trade during Prohibition. In 1922, at his tenth Harvard reunion, Kennedy provided the Scotch. "Joe was our chief bootlegger," said a classmate. "Of course, he didn't touch a drop himself, but he arranged with his agents to have the stuff sent in right on the beach at Plymouth. It came ashore the way the pilgrims did."[27] Decades later, just before his own death, mob leader Frank Costello told a reporter that he and Kennedy had been partners in the liquor-smuggling business throughout the 1920s and early 1930s.[28] Gangster "Doc" Stacher, a lieutenant of archcriminal Meyer Lansky, reported that Joe was involved in a hijacked whiskey shipment being sent from Ireland to Boston in 1927.[29]

Kennedy moved his family from Boston to New York because he was still frustrated by the unwillingness of the Brahmins to take the Kennedys seriously and feared that his children would be barred from elite social events. When Joe applied for membership in the Cohasset Country Club, the summer resort of many old Boston families, he was blackballed. Years later, the incident still rankled him. "Those narrow-minded bigoted sons of bitches barred me because I was an Irish Catholic and son of a barkeep. You can go to Harvard and it doesn't mean a damned thing. The only thing these people understand is money."[30] And Kennedy was determined to make even more of it.

In early 1926 Joe entered the booming movie business. When he heard that an English firm owning Film Booking Offices of America, Inc. (FBO), was in financial trouble, he organized a syndicate to purchase it. FBO produced inexpensive, low-quality American films designed for small-town audiences. Under Kennedy, the company's new president and chairman of the board, production was increased to almost one movie a week, costs were cut, financing was reorganized, and profits rose sharply. By the end of the year the *Motion Picture World* declared, "Joseph P. Kennedy's shadow looms larger every minute."[31]

Kennedy was soon playing a major role in several key film industry mergers. In 1927, with the coming of sound, he struck a lucrative deal between FBO and David Sarnoff's Radio Corporation of America. The next year he and banking associates gained control of the KAO theater chain for $4,200,000. By that fall, Joe was head of the newly created RKO, a holding company with assets of $80,000,000, and he later helped engineer a merger between RKO and Pathé pictures. In thirty-two months in the movies, Kennedy made some $5,000,000 and earned a reputation for shrewdness, boldness, and cunning.[32]

Joe began to be known at this time as an ardent skirt chaser. He was often away from his family for extended periods of time and—like many of the movie moguls—was unable to resist the endless stream of beauties willing to pay any price for a chance at stardom. Joe did not limit his philandering to Hollywood, and he would continue it for decades until debilitated by a severe stroke. He was especially attracted to starlets and showgirls, but no good-looking female—including his sons' girlfriends or the wives of business associates—was off limits. His chauffeur was astonished to see him, in his early seventies, fondling a young hooker brought to a Kennedy party by international playboy Porfirio Rubirosa.[33] One member of his small staff was for years in charge of providing Joe with gossip. "He would not only tell Joe who was sleeping with whom," said an aide, "but also give graphic details, such as the case of the famous star who came home one day and found his wife *in flagrante* on a piano bench with a stunt man.''[34]

During the late 1920s word got out of an affair between Kennedy and glamour queen Gloria Swanson. Joe always denied it, but in 1980 Swanson confirmed the rumor and described it in detail in her autobiography.

When she met Kennedy in 1927, Swanson was one of Hollywood's top stars. In her late twenties, she was beautiful, wealthy, powerful, and married. Her third husband had brought her a European title: Marquise de la Falaise de la Coudraye. On the advice of a friend, the actress had sought out Kennedy when she was faced with several important financial decisions.

Joe was smitten almost instantly with the actress and quickly began to smother her with business advice and personal attention. At dinner that evening the two went on a first-name basis and began to lay plans to make a film together. Swanson recalled: ''He had the most ambitious view of pictures I had ever encountered; in fact, he seemed to see them precisely as a means of attaining not only wealth but also power. Like his father and his father-in-law, whom he mentioned over and over again, he was intrigued by the manipulation of people and events.''

Kennedy soon took over Swanson's extensive financial affairs, creating a new company, Gloria Productions, Inc. The actress enjoyed Joe's solicitude and enthusiasm, and she had complete confidence in his business acumen and character. ''In two months Joe Kennedy had taken over my entire life, and I trusted him implicitly to make the most of it.''

In Palm Beach one evening, Swanson learned something else about Joe. He appeared at the door of her hotel room:

> He just stood there, in his white flannels and his argyle sweater and his two-toned shoes, staring at me for a full minute or more, before he entered the room and closed the door behind him. He moved so quickly that his mouth was on mine before either of us could speak. With one hand he held the back of my head, with the other he stroked my body and pulled at my kimono. He kept insisting in a drawn-out moan, ''No longer, no longer. Now.'' He was like a roped horse, rough, arduous, racing to be free. After a hasty climax he lay beside me, stroking my hair. Apart from his guilty, passionate mutterings, he had still said nothing cogent.

There would be many other intimate hours between the actress and the father of seven when Joe sent Gloria's husband overseas, ostensibly to represent Pathé studios.

In the summer of 1928 Swanson came to New York at Joe's request.

He confided to his stunned guest that he wanted to have a child with her. There had been no Kennedy baby that year. A few days later he begged the actress to visit with Rose and the children. Swanson declined, noting later, "There in that strange situation was all of the man's complexity in a nutshell. While he was in control, he saw nothing as impossible or out of the question." Later, Joe got Gloria and Rose together on a ship returning from Europe. Rose seemed oblivious to the obvious. "Was she a fool . . . or a saint? Or just a better actress than I was?"

According to Swanson, Cardinal O'Connell summoned her to a New York hotel room in late 1929 and warned her to stop seeing Kennedy. Joe, she learned, knowing that divorce was impossible, had approached church authorities seeking permission to live apart from Rose and maintain a second household with the actress.

Kennedy produced a Swanson film called *Queen Kelly*, directed by the eccentric Erich von Stroheim. It was an eight-hundred-thousand-dollar bomb that Joe dared not release in the United States. A second film, *What a Widow*, also flopped at the box office. The relationship between Joe and Gloria ended in 1930, when the actress discovered that her lover had charged numerous items, including a fur coat he had given her, to her personal account. "Once again I had misjudged people and had been deceived by someone I had totally trusted, and I was stunned and in pain." When discovered, Joe simply abandoned the actress, severing all relations. Indeed, he left Hollywood and the movies. He had made millions short-selling stocks during the collapse of the stock market, and in 1930 he was probably worth more than one hundred million-dollars. Now he was beginning to think about Washington and national politics.[35]

→≫≫   ≪≪←

When Rose met Gloria Swanson aboard ship, she rattled on at length about her children. By that time the family had been her principal interest for the past fourteen years. With her husband away for weeks and months at a time, the responsibility for bringing up eight—and in 1932, nine—youngsters was largely hers.

When the first child, Joseph Patrick, Jr., was born in 1915, the Kennedys lived on Beals Street in Brookline. John Fitzgerald, named after his maternal grandfather, arrived in 1917 (May 29), and he was followed by Rosemary in 1918 and Kathleen in 1920. Needing larger quarters, the family moved five minutes away to a rambling house on Naples Road, where three other children were born: Eunice in 1921, Patricia in 1924, and Robert in 1925. In 1926 the Kennedys moved to

New York. (The last two children, Jean, born in 1928, and Edward, born in 1932, were delivered in Boston by Rose's favorite physician.) They first lived in Riverdale, overlooking the Hudson River, and in 1929 they moved to a $250,000 twenty-room Georgian mansion on nearly six acres in the Republican stronghold of Bronxville. That same year, Joe spent $125,000 on a fifteen-room, nine-bath Cape Cod–style home in Hyannis Port, Massachusetts, on Nantucket Sound—the summer home that was to be the family's favorite spot for decades. In 1933 Joe paid $100,000 for a six-bedroom Spanish-style house on fashionable North Ocean Boulevard in Palm Beach, Florida, which became the Kennedy's winter home.

A sizable number of servants (often Irish) took care of the Kennedy homes and did the daily chores. They were a constantly changing cast of characters, as the Kennedys paid very little and were highly demanding. Rose did a little sewing but mostly supervised the labors of the domestic employees. She later said that she considered herself "an executive."[36]

In her autobiography Rose stated that she ate with the children, read to them, took them on outings, helped them with school work, doled out tiny allowances (at ten, Jack wrote a formal letter to his father protesting his forty cents a week), and led them through their prayers and Sunday school lessons. She did some spanking on occasion. She also kept a detailed card file (now at the Kennedy Library) containing her children's medical histories.[37]

Joe and Rose imbued all the Kennedy children with a strong attachment to the Roman Catholic church. Attending weekly mass was a way of life, and there were often private devotions. The girls were the most deeply affected. By stern command and example, Rose (who attended daily mass) supervised their adherence to church teaching. Premarital sex, for example, so common among their upper-class friends, was unthinkable for the Kennedy women.

The boys, too, were compelled to attend church and go through all the motions of proper Roman Catholics. But Joe let them know at an early age, by his own example, that much if not most of this piety need be only superficial. Real men were profane, aggressive, and ruthless; they took what they wanted and broke the rules when necessary. Each of the boys, following in their father's footsteps, would strongly identify with the church and always attend weekly mass, while doing what was to their advantage with little or no regard to its moral content. Lechery, for example, would be a way of life for the Kennedy males. And in politics they would do what it took to win.

As Joe became more blatant about his adultery during the New Deal and war years, Rose grew increasingly distant from everyone, no doubt groping for self-preservation. She was alone much of the time and traveled by herself some seventeen times to Europe during the first six years of the Great Depression to buy the latest fashions. As she grew older, Rose seemed more and more oblivious to all but the most trivial household matters and a prized doll collection. According to one observant employee, Frank Saunders, she was self-centered, stingy, prudish, and often spiteful.

To her children Rose became something of a comic character, barking at the servants (who were ordered to call her "madame") and shuffling around the house with her hair in curlers, her face plastered with brownish cloth bandages ("frownies") to smooth out wrinkles, and her dress covered with notes she had pinned on to remind herself and others of a variety of duties. Her self-absorption kept her at a distance from her children.

Jack was especially sensitive to his mother's frequent absences, exclaiming at age five in front of his brothers and sisters, "Gee, you're a great mother to go away and leave your children alone." He once confided to a close friend that he used to cry each time Rose packed her bag, which only irritated her and made her withdraw from him even farther. Later he told another intimate, "My mother was either at some Paris fashion house or else on her knees in some church. She was never there when we really needed her. . . . My mother never really held me and hugged me. Never! Never!"[38]

Honey Fitz was around the Kennedy house as the children grew up. He took them to baseball games and the zoo and invited them to his house for Sunday dinner. The political talk at the table interested Joe, Jr., at an early age. Jack later claimed to remember when his grandfather took him along on a campaign for governor in 1922. The former mayor especially enjoyed walking the youngsters through Boston and telling them about American history.[39]

The vital force in the family, even when he was away, was Joe, whom Rose called "the architect of our lives."[40] From Hollywood or wherever he was on his travels, he barraged the children with letters, taking an active interest in their personal lives. (In the more than two hundred letters that survived, Doris Kearns Goodwin reported, not once did Joe raise any serious moral principles for his children to ponder.) He kept in touch with Rose by telephone almost daily and on Sundays spoke with each child. "I had them all lined up and waiting, in the order of their ages, so that even the smallest child could hear his voice," Rose wrote. "To them he never seemed far away."[41]

When he was home Joe became deeply involved with the children.

Rose later described him as extremely affectionate, frank, outgoing, and honest. He also tolerated little nonsense and no disobedience. Physical punishment was unnecessary; Rose could not remember a single time when he resorted to spanking. The children knew that their father was the absolute ruler of the house and family. Joe's displeasure was expressed with a stare (inherited from his mother and called by the family "the Hickey look") that a house guest once described as "ice-cold steel blue, piercing right into you and through you and stripp[ing] you to the soul; and you felt naked, shriveled."[42] Joe sometimes supplemented this with outbursts of temper, featuring profanity and cruel sarcasm. And then, often very quickly, his mood would change and a bright smile would relieve the tension.

Rose wrote that her children "grew up with feelings of awe and reverence and respect and friendship and camaraderie and love and duty toward their father." Although a bit overstated, the description rings true: Awe and respect were the primary responses. As Doris Kearns Goodwin has put it, "Joe Kennedy, having achieved an almost primitive dominion over his children's youthful souls, would rule his boys and girls for the rest of their lives."[43]

Many years later Joe's grandchildren were trained accordingly. A family staff member recalled, "The grandchildren had been taught that Mr. Kennedy was the end-all and be-all. They had been taught to revere him, to understand that they were rich because of him." More than once the observer heard a son-in-law lecture his children, "Everything we have we owe to your grandfather. Don't you ever forget it."[44]

Like his brothers and sisters, Jack was never to forget what he owed to his father; not only his wealth, but the early lessons from the patriarch's example and declared values. Indeed, they were lessons that echoed from both the Kennedy and Fitzgerald traditions: Life was primarily about getting what you want, about winning—no matter what the cost, no matter whom it hurt. Pious talk about integrity, humility, and love of one's neighbor was fine in church, but it had little or nothing to do with reality. And so, from their earliest days, the Kennedys were trained to compete, to be second to no one, and to allow no obstacles to stand in their way. The Founding Father thus commanded.

CHAPTER 3

Getting into Shape

⇢⤜ ⤛⇠

BOTH JOE AND ROSE taught their children that the Kennedys were special people, destined for great things. In part this was to protect the youngsters from Yankee discrimination. The great family wealth, of course, also set the children apart. (Joe established a trust fund in 1929 that would provide more than a million dollars for each of his children when they reached twenty-one. Additions to the fund in 1936 and 1949 meant that each Kennedy would be worth more than $10 million without having to work a day.)[1] But more than anything else, the intense demands made on the Kennedy children reflected the elder Kennedy's plans for their future, which required full attention, absolute devotion, and tight teamwork.

Joe Kennedy did not leave the molding of his children's character, intellect, and physical prowess to chance. He knew exactly what he wanted his children to be, to think, and to do, and he would not tolerate resistance. He often put his expectations succinctly: "We want winners. We don't want losers here."[2] Eunice said later that the family motto was Finish First, adding, "I was twenty-four before I knew I didn't have to win something every day."[3]

There were family rules, and the children quickly learned what it took to be acceptable in their parents' sight. "We were computerized at an early age," Eunice said later.[4] The youngsters were required, for example, to be at the dinner table on time. Rose later quoted a favorite maxim: "Promptness is a compliment to the intelligent, a rebuke to the stupid."[5] If the children arrived even seconds late, they did so at their peril. If one of their guests was tardy, Joe would often fly into a rage and administer a tongue-lashing. One such victim, a pal of Jack's who never returned, later recalled, "The other kids, including Jack, sat around the table, heads bowed, apparently frightened to death."[6] The children stood when their mother entered. They were required to listen attentively when their father lectured on any topic (sometimes with a map) and to respond clearly and intelligently when he asked detailed questions about their activities, current events, and matters of general knowledge. There was never to be silliness, irreverence, or even relaxation at a formal family meal.[7]

In the summers Joe ran what were actually family training camps. The children reported at 7:00 A.M. to their physical education instructor for calisthenics. After breakfast, there were lessons in swimming, sailing, and tennis. Joe entered his youngsters in public swimming races as early as six years old. "And if we won," Eunice recalled, "he got terribly enthusiastic. Daddy was always very competitive. The thing he always kept telling us was that coming in second was just no good." Joe followed his children in the family powerboat when they competed in important sailing contests. When his oldest son lost one race, Joe, white with anger, ordered a new mainsail. Joe, Jr., began winning again. Then it was discovered that the new sail was nine inches too high along the mast, giving Kennedy an illegal competitive advantage. Jack named his first sailboat *Victura*, explaining that it meant "something about winning."[8]

The two and one-half acres of lawn at Hyannis Port became football and softball fields, and the tensions of competition between the boys sometimes erupted into fistfights. There was to be no acknowledgment of discomfort or pain. When one injured Kennedy child came to his mother for sympathy and fell to the floor, she ordered, "On your feet!" The youngster obeyed and stood at attention. "Now you know how to behave," she said. "Go out there and behave as you know you should."[9]

To be popular with the Kennedys, visitors at Hyannis Port would have to show reckless courage on the athletic field, especially in football. "It's 'touch,' " said a friend, "but it's murder. If you don't want to play, don't come. If you do come, play, or you'll be fed in the kitchen and nobody will speak to you. Don't let the girls fool you. Even pregnant, they can make you look silly." The visitor was also warned against complaining of pain, criticizing a Kennedy's performance, and being too good. The last rule was especially important for the Kennedys insisted on winning.[10]

Guests were also required to tolerate verbal hazing. "The razzing would begin the minute you stepped inside the house," said another visitor. "Your clothes, your speech, whatever: nothing was sacred. It was like getting constantly pecked by a flock of chickens."[11] One might also be expected to compete in mental games, to know the contents of current magazines, and to be able to tell at least three good jokes.[12] The unforgivable sin was to refuse a challenge of any sort.

The one Kennedy youngster who did not respond to the family regimen was Rosemary, the first daughter. She did badly in kindergarten, was poorly coordinated, and often flew into temper tantrums. By the time she was five, it was obvious that she was mildly retarded. Rose took her to a battery of specialists and hired a nurse and a tutor, but they could do little. The family covered up for the oldest girl, telling others that she was shy and "a little slow."

Rosemary grew more difficult in her teens as the contrast between herself and her siblings became acute. By the time she reached adulthood, her parents were desperate. The young woman was often verbally abusive and even physically violent. She would roam the streets at night, terrifying her mother, who feared she might be attacked or become pregnant. A relative later recalled, "She had the body of a twenty-one-year-old yearning for fulfillment with the mentality of a four-year-old." In 1941 Joe took matters into his own hands. Without telling Rose or anyone else, he had physicians give Rosemary a prefrontal lobotomy, an experimental procedure then thought to work wonders. The operation proved disastrous, leaving Rosemary a shell of a person, unable even to control her bladder.

The now severely retarded Kennedy girl was quietly sent to a nursing convent, St. Coletta School, one mile east of tiny Jefferson, Wisconsin (where she remains to this day). The Kennedys concealed and lied about her condition until after the 1960 presidential election. Some details of the story were made public in 1974 when Rose published her autobiography. Doris Kearns Goodwin, who was given exclusive access by the Kennedys to family papers, claimed in 1987 that Rose did not learn about the prefrontal lobotomy until 1961.

Over the years, Rose and Eunice visited St. Coletta's regularly. Joe, on the other hand, who could barely speak of Rosemary even before the operation, treated his once-adoring daughter as dead. When Gloria Swanson happened to ask about the girl after overhearing part of a telephone conversation, Joe became enraged. "It was frightening," the actress wrote later. "His blue eyes turned to ice and then to steel." Within seconds he was shouting, " 'I don't want to hear about it. Do you understand me? *Do you understand me?*' " Once Rosemary was institutionalized, she did not exist. She was a loser.[13]

→>> <<←

Joe's favorite was his oldest son and namesake, Joe Junior. Young Joe, as he was often called, resembled his father in every way: he was good-looking, athletic, aggressive, daring, worldly, short tempered, and could turn on a magical smile or a steely glare at will. His parents doted on him and trained him to be the model Kennedy.[14]

Joe was determined to help his son reach the highest levels of prominence and power, and he personally designed his formal education to give him every advantage in the inevitable struggles with Yankees. He avoided Catholic institutions (to which his daughters would be sent) and enrolled the boy in Devotion School, one of Boston's best public schools. In 1924 Joe Junior went to Noble and Greenough School (renamed Dexter, a Boston benefactor, after Joe helped save it financially), a Brahmin establishment with close ties to Harvard. Here he excelled in athletics and fistfights. When the Kennedys moved to New York, Young Joe entered Riverdale Country Day School, another Yankee haunt. For prep school the boy was sent to exclusive Choate, north of New Haven and about sixty miles from the Kennedy home in Bronxville. After a shaky start, he became a campus leader, an award-winning varsity football player, and a solid student.

Following Young Joe's graduation in 1933, his father, largely on the advice of Felix Frankfurter of the Harvard Law School, sent him to the London School of Economics for a year to study under the famed socialist economist Harold Laski. Joe wanted the eighteen-year-old to expand his knowledge in the restless depression years, to make contacts, to travel (Laski took him to the Soviet Union), and above all to build a reputation as a young man of the world. Joe Junior startled his roommate and amused Laski by declaring flatly that he was going to be the first Catholic president of the United States. After London the next step was to be Harvard.[15]

→>> <<←

As the oldest, and with his parents away much of the time, Joe Junior played a major role in family affairs while he was growing up. He would sit at the head of the table at times, dispensing meat and orders. He was the cheerleader at athletic events and would set the standards at Hyannis Port for daring. He would play for hours with the smallest children; Teddy was his favorite brother, and he was especially close to Kathleen. He visited siblings in the hospital and at their schools. He also often enforced family rules. "It wasn't the father they were afraid of," said a friend, "It was Joe Junior. The real reason they didn't sneak a smoke here and there was that they were afraid he would find out and beat the hell out of them."[16]

Joe was especially hard on Jack, his younger brother by two years. While he would lob a football to one of his sisters, he would slam it into Jack and grin when the thin boy doubled up in pain. The two fought spirited battles on many occasions over the years. Rose later commented, "Joe Jr. was older, bigger, stronger, but Jack, frail though he was, could fight like fury when he had to." The two once raced around the block on their bicycles in opposite directions, each refusing to veer out of the other's path. The collision sent Jack to the hospital for twenty-eight stitches. His brother was unscathed.[17]

At times, however, the two boys had a close relationship. Joe trained Jack to be a sailor, and they worked together when victory was the goal. Jack later paid a warm tribute to his oldest brother: "He made the task of bringing up a large family immeasurably easier for my father and mother, for what they taught him they passed on to us, and their teachings were not diluted through him, but rather strengthened."[18] Still, Jack grew up mostly afraid and in awe of Joe Junior. A girl who dated Jack in Bronxville during his teens later recalled that his conversation consisted largely of two topics: his health and Young Joe. The latter seemed constantly on his mind. "Joe plays football better, Joe dances better, Joe is getting better grades," she remembered him saying. Later, when Jack arrived at Harvard, he would tell an instructor "I want you to know I'm not bright like my brother Joe."[19]

⇒⇒⇒ ⇐⇐⇐

Jack's poor physical condition magnified the shadows of a domineering father and bullying brother. From birth, he was the most frail and sickly of the Kennedy children. The full extent of Jack's suffering may never be known, as his medical records at the Kennedy Library are sealed. Family members and friends long engaged in a coverup of the health issue. Still, Bobby could recall after his brother's death, "At least one half of the days that he spent on this earth were days of intense physical pain. . . . When we were growing up together we used to laugh about the great risk a mosquito took in biting Jack Kennedy—with some of his blood the mosquito was almost sure to die.''[20] Rose wrote in her autobiography, ''Almost all his life, it seemed, he had to battle against misfortunes of health.''[21]

Jack was born with what a family physician later called an ''unstable back.'' (Later stories about heroic football and wartime back injuries were largely fictitious.) This slight deformity restricted his activities and, in later life, would cause often acute pain that could last weeks. Rest, hot baths, crutches, and a back brace that looked like a corset were all that physicians could prescribe, short of highly risky surgery.[22]

Before he was three, Jack had had scarlet fever, whooping cough, measles, and chicken pox. At eleven he contracted German measles and suffered from occasional bronchitis. In 1931 his appendix was removed and glasses were prescribed. (Jack would always hide his glasses from photographers.) He developed asthma and was severely allergic to dog hair. In 1933 his tonsils and adenoids were removed. There were other problems—''a severe illness,'' for example, was reported by one school official but went unrecorded in Rose's card file—and over the years they would multiply.[23]

For much of his life Jack was extremely thin. Rose described him at nearly six as ''elfin'' in appearance. ''At family meals, if there happened to be an extra portion of food, or perhaps some rich gravy left in the bottom of the pan, I would usually tell the cook to give it to Jack because he needed it.''[24]

Jack's illnesses often confined him to bed, and he envied others who were out on the playgrounds and in their sailboats. He very early got into the habit of reading while bedridden, and he became the only Kennedy youngster seriously interested in books. A friend later remembered him at fifteen lying in a hospital bed surrounded by books. She was impressed because he was reading *The World Crisis* by Winston Churchill. Still, young Jack read mostly for entertainment, and his reading did not influence his grades. Indeed, he would never claim to be an intellectual.[25]

When physically able, Jack was as daring and determined in athletics as any of his brothers and sisters. He fully absorbed his parents' injunctions about winning and refused to accept the fact that he was not as strong or as talented as some of the other Kennedys. He also adhered to the family's abhorrence of self-pity. Bobby later claimed that he had never heard his brother complain about pain. Jack was popular with family members, although his frequent tardiness and sloppiness sometimes riled his parents. He was especially admired for his facility with the family's educational games and contests.[26]

Later it was learned that Jack was among at least several of the Kennedys who suffered emotional damage in their youth. Close friends would tell interviewers that while Jack appeared on the surface to be friendly and concerned about others, he suffered from severe inhibitions. One longtime female friend said, "He was not the kind of person to have self-revealing conversations. Jack had a total lack of ability to relate, emotionally, to anyone. Everything was so surface with him in his relationships with people. All of the Kennedys were blocked, totally blocked, emotionally. Eunice survived best."[27] A lifelong pal spoke often of Jack's aloofness and his inability to love or express feelings. "Mr. Kennedy had never touched them much when they were young. Jack was the same way—didn't touch and didn't want to be touched."[28] Another companion stated, "He was immature emotionally. He had no depth of emotion. The male side of the family were all like that. They came by it naturally—from the father, who chased anything in skirts."[29]

Joe's cruel treatment of Rose surely had an impact on all of the children. The fact that he would proposition their girlfriends and bring mistresses into the home (one stayed for several months and was integrated into the family's activities) conveyed powerful messages to the youngsters about his lack of concern and respect for others. Rose's growing withdrawal into a world of her own and her frequent absences compounded the problem. Jack, perhaps more than the others, resented his mother's indifference. He was later to tell a friend, "My mother is a nothing."[30]

Jack concealed this animosity from the public, of course; in his first authorized biography, by James MacGregor Burns, he described Rose as "a very model mother for a big family."[31] (Theodore Sorensen would declare solemnly, "Rose Kennedy was more quietly devout and less outwardly combative than her husband and sons. From her the latter inherited much of their shy but appealing warmth and spiritual depth.")[32] But Rose knew about her son's true feelings and was aware that they had been shared with others. In her autobiography she twice attempted to counter his charges of neglect, once suggesting that she had been too busy with Rosemary to pay sufficient attention to Jack.[33]

Despite the smiling faces beaming from family photos and the enforced teamwork on the playing fields, there was emptiness and sadness within the Kennedy children. At the root of it were months of loneliness and their parents' often selfish, insensitive behavior. Friends noticed, for example, that Joe Junior often enjoyed visiting pals whose parents were at home and available for a chat.[34] A girl who accompanied Jack a few times to an empty Kennedy house said later, "It was creepy. It wasn't homey, and I just never knew where anybody was unless they had a party."[35] A close friend of Jack's said of the Kennedy youngsters, "They really didn't have a real home with their own rooms where they had pictures on the walls or memorabilia on the shelves but would rather come home for holidays from their boarding schools and find whatever room was available." Jack would say to Rose, "Which room do I have this time?"[36]

Jack grew up with a hostile attitude toward marriage and the family. Women were at best sex objects. "Dad told all the boys to get laid as often as possible," he would say to Clare Boothe Luce. "I can't get to sleep unless I've had a lay."[37] He would tell a writer that he lacked the desire for a large family because he had learned that it involved "institutionalized living, children in a cellblock." In 1932, when he came home from boarding school on vacation, he said sarcastically to companions, "I want to stop by the house for a minute and see if there's anyone new in the family." There was: Teddy.[38]

All this would be papered over later by Kennedy and sympathetic journalists and historians. James MacGregor Burns assured his readers in 1959, "Looking back today, Kennedy cannot remember any unhappy times during his childhood."[39] In 1980 Herbert S. Parmet wrote of Jack, "For warmth, attention, and satisfaction, he turned to his mother, by all accounts a strong woman who gave great attention to the details of routine family needs."[40] Jack himself once stated publicly, "There's no way you can prepare for the presidency. The only things I ever learned from anybody that might have helped were some of the early things I learned from my mother."[41]

>>> <<<

Jack's formal education began at the Dexter School, where Joe Junior had fought as the only Irishman on the rolls. He attended grades four through six at Riverdale Country Day School, where Rose later said his grades averaged about B-minus. In 1930 thirteen-year-old Jack entered the Canterbury School in New Milford, Connecticut, a Catholic institution where he was to get a taste of boarding school before following Joe Junior to Choate the following year. He was weak in Latin and spelling. Rose later published examples of his writing: "I learnt how to play baggamon to-day." (Spelling would always be a problem for him.)[42] Jack turned out for several sports and managed to endure twice-daily chapel. "I will be quite pius [*sic*] I guess when I get home," he wrote to his mother. Appendicitis cut short his studies during Easter vacation, and a tutor helped him pass his entrance examinations to Choate. He had to take the Latin exam twice. Rose assured the headmaster, "He has a very attractive personality—we think—but he is quite different from Joe, for whom we feel you have done so much."[43]

When Jack arrived at Choate in the fall of 1931, his older brother was already a big man on campus. Joe Junior was a highly popular football player who would become editor of the school newspaper and win a trophy for best combined scholarship and sportsmanship. Jack simply could not compete on this level. A year earlier he had taken an Otis Intelligence Test and scored 119. This was above average but not in the same league with many of his gifted classmates. Moreover, Jack lacked motivation and maturity. He stumbled through Latin, French, mathematics, and English but made respectable marks in physics and history (his favorite subject). He would graduate sixty-fifth in a class of 110.

Jack was voted "most likely to succeed" in his senior year. A classmate later explained, however, that the title was Jack's because he wanted it (no doubt to please his father) and campaigned for it, trading votes with boys who wished to be named "the handsomest," "the best dancer," and so on. One researcher, the headmaster's son, later found strong evidence that the vote was rigged.[44]

Jack's health remained a source of serious concern at Choate. A friend later recalled, "He was really very, very delicate."[45] He suffered from colds, mumps, a swollen gland, a knee injury, hives, and also had fallen arches. He was often in the infirmary and was hospitalized once. He was so thin at one point that Honey Fitz offered him a dollar for every pound he could gain. Still, Jack turned out for half a dozen sports, including football. He failed to make the varsity in anything but was a scrappy competitor. His football coach said later, "You take Joe, he was a real athlete. But Jack made up for what he lacked in athletic ability with his fight."[46]

Jack excelled in making friends. He was easygoing, fun loving, a bit shy, and at times charming. His approach to people suggests that lacking physical strength and intellectual prowess, Jack, early on, found charm a potent and seductive attribute to get what he wanted. A pal would say later, "With Jack, nobody really admired what he did or respected what he did but they liked his personality. When he flashed his smile, he could charm a bird off a tree."[47]

His roommate for two years was K. Lemoyne ("Lem") Billings, who would become his closest companion and, in Lem's last years, an invaluable source of information about the Kennedys. Billings, a Pittsburgh physician's son, shared with Jack the burden of having an older brother who had excelled at Choate. Ralph ("Rip") Horton, the son of a wealthy New York dairy owner, was another close friend.

Jack often defied Choate's rigid rules and enjoyed pranks. Billings said later that he had "the best sense of humor of anybody I've ever known in my life. And I don't think I've ever known anybody who was as much fun."[48] One winter when Rose sent him a crate of oranges from Palm Beach, Jack amused himself by throwing them out of his window at friends. He once collected all the pillows in his dormitory and stuffed them into a boy's room. Moreover, his personal sloppiness exasperated his housemaster. Informed of this conduct, Joe wrote a polite but firm letter in Jack's junior year: "I am urging you to do the best you can. I am not expecting too much, and I will not be disappointed if you don't turn out to be a real genius, but I think that you can be a really worthwhile citizen with good judgment and understanding." Jack promised to reform.[49]

Instead, in his senior year, Jack, Lem, and Rip recruited ten buddies and formed a "Mucker's Club," *mucker* being the headmaster's term for everything that was undesirable at Choate. Club members met nightly, devising ways to violate campus rules. The imperious headmaster, Dr. George St. John, was enraged. He suspended the boys and summoned their parents. Jack, the ringleader, was first on his list of troublemakers. St. John recalled years later, "Psychologically I was enormously interested. I couldn't see how two boys from the same family as were Joe and Jack could be so different."

The elder Kennedy, a campus benefactor, came in person for a conference with his son and the headmaster. According to Billings, Jack was "terrified that his father would lose confidence in him once and for all." But when St. John was called from the room by a telephone call, Joe winked and whispered, "My God, my son, you sure didn't inherit your father's directness or his reputation for using bad language. If that crazy Mucker's Club had been mine, you can be sure it wouldn't have started with an M." Joe did not condone Jack's rebelliousness, however, and he spoke sternly in St. John's presence. The Muckers disbanded and young Kennedy was reinstated.[50]

Joe soon wrote to Jack:

Don't let me lose confidence in you again, because it will be pretty nearly an impossible task to restore it—I am sure it will be a loss to you and a distinct loss to me. The mere trying to do a good job is not enough—real honest-to-goodness effort is what I expect. Get yourself into shape so that a man can't write a halfway report on you. You have the goods; why not try to show it? [51]

During vacations Jack enjoyed visiting Rip Horton in New York. The boys went to speakeasies, which, according to his host, Jack liked to do "twenty-four hours a day." Once, Jack and Lem went to a brothel in Harlem, where the seventeen-year-old Kennedy had his first sexual experience. The white prostitute charged him three dollars. Afterward the youngsters panicked at the thought of venereal disease and purchased salves and creams at a hospital. Still worried, Jack woke up a physician in the middle of the night, and the boys went to see him for an examination. There were soon visits to other houses of prostitution and a number of conquests among the unprofessional. "He was very successful with girls," Billings said later, "Very."[52]

In late September 1935, Joe and Rose and seven of their children, including Jack, sailed for London. The elder Kennedy by this time had expanded his financial resources by participating in a lucrative stock market pool and by becoming the exclusive American agent for Haig & Haig and Dewar's Scotch Whiskeys, and Gordon's gin. (FBI files estimate that with the repeal of Prohibition, Joe made a million dollars a year from his liquor franchises. He sold the import business in 1946 for eight million dollars.)[53] He had just resigned as chairman of the Securities and Exchange Commission (SEC) and was an informal adviser and confidential emissary of President Franklin D. Roosevelt. Roosevelt had named Joe to the SEC ("Set a thief to catch a thief," he told critics privately) in return for valuable campaign support. Joe had sought and continued to seek higher positions in the New Deal administration, but the president did not fully trust him and preferred to limit his ambition. By all accounts Kennedy had performed admirably with the commission. His trip to England was part of a six-week European tour of the gold bloc nations.[54]

Jack stayed in London in order to follow the path blazed by Joe Junior at the London School of Economics. He later claimed to have spent the entire year of 1935–36 at the institution. In fact, Jack registered at the school but took ill soon after arriving in London and returned home within a month, not having participated in any academic work. Rose said later that the problem was hepatitis or jaundice, a malady Jack may first have suffered while at Choate.[55]

Instead of resting after his arrival at home, Jack chose to enter Princeton several weeks late. Joe opposed his choice of college, wanting his son to follow Joe Junior at Harvard. But Jack persisted and won a grudging assent. Lem Billings and Rip Horton were at Princeton, and Jack wanted to be with them.

Jack moved in with his two pals, who lived on the fourth floor of a campus dormitory. He remained ill with his blood condition but managed to pass courses in English, history, military science, and French. He failed trigonometry. In early December he gave up and was hospitalized in Boston for two months.[56]

Out of the hospital, Jack went to the Jay Six Ranch near Benson, Arizona, where Joe Junior joined him for a time. Arthur Krock of the *New York Times*, a good friend of the elder Kennedy's, had recommended the 43,000-acre cattle ranch as a good place for Jack to recover his health and for his older brother to work out. Jack stayed four months and took a side trip to Hollywood. "I met this extra in Hollywood that is the best looking thing I have ever seen," he reported to Billings, adding, "The Extra's delight, or how I got my tail in Hollywood."[57]

In the fall of 1936 Jack entered Harvard. His College Board and Scholastic Aptitude Tests had each averaged a mediocre 69. But his father's personal influence, as it had at Princeton, no doubt proved decisive.[58] Young Joe was then a junior at Harvard and had made a name for himself in the classroom, in student government, and on the football field.

Jack's achievements again compared poorly to his brother's. He ran for the freshman class presidency and failed to qualify for the runoff elections. He made the freshman football squad and played end in three games. "Jack wanted to be known in school as a jock," said a classmate.[59] He again showed determination but was not up to the physical demands. At six feet and 149 pounds, he was less than intimidating. "You could blow him over with a good breath," one observer recalled. He played a few more games on the junior varsity in his sophomore year before dropping the sport, no doubt because his back could no longer take it.[60]

Like his father before him, Jack chose to room with football players. One of them, gridiron hero Torbert ("Torby") Macdonald, would become a lifelong friend. "Jack always worshipped athletes," a sympathetic biographer concluded.[61] Not until Theodore Sorensen (an employee), whom he met in 1953, would Kennedy have a close friend who was an intellectual.

Poor health continued to plague Jack in college. He showed promise as a freshman swimmer but illness kept him from trying out for the team. The coach remembered him as "a fine kid, frail and not too strong, but always giving it everything he had."[62] He suffered from asthma during the summer of 1937. In early 1938, the year he turned twenty-one, sickness forced him to miss class, and he apparently was ill on other occasions later in the year. Jack wore a corset during these years, as he would the rest of his life, to ease his back pain.[63]

Jack took a modest interest in extracurricular activities; he worked for the *Harvard Crimson*, joined Winthrop House (the club for jocks that Joe Junior had joined), belong to St. Paul's Catholic Club, and was chosen for membership in Hasty Pudding and the Spee Club. (Like his older brother, he failed to get into Porcellian, the highest ranking club.) Political organizations, then the rage on campus, did not appeal to him.[64]

As at Choate, Jack had many friends. Charles Houghton, a football player–roommate, said later that he was intellectually stimulating and had "the best sense of humor of any of the Kennedys." (Houghton's only complaint, shared by fellow student Torbert Macdonald, concerned Jack's sloppiness. "He never hung up *anything*. He just dropped his clothes where he was, or strewed them all over the suite." A part-time valet, inherited from Joe Junior, eased the situation slightly.)[65] A note attached to a sophomore-year housing application observed that Kennedy was "one of the most popular men in his class." One friend found him "attractive, witty, and unpurposeful."[66]

Chasing women occupied much of the young man's time. "I can now get tail as often and as free as I want which is a step in the right direction," Jack boasted to Lem Billings. Anticipating a visit to his friend at Princeton, Jack advised, "Get me a room way away from all others and especially from your girl as I don't want you coming in for a chat in the middle as usual and discussing how sore my cock is." After being circumcised in 1938, Jack named his penis "JJ" and told Lem that it "has never been in better shape or doing better service."[67] When it came to young women, Jack, like his father, enjoyed variety and quantity.

At one point Jack seriously pursued Frances Ann Cannon, a wealthy North Carolina beauty studying at Sarah Lawrence. He also went with Charlotte McDonnell, the Catholic daughter of a New York stockbroker, and there were rumors of engagement. A McDonnell uncle strongly disapproved of the relationship, labeling Jack a "moral roustabout" and his father a "crook and thorough bounder." McDonnell's father forbade Jack to see her again. The romance would probably have disintegrated in any case. "If the subject of marriage came up," McDonnell later recalled, "Jack would never talk about it directly."[68]

During the summer of 1937, after his freshman year, Jack, accompanied by Lem Billings, traveled in Europe. They were in France, Italy, Germany, and England, sightseeing, wangling dates, swimming, hiking, and gambling. The trip, made largely in Jack's new car, was not entirely frivolous. The two attended public appearances by Mussolini and the pope, interviewed refugees from the Spanish Civil War, and talked with people knowledgeable about fascism and communism. In a diary and in his letters to his father, Jack wrestled with the ideas confronting him on his journey. He came to believe that "Fascism is the thing for Germany and Italy, Communism for Russia and democracy for America and England."[69]

In December 1937 President Roosevelt named Joe Kennedy American ambassador to The Court of St. James's. The year before, Joe had again been instrumental in an FDR campaign, giving speeches, contributing funds, and publishing a book (largely ghostwritten by Arthur Krock) called *I'm for Roosevelt*, in which Joe had declared: "I have no political ambitions for myself or for my children and I put down these few thoughts about our President, conscious only of my concern as a father for the future of his family and my anxiety as a citizen that the facts about the President's philosophy be not lost in a fog of unworthy emotion." In fact, after the election, Joe again sought a top post in the federal government. Though he was led to believe that the coveted Treasury Department might be his reward for able diplomatic service, he was forced to settle for the chairmanship of the Maritime Commission before successfully grabbing the vacant post in London. Kennedy was the first Irish Catholic ever named to the position.[70]

The ambassador (as he would ask to be called for the rest of his life) brought Joe Junior and Jack with him by ship to London in late June 1938. He imposed a midnight curfew on both young men to limit their pursuit of girls. Jack was on the French Riviera in early August.[71]

During the spring semester of 1939, while Europe moved toward war, Jack withdrew from Harvard and spent seven months abroad in a study-travel program supervised by his father. Joe Junior had been engaged in a similar experience since his graduation. Jack traveled widely, sending letters to his father about the economic and political conditions he encountered in places like Prague, Moscow, Istanbul, and Bucharest. James MacGregor Burns wrote later: "The literary quality of his reports was not the highest, and the spelling was still atrocious, but they showed a cool detachment."[72] Foreign Service officer George F. Kennan later recalled receiving Joe's request to get Jack into Prague:

> We were furious. Joe Kennedy was not exactly known as a friend of the career service, and many of us, from what we had heard about him, cordially reciprocated this lack of enthusiasm. His son had no official status and was, in our eyes, obviously an upstart and [an] ignoramus. The

idea that there was anything he could learn or report about conditions in Europe which we did not already know and had not already reported seemed (and not without reason) wholly absurd.[73]

Jack's mind was not always on serious matters. In a letter to Lem Billings he wrote of a girl who had "a cigarette case engraved with Snow White lying down with spread legs and the Seven Dwarfs, cocks in hand, waiting to screw her. Very charming."[74] There were vacations and plenty of time for more fun on the Riviera. Always a reckless driver, Jack overturned a car on the way to a party near Cannes. "There was a big silence," Torby Macdonald later remembered. "We were literally standing on our heads in the overturned car. Jack looked over at me. 'Well, pal,' he said, 'We didn't make it, did we?' "[75]

War broke out in Europe before Jack returned to Harvard in late September for an intensive senior year. By this time his father was drawing fire as an outspoken isolationist and anti-Semite. (The anti-Semitism seems to have made no impression on Jack, and would be a later source of embarrassment). Father Charles E. Coughlin, the famous right-wing "radio priest,"named the ambassador "Man of the Week" in his pro-Nazi magazine *Social Justice*, and ran a full-page picture of his family on the cover.[76] The administration had become uncomfortable about Kennedy's penchant for self-glorification (his staff included a personal public relations man) and his clandestine efforts to build support for his own presidential nomination in 1940.[77]

Not much of a student during his first two years in college, Jack settled for a "gentleman's C" in most of his courses. A tutorial record written after his sophomore year reported that while he showed promise, his mind was undisciplined and "will probably never be very original." His course work concentrated on government, history, and economics.[78]

As a junior Jack took more interest in his studies, perhaps because Joe Junior was no longer on campus to drain him of his self-confidence. He labored over a paper (not available today) on an upstate New York Republican, and years later his government professor remembered it as "a very superior job of investigating" and "a masterpiece." He made the dean's list. Returning from his European travels, Jack earned Bs in all his government and economics courses. Perhaps his firsthand observations of Europe on the brink of war had sparked a new seriousness of purpose. If he submitted an acceptable undergraduate thesis, he could earn a degree with honors in political science.[79]

Jack chose to write about British appeasement at Munich, a topic sup-

plied by his father. The 150-page thesis was written in a few months with
the aid of a personal secretary and, on the day before it was due, the frantic
labors of five stenographers. The paper echoed the ambassador's sympathetic attitude toward Neville Chamberlain, arguing that there were deeper
institutional reasons for the Munich Pact. Joe Junior was unimpressed by
the finished product and reported to his father, "It seemed to represent a
lot of work but did not prove anything." Two faculty readers agreed to
accept it and award Jack magna cum laude standing. They expressed reservations, however, about poor writing and faulty analysis.[80]

The ambassador urged Jack to send the thesis to Arthur Krock of the
New York Times. Krock, who had met the elder Kennedy in 1932, when
both had worked for FDR's election, became a family intimate three
years later. Joe frequently gave the influential journalist information in
return for favorable press coverage.[81] Krock saw numerous difficulties
with Jack's paper but agreed to help the young man turn it into a book.
He gave it a new title, *Why England Slept* (a spinoff of Winston
Churchill's *While England Slept*) and recommended his own literary
agent to find a publisher. Jack liked the idea but told his father, "Whatever I do . . . will depend on what you think is the best thing." With the
ambassador's encouragement, the project got hastily under way.

Krock worked closely with Jack, later stating, "I was an editor, yes,
an adviser, and I may have supplied some of the material as far as the
prose is concerned, but it was *his* book." The ambassador saw flaws in
the argument of the emerging manuscript and recommended that Jack
work more closely with Krock on the shaky writing. He suggested some
specific and significant textual changes that Jack incorporated into the
book almost verbatim. (The book would offer a world view different in
no major way from Joe's in the spring of 1940. Indeed, the following
year, Jack sent one hundred dollars to the isolationist America First
Committee, adding, "What you are doing is vital.")[82] As the publisher's
deadline neared, the ambassador assigned his personal speech writer to
the project. The latter recalled:

> I worked two weeks on it, night and day, delivered it at four o'clock in the
> morning on the day that Eddie Moore [a Kennedy employee] was to go to
> New York and take it to the publisher. When I got it, it was a mishmash,
> ungrammatical. He had sentences without subjects and verbs. It was a very
> sloppy job, mostly magazine and newspaper clippings stuck together. I
> edited it, and put in a little peroration at the end.[83]

The thesis had been submitted on March 15, 1940. Jack graduated
cum laude in June, and the book appeared in late July. Just before it was

published, the ambassador wrote to his son, "You would be surprised how a book that really makes the grade with high-class people stands you in good stead for years to come." Joe got his friend Henry Luce, the *Time-Life* magnate, to write the introduction, and he saw that the volume was well publicized. "I cannot recall a single man of my college generation," Luce wrote, "who could have written such an adult book on such a vitally important subject during his senior year at college."[84]

Why England Slept received favorable reviews in several major newspapers, including the *New York Times*, the *New York Herald Tribune*, and the *Christian Science Monitor*. The *Boston Herald* declared that reading it was "an act of national preparedness." Luce put Jack's picture in *Time* magazine and in a lengthy review called his book "startlingly timely" and "strenuously objective."

To make the book a best-seller, the ambassador quietly purchased between thirty and forty thousand copies, storing them in the attic and basement of his Hyannis Port home. Then, too, the book's timing—it came off the presses on the eve of the Nazi blitz of England—helped sales. By August the volume was in its fourth printing; by September it made several best-seller lists. It was a Book-of-the-Month Club selection. In October, after a deal approved by the ambassador, the book was published in England. By the spring of 1941, eighty thousand copies had been sold, half of them in England. The twenty-three-year-old author, active in bookstores and in the media promoting his book, was something of a celebrity.[85]

The ambassador sent copies to Prime Minister Churchill and Harold Laski. Laski's response was brutally frank:

> For while it is a book of a lad with brains, it is very immature, it has no structure, and dwells almost wholly on the surface of things. In a good university, half a hundred seniors do books like this as part of their normal work in their final year. But they don't publish them for the good reason that their importance lies solely in what they get out of doing them and not out of what they have to say. I don't honestly think any publisher would have looked at that book of Jack's if he had not been your son, and if you had not been Ambassador.[86]

Mrs. Laski thought that in twenty years Jack would be sorry he had written it.[87] She was wrong; he would always be extremely proud of his youthful book, and his authorized biographers would echo that pride. Arthur Schlesinger, Jr., for example, lavished praise on the volume, noting that its tone was "so aloof and clinical, so different from the Churchillian history he loved, so skeptical of the notion that the individual could affect events."[88]

Jack would deny that his father suggested the topic, and he would take full credit for transforming the thesis into the book. When Blair Clark, a former Harvard roommate, reminded him years later that he had once spent six hours rewriting two chapters, Jack exploded: "What do you mean? You never did a goddamn thing on it. You never saw it."[89]

CHAPTER 4

Some Kind of Hero

⇢⟫ ⟪⇠

BY THE END OF 1940, though many envied young Jack Kennedy—he was extraordinarily wealthy, a Harvard graduate, a best-selling author, physically attractive, and capable of considerable charm—few insiders would have predicted greatness for him in any field. He could not equal Joe Junior intellectually or physically, and he seemed to most enjoy a social life in which he could spend family money, travel, and chase girls. Whether or not the elder Kennedy had larger plans for his second son remained to be seen.

With World War II under way, Joe Kennedy became a major voice in the drive to keep the United States out of the struggle. He declared his isolationism publicly, and privately he said that a Nazi victory was inevitable. The clash between the views held by the ambassador and the president grew to such proportions that in late 1940, following Roosevelt's reelection, Kennedy resigned.

In part the ambassador's outlook reflected a passionate desire to protect his sons from the fray. When American involvement became inevitable, however, Joe gave his two oldest boys their wish and let them test their family's valor in the service of the country. The experience would reveal much about Jack's character in his mid-twenties and prove to be a turning point in the young man's life.[1]

→>> <<<

After college, Joe Junior and Jack took different paths. The former, following a year of travel and study in Europe, enrolled at the Harvard Law School. Joe Junior was more than ever a reflection of his father: dashing, smart, amusing, energetic, cruel, penurious, self-centered. A former roommate remembered him as "a very tough guy. Just a little bit unfeeling; he wouldn't have been elected the most popular man in the class." Another roommate recalled, "His whole style was: 'I'm going to do this and you can follow along if you want.' Like the rest of the Kennedys, he never felt he owed anybody anything."[2]

In the family tradition, Young Joe eagerly pursued women; he and Jack competed at times for the favors of several beauties. He enjoyed horseback riding, the stock market, football games, bridge, and leisurely lunches. But Joe Junior was also serious about his studies. He was in the upper 10 percent of his freshman law class and ranked sixty-ninth out of 371 at the end of his second year. "Joe was a born lawyer," a classmate recalled. In the moot-court competitions, "He could cut you apart; the best natural speaker of any of the Kennedys."[3]

Joe Junior began to be active politically in 1940. Only twenty-four, he campaigned successfully for a seat on the Massachusetts delegation to the Democratic National Convention. At the convention, he was one of a handful of delegates who stuck with their instructions and refused to vote for FDR on the first ballot, denying the president renomination by acclamation. (Before voting, he asked Arthur Krock what he thought the ambassador would want him to do.) Afterward Joe Junior worked for Roosevelt's reelection and gave a speech before a huge crowd when the president visited Boston. He led the Harvard Committee Against Military Intervention in Europe and was a defender of his father's isolationism.[4]

Jack, on the other hand, lacked direction after his graduation. He thought about law school and considered Yale, "principally," his father wrote to the dean of the Harvard Law School, "because he felt it would be better not to be constantly in direct competition with his brother, and I rather sympathize with him in that point of view." He abandoned the idea during the summer. Jack had taken ill again, this time with ulcers, and his physicians advised him to take a year off. At the suggestion of one of Joe Junior's roommates, he traveled to California, largely to rest and enjoy the sun. He enrolled at Stanford University as a no-credit auditor in the School of Business Administration.[5]

The *Stanford Daily* heralded Jack's arrival on campus. "Everybody knew who he was," said a date, "son of the Ambassador." Jack had already developed an image. His good looks, great wealth, family connections, education, and reputation as a prominent author caused many to see exceptional qualities in the young man. The image was an appealing one to Americans—good looks combined with brains, youth with wealth—and it made for good press copy.

Jack autographed copies of *Why England Slept* for numerous admirers. ("He autographed one of his books for me," said an attractive coed: 'To Nancy whose [*sic*] heard it all before.' " She later corrected the misspelling with an eraser.) He drove around Palo Alto at recklessly high speeds in a Buick convertible, went to the opera in San Francisco, spent a weekend in Los Angeles, dined with the William Randolph Hearsts at their coastal castle, went to football games, and chased young women. Actor Robert Stack, who shared an apartment with Jack for a time, later recalled, "I've known many of the great Hollywood stars and only a very few of them seemed to hold the attention for women that JFK did, even before he entered the political arena. He'd just look at them and they'd tumble."

Friends later remembered Jack's strong attachment to his father, his charm, his casual Ivy League clothes, his poor health ("I know he had back problems because driving the car a lot made it hurt," a date said later. "I heard him mention it several times"), his keen interest in world affairs, his foul language, and his hot temper ("He had a wild temper," said a girl who once turned off a news broadcast on the car radio and suffered his wrath).[6]

Jack lasted only ninety days as a Stanford auditor, sitting in occasionally on two classes, one in political science and the other in business and government.[7] His landlady later remembered him working on his tan. James MacGregor Burns, on the other hand, would report that Jack "attended business school at Stanford for six months." Rose said that he "enrolled in courses in economics, finance, and business administration" and stayed for a semester.[8]

In mid-December 1940 Jack returned to the East and entered a Boston hospital, perhaps for his ulcer. That winter he relaxed in Charlotte, North Carolina, Nassau, and Palm Beach. In the spring he vacationed in South America for two months and became involved with the two lovely daughters of a distinguished Argentine diplomat. (The girls, who had dated Joe Junior, later visited Jack in New York on numerous occasions.) Jack's physical ills never seemed to interfere with his sexual appetite.[9]

By mid-1941 American participation in the war grew increasingly likely. College men were facing the nation's first peacetime draft, and the president declared a "state of national emergency." Joe Junior joined the Naval Aviation Cadet Program at Harvard, and when the semester ended he was sworn in as a seaman second class in the U.S. Naval Reserve. In June, he, the president's son John, and a number of other elite Ivy Leaguers reported to Squantum Naval Air Facility, near Boston, for training. "Wouldn't you know?" his father said proudly. "*Naval aviation*, the most dangerous thing there is![10]

Burns and Rose Kennedy later contended that Jack tried to join the Army that spring but was rejected due to his back condition. There is no evidence of this. They also claimed that he went through five months of strengthening exercises and then passed the Navy fitness test.[11] Careful research, however, has revealed that the ambassador pulled strings through Capt. Alan Kirk, director of the Office of Naval Intelligence and a former Naval attaché at the American embassy in London, to get both Joe Junior (who had a—no doubt minor—physical problem of some sort) and Jack past Navy physicians. When Young Joe took his physical examination at the Chelsea Navy Hospital, he reported to Kirk, "They took great care of me, and rushed me right through." In August a physician friend of Kirk's gave Jack his physical. Not surprisingly, he passed. Moreover, without any training, Jack was immediately granted a commission as an ensign in the Naval Reserve.[12]

Jack's "unstable" back should alone have disqualified him from military service. Joe Junior was angry that his father had not tried to keep Jack out of uniform for that reason. Jack would be forced, while in the Navy, to wear a corset and sleep on a board. His ulcer and his asthma could have exempted him as well. The scholars who investigated this matter wrote, "Thus, a young man who could certainly not have qualified for the Sea Scouts on his physical condition, entered the U.S. Navy."[13] But Jack, ignoring his physical handicaps, was determined to get into the action. Patriotism was undoubtedly a motive. Then too, the ambassador's boys had been trained since infancy to face a challenge with unflinching courage. The Kennedys were supposed to be tough, heroic, and above all, winners.

Jack's first assignment was a desk job at the Office of Naval Intelligence in Washington. He was there during the Pearl Harbor attack and no doubt saw some of the secret dispatches involving the tragedy. His sister Kathleen was in Washington at the same time, working for the *Times-Herald*, and there were parties and double dates. A friend of Kathleen's said later of Jack, "He wasn't that likable. But he was a fast runner and an interesting operator, a typical Don Juan. You could almost imagine him checking off names in a book." A naval colleague said, "I remember Kennedy quite well. He was a man of high intelligence, with a facile wit—a good writing hand. He also had a heavy social life. In those days he was still more or less in his playboy stage."[14]

Jack lasted only about ninety days in Washington. One of his conquests was Inga Arvad, a gorgeous, twice-married Danish woman about four years older than himself who wrote for the *Times-Herald*. What Jack didn't know was that "Inga Binga," as he called her, was suspected of being a German spy and was under surveillance by the FBI. "We had a microphone planted in her apartment and a tap on her telephone," FBI official William C. Sullivan later commented. In the 1930s Arvad had cozied up to top Nazi leaders, and Hitler had called her a "perfect example of Nordic beauty." She had also been the mistress of a Swedish journalist with Nazi connections. When Jack's relationship with the woman became known to Navy officials, the assistant director of the Office of Naval Intelligence wanted to cashier the young ensign from the Navy. A witness remembered the officer being "really frantic." Reminded of Joe Kennedy's prestige, however, the official eventually calmed down and consented merely to give Jack a speedy transfer to an ONI outpost in Charleston, South Carolina.

In Charleston, where Jack complained loudly about his duties, the affair with Arvad continued. According to Arvad's son, Jack even went AWOL on one occasion to see her in Washington. FBI wiretaps in a hotel room the couple shared frequently discovered that Jack had "disclosed to Mrs. Fejos [Arvad] in general terms his tentative official assignment plans and the fact Presidential adviser Harry Hopkins had gone to the hospital and was expected to leave same." Arvad's son later recalled that Jack wanted to marry the former Miss Denmark, and the two approached J. Edgar Hoover in person to get a formal statement clearing her of charges of espionage. The FBI director acknowledged Arvad's innocence but refused to put anything in writing. (According to a Kennedy legislative aide, Jack tried for years, while he was in Congress, to wrest the incriminating tapes from the FBI. "They must have hung over Jack's public career like a dark cloud," said the investigators who uncovered the story.) Kennedy's official Navy biography, approved while he was in the White House, omitted any reference to his stint in Washington with ONI. Not one of the several books lauding Jack's military heroism mentioned it. Robert J. Donovan's best-selling *PT 109: John F. Kennedy in World War II*, labeled by Kennedy "a highly accurate account," placed Jack in the Pentagon—which had not yet been constructed.[15]

The ambassador was well aware of his son's affair and had met (and personally tried to seduce) Arvad when Jack brought her to Hyannis Port for a visit. Indeed, Joe kept close track of all of his children and had operatives compile biographies of their steady dates.[16] Jack's desire to marry Arvad precipitated his first clash with his father. For all of his twenty-four years, Jack had almost always deferred to his father. Despite his lack of religious convictions, he continued to attend mass regularly; at Harvard he had explained to a friend, "This is one of the things I do for my father."[17] The curvacious, intelligent, and merry Arvad, however, prompted Jack to the point of rebellion.

Arvad, according to her son, thought that the ambassador's authoritarianism had warped his children. "The way she thought of it, the old man would push Joe, Joe would push Jack, Jack would push Bobby, Bobby would push Teddy, and Teddy would fall on his ass. Jack was going through a hell of a crisis about that." At first Jack resisted his father's warnings about marrying a divorced and remarried woman with a highly checkered past. But when Joe finally made his point by using his influence with Under Secretary of the Navy James V. Forrestal to have his son given sea duty status, Jack angrily accepted his fate. Arvad was appalled by the elder Kennedy. "Mother liked Jack and Kathleen," her son said, "but she couldn't figure out how two people who were that bright could stand for all that bullshit. She thought they had to want the money pretty badly."[18]

Arvad left her son vivid memories of the young man she had seriously considered marrying:

> He'd always be walking around with a towel around his waist. That's all he ever wore in the apartment—a towel. The minute he came in, he'd take off all his clothes and take a shower. He was always taking showers. She used to massage his back; he was always in bad shape because of his back. He ate steak, baked potatoes, and milk; gallons of milk and ice cream. She remembered him as very compassionate and somewhat insensitive. If he wanted to make love, you'd make love—now. They'd have fifteen minutes to get to a party and she'd say she didn't want to. He'd look at his watch and say we've got ten minutes, let's go. There was a certain amount of insensitiveness, an awful lot of self-centeredness.

Arvad recalled that Jack sought merely to pursue a very quiet life after the war, do some writing, and live off of his family income. "She felt he was a humanist—he was interested in individual people as they related to the whole. He had a great disrespect for structures, probably because of his family structure."[19]

A man who dated sister Kathleen at this time gleaned a similar insight into the young Kennedys. John White, an editorial assistant at the *Washington Times-Herald*, went out with the lively and ambitious

"Kick" often (he was cleared by the ambassador) and became a close friend. "She loved to cuddle," White later recalled. "I don't think that there had been much of that sort of thing when they were kids." But sex was out of the question; Kathleen referred to it as "the thing the priest says not to do."

One evening, as White was massaging her back, Kathleen turned suddenly and looked at him intently, almost in tears. "Listen," she said, "the thing about me you ought to know is that I'm like Jack, incapable of deep affection."[20]

>>> <<<

In the early spring of 1942, while in Charleston, Jack's poor health again began to plague him. One attack of asthma nearly choked him. His back condition was such that physicians prescribed surgery and ordered Jack to exercise in preparation. He wrote to Billings, "Dear Lemmer: I finished the ATLAS courses and believe I'm well on my way to HEALTH, STRENGTH and PERSONAL POWER, whatever Personal Power is. I can see that this time I will be Powerful, Graceful and Magnetic." Jack requested and was granted six months' inactive duty. He spent a month at the Charleston Navy Hospital and two months in Boston-area hospitals (where he proved healthy enough to visit local nightclubs and date showgirls). Instead of surgery, however, Jack received sea-duty status, courtesy of his father, and was sent to Midshipmen's School at Northwestern University. Perhaps the physicians were satisfied with the progress made by Jack's back-strengthening exercises and called off the operation. (The illness and hospitalization would go unmentioned by Kennedy and his authorized biographers.)[21]

While Jack was still in the hospital, Joe Junior graduated from flight training at Jacksonville, Florida, and received his wings and a commission as an ensign in the Naval Reserve. He had been angry that Jack received a commission first—and without earning it. Now, however, having survived a tough program with an attrition rate of almost 50 percent, Young Joe was a member of one of the most elite groups in the armed forces. The ambassador came from Palm Beach and gave an emotional address to the graduates and pinned on his son's gold wings.[22]

Jack, by contrast, had managed merely to be ill and disgruntled. At Northwestern, no doubt to compensate for his lackluster service record, he signed up for PT-boat duty. PT boats had received much attention in the press for their daring exploits during the early months of the war in the Pacific. In fact, however, the boats were dangerous, vulnerable, and militarily ineffective. Made of plywood, they carried three thousand gallons of gasoline for their three engines; one well-placed bullet could turn a vessel into a firebomb. Their engines often took on water and conked out. Their torpedoes often proved defective. Their radios, originally designed for aircraft, tended to drift off the assigned frequency. Their props produced a phosphorescent wake that could easily be detected by the Japanese. One combat skipper said later, "I think the PT publicity was drummed up mainly for American morale. Things were going badly in the Pacific. The idea of guys on a little PT boat attacking a Japanese battleship was attractive."[23]

Jack was undoubtedly intrigued by the glamour surrounding the boats and by the opportunity to be part of an elite corps—like his older brother. PTs were popular with Ivy Leaguers who had yachting and boating experience and wanted to command their own boats rather than work their way up in the hierarchy of a larger vessel. Jack told recruiters that he wanted to get into combat as soon as possible. A physical was not required, and the executive officer of the PT-boat school, who helped screen applicants, was unaware of Jack's severe back problem. In fact, the pounding absorbed by the frail PT boats meant continuous physical punishment for someone in Jack's condition. But the scrawny ensign was determined to prove himself a true Kennedy.[24]

The ambassador arranged for Torby Macdonald, Jack's Harvard roommate, to join Jack at the PT training school in Melville, Rhode Island, in the fall of 1942. Ironically, the elder Kennedy could not land an important position for himself. Immediately after Pearl Harbor he had wired the president: "In this great crisis all Americans are with you. Name the battlefront. I'm yours to command." But Roosevelt had lost confidence in Kennedy and failed to offer him anything. Wanting some sort of role, Joe secretly enlisted with the FBI as a special service contact. He promised to use Jewish friends in Hollywood as sources of information about Communists and Communist sympathizers.[25]

Most of Joe's energy during the war was to be spent on real estate speculation, including a merciless policy of driving up rents in newly purchased buildings. One realtor-associate estimated that the ambassador made more than $100 million in real estate alone. Joe attracted attention in 1945 by buying Chicago's Merchandise Mart, the world's largest privately owned building. He was frequently in newspaper gossip columns, being spotted in New York's most fashionable nightclubs and at the Hialeah and Saratoga race tracks. Rose was never with him.[26]

While Jack trained for PT duty in Melville, not far from the Kennedy summer home, he spent weekends partying in Boston and New York.

One of his favorites, a stunning starlet named Angela Greene, later remembered her date as "very casual," "very easygoing," and pleasant. She also recalled, as many others did, that Jack never carried any money. "Money meant absolutely nothing to him." The ambassador had outlawed the discussion of finance in the Kennedy home, and Jack grew up thinking very little about the subject. He charged things and borrowed (even a nickel for a candy bar) from friends and acquaintances—who learned, after much frustration, to send a bill for their expenses to the ambassador. Greene said of Jack, "I think he was very dominated by his father, by both his parents, as a matter of fact."[27]

Jack proved to be a good student at Melville, and when he graduated on December 2, 1942, he was ordered to remain as an instructor, though he badly wanted overseas duty. The decision to leave Jack behind appears to have been based on awareness of his back problem. A fellow trainee said later, "Actually, to tell the truth, he had no business being in the military service at all."[28]

In early January 1943, *PT 101*, the boat Jack used in training, was transferred to Jacksonville, Florida, to become part of a squadron permanently assigned to Panama. Jack quickly and quietly got in touch with the ambassador, who contacted Massachusetts Senator David I. Walsh, chairman of the Senate Naval Affairs Committee. Before long Jack's orders were changed and he was on his way to the Solomon Islands in the South Pacific. Kennedy wanted to be where the action was.[29]

Jack's eagerness to be in the thick of things, while courageous, can be seen as somewhat irresponsible. Navy recruiters had sought athletes to be skippers of the brittle, plywood speedboats, and physical fitness was all the more important in combat. Jack's condition was such that he had to be hospitalized during the early voyage of *PT 101* to Jacksonville and was away from his boat for thirteen days. In Donovan's worshipful *PT 109*, we read that Jack caught a cold by diving overboard to release a towline fouled in 101's props. It is just as likely that his back again needed treatment.[30]

At the same time Joe Junior was stuck in Puerto Rico making fruitless antisubmarine flights and relieving his boredom with long nights in San Juan nightclubs. He envied his younger brother for being the first to reach the real action. It meant that Jack had the first opportunity to win a medal. Rose later commented, "In their long brotherly, friendly rivalry, I expect this was the first time Jack had won such an 'advantage' by such a clear margin. And I daresay it cheered Jack and must have rankled Joe Jr."[31]

On March 28, 1943, Jack arrived on an old French liner at Espíritu Santo, a Navy staging base in the New Hebrides Islands (now Vanuatu). He was soon assigned to PT Squadron Two, then based at the village of Sesapi on the small island of Tulagi, in the Solomon Islands near Guadalcanal. By this time the Pacific War had been underway for eighteen months. The Allies had won the Battle of the Coral Sea and the crucial Battle of Midway, and Japanese troops were retreating from Guadalcanal after a bloody five-month struggle. There was a lull in the action as both sides tried to recover from exhaustion. Army and Navy officials had made the defense of New Guinea their top priority in the Pacific and had reduced the Solomon Islands to a secondary concern. There was still combat in the area, however. Japanese planes fired on the ship carrying Jack to Tulagi.[32]

During the months of battle at Guadalcanal, Japan had transported large quantities of men and supplies at night through a passage in the islands Americans called "the slot." The Navy had been unable to seal off the route, and "the Tokyo Express," as Adm. William ("Bull") Halsey labeled it, was currently reinforcing the Japanese base of Vila, on southern Kolombangara Island. PT boats, introduced into the fray in October, proved to be no match for the much-larger Japanese cruisers, destroyers, and troopships, and few believed they would ever again be used as offensive weapons in this way. Some PT men had an even less optimistic view of their boats. At New Guinea they sang:

> Oh, some PTs do seventy-five
> And some do sixty-nine
> When we get ours to run at all
> We think we're doing fine.[33]

The Navy was short of PT skippers when Jack arrived, and he was soon given command of *PT 109*. The eighty-foot boat had seen a good deal of action in the four months it had been at Tulagi, and was covered with grime and infested with rats and cockroaches when Jack took it over. By May the skipper had assembled a ten-man crew and was taking the refurbished boat out on nighttime training patrols.[34]

At Tulagi the officer was well liked and respected; his social position and great wealth, known to almost all the men, did not prove to be an obstacle. One combat-weary skipper recalled how Jack kept seeking information about the boats.

> Always questions, questions—but never in an objectionable way. He had a great sense of humor. I liked him the minute I met him. Generally, he was very quiet. He read and wrote a lot of letters. I remember he had a little

phonograph and was always playing a record, 'My Ship.' He played a lot of bridge for two cents a point. At the end, he owed me two hundred and fifty dollars.[35]

One *109* crewman, a strapping football player named Lennie Thom, became a close friend and confided in letters home that he worried about Jack's health. But the lieutenant kept his pain to himself. His first commanding officer said later, "As far as I can remember, his health was good. I don't remember any illnesses at that point. If there had been any serious problems I would certainly have relieved him of command of the 109." Jack tried to soothe his ulcer with a steady diet of ice cream, pancakes, and toasted cheese sandwiches.[36]

On May 30, the day after Jack's 26th birthday, *PT 109* was one of a contingent of boats moved eighty miles west to the Russell Islands in preparation for a large-scale invasion of New Georgia. Soon Jack and other PT skippers got into the habit of racing for the base refueling dock after all-night patrols. One morning, as Jack roared up to the dock and reversed his engines, all three conked out. The *PT 109* smashed into a corner of the dock, sending men tumbling into the water, jumping for cover, and cussing a blue streak at the embarrassed young lieutenant. The *PT 109* was sent back to Tulagi for three rebuilt engines, and for a time Jack was known as "Crash Kennedy." If he had had a less indulgent commanding officer, Jack might again have found himself in serious trouble.[37]

In mid-July, *PT 109* received orders to head for the base at Lumbari Island. Jack was at last on his way to the front lines. Earlier in the month, the Navy had been waging fierce battles against the Tokyo Express. Admiral Halsey had lost a cruiser and two destroyers in what was essentially a standoff. The fifteen to twenty PTs at Lumbari were to be used in the continuing effort to interdict the enemy's nighttime traffic, attacking vessels—mostly barges—and alerting larger ships to the presence of the Express. The Japanese countered this move with float planes, which watched for the phosphorescent wakes of PT boats and then dropped flares, exposing the PTs both to bombs and the guns aboard ships. A float plane attacked the *109* shortly after its arrival at Lumbari, wounding two Kennedy crew members with shrapnel.[38]

On the night of August 1, *PT 109*, with a crew of thirteen, was part of a fifteen-boat backup force designed to attack an express thought to be headed for Vila. The Express—four destroyers carrying nine hundred Japanese troops and seventy tons of cargo—appeared at midnight in Blackett Strait and drew fire from the assembled PT boats. The skirmish, which included float planes, lasted between thirty and forty minutes. *PT 109*, however, did not participate in the attack. When the destroyers turned on searchlights and began shooting, Kennedy hastily withdrew. Barney Ross, aboard the *109*, said later, "A lot of very strong searchlights came on. What we did was, when the searchlights came on . . . evasive action to get out of the light so we wouldn't get shot." Ross blamed the retreat on lack of training. "We probably should have trailed the thing and attacked." Jack had missed his first exposure to enemy vessels. Apologists would later place him far from the scene of action.[39]

The Express, undamaged by the PT boats, hastily unloaded and headed back through Blackett Strait. Some time after 2:00 A.M., one of the destroyers, *Amagiri*, rammed *PT 109*, sinking much of it and causing a gasoline explosion. No other Japanese destroyer had ever hit a PT boat; none ever would again. When a PT man soon asked how such an accident could have happened, Jack replied "Lieb, I actually do not know. It happened so quickly."[40]

Subsequent accounts of the disaster, some endorsed by Kennedy, would contain numerous omissions and distortions. Donovan, for example, contended that Jack was totally unaware that the destroyers had passed through Blackett Strait.[41] In fact, Jack had a good knowledge of the Express and the battle that had taken place. When it was hit, *PT 109* was part of a three-boat picket line awaiting the destroyers' return.

Available evidence suggests that Jack did not have his crew properly alert at the time. Two men were asleep and two were lying down; the radio man was with Jack and not monitoring the radio. Another PT man at the scene said later, "When I heard the 109 was hit, I asked myself, 'If I could see at fifteen to eighteen hundred yards, why couldn't other people?' I never got an answer. It could have been they were doping off." A nearby PT skipper said later, "It's amazing. You can see it at great distances. We saw that it was more or less headed right at the 109. We radioed Kennedy to look on his starboard bow. There was a bow wake coming directly toward him. No response. Nothing."[42]

Jack had only one of his three engines in gear when the destroyer was sighted, making escape impossible. A PT officer who interviewed Jack said later that this was "a bad thing to do" and strictly against squadron policy. Moreover, if Kennedy turned the wheel to attack as soon as he learned of the danger, as he later claimed he did, data reveal that within that ten-second period he helped the destroyer score a bull's-eye. Squadron Commander Thomas Glover Warfield, who supervised all the PT boats in this action, later said of Jack, "He wasn't a particularly good boat commander."[43]

Two crewmen died in the crash, which deeply disturbed Kennedy. He wrote to his parents, "It was a terrible thing though, losing those two men. One had ridden with me for as long as I had been out here. . . . He had a wife and three kids. The other fellow had just come aboard. He was only a kid himself." Jack must surely have pondered his role in the accident more than once. But he would never admit any personal responsibility. Shortly after being rescued, he bitterly blamed the deaths on other PT-boat skippers for failing to come to 109's rescue immediately.[44]

After the crash Jack ordered all hands to abandon ship. When the gasoline fire on the water's surface died about twenty minutes later, Jack ordered everyone back on the bow of the boat, still afloat. It took about three hours for everyone to be rounded up. Jack personally assisted Patrick McMahon, a forty-one-year-old machinist who was badly burned, and helped another crewman, Charles Harris, get out of his heavy jacket and sweater so he could swim back to the hulk. Several of the survivors helped their fellow crewmen in similar ways. (Only the three officers present would receive medals.) They were all in life jackets. Jack chose not to fire his flare pistol for fear of attracting float planes and enemy troops, a decision that in retrospect seems questionable. In the morning PT 109 and the men clinging to it would be clearly visible to Japanese lookouts on Kolombangara.

The hulk drifted during the night and in the morning appeared to be sinking. After midday the survivors decided to leave it and strike out for a nearby atoll about three and a half miles away. They did not know that the hulk had been spotted by an Australian naval coast watcher, Lt. Arthur Reginald Evans, from a secret outpost high on the volcano at Kolombangara. Evans and his superiors exchanged several messages during the day about 109. Fighter planes searched for the ship, and friendly natives were ordered to explore the islands for survivors. Soon PT officials were receiving urgent dispatches from Admiral Halsey and others— "everybody but the President," one officer said later—to find Kennedy. More planes were sent, and officials stayed in daily contact with Evans.

The survivors improvised a float from a large plank Jack had used to mount a 37-mm gun on the forward deck of 109. (He had removed the boat's life raft to make room for the weapon, technically a violation of Navy regulations.) With nine men clinging to and swimming behind the board, Jack towed McMahon behind him, holding a strap from the wounded man's life jacket in his teeth and doing the breaststroke. The swim took about four hours. Kennedy's effort was heroic, especially in light of his physical condition. McMahon, who had expected to die from his injuries, would be grateful for the rest of his long life.

Once on the deserted atoll, the men hid from Allied fighter planes that flew over—looking for them. A crewman said later, "We didn't do anything to try to signal them. We should have, but we blew it.'' Kennedy later told Evans that he ordered his men to hide themselves on the approach of any aircraft.

Within a half hour of crawling onto the atoll, sick and exhausted, Jack announced that he was going to swim out into Ferguson Passage with a lantern and his pistol and try to flag down a passing PT boat. Several of the men thought the idea absurd and argued against it. Jack surely had little strength left, he knew nothing about water currents in the area, and there might be sharks. Moreover, PT men might well fire at a lantern or a pistol shot in enemy waters. But Jack refused to listen and plunged off into the brush by himself. By 8:00 P.M. he was in the passage, wearing nothing but his life belt and shoes.

The journey, albeit heroic, was impulsive and reckless. Jack traveled between two and three miles in the water just to reach the passage, sometimes swimming, sometimes stumbling along on the sharp and slippery coral. There were no PT boats there that night. On the way back he almost drowned. John Hersey, who later interviewed him, wrote, ''He thought he had never known such deep trouble. . . . He stopped trying to swim. He seemed to stop caring.'' Jack made it back to the atoll at dawn, feverish and nauseated. When he wasn't passing out, he ordered Barney Ross to make the same rescue bid the following night. Ross obeyed half-heartedly, without results.

On the third day, seeking water, the men moved to another island, Jack again towing McMahon and the others using the timber. The trip took three hours. The next afternoon, Kennedy and Ross swam a quarter of a mile to explore another tiny island. Here they found a one-man canoe, some water, and a little food left by the Japanese. (If they had scouted further, they would have discovered the hulk of *PT 109*, washed up on the reef.) They also encountered two natives, sent by Evans to look for *109* survivors. Both parties thought at first they were looking at Japanese and ran for cover. The natives paddled over to where the rest of Kennedy's crew was. They now realized that they had successfully accomplished their mission and gave the nine crewmen water, food, and cigarettes. Lennie Thom, the PT's senior man in Kennedy's absence sent a note back to U.S. forces with the natives asking for immediate assistance. Jack arrived by canoe late that evening, having paddled around Ferguson Passage again trying to hail a PT boat.

On the fifth day, August 6–7, Kennedy and the natives went back to the island where Jack had left Barney Ross. There, according to Donovan, Jack scrawled a note on a coconut to be sent back with the natives, who already had the note from Thom. The natives took both messages to

Evans and then proceeded to alert U.S. authorities. Meanwhile Kennedy and Ross continued to try to rescue themselves, using a newly discovered two-man canoe to go back into Ferguson Passage. A squall almost drowned them.

The next morning seven natives in a large war canoe, sent by Evans, reached Kennedy and Ross. After the entire crew was given food and water, Kennedy returned with the natives to Evans. Two wire service war correspondents were on the PT boats that left Lumbari that night to reach the *109* crew. Tipped off about the rescue of Ambassador Kennedy's son they wanted to make the most of it. In the early hours of the next day, the mission was accomplished. All the *109* crewmen praised their skipper. "There was no question in my mind that Jack Kennedy was a legitimate hero," said one of the reporters.[45]

Navy censors were behind a crucial omission in the initial news stories: There was no mention of Evans, who was actually responsible for the rescue. Kennedy and his men were the source of several distortions. Jack, for example, was credited with three swims into Ferguson Passage, rather than one. The carved coconut received much attention, while Thom's note was ignored. And the skipper was said to have attempted to attack the *Amagiri*. "I'm certain that destroyer was going 40 knots," Jack said. "I summoned the crew to general quarters and tried to get into position for a shot with the torpedoes. But we were too close." The Associated Press story later made the front page of the *New York Times* under the headline KENNEDY'S SON SAVES 10 IN PACIFIC AS DESTROYER SPLITS HIS PT BOAT.[46]

Jack's commanding officer, Albin Peyton Cluster, recommended him for the Silver Star. "The medal was for the survival phase," he said later. "Not the preceding battle." Cluster's statement lauded Kennedy for "heroism," claimed that he had "directed the rescue of the crew and personally rescued three men," and contended that he "finally effected the rescue of his men." These assertions were no doubt investigated up the chain of command and found to be exaggerated. In any case the recommendation was downgraded to the "lifesaving" Navy and Marine Corps medal. Indeed, if the ambassador's friend Undersecretary of the Navy Forrestal had not taken action, Jack might not have received a medal at all. (Jack provided Donovan and Burns with the Cluster citation rather than the more modest and realistic statement signed by Forrestal.) Jack's friend Red Fay said later that the medal was the elder Kennedy's idea from the start. "He was going for the Congressional Medal of Honor and had the Navy Cross in mind as a fallback position."[47]

At the time, the *PT 109* affair was something of a scandal. Within minutes of the crew's rescue, the natives were ribbing the skipper, asking (in rough translation) "Aren't you an old woman for losing your boat?" The shame of losing *109* under highly questionable circumstances helped unite the crewmen behind Jack; they were all in the same jam. PT skipper Leonard A. Nikoloric said later, "There was a lot of criticism in the Navy about the loss of the 109. MacArthur is supposed to have said that Jack should have been court-martialed, but I think he denied it. Jack was actually in a lot of trouble over that, so we never said a word about it." A squadron skipper later recalled:

> This was not a little stream; it was a big strait. Kennedy had the most maneuverable vessel in the world. All that power and yet this knight in white armor managed to have his PT boat rammed by a destroyer. Everybody in the fleet laughed about that.[48]

Barney Ross was astonished to see Jack receive a medal and read an article by Pulitzer Prize–winning writer John Hersey, a friend of Jack's, on *PT 109*. Ross said later of himself and his fellow crewmen:

> Our reaction to the 109 thing had always been that we were kind of ashamed of our performance. I guess you always like to see your name in print and that Hersey article made us think maybe we weren't so bad after all. We'd never gone around saying, hey, did you hear about us? But suddenly your name's in print and Hersey made you sound like some kind of hero because you saved your own life. So I suppose my reaction to the article was to be pleased with myself. I had always thought it was a disaster, but he made it sound pretty heroic, like Dunkirk.[49]

Jack and his father would make much of the *PT 109* episode in the years ahead. Kennedy pressure (and perhaps a timely financial donation) persuaded the *Reader's Digest* to reprint a condensed version of Hersey's *New Yorker* article, which first appeared in mid-1944. (Jack carefully made sure that the *Digest* account of the crash followed Hersey's: "Kennedy saw a shape and spun the wheel to turn for an attack.") Hundreds of thousands of copies of the reprint would be distributed in Jack's campaigns of 1946 and 1952. In the race for the presidency, Jack's wartime courage was to be an integral part of the candidate's publicity. A PT boat would be hauled down Pennsylvania Avenue during the inaugural parade, and the crew of *109* would watch Jack take the oath of office. Robert J. Donovan declared in 1961, "It is even possible that he might never have reached the White House if it had not been for PT 109."[50]

The perpetual inflation of the *PT 109* story for political purposes reveals a basic lack of integrity on Jack's part. The facts of the matter reveal a very young man, in bad physical condition to begin with, who performed poorly on his PT boat and exhibited some recklessness and poor judgment in the subsequent rescue efforts. Still, Kennedy displayed genuine courage after the crash and a willingness to do all in his power to save his men. The bravery was real, however it was exaggerated in campaign literature and in authorized books.

Privately Jack could sometimes admit that he was not much of a hero. In early 1944, back in the United States, he joked about *PT 109* with Inga Arvad. According to her son, "He told her it was a question of whether they were going to give him a medal or throw him out."[51] During his 1946 congressional campaign, he became amused by the embellishments of the *109* affair, telling a friend, "My story about the collision is getting better all the time. Now I've got a Jew and a Nigger in the story and with me being a Catholic, that's great." In the White House, shortly after the Bay of Pigs disaster, Donovan tried to get Jack to talk about the night *PT 109* was hit. The president paused a few seconds, shook his head, and said, "That whole story was more fucked up than Cuba."[52]

CHAPTER 5

In His Brother's Shoes

❯❯❯ ❮❮❮

JACK REMAINED in the South Pacific for the rest of 1943. On September 1 he took command of *PT 59*, soon converted into a gunboat. Jack and his crew made thirteen patrols between October 18 and November 18, looking for Japanese barges. There was little action in the area, however. At one point *59* ran out of gas while coming to the rescue of some Marines, and several planes sent to the rescue were shot down. Jack was not responsible for the mishap but it did little to enhance his reputation. The boat chief later recalled, "There was a big stink about it." On another occasion the skipper gave orders to fire on three beached and deserted barges. This was the first and last time that Kennedy fired at an enemy surface craft during his nine months overseas.

By early November Jack was proposing a daring daylight raid into an enemy stronghold. Several of his men complained to the squadron commander and the idea was scotched. The commander said later, "Jack got very wild. Some of my old guys . . . said he was crazy and would get them killed."[1]

Jack's back suddenly began to act up in mid-November, and a physician ordered him relieved of his command. (Jack would tell John Hersey that the *PT 109* crash was responsible for his back problem. He was more candid with the examining physician.) Jack may also have had

69

malaria. Now a full lieutenant, Kennedy soon received orders to report to the PT school in Melville, and he left for the United States as soon as he was able to arrange air transportation.[2]

In early January 1944, Jack arrived in San Francisco on leave and immediately took a train for Los Angeles and the arms of Inga Arvad. (In late September he had assured the remarried beauty by letter, "knowing you has been the brightest part of an extremely bright 26 years.") Arvad soon published a syndicated newspaper story about Jack's heroics with *109*, and Jack called a press conference to talk about his experiences.[3]

Soon Jack was at home with his family in Palm Beach, where he contacted numerous friends and relatives of his PT pals still in the Solomons. This thoughtfulness would not have been predicted before the war and no doubt stemmed from the camaraderie he had learned in adversity. Jack sent photographs to Barney Ross's father, adding:

> He rode on my boat during a particularly difficult time—and I have been thankful he was with us ever since. He saved one man's life—and contributed to [a] great degree to the rescue of the entire group. For his actions through that week he was recommended for the Silver Star—and he richly deserves [*sic*].[4]

The Kennedys were in turmoil during Jack's two-week visit. Kathleen, Jack's favorite sister, had announced in England that she was going to marry William Hartington, whose father was the tenth duke of Devonshire, a pillar of the Church of England and a Freemason. The ambassador got Francis Cardinal Spellman to try to arrange things with the Vatican, but nothing could be done. Kick, to the horror of her mother (her father was quietly supportive), was prepared to violate Roman Catholic teaching for the man she loved. She would not abandon her church, however, no doubt for the sake of her family, and the result was a compromise: a civil service. The ten-minute ceremony took place in May, and Joe Junior represented the Kennedys. His parents made no public comment.[5]

Joe Junior, stationed in Cornwall and having an affair with a married woman, had defended Kathleen throughout the ordeal. Jack probably gave his support as well. Kick wrote to him in July, "I can't really understand why I like Englishmen so much, as they treat one in quite an offhand manner and aren't really as nice to their women as Americans, but I suppose it's just that sort of treatment that women really like. That's your technique isn't it?"[6]

In late February or early March, Jack was transferred to a PT shakedown unit in Miami. The duties were minimal, and the officers spent much of their time having fun. Jack specialized in the pursuit of women. One observer said later, "Girls were almost an obsession with him. We liked them too, but we didn't make a career of it the way he did." One model he chased recalled, "Jack was very cute, really a darling. He had bristly, wavy, reddish hair. Very coarse. He laughed a great deal. He was very easygoing, happy-go-lucky. I remember one day we had a cold bottle of champagne and went swimming in the ocean and drank it."[7]

In mid-June Jack underwent surgery at the New England Baptist Hospital, where he had spent so many months of his life. The disk operation was unsuccessful. Jack's weight fell to 125 and some of his visitors thought he looked terribly tired and sick. Still, he managed to keep his sense of humor. In time he typed a lengthy letter—filled with grammatical and spelling errors—to his former commanding officer, which said in part:

> I am putting in my eighth week at the hospital where things are fairly grim. Have an advanced case of bed-sores and a slight touch of scurvy—due to our inability to get any limes to mix with the mediacle [*sic*] alcohol. Should be leaving here in a few days for the Old Sailors Home, where I go before a survey board—probably to be issued a rocking chair, a sunny place on the lawn—with the thanks of a grateful Republic wringing [*sic*] in my ears.[8]

Tragedy struck the Kennedys twice during the summer of 1944. On August 12 Joe Junior was killed in the explosion of an experimental bomber designed to knock out V-1 "buzz bomb" launching ramps in France. The twenty-nine-year-old had spent eight frustrating months in England flying patrol bombers without sinking a submarine or shooting down a plane. He courageously volunteered for the top-secret and dangerous V-1 mission. Perhaps, as Arthur Krock and others have suggested, Joe Junior also wanted to disprove the charge, common among the British, that the Kennedys were "yellow." (During the Nazi Blitz the ambassador had spent evenings outside London to escape danger.)[9] Perhaps, too, he had volunteered to equal or better Jack's much-touted feat of a year earlier. The eldest son had to be number one; it was expected of him. His father had warned him in a letter, "Don't force your luck too much." But now, as Doris Kearns Goodwin has observed, "Try as his father might, it was too late to call the demons back." A navigator later recalled, "When I tried to make casual conversation I got the positive impression that I was talking about firecrackers to a man valiantly trying to perfect the atom bomb before an impossible deadline."[10]

Jack was with the family at Hyannis Port on a weekend leave when the news of his brother's death arrived. The loss particularly devastated the ambassador, who was almost never again able to mention his namesake without tears. Arthur Krock wrote that the death "was one of the most severe shocks to the father that I've ever seen registered on a human being." The elder Kennedy took some of his bitterness out on President Roosevelt, asking vice presidential candidate Truman: "Harry, what are you doing campaigning for that crippled son of a bitch that killed my son Joe?"[11]

On September 10 Billy Hartington, Kathleen's husband, was killed in France. The couple had had only slightly more than a month together before he reported to his regiment for the invasion of Normandy. Kick, who was in Hyannis Port when she received the news, soon left for England. Lady Hartington was not to return to her family, except on visits, or to her church. She was heard to remark on the religious difficulties her marriage had caused, "I guess God has taken care of the problem in His own way, hasn't He?" Billy's sister later said of Kick, "I never met anyone so desperately unhappy in my life. I had to sleep in her room night after night. Her mother had tried to convince her that she had committed a sin in this marriage, so that in addition to losing a husband, she worried about losing her soul."[12]

During the fall of 1944 Jack was an outpatient at the Chelsea Naval Hospital. He passed the time resting, exercising his extremely painful back, and collecting eulogies for a little privately printed book on his late brother entitled *As We Remember Joe*. He also continued his pursuit of attractive ladies. One companion, whose wife bitterly referred to the "male prowling thing" in a later interview, said:

> I think the conventional way we Americans look upon women—you know, romantically—escaped him. They were sort of chattel. He treated them that way. In a casual, amiable way. . . . I think he had the feeling it was a war between the sexes, in a sense. A man would always try to conquer a woman. And she was there to be conquered. Sort of a game. It was hard for him to wrap around a woman the American concept of furniture, motherhood, and all that type of thing. I'm sure it must have flowed from his father's attitude toward women.[13]

One date (who soon had to fight off the ambassador's advances) recalled:

> He was a ladies' man, the women loved him, but he didn't have much security in those days. He was very shy, and not sure of himself at all. He said he never knew if a girl liked him for himself or for his money. He said

he had a feeling that every time they look at his face they saw dollar signs.[14]

Unsure about what to do with the rest of his life after his discharge, Jack thought journalism might be a possible career. His friend Charles Spalding later observed that Jack never intended to become a serious writer. "He just automatically thought of writing in terms of current events. . . . He wasn't by nature given to that kind of prolonged introspection."[15]

That Christmas at Palm Beach, the ambassador gave Jack his orders: He was to take Joe Junior's place and enter politics. Jack resisted at first; his poor health, his lack of personal experience in the field, and his desire for a life of ease were serious arguments against a political career. And what about the Inga Arvad caper and the loss of *PT 109*? But the ambassador was not to be defied. Jack later told reporter Bob Considine, "It was like being drafted. My father wanted his eldest son in politics. 'Wanted' isn't the right word. He *demanded* it. You know my father." The ambassador boasted in 1957, "I got Jack into politics; I was the one. I told him Joe was dead and that it was therefore his responsibility to run for Congress. He didn't want to. He felt he didn't have the ability and he still feels that way. But I told him he had to." Red Fay, at Palm Beach that Christmas, remembered Jack saying, "I can feel Pappy's eyes on the back of my neck." When the war was over, Jack told his friend, "I'll be back here with Dad trying to parlay a lost PT boat and a bad back into a political advantage."[16]

Later Kennedy and his followers would try to cover up the ambassador's decisive role. Early in their acquaintance, Theodore Sorensen reported, Jack told him that he entered politics after Joe Junior's death "*not* to take Joe's place, as is often alleged, not to compete subconsciously with him, but as an expression of his own ideals and interests in an arena thereby opened to him." Arthur Schlesinger, Jr., denied what he called the "myth" that the ambassador promoted his second son. "Jack, like so many young veterans, felt the need of doing something to help the world for which so many friends had died."[17]

Jack appeared before a Naval Retirement Board right after Christmas and soon learned that he would be discharged. The final orders arrived in March, transferring him to the retired list "by reason of physical disability." The document, signed by family friend James V. Forrestal, stated, "Your incapacity is permanent, is the result of an incident of the service, and was suffered in the line of duty."[18]

In early 1945 Jack traveled to a mountain resort in Arizona to regain his health. He worked on his brother's eulogy and, on his father's advice, wrote a magazine article about postwar peace. The article was no doubt designed to keep Jack's name in the public eye. Unfortunately the finished product was so lackluster that even the ambassador could not get it published. When asked about his future plans, Jack said that he was to enter "public service." A companion recalled, "He wouldn't say 'politics' to save his life."

Jack enjoyed the swimming pool, took long walks, and, despite his bad back, went horseback riding daily. A friend said later, "He was a wild rider. He would charge his horse down a mountainside. He loved speed. He was a very daring fellow, but not that good a horseman. He was always taking chances." The ambassador, keeping close tabs on his son, called daily at 5:00 P.M., mailed frozen steaks and lamb chops (rationed and highly coveted), and sent Jack a crateful of books on labor relations when the young man expressed an interest in the subject.[19]

After a couple of months, Jack and a pal flew to Hollywood, where Jack visited Inga Arvad, among others, and went to numerous parties. One afternoon he tried to woo actress Olivia de Havilland. His friend Charles Spalding recalled, "He leaned toward her and fixed her with a stare and he was working just as hard as he could, really boring in." Apparently unimpressed, the actress said she had another engagement. "Then, taking his leave, Jack, unable to take his eyes off Olivia, put his hand on the doorknob and walked straight into the hall closet! Tennis rackets and tennis balls and everything came down on top of his head." Jack could later laugh, among friends, about his gaffe; Spalding found his self-deprecation very appealing.[20]

With Jack feeling a bit better, the ambassador wangled him a three-month stint with the Hearst newspapers as a special correspondent. He was to cover the first United Nations meetings in San Francisco and the elections in England. This was Jack's first civilian job, and he earned $750. The Hearst chain lavished praise on its new writer; the *Chicago Herald-American* declared: HERO COVERS PARLAY FOR H-A. The daily photos (in uniform) and references to his best-selling book and *PT 109* were designed to keep Jack in the public spotlight and place him at the scene of highly significant international decision making. He told Charles Spalding, "You know, as soon as I can, I'm going to run for office."

Jack's articles, labeled "a serviceman's point of view," were only about three hundred words apiece, and all of them together amounted to about one magazine article in length. Their intellectual content was very modest, and the writing was filled with references to sports. At one point

Molotov was identified as the "key man" at the conference: "This would have been true even if he had thrown the ball straight—it was particularly true when he started throwing curves."

Jack spent much of his time and energy in the social whirl surrounding the conference. He met many women in the course of many parties, including Mary Pinchot Meyer, a wealthy and talented beauty he had first encountered during her Vassar days. She was newly married, and her husband, Cord Meyer, Jr., a military aide to Commander Harold E. Stassen, had a falling-out with Jack, perhaps over the attention he paid to Mrs. Meyer. Many young women found the nearly twenty-eight-year-old bachelor intensely attractive, including columnist Austine ("Bootsie") Cassini (later Mrs. William Randolph Hearst, Jr.), who said later that Jack "looked awfully boyish and helpless, like a kid." One night at a party, lovely Anita Marcus (later Mrs. Red Fay) was swept away by the Kennedy treatment:

> I think that the main thing was that when he talked to you, he looked you straight in the eye and his attention never wandered. He was interested in finding out what I was doing there—why I was there. It was a drawing-me-out thing. It was undivided attention. I was the most envied girl in the room. He had a way with women. There's no question about it."[21]

In mid-June, Jack flew to London to cover the British elections. Kathleen greeted him and loaned him a car. Three weeks later, despite strong indications to the contrary (he heard Churchill booed mercilessly in public), Jack predicted a Conservative victory. The Tories were buried in a Labour landslide. In his election report, marking the end of his career as a journalist, Jack declared, "People are already saying 'I told you so,' which they may have done, but if they did I do not remember it."[22]

Jack also went to Ireland and traveled in Secretary Forrestal's plane to Potsdam, Germany, site of the Big Three Conference. As usual he was busy with the ladies. A beautiful British tennis star who began a lengthy affair with the young American at this time said later, "Jack had much more of an Englishman's attitude toward women. He really didn't give a damn. He liked to have them around and he liked to enjoy himself but he was quite unreliable. He did as he pleased."[23]

In London, in early August, Jack became violently ill. "I've never seen anyone so sick in my life," a friend said. "He had a hell of a high temperature. It scared hell out of me." Jack said that the attack was a recurrence of malaria, and several Navy doctors agreed. It may well have been, however, the early stages of Addison's disease, diagnosed officially two years later. This failure of the adrenal glands, often confused

by physicians with malaria or jaundice, comes on slowly, and its symp-
toms are general weakness, poor appetite, weight loss, and a yellowish or
brownish pigmentation of the skin. Jack was gaunt, appeared to be deeply
tanned, and was barely able to digest anything. In any case, he was back
on his feet in a few days and returned to the United States with Secretary
Forrestal.[24]

→≫≫   ≪≪←

The ambassador was determined that Jack should bear the full responsibility he had assigned to Joe Junior. James Reed, a family friend,
recalled an evening with the elder Kennedy, Honey Fitz, and Jack. Fitzgerald:

> proposed a toast to the future President of the United States—he looked
> right at Jack—to which everyone joined in. It was not really said in any
> degree of levity or frivolity. It was a serious toast, really, that was pro-
> posed to Jack, and I think everyone there thought that one day Jack would
> be President of the United States.[25]

The ambassador thought that Massachusetts was the best place to
launch Jack's career, even though the Kennedys spent only the summers
there. "I'm willing to come back [to Massachusetts] to live," he told
Time magazine, "because this is where my heart is." In April 1945 he
got his friend Governor Maurice J. Tobin to appoint him cochairman of
a committee making an economic survey of the state. While on the road
collecting data and portraying himself as the champion of the state's
prosperity, the elder Kennedy made contacts, lined up supporters, and
organized a group of experienced advisers. He also made sure that Joe
Junior's Navy Cross received maximum publicity (he had pushed for the
Congressional Medal of Honor), he had Secretary Forrestal name *Destroyer 850* the USS Joseph P. Kennedy, Jr., he created a scholarship in
Joe Junior's name, and he gave newly released details of his son's death
to the press. Before long, a new VFW post bearing Joe Junior's name
would be founded in Boston, and Jack would be its president. Heroism,
sacrifice, and generosity seemed indelibly linked with the name
Kennedy.[26]

Joseph Francis Timilty, a close associate of the ambassador's and a
former Boston police commissioner, said later that the ambassador was
"*the* mastermind" of all of his son's political campaigns. "And he was
completely in charge of everything, every detail." Edward M. Gallagher,
a longtime business assistant and personal friend (Ted was named for
him), later commented on the ambassador's role in 1945–46: "He was,

without question, the manager of that political campaign in every sense of the word. The mastermind." Mark Dalton, the official head of Jack's 1946 effort, said later, "the Ambassador was the essential, real campaign manager."[27]

Jack and his partisans would later attempt to dismiss the elder Kennedy's importance. "Kennedy won his first big race mainly on his own," Burns wrote, and his father's activities "probably had only a small effect on the outcome." Dave Powers contended that there was practically no Kennedy money in the campaign and that Jack "deftly moved his father's old political cigar-smoking friends into the background and replaced them with new young faces." Kenny O'Donnell said in 1976 that Joe Kennedy "no longer knew a goddamn thing about what was going on in Massachusetts."[28]

The ambassador was soon directing his attention toward the congressional seat from the Eleventh District, a predominantly blue-collar, Irish and Italian area centered in Cambridge and portions of Boston and including Somerville, Charlestown (home of the Boston Navy Yard), and a part of the suburb of Brighton. P. J. Kennedy and Honey Fitz had started their political careers in the District, and the latter had represented it in Congress. Both Joe and Rose were born there, and Joe had gone into banking within it. Many people might identify with the name John Fitzgerald Kennedy.

The seat was currently held by James Michael Curley, the shady (he was under federal indictment) old pol who had long been Honey Fitz's nemesis. In May 1945 the congressman stunned political observers by announcing that he would run for mayor of Boston, an office he had held from 1922 to 1926 and again from 1930 to 1934. The Kennedy strategy was that if Curley won in the fall election, Jack would pursue his vacated position. In the meantime Jack would move to Boston and spend several months getting acquainted with the district's people. His political ambition was not to be discussed publicly.

Without an occupation, Jack had ample time to prepare himself for his new career. He wrote a speech entitled "England and Germany: Victor and Vanquished" and tried it out at the Hyannis Rotary Club (where the ambassador had spoken two months earlier). Leo Damore, who would write *The Cape Cod Years of John Fitzgerald Kennedy*, recalled:

> The speech was not a memorable one. . . . In a voice somewhat scratchy and tensely high-pitched, Jack Kennedy projected a quality of grave seriousness that masked his discomfiture. No trace of humor leavened his talk. Hardly diverging from his prepared text, he stood as if before a blackboard

addressing a classroom full of pupils who could be expected at any moment to become unruly. Although he was not a natural speaker, some of his own personality irrepressibly shone through. Stumbling over a word, he flashed a quick, self-deprecating grin that, a member of his audience remembered, "could light up the room." An appealing waif-like quality showed through, and above all a winning sincerity impressed his audience more than did the frequently high-flown language of his speech.

Jack was extremely thin; his shirt collar and suit seemed too large. One Rotarian thought he looked like "a little boy dressed up in his father's clothes." Damore recalled, "Jack Kennedy more closely resembled a high-school senior chosen as Boys' State representative . . . than a young man on the threshold of his political career." Jack gave the same speech many times that fall in appearances arranged by the ambassador's advertising agency.[29]

Curley won in November, but the ambassador delayed the announcement of his son's candidacy. He was toying briefly with an offer to run Jack for lieutenant governor. Moreover, an early declaration would only solidify the opposition. Jack already had one formidable opponent, Michael Neville, the highly popular mayor of Cambridge, and there would be others. Several Democratic insiders knew what the ambassador was up to, but few gave his son much of a chance. Democratic state legislator (later Speaker of the House) Thomas P. ("Tip") O'Neill said that he was among those who were "pooh-poohing Kennedy because he was a young, skinny, frail-looking kid, a carpetbagger whose father lived in Palm Beach."[30]

Jack established his legal residence in the Eleventh District in early January 1946 by renting a room at the Bellevue Hotel on Beacon Street next to the State House. (Eighty-three-year-old Honey Fitz was living in retirement in the building.) Here Jack was instructed in the art of practical politics by Joe Kane, a cousin of the ambassador's who, at sixty-six, had long been known as one of the city's shrewdest politicos. (Rose would call him an "experienced realist.") Kane coined a campaign slogan, "The New Generation Offers a Leader," and helped make the decision to run Jack as a war hero. Given the fact that the twenty-eight-year-old had never held a regular job or run for office, the options were limited.[31]

Kane and Joe Timilty recruited a group of young working-class volunteers from the district. The Kennedy public relations men dubbed them the "junior brain trust" and portrayed them as the vital force behind Jack's campaign. One was Billy Sutton, who became Jack's secretary and helped recruit Dave Powers. James F. Kelley turned out to be an invaluable loyalist. Another was Peter Joseph Cloherty, who was soon putting in twelve-hour days handling Jack's appointments and correspondence. Cloherty's activities, like those of the other leading volunteers, were carefully monitored by the ambassador. Cloherty said later that Jack's father "was the number one political expert around there. Very serious—the most serious of all."[32]

Scores of volunteers from throughout the district were attracted to the still-undeclared Kennedy campaign in large part by Jack's good looks and charm. Anthony Galluccio of Cambridge said later, "Kennedy was very personable, very relaxed, casually dressed with his hair all tousled. He had a very easy manner. People liked to help him. He could win people over." Women often responded viscerally. John J. Droney, another Cambridge volunteer, recalled, "The older ladies seemed to mother him; all of the young ones fell in love with him." There were also a few old friends from Choate, Harvard, and the Navy on hand. Others, of course, sought jobs and favors. One old pol, Patrick J. ("Patsy") Mulkern, blurted out to Jack one day, "I'll tell ya da troot. Every guy tells ya dere witcha. Well, I'll tall ya da troot. I don't know if *I'd* be witcha if ya wasn't a millionaire."[33]

By early February Jack was working full-time in the district, giving speeches and walking the streets introducing himself, "He got no more than four and a half hours' sleep every night for four months," Billy Sutton recalled. At first, it was exceedingly difficult for the inexperienced young millionaire to rub elbows with the voters. An older adviser from East Boston said later, "He was very retiring. You had to lead him by the hand. You had to push him into the poolrooms, taverns, clubs, and organizations. He didn't like it at first. He wanted no part of it."[34]

In time Jack improved. A young veteran later observed, "Billy Sutton brought Jack around. He was very, very thin, sort of shy, but easy to meet." Still, Kennedy would not develop into the aggressively gregarious Irish politico familiar to Bostonians. O'Neill recalled, "He hated crowds. When we went into a hall together, he'd inadvertently look for the back door. It was said that Jack Kennedy was the only pol in Boston who never went to a wake unless he had known the deceased personally."[35]

Although he worked on his delivery with a tape recorder, Jack was still an ineffective public speaker. Anthony Galluccio recalled, "He was a lousy speaker when he started. He wasn't forceful. It was pathetic. . . . The only thing, he was *quick*. And relaxed and smiling and informal." When Joseph de Guglielmo first encountered Kennedy, he thought he looked like "an underfed, scrawny baby" and did not sound much better. "He wasn't so suave in those days." Years later, Eunice recalled her father carefully going over speeches with Jack, giving the young man much-needed encouragement and praise. "I can still see the two of them sitting together, analyzing the entire speech and talking about the pace of delivery to see where it had worked and where it had gone wrong."[36]

Many opposed Kennedy's bold effort, of course. One Boston pol made the press by saying that Jack ought not to run for Congress when he had never even held a seat in the Boston City Council. Daniel F. O'Brien, a Mike Neville lieutenant, told Jack to his face that he was an interloper and carpetbagger. When O'Brien and some colleagues confronted the ambassador with the charge and offered to "give Jack a shot later on," Joe "coldly sat back in his chair" and said, "Why you fellows are crazy. My son will be President in 1960." Harvard historian Arthur Schlesinger, Jr., flatly turned down a bid to support Kennedy (a decision he chose not to mention in his books on JFK). Anthony Galluccio later recalled, "He gave me the intellectual stuff. He said Jack's father never did anything creative." and that the ambassador "was only interested in making money, and this sort of stuff."[37]

Jack's back gave him much trouble during the campaigning. "The guy was in agony," Patsy Mulkern said later. He had a hot bath, a rubdown, and a nap daily—and kept going. He frequently looked ill. One Charlestown worker recalled, "He was very yellow." State Senator Robert L. Lee said, "My first impression was that he was a very sick boy." Jack made it clear to John Droney that he was in the race only because of his father. "Sometimes we all have to do things we don't want to do." He told a group of campaign workers during a rare moment of discouragement, "I'm just filling Joe's shoes. If he were alive, I'd never be in this." One afternoon, a veteran journalist found Jack in the back room of his Bellevue Hotel campaign headquarters weeping with fatigue and expressing disgust at what he had been forced into.[38]

On April 10 the *New York Times* announced that Jack's nomination papers were circulating, "but Mr. Kennedy said the action was without his consent." The formal candidacy was declared on April 22. The primary that year was in June, to give men in the armed services more time to mail absentee ballots for the November elections. The winner of the primary in the heavily Democratic Eleventh District was almost certain to be Curley's successor.[39]

Jack made some 450 speeches (written by the ambassador's public relations firm), climbed endless flights of tenement house stairs, walked the streets for thousands of hours, and appeared at scores of well-planned rallies, forums, and house parties. (He tried to cover at least a half dozen house parties in one evening.) He lived largely on candy and ice cream.

After a five-mile walk on a hot day in Charlestown in the annual Bunker Hill Day parade, Jack collapsed. "He appeared to me as a man who had probably had a heart attack," said Robert L. Lee. "Later on I found out it was a condition which he picked up, probably malaria or yellow fever." The public did not see the collapse. (Dave Powers, in his later account of the parade, did not mention it.) Later that night, Jack was pumping hands all over Charlestown.[40]

All the Kennedys pitched in to help the candidate. Rose gave a few talks and presided over a reception and tea that attracted fifteen hundred Cambridge women. Eunice, the most aggressive of the Kennedy girls ("If that girl had been born with balls," said the ambassador, "she would have been a hell of a politician"), labored in Cambridge and in the main campaign office in Boston. She also appeared at house parties, as did Pat and Jean. Bobby, just out of the Navy and a stint on the *Joseph P. Kennedy, Jr.*, worked in three wards in tough East Cambridge. Even fourteen-year-old Teddy ran errands. Bobby drafted his Harvard friend Kenny O'Donnell to perform an assortment of duties. Jean brought her college roommate Ethel Skakel (later Mrs. Robert Kennedy) along to lend a hand.[41]

The ambassador quietly orchestrated the entire campaign. He was constantly on the telephone with aides and others useful to the cause. "He'd keep you on the phone for an hour and a half, two hours," said Mark Dalton. He had total control of financial disbursements and spent lavishly—perhaps as much as three hundred thousand dollars. There were five campaign offices in the district. At one point professional pollsters were employed. Kennedy billboards and posters were everywhere (a single streetcar might have as many as four placards), and the radio advertising was intensive. Leaflets and pamphlets stressing the candidate's wartime heroism (Jack was the only veteran in the race) were distributed by the thousands, and one hundred thousand reprints of the *Reader's Digest* version of John Hersey's *PT 109* article reached voters the day before the election.

Tip O'Neill later recalled that the Kennedys offered a number of large families fifty dollars in cash to help out at the polls. "They didn't really care if these people showed up to work. They were simply buying votes, a few at a time, and fifty bucks was a lot of money." The hosts of cocktail parties and teas were given a hundred dollars, ostensibly to cover the cost of housecleaning.

Joe was said to have bragged that with the money he was spending he could elect his chauffeur to Congress. Perhaps not, but some wags wore a twenty-dollar bill in their lapel, calling it a Kennedy campaign button. Jack would report to the Massachusetts secretary of state that there were no campaign contributions or expenditures. (The ambassador later suggested to publisher Henry Luce that he buy a safe congressional seat for his son Hank. When Luce said that he doubted the possibility of such an action, the elder Kennedy replied, "Come on, Harry, you and I both know how to do it. Of course it can be done.")[42]

Opponents learned that the ambassador could be rough. When former Boston City Councilman Joseph Russo declared his candidacy, the Kennedy forces recruited another man with the same name to run, thereby reducing the councilman's vote. Another candidate was paid $7,500 to "stay in or get out," depending on what was later needed.

Kennedy opponent Mike Neville discovered that William Randolph Hearst's *Boston American* refused to mention him during the last sixty days of the campaign and would not even accept his paid advertising. Tip O'Neill later explained that the ambassador had given financial assistance to the Hearst empire a decade earlier and was now requesting a favor in return.[43]

There were no authentic issues in the campaign. Jack stressed his military record, saying in one speech that he recalled a promise made in the Solomons: "When ships were sinking and young Americans were dying . . . I firmly resolved to serve my country in peace as honestly as I tried to serve it in war." (O'Donnell and Powers would later assert, "Although Kennedy's supporters played up his war record during the primary campaign, Jack himself seldom mentioned it and squirmed uncomfortably when he was introduced as a war hero.") He publicly favored things that the voters clearly wanted, such as veterans' housing, a strong U.S. military, an extension of Social Security benefits, a rise in the minimum wage to sixty-five cents, and the modernization of Congress. He opposed communism, fascism, Nazism, and socialism.[44]

Selig H. Harrison, then editor of the *Harvard Crimson*, recalled that Jack did not like to be pinned down to a specific platform. He preferred merely to be labeled a Massachusetts Democrat. "I'm not a doctrinaire. I'll vote the way I see them." Billy Sutton said later that deep down, Jack was "an ultraconservative" like his father. A story in *Look* magazine, part of a national media campaign sponsored by the ambassador, called Jack a "fighting conservative."

Tip O'Neill later wrote, "Looking back on his congressional campaign, and on his later campaigns for the Senate and then for the presidency, I'd have to say that [JFK] was only nominally a Democrat. He was a Kennedy, which was more than a family affiliation. It quickly developed into an entire political party, with its own people, its own approach, and its own strategies."[45]

Jack's opponents added little to the quality of the rhetoric. John F. Cotter of Charlestown used the Reds-in-government issue popular in 1946 and implied that the ambassador favored British-style socialism. The "real" Joseph Russo attacked the Kennedys as carpetbaggers and spendthrifts. One newspaper ad declared:

CONGRESS SEAT FOR SALE
No Experience Necessary.
Applicant must live in
New York or Florida
Only millionaires need apply.[46]

Jack was the favorite as the primary neared, and on June 18 he won by a landslide, taking 42 percent of the vote. He outpolled his nearest rival, Neville, two to one. Others were in statewide battles for governor and senator, but it was Jack who made the headline in the *New York Times*, "Kennedy Makes Political Bow," and who was awarded a large photograph showing him walking to the polls with his grandmother, Mrs. Fitzgerald. The ambassador also saw to it that *Time* magazine ran a sizable story on the race in its National Affairs section, stressing Jack's military heroism and describing him as "grave, earnest, teetotaling" and yet quite folksy. "A boyish-looking bachelor of 29, he worked hard to prove he was no snob."[47]

Jack soon left Boston for a six-week vacation. He went first to New York (and Inga Arvad) and then to Los Angeles, where he visited a few celebrities (he bragged to Red Fay about seeing Sonja Henie) and dated starlets. He started an affair with the lovely actress Gene Tierney—then married to fashion designer Oleg Cassini—that would last for about a year, until Jack announced that he could not marry her. Tierney later had difficulty explaining Jack's charm, but her attempt made it clear that she was another victim of the Kennedy treatment:

He made you feel very secure. . . . Gifts and flowers were not his style. He gave you his time, his interest. He knew the strength of the phrase, "What do *you* think?"[48]

Jack's friend Charles Spalding was with him in Los Angeles and later recalled how intensely concerned Jack was with his public image. He began to ponder the attraction of stars like Gary Cooper, Spencer Tracy, and Clark Gable and wonder if he had the same kind of personal magnetism. "We'd spend hours talking about it."[49]

The fall election was largely a formality, and Jack's campaign activities were minimal. The ambassador further elevated the Kennedy name by donating six hundred thousand dollars to Archbishop Richard Cushing—through the Joseph P. Kennedy, Jr., Foundation (John Fitzgerald Kennedy, president)—for a children's hospital in Boston. In early September Jack served as chairman of a thirty-thousand-member VFW convention in Boston and made headlines by backing a resolution endorsing a public housing bill. He marched in a Columbus Day parade and gave a few speeches. On November 5, Jack polled 60,093 votes to his Republican opponent's 26,007. Elsewhere in the state, as in the nation, the GOP was scoring huge victories.[50]

This frail, frolicsome young man had proved beyond a doubt that he was worthy of the Kennedy name and that—with his father's extraordinary assistance, to be sure—he was a winner.

The loser, however, was the voter, who was unable to tell the difference between the handsome young war-hero candidate and the reality of the forces that assured his election. This political debut revealed a pattern of conduct by the Kennedys that would be displayed in all of Jack's future campaigns: control by the ambassador, extravagant expenditure, shady tactics, fuzzy issues, and unlimited energy.

It is doubtful that this first campaign engaged Jack on a deep level, either intellectually or morally. He was not forced to devise a meaningful political agenda or develop the moral qualities that have historically been associated with effective leadership. The candidate was responsible chiefly for the charm. Others took care of the rest.

Jack would soon tell a close friend, Congressman George Smathers, that he wanted to be a writer and had gone into politics only because his father had ordered him to stand in for Joe Junior.

> He told me the agony he suffered in going around sticking out his hand to people he'd never met, never seen, and saying, 'I'm Jack Kennedy. I'm a candidate for Congress.' And they'd look at him [and think] 'Why, you're not old enough to be the babysitter.'[51]

CHAPTER 6

His New Career

⇥⟫ ⟪⇤

THE MANTLE had fallen to Jack. Although few Kennedy insiders expected him to wear it with the same intellect, ambition, and drive as Joe Junior would have, he had proved in the Massachusetts campaign that he would work hard to win and that the voters could respond warmly to him. At the age of twenty-nine, Jack faced a new career with the clear understanding that this was only the first step in fulfilling his father's desire to place a son in the White House.

After the election Jack visited friends in New York, including Inga Arvad. Back in Palm Beach, he courted twice-divorced socialite Durie Desloge, one of Joe Junior's favorites. (A later story would erroneously report their marriage.)[1] Inevitably, as 1946 came to a close, the congressman-elect had to think less about his social life and begin turning his attentions to his new career.

Jack had a residence and office in both Boston and Washington. He rented a three-room apartment on Bowdoin Street in an older building facing the State House and used it for the rest of his life as his legal address. In the nation's capital Jack rented a three-story row house in Georgetown, sharing it with twenty-four-year-old Eunice, a Justice Department employee (and now his official hostess); Billy Sutton; one of the family cooks; and a black valet provided by Arthur Krock.

To keep control of things, the ambassador placed Frank Morrissey, widely thought to be his "eyes and ears," in charge of Jack's Boston office. Grace Burke, the office secretary, kept a log of every visitor and gave it to the elder Kennedy. Timothy ("Ted") Reardon, Joe Junior's ever-loyal Harvard roommate, was put in charge of the Washington office, and the ambassador offered him money to report on Jack's activities. There was even a maid in Jack's Georgetown home who reported to the ambassador.[2]

Joe Kennedy heralded his son's entry into politics by engineering (a press agent and other friends quietly lobbied at least one judge) his selection by the United States Chamber of Commerce as one of the "ten most outstanding young men of the year." The award was given "for civic responsibility and fighting for veterans' housing." In a ceremony in Chicago, Jack shared the stage with Arthur Schlesinger, Jr., among others.[3]

In the postwar world Americans faced enormous problems involving housing, labor, inflation, farm prices, education, civil rights, and the containment of communism overseas. Republicans, stressing President Truman's initial inadequacies and failures, carried both houses of Congress in 1946 and won governorships in twenty-five states. The Eightieth Congress, which Congressman Kennedy entered, promised to be in harmony with a new mood of conservatism sweeping the country.

Jack was one of fifteen Massachusetts members of the House. Appointed to the District of Columbia Committee, he also gained a seat on the more prestigious House Committee on Education and Labor (perhaps because of the friendship between Rose and minority whip John McCormack). He was soon asked to serve as well on a subcommittee of the House Veterans' Affairs Committee. With labor and veterans' housing two of the hottest issues in the country, Kennedy's opportunities for making headlines were considerable, despite his junior status.[4]

Instead, Jack took little interest in his work. Mary Davis, his highly experienced and efficient Washington secretary, later recalled that the congressman was "rather lackadaisical" and "didn't know the first thing about what he was doing." The situation would improve only very slightly. In the six years Davis worked for Kennedy, she said, "he never did involve himself in the workings of the office. He wasn't a methodical person. Everything that came into the office was handed to me." When she would complain about the backlog of business, Jack's response was often, "Mary, you'll just have to work a little harder."[5]

Jack's poor health was part of the problem. Davis recalled, "He had malaria, or yellow jaundice or whatever, and his back problem." His friend Congressman George Smathers later recalled that he was "constantly laid up." Billy Sutton said that on one of Jack's frequent trips to Boston, "He got very, very sick. I never saw anything like it." Richard Bolling, later a Missouri Congressman, remembered, "He was a frail, sick, yellow man when I saw him in 1947."[6]

It was obvious to insiders that Jack did not like being a congressman. He felt uncomfortable with many of his older, more experienced and knowledgeable colleagues. He was often mistaken for a House page and was once thought to be an elevator operator. More than a few congressmen grumbled at the casual, sloppy, and unmatched clothes he wore on the House floor. Jack especially disliked the backslapping that went with politics. Smathers recalled, "he was very, very shy and diffident by nature." Jack was clearly not at ease in his new position. Supreme Court Justice William O. Douglas said later that time was heavy on Jack's hands: "he had nothing of all-consuming interest. . . . He never seemed to get into the mid-stream of any tremendous political thought, or political action, or any idea of promoting this or reforming that—nothing."[7]

Jack spent many long hours fantasizing about being a heroic athlete. "Football!" Billy Sutton said later. "If you could figure that out, you'd have the real key to his character. He really cherished this dream of being a great football star. He was always talking about Otto Graham of the Cleveland Browns and people like that." Despite his physical problems, Jack spent much time in a Georgetown park playing a rough game of touch football. Said Sutton, "I honestly think he'd rather have been a pro football quarterback than president."[8] Jack would have to mature considerably in the years ahead to convince insiders that he possessed the qualities of mind and character to be an effective chief executive.

While Jack cared little for the formal social life in Washington, he and Eunice gave scores of parties in their Georgetown home. One guest later thought the affairs "wonderful." "We played a lot of games—charades, murder, sardines, twenty questions, and so on." Young veterans Richard Nixon and Joe McCarthy, both elected to Congress for the first time along with Jack, got along well with the Kennedys and were frequent guests. Eunice especially enjoyed McCarthy's company.[9]

Jack continued to spend much of his time pursuing attractive young women. Tip O'Neill later recalled that "he had more fancy young girls flying in from all over the country than anyone could count." Anthony Galluccio, a friend, thought Jack emotionally immature. "He had no depth of emotion. . . . He was like a kid. He really liked girls. . . . But Kennedy never got emotionally involved. He'd sleep with a girl and then he'd have Billy take her to the airport the next day." One woman close to Jack and Eunice said later, ''The young girls—the secretaries and the airline hostesses—they were safe grounds. They were not going to make intellectual or strong demands on him which he wasn't ready to fulfill.'' She thought Jack ''capable, but not ready for deep commitment, either politically or romantically.''[10]

The ambassador kept a sharp eye on his son. He fretted about his health, filled his head with opinions and information, and recommended advisers. Jack told Lem Billings at one point, ''I guess Dad has decided that he's going to be the ventriloquist, so I guess that leaves me the role of dummy.''[11]

The ambassador also went after many of his son's girlfriends. ''He asked a lot of personal questions—*extraordinarily* personal questions,'' said one young woman who accepted an invitation to dinner. Joe later appeared in her bedroom one night while she was visiting Eunice at the Cape and gave her a romantic kiss goodnight. The doors to Eunice's room were open. ''I remember thinking, 'How embarrassing for Eunice.' '' Jack told friends about the time a sister's friend awoke one evening at Hyannis Port and found the ambassador taking off his robe as he whispered, ''This is going to be something you'll always remember.'' Jack would smile as he told women visitors, ''Be sure to lock the bedroom door. The Ambassador has a tendency to prowl late at night.''[12]

The ambassador was paying most of Jack's personal and office expenses. Congressmen earned only twelve thousand dollars a year at the time plus a small expense allowance. Jack continued to have virtually no understanding of his own finances, almost never carried money, and was constantly mooching ''loans'' from friends, staff members, and dates. At the ambassador's request George Smathers tried to talk to Jack about the matter, but without success. ''His mind was just not geared to that sort of thing,'' Smathers said later. When Jack did think about money, often, like his parents, he was extremely penurious, complaining about such small items as the price of gasoline. He once chewed out Patsy Mulkern for eating peaches from the Hyannis Port icebox. He went shopping with Smathers and selected a suit ''with cloth so cheap and inferior it was embarrassing.'' Hardworking Mary Davis labored for a modest sixty dollars a week and was unable to persuade her boss even to discuss a raise. ''He'd say, 'Mary, I can get any number of secretaries from Boston for sixty dollars.' ''[13]

Jack's close friends in Washington, Smathers aside, were the old buddies, pranksters, and ex-athletes he liked around him and whose loyalty was total. They especially liked Jack's earthy sense of humor, and his passion for gossip and intrigue. Columnist Rowland Evans said later,

"Jack was simply the most appealing human being I ever met. He loved people—not in the intimate sense perhaps, but he loved their humanness. He loved conversation. The more personal and gossipy the more he loved it. Whenever you had inside, salacious stuff, he wanted to hear it." George Smathers thought that Jack "had a great sensitivity and was aware of who was happy, who was unhappy. I've never seen Jack Kennedy do an unkind thing, unless he intended to do it and thought about it and wanted to do it, and tell somebody else."[14]

The dark side of these relationships was the fact that members of Kennedy's inner circle were required to be obsequious; it was an ironclad condition of friendship—another sign of Jack's immaturity and insecurity. If he was not the tyrant his father was, he was nevertheless, in his own way, a bully. Jack called on the likes of Billy Sutton, Lem Billings, Dave Powers, Red Fay, and Kenny O'Donnell to brighten his spirits, entertain at parties, join him in athletic events, and run errands. Sutton, for example, was often asked to tell funny stories and do impersonations. Mary Davis called him "the court jester." Jack would introduce him to visitors as Billy Sutton "of the Suttons from Boston" and would add, "Billy, please don't tell them how you made all your money." For years Red Fay would be ordered to bellow the song "Hooray for Hollywood" at gatherings of all sorts. Ted Reardon spent hours tossing and catching footballs in the Washington office. Dave Powers fixed breakfasts on the campaign trail.

Jack's pals were often the butt of his jokes, and they sometimes felt the sting of his temper. Pierre Salinger later wrote of "his bristling temper, his cold sarcasm." Reardon was later described as "awfully kind of beaten, you know?. . . He should have gotten out. But he never did." Patsy Mulkern later complained of the Kennedys' impersonal approach toward everyone—"Take it from me, there's nobody close to them"— and noted that Jack's close friends "never went anyplace in public life." Few members of the inner circle (Sutton was an exception) rebelled. In return for their loyalty, Jack gave them modest jobs, travel, entertainment, and what Fay called "the pleasure of his company." It was this "pleasure" experienced by his inner circle—the aura of his charm, humor, good looks, wealth, and political office—that would ultimately attract and engage a far wider audience that would also be willing to overlook the indiscretions and inadequacies in order to bask in Kennedy's light.[15]

Many noticed the impersonal or insensitive side of Jack's behavior. A labor leader who had drinks in a Washington hotel with the congressman was startled by what he considered to be the young man's selfcenteredness. In the middle of a story about Honey Fitz, Jack interrupted with a question about a floor vote. It was obvious that his mind was elsewhere. A few minutes later he again interrupted the story with an unrelated question. A colleague who was present said later, "The thing is that if you had told Kennedy he had hurt the man's feelings, he honestly wouldn't know what you were talking about, any more than you had walked and stepped on an ant."[16]

On the Hill Jack's friends tended to be conservatives. According to Smathers (himself a conservative), he got along well with Southern Democrats Richard Russell and Spessard Holland and greatly admired Republican Robert A. Taft of Ohio (one of the ambassador's favorites). Jack also liked Charles Kersten, a right-wing Republican from Milwaukee who was a close friend of Joe McCarthy and Richard Nixon.[17]

Kersten, Kennedy, and Nixon were members of the highly conservative Education and Labor Committee. In March the Committee looked into the charge that a lengthy strike at Milwaukee's huge Allis-Chalmers corporation had been instigated by Reds in the United Auto Workers local. Harold Christoffel, honorary president of the striking local, and Robert Buce, president, testified that they were not and had never been members of the Communist party. Both charged that the committee was engaged in strikebreaking—which it no doubt was.

Jack interrogated Christoffel at length, revealing a competent grasp of the evidence against the witness. In an exchange with Buce, he was less impressive, revealing a sophomoric approach to political ideology: "I think I would like to inform you what I believe to be the main difference between socialism in England and socialism in Russia. They have a freedom of opposition which they do not have in Russia."

The committee then summoned ex-Communist Louis Budenz, who repeated charges made earlier to the *Milwaukee Journal* that the two officials had been Communists and that the party had ordered a 1941 strike at the same plant. Jack quickly moved that the labor leaders be cited for perjury. The motion was ruled out of order, but a subcommittee chaired by Kersten and including Kennedy was sent to Milwaukee to investigate possible perjury charges. Kersten would later describe Jack's motion as "like one of the shots fired at Concord Bridge. It was the opening skirmish between Congress and the American Communist conspiracy." Adlai Stevenson, campaigning in 1960, would ask, "I wonder how many of you know that it was Congressman Kennedy and not Senator Nixon who got the first citation of a Communist for perjury?"

In fact, Congressman Kersten was largely responsible for the research and the hearings that followed, as well as for Christoffel's eventual conviction. (He would later recommend Louis Budenz to Joe McCarthy, and the two joined hands in promoting the second Red scare.) Jack arrived late in Milwaukee and said little. But the impression he had given as a hard-line anti-Communist was undoubtedly popular with his constituents. And it was certainly greeted with approval by the ambassador, whose ultraconservative outlook on internal subversion helped cement his friendship with FBI Director J. Edgar Hoover.[18]

On the Education and Labor Committee and elsewhere, Jack responded largely to the sentiments of the people who had elected him. The great majority of his constituents, as James MacGregor Burns described them, were "immigrant Catholic, liberal on economic and social matters, conservative on issues of public education and civil liberties, rigidly anticommunist, somewhat isolationist." Jack was active in the fight for public housing, favored federal aid to parochial schools, sought to broaden Social Security, wanted higher minimum-wage provisions, voted for liberalized immigration laws, and backed price and rent controls. He opposed the antiunion Taft-Hartley Act, backing Truman's veto. Burns pointed to "his solid support of market-basket liberalism" as the explanation for Jack's high rating among liberals.[19]

But Jack was not a liberal and did not seek the label. The ambassador was still the dominant force in his life, and Jack's views on most things differed only superficially from his father's. (The ambassador, in turn, knew what Jack had to give his constituents in order to have a political future.) Congressman Kennedy repeatedly favored fiscal conservatism and often expressed wariness about big government. In a speech at Notre Dame University he warned students about the "ever-expanding power of the federal government" and agreed with the Irish statesman Henry Grattan, who declared that "control over local affairs is the essence of liberty." A Chamber of Commerce tabulation in late 1951 showed Jack to be more fiscally conservative than eleven other Massachusetts Democrats.[20]

One of the ambassador's attorneys helped Jack formulate his moderate position on what became the Taft-Hartley Act. Joe's publicist assisted the congressman's push for public housing. When Jack was asked to add his name to a petition for the commutation of aging Jim Curley's prison sentence for mail fraud, the ambassador advised against it, and the congressman did not sign. When Jack became seriously ill before the end of his first year in the House, the ambassador appointed James Landis, dean of the Harvard Law School and former chairman of the Civil Aeronautics Board, to assist the young congressman.[21]

Jack and his father disagreed mostly about foreign policy, which

Jack had long been interested in, perhaps due to his travels, and followed carefully in newspapers and magazines. The congressman supported the Truman Doctrine at a time when the ambassador was still defending isolationism, and he backed the Marshall Plan, Point Four, and other aid programs. But both men were ardent cold warriors who condemned President Roosevelt for the Yalta agreements and blamed Reds in the State Department for the loss of China. In November 1950, in a speech at Harvard, Jack echoed his father's disenchantment with the Korean War, criticized President Truman and Secretary of State Dean Acheson, endorsed the ultra-conservative and anti-Communist McCarran Act, and expressed support for Red-scare leaders Joe McCarthy and Richard Nixon. (Jack had personally delivered his father's campaign contribution to Nixon for the Californian's Senate race. The ambassador told Tip O'Neill that the contribution totalled $150,000.) In 1951 he sought to slash economic aid to Africa, the Near East, and Europe. Kennedy biographer Herbert Parmet observed that Jack's position on foreign policy "relative to his father's resembled two roads diverging from time to time and merging every now and then, but essentially going in the same direction."[22]

Jack would always deny any direct influence by his father. He assured one writer that he and the ambassador were "far apart" on foreign affairs. "I've given up arguing with him. I make up my own mind and my own decisions." In 1959 Burns wrote, "his father states flatly today that he never asked his son to vote for or against any bill in Congress."[23] To accept such an assurance requires extreme credulity.

→» «←

It was later disclosed that during his listless career in the House, Jack was suffering from Addison's disease, a chronic insufficiency in the production of hormones by the cortex of the adrenal glands. The mysterious and relatively rare affliction brought Kennedy close to death in the fall of 1947 and helps account for the lack of initiative and involvement in his legislative work.[24]

Jack covered up his condition in an interview in 1959:

The facts are these. . . . During the war I contracted malaria in the South Pacific, along with water exposure and a series of fevers. Diagnosis showed that this stress was accompanied by a partial adrenal insufficiency, though there was no tubercular infection or other serious problem.

From 1946 through 1949 I underwent treatment for the malaria—the fevers ceased—there was complete rehabilitation and I have had no special medical care, no special checkup, no particular difficulty on this score at all, while meeting a very full schedule of committee work, Senate responsibilities and speaking engagements.[25]

The issue of JFK's health and ability to carry out his responsibilities emerged again in July 1960, as the Democratic party was about to select a presidential candidate. Two Lyndon Johnson aides, John B. Connally and Mrs. India Edwards, called a press conference and made the medical question a political issue. Edwards told reporters that Kennedy was so ill from Addison's disease that he "looked like a spavined hunchback." She added, "Doctors have told me he would not be alive if it were not for cortisone." Jack, his associates, and a physician, Dr. Janet Travell (who would play an active role in the cover-up), denied the charge, again referring to an adrenal insufficiency of no consequence. Ted Sorensen, who three weeks earlier had denied that Jack took cortisone, said now, "I don't know that he is on anything anymore than you and I are on." After the election, Jack declared flatly, "I have never had Addison's disease." Sorensen and Schlesinger would repeat this contention in their books on Kennedy. However, careful research by Joan and Clay Blair, Jr., among others, has now provided us with a more accurate account of Jack's first flare-up of Addison's disease.

During the summer of 1947, Charles Kersten's labor subcommittee organized a European junket designed to study overseas labor problems. Jack arrived in Ireland on September 1 for a three-week reunion with Kathleen before meeting Congressional colleagues elsewhere. Kick had tried living at home in 1946 but found her parents oppressive (she was kept out of sight during Jack's campaign for fear that news of her marriage might lose Catholic votes) and returned to her late husband's estates, where she was having an affair with a married Protestant, the handsome, roguish aristocrat Peter Milton, Lord Fitzwilliam.

Jack was not well while in Ireland and sent a coded message to Ted Reardon requesting medicine. (The wire would pass through the House telegraph office, and Jack did not want such requests made public.) On his arrival in London with Kathleen, he became so ill that a physician hospitalized him. Addison's disease was discovered, apparently for the first time, and a doctor told Jack's friend Pamela Churchill, "That young American friend of yours, he hasn't got a year to live."[26]

The ambassador quickly dispatched a registered nurse to London, and she and Jack soon sailed for home on the *Queen Mary*. When the ship docked in New York, a priest came aboard and gave Jack extreme unction. Jack was then carried off on a stretcher and flown to the New England Baptist Hospital in Boston. There physicians confirmed the British diagnosis and administered DOCA, a synthetic substance developed in 1939 that possessed cortical-hormonelike activity. Later Jack would have DOCA pellets implanted in his thighs every three months to eliminate the need for constant injections.

In about 1949 Jack began taking oral doses of cortisone, a newly developed hormone that, with DOCA, enabled him to live a fairly normal life. Telling everyone that Jack's bouts with illness were related to his South Pacific experiences, the Kennedys quietly placed emergency supplies of cortisone and DOCA in safe-deposit boxes all over the country. Although these drugs lacked curative power and did not decrease the danger of infections or illness, they could keep Addisonians alive and increase appetite, strength, and stamina.[27]

→→→   ←←←

In the spring of 1949, tragedy again visited the Kennedys with the deaths of Kathleen and Fitzwilliam in the crash of a light plane in France. A few weeks earlier, during a visit to the United States, Kick had broken the news of her romance to her parents. Rose threatened to disown her if she married a divorced man and warned that she would have the ambassador cut off her allowance. Now twenty-eight, Kick defied her mother and returned to England. Soon Rose appeared at her door, angrily invoking Roman Catholic dogma and again threatening to banish her from the family.

Kick hoped to win over the ambassador. "I'd like to get Dad's consent," she told a friend. "He matters." In mid-May, the elder Kennedy was scheduled to be in Paris on a fact-finding tour for the Marshall Plan. He also intended to travel to the Vatican to see what could be done on his daughter's behalf. Kick and her lover arranged to meet the ambassador in Paris for lunch. En route to Cannes for a brief holiday before proceeding to Paris, both young people were killed when their small plane encountered a violent storm and crashed into a mountain.

The ambassador identified his oldest daughter's body and devised a cover-up story for the press. He was badly shaken and depressed. He wrote to a British friend, "The sudden death of young Joe and Kathleen within a period of three years has left a mark on me that I find very difficult to erase." Rose, on the other hand, refused to attend the funeral and dispatched memorial mass cards that made it clear she thought Kathleen was in purgatory. Lem Billings said later, "For her that airplane crash was God pointing his finger at Kick and saying *no!*"[28]

Jack took the loss of his favorite sister terribly hard. For the next several years, haunted by Kick's death and fears about his physical condition, Jack spoke often of death. George Smathers thought him "deeply preoccupied by death'' and later recalled a fishing trip in which Jack pondered the best ways to die. Journalist Joseph Alsop said later, ''In those days, he impressed me as totally unambitious—frankly, I think, because he expected to die.'' Jack once told Alsop, ''They keep giving me these chemicals because I have this disease. It'll finish me off by the time I'm 45. . . .'' He said to Smathers, ''The point is that you've got to live every day like it's your last day on earth. That's what I'm doing.''[29]

So Jack accelerated his pursuit of pleasure. Especially after Eunice moved out of the Georgetown house in 1948, girls went in and out of Jack's bed in such numbers that he often neglected to learn their first names, referring to them the next morning merely as ''sweetie'' or ''kiddo.'' One woman later recalled, ''He was as compulsive as Mussolini. Up against the wall, Signora, if you have five minutes, that sort of thing. He was not a cozy, touching sort of man. In fact, he'd been so sick so long that he was a sort of touch-me-not.''[30]

Charles Spalding later told of Jack's identification with Lord Byron: ''he also had the disability—the club foot—and the conviction of an early death; and most of all he had the women. In that regard most of all Jack was Byronic. He had the hunger for women and the realization that the hunger was displaced, which led to a fedupness with women too.'' Lem Billings said, ''He knew he was using women to prove his masculinity, and sometimes it depressed him. I think he wanted to believe in love and all that but what he'd seen at home didn't give him much hope.''[31]

Jack confided a bit in one woman who resisted his advances, and asked questions about women and marriage as though they were totally foreign topics:

> During one of these conversations I once asked him why he was doing it—why he was acting like his father, why he was avoiding real relationships, why he was taking a chance on getting caught in a scandal at the same time that he was trying to make his career take off. He took a while trying to formulate an answer. Finally he shrugged and said, ''I don't know, really. I guess I can't help it.'' He had this sad expression on his face. He looked like a little boy about to cry.[32]

Of course, being a Kennedy and continuing to live under the will and domination of the ambassador had more to do with Jack's immature and insensitive behavior than did his fear of death. A date once watched the congressman prowl through the Hyannis Port house in his father's absence, peering into the ambassador's dresser drawers and sitting in his Cadillac convertible, putting the top up and down ''like a kid without a license, not daring to drive it out onto the highway.''[33]

Some of his male friends thought that Jack's new view of his mortality made him more companionable and interesting. Charles Spalding later spoke of Jack's "heightened sense of being."[34] However that may be, it is certain that Jack's sense of impending doom further dampened his interest in politics. His rate of absenteeism in the House was extremely high. ("Sometimes we didn't have the pleasure of Jack's company for months at a time," said a Labor and Education Committee colleague.) In his third term, he ranked among the bottom four members in the entire House in attendance. Moreover, he failed to distinguish himself or ingratiate himself with congressional or Democratic Party leaders.[35] And, although a fairly avid reader, he had yet to work out a meaningful political philosophy. Jack told a television panel in 1951, "I think that's the difficulty in politics; you are always bound to lose supporters once you take a stand on an issue."[36] (Burns would later contend that in these years Jack "rejected the ideologies and stereotypes of both conservatives and liberals, both isolationists and interventionists. . . . Committed to neither world, though related to both, he could sit back and regard each with a cool and judicial eye.")[37] Mary Davis later recalled, "I don't think he really knew if he wanted politics—if he was going to remain with it—or what politics was going to do with him."[38]

Jack ran for reelection in 1948 unopposed, and two years later he easily defeated token GOP opposition. By this time the ambassador was carefully planning his son's entry into the 1952 senatorial race. Arthur Krock said later that Jack's move to the Senate "was inevitable in the pursuit of the ambition that Kennedy's father conceived before the future President [did]."[39]

Jack responded to his father's decision with resignation and determination. He would, as trained, earn his father's respect. He would meet the challenge, and do it with everything in his power. Moreover, Jack welcomed the change of scenery. He later told Burns, "We were just worms over in the House—nobody pays much attention to us nationally."[40]

Soon after his second reelection, the thirty-three-year-old congressman began a strenuous tour of Massachusetts, crisscrossing the state for months on end, giving speeches and shaking hands. He rarely discussed political issues and was not openly running for office. He was again advancing the Kennedy name. Aide Frank Morrissey, who accompanied him, later commented, "I'll bet he talked to at least a million people and shook hands with seven hundred and fifty thousand."[41] George Smathers, who knew of Jack's precarious health, asked him at one point, "For Chrissakes, Jack, wait until you're better. You can't do this now. You won't survive it. What in God's name is the rush?'' Jack replied, ''I can't wait. I don't have time. I've got to do it *now*.''[42] No effort would be spared to assure victory.

To give the impression of being an authority on international issues, Jack went on a five-week fact-finding tour of Europe in early 1951. The ambassador made sure that the trip was highly publicized, including an interview with Marshal Tito in Yugoslavia and an audience with the pope. After returning Jack testified before the Senate Foreign Relations Committee, urging Europeans to do more in their own defense against Soviet aggression, and he spoke over a national radio hookup. One Boston newspaper ran a front-page portrait of Jack under the heading KENNEDY ACQUIRING TITLE ''AMERICA'S YOUNGER STATESMAN.''[43]

By this time Jack's congenitally bad back was causing such pain that he was forced to use crutches. Constant travel and walking on the marble floors of the House Office Building intensified his discomfort. Burns wrote, ''He could climb upstairs only by dragging his leg, when he thought people were looking the other way.'' Jack took hot baths each day and slept with a stiff board under his mattress. Daily doses of cortisone helped him survive extremely long days.[44]

That October, Jack, brother Bobby, and sister Pat embarked on a seven-week, 25,000-mile tour of Israel and the Far East. (Jack and Bobby first became closely acquainted during the trip. Bobby, eight years younger and often away at school and in the service, had had few chances to spend time with his brother.) This was another effort to give the congressman international credentials. The youthful trio met, among others, Israeli Prime Minister David Ben-Gurion, Indian Prime Minister Nehru, and the Vietnamese chief of state Bao Dai.

In Japan Jack became seriously ill. At the military hospital in Okinawa his temperature reached 106, and physicians doubted he would live. The problem—covered up by the family and unmentioned by friendly historians—was undoubtedly related to Addison's disease. A family doctor told the Blairs years later that Jack had not been properly taking care of himself on the trip and had come down with a severe fever. By telephone the physician prescribed penicillin and adrenal hormones.[45]

Jack recovered after returning to the United States and resumed his speechmaking in late November. He now made solemn declarations concerning the nation's foreign policy, broad-ranging statements befitting a senator. He condemned French colonialism in Vietnam, for example, and argued that the task was ''to build strong native non-Communist sentiment within these areas and rely on that as a spearhead of defense rather than upon the legions of General de Lattre, brilliant though he may be, and to do this apart from and in defiance of innately nationalistic aims spells foredoomed failure." Of American diplomats, he said harshly, "One finds too many of our representatives toadying to the shorter aims of other Western nations, with no eagerness to understand the real hopes and desires of the people to whom they are accredited."[46]

The Senate seat the Kennedys coveted was held by Henry Cabot Lodge, Jr., grandson of the famed scholar-politician who had defeated Honey Fitz in a bitter struggle in 1916 and led the fight in 1919 against Woodrow Wilson's rigid postwar visions of peace and international cooperation. The younger Lodge, handsome, urbane, Harvard-educated, and a Yankee Brahmin of the sort likely to irritate Joe and Rose Kennedy, was first elected to the Senate in 1936 at the age of thirty-four. (He had been a college hero of Jack's.) A liberal on domestic matters with close ties to the New Deal, he won reelection in 1942. Two years later he resigned in order to serve full-time in the Army. He returned with a Bronze Star and other decorations, and in 1946 crushed a popular Democrat by 330,000 votes. By 1952 a perceptive article in the *Reporter* described the fifty-year-old incumbent as "at the peak of his power, prominence and experience."[47]

When Lodge first heard about Jack's candidacy, he sent word to the ambassador through Arthur Krock not to waste his money. "I'm going to win by 300,000 votes."[48] Others also thought the challenge hopeless. Evelyn Lincoln, a new Kennedy office employee, heard a friendly Democratic congressman say of Jack, "Why, he's nothing but a playboy." And there were whispers about Kennedy's health. "Did you know that he walks around on crutches most of the time?" "I heard he has only six months to live."[49]

But such talk only made the ambassador more eager for combat. Lodge—a Yankee blueblood, a liberal, and an Eisenhower internationalist—was a highly tempting target. He advised Jack, "When you've beaten him, you've beaten the best. Why try for something less?"[50]

For a year and a half before the 1952 campaign formally got under way, the ambassador had a pair of full-time advance men comb the state, quietly taking public opinion polls and sounding out potential supporters. When he was persuaded that victory was possible, he put the full force of his energy, power, and wealth behind Jack. Lodge would tell a reporter that the ambassador was his son's true campaign manager, and the reporter observed, "I picked up the former Ambassador's tracks everywhere I went." The elder Kennedy wrote to a friend, "You know me well enough to know that we wouldn't be in it if we weren't going to win."[51]

In early April 1952, the ambassador had a private meeting with Governor Paul Dever, a possible rival for the Democratic nomination. When it concluded, Dever had decided to run for a third term, and certain of his reelection expenses were to be pooled with the Kennedy campaign. The suggestion of a payoff was unavoidable.[52] Jack soon called Larry O'Brien, a new campaign worker, exclaiming excitedly, "I've just talked to Dever. He's running for governor again. Here we go, Larry—we've got the race we want."[53] (Jack would say later, "The choice was Dever's . . . and I was prepared to defer to him. Dever finally decided to run for a third term because he considered Lodge unbeatable. He was afraid to take on Lodge.")[54]

On Sunday evening, April 6, Jack read the formal announcement of his candidacy. "Other states have vigorous leaders in the United States Senate, to defend the interests and principles of their citizens—men who have definite goals based on constructive principles and who move toward these goals unswervingly. Massachusetts has need for such leadership."[55]

A participant in early strategy sessions at Hyannis Port later said of the ambassador, "He dominated everything, even told everyone where to sit. They [were] just children in that house."[56] Later that spring, from an apartment in central Boston, he assumed control of the campaign. Rose, who was with him, said later, "he kept a close supervisory eye on everything and did many things to smooth the way for Jack."[57] When the ambassador humiliated Mark Dalton at a meeting ("Dalton, you've spent ten thousand dollars of my money and you haven't accomplished a damn thing"), the 1946 campaign manager approached Jack for a vote of confidence. Jack just shrugged, and Dalton quit in disgust.[58] One participant in the morning conferences at the ambassador's apartment later recalled Jack being bawled out by his father for taking an action that hurt his chance for victory. "You don't argue with Joe Kennedy," said the observer.[59] (Jack would later discount his father's influence. "The rest of the family was in Boston helping me, but my father stayed up at the Cape the whole time." Burns portrayed the candidate as listening to his father, among others, and then making his own campaign plans.)[60]

The ambassador brought key personnel into the campaign, including James Landis, attorney Lynn Johnston, journalist Ralph Coghlan, financial writer John Harriman, fiscal expert John J. Ford, and the young Merchandise Mart executive R. Sargent Shriver, Jr. This "brain trust" developed issues, wrote speeches, and advised the ambassador and the candidate on campaign strategy.

Veteran New Dealer Gardner ("Pat") Jackson was named to win over the liberals, who initially had strong misgivings. After the GOP convention, Boston banker T. Walter Taylor was asked to form "Independents for Kennedy," an organization designed to appeal to Taft conservatives, smarting over Lodge's successful management of Eisenhower's bid for the presidential nomination. In a letter to Taft supporters, Taylor noted that the ambassador was a close friend and ardent backer of the Ohio senator.

The two-pronged strategy proved successful, in large part of course because of the malleability of Jack's ambivalent voting record and amorphous political philosophy. Jackson brought labor unions and the liberal Americans for Democratic Action into the fold. Kennedy was a Democrat, after all, and seemed to be more liberal than his opponent. Adlai Stevenson, in Massachusetts, endorsed Jack as "my type of guy." (This action also no doubt reflected Stevenson's gratitude for receiving an ample financial contribution for his presidential aspirations from the ambassador.) On the other hand, Taft's state manager, Basil Brewer, swung his influential *New Bedford Standard-Times* into the Kennedy camp and labeled Lodge "a Truman socialistic New Dealer." Jack and his father had many friends on the Right, and shared their views of the Cold War and fiscal responsibility.[61]

The elder Kennedy spent a vast sum of money on the campaign. Burns declared that the family contributed $70,000, but the actual figure was certainly far greater. The various Kennedy committees, operating independently of the Democratic party's fund-raising organizations, reported expenses of just under $350,000. The full cost of the campaign was surely well over $500,000, and some estimates ran into the millions. One labor leader told a professor, "You could live the rest of your life on the billboard budget alone."[62]

The Kennedy publicity blitz left veteran observers gasping. The mayor of Boston observed that at the rally launching the campaign, all of the speeches were televised, a rarity at the time, and that two Teleprompters were on hand, the second one taking over when the first broke down. Late in the campaign, 900,000 copies of an eight-page tabloid touting Jack's wartime heroism were distributed across the state.[63] Everywhere one encountered the image of Jack Kennedy—youthful, attractive, heroic, idealistic.

The ambassador won a ringing endorsement from the conservative *Boston Post* after quietly loaning its editor, John Fox, $500,000. (When word of the transaction got out in 1958, Joe said that the loan was a purely financial matter. Fox claimed that the endorsement slightly preceded the loan.) Jack later admitted to journalist Fletcher Knebel, "You know, we had to buy that fucking paper or I'd have been licked."[64]

The ambassador also took care of the Joe McCarthy problem. The junior senator from Wisconsin, nearing the peak of his fame, was highly popular in Massachusetts, especially among the state's 750,000 Irish. As an influential Republican and in great demand, McCarthy was expected to enter the state and campaign for Lodge. Moreover, Lodge had defended McCarthy two years earlier when the Tydings Committee investigated early charges by the Wisconsinite of internal subversion in the federal government.

Although he would later deny it, Lodge pleaded with McCarthy to help him out, especially to quell Kennedy charges that he was soft on the Reds. One forty-page expose prepared by Ted Reardon condemned Lodge for "straddling" on the guilt or innocence of McCarthy victims Owen Lattimore, John Stewart Service, and Philip Jessup. Another document contrasted Kennedy's hard-line record with Lodge's "100 percent" support of the Truman administration's "conciliatory and appeasing" Far Eastern policy.[65] The ambassador scotched Lodge's request with a personal plea to McCarthy and a sizable donation to the Senator's own election campaign. This in part was responsible for the assurance that the Commonwealth could not be on the spy hunter's itinerary.[66] The elder Kennedy later boasted to Hearst columnist Westbrook Pegler that McCarthy's absence had been helpful and possibly decisive in the campaign. (The ambassador would claim that he contributed "only a couple of thousand dollars" to McCarthy and strictly "because a mutual friend of ours, Westbrook Pegler, asked me to give it to him." Pegler denied this. Jack would state categorically, "My father at no time asked Senator McCarthy for any assistance.")[67] The ambassador also persuaded Adlai Stevenson not to give an anti-McCarthy speech while campaigning in Massachusetts, fearing that the attack might hurt Jack's chances at the polls.[68]

At one point in the campaign, Pat Jackson tried to get Jack to behave like a liberal by taking a stand against McCarthy. He prepared a newspaper advertisement featuring the headline COMMUNISM AND MCCARTHY: BOTH WRONG and containing statements by ninety-nine faculty members of Notre Dame University. Jack agreed to sign it if Congressman McCormack would. McCormack assented.

The next morning Jackson took the ad to Jack's apartment and discovered the ambassador and three of his brain trusters present. The candidate asked Jackson to read the ad aloud and then quickly left the room. When two sentences had been completed, the ambassador was on his feet, angrily shouting, "You're trying to ruin Jack. You and your sheeny friends are trying to ruin my son's career." Jackson recalled, "I can't estimate how long he poured it out on me. It was just a stream of stuff—always referring to 'you and your sheeny friends.' " Finally, the ambassador stalked out of the apartment. The anti-McCarthy ad was dead. Jack pretended during the campaign that family friend McCarthy did not exist.[69]

The ambassador no doubt selected twenty-six-year-old Bobby Kennedy to supervise the details of the campaign. "When Bobby came in," an insider said later, "we knew it was the old man taking over. What had Bobby done up to that time politically? Nothing. Not a damn thing and all of a sudden he was there as campaign manager, waving the banners."[70] Bobby indeed had had no political experience. After marriage to wealthy and energetic Ethel Skakel and graduation from the University of Virginia Law School (placing fifty-sixth in a class of 124), he had worked for the Department of Justice for a few months before being summoned to enter his brother's campaign. When first asked, his response was negative, "I'll screw it up."[71]

But Bobby proved to be efficient, demanding, and effective. He was also imperious, ruthless, and unpopular. He shooed one labor leader out of a campaign office with, "If you're not going to work, don't hang around here." He almost got into a fistfight with one state legislator. Tip O'Neill thought him "a self-important upstart and a know-it-all." Governor Dever telephoned the ambassador at one point and demanded, "I know you're an important man around here and all that, but I'm telling you this and I mean it. Keep that fresh kid of yours out of sight from here on in." Old pol Patsy Mulkern later called Bobby "very tough" and a "slave driver."[72]

The ambassador greatly admired Bobby's performance; the youngster was proving himself a Kennedy. Soon he would describe his son as "a tough one" and "as hard as nails." He would tell Charles Spalding, "Bobby is like me." On one occasion the ambassador complained to Tip O'Neill that Jack was too soft. "You can trample all over him," he said, "and the next day he's there for you with loving arms. But Bobby's my boy. When Bobby hates you, you stay hated."[73]

Jack and Bobby were unalike in several ways, Bobby being more intense, ambitious, abrasive, and less inclined toward lechery. (Schlesinger would rhapsodize, "John Kennedy was the more secure, the freer, of the two—freer of his father, of his family, of his faith, of the entire

Irish American predicament.'')[74] But, despite the difference in personality, their similarities were striking. Both loved, admired, and at times feared the ambassador, and they shared his basic determination to use any means to get what they wanted, whether it be political office or personal desires.

Like Jack, Bobby disliked political campaigning. Larry O'Brien said later, "The entire hand-shaking, small-talking side of politics was repugnant to him; he often said to me, 'Larry, I don't know how you stand it.'"[75] But, also like his older brother, Bobby wanted to win, and so he did as told, giving his all for the Founding Father, for the family, for victory.

Jack deeply appreciated Bobby's eighteen-hour days and his firm grasp of administrative detail. (Once, when he could not find anyone to nail up a huge poster on the side of a building, Bobby obtained a long ladder and did it himself.)[76] One afternoon the candidate gave a tongue-lashing to a distant cousin in charge of outdoor advertising because the Lodge camp had revealed that Kennedy billboards were printed out of state by nonunion labor. "Look at what a Christly mess you've made of things." When the campaign worker replied that he was only obeying Bobby's dictum to "save a dime of your father's money," Jack exploded. "Oh, bullshit, everybody bitches about Bobby, and I'm getting sick and goddamn tired of it. He's the only one who doesn't stick knives in my back, the only one I can count on when it comes down to it.''[77]

The other Kennedy family members, plus numerous relatives, participated actively in the campaign. The family had already assumed a popular public image as a close, caring clan who all pulled together for any one of its members. The opportunity of seeing the handsome family of tanned, healthy, and wealthy young men and women in person proved irresistible to many voters; it was like being summoned to a Hollywood celebrity party. Some 70,000 women responded to hand-addressed, engraved invitations to thirty-three tea parties. There they met the candidate, his mother, and one or more of her three daughters. The first such event, in Cambridge, drew 7,500 to a hotel that could hold only 400. An informal, chatty, call-in program entitled "Coffee with the Kennedys" was shown twice on television. Rose gave numerous little talks about bringing up her children and always mentioned her oldest sons' military records. ("Her eloquently moving account of her two sons' adventures in the war," a pro-Kennedy reporter wrote later, "is said to have reduced to tears some of Massachusetts' most blasé citizens.") Eunice, Pat, and Jean rang doorbells for months, gave house parties, and showed films of a "Meet the Press" interview with their brother. At one point the campaign almost ran out of Kennedys, and Bobby gave that fall's most succinct political speech: "My brother Jack couldn't be here, my mother couldn't be here, my sister Eunice couldn't be here, my sister Pat couldn't be here, my sister Jean couldn't be here, but if my brother Jack were here, he'd tell you Lodge has a very bad voting record. Thank you."[78]

One Lodge supporter moaned, "I don't worry about Jack Kennedy. I don't worry about Kennedy's money. It's that family of his . . . they're all over the state." After the election, Lodge would growl, "It was those damned tea parties."[79]

No one worked harder than Jack. Despite constant back problems and bouts with exhaustion and nausea, he labored on through the spring, summer, and fall. By election time he had covered all of the Commonwealth's 351 cities and towns. At a Springfield fire station, he slid down two floors on a fire pole, doubling up with pain on landing. At a tea in Fall River, he leaned on his crutches while shaking hands with more than two thousand women. Usually, however, he was able to conceal his pain and discomfort, handing his crutches to associates or concealing them in the car before striding into a hall or auditorium appearing to be in perfect health.[80]

Jack continued to dislike handshaking, backslapping, and the entire process of thrusting himself on others with pleas for votes. But he did what was necessary, pretending to all but his traveling companions (with whom he was often tense and irritable) that he was enjoying the campaign. He was only "all right," in Patsy Mulkern's eyes, at remembering faces and names, and he would often have to be prodded to meet and greet people. Larry O'Brien later noted how difficult it was for Jack to shake hands at a factory gate. But he did his duty; he was Kennedy-tough. One close observer said later, "I didn't think he was going to live through the campaign." But he "absolutely had to; he had to show his father."[81]

The candidates closely resembled each other, and there were virtually no substantive issues raised during the campaign. One commentator said later, "The Kennedy-Lodge campaign finally came down to a question of who had the less embarrassing absentee record."[82] The rivals held two television debates, and Jack appeared to hold his own against the urbane and smooth-talking incumbent. Despite his inexperience and lack of knowledge, Jack came across as an appealing, handsome young man with warmth and humor. Television would always be good to him, magnifying his surface attributes.

When the candidates met for a debate in a school auditorium in Waltham, the ambassador was observed high in the balcony scribbling informative notes and arguments for delivery by two runners to his son on the platform.[83]

Jack's gaunt and boyish appearance, his informality, his studied charm ("He always made every girl feel he was really interested in talking to them," a campaign secretary said later), his wealth, and his unmarried status made a huge impact on young women. Patsy Mulkern recalled, "The girls went for him. Every girl you met thought she was going to be Mrs. Kennedy." At a rally in Lynn, a clothier told Mulkern that girls had been buying gowns all day in order to impress the candidate.[84] In receiving lines some women could not resist giving Jack a kiss on the cheek. One Republican who watched Kennedy female workers hand out pamphlets at the entrance of an Eisenhower rally was overheard asking, "What is there about Kennedy that makes every Catholic girl in Boston between eighteen and twenty-eight think it's a holy crusade to get him elected?"[85]

The Kennedy campaign recruited thousands of others as well, attracted not only by Jack but by the vitality and zeal of the entire Kennedy family ("The Kennedys were so glamorous and so exciting," Rose's biographer wrote, "that it became a status symbol to support them") and by the promise of vigorous new leadership. Jack's slogan was "Kennedy will do MORE for Massachusetts," and many believed it. Volunteers helped collect a record 262,324 signatures on the candidate's nominating petition (only 2,500 were required by law). A statewide network of 286 committee secretaries, led by Larry O'Brien and Kenny O'Donnell, organized 21,000 regular volunteers, and another 30,000 workers helped out. The youthfulness of the volunteers prompted one writer to conclude that Kennedy's campaign "was in the hands of boys and girls."[86]

The Lodge campaign was well financed, but it started to roll only two months before the election, due to the senator's involvement with Eisenhower, and lacked enthusiasm. By late September Lodge was worried, and Sherman Adams, Eisenhower's chief strategist, had reportedly said "Cabot is in trouble." But the senator chose not to stress the Korean War, a prime GOP target, and did not capitalize on the second Red scare, as Eisenhower and most other Republicans were. Burns later labeled Lodge's reelection bid "remarkably mild and gentlemanly."[87]

On election night, according to Rose, Jack was "really nervous." At his father's Beacon Street apartment, he paced the floor and kept taking his jacket on and off, oblivious to the fact that his sleeves were inside out part of the time. The race was close all evening. When Jack finally went ahead by a comfortable margin and heard that Lodge was leaving his nearby headquarters, he expected a gracious concession speech and alerted his campaign workers to greet the senator with applause. When the Lodge limousine sped by, Jack muttered, "Sonofabitch. Can you believe that?" The Yankees would apparently always be imperious.[88]

Despite a massive Eisenhower victory in Massachusetts and the GOP conquest of the State House, Jack defeated Lodge by more than 70,000 votes. By holding onto the Catholic immigrant Democrats and winning over some Taft Republicans, Jack took 51.5 percent of the senatorial votes.

The ambassador was ecstatic over the results; Jack was now firmly on the road to the White House. Rose could not resist the temptation to crow, "At last, the Fitzgeralds have evened the score with the Lodges!"[89]

The following night, at a huge victory party, Jack fulfilled a campaign pledge by reluctantly singing "Sweet Adeline." John J. Droney, a leading campaign worker, recalled, "He sang it alone. Of course, he had a terrible voice—he had no tone—and then Bobby sang. I think Bobby was worse."

A short time later, Droney attended another party for Jack. He noticed while standing in the reception line that Jack "looked pretty pale." After introducing Droney to Jacqueline Bouvier for the first time, he "sort of put his arm on my shoulder, and he said, 'John, get me out of here. I'm awfully sick.'" Jack was quietly whisked away to a hospital.[90]

>>> <<<

The Kennedy image portrayed in the campaign of 1952 was dazzling. Here was youth, energy, intelligence, warmth, and selfless devotion to principle. Few of the cheering voters knew that beneath that surface was a much less substantial reality. There was indeed intelligence, discipline, and determination. All the Kennedys fought hard and tirelessly. But behind the whole effort was the will and ambition of the Founding Father, Joe Kennedy, who cared little for any principle beyond the advancement of his family's power and prestige.

Jack lacked the full measure of his father's ambition, cruelty, and will to dominate. He was a more amiable, less focused man; his personality was not the almost carbon copy of the ambassador's that Bobby's was at the time. Still, Jack, like his father and his brother, was without any guiding intellectual, philosophical, or moral vision in his pursuit of office. Politics, like life, was about winning, and little else.

Kennedy energy, grit, money, and skulduggery had taken Jack to the United States Senate. In the process, the gap between the imagery and the reality had grown larger. Beneath the Kennedy clan's vigor, the expensive signs, and the slick slogans lay little more than the desire to wrest power from a Boston Brahmin. The moving generalities expounded in well-crafted speeches were designed to appeal to the maximum number of voters. To Jack there was no reward more profound than election returns, no principle higher than winning the game and, ultimately, his father's favor. Kennedy biographer Herbert Parmet observed an essential truth when he wrote, "Jack Kennedy never thought of the world as a moral place."[91]

CHAPTER 7

Full of Ideals

⇥≫ ≪⇤

JACK'S FRIEND Charles Bartlett first introduced him to Jacqueline Bouvier in May, 1952 at a dinner party in Bartlett's home. The meeting was uneventful. By that fall, however, gossip columnists were hinting that Jack and Jackie were serious about each other. Right after the election Jackie's cousin John H. Davis asked her about the rumors. The dark, attractive, twenty-three-year-old *Washington Times-Herald* "inquiring photographer" laughed and began describing the senator-elect.

"You know, he goes to a hairdresser almost every day to have his hair done," she said, in that low, breathless whisper of hers, "so it'll always look bushy and fluffy?"

I nodded, without saying anything.

"And you know," she went one, "if, when we go out to some party, or reception, or something, nobody recognizes him, or no photographer takes his picture, he sulks afterwards for hours."

"Really?"

"Really. He's so vain you can't believe it."

"Maybe he's just ambitious," I said.

"Oh sure, he's ambitious all right," she said, "he even told me he intends to be President some day," and she tossed her head back and laughed again.

Jackie also had qualms about the social status of Jack's family. "Wait 'till I introduce Jack Kennedy to Aunt Edie," she told Davis. (Aunt Edith Bouvier Beale was an eccentric who owned forty cats.) "You know, I doubt if he'd survive it. The Kennedys are terribly bourgeois."[1]

The first Bouvier to arrive in America was a cabinetmaker who fled France in 1815 as a refugee from the Napoleonic wars. Through the mass production of furniture, an import business, and real estate speculations, Michel Bouvier became one of Philadelphia's wealthiest citizens. At his death in 1874 he left approximately $1 million. His three sons continued to prosper, and by the mid-1920s the youngest, Michel C., had amassed $10 million. The large Bouvier family moved in a world of luxury, beauty, and the social graces.

The Bouvier wealth declined after the Great Depression, and by 1953 Jackie's father, John Vernon ("Black Jack") Bouvier III, was only worth $250,000—a sum at least a thousand times smaller than the fortune built by the elder Kennedy. Still, the Bouviers continued to travel in aristocratic circles.

Jackie's mother was a Lee, a family as Irish as the Kennedys. (Jackie did everything possible to conceal her Irish background, choosing to be seen as French—although in fact she was only one-eighth French.) The first Lee left Ireland during the 1840s and settled in a rough neighborhood in New York City. His son, James, became an attorney and a multimillionaire real estate speculator. He married a daughter of Irish immigrants, and one of their daughters, Janet, was Jackie's mother.

The Lees were not in the same social set as the Bouviers. People with older fortunes snickered at James's awkward clothes, his wife's Irish domesticity, and his mother-in-law's thick brogue. Their values also clashed. Like the Kennedys, the Lees prided themselves on their drive and tenacity. Janet was a strong, athletic, and deeply competitive person who sought victory in whatever she undertook, from horseback riding to romance. Her passion for social climbing was part of what led to her marriage to Black Jack Bouvier and brought the Lees into high society.

Jackie drew on qualities found in both families. John H. Davis, who knew his cousin well, wrote, "Just as the Bouviers transmitted their highly developed sense of style to Jacqueline, so the Lees transmitted their toughness and ambition to her."[2]

Born in 1929, Jackie grew up in considerable luxury in family estates and apartments. She began riding horses at four and quickly became a ribbon winner at horse shows. She was an above-average student at a private school in New York, and she excelled at her ballet lessons.

But Jackie had a disturbed childhood. Her parents fought bitterly, largely over Black Jack's continuous philandering. After their parent's separation in 1936, Jackie and her younger sister Lee stayed with their mother, who grew increasingly aloof and was often absent. Black Jack, an adoring father, visited on weekends and gave his daughters everything they asked for. The girls would weep as they were returned to their mother. Davis later observed, "Jacqueline learned to play one parent off against the other. And as she succeeded admirably, especially with her father, she learned the great lessons of her life: that with a little charm, and a little cunning, you could get almost anything you wanted out of a man."[3]

In 1940 Janet filed for divorce, publicly charging her husband with adultery. Jackie suddenly became the daughter of a black sheep and for years endured the petty cruelties inflicted by other family members. Jackie still loved her father deeply. She made little secret of her dislike for her mother. The two, in the words of a witness, "frequently had yelling spells." Both Bouvier girls, she said, "seemed very happy when they were allowed by their mother to go see their father, in fact it was almost pathetic."[4]

Janet obtained a Nevada divorce in 1940 and two years later married Hugh D. Auchincloss, a twice-divorced millionaire with the highest social standing. The Bouvier girls went with their mother to live at an Auchincloss estate. Jack Bouvier, meanwhile, tried desperately to retain the affections of his daughters. At times, when they were with him, they grew accustomed to the presence of his "lady friends." (One British married woman had twins by him. Jackie was later astonished to discover that they were almost replicas of herself.) They also watched him grow increasingly alcoholic.

Janet and "Hughdie," as her husband was called, were tightfisted, and they wanted Black Jack, who had fallen on hard times financially, to pay all of his daughters' expenses. The fighting over money affected Jackie negatively. On many occasions, much to her father's anguish, she spent money on herself recklessly. More could always be had, however, by smiling and cooing sweetly in a little-girl voice.[5]

Jackie studied at Vassar and the Sorbonne, traveled widely in Europe, and graduated from George Washington University in 1951. She won first prize, beating out 1,280 other entrants, in a *Vogue* magazine contest requiring an essay on "People I Wish I Had Known" and four technical papers on haute couture. Her longtime private secretary wrote later, "What most people didn't know . . . was that behind that pretty face was a steel-trap mind." Arthur Krock helped her get the *Washington Times-Herald* job, the same post Inga Arvad and Kathleen Kennedy had held.[6]

When she fell in love with New York stockbroker John G. W. Husted, Jr., her mother discouraged marriage. The young man was insufficiently wealthy; Jackie could do better, perhaps much better, as she had. For all her difficulties with her mother, Jackie accepted the advice. On her scale of values, money and position ranked far above romance. She had long been thought somewhat aloof and cold. Davis recalled, ''As a young girl she was the classic virgin princess.''[7] Her close friend Betty Spalding thought that as an adult she was as emotionally blocked as Jack Kennedy.[8] A *Look* magazine photographer who knew her well a few years later recalled, ''She was a very strong-minded girl and very tough. . . . I think this is one thing that old Joe Kennedy liked about her, that she was a tough babe.''[9]

By 1952 Jackie had almost no money of her own—her newspaper job paid $42.50 a week—and she stood to inherit virtually nothing. (Black Jack had gone through several fortunes. Auchincloss intended to leave his millions to several children of his own.) Thus, when the junior senator from Massachusetts began to pay his respects after defeating Lodge, she became highly attentive. Jack had personal charm, of course, but also position and a nationally recognized name, and he was worth about $10 million. ''Essentially,'' Nancy Dickerson wrote, ''she was motivated by a desire for money.''[10]

Jack turned thirty-six in 1953. Marriage was undoubtedly his father's idea. Jack told George Smathers that the ambassador had said it was time to take a spouse; a wife and a family were political necessities.[11] Jack himself was in no way ready to settle down to a monogamous, self-denying relationship. He remained unable to become emotionally involved.

Jack liked Jackie. He was fascinated by her facility with foreign languages (which he lacked), he admired her knowledge of ancient history (which surpassed his own), he respected her love of the fine arts (in which he had little interest), and he appreciated her elevated vocabulary. (Kennedy himself used vulgarities regularly. His close friend Ben Bradlee would write later, ''He used 'prick' and 'fuck' and 'nuts' and 'bastard' and 'son of a bitch' with an ease and comfort that belied his upbringing.'')[12] Jack thought of Jackie as a woman of ''class,'' someone who would elevate the Kennedys' social as well as political standing. (''Jackie always managed to look rich,'' Davis recalled, ''so that Kennedy never dreamed she was virtually penniless.'') But he could go no deeper. The courtship would lack candy or flowers or any sign of serious affection. Jack would propose by telegram.[13]

Jack escorted Jackie to Eisenhower's inaugural ball in January 1953. During the evening Lem Billings took Jackie into a corner and tried discreetly to warn her about Jack—his illnesses, his amours, and the fact that, being twelve years older, he was "set in his ways." But Jackie was not impressed; she knew what she wanted. Charles Spalding said later, "She wasn't sexually attracted to men unless they were dangerous like old Black Jack."[14] Her private secretary later wrote, "She was completely organized, always planning her life, always looking ahead. . . . She was never naive."[15] When *Times-Herald* editor Frank Waldrop warned her about Jack's womanizing, Jackie merely replied that she would be "the luckiest girl in the world" if Jack would marry her.[16] Jack sent his telegram in May while Jackie was in London, and she soon accepted.

Jack got along well with Black Jack Bouvier. They both fancied themselves worldly sophisticates, and they enjoyed chatting about politics, sports, and girls and sharing off-color jokes. Jack was less comfortable with Janet Auchincloss, who considered the Kennedys *nouveaux*. (In April Jackie's sister Lee married a wealthy publisher's son said to have royal blood; her second marriage would make her a princess.) When negotiations got sticky, the ambassador stepped in. Preparations for the wedding would require three and a half months, and in the end the ambassador would have his way in almost every detail.[17]

Jackie and the ambassador hit it off well from the start; indeed, Joe undoubtedly played a major role in her selection from the many scores of applicants for Jack's affections. (When it came to marriage, he advised, the choice should be made carefully and "not related to the groin.") The ambassador liked Jackie's aristocratic bearing, strong will, and often acid wit. Jackie, in turn, came to depend on the ambassador for encouragement and protection.[18]

Jackie's relations with Rose, on the other hand, were never good. Jackie disliked Rose's selfishness and said she was "scatterbrained." Rose was angered by the younger woman's frequent tardiness and displays of independence. Once in Palm Beach, Rose asked Jackie's secretary, "Do you think Jackie is getting out of bed today?" The secretary was unsure. "Well, you might remind her," Rose said icily, "that we're having some important guests for lunch. It would be nice if she would join us." When informed of the request, Jackie mimicked her mother-in-law's words and voice and stayed in her room.[19]

Jackie's introduction to Jack's siblings at Hyannis Port left her exhausted and irritated. She disliked the boisterous teasing about her name (the girls joked that she pronounced her name "Jacklean" to rhyme

The Kennedy family (minus Joe Junior) in 1934. Over the next decades, this group would rally to the defense of any of its members, against personal or political attack. Front row—left to right—Patricia, Mr. and Mrs. Kennedy with baby Edward, Rosemary, Kathleen, Eunice. Back row—John, Jean, and Robert. *(Bettmann)*

Jack graduating from Choate, where he was popular and rambunctious. A friend said that with his smile "he could charm a bird off a tree." *(JFK Library)*

Kennedy, plagued with back pain from youth, swims at Harvard. True to the family devotion to sports and fitness, he privately aspired to the role of football hero. *(AP/World Wide)*

Jack on the liner Bremen, returning from summer vacation in Europe. At 21, Jack began to be serious about his studies for the first time. *(AP/World Wide)*

The new Ambassador to Great Britain sails to England with his oldest sons. With the wartime death of Joe Junior, the father's expectations fell on Jack. *(Bettmann)*

All of their lives, the Kennedys would love football and other aggressive sports. They had been taught as children to compete, to give their all, and to win at any cost. *(JFK Library)*

The frail young lieutenant poses for a photograph in 1944, proudly displaying his lifesaving medal. The PT-109 incident, something of a scandal initially, was soon interpreted to make Jack a hero. *(Bettmann)*

Congressman Kennedy in 1950. Cortisone had restored some of the energy and vitality Jack was losing to Addison's Disease. *(Bettmann)*

Kennedy labors on in the 1952 campaign in Massachusetts for the Senate. Rose, in the background, was one of several family members who helped with the election. *(JFK Library)*

The wedding party in September, 1953. The new Mrs. Kennedy would soon learn that marriage to Jack brought unanticipated frustrations. *(National Archives)*

Kennedy and journalist Russell Jones congratulate each other on their Pulitzer Prize awards in 1957. Jack took full credit as author of *Profiles in Courage.* *(AP/World Wide)*

OCRATIC NATIONAL CONVE
1960

Jack's 1960 acceptance speech as the Democratic presidential candidate was a battle cry for fresh energy, ideas, and ideals. The New Frontier, said the candidate, required self-sacrifice by all Americans. *(Bettmann)*

Kennedy and Nixon after their second presidential campaign debate, 1960. Jack's telegenic appeal was an important element in his eventual success. *(Bettmann)*

A crowd in Elgin, Illinois, flocking to see and touch the Democratic candidate. Kennedy's personal magnetism was extraordinary. *(AP)*

with "queen"), her clothing, and her large (size-ten) feet. She was also turned off by the intense athletic competition. She tried at first to participate in the roughhouse games but quickly realized that she could not take the physical punishment. "They'll kill me before I ever get to marry him," she told her sister. "I swear they will." She later broke an ankle playing touch football with Teddy. Jackie termed the Kennedy women "the rah-rah girls." They in turn referred to her as "the Debutante," and made fun of what they called her "babykins voice."[20]

George Smathers later recalled, "Jack's sisters were unbelievably overbearing. God, those women were always talking about how much money they had, how influential Joe was, and how much money the family possessed. They'd drive you crazy with that kind of talk. . . . I think it really got to Jackie after a while."[21]

During her first Christmas at Palm Beach, Jackie was appalled to see an oil-painting set she had given Jack appropriated by family members, who madly painted away for hours, even after Rose banished them to the bathrooms.[22]

Jack delayed announcing his engagement until after the *Saturday Evening Post* published a major article in mid-June entitled "The Senate's Gay Young Bachelor." The piece focused on the recent election and was undoubtedly based on materials provided by the ambassador's public relations men. It contained the now-standard accounts about Jack's education and war record and claimed that the senator read six to eight hardcover books a week. Rosemary Kennedy was described as "a school-teacher in Wisconsin." Not a hint of Jack's sexual exploits appeared, of course, but the subject of his marital status was prominent. "Many women have hopefully concluded that Kennedy needs looking after. In their opinion, he is, as a young millionaire senator, just about the most eligible bachelor in the United States—and the least justifiable one."[23]

Between the official announcement and engagement party, on June 25, and the wedding, set for September 12, Jack and Torby Macdonald took off on a European vacation. Many were puzzled by this apparently callous action. A Washington society editor said, "No man in love does that. If you're in love with somebody, you want to be with them."[24]

At the bridal dinner given by the Kennedys, Jack and his fiancée teased each other in toasts and speeches. Jackie pointed out that Jack had neglected to send her a single love letter during his courtship. She held up the only written record of his affection: a postcard from Bermuda containing the message, "Wish you were here, Jack."

The wedding, at St. Mary's Roman Catholic Church in Newport, Rhode Island, was an extravaganza designed by the ambassador for maximum publicity. (It was prominently featured on the front page of the Sunday *New York Times*.) Three thousand people milled outside the church. The eight-hundred-person guest list included the entire Senate, House Speaker Joe Martin, most of the Newport summer colony, and other celebrities from politics, journalism, business, and show business. Distinguished clergy, led by the archbishop of Boston, Richard Cushing, celebrated the high nuptial mass. The pope sent a special blessing. A well-known tenor sang three popular selections. The five-tier wedding cake was described by its creator as his masterpiece. The ambassador also provided two truckloads of champagne.

Bobby Kennedy was the best man, while Jackie's sister Lee served as matron of honor. Only a few people noticed the long red scratches on the groom's face, a result of the previous day's touch football game.

The only hitch in the ceremony was Black Jack Bouvier's absence. Having been snubbed cruelly by his ex-wife on two recent occasions, he drank too much and, at Janet's insistence, was kept away by anxious relatives. Jackie's stepfather escorted her down the aisle. Janet also gave orders that Black Jack was not to attend the huge reception at Hammersmith Farm, the three-hundred-acre Auchincloss estate overlooking Narragansett Bay. Jackie endured this parental warfare with a smile. Acting would henceforth be an integral part of her life.[25]

At the reception, where more than twelve hundred guests lined up to shake hands with the newlyweds, a friend told Jack that the next major step in his life should be the White House. Jack paused for a few seconds and replied, "I think you're right." As the two men walked out of the mansion to enjoy the view of the bay, Jack said, "That'd be a helluva place to sail in with the presidential yacht."[26]

After their wedding night at the Waldorf-Astoria in New York, the John F. Kennedys enjoyed a few weeks in Acapulco. Jack caught a nine-foot sailfish that he later had stuffed and mounted and hung in his Senate office. The couple concluded their honeymoon with a visit to Red Fay and his wife Anita in Monterey. On the newlyweds' last day on the West Coast, Jack and Red went to a pro football game, leaving their wives to fend for themselves. Fay later commented, "I'm sure this didn't seem a particularly unusual arrangement to Jack." Back at the Cape, Jack left his bride with the Kennedy family for several weeks while he looked for a house and caught up with his Senate duties. He visited on weekends.[27]

The Kennedy marriage was severely strained almost from the start. Jack was often away, and even when he was home the couple had difficulty communicating. Jack's world by this time was almost completely politics, a subject that bored Jackie. "Asking Jackie to get interested in politics was like asking Rocky Graziano to play the piano," Betty Spalding said. "She just didn't have any desire in the world to do it. She was smart enough, but it was out of her field. She didn't have the taste or stomach for it. Her nature was literary and artistic. Let's face it, he loved politics and she hated it." Reporters' wives watched her at parties, often sitting by herself, her husband ignoring her. At one party, when the subject of politics came up, "she almost literally took a chair, turned it towards a corner, and sat there for the entire evening without bothering to talk to anybody." A course in American history at Georgetown University in the spring of 1954 (she earned a B) failed to change her attitude.[28]

Jackie also resented the fact that she and her husband were rarely alone together. Jack's buddies were around constantly, frequently living in the Kennedy home. Lem Billings, for one, seemed to be a permanent fixture. And Jack's political associates seemed forever underfoot. "I can understand the way she felt about those politicians," Letitia Baldrige said. "They sprawled all over her furniture, broke her Sevres ashtrays, dropped their cigarette butts in her vases, and, most of all, took up her husband's time."[29]

Jackie's extravagant spending soon became a sore point between the couple. Jack, strongly given to parsimony, was often stunned by the bills pouring in after one of his wife's frequent shopping sprees. In mid-1955, the couple moved into a beautiful old $125,000 house called Hickory Hill in McLean, Virginia, which Jackie never tired of redecorating. By mid-1957 Jack had required Jackie's personal secretary, Mary Barelli Gallagher, to provide him with a complete list and description of all checks written. Gallagher later recalled, "That was just the beginning. Jackie's finances would haunt my nights and days from then on, all through the White House years and even after." At the same time, Jackie, like her in-laws, paid her help as little as possible.[30]

The most difficult problem Jackie faced was her husband's flagrant philandering. She had not expected total devotion; she had known about her father's many affairs and had no doubt grown to accept a measure of such conduct as characteristic of upper-class males. But she had not dreamed of the extent to which Jack would pursue other women. He and his pal George Smathers, for example, kept an apartment at the Carroll Arms in Washington where they met young women. "Jack liked to go over there and meet a couple of young secretaries," Smathers said later. "He liked groups."[31] Jack often attended parties accompanied by other women. At times, like his father, he brought along a "beard," another man on a date to pretend to be with the woman and to make the necessary hotel reservation. Actor Peter Lawford, who married Pat Kennedy in June 1954, sometimes played the part.

Jackie quickly learned what was going on. A friend recalled, "Jack kept assuring us that she didn't suspect, when it was obvious that she knew exactly what was happening." Another friend said later, "After the first year they were together, Jackie was wandering around looking like a survivor of an airplane crash."[32]

Still, a sort of friendship grew between the two. They learned to enjoy each other's company. Jackie, her secretary later reported, took delight in surprising Jack with small gifts.[33] Jack, when he paid attention, found his wife consistently interesting. Charles Spalding recalled, "He really brightened when she appeared. You could see it in his eyes; he'd follow her around the room watching to see what she'd do next."[34] Ted Sorensen wrote later, "Jacqueline possessed a quality of strong independence and, occasionally, saucy irreverence that made him all the more pleased to impress her in his work."[35]

In public, of course, the John F. Kennedys portrayed themselves as models of domestic bliss. Lem Billings considered them both excellent actors. Anita Fay later said of Jackie, "From the first time I met her I felt I was in the presence of a very great actress."[36] Edward R. Murrow's popular CBS television program *Person to Person* visited them a month after their marriage. Jackie seemed a bit nervous and Jack's responses were obviously prepared in advance, but both came across as attractive, sincere, and devoted to one another. In feature stories in several newspapers they were made to appear "as a modest, hardworking, and romantic collegiate couple."[37]

->>> <<<-

In early January 1953, even before his Senate offices were available, Jack took a momentous step in his political career by employing Ted Sorensen as a legislative assistant. The twenty-four-year-old Sorensen was a brilliant attorney who, since leaving his home state of Nebraska in 1951, had worked for the Federal Security Agency; and for the past eight months, a Senate subcommittee studying the railroad retirement system. Senator Paul Douglas of Illinois, the subcommittee chairman, had recommended him to a large number of Democratic senators and senators-elect. Following two five-minute interviews, conducted a few days apart, Kennedy hired him for a trial period of one year. Jack apparently had little idea of the young attorney's ideological credentials.

Like Douglas, Sorensen was a liberal. His father had been a crusading Nebraska Progressive, an insurgent Republican attorney general, and a supporter of Franklin D. Roosevelt. His mother had been a dedicated feminist. Young Ted had helped organize an Americans for Democratic Action chapter in Lincoln, had been involved in civil rights, and was a pacifist. He knew that Kennedy had shaky credentials as a liberal, and in his second interview he asked Jack about Joe McCarthy and related matters. This did not bother the senator-elect ("He was not pro-McCarthy, he said, but he did doubt Owen Lattimore"); he needed an experienced attorney who could frame legislation to boost the New England economy.

Sorensen—ambitious and eager to please—quickly proved indispensable. Evelyn Lincoln later wrote, "From the very first he was like the Rock of Gibraltar." Sorensen was extremely hardworking, would do as told, and was almost fanatically loyal.

The tall, serious young intellectual with hornrimmed glasses and a Phi Beta Kappa key could seem cold and disagreeable to some, including his fellow office employees. According to them, his concern for humanity was often left in the abstract and did not extend to individuals. The receptionist said later, "He really didn't know how to get along with people—maybe he was too smart." But Jack liked and trusted Sorensen and soon grew to depend on him, calling him at one point his "intellectual blood bank." Herbert Parmet later wrote, "As Dwight Eisenhower learned about Sherman Adams, Wilson about Colonel House, and FDR about Harry Hopkins, Kennedy needed Sorensen."[38]

Despite his youth, Sorensen had probably read as much as Jack and he wrote a great deal better. Moreover, he had the intensity and discipline his employer had always lacked. Soon Sorensen, surely with the ambassador's blessings, was cranking out first-rate speeches and articles on a wide variety of topics under Jack's name. Within little more than a year of his employment, "Kennedy" articles were published in *American Magazine*, the *New Republic*, the *New York Times Magazine*, and the *Atlantic Monthly*. The junior senator from Massachusetts began gaining a national reputation as an important intellectual and an expert on public affairs.[39]

From this point on, historians have difficulties distinguishing Sorensen's consistently gifted rhetoric from Jack's. What is certain is that prior to Sorensen's employment, one searches Kennedy's writings and speeches in vain for the beautifully flowing sentences, rich historical allusions, and often brilliant wit seen and heard afterward. Sorensen later acknowledged the difference and attributed it to JFK's capacity for growth. He "was not the same man" in 1963 that he had been a decade earlier, Sorensen claimed. His intellectual curiosity was greater, his reading more rapid, and his retention "amazing"; he "enjoyed listening at length to anyone with new information or ideas on almost any subject, and he never forgot what he heard." Moreover, changes in his personality and philosophy were even "more profound." He lost most of his public shyness, was kinder and more considerate, better organized, more liberal.[40]

Amid the typical Sorensen adulation, there is clearly some truth. Kennedy certainly had a greater sense of physical and intellectual well-being. Though some of this undoubtedly came from experience, it is clear that his regular doses of cortisone contributed. Campaign victories, a new office, and marriage also helped Kennedy mature. Jack took a speed-reading course in early 1954, and he thereafter impressed people by glancing at documents and claiming to have absorbed them. (At least some of the time, certainly, he was bluffing.) Moreover, Jack learned to handle himself in public with greater self-confidence, and in time he excelled at sparring with reporters. Many people later testified about his eagerness for information.

Still, the most plausible and at times provable explanation for the huge gap between the rhetoric of the "old" and "new" Kennedy is that Sorensen himself was largely responsible for the wit, sophistication, and literary prowess linked in the public's mind with JFK after his entrance into the Senate. Sorensen later made several admissions about Jack, including his difficulties with English grammar, his need for the complete text of a speech, and his initial poor delivery. "Often his tone was monotonous. Often his emphasis was on the wrong word." He wrote of "the Kennedy style of speech-writing—our style," asserting, "As the years went on, and I came to know what he thought on each subject as well as how he wished to say it, our style and standard became increasingly one." Kennedy's image owed much to the wisdom and words of Ted Sorensen.[41]

>>>   <<<

Although Jack showed more interest in the Senate than in the House, most of his work was still done by others; a staff member was trained to sign all his official outgoing mail. The Senate office, across from Vice President Nixon's Capitol Hill office, was a happy and informal place. The door to the outer office was always open. Jack was a demanding but friendly and considerate employer. One staff member later recalled her boss's wit. "You could get away with anything if you could turn it into a witticism, somehow. His own humor was sometimes sophisticated, but it could also be quite earthy, as when he would say, 'As the cow said to the farmer, "Thank you for a warm hand on a cold morning." ' "

When singers dropped by the office, Jack would close the outer office door and compel them to perform. Sometimes the office staff would sing along. Famed tenor Morton Downey, a friend of the ambassador, once sang "Danny Boy," leaving his audience in tears. Jack inevitably tried to persuade each musical guest to sing his favorite, "Bill Bailey, Won't You Please Come Home?"[42]

Jack readily admitted lacking any firm ideological leaning. He told one writer in early 1953 that he especially disliked letters that chided him for failing to be a true liberal. "I'd be very happy to tell them I'm not a liberal at all. I never joined the Americans for Democratic Action or the American Veterans Committee. I'm not comfortable with those people." At the same time Jack claimed to disagree with his father on most major issues.[43]

In fact the ambassador and his staff worked closely with the new senator from the start, developing a strategy that would pave the way for a later Presidential bid. At first Jack was to build a reputation as a concerned expert on New England affairs, carefully balancing the interests of his constituents with national considerations. In May 1953, he delivered three Senate speeches calling for a variety of federal aid to the depressed New England economy. He later became a leader of the New England Senators' Conference, created to promote the economic interests of his region. And at the end of his first two years in office he could boast of numerous special-interest activities.

In January 1954 Jack abandoned a 1952 campaign pledge and gave a major speech backing construction of the St. Lawrence Seaway. This move, objectionable to many New Englanders, who feared the seaway's economic influence, made Jack a national figure. Kennedy now seemed more a man of principle, concerned primarily with the larger issues of national life. (An opponent would later say that his vote was designed to help the ambassador's Merchandise Mart in Chicago.) "The speech," Sorensen (its author) wrote later, "was regarded as a turning point in the Seaway debate as well as in the Senator's career."[44]

Jack gained more attention, however, for his foreign policy views (which echoed his father's hard-line approach). He repeatedly condemned the Eisenhower administration for its dependence upon "massive retaliation" and sought increases in military spending. He took a special interest in French Indochina, and in the Senate tried unsuccessfully to tie American aid to the French with the eventual independence to the Vietnamese. Even before President Eisenhower mentioned the "domino" principle, Kennedy linked the existence of a non-Communist regime in Vietnam to the security of all Southeast Asia.

In the spring of 1954, Jack toured the country, campaigning for Democrats and expounding his Cold War positions. The *Brooklyn Eagle* exclaimed, "Keep your eye on young Democratic Senator John Kennedy. He's been getting a build-up for a nationwide campaign such as a Vice Presidential candidate." At the Democratic state convention in Connecticut, he charged that the Free World's security was "rapidly dissolving under the heat of Communist intimidation and subversion."[45]

Like a great many politicians of the period, Jack tried to avoid the raging controversy surrounding Senator Joe McCarthy. For one thing, the junior senator from Wisconsin was a personal and family friend. He had visited Hyannis Port on several occasions, enjoying long conversations with the ambassador, and he had dated two of the Kennedy girls. In early 1953, at the ambassador's request, McCarthy gave Bobby a job with his subcommittee. In addition, the headline-hunting leader of the second Red scare continued to enjoy strong support in Massachusetts. The state's senior senator, liberal Republican Leverett Saltonstall, up for reelection in 1954, dared not oppose McCarthy publicly, although he privately detested him. Moreover, of course, Jack and his father shared many of McCarthy's basic assumptions about Reds at home and abroad.[46]

Jack, perhaps to placate liberals, opposed McCarthy from time to time on minor issues. He voted to approve the president's nominees James B. Conant as ambassador to Germany and Charles Bohlen as ambassador to Russia; he opposed the appointment of McCarthy's friend Robert E. Lee to the Federal Communications Commission; he voted to restrict the political activities of McCarthyite State Department Security Chief Scott McLeod. On the whole, however, Jack tried to be noncommittal, avoiding criticism from both the Left and Right. In an undelivered speech on McCarthy's proposed censure, he would later declare, "I am not insensitive to the fact that my constituents perhaps contain a greater proportion of devotees on each side of this matter than the constituency of any other Senator."[47]

After McCarthy's public humiliation during the nationally televised Army-McCarthy hearings in the spring of 1954, there was a serious effort in the Senate to censure him. The ambassador, undoubtedly opposing his son's involvement in such a move, sent him a packet of clippings from European newspapers to discredit liberal claims that McCarthy had damaged America's image abroad. "As far as strained relations which we have heard so much about, that's a lot of bunk."[48] When a reporter asked

Jack what he thought about McCarthy, he replied: "Not very much. But I get along with him. When I was in the House I used to get along with Marcantonio and with Rankin. As long as they don't step in my way, I don't want to get into personal fights."[49]

On July 30, 1954, the Senate debated a motion by maverick Republican Ralph Flanders to censure McCarthy. By the end of the following day, forty-six charges were in the record. On August 2, the Senate voted to create a select committee to study the matter—and report after the fall elections. Still, much of the fear of McCarthy and his allies had dissipated, along with the senator's standings in public opinion polls. Democratic Minority Leader Lyndon Johnson virtually handpicked the committee to assure censure. By this time most senators on both sides of the aisle were fed up with McCarthy's often irresponsible and disruptive behavior.[50]

Jack did not participate in the heated debates. Ted Sorensen drafted a speech for the occasion, but when the Senate, with Jack's support, voted to establish a select committee, it went into the files.[51]

The speech reflected Jack's effort to conciliate both McCarthy's friends and foes. Kennedy came out for censure, but on extremely narrow grounds—McCarthy's support of his chief counsel Roy Cohn, an easy target whose flagrant official misconduct and obnoxious personality had been exposed by the Army-McCarthy hearings. One would never know from the speech that McCarthy was guilty of anything else. No abuses of civil liberties were mentioned. Accepting his father's advice, Kennedy denied that McCarthy had caused significant dissension at home or abroad. Indeed, he warned, the Flanders censure proposal would likely "have serious repercussions upon the social fabric of this country and must be so recognized."

The speech stressed JFK's consistent support for McCarthy:

This issue involves neither the motives nor the sincerity of the Junior Senator from Wisconsin. Many times I have voted with Senator McCarthy, for the full appropriation of funds for his committee, for his amendment to reduce our assistance to nations trading with Communists, and on other matters. I have not sought to end his investigations of Communist subversion, nor is the pending measure related to either the desirability or continuation of those investigations.[52]

By this time letters sympathetic to McCarthy were pouring into Jack's office, and the *Boston Post* was questioning Kennedy's patriotism. To further immunize himself from any possible suspicion of being "soft on the Reds," Jack teamed up with Hubert Humphrey of Minnesota and

Wayne Morse of Oregon in backing the Communist Control Act of 1954. This hastily devised and poorly thought out response to the ultraconservatives virtually outlawed the Communist party in the United States. There was clearly a link between the act and the impending study and vote on McCarthy. Humphrey said later that he was "so damn sick and tired with having Joe McCarthy bring up communism every fifteen minutes in the Senate that I said, 'If you really want to deal with this issue, let's deal with it across the board, come on, boys.' "[53] The measure swept through the House almost without dissent and passed the Senate in two forms by votes of 85 to 0, 81 to 1, and 79 to 0. Irving Howe wrote of "this Congressional stampede to prove that each party was as ready as the other to trample the concept of liberty in the name of destroying its enemy."[54] How exactly this expedient action would effect the McCarthy matter remained to be seen. In the meantime Jack had other worries.

By the summer of 1954, Kennedy was in constant and often severe physical pain. His Addison's disease had apparently been acting up for at least a year, and by May his back condition required him to use crutches almost full-time. Jack cut down on his travel and cancelled many appointments. He sometimes spent long hours at his Senate desk to avoid having to leave the floor and return. He became so irritable that Evelyn Lincoln seriously considered looking for another job.[55] Jack's condition caused further strains on his marriage.[56]

In early October Jack's temper flared before, during, and after a television program designed to boost two prominent Massachusetts Democrats, Robert Murphy and Foster Furcolo. State Treasurer Furcolo was a young, articulate, and well-educated senatorial candidate whom the Kennedys feared as a future rival. After a prebroadcast altercation concerning the strength of Kennedy's prepared remarks, Jack did not endorse Furcolo directly on the air. An aide soon declared publicly that the omission was intentional. With Jack's support and the ambassador's financial backing, Murphy won the gubernatorial race in November. Furcolo lost to Senator Saltonstall by some thirty-thousand votes. Almost a quarter century later, Furcolo remained bitter about the election, charging that Jack had actually supported the incumbent and was wooing Republicans. (Kennedy and Saltonstall issued a joint communiqué during the campaign describing their bipartisan achievements.) Furcolo also stated that Jack "didn't like people to take a position contrary to him in any way. He didn't like that at all. I don't know whether you'd call it vindictive or not. . . . He just couldn't be aware of the fact that anyone could have a position different from his."[57]

Jack's back pain became so intense that on October 10 he entered the New York Hospital for Special Surgery to undergo a "double-fusion" operation. He was warned that, due to his Addison's disease, the operation was extremely risky. But Jack was desperate; his weight had dropped from 180 to 140, and he could barely walk, even with crutches.[58]

Rumors of Jack's serious illness soon spread. A Boston reporter asked Ted Reardon to issue a public medical history. "No," Reardon replied sadly, "old Joe doesn't want that to be done. We can't do it now."[59]

The operation took place on October 21, with two teams of physicians on hand, one skilled in endocrinology and the other in surgical physiology. Three days later, infection set in, and Jack fell into a coma and was placed on the critical list. He received the last rites. At one point the ambassador came into Arthur Krock's office at the *New York Times* and slumped into a chair weeping: "He told me he thought Jack was dying." He would later tell reporters that his son had twice come within twenty minutes of death.[60]

Details of the operation were covered up, of course, to conceal Addison's disease. The press attributed Jack's back problems to his wartime service, thus linking the surgery with military heroism. Also concealed was the fact that as Kennedy recovered over the next few weeks, he was conscious and alert much of the time, and in fact was perfectly capable at some point of reaching Ted Sorensen and taking a position on the censure of Joe McCarthy. Kennedy and his apologists argued for years that he was too ill on December 2, when the vote was taken, to take a position. Besides, O'Donnell and Powers declared, "everybody in the Senate knew that Kennedy had been planning to vote for McCarthy's censure."[61] But Sorensen admitted in 1971, "I think he deliberately did not contact me."[62]

In fact, Kennedy intentionally avoided the vote, largely in deference to his father and with a keen eye on the Massachusetts electorate and his own political future. He was the only Senate Democrat who failed to vote or pair against McCarthy. While still in the hospital, he predicted to his friend Charles Spalding what awaited him on his release. " 'You know, when I get downstairs I know exactly what's going to happen.' He said, 'Those reporters are going to lean over my stretcher. There's going to be about ninety-five faces bent over me with great concern, and everyone of those guys is going to say, "Now, Senator, what about McCarthy?" And he said, 'Do you know what I'm going to do? I'm going to reach back for my back and I'm just going to yell, "Oow," and then I'm going to pull the sheet over my head and hope we can get out of there.' " Spalding said later, "Well, what could he do? He'd ducked the vote. . . . All he could think of was he was going to avoid it by not saying anything."[63]

It would not be until 1956, a few weeks before the Democratic National Convention, that Kennedy publicly endorsed McCarthy's censure. Later, under heavy fire from liberals, he declared that he would have voted for censure. Before that, however, he told a close associate, "Even my Dad is against McCarthy now, and if he is, then McCarthy has nobody left."[64]

While running for the White House, Jack would continue to use physical incapacity as the reason he failed to vote in 1954, and would admit that he still could not see McCarthy and his "ism" as a moral problem. Still, James MacGregor Burns quoted him as saying that he was "completely out of sympathy with McCarthy and had no close relationship with him, particularly after I voted against him on several occasions."[65]

Jack's New York hospital room reminded one visitor of a college dorm. A poster of Marilyn Monroe in blue shorts had been placed upside down on the wall so that her well-spread legs were up in the air. A Howdy Doody doll lay on the bed. Young women, described as "cousins," visited. Jackie appeared often, passing along gossip, evaluating nurses who had caught Jack's eye, bringing along balloons for him to shoot at with a popgun, and trying in numerous other ways to revive her husband's spirits. She was also part of a prank that hired actress Grace Kelly to pose as a night nurse. "When Jack opened his eyes, he thought he was dreaming."[66]

→>>   <<←

During long weeks Jack tried hard to conceal his pain. "The marvel was that he could make jokes about his own pain," Charles Spalding said later. "He'd turn everything into a funny remark, sometimes at the expense of the doctor or the nurse or himself or the hospital or science or anything."[67] A Harvard researcher who visited later recalled, "He'd be on his stomach and the doctors would be doing all this horrid stuff to him and he'd be on the phone to someone getting the latest gossip. The hospital staff couldn't believe it." The researcher brought Jack some serious books, and she later commented, "Jack had a voracious curiosity, but it really didn't have much to do with abstract ideas. He had a very precise sense of what was useful and what wasn't, and that determined how far he pursued things."[68]

Jack was released from the hospital temporarily to spend Christmas with his family at Palm Beach. He was carried out on a stretcher, and there was uncertainty whether he would ever walk again. Years later Jackie said of the holiday, "It was horrible. We spent the whole time hovering around the heir apparent.'' All her energy was devoted to devising ways to cheer him up.[69] She and the ambassador grew increasingly close during these dark days. They told jokes and played games, one involving throwing lamb bones at the housekeeper whenever the ambassador made his favorite lamb stew.[70] Lem Billings later remarked, ''It was a terrible time.'' Jack ''was bitter and low. We came close to losing him. I don't just mean losing his life. I mean losing him *as a person*.''[71]

When the infection was discovered in early February 1955, Jack returned to the hospital for the removal of a silver plate used in the first operation. He again received the last rites. This time, however, he rallied. Dave Powers watched the surgical dressing being changed and later observed that Jack ''had a hole in his back big enough for me to put my fist in it up to the wrist.'' Two weeks later, Jack was again in Palm Beach to recuperate. Powers recalled that he was in constant pain and unable to sleep more than an hour or two at a time. ''The Ambassador, who was there with us all the time, would say to me often, 'Dave, don't try to give him anything for the pain—it's something he has to go through.' ''[72]

By early March Jack was able to walk fifty feet without his crutches. The next morning, he made it down to the beach. The ambassador watched approvingly and said to Powers at lunch, ''God, Dave, he's getting stronger all the time. Did you see the legs on him? He's got the legs of a fighter or a swimming champion.''[73]

Jack's recovery was steady, despite a fall in April when one of the screws in a crutch worked loose. He boasted to a reporter in May that since March he had been recorded on 73 percent of all legislative votes by the process of pairing (agreeing with a colleague not to vote on a specific issue about which the two held opposing positions), and that since March 16 the level had reached 100 percent. ''We've sponsored or co-sponsored 24 bills since January,'' he said proudly, putting to rest rumors that his health would force him to resign.[74]

Jack's misery remained, however, and his surgical would healed very slowly. Charles Spalding later recalled, ''I think the pain was constant and he had to literally fight against it. . . . I would walk up the beach with him with the back, still open, and he'd say, 'How is it now? Is it open?' or 'Is any stuff running out of it?' '' Spalding thought that Jack's pain ''had a shaping effect on his personality.''[75]

Jack's struggles with surgery and pain added a new dimension to his public aura. The handsome young war hero was overcoming his disability with courage and determination. Americans had always cherished stories about the successful conquest of adversity, and Kennedy added to his appeal by tapping into this national predilection.

On May 23, six days before his thirty-eighth birthday, Jack returned to Capitol Hill. The *New York Times*, in a front-page story with a photograph, reported, "The surgery was required by wounds he suffered during World War II as commanding officer of a motor torpedo boat." Intent on proving himself Kennedy-tough, Jack told newsmen at a press conference that he had thrown away his crutches a few days earlier. To make his point he climbed the front steps of the Capitol and strolled over to the Senate Office Building. Richard Nixon had had a basket of fruit and candy placed on his office desk with a note reading "Welcome Home." The next day Senate leaders formally welcomed their long-absent colleague. The *New York Herald Tribune* declared, "Young Jack Kennedy comes from a bold and sturdy breed, and he's back on the job again."[76]

Shortly after his return to Washington, Jack consulted Dr. Janet Travell, a New York pharmacologist. Dr. Travell later revealed that Jack had to be helped by two men to navigate the few steps down to her ground-floor office. He could barely place any weight on his left leg, which was three-quarters of an inch shorter than his right. His right knee was stiff. "He looked thin; his weight of about 155 pounds did not adequately cover his generous frame and stature of six feet." He was pale and anemic and had to turn his entire body to address different people. "When I examined him, the reality of his ordeal was brought home to me by the callus under each armpit toward the shoulder blade where the skin had borne his weight on crutches for so long," Dr. Travell urged him to enter a New York hospital for further treatment, and Jack reluctantly agreed.[77]

Kennedy remained in the hospital for a week, and for the next few months he made weekend trips to New York for physiotherapy. In July he entered two different hospitals, not only for back treatments but also no doubt because of his Addison's disease, which physicians were still trying to control. Improvements by endocrinologists in cortisone and its "relations" were to give Jack much of the strength he needed to pursue higher office.[78]

After a nine-week European trip with Jackie that late summer and early fall, Jack admitted to Dr. Travell that his discomfort had increased. He then began receiving weekly Novocaine treatment for muscle spasms. That Christmas Dr. Travell visited the Kennedys in Palm Beach. Looking back, she pondered, "My host and his beautiful bride of two years had that health-giving world to hold forever. What forces drove him to leave it for the ravages of politics?"[79]

>>> <<<

In early 1954, Jack had an idea for an article: a piece depicting courageous stands taken by American politicians in the best interests of the public. During the rest of the year, he and Ted Sorensen solicited names and events from a variety of journalists and professors. While Jack recuperated from surgery, the concept of a book emerged, and a contract was signed with a prestigious New York publisher. Jack's survival meant the continuation of the drive for the White House. A book, as the ambassador had long advised, would provide credentials.

Sorensen worked almost full-time on the project during the first half of 1955, aided by Georgetown historian (and Jackie's former professor) Jules Davids; James Landis of the ambassador's staff; William R. Tansill of the Library of Congress; and a number of well-known scholars including Arthur Schlesinger, Jr., James MacGregor Burns, and Allan Nevins. Sorensen and Davids did most of the research and drafting of chapters for what became known as *Profiles in Courage*. Sorensen was responsible for the book's lucid and compelling style.

Jack supervised the project during his convalescence and European travels. He arranged to finance publicity for the book and had a hand in its design. (He specifically asked that laudatory comments by Schlesinger be kept off the cover, no doubt to avoid offending conservatives.) He also did a bit of writing, probably in bed in Florida.

This handwritten contribution to *Profiles in Courage*, now in the Kennedy Library and frequently cited as proof of Jack's authorship, in fact bears little resemblance to the finished product. Herbert Parmet, whose careful research has best illuminated the origins of *Profiles in Courage*, accurately described Jack's writing as a "disorganized, somewhat incoherent, melange from secondary sources." One finds "very rough passages without paragraphing, without any shape, largely ideas jotted down as possible sections, obviously necessitating editing." Existing tape recordings of dictation by Kennedy, Parmet notes, "duplicate the pattern of the nearly illegible scrawls on those canary sheets."

Rather than actually writing a book, therefore, Jack was transmitting thoughts and information to Sorensen and his helpers, who chose largely to organize and write things their own way. Parmet concluded that "the Senator served principally as an overseer or, more charitably, as a sponsor and editor, one whose final approval was as important for its publication as for its birth."[80]

In the Preface to *Profiles*, Jack paid tribute to Sorensen ("my research associate"), Davids, Landis, and others, but he claimed unequivocally to be the volume's author. "A long period of hospitalization and convalescence following a spinal operation in October 1954, gave me my first opportunity to do the reading and research necessary for this project,'' For the rest of his life, Kennedy's wrath could be roused by few things like the persistent suggestion that others had written or helped to write *Profiles*. In 1957 he and family attorneys got columnist Drew Pearson to recant the charge that Jack had employed a ghostwriter. That same year the ambassador asked the FBI to probe a group of New York critics.[81] Sorensen, Schlesinger, Burns, and other Kennedy loyalists would give Jack full credit for the book.[82]

The politically balanced, highly readable, two-hundred-and-sixty-six-page volume proved to be exceedingly popular. Chapters describing heroic deeds by John Quincy Adams, Daniel Webster, Thomas Hart Benton, Sam Houston, Edward G. Ross, Lucius Q. C. Lamar, George Norris, and Robert Taft contained something of interest for almost everyone. It was a book about faith in democracy, undaunted courage, and ''unyielding devotion to absolute principle.'' Reviewers applauded, and more than one identified Senator Kennedy with the idealism he extolled. A sober photograph of Jack made the cover of the *New York Times Book Review*, and reviewer Cabell Phillips exclaimed, ''it is refreshing and enlightening to have a first-rate politician write a thoughtful and persuasive book about political integrity.'' Jack, he said, was ''a solid journeyman full of ideals but few illusions.''[83]

Prepublication sales of *Profiles* to major magazines were brisk; advertising, subsidized by a percentage of Jack's profits, was extensive. Sorensen boasted in late 1955 that ''more people will have heard of this book by January than any other.'' *Profiles* was published on the first day of 1956 and quickly became a best-seller. Television rights were arranged; foreign-language editions proliferated. By March 1958, 124,665 copies had been sold. Drew Pearson later reported that the Senator made fifty thousand dollars in royalties. (Sorensen, according to Pearson, received six thousand dollars. Davids, according to Parmet, received a fee of seven hundred dollars.) Jack told Pearson, on the other hand, ''I never expected the book to sell, and I was surprised that it did.''[84]

The young senator was now more widely recognized and highly regarded than ever. He was thought to be a deep thinker, an important writer, a champion of principle, a conquerer of adversity, and a politician of the highest promise. *Profiles in Courage* had celebrated his image, and the Democratic National Convention was only a few months away.

CHAPTER 8

The Upstart

>>> <<<

As THE NATION edged toward the election of 1956, the American people on the whole thought well of themselves. The country was prosperous (the gross national product had grown from $167 billion in 1945 to $400 billion in 1955) and at peace; technological innovations were flourishing; higher education was expanding at a record pace; big families were in fashion, and the suburbs were booming; church membership was growing rapidly; radicalism of all sorts seemed dead; the Eisenhower administration enjoyed widespread confidence as it moved successfully to stop communism abroad and bring healing and moderation at home.

In these good times, greatly romanticized as they were (then and subsequently), the nation saw itself as young, rich, brash, idealistic, and beautiful. This self-image bore a striking similarity to the public image projected by John F. Kennedy. Indeed, to many JFK would soon seem to personify the best features of American civilization, and they would rally with great enthusiasm behind his efforts to attain a position of national leadership.

As early as 1953 the ambassador and Jack had discussed the vice presidency. By the following year they were giving serious thought to a Stevenson-Kennedy ticket. The ambassador had backed Adlai Stevenson in 1948 when the ambitious and articulate attorney captured the governorship of Illinois. "I discovered Adlai Stevenson," he sometimes boasted. In 1952, the elder Kennedy quietly contributed some $25,000 to the Stevenson presidential campaign (while telling Republican friends that he supported Eisenhower). Stevenson was considered the likely candidate in 1956, and Kennedy backers asserted that an alliance with the Massachusetts senator would lend geographical balance to the ticket, win Catholic votes, reduce controversy over Stevenson's divorce, and help ward off inevitable GOP charges that Democrats were "soft" on the Reds. One Stevenson associate said later, "We were lobbied to death" by Jack Kennedy. Stevenson later admitted that the ambassador "came to see me several times—he had contributed to my campaign—and we talked about Jack in a general way."[1]

But the former governor did not like or trust the ambassador and was not overly fond of his son. Many Stevenson supporters, moreover, thought Jack a potential liability. His Catholicism, they argued, would repel a great many voters, and his poor health, youth, and inexperience could prove detrimental. Stevenson's manager, Jim Finnegan, said, "I like Jack, for what I've seen about him. I don't really know him. But he's a kid."[2]

President Eisenhower's heart attack in September 1955 cast doubt on his political future and thus made the Democratic presidential nomination more attractive. Stevenson soon had challengers, and the second place on the ticket attracted a crowd of aspirants.

Profiles in Courage boosted Jack's visibility in early 1956. He and Sorensen were soon pestering Senate Majority Leader Lyndon Johnson for more important committee assignments. Johnson resisted, not caring for Jack personally and resenting the young man's independence and consistent support for the political and economic interests of his own region. In early February Kennedy made headlines by calling on the Democratic party to support unequivocally the Supreme Court decision ending segregation in the public schools, even if that meant alienating many Southern Democrats. Stevenson was saying similar things at the same time, and Jack, hoping to link himself with the front runner, was undoubtedly trying to attract national attention. Kennedy won more notice from journalists and colleagues that spring by playing an active role in the defeat of proposals designed to alter the structure and functions of the Electoral College.[3]

On March 8 Jack formally endorsed Stevenson, telling reporters that he was not a candidate for the second spot. Stevenson people knew better, however, and understood that Kennedy hoped Stevenson would name him his running mate. In mid-February, Jack had sent a private poll to one of the candidate's law associates showing that in Massachusetts Stevenson led Tennessee Senator Estes Kefauver by a huge margin. It also revealed that Jack led Congressman McCormack as a favorite-son candidate for the presidency by an even larger margin.[4]

Veteran Congressman McCormack was the major obstacle in Massachusetts to a Stevenson-Kennedy endorsement. McCormack did not believe that Stevenson could defeat Eisenhower, and he and several allies, including state Democratic committee chairman William ("Onions") Burke and right-winger John Fox of the *Boston Post*, had little use for the aloof and often unreliable Kennedy. In the Massachusetts Democratic primary in April, McCormack, running as a favorite son, garnered 20,969 votes to Stevenson's 13,377. Jack won 845 votes.[5]

Jack was forced, with great reluctance, to become directly embroiled in an internal party struggle. In early May he and supporters, led by Kenny O'Donnell and Larry O'Brien, worked actively to elect their own man, Pat Lynch, to the position of state committee chairman. McCormack backed Burke "one thousand percent." Former Governor Paul Dever gave his support to Lynch. The senator toured the entire state, visiting each of the eighty members of the committee. After a bitter struggle, Lynch defeated Burke. O'Donnell later called it "the most vicious fight I have ever experienced in all the years I have worked in politics." The loser, without producing evidence, declared that Jack had bought votes. "He and his millions don't know what decency and honor mean." Kennedy assured reporters that the battle had not been directed at Congressman McCormack. He quickly telephoned Stevenson with the news of his triumph. A Boston reporter observed, "Jack is as hard as nails; he is mean and tough. Nobody—short of the voters—is going to stop him from getting what he wants."[6]

Kennedy eulogists later claimed that the ambassador opposed Jack's direct involvement in state political warfare and was against his bid for the vice presidency after Eisenhower declared his candidacy.[7] The assertion, although widely accepted, is unconvincing. That Jack would enter a dangerous factional struggle on his own and against his father's wishes is contrary to what we know about the relationship between the two men, before and after 1956. And given the ambassador's carefully laid plans for his son to this point, and the Kennedys' long-established and widely known (among insiders) designs on the 1956 ticket, it seems highly unlikely that the elder Kennedy suddenly failed to support his son's bid for national prominence.

Kenny O'Donnell and Ted Kennedy later claimed that Jack defied his father at a crucial point during the Democratic National Convention, asserting that when Bobby telephoned the ambassador to announce that Jack had decided to continue seeking the vice presidency, "The Ambassador's blue language flashed all over the room. The connection was broken before he was finished denouncing Jack as an idiot who was ruining his political career." Doris Kearns Goodwin claimed that Jack's defiance "was an important rite of passage."[8]

If the incident did occur, it could only have been a temporary flare-up, brought about by specific developments during the convention proceedings and quickly abandoned. We now know that, for weeks before the convention, Jack kept his father informed in detail of his efforts to win the second spot on the ticket. In mid-June, the ambassador privately predicted that Stevenson would win the nomination "with possibly Jack Vice President." A month later, Sargent Shriver told the senior Kennedy he had assured Stevenson that "you were 100% behind Jack, that you gave him and his campaign everything you had even if perchance you might disagree with the basic wisdom of a decision Jack might make."[9] About the same time, the ambassador was giving serious thought to attending the convention himself and working on Jack's behalf. Instead James Landis, the Ambassador's trusted speechwriter, accompanied Jack to the convention and tried to persuade Eleanor Roosevelt to back his young friend. During the convention, the ambassador made telephone calls on behalf of his son to influential friends. We know that he reached Landis and sent him to Congressman Sam Rayburn. Mayor Richard Daley of Chicago, a friend and ally, came out for JFK during the convention and may well have been contacted.

The elder Kennedy's decision to be on vacation in Southern France before and during the convention (the *New York Times* ran a photograph of him at his villa on the second day of the proceedings) no doubt reflected his desire to encourage the view—already the official line for years—that Jack was entirely independent. After 1956 the ambassador would retire from public life completely to foster that illusion. (Moreover, in later interviews he no doubt dissociated himself entirely from Jack's vice presidential effort because the drive had been unsuccessful. He contended that he knew Stevenson would lose. Jack's boosters, however, had argued that even if Stevenson lost, his running mate would be nationally known and in good shape to try for the presidential nomination in 1960. The evidence seems conclusive that the Founding Father held the same view.)[10]

The Kennedy campaign went into high gear after the victory in Massachusetts. Leading Democrats around the nation began receiving autographed copies of *Profiles in Courage*.[11] Two local Memorial Day celebrations were turned into Kennedy rallies attended by more than forty-thousand cheering spectators. Democratic Senator Albert Gore of Tennessee was on hand to endorse JFK for first or second place on the national ticket, and telegrams bearing tributes poured in from Capitol Hill.[12]

The June 12 issue of *Look* contained an article by Fletcher Knebel entitled "Can a Catholic Become Vice President?" The answer was predictable given the fact that the piece had been quietly suggested by Kennedy and Sorensen and that the data Knebel employed came from Sorensen. At the same time Kennedy supporters were distributing the "Bailey Memorandum," a document named after John Bailey, the state chairman from Connecticut, but actually prepared by Sorensen. The memo was designed to allay fears that a Roman Catholic on the national ticket would cost votes. Indeed, the memo argued *for* a Catholic candidate, citing valuable areas of Catholic strength. It received national attention, and the Gallup Poll soon noticed a marked decline since 1940 in voter prejudice against having a Catholic president. Bailey and others quietly urged Stevenson to name Kennedy his running mate.[13]

Two Stevenson supporters, Governor Abraham A. Ribicoff of Connecticut and Dennis J. Roberts of Rhode Island, backed Kennedy at the annual governors conference in late June.[14] Jack informed his father of this support and noted that Stevenson adviser Arthur Schlesinger, Jr., now an ally, would work for the cause inside Stevenson headquarters.[15] Jack appeared on the nationally televised program *Face the Nation*. He sent letters to convention delegates and alternates urging them to watch a televised dramatization of his *PT 109* heroics. He worked at a studio narrating a film that would be shown at the convention. One Washington columnist, John O'Donnell, reported that Stevenson was ready to pick Kennedy.[16]

The former Illinois governor resisted the pressure, however, and remained noncommittal. Senators Hubert Humphrey of Minnesota, former presidential aspirant Senator Estes Kefauver of Tennessee, and several others were also campaigning actively for the second spot. In a private huddle with top advisers in late July, Stevenson noted that former President Truman thought Humphrey "too radical," had no use for Kefauver, and dismissed Kennedy because of his Catholicism. Stevenson may well have accepted Truman's evaluation of Kennedy; veteran New Dealer James Farley had advised him, he said, that "America is not ready for a Catholic yet." And powerful Texas Congressman Sam Rayburn had told him, "Well, if we have to have a Catholic, I hope we don't have to take that little piss-ant Kennedy. How about John McCormack?"[17]

On August 9, four days before the Democratic National Convention was scheduled to open in Chicago, Jack told the annual convention of the Massachusetts Federation of Labor that he was not actively seeking the vice presidential nomination and thought that the candidate should be "someone from another area of the country." At the same time the Kennedy forces were establishing a convention headquarters at Chicago's Palmer House hotel, and a team of strategists, including Bobby Kennedy, Larry O'Brien, Kenny O'Donnell, Torby Macdonald, and Ted Sorensen, was hard at work. Two of Jack's sisters, Eunice and Jean, were soon on hand, along with Ethel Kennedy. Jackie, noticeably pregnant, was also in Chicago but kept out of the action. She said later, "During the whole five days of the convention I never saw [Jack] except when he wandered by our box."[18]

Jack, now head of the Massachusetts delegation, arrived in Chicago on August 10, telling reporters, "I am not a candidate, and I am not campaigning for office." He admitted, however, that he would accept the vice presidential nomination should Stevenson select him. (Kefauver, Humphrey, and other contenders were playing the same game.) By this time, most of New England's delegates were in the Kennedy camp. Jack visited receptions and pumped hands for hours, while his backers wooed scores of delegates from across the nation.[19]

On the first evening of the convention, delegates noisily approved the campaign film *The Pursuit of Happiness*, produced by Dore Schary. Jack had been selected to narrate the film because he had performed well during television appearances and because *Profiles in Courage* was a best-seller. Kennedy appeared at the rostrum soon after the film's showing, prompting a placard-waving demonstration by the Massachusetts delegation. The movie and the convention proceedings were televised nationally, and Jack became known to tens of millions. (When Jack's Georgetown neighbor and friend, television newsman Charles Collingwood, kidded him about the failure of CBS to air the film, Jack shot him a hateful look and said, "I know, you bastards.")[20]

The next day Jack met with Eleanor Roosevelt, hoping to win her support. The effort was unsuccessful. O'Donnell and Powers later recalled that the former first lady "berated him before a room of people for not taking a firmer stand against Joe McCarthy." A private meeting with Harry Truman followed. Insiders soon reported that the former president was wary about having a Roman Catholic on the ticket.[21]

When Jack met with Stevenson on the third day of the convention, he came away with nothing more than an invitation to make the nominating speech. This move was thought by many to be a sop to Kennedy and a clear signal that another candidate would be named. Jack and Ted Sorensen were determined to make the most out of the situation, however. They chose not to use an address written by Arthur Schlesinger, Jr., and the distinguished journalist John Barlow Martin and stayed up all night working on a speech of their own. The finished product bore traces of haste ("Mr. Kennedy was obviously caught off-balance," a *New York Times* reporter observed. "He was forced to fall back on his cliché dictionary") and was slightly self-serving, but it enhanced his image as an attractive, idealistic, and articulate party leader and was well received by delegates.[22]

The next day Stevenson won the nomination easily on the first ballot. He then stunned veteran politicos by declining to select a running mate. "The choice will be yours," he told the delegates. "The profit will be the nation's." Stevenson had been unable to make up his mind. Moreover, throwing the convention open stood in sharp contrast to the GOP convention, which had forced Nixon on the delegates. The tactic also focused attention on the vice presidency, which, in a roundabout way, raised the issue of Eisenhower's health.[23]

Lyndon Johnson later called this "the goddamned stupidest move a politician could make." The leading candidates, Kefauver, Humphrey, Kennedy, and Gore, were disappointed and angry. They had only twelve hours to fight for a place on the ticket. Governor Robert B. Meyner of New Jersey said wearily, "This will be one of the busiest nights in history."[24]

Jack, Bobby, Eunice, and Jean were up to the challenge, and they and others worked through the night corralling delegates. "There were just an awful lot of Kennedys around," an observer said later. Jack talked with Governor Earl Long of Louisiana and Lyndon Johnson. He caught up with Robert F. Wagner, Jr., of New York City at midnight in a men's room. At 2:00 A.M. he was lining up nomination speakers. He got his brother-in-law, actor Peter Lawford, out of bed in Las Vegas to work on Nevada delegates. (The head of the Nevada delegation later said that Lawford's telephone calls helped win thirteen and a half of the state's fourteen votes.) At 5:00 A.M., rushing to another meeting, Jack tripped over a television cord and almost landed on Kefauver, who was doing an interview in a hotel corridor. By sunrise Kennedy for Vice President buttons, banners, and signs were available. Later that morning, with hardly any sleep, Jack took a cab to the convention hall. A Boston reporter with him noticed that during the ride Jack clenched his fist and kept whispering to himself, "Go! Go! Go!" The competitive drive and endurance that the Kennedys had perfected in touch football served them well in the political arena.

The other candidates were working with almost equal fury, of course, but there was something in the Kennedy drive that irritated certain people and caused resentment. Abraham Ribicoff later recalled that many leading Democrats sought to block the Kennedy effort. "He wasn't a great senator. They looked on him as a whippersnapper. I know I remember the remarks of Lyndon Johnson, Sam Rayburn, and Harry Truman—all these men—that just looked on him as a young rich upstart who didn't have the intellectual qualifications to be president." Johnson later told Doris Kearns Goodwin, "It was the goddamndest thing, here was a young whippersnapper, malaria-ridden and yallah, sickly, sickly. He never said a word of importance in the Senate and never did a thing. But somehow, with his books and his Pulitzer Prizes, he managed to create the image of himself as a shining intellectual, a youthful leader who could change the face of the country."[25]

The following day delegates placed thirteen names in nomination. Estes Kefauver, who had been running for office nationally since January, led on the first ballot with 483½ votes of the necessary 686½. Jack, with 304, placed second, thanks largely to New England support and anti-Kefauver votes from Southern delegates. The resistance to Kefauver grew stronger when the second ballot was taken, and Jack was the major beneficiary. Lyndon Johnson, who hated Kefauver more than he did Kennedy, shouted into a microphone, "Texas proudly casts its fifty-six votes for the fighting sailor who wears the scars of battle." (Johnson was soon in touch with the ambassador, explaining his vote.) Kennedy's strength grew to 646 votes to Kefauver's 551½. After the ballot, elated by his Southern support, Jack visited Arthur Krock. "His face was bright and shiny," Krock later recalled. "He was a very happy-looking boy. He said to me, 'I'm going to sing "Dixie" for the rest of my life.' "[26]

On the third ballot, however, after Gore withdrew, Kefauver recovered his momentum. A Kennedy vote in 1956 against 90 percent parity prevented several farm states from aiding the Bay State Senator. The turmoil ended with Kefauver taking the nomination 755½ to Kennedy's 589.

Jack was bitterly disappointed by his defeat and would feel an intense distaste for Stevenson for the rest of his life, saying privately that Adlai was weak, indecisive, and even effeminate. George Smathers later remembered Jack sitting in a hotel room for an hour and a half after his defeat, talking over what he might have done differently. "He was hurt, deeply hurt." O'Donnell and Powers later wrote that Jack was "furious" and full of "anger and frustration." "He hated to lose anything, and he glared at us when we tried to console him by telling him that he was the luckiest man in the world." Jack thought he had been "jobbed and

double-crossed by the party's bosses.'' Bobby expressed similar sentiments to friends. Many Kennedy supporters would long blame convention chairman Rayburn for failing to recognize delegates seeking to switch
to Kennedy on the second ballot.[27]

In public, however, Jack appeared gracious, humble, and supportive. He received a thunderous ovation for quickly making his way to the
podium after the decisive ballot and asking delegates to make the Kefauver nomination unanimous. He thanked the convention for its generosity
and kindness and said that the nomination of Kefauver revealed the party's strength and unity. He praised Stevenson's ''good judgment'' in
bringing the vice presidential nomination to the floor.[28]

Some observers thought that the attractive and photogenic young
senator was the only true victor of the entire convention. James Mac-
Gregor Burns wrote later, ''The dramatic race had glued millions to their
television sets. Kennedy's near-victory and sudden loss, the impression
he gave of a clean-cut boy who had done his best and who was accepting
defeat with a smile—all this struck at people's hearts in living rooms
across the nation.''[29]

→≫≫ ≪≪←

Soon after his convention loss, Jack telephoned his father in France.
Within a few hours, he was on a plane headed for the ambassador's villa
and a vacation. Jackie, eight months pregnant, was left behind at the Auchincloss estate in Newport. She had suffered a miscarriage in her first year
of marriage and was in considerable discomfort following the excitement
of the convention. Jack might have spent some time with his wife, offering
sympathy and companionship, but instead, he went on his own way.[30]

Jack relaxed for a short time at the ambassador's rented mansion on
the Riviera. Whatever, if any, disagreements the two men had had over
strategy during the Democratic Convention were quickly forgotten. Both
knew that Jack's presidential campaign would begin in the near future.
Bobby would soon be assigned to travel with Stevenson to learn the
mechanics of a national effort. While sunbathing one afternoon, a friend
asked Jack why he wanted to be president. Without opening his eyes,
Jack replied, ''I guess it's the only thing I can do.''[31]

Jack then joined George Smathers and several young women for a
bacchanalian yachting trip on the Mediterranean. Smathers later told of
one stunning but not especially intelligent blond aboard who referred to
herself in the third person as ''Pooh.'' ''She fascinated Jack, who was
wound very tight when he arrived in Europe and almost completely
unwound a few days later.''[32]

While at sea, word was received that Jackie had undergone an emergency cesarean operation and given birth to a stillborn child. For several hours her condition was listed as critical, and a priest was summoned. Jack only agreed to return home three days later, after Smathers convinced him that a shattered marriage would harm his political career. (This callousness was later covered up by the contention that Jack could not be reached aboard ship.) Smathers recalled, "I told him I was going to get him back there even if I had to carry him. Joe Kennedy agreed, so we went back together."[33]

The Kennedy marriage was indeed damaged by the incident. Jackie was furious, especially after learning what Jack and George Smathers had been up to during her suffering. (A *Washington Star* reporter revealed the presence of girls aboard the yacht.) She would never forgive Smathers. "Even after they were in the White House," Smathers said later, "She'd bring it up. . . . When I danced with her, she always said in that affected little whisper of hers, 'I bet you and Jack wish you were over in Vendome, France, right now, don't you?' She was always sticking it to me."[34]

Jackie moved to the Auchincloss estate after leaving the hospital and soon urged Jack to sell their Virginia home, recently equipped with a luxurious nursery. Rumors of marital discord spread throughout Washington, and *Time* reported that the ambassador made a million-dollar deal with Jackie to avoid scandal. Family friend Igor Cassini later revealed that the elder Kennedy told him he had offered Jackie a million dollars not to divorce Jack, acknowledging that the break would mean political suicide for his son.[35]

While it is clear that the ambassador stepped in to smooth things over, it seems unlikely that a significant monetary arrangement was made. By all accounts, however, Jackie was far from happy, and she found ways of expressing her displeasure, including going on extravagant shopping sprees, making barbed comments about pretty girls, and arousing Jack's jealousy by being seen in public with male friends. Betty Spalding recalled, "Believe it or not, Jack was jealous of Jackie seeing any other man, even a pal like Bill Walton, because he was convinced that she was doing the same things he was doing." And it upset Jack to be jealous, "because it threatened his macho image of himself as a husband and a man who must be all things to his wife and every woman in the world."[36]

That fall the Kennedys moved into a rented home in Georgetown. Friends noticed that Jackie, like Rose, had an ability to seal herself off from the pain of having an often absent and unfaithful husband and live in a private world. Ben Bradlee later recalled that in disturbing situations,

Jackie could "pull some invisible shade down across her face, and cut out spiritually. She was physically present, but intellectually long gone." With close friends, Jackie could be quite cynical about marriage. "I don't think there are any men who are faithful to their wives. Men are such a combination of good and bad."[37]

→›› ‹‹←

Jack made about 150 public appearances in twenty-six states and traveled some thirty-thousand miles on behalf of the Stevenson-Kefauver ticket. His televised struggle for the vice presidential nomination had made him something of a celebrity, and crowds flocked to see and hear him. Women seemed especially moved. At Ursuline College in Louisville, Kentucky, female students caused a near riot by blocking the senator's car and shouting and screaming their approval. "We love you on TV," the young women yelled. "You're better than Elvis Presley."[38] No one could have said that about Stevenson or Kefauver.

As many leading Democrats knew or suspected, Kennedy was also making contacts and laying plans for his own presidential campaign. Jack's speeches carefully skirted controversy (Sorensen vetoed a plea by Stevenson supporters that Jack should attack Joe McCarthy in Boston) and portrayed the senator as a sort of high-minded moderate, little interested in electioneering. Southerners took a special liking to him.[39]

In the meantime, at his brother's request, Bobby was traveling with Stevenson and taking copious notes. Arthur Schlesinger, Jr. later wrote, "From my own viewpoint on Stevenson's staff, Robert Kennedy seemed an alien presence, sullen and rather ominous, saying little, looking grim and exuding an atmosphere of bleak disapproval." Bobby became extremely critical of the presidential candidate and later told Kenny O'Donnell that the campaign was "the most disastrous operation you ever saw." Adlai's basic problem, he thought, was his distaste for politics and politicians. On election day, Bobby quietly voted for Eisenhower.[40]

Stevenson lost by a larger margin than he had in 1952, carrying only seven states and collecting a mere seventy-three electoral votes. However, the election was only a personal victory for the president, the Democrats retaining control of both houses of Congress and gaining one governorship. Though Massachusetts joined the rest of New England in going for Eisenhower, Stevenson graciously acknowledged Jack's efforts on his behalf, saying: "I can think of no one to whom we should all be more grateful than to you," and adding, "I have confident hopes for your future leadership in our party." Within the week a veteran Democrat announced in Los Angeles the formation of a Kennedy organization.[41]

Jack spent the Thanksgiving weekend at Hyannis Port, relaxing and consulting with his father. (In 1956 he had purchased a small house of his own on his father's property.) He was already planning the 1960 campaign. Dave Powers later remembered him pondering how close he had come to the vice presidential nomination and exclaiming, "If I work hard for four years, I ought to be able to pick up all the marbles."[42]

In early 1957, hundreds of speaking invitations poured into Kennedy's office, and Jack and Ted Sorensen were soon traveling throughout the country, writing and delivering scores of speeches, meeting thousands of people, and collecting names of important party leaders. (They would eventually have some seventy thousand names on file.) Jack was sometimes making as many as seven speeches a week outside Washington by midyear; by year's end he had made some 150 personal appearances, and Sorensen was seeking additional speechwriters.[43]

Jack was especially intent on winning support in the South, a region certain to object to his Catholicism. While defending the Supreme Court's position on racial integration following the Little Rock crisis, he made much of his "moderate" stand on civil rights. He worked hard at charming Southerners in numerous speeches and labored to ingratiate himself with leading Southern politicos. These efforts proved strikingly successful.

Senate Majority Leader Lyndon Johnson awarded him a much-coveted seat on the Foreign Relations Committee, choosing him over Estes Kefauver, who had more seniority. (The move, Johnson later admitted, was in direct response to pressure from the ambassador.)[44] Governor James Coleman and Senator James Eastland of Mississippi were early backers of Kennedy for president, as was powerful Senator John McClellan of Arkansas. Later in the year, a political analyst for the *Christian Science Monitor* reported "a growing feeling throughout the region that the Bay Stater may be the one to head a third party in Dixieland." Sorensen later admitted that Jack's views on racial discrimination at this time were still "shaped primarily by political expediency instead of basic principles."[45]

At the same time Jack's Senate votes increasingly appealed to Eastern liberals. Kennedy backed the most controversial and liberal section of the Civil Rights Bill of 1957, which sought to give the attorney general broad enforcement authority over individuals violating the civil rights of others. (Illustrating his pragmatic approach to the issue, he then voted for a controversial amendment favored by Southerners. A colleague reportedly wondered, "Why not show a little less profile and a little more courage?") He championed immigration reform and came out for health care for the elderly, a higher minimum wage, and federal aid to education. Liberal columnist Drew Pearson praised the senator's "growth line," declaring, "The vacillations have been ironed out. And it has consistently followed a left-of-center direction."[46]

Still, Jack continued to avoid calling himself liberal or conservative. "I'll stick to being a Democrat," he told one interviewer. He was especially eager to shun identification with the Left. A *Time* cover story in late 1957 described Kennedy as "in many aspects, a conservative," and quoted him as saying, "In a militantly liberal Convention, I wouldn't have a ghost of a chance." Jack was embarrassed when the liberal Americans for Democratic Action applauded his voting record. He declared himself "a moderate Democrat who seeks on every issue to follow the national interest, as his conscience directs him to see it." Jack was saying that character was more important than ideology, and yet there was little indication of any abiding moral vision directing his conscience, much less his vote.[47]

Some commentators thought Kennedy merely cynical; his father's son, he would do and say whatever was necessary to win votes. Many others, however, were simply puzzled by the ambiguities in the young senator's voting record and public pronouncements. In an *American Mercury* article entitled "Senator Kennedy: The Perfect Politician," conservative Russell Turner likened Jack to Richard Nixon: "Nixon probably is basically a moderate conservative, but with some liberal tendencies. Kennedy is basically a moderate liberal, but with many conservative leanings. Neither is an extremist in any sense."[48]

In the spring of 1957 Jack received much favorable publicity for chairing a special Senate committee to name the five greatest senators in American history. Conservatives were especially pleased that of the five selected the most recent was Robert A. Taft, the same "Mr. Republican" Jack and his cohorts had chosen to lionize in *Profiles in Courage*.[49]

Jack's reputation as a thinker and scholar soared on May 6 when he won the Pulitzer Prize for biography. Other winners included the late playwright Eugene O'Neill, historian and diplomat George F. Kennan, poet Richard Wilbur, and journalist James Reston. Media all over the nation trumpeted Kennedy's new triumph. Jack's official photograph, now seen by millions, was the most attractive he had ever released. (The cortisone was filling out his face, and he now weighed 160 pounds.) A laudatory *New York Times* biography reported that *Profiles* "was written during a year's convalescence from World War II injuries." Not only was Jack known as a war hero, glamorous personality, kindly benefactor, and prominent political leader (a feature article in the *Saturday Evening Post* declared, "Mr. Kennedy is the clean-cut, smiling American boy, trustworthy, loyal, brave, clean and reverent, boldly facing up to the challenges of the Atomic Age''), he was now one of the nation's most distinguished men of letters. And he took the accolade seriously. Sorensen would later recall, "Of all honors [Jack] would receive throughout his life, none would make him more happy than his receipt in 1957 of the Pulitzer Prize for biography."[50]

In fact the Pulitzer Prize may well have been another quiet triumph for the ambassador. Careful research has revealed that the judges for biography made no mention of *Profiles* in their recommendations to the Pulitzer Advisory Board. The board, consisting largely of journalists, ignored the two distinguished historians who lauded volumes by such well-known scholars as Alpheus T. Mason, Irving Brant, and Samuel Flagg Bemis. It is also known that influential Arthur Krock lobbied for Kennedy among his professional brethren. He later told William Manchester, "I worked as hard as I could to get him that prize." Herbert Parmet concluded, "Keeping hands off would have been out of character for the ambassador. Allowing the Pulitzer Prize to be decided by chance would have been especially unique for a man who placed so much importance on having his son gain literary respectability en route to power."[51]

In late May the *Wall Street Journal* proclaimed, KENNEDY MOVES OUT FRONT. The following month the Gallup Poll showed Jack ahead of Kefauver as a presidential preference by 50–30. Endorsements began to appear, and honorary degrees were offered. To the ambassador's delight, Jack was elected to Harvard's Board of Overseers by the highest vote ever polled, and requests for interviews and public appearances overwhelmed Kennedy's office staff. Jack was hot copy for newspapers, magazines, and television stations all over the country.

In 1957–58, Kennedy's presence on the McClellan Committee, the Senate "rackets committee" probing Teamsters Union skulduggery, earned extensive media coverage. Bobby served as chief counsel and began his zealous and prolonged war against Teamsters boss Jimmy Hoffa. A veteran journalist later observed, "Those hearings gave the Kennedy brothers entree into every newsroom in this country that had an investigative reporting group."[52]

Not long after the Russian launching of Sputnik, the *New York Times* published a Kennedy article that called for sacrifices and proposed a variety of dramatic changes, from increased weaponry (the alleged "missile gap" was becoming a favorite theme) to a "reappraisal of our intellectual and moral atmosphere." The forty-year-old Senator declared: "This is not time for panic, for partisan politics, for business as usual.

We must re-examine, revise—and get to work. For as Goethe reminded us: 'He only earns his freedom and existence who daily conquers them anew.' ''

At the same time, what Collier and Horowitz have called Ted Sorensen's "literary cottage industry" continued to crank out learned articles under the Kennedy by-line for prestigious magazines and journals. Increasingly, the junior senator from Massachusetts was becoming recognized as a national leader whose pronouncements (consistently strong on generalities and calls to action) on political, international, intellectual, and moral matters were to be taken very seriously.[53]

Still Jack insisted publicly that he was not a presidential candidate. "I'm not thinking about 1960," he said in November, 1957. "I'm tremendously interested in my Senate job and want to stay there."[54]

Few serious political observers accepted the disclaimer. At year's end *Time*, in a cover story, called Kennedy "the Democratic whiz of 1957." (Owner Henry Luce and the ambassador were longtime friends.) During the year Jack began negotiations with a Democratic chieftain in the Bronx to capture New York's convention votes. He kept in touch with Chicago's all-powerful Mayor Richard Daley. He attracted crowds and publicity wherever he went, and he continued to learn the names of leading Democrats across the country. One day in Palm Beach, Jack and a well-traveled writer concentrated on a large map of the United States spread out on the floor of the senator's living room. Each tried to outdo the other by placing a finger on the map and reeling off the names of influential people who resided in the area. Jack won easily. His aides were, in Ken O'Donnell's words, "amazed by the amount of detailed information that he had picked up in his travels."[55] Clearly, Jack was becoming politically astute and totally engaged.

He was not yet, however, the master of his fate. The ambassador was still in charge, and at this time was creating what Richard Whalen has called "a publicity buildup unprecedented in U.S. political history." He fed information and granted interviews to sympathetic journalists. (He said of Jack to one reporter, "I've never tried to influence his thinking and never shall. That's the truth and he'll tell you.") He wooed publishers. He attempted to recruit syndicated columnist Marquis Childs to write Jack's biography. Ever mindful of his son's image in the media, the elder Kennedy confided to a friend, "We're going to sell Jack like soap flakes."[56]

One evening at dinner in Palm Beach, Jack and Lem Billings were trading friendly insults when Billings made a crack about one of his pal's sexual exploits. As others at the table began to laugh, the ambassador slammed down his fork, glared at Billings, and commanded:

You're not to speak like that any more. There are things that you just can't bring up any more, private things. You've got to forget them. Forget the "Jack" you once knew. From now on you've got to watch everything you say. The day is coming, and it's coming soon, when he won't be "Jack" any more at all—not to you and not to the rest of us either. He'll be "Mr. President." And you can't say or do anything that will jeopardize that.[57]

While her husband traveled frantically throughout the country seeking political allies, Jackie grew increasingly unhappy. Detesting politics, lonely, and suffering from occasional black moods, she was hurt by continuous stories of Jack's extramarital affairs.[58] And yet, as much as Jackie valued her privacy ("I need to sulk," she said privately), some interviews with reporters and photographic sessions were inevitable to help Jack's career. She played the adoring wife and said the expected things. Jackie boosted her husband's image as an intellectual, for example, declaring, "If I were drawing him, I'd draw a tiny body and an enormous head." She also defended the ambassador against charges that he ran his children's careers. "You'd think he was a mastermind playing chess, when actually he's a nice old gentleman we see at Thanksgiving and Christmas."[59]

In late November Jackie gave birth by cesarean section to Caroline Bouvier Kennedy. This time Jack was on hand. "Jack was more emotional about Caroline's birth than he was about anything else," Lem Billings later recalled. "I remember how his voice cracked when he called to tell the news, and when he showed me the baby he looked happier than I had seen him look in a long time. With this child, he finally had a family of his own." Still, there was little time to enjoy the family; campaigning came first. Friends observed later that of Caroline's first six words—*Daddy, airplane, car, shoe, hat,* and *thank you*—at least three had something to do with motion.[60]

Three weeks after Caroline's birth, the Kennedys purchased a three-story, red-brick house in Georgetown. Soon Jackie was working out schedules for her cook, English nanny, maid, valet, chauffeur, and visiting gardener. She was an exacting employer, and there was a rapid turnover of servants. "Considerable friction of personalities existed," Mary Gallagher, her private secretary, wrote later.

Jackie did almost nothing of a domestic nature herself. The nanny, Maude Shaw, had virtually complete responsibility for Carolyn. Even Jackie's daily diary was filled out by someone else. She arose late (Jack, when home, ate breakfast alone), spent much of her day in solitude, and devoted most of her energy to her appearance. Gallagher best remembered the silence that filled the house. "Never, in fact, have I ever remembered hearing Jackie herself as much as *hum* a little tune as she went about her daily business, or indulge in a really hearty laugh. Perhaps one explanation for this could be attributed to her rather 'reserved' personality." Gallagher, with a touch of bitterness, thought her employer "born and groomed to a queenly role."[61]

Much to her husband's annoyance, Jackie constantly redecorated the first permanent home she had known in her four-year marriage. "It seemed to me," wrote Gallagher, "there were just two things that John F. Kennedy wanted—a comfortable, familiar, *unchanging* place to read in peace and quiet, and second, no money worries." Both goals were to elude him. The wallpaper in the study changed three times within a few months. Jack was never sure what would await him when he returned from a trip. He once hollered, "Dammit, Jackie, why is it that the rooms in this house are never completely livable all at the same time?" Jackie thought her efforts unappreciated. At one point, after having the living room painted, she complained to a friend that Jack had failed to notice the difference. "He has no feeling about any possessions."[62]

Still, a friend later recalled that on the whole Jack was happy with the way his wife organized and fixed up the new house. "Jack was so pleased," said Bill Walton, "that he could actually get his laundry done and everything else taken care of."[63]

→>> <<←

Kennedy continued his frenetic pace in 1958. Jackie remarked, "If Jack didn't run for President, he'd be like a tiger in a cage." In the first five and a half months of the year, he received 2,568 invitations and accepted 96. Speeches in Bismarck, North Dakota; Eugene, Oregon; and Morgantown, West Virginia, were deliberately designed to increase his nationwide exposure. One week he flew to Casper, Wyoming to speak about water and then traveled to Billings, Montana to be made an honorary member of the Crow Indian tribe. "If I decide to run in '60," Jack said publicly, "I will at least have been around and met a lot of people in different parts of the country."[64]

Jack was at last developing into an above-average public speaker, and his witty and often beautifully crafted addresses, written by Sorensen and a battery of East Coast professors, roused audiences all over the country. Kennedy and Sorensen kept a humor file for speech openings and a collection of appropriate endings Jack knew by heart. A favorite closing quotation was a paraphrase of a Robert Frost poem:

Iowa City is lovely, dark and deep
But I have promises to keep
And miles to go before I sleep.

While Jack was becoming sufficiently self-confident to engage in some off-the-cuff remarks, he still required a complete text of every speech. Sorensen wrote later, "He wanted the reassurance a manuscript gave him."[65]

Jack won approval offstage, as well. Interviewers often found him, as a *Newsweek* story put it, "candid, informal, and disarmingly relaxed." (The Kennedy charm could at times be intense, especially in the presence of desirable women and politically valuable journalists.) Increasingly, the media touted Kennedy's credentials as a scholar (a *New York Times Magazine* piece reported that he had "a year each at Stanford and the London School of Economics"), prizewinning author, war hero, athlete, statesman, political whiz, and moral idealist. The Kennedy image was looming large in America, prompting a boom in the candidate's popularity.[66]

In midyear, a Roper Poll showed Jack, in the eyes of the public, to be the most admired man in the Senate. A survey of delegates to the 1956 Democratic National Convention revealed Kennedy ahead of his nearest rival for the 1960 nomination by more than two to one. One Democratic strategist said flatly, "If the Convention were held tomorrow, Kennedy would get it hands down." GOP leaders were aware of Jack's looming stature, and the Eisenhower administration took several steps to hinder the Senator's legislative proposals.[67]

Still, there were doubts. Some questioned Jack's youth and what Cabell Phillips called "a certain glibness of speech and manner." Some frowned upon Kennedy's inexperience outside Congress. Others argued that a Roman Catholic could not be elected. Eleanor Roosevelt indirectly raised the issue of character by again pointing to Kennedy's dodging of the McCarthy matter. (Jack replied that he had repeatedly described McCarthy's censure as "reasonable and proper.") Many political experts thought the senator was "pressing too hard" to stay in the limelight, and that his popularity might fizzle out by 1960. The ambassador, in a rare moment of candor, scoffed publicly at the latter suggestion: "The only way we can win this is to wrap it up very, very early."[68]

The Kennedy strategists were convinced that an overwhelming victory in Jack's reelection campaign of 1958 would quiet the most severe critics. Some newspapers predicted that Jack would have to win by two hundred thousand votes or more to maintain his national prestige.

The ambassador was aiming higher. "If we can get a plurality of a half million," he told friends, "they can't stop us for the Presidency."[69]

Massachusetts Republicans knew that Kennedy was certain to win reelection. One of the senator's boosters crowed, "He couldn't lose if he came out against the Pope." Jack's opponent was thirty-four-year-old Vincent J. Celeste, a scrappy, working-class Italian whom Kennedy had defeated in 1950. Celeste specialized in attacking the Kennedy family and its wealth. "What right do Kennedy and his brother Bobby have to sit in judgment on labor without even doing a day's work in their whole lives?" he demanded. The ambassador was a regular target. "Look how my opponent voted for the St. Lawrence Seaway—it starts right at the front door of the Merchandise Mart in Chicago, which is owned by old Joe Kennedy."[70]

Behind the scenes the ambassador was again playing a vital role. "It was the old man who really ran those goddamned campaigns, you know," an insider said later.[71] The elder Kennedy quietly took an apartment in Boston, avoided reporters, and tried not to be seen in public with his son during the electioneering. But the inner circle knew that he was pulling strings, giving advice (twenty-six-year-old Teddy was the official campaign manager), and spending money—an estimated $1.5 million. Campaign leaders, sensitive to Celeste's charges, attempted to avoid the appearance of being well-heeled. The television budget was modest, and there was only a single downtown office in Boston.[72]

Jack ran unopposed in the primary and spent some time in Europe with Jackie on Senate business. He was angered to learn that he had won 6,733 fewer votes in Boston that Governor Foster Furcolo, an old rival with whom, with the ambassador's approval, he was running something of a joint campaign. "Damn, it, Larry," he barked at Larry O'Brien, "I didn't go into politics to run behind Foster Furcolo. We've got to do better in the general election." The ambassador was furious and began to suffer from the nervous irritation he called "the itch." Dave Powers said later that the only misfortune that blackened the first year of Caroline's childhood was the Furcolo vote in Boston.[73]

While continuing to make cross-country trips, Jack spent seventeen days in Massachusetts traveling at a physically punishing pace. When the ambassador first looked at the schedule, he exploded, "What are you trying to do to him? Kill him?" Larry O'Brien soon boasted, "We ran the Senator in one day through fifteen speaking appearances in fifteen cities and towns, from Chelsea to Gloucester, and had him in bed by eleven o'clock at night."

Jackie accompanied her husband on several journeys within the state. While Jack shook hands, gave speeches, and huddled with local politicos, she smiled tirelessly, entertained wives, and tried not to look "too rich" or "too New York." Her biographer wrote later, "Jackie accomplished this with white gloves, little hats, a simple and short blown-out hair style, very little jewelry, and very little makeup." Kenny O'Don-nell observed, "When Jackie was travelling with us, the size of the crowd at every stop was twice as big as it would have been if Jack was alone."[74] The candidate's wife played a vital role in the image making; to many she was the model of good looks, good taste, modesty, femininity, poise, and dignity.

One day Jack toured a Boston sausage factory and fell into conver-sations with several black workers. Driving away amid cheers, he told O'Donnell, "Well, you just wasted an hour of my time. They gave me a great reception but not one of them is a registered voter in Massachusetts who can vote for me."[75]

The day before the election, Jack spied an elderly woman in South Boston about to cross a street alone. He ordered his car stopped, got out, introduced himself to the woman, and escorted her across the street. Powers watched in amazement, and said, "You really want *all* of the votes, don't you?" Jack replied, "How would you feel if you lost South Boston by one vote, and then remembered that you didn't bother to help this lady across the street?"[76]

The senator and his wife awaited the election returns at the ambas-sador's Boston apartment. The news was good from the start, and the ambassador personally answered telephone calls from precinct workers, repeating data to Dave Powers, who had a calculating machine. When the elder Kennedy discovered that Jack had carried a Charlestown ward 1,271 to 85, he asked Powers, "Say, Dave, that's your neighborhood. Have you got any idea who those eighty-five are?"[77]

In a record turnout for an off-year election, Kennedy received 73.6 percent of the votes and rolled up a majority of 874,608 over Celeste. It was the largest majority ever won by a candidate for any office in Mas-sachusetts. The ambassador soon wrote to a friend, "The vote was be-yond our fondest dreams."[78]

Jack, Jackie, Ethel, Jean, and Ted greeted a noisy crowd in Boston. Some well-wishers cheered "our next President." O'Donnell later re-called that few of the Kennedy lieutenants showed much excitement. "We were already thinking about the next ball game."[79]

On November 9 Kennedy appeared on the nationally televised *Meet the Press* program. *New York Times* correspondent James Reston asked, "Are you now seeking delegates to the 1960 Presidential

Convention?'' Jack replied, ''I am not.'' Reston continued, ''Have you established or will you establish headquarters looking to 1960?'' Jack answered, ''No.'' Reston persisted, ''Do you have any plans to go into the preferential primaries of 1960?'' Jack said flatly, ''I don't.''[80]

CHAPTER 9

The Center of Moral Leadership

→≫ ≪←

JAMES RESTON, a thoughtful and experienced journalist, was deeply concerned about the superficiality he perceived in Kennedy and several other presidential aspirants. Professional politicians and the press, he wrote, seemed primarily interested in glamorous candidates "rather than men of vitality and character who can grapple effectively with an increasingly intricate and exhausting job." Democrats especially, he thought, were thinking about 1960 simply "in terms of a personality who can win." The Associated Press soon reported that state Democratic party chairmen ranked Kennedy first among the candidates in the race for the nomination.[1]

Reston's reluctance about Kennedy was shared by Eleanor Roosevelt and others in the liberal community. In early December 1958, the former first lady told a television interviewer that Minnesota Senator Hubert Humphrey was the only candidate who came close to having "the spark of greatness" needed in the White House. Kennedy, while young and charming, was far too much in his father's control. The ambassador, she said, had been spending "oodles of money all over the country" on Jack's behalf and "probably has paid representatives in every state by now." (Jack replied, "There are no such expenditures, and no such agents.'') In an interview with *Look* magazine, she expressed her continuing unhappiness with the Massachusetts Senator for lacking the courage to speak out against Joe McCarthy.[2]

When Franklin D. Roosevelt, Jr., was invited to dine with Kennedy, he knew that the purpose was to reach and win over his mother. Afterward Roosevelt said to his wife, ''How can a guy that politically immature seriously expect to be President?'' He later told an interviewer, ''The only thing Jack could talk about at that dinner was himself and his political problems. I'd never met somebody so completely obsessed in himself.''[3]

Others had similar thoughts. *Chicago Sun-Times* Washington correspondent Peter Lisagor heard Kennedy speak to a group of journalists at Harvard and was astonished when Jack said of labor leaders George Meany and Walter Reuther, ''I wouldn't give them the time of day, but in politics you simply have to.'' One journalist in the audience commented afterward, ''Can you imagine that young fellow thinking that he could be President of the United States anytime soon?'' Lisagor recalled, ''I must say the thought occurred to me, too.''[4]

Former Secretary of State Dean Acheson reacted angrily when Kennedy gave a speech advocating Algerian independence from France, calling the senator ''still wet behind the ears.'' (Jack later developed reservations about his proposal.) Acheson backed Lyndon Johnson for the presidential nomination.[5]

While liked by numerous colleagues, Kennedy was not a member of the Senate's ''inner club.'' He was often absent, not extraordinarily productive, and his voting record was correctly thought to be basically pragmatic and consistent with his well-known desire to be president. *Newsweek* accurately labeled Kennedy ''an authentic moderate without excessive party loyalties,'' adding that he ''has constructed a voting record that is a veritable department store in which almost anyone can find much to like and dislike.''[6]

Kennedy's flexible political principles helped him appease many of his liberal critics. He courted liberals by challenging loyalty oaths for labor leaders and academics. After initial misgivings, he joined the liberal Democratic Advisory Council and attended a dinner honoring Mrs. Roosevelt. He defended civil liberties in an appearance before the Philadelphia chapter of Americans for Democratic Action. In a review of Richard Rovere's hostile *Senator Joe McCarthy* for the liberal *Washington Post*, Jack spoke out against the second Red scare. (He sought unsuccessfully to block publication of the favorable review by the *Boston Globe*.) His staff released his undelivered speech of 1954 containing the sentence: "I shall vote to censure the junior senator from Wisconsin."[7]

For those, like Mrs. Roosevelt, who worried about his Roman Catholicism, Jack expressed his belief in the total separation of church and state, and he opposed the appointment of an ambassador to the Vatican. He was elated when Paul Blanshard, a severe critic of the Catholic church in America, applauded his position. Several diocesan newspapers, however, were less than pleased, and Cardinal Cushing, a longtime friend of the Kennedys, said it was "a great pity" that constitutional questions of this sort had to be raised. Many Protestants remained wary. Martin Marty, associate editor of the *Christian Century*, thought Jack "spiritually rootless and politically almost disturbingly secular." Many fundamentalists simply could not believe the candidate.[8]

Jack knew that much of his opposition within the Democratic Party came from people, again like Mrs. Roosevelt, who were still loyal to Adlai Stevenson. He remained bitter about the 1956 convention experience and often spoke disparagingly—in private—of the former presidential candidate. When Peter Lisagor raised the possibility of Stevenson's nomination in 1960, Jack became angry and said, "Why, that's impossible. Adlai Stevenson is a bitter man. He's a bitter, deeply disillusioned, deeply hurt man." Kennedy's view of Stevenson's masculinity was expressed to a congressional colleague when Jack sneered, "He must be a switcher."[9]

In December 1958, an "Academic Advisory Committee" consisting largely of liberal intellectuals from Harvard and MIT met for the first time. Participants included Archibald Cox, Jerome Weisner, Arthur Schlesinger, Jr., John Kenneth Galbraith, Abram Chayes, Walt Rostow, Paul Nitze, Paul Samuelson, and Seymour Harris. This Kennedy "brain trust" was recruited by Ted Sorensen largely to persuade people of similar bent across the country to abandon Stevenson and Humphrey for Kennedy. It connected Kennedy, by association, to the intellectual elite, individuals and institutions whose power and prestige would now redound to him in the eyes of the public.

The New England intellectuals, who in general liked Jack and saw him as the likely Democratic nominee, were asked for public policy ideas during the next two years and given papers to write. Their actual significance, however, was minimal. Ted Sorensen later wrote, "Not all of their material was usable and even less was actually used." Abram Chayes later recalled, "I just remember a terrible sense of inadequacy in the response of this collection of brains; nobody really was able to come up with anything terribly important." Jack met with the committee several times, successfully concealing his—and his father's—lifelong distrust of liberals and intellectuals. "Jack has conned them," said an important Washington liberal. Sorensen later claimed that those scholars who talked personally with Kennedy "were deeply impressed."[10]

By April 1959 the Kennedy forces had organized formally for the presidential contest. Their first meeting was held at the Kennedy home in Palm Beach in the presence of the ambassador. The list of full-time campaigners included brother-in-law Steve Smith, longtime pals Kenny O'Donnell and Larry O'Brien, and Bob Wallace from Kennedy's Senate staff. Several others, including Teddy Kennedy, Sargent Shriver, Torby Macdonald, and Dave Powers, were at work part-time. Bobby Kennedy, writing *The Enemy Within*, a book about his Senate rackets probe, could not devote his full energies to the campaign until the fall. The same was true of former newsman Pierre Salinger, who worked with Bobby as an investigator.[11]

Planning the candidate's travels occupied much of the staff's time, as Jack continued to tour the country at a breakneck pace. In July 1959 Kennedy officials announced that the Kennedy family had purchased and leased to Jack a luxurious $385,000 Convair plane. The *Caroline* logged 110,000 miles in 1959 and 1960. In the fall of 1959 alone, Jack made appearances in twenty-two states. By October, Kennedy and Sorensen had met more than half of the potential delegates to the 1960 convention. Moreover, Jack and Teddy showered important Democratic leaders with telephone calls, personal notes, and anniversary cards. Tens of thousands of Christmas cards were mailed with "Best wishes, John" written in ink at the bottom.

Kennedy strategist Hy Raskin soon said, "If somebody tells me that they think some other candidate will win, I say to them, 'Tell me how? Where are their votes coming from? On what ballot? Where are the numbers . . . where are the numbers?' " To Raskin, "Politics is arithmetic."[12]

No other Democrat was making half the effort to win the presidential nomination. Of course, no other Democratic hopeful had Kennedy's money. One writer observed that Kennedy's staff was larger and better run than any of his competitors' and noted that prominent pollster Lou Harris was in the Kennedy employ, conducting constant surveys of crucial states. One Hubert Humphrey adviser contended that Kennedy campaign costs were twenty times the Humphrey costs. Syndicated columnist Marquis Childs asserted that at least a million dollars had been spent by July 1959 and that the ambassador was masterminding the entire effort.

Kennedy managers denied the Childs charge, even claiming that the elder Kennedy had no connection at all with the campaign. In fact, as always, the ambassador was the major contributor to his son's political strategy. He recruited speech writers, wooed and pressured influential politicians, got *U.S. News & World Report* to publish unauthorized excerpts from John Hersey's article on *PT 109*, and tirelessly flattered FBI Director J. Edgar Hoover, whose files contained the Inga Arvad story and no doubt much additional information potentially damaging to the candidate. Tip O'Neill recalled how the elder Kennedy began successfully courting an influential Pennsylvania Democrat within two days of learning his name.

Powerful New York Congressman Eugene Keogh later said of the ambassador, "He knew instinctively who the important people were, who the bosses behind the scenes were. From 1958 on he was in contact with them constantly by phone, presenting Jack's case, explaining and interpreting his son, working these bosses."[13] According to Richard Whalen, the ambassador spent at least $1.5 million on Jack's preconvention campaign; other estimates put the figure much higher.[14]

By this time, cortisone had fully filled out Jack's face, giving him the extraordinarily handsome appearance he was to have for the rest of his life. (Kennedy was never comfortable with his new look, however. Ben Bradlee wrote later, "Vain as always, it bugged him if he appeared a little jowly at press conferences, which he often did, not because he overate, but because he was taking some form of cortisone." Judith Campbell Exner would write of Jack's exceptional vanity and note that when he took cortisone, "His face would puff up until his features were distorted.")[15] Though he was concerned about its effects, the youthful-looking results served him well. Kennedy's solicitous charm, good looks, and almost boyish earnestness made such an impression on the campaign trail that his personal appeal was being compared to that of Charles A. Lindbergh in 1927.[16]

Cabell Phillips, traveling with Jack in the fall of 1959, wrote in the *New York Times Magazine*, "Jack Kennedy is a singularly gifted young man in looks, bearing, intelligence and personality. There is about him a subtle blending of deference and self-confidence, of engaging shyness and mature forthrightness. He radiates a gentle, honest warmth and people are instinctively at ease with him."[17] Kennedy had emerged as a mature and persuasive politician.

In a tour of Wisconsin in late 1959, Jack opened his speeches before student gatherings with quotations from Goethe, Homer, Hitler, Daniel Webster, Robert Frost, William Pitt, Clement Attlee, and several queens of England. (The publishers of *Bartlett's Familiar Quotations* soon advertised, "Sen. John F. Kennedy owns the modern Bartlett's. Do you?")

At other times, Jack was far more folksy. For testimonial dinners and box suppers, he began with a surefire gag: "Actually, I am not campaigning for votes here in Wisconsin. The Vice President [Nixon] and I are here on a mission for the Secretary of Health, Education, and Welfare to test cranberries. Well, we have both eaten them, and I feel fine. But if we both pass away, I feel I shall have performed a great public service by taking the Vice President with me."[18] Whatever followed often made little difference; audiences were almost always captivated. Ted Sorensen, the author of most of what Jack had to say, sat in the front row during many speeches, watching every gesture and taking careful notes on what people especially liked to hear.[19]

Jack had never been an impressive orator; he spoke in what Cabell Phillips called a "hurried monotone" and had little feeling for the emotions of his audience, often even failing to wait for applause to die down before continuing. But with all his experience and coaching, he was becoming quite effective in question-and-answer sessions and with small groups. When asked about his religion, for example, he would reply that he welcomed the question and state dispassionately, "I have enough confidence in the judgment of the American people to believe that they will vote for what they think is good in a man seeking office, and not for what church he happens to go to on Sunday." This flattering appeal for trust in his character always won a burst of applause.

Sorensen told an interviewer, "We both had much to learn, and we learned together. I think we improved 100 percent. I know that people even now keep telling Jack, 'Boy, you're sure a lot better than you were last time.' "[20]

Above all Jack's appearance and image made an impact on his audiences. In Marshfield, Wisconsin, as Jack shook hands with twelve hundred guests following an address, one young woman burbled, "Oh, those pearly teeth." One teenage girl told the candidate, "If I only had a vote, you'd have it," and then fled to her high school locker room in embarrassment. An elderly couple next in line was equally supportive. "We have the vote," the grandmother told Jack, "and you've got both of them."[21]

At about the same time, the ambassador was boasting of his son, "You advertise the fact that he will be at a dinner and you will break all records for attendance. He can draw more people to a fund-raising dinner than Cary Grant or Jimmy Stewart. Why is that? He has more universal appeal. That is why the Democratic Party is going to nominate him."[22]

Kennedy's appeal was enhanced that fall by the presence of his wife during many of his travels. Jackie's intense distaste for politics and campaigning was unchanged, but she did her duty and concealed her true feelings.[23] Cabell Phillips described her as "braving the handshaking, the frequently indigestible luncheons and dinners and the interminable speechmaking with a wan but courageous smile."[24] Crowds were consistently awed by the handsome young couple, obviously supportive of each other and committed to the values of family, church, and flag that dominated much of American life during the Eisenhower years.

The Kennedy forces were able to produce a flurry of newspaper and magazine articles on the candidate and his family. *Look* magazine, for example, ran a series of highly sympathetic pieces written by journalist Joe McCarthy that featured such subheadings as: "They are a proud and close clan," "He is acceptable to Southern politicians," "Each Kennedy has a mind of his own," "Jack refused to live on crutches," "Kennedy's nonstop campaigning has silenced talk about his ill health," "He has an independent voting record in the U.S. Senate," and "He refused to duck integration problem in Mississippi speech."

The McCarthy articles, which had the blessing and cooperation of Jack and his parents, contained numerous distortions. Jack was alleged to be in excellent physical health: "He says that he feels no pain worth mentioning . . . and he denies that he takes any injections. . . . A physician who has treated the Senator says that Kennedy no longer has an adrenal depletion."[25] Rose was reported to have "none of the supercharged competitiveness" of the Kennedys and was said not to understand why Jack was running for the presidency: "After all, he could have a nice, interesting life if he stayed in the Senate."[26] The ambassador was alleged to have little influence on his son and little inclination to spend money on his election campaigns: "In political circles, the Kennedys are not regarded as big spenders."[27]

The photographs in the *Look* articles probably made the greatest impression. The first was a shot of Bobby, Jack, and Teddy in bathing suits, smiling and laughing as they emerged from the surf—handsome, manly, self-confident. There were historical photos of the Kennedy family, a wartime shot of Jack in the South Pacific, scenes of Jack campaigning and in deep thought, and several skillfully posed photos featuring Jack, Jackie, and Caroline. (One can imagine how Jack suffered to pose for a shot of his daughter riding on his shoulders.) Modern American politics had not known such young, physically attractive—and apparently noble and heroic—people.[28]

The Kennedys had been planning an authorized campaign biography for some time. After a considerable struggle involving the ambassador, Ted Sorensen, and several editors and writers, liberal political scientist

James MacGregor Burns was selected. Burns learned that the Kennedys were more interested in their image than in historical accuracy. The entire manuscript was submitted to Sorensen and Kennedy, who pressured the author repeatedly to make concessions. They were especially sensitive about the McCarthy issue, Jack's relationship to his father, and the depiction of the senator as lacking conviction about specific issues. The final product, *John F. Kennedy: A Political Profile*, proved satisfactory to the candidate and his family.[29]

All the while Kennedy was campaigning and tending to his Senate duties, a growing stream of books, articles, book reviews, and guest editorials continued to appear under his name. The products included *A Nation of Immigrants*, published by the Anti-Defamation League of B'nai B'rith, and *The Strategy of Peace*, sent "personally" to 250 intellectuals in primary states. Articles on numerous topics appeared in such varied periodicals as the *Georgetown Law Review*, the *Reporter*, the *Progressive*, the Standard Oil Company's *Plant Council News*, *Life*, *Look*, *McCalls*, the *General Electric Defense Quarterly*, and the *Chatterbox*, the organ of the Delta Zeta Sorority.

In these often highly impressive publications, Jack appeared to be something of a political centrist, an internationalist, an anti-Communist, a moralist, and an activist. Above all, he seemed to be an expert on a dazzling variety of subjects. Herbert S. Parmet has observed, "Correspondents learned how easy it was to get an article out of Kennedy's office, properly revised, if needed—made-to-order—to suit almost any need."[30]

It now seems clear that Ted Sorensen wrote and supervised the creation of these publications. (At the last minute, he and Jack removed a potentially damaging Kennedy interview on Joe McCarthy from *The Strategy of Peace*.) But the public had no way of knowing that the author was anyone other than the remarkable, Pulitzer Prize–winning senator from Massachusetts. And, as James MacGregor Burns made clear, Jack took full credit.[31] While public figures almost always, of course, employ ghost writers at times to express their ideas, no national figure had ever so consistently and unashamedly used others to manufacture a personal reputation as a great thinker and scholar.

→>> <<←

Kennedy formally announced his candidacy on January 2, 1960. Facing three hundred cheering supporters in the Senate Caucus Room, the forty-two-year-old Senator flatly ruled out the possibility of accepting the vice presidential nomination, said that he would enter several primaries,

and predicted that "by April or May we will have a pretty good idea of
who is going to get nominated in July." Among the real issues of 1960,
he said, were:

> How to end or alter the burdensome arms race, where Soviet gains already
> threaten our very existence. How to maintain freedom and order in the
> newly emerging nations. How to rebuild the stature of American science
> and education. How to prevent the collapse of our farm economy and the
> decay of our cities. How to achieve, without further inflation or unem-
> ployment, expanded economic growth benefiting all Americans. And how
> to give direction to our traditional moral purpose, awakening every Amer-
> ican to the dangers and opportunities that confront us.[32]

With an agenda emphasizing moral ideals and global concern, Kennedy
tossed his hat in the ring.

Less than two weeks later, in a speech before the National Press
Club, Jack promised to be a "strong" president in the tradition of Lincoln, Jackson, the two Roosevelts, and Truman. (The implication was,
of course, that Eisenhower was "weak.") He also returned to the issue
of "moral purpose," declaring that the White House "must be the center of moral leadership." Character was to be an important campaign
issue. [33]

Jack intended to enter state primaries in every part of the country.
Even though to this time no Democrat had ever won the nomination
solely because of primaries, there was no better way to impress party
leaders. In several states he was without real opposition. He won an easy
victory in New Hampshire—where Rose campaigned and proved to be a
popular attraction. He made favorable deals with politicos in California
and Ohio, freeing him from intensive campaigns there. Wisconsin promised to be a meaningful challenge because popular Hubert Humphrey
from neighboring Minnesota was his opponent.

This gabby, bright, sentimental, Protestant, forty-eight-year-old
populist ("If Muriel and I ever move to sixteen hundred Pennsylvania
Avenue, it will be a real family place, and you folks would always be
welcome. We'd keep the coffee pot on all the time") was sometimes
called Wisconsin's "third Senator." A private poll by Lou Harris, however, showed Kennedy leading Humphrey 60–40. (Harris's final bill for
his intensive and pioneering services in the state was three hundred thousand dollars.) That, plus the ambassador's insistence, persuaded the candidate to go all-out in the Badger State.

Privately, Jack began the grueling contest with the same sort of grim
determination that had sustained him since his entry into politics fourteen

years earlier. On one frigid morning, before appearing at a factory gate to shake hands, Kennedy sipped coffee in a diner and told a companion, "You think I'm out here to get votes. Well, I am. But not just their votes. I'm trying to get the votes of a lot of people who are sitting right now in warm, comfortable homes all over the country, having a big breakfast of bacon and eggs, hoping that young Jack will fall right on his face in the snow. Bastards." Reluctantly getting off his stool, he added, "What the hell. They'll take me if they have to. Let's get started."[34]

Jack's day often began at 5:30 A.M. and ended at 1:30 the next morning. James Reston called it "his dawn to exhaustion schedule." (Dave Powers quietly reported to the ambassador daily on Jack's health.) Dozens of Kennedy campaign leaders and friends fanned out across the state. There were Kennedy personnel in eight of the state's ten congressional districts. Humphrey could afford only two offices in Washington, staffed with weekend help.

Family members, including Jackie and Rose, seemed omnipresent, making headlines, shaking hands, and giving talks. (Only the ambassador stayed behind the scenes.) Bobby, the blunt and demanding campaign manager, asked his three sisters to attend nine house parties a day, a total of twenty-seven parties a day, over a two-week period. Humphrey wrote later of the Kennedy women, "They were queen and queen mother among the commoners, extracting obeisance, awe, and respect. They lacked only tiaras, and you knew that if crowns were needed, Joe Kennedy would buy them. I felt like an independent merchant competing against a chain store." Humphrey's own efforts, which included some accordion playing, seemed comparatively meager and ineffective.[35]

Journalist Peter Lisagor traveled briefly with Kennedy in Wisconsin. Sitting in a car with the candidate as it pulled up to a supermarket, Lisagor asked, "Do you like these crowds and this sort of thing?" Jack turned and said, "I hate it," and then opened the door to greet voters. Lisagor recalled, "You'd think that this man loved above all other things the contacts he had with the crowd. He lit up and smiled. . . . The empathy with the crowd was so plain and so clear." A local reporter observed, "He gives the impression of truly liking to shake hands. . . . After each fifteen minute talk he races for the exit ahead of his departing audience and offers each member a firm grip, a warm smile and a murmured 'Thank you for coming.' Babes in arms and small fry get pats and teasing compliments." Jack told a Milwaukee audience that politics is "the most rewarding and stimulating of lives."[36]

Not everyone was convinced, however. Stewart Alsop, traveling with the candidate, wrote in the *Saturday Evening Post*, "When Kennedy is campaigning, it is obvious that a good deal of the time he would just as soon be doing something else." Alsop thought Jack "unexpectedly self-conscious" and "diffident."[37]

Kenny O'Donnell and Dave Powers later recalled Kennedy's exhausting campaign. After one early-morning appearance at a factory gate in fifteen-degree weather, they noticed that "Jack's bare right hand, swollen and blue from the cold, was scratched and bleeding. Its flesh had been torn in many places by the fingernails scraped against it in hurried handshakes. During one drive to a factory in frosty Ashland, on Lake Superior, Jack said to Powers, "What a hell of a way to spend Saint Patrick's Day."[38]

In hundreds of small towns, Jack would enter with his sound truck playing a recording of "High Hopes," sung by his friend Frank Sinatra. Aides would pass out posters and pamphlets, and Jack would shake hands furiously wherever people could be found. Alsop noted that the candidate, after marching up to a potential voter, pumping his hand and announcing, "I'm Jack Kennedy," would then be at a loss to keep the conversation going. Jack would give a brief speech that usually included, "I come from 1,000 miles from here. I am not your neighbor, but I don't think that has anything to do with it. What counts is the quality of a man and his good judgment."[39]

Jackie was in Wisconsin occasionally. At one of several well-financed and highly organized public receptions, some four thousand turned out in Milwaukee to shake hands with the candidate and his wife. (Jackie stayed only briefly, pleading illness.) At times Jack and Jackie took opposite sides of the street in a small town and shook hands with everyone they could find. Alsop observed, "Kennedy and his beautiful wife Jacqueline wander up the street with an uncertain and faintly embarrassed air, a little like a pair of lost children." Jackie gave many brief speeches (at first whispering, "Oh *God*, do I *have* to?") and dutifully followed instructions not to discuss issues or smoke in public.[40]

Though Jackie lost some of her reserve during the campaign, her impact was largely visual. "Isn't she gorgeous" was a frequent comment. Reporters described her apparel in detail. (Muriel Humphrey, also campaigning, did not receive such careful attention.) On the last weekend of the primary race, a Milwaukee reporter watched Jackie on television and said that she looked "like a cover girl."[41]

On election night a reporter observed Jackie sitting in a corner of the Kennedy headquarters in Milwaukee "looking undernourished, beautiful and bored." It had been predicted that Jack would win the April primary easily; some Democrats in the governor's office were of the opinion that he might take all ten districts and wrap up the nomination on the spot. Jack won, taking 40 percent of the popular vote and 56 percent of the Democratic vote. (Wisconsin had an open primary, and many Republicans voted for Kennedy.) But his strength came almost entirely from three heavily Catholic districts. He lost all four predominantly Protestant districts and barely carried an unclassified one.

Jack realized that his victory would not persuade party leaders that he was a winner. Political observers almost unanimously agreed. Walter Lister, Jr., of the *New York Herald-Tribune* wrote, "Wisconsin, despite all the time, money and hoopla, has proved virtually nothing." When a sister asked Kennedy what the final tally meant, he replied—"quietly yet bitterly," according to Theodore H. White—"It means that we have to do it all over again. We have to go through every [primary] and win every one of them."[42]

The candidates traded barbs in Wisconsin and left the state at odds. Jack railed privately about Hubert Humphrey's "smear tactics," exclaiming at one point, "It's just one fucking lie after another." Humphrey said later that he saw in the Kennedy campaign "an element of ruthlessness and toughness that I had trouble either accepting' or forgetting."[43]

After Wisconsin Humphrey claimed a moral victory over the "chain store" Kennedys and openly challenged Jack to campaign against him in West Virginia, which was 95 percent Protestant. Bobby and two other campaign leaders arrived in Charleston the next morning, where they learned immediately that Jack's Catholicism was a grave obstacle. A December Harris poll showing Kennedy ahead 70–30 had been taken before local people learned he was a Catholic.

Humphrey, gaining support from other Democrats eager to knock Kennedy out of the race, resisted efforts to persuade him to withdraw from the primary and avoid an ugly religious battle. The Kennedy forces then entered the fray with all the energy and money at their disposal. Some fifty Kennedy friends invaded West Virginia to lend their services. Kennedy volunteer organizations were soon in thirty-nine of the state's fifty-five counties. Bobby nervously made campaign speeches, and twenty-seven-year-old Teddy showed up at factory gates, dance halls, and coal mines to shake hands. (When Jack's voice gave out at one point, Teddy took over the oratorical work while his brother looked on.) The Kennedy women were again active, ringing doorbells, making telephone calls, appearing on television, and giving speeches. (Rose, a papal countess, was asked to stay out of Protestant West Virginia.) Jackie, according to O'Donnell and Powers, visited miners' wives, shook hands on street corners, passed out bumper stickers at shopping centers, and chatted with a gang of railroad laborers as they ate lunch.[44] The Kennedy entourage would, as usual, give their all to win the game.

The ambassador recruited Franklin D. Roosevelt, Jr., then a Washington car salesman, to campaign all over the state, reminding voters of what the former president had done for coal miners during the Great Depression. When introducing the candidate, FDR Junior frequently held up two fingers tightly pressed together and said, "My daddy and Jack Kennedy's daddy were just like that." Hearing that bit of historical perversity for the first time, Jack turned to Powers and O'Donnell and muttered, "This is a hard act to follow." Letters to voters in West Virginia signed by FDR Junior were shipped to Hyde Park to be mailed.[45]

Kennedy's tacticians agreed to stress Jack's military record in this state with a high percentage of war veterans. (Five *PT 109* buddies had showed up in Wisconsin for a last-minute televised rally.) Tens of thousands of copies of the *Reader's Digest* article on *PT 109* were distributed, and Kennedy workers sported lapel buttons and tie clasps shaped like PT boats and bearing the legend "Kennedy in '60." FDR Junior incorporated the approach enthusiastically. "You know why I'm here in West Virginia today?" he asked at one point. "Because Jack Kennedy and I fought side by side in the Pacific. He was on the PT boats and I was on the destroyers." (Sorensen later wrote, "Kennedy discussed with his campaign team whether to capitalize on his war record. Upon more sober reflection, he decided in the negative.")[46]

Jack wisely decided early to meet the religious issue head-on. (Humphrey was using the music of "Give Us That Oldtime Religion" for his campaign song.) In a speech at Morgantown, he raised the delicate subject openly, cleverly trying it to his military record: "Nobody asked me if I was a Catholic when I joined the United States Navy." He went on to ask if forty million Americans had forfeited their right to run for president the day they were baptized Catholics. "That wasn't the country my brother died for in Europe," he said, "and nobody asked my brother if he was a Catholic or a Protestant before he climbed into an American bomber to fly his last mission."

The speech, which O'Donnell later claimed was impromptu, was clearly a hit. One man was overheard saying, "Pretty good talker." A companion nodded and replied, "Good-looking feller, isn't he?" During the remainder of the campaign, Jack spoke often of his Catholicism. In one talk in the southern coalfields, he said that he did not "take orders from any Pope, any Cardinal, any Bishop or any priest—not that they would try to give me orders." "The American Catholic Church," he declared (no doubt to the surprise of many students of the issue), "is devoted to the separation of church and state."[47]

Liberal journalist Theodore H. White labeled one such speech, delivered the night before the election, "the finest TV broadcast I have ever heard any political candidate make." Looking straight into the camera and using every ounce of sincerity he could produce, Jack said:

> So when any man stands on the steps of the Capitol and takes the oath of office of President, he is swearing to support the separation of church and state; he puts one hand on the Bible and raises the other hand to God as he takes the oath. And if he breaks his oath, he is not only committing a crime against the Constitution, for which the Congress can impeach him—and should impeach him—but he is committing a sin against God.

Jack then raised his hand from an imaginary Bible, as if lifting it toward God, and repeated softly, "A sin against God, for he has sworn on the Bible."[48]

While Jack focused on pieties, his lieutenants were quietly threatening his opponents for aiding Humphrey. (Kennedy complained repeatedly in speeches that he was being "ganged up on.") In New York Stevenson backers were warned that their man would not even be *considered* for secretary of state unless they cut off all support to Humphrey. In Connecticut Senator William Benton was told sternly that if he continued to give money to Humphrey, his political future in the state was over.[49]

As the election neared, the Kennedys played an even rougher game. A large advertisement showed votes cast for Humphrey landing in a garbage can beside a road heading back to Minnesota, while votes for Kennedy would drop through the roof of the White House. Bobby, moreover, got FDR Junior to release press material charging Humphrey with being a "draft dodger." (In fact, the Minnesotan had been rejected for service in World War II because of a physical disability.) On April 27 Roosevelt said: "There's another candidate in your primary. He's a good Democrat, but I don't know where he was in World War II." An announcer said just before a Kennedy television documentary: "Kennedy is the only veteran in the West Virginia primary."

Jack publicly repudiated the charge that Humphrey had been a draft dodger. But, as Doris Kearns Goodwin later observed, Kennedy perfectly understood that "the deed was already done, the contrast had been drawn between a young decorated veteran and a politician who didn't even want to be a soldier." (The ambassador had sanctioned a similar tactic in Honey Fitz's 1942 Senate campaign.)[50]

Unlike Humphrey, who had little money and still owed seventeen thousand dollars on his Wisconsin effort, Kennedy was on television frequently. Theodore H. White recalled, "Over and over again there was the handsome, open-faced candidate on the TV screen, showing himself, proving that a Catholic wears no horns." The Kennedys could also afford to produce a documentary, shown statewide. As White described it, the film:

> opened with a cut of a PT boat spraying a white wake through the black night, and Kennedy was a war hero; the film next showed the quiet young man holding a book in his hand in his own library receiving the Pulitzer Prize, and he was a scholar; then the young man held his golden-curled daughter of two, reading to her as she sat on his lap, and he was the young father; and always, gravely, open-eyed, with a sincerity that could not be feigned, he would explain his devotion to the freedom of America's faith and the separation of church and state.[51]

The Kennedy forces, along with a growing number of allies in the nation's major newspapers, let West Virginia voters know in several ways that a vote for JFK was a vote for tolerance; a vote for Humphrey, therefore, revealed intolerance. (Sorensen cooked up an open letter signed by thirteen liberal Protestant leaders calling for "charitable moderation" toward both candidates. A copy was sent to every Protestant minister in West Virginia.) A Charleston newsman wrote, "The constant din is calculated, it would seem, to shame West Virginia Democrats into voting for Kennedy. I regard this as very poor strategy and an almost personal insult." But the tactic was undoubtedly effective. One woman, who switched from Humphrey to Kennedy just before the election, told White: "We have enough trouble in West Virginia, let alone to be called bigots, too."[52]

The Kennedy strategy also focused on the economic difficulties facing West Virginians. (Both Jack and Jackie were genuinely shaken at times by the squalid poverty they encountered in the state.) Jack now portrayed himself to be what pollster Lou Harris called "an all-out New Deal Democrat—a fighting liberal." In depressed mining areas, he evoked the memory of FDR's Hundred Days and called for greater federal aid. Still, it was the candidate's appearance that again seemed to make the greatest impression, even among the poor. A *New York Times* reporter heard one woman in White Sulphur Springs exclaim, "How could anybody vote for anyone else after looking at him?"[53]

Humphrey fought back as well as he could, blasting Kennedy for spending money "with wild abandon" and attacking Bobby for using

McCarthyite tactics. When Bobby declared that Jimmy Hoffa had ordered West Virginia Teamsters to back Humphrey, the Minnesotan snarled, "This is just cheap, low-down, gutter politics." He referred to Jack as "the spoiled candidate" and "papa's pet" and called his brother "that young, emotional, juvenile Bobby." Jack moaned publicly, "I have never been subject to such personal abuse."

But Humphrey was no match for the Kennedys. He could not, above all, begin to compete with their financial resources. He traveled in a rented bus (OVER THE HUMP WITH HUMPHREY read the bus's sign); he rode commercial airlines and carried his own luggage; he had to write a personal check for a half hour of television time just before the election. A *Newsweek* editor on the scene reported, "Almost everywhere, the Kennedy posters in the store windows outnumbered the Humphrey posters by 10 to 1. The Kennedy stickers on the parked cars outnumber the Humphrey stickers by even more." (On May 3 Kennedy backers made the absurd claim that they were $2,500 in debt and told reporters they had spent 20 percent less than the Humphrey supporters.)

Moreover, Larry O'Brien negotiated what he later called "payments for campaign expenses" from the Kennedys to local politicians—an ancient West Virginia custom. (Theodore H. White would list West Virginia as one of the four most politically corrupt states in the nation.) Humphrey could offer only what he termed "peanuts."

There were other quiet expenditures. In 1966 Richard Cardinal Cushing of Boston said to Humphrey, "I'll tell you who elected Jack Kennedy. It was his father, Joe, and me, *right here in this room*." The prelate explained that he and the ambassador had decided which Protestant ministers should receive "contributions" of $100 to $500. Cushing smiled as he described the tactic. "It's good for the Lord. It's good for the church. It's good for the preacher, and it's good for the candidate."[54]

No doubt most of the undercover funds belonged to the Kennedys. We now know that an undetermined amount of money also came from the Mafia. Judith Campbell (later Exner) had begun her affair with Jack in early March. Frank Sinatra had introduced them a month earlier in Las Vegas. In mid-March Sinatra introduced Campbell to Sam Giancana, the Chicago "godfather," then calling himself "Sam Flood." In early April Campbell visited Jack at his Georgetown townhouse (Jackie, pregnant, was in Florida) and listened attentively as the candidate discussed the West Virginia primary with a lobbyist. In the middle of the conversation, Jack asked Judith if she could arrange a meeting with "Sam," adding, "I think I may need his help in the campaign." Campbell, not knowing who "Flood" was, complied. Kennedy and Giancana met secretly on April 12.

FBI wiretaps later revealed large Mafia donations to the Kennedy campaign in West Virginia that were apparently disbursed by Frank Sinatra. The money was used to pay off key election officials. Paul (''Skinny'') D'Amato, an Atlantic City casino owner and Giancana henchman, distributed more than fifty thousand dollars to local sheriffs to get out the vote for Kennedy—by any means possible.[55]

The mobsters were, of course, after influence at the highest level. Giancana's daughter later reported that the ambassador had promised them assistance against federal probes. FBI documents secured under the Freedom of Information Act support this contention.[56]

Humphrey hoped that a television debate with Kennedy would be helpful. Jack had declined such an invitation in Wisconsin, and he privately considered the West Virginia challenge ''stupid.'' The hour-long event indeed proved dull; the two candidates seemed to agree on most things. At one point Jack held up a skimpy surplus food package and cited cases of economic hardship in the state. In the question-and-answer period, he incorrectly claimed to have spoken out in favor of Senator McCarthy's censure.[57]

Jack awaited the election returns in Washington. After dinner he and friends attended a pornographic movie in a downtown theater. Jack got out of his seat every twenty minutes to call Bobby in West Virginia. ''He wondered aloud,'' Ben Bradlee later wrote, ''if the movie was on the Catholic index of forbidden films (it was), and whether or not there were any votes in it either way for Kennedy in allegedly anti-Catholic West Virginia if it were known that he was in attendance.''[58] The contrast between the idealistic candidate who had presented himself to West Virginian voters and the cynical viewer of the porno movie on election eve was considerable, of course, but was unknown outside the Kennedy inner circle.

Kennedy swept West Virginia by 3–2, collecting 219,246 votes to Humphrey's 141,941. The winner carried forty-eight of the state's fifty-five counties. The *New York Times*, embracing Jack's contention of underdog status, called the victory a ''smashing upset.'' It reported ''unanimous agreement'' that Kennedy was a winner, and carried numerous stories pointing to a Kennedy bandwagon.

Humphrey tearfully dropped out of the presidential race. To his surprise Bobby proved gracious after the announcement, kissing Mrs. Humphrey on the cheek. Humphrey later wrote: ''Muriel stiffened, stared, and turned in silent hostility, walking away from him, fighting tears and angry words.'' The Minnesotan told a GOP colleague: ''You can't beat a billion dollars. The way Jack Kennedy and his old man threw the money around, the people of West Virginia won't need any public relief for the next fifteen years." Jack told a press conference: "I think we have now buried the religious issue once and for all," and he predicted his nomination.[59]

When Jackie was asked to make some comments at the noisy victory celebration, she asked columnist Rowland Evans, Jr., standing next to her: "Do I have to go up there? I don't have to, do I?" He assured her that she did. And he observed how difficult it was for her to face the public—and how well she performed. After that, Ben Bradlee recalled: "Jack ignored Jackie, and she seemed miserable at being left out of things." The candidate went on television while his wife quietly disappeared, went out to the car, and sat by herself until Jack was ready to fly back to Washington.[60]

Kennedy's victory in West Virginia impressed Democrats all over the country. By the end of May the young senator, with the help of a well-oiled campaign staff, had swept seven primaries, backed at least in part by those eager to rally behind the front runner. Kennedy's opponents, who had helped Humphrey in small ways, were now forced to be more open and active in order to prevent a preconvention landslide.

Adlai Stevenson's liberal backers labored at length, but the former presidential candidate himself wavered constantly and kept aloof from the political struggles. Missouri Senator Stuart Symington had numerous supporters, but he lacked the personal drive necessary to be an effective campaigner. Senate Majority Leader Lyndon Johnson hoped that he might wrap up the nomination by creating an impressive legislative record, and he rarely left Washington.

Only Jack Kennedy had the passion, the time (by June 29 he had missed 120 of the previous 159 Senate roll calls), the energy, the money, and the organization necessary to win large numbers of delegates. (Rowland Evans, Jr., observed, "The Kennedy organization doesn't run, it purrs. It has the smooth rhythm of a delicate watch.") After the convention, Symington would say diplomatically, "He had just a little more courage . . . stamina, wisdom and character than any of the rest of us."[61]

Lyndon Johnson despised Kennedy. When asking Tip O'Neill for his support, the Texan referred to Jack exclusively as "the boy." In a conversation with Peter Lisagor, he called his colleague a "little scrawny fellow with rickets." Lisagor later recalled, "He said, 'Have you ever seen his ankles? They're about so round.' And he made a gesture with his fingers. And he said, 'If he ever got elected President of the United States, his father, old Joe Kennedy, would run the country.' "[62]

After the U-2 spy plane incident in early May, Jack told reporters that he would "express regret" to Soviet Premier Khrushchev "that the flight did take place." (He later repeated it, regretted saying it, and then denied having said it.) Johnson charged Kennedy with appeasement and asked audiences, "I am not prepared to apologize to Mr. Khrushchev— are you? I am not prepared to send regrets to Mr. Khrushchev—are you?" Audiences invariably shouted "No!"[63]

When Johnson formally announced his candidacy five days before the convention opened, he criticized Kennedy's youth and comparative lack of experience. The "forces of evil," he said, meaning international communism, "will have no mercy for innocence, no gallantry toward inexperience." Privately, he said bitterly, "Jack was out kissing babies when I was passing bills."[64]

Both Jack and Bobby saw the tall Texan as their most formidable opponent. Jack told Arthur Schlesinger, Jr., that Johnson was "a chronic liar" and called him "a riverboat gambler." Stevenson said of Kennedy and Johnson, "Obviously the feeling between the two of them is savage."[65]

As Jack continued his furious pace across the country prior to the convention, he made much of his victories in Wisconsin and West Virginia, noting that Johnson, Symington, and Stevenson had failed to confront him before the voters. "No convention," he told a gathering of New York Democrats, "has ever nominated a man who avoided the primaries and elected that man President. And the 1960 Democratic Convention at Los Angeles is going to be no exception."[66]

In late June Jack assured New York's Liberal party policy committee that he hoped to win the nomination without a single Southern vote at the convention, and he promised to be stronger on civil rights than Eisenhower. When word of this reached the press, a storm arose because Bobby and Teddy had been quietly visiting Southern politicos for weeks, and Kennedy was "personally" soliciting support from Southern delegates by letter. Johnson campaign leaders called the Kennedy statement "incredible." Publisher John S. Knight commented, "Apparently, Kennedy wants the New York eggheads to believe that he has no truck with the 'benighted South.' And yet Kennedy, with private blandishments, pressure and cash is slickering up to every impressionable political leader below the Mason-Dixon line. . . . So 'John Boy' is neither as noble nor as agile as we had thought."[67]

Others were also critical of the young front-runner. Senator Wayne Morse, who ran in Oregon and Maryland, condemned Jack's "highly reactionary voting record in the fields of agriculture, military and taxes," and declared, "We must change this campaign from a contest of political sex appeal to a discussion of the issues.'' A *Congressional Quarterly* poll of senators and representatives showed that 54 percent of the members responding thought Lyndon Johnson was the Democratic party's ''strongest possible'' candidate, while only 20 percent named Kennedy. Former President Truman publicly endorsed Stuart Symington.[68]

But the front-runner continued to attract Democrats, including intellectuals. In early June an impressive group of liberals, including John Kenneth Galbraith, Henry Steele Commager, Arthur Goldberg, James MacGregor Burns, Joe Rauh, and Arthur Schlesinger, Jr., publicly endorsed Kennedy. Some of this support surely stemmed from the fact that Adlai Stevenson seemed out of the race, and the liberal intellectuals, needing someone to support, chose the man who had himself shown intellectual tendencies and who, in addition, was likely to win. Some of these leading liberals indeed became convinced that Kennedy was actually one of them. He was a Harvard man, after all, with an extremely impressive bibliography.[69]

Theodore H. White, a brilliant Harvard graduate who had enjoyed a rich career as a diplomat and writer, traveled with Kennedy for a short time before the convention and was completely won over by him. White observed Jack's hot temper (''His anger was cold, furious. When Kennedy is angry, he is at his most precise, almost schoolmasterish''), and listened attentively as the candidate lambasted his opponents (''the words sharp, his personality portraits merciless''). But what struck him most was the candidate's mind.

As Jack rattled on about a variety of topics during plane trips, asking many questions, spewing forth rapid-fire opinions, and reciting the quotations he had been memorizing and delivering on the stump for years (as Ben Bradlee would point out, Jack could often be something of a chatterbox), White, disposed by partisanship and impressed by Kennedy's intellectual credentials, was persuaded that he was in the presence of a first-rate mind. ''It was the range, the extent, the depth and detail, of information and observation that dazzled, then overwhelmed, the listener.'' White was particularly excited when Jack, surely knowing what he was doing, pressed White for information about China, White's specialty. Kennedy, White later wrote, ''was playing President,'' and the journalist was enchanted and flattered.[70]

By early July Kennedy's lead was such that Truman resigned as a delegate, not wanting, he said, to be a party to ''proceedings that are taking on the aspects of a prearranged affair.'' The seventy-six-year-old former president asked Kennedy to ''put aside'' his personal ambitions in light of current world turmoil and the need to nominate ''someone with the greatest possible maturity and experience.'' (In referring to Kennedy, he once spoke of the senator as ''Joseph'' rather than ''John.'' Later, he would say that it was the pop, not the pope, that bothered him about Jack's candidacy.) Truman called for an open Convention and said he knew first hand of instances of delegates being ''pressured into preconvention commitments against their better judgment.'' Johnson and Humphrey applauded the statement.[71]

By this time, however, Kennedy backers believed they had the votes necessary to win the nomination on the first ballot. Seven primary victories were only part of the story. Jack had won supporters throughout the country by shrewdly hinting that the local politico was just the sort of person he was looking for as his running mate. Bobby had been quietly cutting deals for months. The ambassador had also been extremely active behind the scenes. ''I saw him and heard him,'' George Smathers said later. ''He worked his tail off. He had an enormous influence with all kinds of people all over the United States.'' Frank Morrissey insisted, ''it was the ambassador who made sure that the votes of the various delegations in the big states like New York, Pennsylvania, Illinois, and New York all went for Jack.'' Sympathetic *New York Times* columnist James Reston observed, ''Senator Kennedy, and particularly his brother Robert, have run a very tough campaign. They have been as ruthless in their own way behind the scenes in gathering delegates as Mr. Truman was in the open this afternoon.''[72]

On July 4, with Jackie beside him (''she arrived looking very much like a movie starlet,'' wrote one reporter), Jack replied to Truman at a televised news conference. He claimed he had made no commitments to anyone and said, ''I do not want any votes that have been pressured.'' (Sorensen would later declare of JFK, ''He had made no promises he could not keep and promised jobs to no one.'') He added his naval service to his years in Congress to counter Truman's assertion about inexperience. He noted the youth of several historical figures at the height of their careers, including Alexander the Great, Napoleon, Columbus, and Jefferson, and he called for youth, vigor, and strength in the White House. ''It is true, of course, that almost all of the major world leaders today on both sides of the Iron Curtain are men past the age of 65.'' The *Wall Street Journal* labeled this ''a sophomoric argument.'' The *New York Herald-Tribune* commented, ''in plugging youth for youth's sake, Kennedy has missed another magnificent opportunity to answer a growing number of doubts about his qualifications for the nomination and the tactics he is using to seek it.'' Other observers, however, including the increasingly partisan *New York Times*, were pleased with the candidate's response.[73] After years of old men at the helm, America was ready for a young and energetic new leader.

Jack then retreated to Cape Cod for a few days of rest before the convention. Sorensen observed that his employer was "tired, almost haggard." The ambassador remarked, "He would be a lot more tired if he'd lost."[74]

Johnson backers thought that Kennedy's call for strength and vigor was a subtle shot at LBJ, who had suffered a severe heart attack in 1955. John B. Connally and Mrs. India Edwards, of Citizens for Johnson, quickly summoned reporters and told them that Kennedy had Addison's disease, which had been whispered by hostile Democrats for at least a year.

Bobby flew into a rage, charging the Johnson backers with malice and irresponsibility. He claimed that while his brother had suffered an "adrenal insufficiency" during the war ("Doctors have stated that this condition he has had might well have arisen out of his wartime experiences of shock and continued malaria"), he was now in excellent health. Bobby produced a vaguely worded and highly partisan medical report confirming this view and told reporters to consult the James MacGregor Burns biography for further information.

Ted Sorensen denied that Jack took cortisone. Jack, however, soon told *Time* reporters that he had taken cortisone periodically after the war for "partial adrenal insufficiency" and now took a cortisone-type medication "frequently, when I have worked hard." These inconsistencies, though rarely questioned by the press, were duly noted by several Republican leaders.[75]

Lyndon Johnson formally entered the race on July 5. He simply refused to believe that Kennedy could be nominated. "He's winnin' those beauty contests," he told aide Bobby Baker, "but when it gets down to nut-cuttin' he won't have the bulls with him."[76] Johnson dissociated himself from the Addison's disease issue, expressing confidence that both he and Kennedy were in good health. When asked about his political bent, he described himself as a centrist, then noted, "I was a voting liberal when McCarthyism was an issue in the Senate of the United States." No one missed the jab at Kennedy. Publicly Johnson hedged about taking second place on the ticket, but anyone who knew his love of power seriously doubted that he would trade the majority leadership for the vice presidency. Television reporter Nancy Hanschman (later Dickerson), a Johnson confidante, wrote later that LBJ "had sworn to me a dozen times, both on the air and off, that he would never take the vice-presidency."[77]

On July 7, in Chicago, Johnson sharply criticized Bobby for predicting publicly that the outcome of the convention would be decided before the official opening. "There are countries in the world where such arrogance is customary in politics," he said. "This is not that kind of country." He asked angrily, "Is this Convention open or has the outcome been determined somewhere in a back room, with the result only now being announced to the delegates?" Johnson backers soon condemned the ambassador for being anti-Semitic and soft on Hitler, and they made much of the contrast between Johnson and Kennedy on Joe McCarthy. Kennedy supporters countered with the false accusation that Jimmy Hoffa and the Teamsters Union were backing LBJ.[78]

As delegates began to gather in Los Angeles, several black leaders questioned Kennedy's commitment to civil rights, and black Congressman Adam Clayton Powell, Jr., declared that he could not support the senator. (Powell soon revealed that Jack had had a secret breakfast meeting in 1959 with Governor John Patterson of Alabama, a militant segregationist, and Sam Englehardt, a former head of the White Citizens Council in Alabama, obviously seeking their support.)[79] Jack quickly traveled to Harlem to confer with black spokesmen and agreed to head a rally sponsored by the National Association for the Advancement of Colored People (NAACP), scheduled for the eve of the convention.

Before a crowd of six thousand in Los Angeles, Jack spoke favorably of the sit-in demonstrations in the South and said that the president should use his "immense moral authority" and "legal authority" to help end discrimination. He disappointed the crowd, however, by failing to make any specific pledges on black rights. Hubert Humphrey was more forceful. "I didn't come to Los Angeles to get elected to anything," he told the crowd. "I came to make sure the Democratic Party was worthy of its victory."

At the same time, Bobby was quietly wooing Southern delegates by telling them that his brother approved of sit-in demonstrations only when they were "peaceful and legal." Since the sit-ins were already illegal, for the most part, Southerners got the message and were pleased. (During the balloting at the convention, Bobby would have Alabama Governor Patterson withhold nine out of the fourteen votes that could have been delivered to Kennedy, not wanting others to know immediately the strength of Jack's Southern support.) Both Senator James O. Eastland of Mississippi, an archsegregationist, and crusading liberal senator Paul H. Douglas of Illinois were favorable toward Kennedy. They had been told what they wanted to hear.[80]

Some twenty Kennedy family members were in Los Angeles before the convention. Jackie, expecting in November, stayed at Hyannis Port. The ambassador was among the first on the scene, renting a Spanish-colonial villa in Beverly Hills, belonging to retired actress Marion Davies. (He stopped in Nevada on his way to the Convention and placed a substantial wager on his son to ensure that the gambling odds on the nomination would favor Jack.)[81] Rose arrived later, telling reporters, "My son was rocked to political lullabies." One newsman observed, "Even the in-laws in this phalanx have youth, health, good teeth and the bone-crushing grip of Japanese wrestlers. They seemed to be everywhere—at the Biltmore Hotel's convention headquarters, on television, on the street, at the airport greeting relatives." A Johnson supporter complained, "You can't move ten steps in the headquarters hotel without encountering a Kennedy poster, a Kennedy brother or a Kennedy staff man."[82]

Jack's principal residence was at the Biltmore, but he also rented a secret retreat, a three-bedroom suite in an apartment house owned by actor Jack Haley. When the press discovered the hideaway, Kennedy evaded reporters by climbing down a fire escape and scaling a neighbor's fence to a waiting car. Caught in the act during the convention, Jack shouted to reporters that he was going off "to meet my father." Further investigation indicated that the stealthy visit was to a nearby home of a former diplomat's wife.[83]

➢➢➢   ≪≪≪

In the midst of these final days in his grueling campaign to become his party's presidential candidate, Jack found time to spend in Peter Lawford's suite at the Beverly Hilton Hotel. It was there, on the evening of July 11, that Jack summoned beautiful Judith Campbell to a late-night party. When all the guests were gone except Kenny O'Donnell, Jack asked Judith to join him in a bedroom. She was quickly shocked to find another woman waiting for them. "He assured me the girl was safe, that she would never talk about it to a single soul, that there was nothing wrong with a *ménage à trois*, that it was practiced widely, and, over and over again, that I would enjoy it—'I know you, I know you'll enjoy it.' " (Joan Lundberg Hitchcock, a Kennedy mistress in the late 1950s, wrote of Jack, "He loved threesomes—himself and two girls. He was also a voyeur.")[84] When Campbell tearfully rejected the arrangement, Jack pursued her with apologetic telephone calls and flowers. He also got Evelyn Lincoln to reserve convention tickets for his twenty-five-year-old friend. (Campbell, declining to attend, sent her mother, who sat next to the Kennedy family during the proceedings.)[85]

Earlier Jack had assured Judith that if he failed to win the nomination the two of them would retreat to some far-off place together "and never wear clothes." Jack rarely mentioned Jackie. (At least once Judith felt uncomfortable about making love in the Kennedy bedroom at Georgetown.) "The most he ever said was that their marriage was not a happy one. It hadn't worked out as they had hoped." He did not criticize his wife, however. "I got the impression," Campbell wrote later, "that it was Jackie who was planning to leave him if he didn't become President."[86]

→≫≫ ≪←

Bobby could usually be found directing strategy from the nerve center of the Kennedy campaign on the eighth floor of the Biltmore. Here an expensive and tightly organized communications network, unprecedented in American politics, linked Bobby with representatives in all parts of the convention hall. Some forty agents assigned to specific state delegations counted and reported votes hourly around the clock. Delegates were visited, cajoled, and pressured by Kennedy staff members and volunteers. Theodore H. White wrote, "Control as exercised from 8315 was precise, taut, disciplined—yet as casual as that of a veteran combat army, blooded in battle, which has learned to know all its component parts and recognizes the full reach of its skills and courage."[87]

A less sympathetic observer, columnist Jim Bishop, called Bobby "an irritable and irritating little man" who was "tactless, impatient, ruthless. . . . When he concludes a short, confidential chat with a political leader, the man is left with the feeling that his suit is hanging in tatters and, if he doesn't do exactly as Robert tells him, God will strike him dead." The *New York Times* referred editorially to "the brash young man who is fighting with no holds barred for his brother's nomination." Arthur Schlesinger, Jr., later remembered thirty-four-year-old Bobby in his shirtsleeves, his tie loose, rallying his staff to action, chewing out an exhausted worker, and demanding the name, address, and telephone number of every half vote. ("Bobby always spoke in commands," Nancy Dickerson recalled.) " 'I don't want generalities or guesses,' he would say. 'There's no point in our fooling ourselves. I want the cold facts.' "[88]

Two days before the convention opened, reporters observed a stampede for Kennedy. When Symington backers began to lean toward Johnson to turn things around, Jack countered by letting it be known that Symington was his favorite for the vice presidential nomination. Stevenson continued to play coy, saying that he would accept the nomination but would not work for it. He refused all invitations to endorse Kennedy and preferred to remain "neutral." When Stevenson aide Bill Blair introduced himself to the ambassador just before the proceedings began, the elder Kennedy became enraged. "He shook his fist and waved it in my face and said, 'You've got twenty-four hours!' " Soon Bobby telephoned Blair, offering Stevenson the opportunity to place Kennedy's name in nomination. "I'm calling now for the last time." When Blair hedged slightly, Bobby slammed down the phone.[89]

The convention opened on July 11 in the new Sports Arena. The *New York Times* greeted delegates with a front-page headline that began: KENNEDY NOMINATION SEEMS SURE. *Time* celebrated the certain victory with a lavish spread on the Kennedy family. "The Kennedy clan is as handsome and spirited as a meadow full of Irish thorough-breds, as tough as a blackthorn shillelagh, as ruthless as Cuchulain, the mythical hero who cast up the hills of Ireland with his sword." The article contained a revealing statement by the ambassador about the possibility that his son might accept the vice presidential nomination: "Not for chalk, money or marbles will we take second place. Nobody's going to make a deal with us in a back room somewhere for second place on the ticket."[90]

Still, Jack continued to work furiously, rushing from hotel to hotel and speaking to nine state caucuses in one day. He also made a gesture of conciliation toward Johnson, his only viable opponent, telling a news conference that if nominated he would consult with the majority leader and Speaker Sam Rayburn, a Johnson backer, about the choice of a new national party chairman. The current chairman, Paul M. Butler, had been strongly criticized for allegedly rigging the convention procedures to favor Kennedy.[91]

Johnson made a last-ditch effort to gain the nomination by calling for a nationally televised debate with Kennedy. The ambassador thought a debate unwise, and Jack declined. When Johnson proceeded to make the arrangements, however, Jack had no choice but to participate. Jean Smith was overheard telling her father, "But, Daddy, how can Jack say no? That man challenged us."[92]

Johnson sarcastically described Kennedy's frequent absences from the Senate during debate on the Civil Rights Act of 1957, stressed his own maturity and legislative experience, and brought up the religious issue by noting Protestant support for Kennedy in West Virginia and declaring, "What we want is equal proof that a Catholic state will go for a Protestant." Johnson introduced his rival as "a man of unusually high character" and "great intellect."

Jack, so nervous that some reporters noticed his knees shaking, stuck to pleasantries—"I don't think Senator Johnson and I disagree on the great issues that face us"—and resorted to his usual litany of generalities. "I think that this is the responsibility of our party—to help build in this country a society which serves our people and serves as an attraction to those who determine which road they shall take." Both candidates promised to campaign vigorously for the winner. Few thought that the debate was of any consequence.[93]

Johnson continued his fight, however, to the bitter end. He condemned the ambassador in an appearance before the Washington State caucus, shouting, "I was never any Chamberlain umbrella policy man. I never thought Hitler was right." He railed against Jack's wealth. "I haven't had anything given to me. Whatever I have and whatever I hope to get, will be because of whatever energy and talents I have." Johnson said also that when Joe McCarthy was on the march, "I was not contributing comfort to his thinking or contributions to his campaign. Every Democratic Senator stood up and voted with their leader. That is, all those who were present." On a new tack, he raised the issue of "bossism," contending that Kennedy was in the clutches of a half dozen big-state bosses. But this effort, like the massive demonstrations for Adlai Stevenson outside and inside the arena, was futile. Kennedy had the votes.[94]

The number needed to win was 761, a majority of the 1,520 delegates votes. The Wyoming delegation—with Teddy working in its midst—secured the nomination for Kennedy on the first ballot. The final tally was Kennedy, 806; Johnson, 409; Symington, 86; Stevenson, 79½; and all others, 140½. Russell Baker of the *New York Times* observed, "The political connoisseurs here are talking in awe of the Kennedy machine's efficiency in coolly eliminating every element of contest before the convention opened." It was a dull gathering he wrote, "in which all the battles were sham and all the hullaballoo synthetic."[95] Cynical and calculated, the Kennedy organization had pulled all stops to get their candidate to win. The contrast between the candidate's public persona of warmth, sincerity, and ideals and the ruthless, heavily financed campaign that secured his victory could not have been greater.

Jack first telephoned his father and then Jackie. Jackie told reporters several times, "I'm so excited," and soon described her husband as "strict—but very affectionate." When asked if she had any preference for second place on the ticket, she replied, "I like everyone."[96]

→>> <<←

An exact account of Kennedy's selection of Johnson cannot be written; several crucial conversations were held in private, confusion and stress surrounded all the events, Kennedy later told different things to different people, and his partisans again muddied the historical record with dubious stories. Johnson, too, was secretive, keeping even his aide George Reedy in the dark about the details of his selection. Still, we have a reasonably clear idea of what transpired. And it is certain that Kennedy's first act as his party's leader was far from noble.

In early June Jack had assured liberal leader Joe Rauh that his preference for a running mate would be Hubert Humphrey or "another Midwestern liberal." A month later, he told a national television audience that he favored a person familiar with the agricultural problem, "somebody from the Middle West or Far West." Bobby and Kenny O'Donnell told liberals and labor leaders that a "Midwestern liberal" would likely be chosen.[97]

Just before the convention, in Jack's hideaway suite, JFK offered the vice presidency to Stuart Symington, who could roughly qualify as a Midwesten liberal. Symington adviser Clark Clifford, who completed the negotiations, said later, "There were no strings attached. It was a straight offer." Symington approved the arrangement. "We had a deal signed, sealed and delivered," Clifford told Nancy Hanschman.[98]

At about the same time, *Washington Post* publisher Philip Graham and columnist Joseph Alsop visited Kennedy and urged him to select Lyndon Johnson. Jack agreed immediately, Graham later wrote, "so immediately as to leave me doubting the easy triumph." Graham was especially surprised because Bobby had told him that Johnson would not be considered. When Alsop urged Kennedy not to consider Symington, saying, "You know perfectly well he's too shallow a puddle to dive into," Jack grinned and replied, "You know damn well I would never do that."

The day before the convention vote, realizing that Kennedy had the nomination in his grasp, Speaker Sam Rayburn and Texas Congressman Wright Patman endorsed Johnson for the number-two spot. When Tip O'Neill approached Jack with this news, the front-runner was delighted. "Of course I want Lyndon," he said. "But I'd never want to offer it and have him turn me down. Lyndon's the natural choice, and with him on the ticket, there's no way we could lose." Jack telephoned Rayburn that night, confirming the choice.[99]

Johnson was at first wary of Jack's enthusiasm, thinking that the Kennedys were saying the same thing to other candidates and influential party leaders, as indeed they were. Bobby told the Washington State delegates that their own Senator Henry Jackson was his personal favorite. When Jack visited the Minnesota delegation, he put his arm around Orville Freeman and said that the liberal governor was just the kind of man he would like to run with. Hours before the first ballot, Jack again consulted Graham, asking if a vice presidential offer to Johnson might be worth some votes.[100]

After winning the nomination, Jack faced the problem of choosing between the several contenders mentioned as possible running mates. He decided on Johnson. Several Southerners had advised Jack that he needed the Texan to carry their region and the election, a position that made sense to many Democratic strategists. There was ample precedent: Al Smith had picked Joseph Robinson; Franklin Roosevelt had named his earlier opponent, John Nance Garner; and Adlai Stevenson had taken John Sparkman. But the decisive factor was that the ambassador favored the majority leader. Bobby and Teddy later admitted, in the words of an interviewer, that their father "vigorously approved" the selection. Johnson later told Henry Jackson, "Hell, Scoop, they didn't want me. They wanted you. It was the old man who wanted me."[101]

Kennedy apologists later covered up the ambassador's role. O'Donnell and Powers contended that Jack first thought of making the offer to Johnson after the nomination when he was moved by the Texan's congratulatory telegram. Schlesinger claimed that the offer was made only halfheartedly, "to restore relations with the Senate leader," with the near certainty that Johnson would decline. Sorensen denied all but the highest motives for the selection: "Above all, Kennedy respected him and knew he could work with him. Lyndon Johnson was, in his opinion, the best qualified man to be President."[102]

Kennedy called Johnson in the middle of the night, could not reach him, and left a message that he wanted to see him. In the morning Jack learned from Sargent Shriver that a man close to Johnson had telephoned during the night to say that the majority leader would accept the vice presidential nomination if it was offered.[103]

Jack then huddled with Shriver, Bobby, Salinger, and several other intimates, talking at times heatedly about the second place on the ticket. Bobby was especially incensed by the selection of Johnson, a man who had publicly questioned his brother's health and smeared his father. When the decision was made to obey the elder Kennedy, Jack telephoned Johnson, saying he would like to chat later that morning.

Johnson knew what to expect and began consulting advisers. Lady Bird Johnson strongly urged her husband not to be part of the Kennedy ticket. By the time Jack arrived, however, shortly before 11:00 A.M. (taking a back stairway down two flights of stairs to avoid reporters), Johnson was favorably disposed toward the offer. He had long wanted to be a national political figure. And he may have become weary of his demanding Senate duties. There was also a darker side to his decision. He soon told Clare Booth Luce, "Clare, I looked it up: One out of every four Presidents has died in office. I'm a gamblin' man, darlin', and this is the only chance I got.' "[104]

When Jack offered the nomination, Johnson asked several questions and wanted to know who favored his selection. Jack listed his father, Alsop, and Philip Graham.[105] While Johnson said that he would like to think over the matter for a short time, he left the clear impression that he wanted the vice presidency. According to Schlesinger, Kennedy later told a friend, "He grabbed at it."[106] When Jack returned to his suite, he was handed a message to call the ambassador. Evelyn Lincoln heard Jack tell his father "accepted." Lincoln asked an aide, "What did Johnson say?" She was told, "He said yes."[107]

A group of Southern governors quickly approved Johnson's selection. Others were less than pleased. Bobby, Shriver, and Salinger were glum. Kenny O'Donnell was enraged. (In 1964 he told an interviewer that Jack cut him off when he objected. "He wanted no back talk." In his book on JFK he told a far-less-believable story about Jack taking him into a bathroom and explaining his decision at length. "I'm forty-three-years old, and I'm the healthiest candidate for President in the United States. I'm not going to die in office. So the Vice-Presidency doesn't mean anything. I'm thinking of something else, the leadership in the Senate.")[108] Three top labor leaders complained bitterly and threatened a floor fight. Liberal Michigan Governor G. Mennen Williams shouted that he would personally lead a floor fight against Johnson's nomination.[109]

As the criticism mounted, Jack wavered. After considerable debate he sent Bobby down to Johnson to try to talk to him out of accepting the nomination. It was a foolish move that could only alienate the majority leader and reveal the party's standard bearer to be weak and untrustworthy.[110]

Lady Bird advised her husband to deal only with the candidate himself, so Bobby spoke with Rayburn, bluntly warning the veteran House Speaker of the possible floor fight and implying that Johnson should bow out. Rayburn, who considered Bobby a "kid" and a "punk," was furious. Phil Graham, close to both Johnson and Kennedy, was asked to telephone JFK in an effort to find out what was going on. Bobby returned upstairs.

The anguish in the Kennedy suite continued, even after Jack had assured Graham that all was well. "We just vacillated back and forth as to whether we wanted him or didn't want him," Bobby said later. Finally the decision was made to dump Johnson. At a time of triumph and with the ambassador not physically present, the young Kennedys were choosing to defy their father.

Bobby returned to the Johnson suite and met with the majority leader and Rayburn. He offered Johnson the chance to be Democratic national chairman if he would withdraw. Rayburn simply said, "Shit, sonny," and stomped out of the room. When Nancy Hanschman encountered him in a hallway, he was muttering about "the goddamn Kennedys" and how "we'll teach them how to do things." Johnson burst into tears ("You know," LBJ once told a friend, "a man ain't worth a damn if he can't cry at the right time"), and told Bobby unequivocally that he was determined to fight for the nomination. (According to George Reedy, the majority leader had a shorthand expert hidden in a closet taking notes of the conversation.) At that point Bobby caved in. "Well, it's Jack and Lyndon." After Bobby left the suite, LBJ referred to him as "that little shitass" and worse.

When Graham again telephoned Jack to discuss Bobby's visit, the candidate responded calmly and replied that Bobby was "out of touch and doesn't know what's been happening." He then reassured Johnson of his support. Of course, Jack may have been attempting to separate himself from his brother's visits. But that seems highly unlikely given the relationship between the two men. A few have argued that Bobby in fact acted on his own, but the contention is unconvincing. Bobby said in 1964, "I was not operating independently. I was Senator Kennedy's agent." Far more likely is the theory held by Herbert Parmet that in the interval between Bobby's second mission and Graham's call, the ambassador intervened and ended his sons' embarrassing and destructive escapade. John McCormack told Burton Hersh that the elder Kennedy personally telephoned Johnson to urge him to join the ticket.

Only hours after Johnson's selection, unnamed sources told the *New York Times* that the offer to Johnson was a mere courtesy and that Kennedy was surprised when it was accepted. Jack later told Henry Jackson and Wisconsin Senators Gaylord Nelson and William Proxmire a yarn about Sam Rayburn forcing him to put Johnson on the ticket, threatening to destroy Kennedy's legislative program if Johnson had to remain in the Senate. Bobby spread the tale to other Democratic leaders.[111]

Numerous liberals and labor leaders were deeply upset by the selection of Johnson, thinking the move supremely cynical and a betrayal of the party's staunchly liberal platform. "I'm sick," Arthur Schlesinger, Jr., announced. "I'm shocked," gasped Robert Nathan, former head of Americans for Democratic Action. "The liberals that I have talked to here feel that this is a complete violation of an understanding." Joe Rauh spoke of a "double cross," and G. Mennen Williams called the Johnson selection a "mistake" and a "disappointment." Max Lerner thought that this first act of Kennedy as candidate was a crucial symbolic one. If he capitulated to pressure, his courage must be questioned. If he took the initiative, then his basic drive toward liberalism must be questioned.[112]

Many Johnson loyalists were equally shocked. On first hearing the news, Oklahoma Senator Robert Kerr glared at LBJ, his wife, and Bobby Baker and yelled, "Get my .38. I'm gonna kill every damn one of you. I can't believe that my three best friends would betray me." Lady Bird wept when Senator Jackson made the announcement on television, telling aide Bill Moyers, "But I was so happy being the wife of the Senator from Texas."[113]

Tempers quickly cooled, however, as Democrats of all shades of opinion began to realize that they would soon be facing a GOP ticket probably led by Richard Nixon. ("I don't want a man who calls me a traitor to be President of the United States," Sam Rayburn bellowed during the turmoil surrounding Johnson's selection.) Moreover, Johnson made peace with several major liberals and labor leaders by quietly writing a letter promising to support the platform's civil rights plank. Still, resistance at the convention was certain. To quell any possibility of rebellion, the Kennedys made an arrangement with the convention chairman to gavel through a motion nominating Johnson by acclamation. When this was done, hundreds booed, but to no avail.[114]

Back at the ambassador's villa, Jack and Bobby sat gloomily by the swimming pool, bemoaning the selection of Johnson. "Jack was in a low state of mind," said an observer. "Bobby was in near despair," exclaiming, "Yesterday was the best day of my life; today is the worst." Then the ambassador strolled by in a fancy smoking jacket and said cheerily, "Don't worry, Jack. In two weeks everyone will be saying that this was the smartest thing you ever did."[115]

Some fifty thousand people were on hand at the Los Angeles Coliseum to hear the presidential candidate's acceptance speech. Entertainment preceded the address, and comedian Mort Sahl was irreverent. The candidate, he said, was "on his way back to school to take care of his affairs and write a term paper called 'What I did on my summer vacation.' " Vice President Nixon, he continued, had just sent a telegram to Joseph P. Kennedy offering congratulations and declaring, "You have not lost a son. You have gained a country."[116]

>>>   <<<

The Kennedy image was now widely perceived and appreciated by the American people. This handsome, brilliant, idealistic young statesman, who enjoyed and empathized with people, who loved his charming wife, who was blessed with caring and sacrificing parents and siblings and surrounded himself with some of the most impressive thinkers from elite institutions, had boldly persuaded the nation's leading Democrats that he was the right man to lead the country toward greatness. Behind the scenes, however, there was a less pleasant and unpublicized reality involving money, bribery, manipulation, adultery, and a consistent lack of propriety. The gap between the Kennedy image and reality had grown larger, and in the ensuing campaign it would widen even more.

CHAPTER 10

Moving Ahead

➤➤➤ ⫷⫷⫷

IT TOOK JACK KENNEDY only fourteen years to rise from being a first-term congressman to being his party's presidential nominee. The ambassador's passionate devotion to his son's career was the principal reason for the rapid progress. But Jack's willingness to assume his responsibilities as the oldest family male and his tireless and often painful labors to win the nation's highest office were crucial to his success.

There were still many doubters in 1960; millions would have to be persuaded that the young Democrat's image and reality were one, and that America, with his election, would become a far greater place. But the Kennedys were ready for the struggle, willing to spend whatever money and energy it took to grasp the prize the Founding Father had long sought. They were also prepared to make any deals and cut any corners that would be to their advantage. They looked forward to the campaign, confident that victory would follow, as it always had.

Jack's acceptance speech, largely a Sorensen product, was designed, among other things, to accept the nomination, to heal party wounds, to criticize Republican leadership, and to attack Richard Nixon. At the heart of it was a battle cry, a call for fresh energy, ideas, and ideals. The New Frontier, a label (apparently devised by aide Walt Rostow) Jack hoped would rank with Wilson's New Freedom and Roosevelt's New Deal, was an appeal for public sacrifice to combat poverty, ignorance, and war. It was a "set of challenges" that "sums up not what I intend to offer to the American people, but what I intend to ask of them."

The forthcoming election, Jack said, was a "turning point in history," for the American people faced a choice "not merely between two men or two parties, but between the public interest and private comfort, between national greatness and national decline, between the fresh air of progress and the stale, dank atmosphere of 'normalcy.' "

Kennedy quoted from Isaiah and added, "As we face the coming great challenge, we too shall wait upon the Lord and ask that He renew our strength. Then we shall be equal to the test. Then we shall not be weary. Then we shall prevail."[1]

All this assumed, of course, there was much truth to the overall charge—gospel to liberals and seen often in the media—that the Eisenhower administration was witless, insensitive, and backward, and that the public was dissatisfied and eager for change and challenge. The facts did not encourage such assumptions. Eisenhower remained enormously popular; the public endorsed his moderate conservatism at home and firm anticommunism abroad. Moreover, public confidence in the American political and economic system was extremely high. Middle-class prosperity, thought limitless, spawned the "consumer culture" of the 1950s. Peace prevailed overseas. The second Red scare had ended. And billions of dollars were being spent on higher education and the space race in order to catch up with technological advances made by the Soviet Union.

Kennedy and his advisers could point to numerous national shortcomings in such areas as the arms race, civil rights, farm prices, and urban blight. They believed, or at least said they believed, that government could help right the wrongs of the past and meet the needs of the present. Still, it was highly questionable whether the Democrats could convince most voters to replace self-satisfaction with some as-yet-vague summons to self-sacrifice.

Some experts predicted that the only way Kennedy could defeat Nixon would be on the personal level: He would have to prove that he was more intelligent, honest, and charming than the vice president. Jack and his advisers were well aware of this line of thought and from the start were eager to enhance the Kennedy image. Thousands cheered as the handsome young presidential candidate cried out in his stirring acceptance speech: "A whole world looks to see what we will do. We cannot fail their trust. We cannot fail to try. . . . Give me your help and your hand and your voice and your vote."[2]

Nixon watched the address on television and gained confidence from Kennedy's performance. Jack read the speech rapidly and was obviously nervous and exhausted. Moreover, the often-lofty rhetoric seemed beyond the public's comprehension. Talks were already underway about televised debates between the candidates, and the vice president relished the thought.[3]

The ambassador also watched the speech on television. Wanting to avoid public attention, he had left Los Angeles soon after Johnson's selection as his son's running mate and had flown to New York. At the home of publisher Henry R. Luce, he watched scornfully as Stevenson, Humphrey, and others preceded Jack to the platform to urge party unity. "There was no respect for any of these liberals," Luce's son later recalled. "He just thought that they were all fools on whom he had played this giant trick."[4]

⇢⟫⟫   ⟨⟨⟨

Many Democrats remained uninspired by the convention's outcome. James Reston reported, "To the very end, doubt persisted in every honest mind." Associated Press news analyst James Marlow observed, "To this writer, who has seen every political Convention since 1944, the nomination of Kennedy seemed the least enthusiastic of the past sixteen years. The answer may be that it is difficult to get emotional about a technician." Even the friendly *Washington Post* said that "the nomination was more of a triumph of organization and evaluation than of deep dedication."[5]

Many liberals, eager to expand the welfare state that developed under Roosevelt and Truman, and committed to greater economic and racial equality, were unhappy and apathetic. They smarted over Johnson's nomination, and the very thought of Bobby Kennedy provoked invective. (Stevenson took to calling him the "Black Prince." His friend Agnes Meyer privately labeled Bobby "that incipient dictator.") When the national board of Americans for Democratic action met, half the representatives favored making no endorsement. One delegate complained, "It isn't what Kennedy believes that worries me. It's whether he believes anything." *New York Post* columnist Joseph Barry wondered if 1960 would be remembered as "the year nobody voted."[6]

Many Catholics were cool toward the ticket. All through the 1950s Catholics had been deserting the Democratic party, their traditional political home. In 1952 Stevenson received only 56 percent of the Catholic vote; four years later, he won only 51 percent. Theodore H. White observed: "In many of the most important dioceses of the nation it was known in 1960 that if the Catholic Church had any silent inclination, it leaned to Richard M. Nixon rather than to John F. Kennedy.'' (When Francis Cardinal Spellman refused to support JFK and escorted Eisenhower and Nixon in a parade down Fifth Avenue, the ambassador vowed never to speak to Spellman again and never to contribute a cent to the church.) Others, including several urban bosses, feared an anti-Catholic backlash against Kennedy's candidacy that would hurt local politicians.[7]

There was considerable Democratic disarray in the South. The party's liberal platform, especially its strong civil rights plank, turned off many Southerners. And Johnson's presence on the ticket did not seem to appease great numbers of Dixie conservatives. James Kilpatrick, editor of the *Richmond News-Leader,* branded the majority leader a "counterfeit Confederate."[8]

Of course, Kennedy's religion was a major obstacle. In May thirteen thousand delegates to the Southern Baptist Convention's annual meeting voted unanimously for a resolution expressing strong fears about electing a Roman Catholic president. The best-known minister in the 9.5-million-member denomination, Billy Graham, hinted that he favored Nixon. "This is a time of world tensions, and I don't think it is the time to experiment with novices." On July 14 the Rev. Dr. W. A. Criswell, pastor of the First Baptist Church of Dallas, the nation's largest (twelve thousand members) all-white Baptist congregation, declared that the election of a Catholic would "spell the death of a free church in a free state and our hopes of continuance of full religious liberty in America."[9]

There were also whispers among insiders about Jack's penchant for adultery, an issue that had the potential to explode. When, in the course of a strategy session on the problem of JFK's Catholicism, a Johnson adviser referred to Kennedy's sexual exploits, Lady Bird responded with horror, "Oh, no! Not that too!" After a ten-day visit to the East Coast, Adlai Stevenson wrote privately, "Much too much talk about Jack's girls."[10]

After the convention Jack flew to Hyannis Port for some badly needed relaxation. An eight-foot wooden fence was built around the Kennedy home to fend off the curious, and a squad of policemen ordered tourists to keep moving. Jackie soon said softly to Adlai Stevenson, "I can't bear all those people peering over the fence. Eunice loves the whole horrible business. I may abdicate."[11]

When not boating, sunbathing, and partying, Jack consulted advisers, helped create elaborate campaign machinery, and visited with a number of leading Democrats to solicit their support and plan their participation in the campaign. Stevenson, widely thought to be Kennedy's choice for secretary of state, came away from Hyannis Port dejected. He confided to Arthur Schlesinger, Jr., that he found the presidential nominee cold and ruthless (although less so than Bobby), and that he was not sure he could serve or even wanted to serve in a Kennedy administration. He would support the ticket, of course, but he did not want to campaign as actively as the Kennedy people requested.[12]

Another guest, W. Averell Harriman, the ambitious millionaire who had served as wartime ambassador to the Soviet Union, was far more positive. At a press conference with the candidate, he blasted the Eisenhower foreign policy and said, "I thank God we will have a President in Senator Kennedy who is not afraid to act." Allen W. Dulles, director of the Central Intelligence Agency, paid a call to Hyannis Port to brief the candidate on international affairs. The Johnsons also turned up, and Jack and Lyndon held a press conference that included some jibes at the Republican ticket of Richard M. Nixon and Henry Cabot Lodge.[13]

On August 8 Kennedy, Nixon, and Johnson found themselves stuck in Washington during a special session of Congress, called earlier, before the Democrats convened, in the hope of pressuring support for Johnson's presidential bid. Both Democrats and Republicans used the session for political posturing and the presentation of an array of proposals they allegedly favored but could not pass. Eisenhower dropped a twenty-one point legislative program in the lawmakers' laps, which included civil rights legislation, a farm bill, federal aid for schools, an increase in the minimum wage, and medical benefits for the elderly. Kennedy called for a three-stage increase in, and extended coverage of, the minimum wage, aid for schools, and medical care for the aged. The failure of Jack's proposals was especially noticeable because both houses of Congress were controlled by Democrats. Coming away empty-handed did little to enhance his image as a vigorous leader. When Kennedy addressed the Senate on the minimum wage, the chamber was almost empty.[14]

Senate leaders had long considered Kennedy a mere playboy, and this impression had not changed dramatically since the convention. Throughout the special session the Senate powers were condescending. At one private luncheon Jack rushed in late to greet powerful Southern Democrats Richard Russell, Harry Byrd, John Stennis, and other with "Hello, Senator." They all replied, "Hello, Jack." Nancy Dickerson recalled, "The atmosphere was stiff from the start and got stiffer." Meaningful conversation did not develop. Kennedy kept calling them all "senator" and they kept calling him "Jack." The candidate left early, hardly a sign that he had endeared himself to them. Lyndon Johnson sidled up to a couple of his old friends and said, "See, I told you he really was a nice boy." His colleagues, however, remained unimpressed.[15]

Many senators and congressmen, eager to get on with the campaign, grew tense and irritable during the special session. By mid-August, Republicans were attacking Kennedy's spending during his preconvention and convention activities. Senator Hugh Scott of Pennsylvania declared, "Estimates vary between $1,500,000 and $7,000,000 already used, and I am sure that millions more will be used if means can be found to evade the election laws." Kennedy Press Secretary Pierre Salinger insisted that the Democratic candidate had spent only $912,500—a figure as unbelievable as the upper range of Scott's contention.[16]

Jack was reportedly in a bad mood throughout the session. After the convention triumph, the petty sniping on and off the Senate floor was discouraging, and he was impatient to go out and win. Bobby was frantic to be out on the road. Kennedy and Johnson campaigned together in Des Moines, and Jack gave a speech by telephone to a labor convention (portraying himself as FDR's successor). But Nixon was able to free himself more and gain a head start in the campaign.[17]

In mid-August Jack traveled to Hyde Park, New York, in an attempt to win over Eleanor Roosevelt. The two got along well, and the first lady of the party agreed to back the ticket. But Jack had to grovel a bit to win her favor. Mrs. Roosevelt reported to Stevenson that Kennedy left "somewhat chastened" and was "in awe" of her judgment and experience. Moreover, he was obviously "hungry" for her help. Dave Powers, who was present, said, "The Senator came out of there like a boy who has just made a good confession. It was a great load off his mind."[18]

In her syndicated newspaper column Mrs. Roosevelt wrote: "Kennedy has a quick mind, but I would say that he might tend to arrive at judgments almost too quickly." She hoped that he would lean on Stevenson's "more judicial and reflective type of mind." She added, "I think Kennedy is anxious to learn. I think he is hospitable to new ideas. He is hard-headed. He calculates the political effect of every move."[19] And so he had with Eleanor.

A trip to Independence, Missouri, also won him the grudging support of former President Truman. When asked by reporters what had caused him to back Kennedy, Truman snapped, "When the Democratic National Convention decided to nominate him for President. That is all the answer you need." Privately, Truman complained about "this immature boy" and credited "Kennedy's Pa" for the convention victory. Jack soon smirked to Judith Campbell, "That old bastard has no other option. I'm the only game in town. I think he'd support the devil before he would Nixon."[20]

Congress adjourned on September 1, and Kennedy took off the next day in a race across the United States and north to Alaska to make up for lost time. The Gallup poll had recently showed Nixon ahead by a margin of 6 percent.[21] For the next two months, Jack would put in many twenty-four-hour days and make speaking appearances at rallies in 237 cities. Nixon would travel to 168 cities. In one week JFK visited twenty-seven states. Theodore H. White observed the grueling pace set by both candidates with astonishment and later wrote that the contest "seemed to rest more on pure glands and physical vitality than on qualities of statesmanship, reason or eloquence."[22]

Jack was able to handle the physical pain of his ordeal with a minimum of complaint. His back ached, his voice gave out from time to time, he missed meals, and he never got enough sleep. His right hand often throbbed with pain. Once, after touring a Pennsylvania coal-mining area, Jack's hand was bloodied. He commented to a young reporter, "Those fuckers. When they shake hands, they *really* shake hands."[23]

Most of Kennedy's speeches were five-minute performances in which he repeated his generalities about "moving ahead" and the need for a return to national greatness. Despite the presence of a vocal coach provided by the ambassador and much attention to the oratorical techniques of Winston Churchill, Jack at first spoke too rapidly, his gestures were awkward, his tone was mechanical, and he seldom smiled. Slowly, however, the training and experience led him to relax and become more effective. Personal comments about Jackie's pregnancy proved popular during a swing through Oregon and California. Sorensen, Richard Goodwin, and a team of speechwriters worked frantically to prepare material on a wide variety of topics, and the candidate, as a result, had a vast quantity of data at his fingertips.

At times Jack and his writers came up with some winning humor. In the South, for example, where Nixon was portraying himself as Jefferson's heir, Jack quoted one of Jefferson's contemporaries describing the Virginian: "He is a gentleman of thirty-two who can plot an eclipse, survey a field, plan an edifice, break a horse, play the violin, dance the minuet." "Now what," Kennedy would ask, "has *he* got in common with Mr. Nixon?"—and the audience would roar: "Nothing."

Jack grew to dislike Nixon, who was given to personal attacks, bad taste, and self-pity. Many of Jack's speeches contained evidence of his contempt. "The first living creatures to orbit the earth in space and return," Jack said at one point, "were dogs named Strelka and Belka [a reference to the Russian lead in space exploration at that time], not Rover or Fido—or Checkers" (a reference to Nixon's maudlin 1952 television explanation of his campaign financing in which he spoke of his wife's plain cloth coat and his little dog Checkers.). When contending that America was neglecting the world's nationalist movements, he would say, "There are children in Africa named Thomas Jefferson, George Washington and Abraham Lincoln. There are none called Lenin or Trotsky or Stalin—or Nixon." Privately, Jack was even more adamant. Richard Goodwin later recalled that "He's a filthy, lying son-of-a-bitch, and a very dangerous man" was one of Kennedy's "kinder descriptions" of his opponent late in the campaign.

Jack answered familiar audience questions (usually screened by Sorensen and Goodwin) with considerable skill. He handled hecklers well. "Just listen," he told a group of young Republican hecklers. "You won't learn anything if you are talking." He was able to smile through many mishaps, although when a microphone stopped working during a Pennsylvania rally he was unable to speak impromptu to hold the crowd. "I can't do that," he told Governor David Lawrence tersely. "I can't *do* that."

Kennedy's anger appeared only in private. Once, in the middle of a motorcade in a working-class district, he saw two well-dressed men in silk suits making a contemptuous gesture. Jack confided to Sorensen that he felt like leaping out of the car and slugging them. Instead he smiled and waved.[24]

At the core of Jack's entire campaign was the repeated contention, usually expressed in sweeping generalities, that America's values were all wrong and that a Kennedy administration would set them right. Stale, unimaginative, and greedy Republicans had, for eight years, lulled America into a dangerous passivity in domestic and global affairs, and now it was time to opt for renewed vigor, brains, morality, and self-sacrifice. "Ours is a great country," he told an audience of South Dakota farmers:

> but we can make it a greater country. It is powerful, but we must make it more powerful. I ask your help. I promise you no sure solutions, no easy life. The years ahead for all of us will be as difficult as any in our history. There are new frontiers for America to conquer in education, in science, in national purpose—not frontiers on a map, but frontiers of the mind, the will, the spirit of man.

(Privately Jack admitted that he had no interest in agricultural issues. After presenting his "farm policy" speech to an unresponsive audience at a South Dakota fairground, he said to aides, "Well, that's over. Fuck the farmers after November.")[25]

The first hurdle Kennedy faced in the campaign was the religious issue. Many Protestants all over the country were extremely wary of the

Democratic presidential candidate. As recently as 1944, the *Christian Century*, a liberal Protestant magazine, had published a series of eight articles entitled "Can Catholicism Win America?," and the author's worried answer was yes. In 1949 Paul Blanshard's militantly anti-Catholic *American Freedom and Catholic Power* became a best-seller, and throughout the next decade it sold in the hundreds of thousands. In late August 1960 the Minnesota Baptist Convention declared in a resolution that Roman Catholicism posed "as serious a threat to America as atheistic communism."[26]

In early September a group of 150 ministers and laypeople under the leadership of Rev. Norman Vincent Peale, a well-known lecturer, author, and minister of New York City's Marble Collegiate Church, declared, "It is inconceivable that a Roman Catholic President would not be under pressure by the hierarchy of his church to accede to its policies with respect to foreign relations in matters, including the representation to the Vatican." Eschewing all forms of religious bigotry, the statement calmly argued that a Catholic chief executive would be unable to honor the separation of church and state embodied in the Constitution. Catholic canon law and practice concerning interfaith gatherings, birth control, public schools, and religious liberty, at home and abroad, were cited to buttress the contention.[27] (Those worried that Kennedy might bow to the papacy on great *public* issues did not know that he ignored the church even on *private* issues, such as his marriage vows.)

Bobby simply equated the entire religious issue with bigotry and dismissed Peale as a Nixon supporter. Scores of liberal Protestant, Catholic, and Jewish leaders quickly agreed in often emotional public statements. Jack likened attacks on his religion to attacks on his patriotism. In Los Angeles he said: "The great struggle today is between those who believe in no God and those who believe in God." Johnson, in New York, lashed out at what he called a "hate campaign," declaring piously, "I abhor intolerance in any form." Nixon, knowing that the Democrats were scoring points with the issue, called for an end to all talk about religion in the campaign.[28]

Instead the Kennedys accepted an invitation from the Greater Houston Ministerial Association to explore the matter further—even paying for the ballroom in which the meeting was held. The liberal Catholic journalist John Cogley was recruited to coach Jack to handle questions from his audience.

On September 12, in a highly publicized appearance televised across the nation, Jack again declared his commitment to the absolute separation of church and state and his independence from Catholic pressures of any kind. He also repeated his pledge to resign from the presidency if he could not make every decision according to his conscience and in the national interest. The religious issue had enabled him to project an image of high moral conscience and responsibility.

In the brief address, written by Sorensen, Kennedy blasted those who had even raised the religious question: "The real issues in this campaign have been obscured—perhaps deliberately, in some quarters less responsible than this." At the conclusion of a question-and-answer session, however, he declared, "I don't want anyone to think because they interrogate me on this very important question that I regard that as unfair questions, or unreasonable, or that . . . somebody who is concerned about the matter is prejudiced or bigoted."[29]

By all accounts Kennedy's performance in Houston was a great success. The Rev. Daniel Poling, one of those who joined Peale in questioning Kennedy's objectivity, called the candidate's statement "magnificent."[30] Jack had told the ministers what they wanted to hear (although several, brandishing historical documents, still wondered if the Roman Catholic church approved of Kennedy's stand), and had come across as sincere and forceful. The political dividends seemed bright, for few Americans could fail to sympathize to some extent with a national figure being grilled about his personal faith.

One liberal minister, embarrassed by the entire meeting, soon wrote, "Might not the world see with alarming clarity the contrast between his unfailing patience, dignity, honesty, intelligence, and courtesy, and our own bumbling, strident, and often hopelessly irrelevant interrogation?"[31]

Republicans again attempted to bar the issue of religion from the campaign. Vice presidential candidate Lodge told an Ohio audience: "The candidates should agree among themselves not to raise it."[32] Senator Henry Jackson, however, chairman of the Democratic National Committee (and completely under the authority of the Kennedys), began calling for the press to investigate an "organized and planned" hate campaign, and he demanded that Nixon repudiate Peale "by name." Peale's book, *The Power of Positive Thinking,* Jackson said, should be changed to *The Power of Positive Prejudice.*[33]

Democrats showed selected portions of the film of Kennedy in Houston to millions all over the country to drum up sympathy and support. Theodore H. White called the film the "basic document" of the Kennedy volunteers.[34] Johnson began embellishing his campaign speeches with a story about the wartime heroism of Joe Junior, "a young Catholic boy." LBJ would ask solemnly in a near whisper, "Did anyone ask *his* religion when he gave *his* life for our country?'' Audiences would roar back, ''No!''[35]

Bobby Kennedy raised the religious question in a well-publicized speech at the opening of Kennedy headquarters in Cincinnati. ''Did they ask my brother Joe whether he was a Catholic before he was shot down?'' he asked. His eyes seemed to fill with tears, and he could not continue. The audience burst into applause. Soon Bobby was touring New York's Catskills, constantly bringing up the religious issue in order to urge voters to forget it. FDR Junior, with Bobby, reminded the largely Jewish audiences that ''If religious prejudice is raised against one minority today, it can be raised against another minority tomorrow.''[36]

In October Bobby told a national television audience that Republicans were distributing anti-Catholic literature across the country. Senator Jackson charged that the Nixon campaign in at least one state was ''based on religious prejudice.'' The nonpartisan Fair Campaign Practices Committee later studied the charge and said that it was without foundation. In fact, the committee reported, ''The Republicans—with only rare and short-lived exceptions—were scrupulously careful to avoid abuse of the religious issue.'' But the cynical use of this issue was fundamental Democratic campaign strategy. A party spokesman in Chicago told *U.S. News & World Report,* ''Our workers go in and talk about the candidates for Governor and Senator. Finally, they raise the question: 'Do you think they are going to keep Kennedy from being President just because he is Catholic?' It gets a good response. We are winning lots of new votes.'' The United Auto Workers Union issued a campaign pamphlet depicting a Ku Klux Klan member in contrast to the Statue of Liberty, clearly implying that a vote for Nixon was a vote for bigotry. The influential *New York Times* ran numerous stores on anti-Kennedy extremists that carried the same message.[37]

The first of four nationally televised debates between the two presidential candidates was scheduled for September 26. The confrontation was novel and its details long negotiated by both sides. (In 1952 Eisenhower had flatly refused to debate Stevenson.) Nixon apparently thought he could destroy Kennedy quickly. Kennedy representatives, seeking maximum media exposure in their battle against the favored Republican, argued for five debates and settled for four. Some 60 million Americans saw the first debate, and later estimates had between 85 and 120 million people watching one or all of the debates. Theodore H. White commented: ''No larger assembly of human beings, their minds focused on one problem, has ever happened in history.''[38]

Jack was coached by Bobby, Sorensen, Goodwin, and Myer

("Mike") Feldman, chief of the senator's Legislative Research staff. Nixon, on the other hand, spent the day alone, consulting at times with his wife. Arriving early at the studio, he accidentally struck his knee on the car door—the same knee that had been infected by a similar mishap in late August and had put him in the hospital for eleven days.[39]

Before the cameras went on, Jack attempted to rattle his adversary, already in pain and visibly nervous, by striding into the studio with only moments to spare, barely glancing at him. Larry O'Brien later wrote, "Kennedy had played the clock perfectly. He had thrown his opponent off stride. Nixon was ill at ease throughout."[40]

The first debate was restricted to domestic issues. Jack's opening statement contained a predictable and well-worn litany of national woes, praise for the New Deal, and pleas for America to get moving again. Much of the rhetoric was not designed to appeal to the intellect.

> I don't believe in big government, but I believe in effective governmental action. And I think that's the only way that the United States is going to maintain its freedom. Its' the only way that we're going to move ahead. I think we can do a better job. I think we're going to have to do a better job if we are going to meet the responsibilities which time and events have placed upon us. We cannot turn the job over to anyone else.

Nixon, just as predictably, argued that America had enjoyed peace and prosperity under Eisenhower while stressing fiscal responsibility. He said that he favored all Kennedy's lofty goals, including "the spirit that the Unites States should move ahead." The difference between the candidates, he contended, was not compassion—"I know what it means to be poor"—but a disagreement about the means to reach full employment and have good schools, decent medical care, and the other things all Americans wanted.

Questioning by four network journalists confirmed the suspicion that there were few if any meaningful issues on which the two men disagreed. Neither said anything eloquent, controversial, stimulating, or even particularly informative. At times the rhetoric almost became gibberish. When asked about federal agricultural price supports, for example, Jack replied in part:

> The farmer plants in the spring and harvests in the fall. There are hundreds of thousands of them. They really don't—they're not able to control their market very well. They bring their crops in or their livestock in, many of them about the same time. They have only a few purchasers . . . that buy their milk or their hogs—a few large companies in many cases—and there-

fore the farmer is not in a position to bargain very effectively in the market place.

When Nixon was asked about Communist subversion in the United States, he agreed with Kennedy's reply, which lauded the FBI, and soon was saying:

> And, in this connection, I think that uh—we . . . must look to the future having in mind the fact that we fight Communism at home not only by our laws to deal with Communists, uh—the few who do become Communists and the few who do become tra—fellow travelers, but we also fight Communism . . . at home by moving against those various injustices which exist in our society which the Communists feed upon. And in that connection I again would say that while Senator Kennedy says we are for the status quo, I . . . do . . . believe that he, uh—would agree that I am just as sincere in believing that my proposals for federal aid to education, my proposals for health care are just as sincerely held as his.[41]

CBS commentator Eric Sevareid called both candidates "tidy, buttoned-down men . . . completely packaged products." Both, he said, were "sharp, opportunistic, devoid of strong convictions and deep passions, with no commitment except to personal advancement." Abe Fortas, a Johnson adviser and future Supreme Court justice, said, "They're both hardworking, both intelligent, and I think neither has a core. I think there is nothing that either man wouldn't compromise on to get the job."[42] Sevareid and Fortas were exactly on target; both candidates largely defined right and wrong by what scored at the ballot box, and were devoted above all else to winning. The presidential election of 1960 was not essentially about ideas or ideals; it was anything but a moral crusade.

What mattered to most people was the visual image that emerged from the debate. Those who listened to the program on radio thought that Nixon had won. The vice president's voice was deeper and more resonant than Kennedy's and seemed to carry more authority. Lyndon Johnson, listening on the radio and keeping verbal score—"One for Nixon" or "One for the boy"—was sure that Nixon was the winner.[43] But those who saw the debate on television favored Kennedy. Jack appeared poised and self-confident; Nixon was tense and hesitant. Kennedy's good looks came across well; Nixon seemed to need a shave, the powder he wore to hide his beard was slightly streaked with sweat, and, in White's words, his eyes were "exaggerated hollows of blackness, his jaw, jowls, and face droop[ed] with strain." Harvey Wheeler later observed, "What one's face looks like—how one's face corresponds to television's laboriously created stereotypes for good guys and bad guys—becomes critical." To many Americans Kennedy became the hero, Nixon the villain.[44]

From his television debate on, Jack was a star. Crowds flocked to see him. Journalists began writing about the frenzy that swept through audiences and of the female "jumpers," "leapers," "clutchers," "touchers," "screamers," and "runners" who worshipped the new celebrity. "One remembers," White wrote, "the groans and moans; and a frowzy woman muttering hoarsely as if to herself, 'Oh, Jack I love yuh, Jack, I love yuh, Jack—Jack, I love yuh'; or the harsh-faced woman peering over one's shoulder glowering, 'You a newspaperman?—You better write nice things about him, or you watch out' (and she meant it)."[45]

After the debate support emerged everywhere and cash poured into party coffers. The GOP contention that Kennedy was merely an inexperienced youth would no longer wash. He had faced the vice president and proven himself to be at least his equal. A Vermont cab driver was quoted in *Newsweek:* "Why did Nixon look so scared if he's the only one tough enough to face Khrushy?"[46] Kenny O'Donnell said later, "After the first debate, the 1960 campaign was an entirely different ball game." Democrats soon began distributing a five-minute television film of the debate edited so that Nixon appeared to be nodding agreement to things said by Kennedy.[47]

On October 1 at Hyannis Port, Jack huddled with his father, Bobby, Sorensen, O'Donnell and several others of the inner circle to evaluate the first debate and draw plans for the remainder of the campaign. "All of us," O'Donnell said later, "except Kennedy himself, were basking in optimism," and the talk was of tactics. The group concluded, among other things, that Jack would have to stress differences between the goals of Republicans and Democrats, not just methods, and hammer harder on the theme, made in the first debate and in countless speeches, that Nixon was the spiritual descendant of McKinley, Harding, Hoover, Landon, and Dewey.[48]

The second debate, six days later, concerned itself with foreign as well as domestic policy. Both candidates were more at ease, more lucid, and in better command of factual material than they had been during the first encounter. Nixon, having gained a little weight and wearing theatrical makeup, looked healthy, and his aggressiveness cheered Republicans all over the country.

Jack defended his view that the president should have apologized to Russian Premier Khrushchev over the U-2 spy plane incident in May, which, he claimed, prevented an important summit meeting. He argued that Quemoy and Matsu, tiny islands between China and Formosa, were not strategically defensible and thus were unwise places to draw a line of defense. On civil rights, he called for moral leadership and said—in a sentence that would haunt him—that equality of opportunity in federally assisted housing could be achieved "by a stroke of the President's pen."

Nixon, defending the administration, said he would not apologize to Khrushchev, defended the U-2 flights, and argued that Quemoy and Matsu should never be surrendered. "It's the principle involved. These two islands are in the area of freedom. The Nationalists have these two islands. We should not uh—force our Nationalist allies to get off of them and give them to the Communists." On civil rights, the vice president defended the Southern sit-ins and chided Kennedy for having chosen Johnson as his running mate. "I selected a man who stands with me in this field and who will talk with me and work with me on it."

Each candidate, drawing on his McCarthyite background, implied throughout the debate that the other was soft on the Reds. (This poison was still in the political air. Minnesota Congressman Walter H. Judd employed McCarthyism blatantly in his keynote address to the GOP National Convention. Senator Thruston Morton of Kentucky, the Republican National Chairman, would soon label Kennedy an "apostle of appeasement.") Jack blamed the Eisenhower administration for losing Cuba to Fidel Castro. He also claimed that Republicans had let the Armed Forces deteriorate and had lost support in the United Nations. Nixon linked Kennedy with Truman, claiming that under the last Democratic administration 600 million people had gone behind the Iron Curtain. "In this Administration we've stopped [Communists] at Quemoy and Matsu; we've stopped them in other parts of the world."

Nixon clearly held his own against Kennedy and no doubt regained much public confidence. He was even slightly more articulate than Kennedy, who said during a discussion of hunger in America:

> Now I've seen a good many hundreds of thousands of people who are, uh—not adequately fed. You can't tell me that a surplus food distribution of five cents po—per person—and that n—nearly six million Americans receiving that—is adequate. You can't tell me that any one who uses beans instead of meat in the United States—and there are twenty-five million of them according to Mr. Benson—is well fed or adequately fed.[49]

In the third debate Kennedy spoke from New York and Nixon from Los Angeles. Three newsmen asked questions from a third studio. The candidates again contributed little of value to the campaign. Nixon came

out swinging with a smear against the Democratic party ("I would remind Senator Kennedy of the past fifty years. I would ask him to name
one Republican President who led this nation into war") and was soon
charging Kennedy with appeasement over Quemoy and Matsu. At times,
the vice president spoke harshly to his opponent. Responding to a shaky
charge of administration neglect of disarmament, he said sternly, "when
Senator Kennedy suggests that we haven't been making an effort, he
simply doesn't know what he's talking about." Nixon dismissed
Kennedy's campaign theme with:

> America has not been standing still. Let's get that straight. Anybody who
> says America's been standing still for the last seven and a half years hasn't
> been traveling around America. He's been traveling in some other country.
> We have been moving. We have been moving much faster than we did in
> the Truman years.

Jack was equally sharp tongued at times ("I don't think it's possible
for Mr. Nixon to state the record in distortion of the facts with more
precision than he just did"), but chose merely to repeat well-known
positions on issues raised by the newsmen. Without a manuscript (although, unlike Nixon, he used notes), he uttered such bromides as "There
have been many wars in the history of mankind," and "I think the fate
not only of our civilization, but I think the fate of the world and the future
of the human race is involved in preventing a nuclear war."

Kennedy lost points when the issue of the oil depletion allowance
came up. This tax break was dear to Senator Johnson and his Texas
backers but made Northern liberals extremely uneasy. Jack evaded the
question, saying it deserved study. Nixon said flatly that he was for the
allowance and chided Kennedy for failing to support the economic growth
he claimed to favor. The vice president also dismantled Kennedy's often-
made charge that the Soviet Union's economy was growing faster than
America's, and he scolded his opponent for damaging national confidence. Sample surveys revealed that Nixon made his greatest audience
impact in this debate.

Still, millions found the GOP candidate's style less than inspiring.
When a newsman raised the mini-issue of Harry Truman's hot temper and
profanity, Kennedy dismissed the matter quickly, saying that the former
president's style was not his. Nixon, on the other hand, launched into a
mawkish sermonette on the need for presidential dignity that began, "We
all have tempers; I have one; I'm sure Senator Kennedy has one." When
the religious issue appeared, Nixon again became sanctimonious: "I have
seen Communism abroad. I see what it does. Communism is the enemy

of all religions; and we who do believe in God must join together. We must not be divided on this issue."[50]

Nothing significant emerged from the fourth debate, devoted to foreign affairs and held in New York on October 21. Each candidate tried to portray himself as more anti-Communist than his opponent. Nixon said, "I know Mr. Khrushchev. I also have had the opportunity of knowing and meeting other Communists in the world." Kennedy asked, "Will the Congo go Communist? Will other countries? Are we doing enough in that area? And what about Asia? . . . Do people want to be identified with us? Do they want to follow United States leadership? I don't think they do, enough." The two men wrangled again about Quemoy and Matsu, about which they had no genuine difference, they exchanged platitudes about freedom and democracy, and they argued about the alleged level of American prestige in the world. (Kennedy said it was down, and Nixon said that the repeated contention drove it down.)

Both candidates were in favor of "moving ahead." Kennedy, invoking the memory of Franklin D. Roosevelt, said that America had "a rendezvous with destiny" in 1961. Nixon concluded on a pious note: "Keep America's faith strong. See that the young people of America, particularly, have faith in the ideals of freedom and faith in God, which distinguishes us from the atheistic materialists who oppose us."[51]

Russell Baker of the *New York Times* called the debate "comparatively tepid." James Reston thought it "highly repetitive." Comedian Mort Sahl said of the election, "Neither candidate is going to win."[52]

The only discussion of any interest centered around Castro's Cuba. Just before the debate Kennedy headquarters issued a statement declaring, in part, "We must attempt to strengthen the non-Batista democratic, anti-Castro forces in exile, and in Cuba itself, who offer eventual hope of overthrowing Castro. Thus far, these fighters for freedom have had virtually no support from our government." In the debate, Nixon branded this proposal "dangerously irresponsible" and argued that if followed it would lose friends in Latin America and the United Nations and serve as "an open invitation for Mr. Khrushchev to come in, to come into Latin America and to engage us in what would be a civil war, and possibly even worse than that."[53]

In fact, Nixon was privy to a covert administration program, under way since early in the year, to prepare and arm anti-Castro exiles for an invasion of Cuba. In *Six Crises,* published in 1962, Nixon claimed that between the Kennedy press release and the debate, he checked with the White House and was told that Kennedy had been briefed on the operation by CIA Director Dulles. That meant that the Democrat was jeopardizing the secret operation for his own political gain. "For the first and only time in the campaign," Nixon wrote, "I got mad at Kennedy—personally." To protect the covert action, Nixon had to oppose Kennedy's proposal publicly. "I was in the ironic position of appearing to be 'softer' on Castro than Kennedy—which was exactly the opposite of the truth, if only the whole record could be disclosed."[54]

Kennedy denied the charge in *Six Crises*. Dulles supported him, stating that the controversy was due to an "honest misunderstanding." Ten Sorensen later declared that Kennedy had not been briefed about the invasion during the campaign. Chester Bowles, Kennedy's foreign policy adviser, wrote in his autobiography that Secretary of State Christian Herter, in the course of weekly briefings, never mentioned the planned invasion to him.[55]

In fact, as Richard Goodwin explained in 1988, Kennedy had indeed been briefed by the CIA about the anti-Castro military force. The statement issued by Kennedy headquarters had been written by Goodwin, who did not understand its implications, and released without the candidate's knowledge. "I called Kennedy at the Hotel Carlyle," Goodwin wrote, "to read him the statement. He was asleep. I consulted with other staff members. None of us had the heart to wake the weary candidate. . . . It was the only public statement by the candidate in the entire campaign that he had not personally reviewed."

Jack handled the issue awkwardly during the debate because he was unsure of the contents of the statement Nixon was attacking. The next evening, aboard the *Caroline,* Kennedy pointed to Goodwin and Sorensen and said, "If I win this thing, I won it; but if I lose it, you guys lost it."[56]

The following day, Kennedy formally "clarified" his position on Cuba, declaring: "I have never advocated and I do not advocate intervention in Cuba in violation of our treaty obligations. . . . We must use all available communications—radio, television and the press—and the moral power of the American Government, to let the forces of freedom in Cuba know that we are on their side." Both candidates were now actively concealing the surprise the CIA was planning for Cuba.[57]

Goodwin's controversial press release was merely another attempt to show that the Democratic candidate was tough on the Reds. Just before the fourth debate, the liberal and normally dovish Bowles wrote to Jack, "You have been brilliantly successful in building up our position in regard to American military strength to a point where no one can call us 'soft on Communism.' "[58]

Despite their lack of intellectual substance, the debates stirred public interest in the election and clearly helped Kennedy's campaign. Nixon admitted in *Six Crises,* "'There can be no question but that Kennedy had gained more from the debates than I.'"[59] Jack became better known to the nation and impressed millions with his ability to stand toe-to-toe with the more famous vice president. His emerging charisma—stemming from a blend of good looks, a forceful speaking manner, and a seeming abundance of self-confidence, charm, and sincerity—was no doubt an even more powerful influence. In Detroit, where Kennedy made strong gains, voters told a reporter that the Democratic candidate had projected a more favorable image than his opponent. "It's not so much the issues but the way he talks," said one housewife. "He just seems more for me." The wife of a building contractor said that the debates had strengthened her feeling that Kennedy was the better man. "He's so emphatic. He makes a lot of sense and he seems very sincere."[60]

Of course, Nixon fans described Kennedy's appeal in different terms. Robert H. Finch, Nixon's publicity director, soon said, "Kennedy obviously was attractive, articulate and glib. Superficially, Kennedy appeared to stand on a par with Nixon, and, while it has no rational basis, these qualities were equated with maturity, judgment and experience."[61]

Many neutral observers were less than enthusiastic about the debates in general. Pollster Samuel Lubell, for example, soon wrote, "The real 64-million-vote question is what is it that comes through the TV screen—the real man or the actor?" Some voters, he reported, shared the view of a Detroit auto worker who said, "It's all phony. This has become an actor's election." Lubell was inclined to agree with the highly perceptive auto worker.[62]

Still, by early November, James Reston reported Kennedy in the lead and added, "there are those who feel that Mr. Nixon blundered it away by going on television with Young Lochinvar, and there may be something in this."[63]

>>> <<<

Between the third and fourth debates Kennedy gave what aides described as a major policy speech in Columbus, Ohio. Alluding to recent minor scandals in the Eisenhower administration, Jack presented eight ethical guidelines to be followed in his administration and pledged to "restore" an atmosphere of "moral leadership" in the White House. The next president himself, he said, "must set the moral tone—and I refer not to his language but to his actions in office."[64]

Insiders knew, however, that Kennedy's definition of moral leadership had its limits, for throughout the campaign, as time and energy permitted, Jack continued his liaisons with young women. Peter Lawford played a role in some of this activity, and his home north of Santa Monica would become a favorite vacation spot of the President's. Singer Dean Martin's former wife later told writer Anthony Summers, "I saw Peter in the role of pimp for Jack Kennedy. It was a nasty business—they were just too gleeful about it, not discreet at all. Of course there was nothing discreet about either of the Kennedys, Bob or Jack. It was like high school time, very sophomoric. The things that went on in that beach house were just mind-boggling."[65] Lawford told an interviewer in 1983, "I'm not going to talk about Jack and his broads . . . but . . . all I will say is that I was Frank's [Sinatra] pimp and Frank was Jack's. It sounds terrible now, but then it was a lot of fun."[66]

In early and mid-August, Jack spent several evenings with Judith Campbell. He stopped at Las Vegas at one point to party with his friend and campaign supporter Frank Sinatra. On an envelope he handed to an aide aboard the *Caroline* when his voice gave out, he wrote, "I got into the blondes [or blonde]." There were rumors about the beautiful brunette Janet des Rosiers, Kennedy's "girl Friday," who traveled on the *Caroline* (Evelyn Lincoln later called her "our stewardess") and massaged the candidate and combed his hair in the private compartment. She had earlier worked in the same capacity for the ambassador.[67]

Just before the first televised debate with Nixon, Jack asked aide Langdon Marvin, "Any girls lined up for tomorrow?" Ninety minutes before airtime, Kennedy was in a hotel room with a call girl. The candidate was so pleased by the result of the debate, Marvin later recalled, that "he insisted we line up a girl for him before each of the debates."[68]

In another of the profanity-filled notes written aboard the *Caroline*, Jack said, "I suppose if I win—my poon days are over," using an expression for sexual activity he had picked up in the Navy. He even wondered if Nixon would reveal his lubricity. "I suppose they are going to hit me with something before we are finished." Republicans had heard the stories, of course, but elected not to use them. Many reporters, in Washington and around the country, were aware of Kennedy's extramarital affairs. "We knew," George Reedy said later. "We all knew." And they chose to keep the information out of the press.[69]

The largely all-male press corps at the time permitted certain misconduct by major public officials to go unreported. Drinking, womanizing, and homosexuality were on the list unless these activities became unusually blatant or could be shown to affect the officeholder's public duties in a direct and pronounced way. Numerous reporters had known, for example, of Franklin D. Roosevelt's longtime mistress, Lucy Mercer Rutherford.[70]

Kennedy's sexual adventures, then, were off-limits to reporters in 1960, and Jack would enjoy that immunity for the rest of his life. In early 1963 a *New York Times* reporter told his editor that he had observed a prominent actress repeatedly visiting President Kennedy's New York hotel suite. "No story there," said the editor, and the matter was dropped.[71]

But there was more to this selective treatment of Kennedy than general editorial policy. The great majority of reporters on the influential newspapers and magazines were liberally inclined in their politics and pro-Kennedy. (The nation's publishers, on the other hand, favored Nixon 4–1.) Like his father, who had wooed reporters for decades, Jack went out of his way during the campaign to be friendly and helpful to the press. Pierre Salinger made arrangements for their luggage, transportation, and accommodations, and he provided them with instant speech transcripts. Reporters responded in kind. Salinger later recalled, "In analyzing the role of the press in the general election, I cannot help but feel that Senator Kennedy—on balance—got the best of the coverage."[72]

Nixon, sensing that the press was his enemy, was aloof and often hostile. A Nixon aide told Theodore H. White, *"Stuff* the bastards. They're all against Dick anyway. Make them work—we aren't going to hand out prepared remarks; let them get their pencils out and listen and take notes." White observed, "To be transferred from the Nixon campaign tour to the Kennedy campaign tour meant no lightening of exertion or weariness for any newspaperman—but it was as if one were transformed in role from leper and outcast to friend and battle companion."[73] This friendship between Kennedy and the reporters would continue through the White House years. Jack and his staff knew well the power of the image in the press.

→>> <<←

Almost all members of the Kennedy family were highly active in the campaign. With hundreds of newspaper and magazine articles extolling their virtues and two family-approved books on the market (Joseph Dineen's *The Kennedy Family* and Joe McCarthy's *The Remarkable Kennedys*), they were widely recognized throughout the country and often greeted by large, adoring crowds.

Teddy led motorized cavalcades in the Far West, giving a pat speech, passing out *PT-109* tie clasps, shaking hands at factory gates, and belting out "Jalisco" in Spanish and "Sweet Adeline." Although personable, the twenty-eight-year-old was generally ineffective as a campaigner; Nixon carried ten of the thirteen states assigned to Teddy. His wife, Joan, visibly pregnant, joined him during the last month of the campaign. (Rumors of Teddy's roving eye were already circulating. Earlier in the year, he had aggressively pursued Judith Campbell. She later wrote, "He was the baby brother walking in his older brothers' shadow.")[74]

Eunice campaigned with Ethel in Texas (where they refused Lady Bird's request to wear ten-gallon hats) and elsewhere. She told a *Chicago Tribune* reporter, "All we talk about is winning" and then picked up her year-old son, held him aloft, and cooed, "Win, win, win."[75]

Pat and Jean toured women's clubs across the country. Ethel traveled widely, telling an audience in Aberdeen, South Dakota, that her husband had told her, "Whatever you do, don't speak." Rose, at seventy, traveled in fourteen states and made forty-six appearances. In one evening in the Bronx, she spent twelve hours campaigning: attending three "coffee get-togethers," visiting several educational institutions, and giving a speech. (She said that Jack's political education had begun when he was only "knee high" and that he was intimate with world affairs at an age "when most young men were spending their time in just the irresponsible outdoor sports.") When one veteran politico invited some Kennedys to a rally, he was stunned: "They pounced on the meeting like a squad of Marines in a commando operation."[76]

Although Jackie, pregnant and due in mid-December, did not travel with her husband, she played an active role in the campaign. She wrote a newspaper column, made radio tapes in four foreign languages, organized women's discussion groups, sponsored a program to collect women's opinions on campaign issues, hosted teas, appeared with Jack in a New York City parade, and made several television appearances. When asked on the "Today" show what the basic duties of a first lady were, she replied, "I have always thought the main duty is to preserve the President of the United States so he can be of best service to his country, and that means running a household smoothly around him, and helping him in any way he might ask you to." When later asked if she thought being the first lady would change her, she said, "I wouldn't put on a mask and pretend to be anything that I wasn't."[77]

In a *Life* magazine article on the wives of the presidential candidates, Jackie portrayed herself as a full-time mother without a nurse. In fact, the full-time, live-in nurse, Maude Shaw, had almost complete responsibility for Caroline's every need. Jackie also claimed that she answered her letters personally with only the assistance of a part-time secretary. Actually, she had a full-time secretary, Mary Gallagher, who worked tirelessly to keep up with the voluminous correspondence. Both Gallagher and Shaw were kept out of sight when reporters and photographers drew near. Gallagher wrote later, "Maude Shaw and I continued to learn that the way to stay on the good side of Jackie was to stay on the side *away* from the cameras."[78]

When a New York trade paper contended that Jackie was "too chic" and claimed that she and Rose spent thirty thousand dollars a year buying Paris clothes, Jackie reacted angrily, saying, "I couldn't spend that much unless I wore sable underwear," and expressing certainty that Pat Nixon spent more than she did. She also employed a little political strategy to win sympathy: "They're beginning to snipe at me about that as often as they attack Jack on Catholicism. I think it's dreadfully unfair." In the presence of a reporter, she tried on dresses that cost thirty and forty dollars apiece. In fact, Jackie devoted much attention to high fashion. According to Gallagher, who kept the accounts, she spent more than forty thousand dollars on apparel in 1961. Since the ambassador personally paid for her couturier-designed clothing, her actual expenditure was far higher.[79]

Privately, Jack was often less than pleased with press stories about his wife, and considered her to blame. Jackie's high-society image, her sometimes snide comments to reporters, and her often condescending attitude toward the woman reporters assigned to her did little to win friends and votes. When Dorothy Schiff, publisher of the *New York Post*, told him that she thought Jackie had been very effective on a recent broadcast, Jack agreed that his wife was much better on television than in her personal interviews. Schiff later reported, "He was utterly cold in his remarks about her, and I had a feeling he had very little interest in her except as she affected his campaign."[80]

The principal catalyst in the entire campaign was its manager, Bobby. Stories of his zealous and frequently offensive behavior for the cause were legion. Early in the campaign, for example, he caused a minor storm by publicly attacking several Southern congressmen for blocking legislation at the special session and blasting baseball great Jackie Robinson for daring to question his brother's commitment to civil rights. Jack was forced to intercede with the Dixie Democrats, apologizing for his brother's remarks and promising to keep him out of the Florida and South Carolina campaigns.[81]

Privately Bobby traveled from state to state lashing local Democrats into action and accepting no excuses. In New York, for example, he ordered feuding Democrats to come together and back the ticket. "Gentlemen,'' he said to one faction, ''I don't give a damn if the state and county organizations survive after November, and I don't give a damn if *you* survive. I want to elect John F. Kennedy.'' Weary party members all over the country warned each other: ''Little brother is watching you.'' Arthur Schlesinger, Jr., later wrote, ''John Kennedy recognized that a campaign required a son of a bitch— and that it could not be the candidate. Robert was prepared to do what the candidate should not have done.''[82]

The ambassador was kept out of sight to perpetuate the myth that he lacked influence on the candidate. Following the convention, the elder Kennedy traveled to a rented villa at Cap d'Antibes on the French Riviera. He told a *Newsweek* reporter, ''There'll be no questions about whether Jack is doing things himself if nobody else is around. Jack has already proved he is doing a fantastically good job.''[83] He was stepping aside in deference to the young people, the seventy-two-year-old patriarch told a *U.S. News & World Report* writer. ''Since 1952, when Jack went to the Senate, I've never campaigned for him, never made any speeches. You know, I've never even heard Jack make a speech on television.''[84]

Leaflets and at least one newspaper ad appeared during the campaign condemning the ambassador's anti-Semitism. Some fundamentalists called him ''the world's richest bootlegger.'' Jack assured reporters that he and his father were now in total disagreement. ''Dad is a financial genius, all right, but in politics, he is something else.'' The ambassador, who returned to the United States in mid-September, said that he could best help his son by staying out of the campaign. One skeptical Republican wag penned this timely couplet:

> Jack and Bob will run the show
> While Ted's in charge of hiding Joe.[85]

Earlier in the year, when Hugh Sidey of *Time* was interviewing Jack for a cover story, Red Fay, seated nearby, was asked about Joseph P. Kennedy's influence on his children, particularly on Jack. When Fay began to respond honestly, ''Hugh, I think that Mr. Kennedy has been the most vital force in the careers of the Kennedy men and women . . . ,'' Jack grimaced and drew his finger across his throat to signal Fay to be quiet. When Sidey left, Jack flew into a rage. ''God, if I hadn't cut you off, Sidey could have headed his article, 'A Vote for Jack is a vote for Father Joe.' '' Fay groveled sufficiently to get back in his old friend's graces, but it took some time. The ambassador's influence, Fay wrote later, ''was a subject on which he was highly sensitive.''[86]

The full extent of the ambassador's contribution to the campaign may never be clear, but his role was certainly far more important than Jack and his partisans wanted known. Just before and immediately after the first debate with Nixon, the elder Kennedy was on the telephone giving advice and encouragement to his son. After the debate he telephoned people around the country to test their reactions. When newspaper columnists suggested that the debate was a draw, the ambassador stormed, "If that wasn't a clear victory for Jack I never saw one." Then he paused, grinned, and said, "We'll knock their brains out."[87]

The ambassador participated in at least one important strategy meeting at Hyannis Port. He gave advice to Jack on the economy. He arranged a meeting with Teamster official Harold Gibbons to soothe relations with Jimmy Hoffa and his followers. "I don't think there's much of a war going on between the Kennedys and Hoffa," he said. "I hardly hear the name Hoffa in our house any more." He quietly gave assurances to Hoffa's allies in the Mafia. Then too, in Walter Trohan's words, "Papa Joe cultivated the bosses of the city machines." One such boss, Mayor Richard Daley of Chicago, would prove extraordinarily valuable in the election.[88]

The ambassador's financial contributions were no doubt of major significance, although the amount of funds available to both parties seems to have been approximately equal. The Founding Father was willing to spend any amount necessary to win the election. He asked James M. Landis, "What's a hundred million if it will help Jack?"[89]

Lyndon Johnson worked hard for the ticket, but he made few headlines and failed to integrate himself with the Kennedys. Jack almost never mentioned him in public. Some Northern liberals like Arthur Schlesinger, Jr., dismissed him as unimportant, especially after he defended oil depletion allowances and waffled about repealing anti-union right-to-work laws. The Kennedys tried to keep Johnson out of certain parts of the North where his presence might lose votes. At one point the friction between the two camps was such that peacemakers brought LBJ to Hyannis Port for a weekend to smooth things over. Theirs "was never a marriage of love," Nancy Dickerson recalled, "only of mutual dependence."[90]

→>> <<←

Civil rights was a touchy issue for both parties as they attempted to win black votes without alienating conservatives and segregationists. Kennedy was particularly sensitive to the integration question because he had to hold together the shaky Democratic alliance of fiery Northern liberals and die-hard Dixiecrats. His own record on civil rights prior to his nomination showed him to be mildly positive, but many doubted that he possessed convictions on the matter that superseded his desire for the White House. They were almost certainly correct.[91]

The selection of Johnson was an obvious message to Southerners that they could discount, at least to some degree, the strong civil rights plank in the party platform. In the special session of Congress, both Kennedy and Johnson voted against GOP-sponsored civil rights legislation designed to embarrass Democrats. In his campaign, however, JFK defended sit-ins in the South and spoke of implementing desegregation in schools and housing. Kennedy leaders ruled out participation in segregated meetings, and they organized black voter registration drives. In October the Civil Rights Section of the Kennedy campaign sponsored a conference of civil rights activists. (It was given an innocuous name, however, and Jack personally held up its report until after the election.) That same month, on NBC's nationally televised "Meet the Press," Lyndon Johnson pledged his full support for the Democratic platform position on civil rights.[92]

The most widely followed black leader in the country was The Rev. Martin Luther King, Jr., the thirty-one-year-old head of the Southern Christian Leadership Conference (SCLC). While King's preacher-father declared for Nixon, solely on religious grounds, King favored Kennedy. Jack, of course, eagerly sought the civil rights leader's endorsement, but King chose to remain officially neutral in keeping with his organization's public posture.[93]

In a private meeting after the Democratic Convention, King urged Kennedy to do "something dramatic" to assure blacks of his commitment to equality. King soon attempted to arrange a public meeting between Kennedy and himself in the South, but the plan fell through, in large part because Kennedy feared white backlash. King stayed in Atlanta, reluctantly participated in a sit-in he had wanted postponed until after the election, and, on October 19, two days before the final Kennedy-Nixon debate, was jailed, along with fifty-one others.

Three days later Harris Wofford, Kennedy's liberal civil rights coordinator and a personal friend of the Kings, telephoned from his home in Virginia to Morris Abram, a leading attorney and civil libertarian in Atlanta. Without Kennedy's knowledge, Wofford expressed concern for King. Abram then went to a meeting with moderate Mayor William Hartsfield and a group of black leaders, and in a few hours the mayor brazenly announced to reporters that because of Kennedy's personal intervention, he had reached an agreement with the blacks for the release of

King and the other sit-in prisoners. In fact, Kennedy had not played any role in the matter. Hartsfield soon told Wofford privately, "You tell your Senator that he and I are out on the limb together, so don't saw it off. I'm giving him the election on a silver platter, so don't pull the rug out from under me."

Wofford quickly telephoned Kennedy aides, who were startled and angered by the news. After a consultation with the candidate, Pierre Salinger contradicted Hartsfield and issued a bland statement requesting facts and declaring merely that "the Senator is hopeful that a satisfactory outcome can be worked out." Kennedy's Georgia campaign chief, Griffin Bell, on behalf of the governor and the local congressmen, defended King's arrest and stated, "We know that Senator Kennedy would never interfere in the affairs of a sovereign state."

The issue became more volatile when Judge Oscar Mitchell declared that King's actions had violated his probation for an earlier traffic conviction. King was sentenced to four months in a state prison at hard labor. Wofford, reflecting worldwide dismay at the sentence, prepared a draft of a strong public statement. Kennedy at first approved it but yielded to pressure from Southerners. Finally Governor Ernest Vandiver, no doubt eager to thwart a Nixon charge that all Southern Democrats were racist reactionaries, promised to get "the son of a bitch" released if Jack would say nothing in public. The candidate agreed. When King remained in jail three days after the others were released and was moved to a rural prison farm, Coretta King tearfully telephoned Wofford, expressing fear for her husband's life.

Over a drink with a fellow campaign worker, Wofford came up with the idea of having Kennedy make a personal call to Mrs. King to express his sympathy. Unable to reach the candidate (aides did not return his calls, "probably fearing more pressure for public action," Wofford wrote later), Wofford called Chester Bowles, who immediately telephoned Mrs. King. Wofford then reached Sargent Shriver, who was in charge of civil rights in the campaign, and persuaded him that Kennedy should follow Bowles's action. Shriver sped to Kennedy's Chicago hotel room, waited until aides such as Kenny O'Donnell were elsewhere, and posed the idea to the candidate, noting the political as well as the humanitarian qualities of the gesture. "Negroes don't expect everything will change tomorrow, no matter who's elected. But they do want to know whether you care." Jack quickly agreed, and he spoke comfortingly for about a minute and a half with Mrs. King, who was deeply moved.[94]

Bobby flew into a rage on learning of the call, predicting that it might cost three Southern states and the election. He ordered Kennedy workers to say nothing further on the matter, hoping that the story could be contained and the damage minimized. But by this time, with Wofford's approval, Mrs. King had already alerted the *New York Times*.

The next morning Bobby changed his tune. Without consulting his brother he telephoned Judge Mitchell and requested King's release. "I called him," Bobby told an aide, "because it made me so damned angry to think of that bastard sentencing a citizen to four months of hard labor for a minor traffic offense and screwing up my brother's campaign and making our country look ridiculous before the world." Later Bobby said that the suggestion for the call had come from Governor Ernest Vandiver of Georgia. (To cover his tracks Vandiver soon criticized JFK's call to "the foremost racial agitator in the country" but said he would support the ticket. He was later offered a position in the Kennedy administration.)

It now seems reasonably clear that the motivation for Bobby's call was, as in Jack's case, both humanitarian and political. The request was risky: It violated the Canons of Professional Ethics of the American Bar Association (prohibiting an attorney from communicating with a judge privately about the merits of a pending cause), and its political implications were unpredictable. Yet within a short time, the judge yielded, King was out on bail, and political dividends began to pour into the Kennedy camp.[95]

Outside the prison, King erroneously gave Jack full credit for his release. He lauded the Democratic presidential candidate as a man of principle and predicted that he would enforce his party's civil rights plank. This was still not an official endorsement, but, as the *Atlanta Journal* commented, King "did just about everything short of it." King's father publicly switched his support from Nixon (who had refused to comment about the arrest) to Kennedy. "I had expected to vote against Senator Kennedy because of his religion. But now he can be my President, Catholic or whatever he is. It took courage to call my daughter-in-law at a time like this. He has the moral courage to stand up for what he knows is right."[96]

In a private conversation with Wofford, Jack asked, "Did you see what Martin's father said? He was going to vote against me because I was Catholic, but since I called his daughter-in-law, he will vote for me. That was a hell of a bigoted statement, wasn't it? Imagine Martin Luther King having a bigot for a father!" Soon, however, he grinned and added, "Well, we all have fathers, don't we?"[97]

Wary of the political ramifications, Kennedy issued no public statement about his telephone call. When asked by a reporter if he had made it, Jack muttered something under his breath about having a traitor in his camp and admitted his action. "She is a friend of mine and I was concerned about the situation." That was to be his only public comment.[98]

Many Northern blacks and liberals were soon ecstatic over Kennedy's gesture. The *New York Post* declared that the senator had responded "with full awareness that his words and deeds would inflame the Southern racists and multiply his difficulties in Dixie." Rev. Gardner Taylor, president of the Protestant Council of New York, proclaimed, "This is the kind of moral leadership and direct personal concern which this problem has lacked in these last critical years." Wanting to reach larger numbers of blacks, Wofford suggested to Shriver that they violate Bobby's ban on new statements and distribute a pamphlet on the King case. Shriver approved: "Let's do it. If it works, he'll like it. If we don't do it, and we don't get enough Negro votes, he and Jack wouldn't like that, and we would all be kicking ourselves for a long time."[99]

Within six hours a pamphlet went to press entitled *The Case of Martin Luther King,* sporting a cover that read: " 'No Comment' Nixon versus a Candidate with a Heart, Senator Kennedy." It contained statements by the Kings, Gardner Taylor, King associate Ralph Abernathy, and others. Abernathy was quoted as saying that it was "time for all of us to take off our Nixon buttons." The "blue bomb," as it was dubbed, quickly won Bobby's approval. During the last days of the campaign, nearly two million copies of the pamphlet were distributed all over the country. On the Sunday before the election, they were handed out outside black churches. Wofford heard reports that "whole congregations of Negro Baptists and Methodists [were] standing up and pledging to vote for Kennedy." To reach blacks not in church, runners were sent to tell them of Kennedy's character and courage. Wofford sensed "a tide running for the Senator in practically every Negro community, North and South."

James Michener later called the King affair "the single event which came closest to being the one vital accident of the campaign." In a conversation with John Kenneth Galbraith, Jack said, "The finest strategies are usually the result of accidents."[100]

→>> ‹‹←

In late October Nixon brought President Eisenhower into the campaign, and he soon promised to tour Communist nations if elected, contended that his opponent was a "barefaced liar" and a captive of labor leader Walter Reuther, and starred in a last-minute media blitz that cost about $2 million.

Kennedy proposed a Peace Corps, said Nixon feared a fifth debate, made numerous jests about the vice president ("Having seen him in close-up—and make-up—for our television debates, I would never accuse Mr. Nixon of being barefaced"), and accused him of making reckless and dangerous foreign policy decisions, including one in 1954 that "tried to get us involved in a hopeless colonial war" in Indochina. "I think we need leadership that is better informed."[101]

Within only ninety days of taking office, Jack pledged, he would reassert American leadership at home and abroad, proposing plans to wipe out American poverty, end the "missile gap" that left us vulnerable to Soviet aggression, and develop programs to pour capital into underprivileged nations, helping to prepare them for democracy.[102]

Above all, Kennedy made promises—scores of them daily—telling people wherever he went that he and big government would cure their ills. In a Los Angeles speech on education, for example, he called for federal aid to school construction, federal assistance to increase teachers' salaries, a large federal educational service, a federal student-loan insurance program, and a federal loan program for the construction of college classrooms and dormitories.[103] The Congressional Quarterly later added up 220 Kennedy "musts," priorities, and pledges of action made during the campaign.

"Kennedy has got away with murder on his domestic program," sympathetic James Reston commented. "His promises to the farmer, to labor, to old people, are all very exciting, but he has not given anybody the slightest idea of how they are to be financed." Nixon estimated the cost of the various proposals at between 13 and $18 billion over what was currently spent annually. Jack termed this figure "wholly fictitious" but declined to offer his own estimate. He spoke often of his commitment to low taxes and balanced budgets.[104]

Another insight into the Democratic candidate emerged in the last week of the campaign. Democrats had been showing a filmed interview between Kennedy and Mr. and Mrs. John McNamara of Newport, Kentucky. McNamara, sixty-eight, had suffered a fractured hip, and Jack spoke sympathetically with the retired couple, making a point of his compassion and his concern for the high medical costs facing the elderly. On film McNamara said that his hospital bills amounted to $619.60 and added that he felt Kennedy's Medicare plan based on Social Security would have helped him. On November 2 McNamara revealed that he had told Kennedy before the film was made that Blue Cross and Blue Shield health insurance plans had paid most of his health costs. Kennedy replied, "We won't talk about that now," and the program went on as scheduled.[105]

Some Republicans, eyeing the polls nervously, were willing during the last week of the campaign to reopen the issue of Kennedy's physical health. John Roosevelt, a son of the late president who was supporting Nixon, challenged both candidates at least twice to disclose any medical difficulties they had that might impair their ability to serve as chief executive. He sent a telegram to Nixon inquiring about his knee injury, but the obvious target was Kennedy and the allegation that he had Addison's disease. A telegram to the Democrat noted that an earlier medical report, issued at the Democratic National Convention, "notably failed to disclose the extent of your adrenal insufficiency and what drugs you are taking to compensate for this insufficiency." Jack did not respond until after the election when he told reporters flatly, "I have never had Addison's Disease." The *New York Times,* in a postelection summary, declared, "His only physical weakness is an occasional glandular deficiency, caused by his malaria, which requires him occasionally to take cortisone tablets."[106]

At the conclusion of the campaign, three of four major public opinion polls gave Kennedy a slight lead. Pollster Elmo Roper said, "It can go either way. This has been the most volatile campaign since we began taking samplings in 1936. I have never seen the lead change hands so many times." Before cheering crowds, Jack expressed both optimism ("The door at the White House is going to click on Dick") and caution ("This will be a very close election. It will be decided by 1 to 2 per cent of the voters in most of the close states"). On election day, November 8, he and Jackie voted in Boston and then flew to Hyannis Port to be with family and friends.[107]

To kill time Jack opened some of the hundreds of telegrams that had swamped the local post office. Most expressed best wishes, but a few were nasty. ("Dear Juvenile Jack," said one, "God help us if you are elected tomorrow.") When Jack encountered one that said *"Vaya con Dios,"* he asked a person near him what that meant.[108]

Hour after hour passed that night without the election data showing a clear lead by either candidate. Bobby, heading a large staff at the election headquarters established in his home, was extremely concerned and stayed up all night checking returns. The long-distance telephone bill from the Kennedy compound that evening was estimated at ten thousand dollars. When bad news happened, Bobby would groan and his sisters would wail. Jack, never flinching, would just mutter "shit" or "fuck it."[109]

By the early morning hours, when Jack went to bed, California, Michigan, Minnesota, and Illinois were still uncertain. Before retiring,

Jack telephoned his father's longtime friend Mayor Richard Daley of Chicago. (Daley later told Kenny O'Donnell that he received at least fifteen calls from various Kennedy friends and relatives before the polls closed in Illinois.) Soon the ambassador sent a message to his son, telling him not to worry about Illinois: it was his. Later that day Illinois officially went for Kennedy by a slight margin. Jack surely knew what Daley had undoubtedly done; vote fraud was a was of life in Cook County. He soon told Ben Bradlee of his call to Chicago and of the mayor's knowing reply: "Mr. President, with a bit of luck and the help of a few close friends, you're going to carry Illinois."[110]

Later it was discovered that Nixon had carried 93 of the state's 102 counties yet lost Illinois by 8,858 votes. The huge Democratic turnout in Cook County had provided the winning margin. Republicans made an unofficial check of only 699 paper-ballot precincts in the county and came up with a net gain of 4,539 votes for Nixon. The Daley machine blocked an official recount.[111]

Chicago Mafia chieftan Sam Giancana also played a role of some kind in the Cook County victory. Since July, at Jack's request, Judith Campbell had arranged several clandestine meetings between the candidate and Giancana. (She would arrange some ten meetings in all between the two men and later thought that one of them took place in the White House. In 1961 Campbell would become a secret courier between the president, Giancana, and mobster John Roselli, carrying unmarked nine-by-twelve-inch envelopes across the country by airplane. "I didn't know what they contained," she later revealed, "but I knew that the contents were very important to Jack.") The syndicate dominated the important West Side river wards that had given Daley his initial victory in 1955. After the election Giancana often bragged to Campbell, "Listen, honey, if it wasn't for me your boyfriend wouldn't even be in the White House."[112]

But Illinois was not decisive; the Michigan returns put Kennedy over the top. Nixon did not concede until midday. He sent a telegram to Kennedy but had his press secretary appear before the television cameras and read a terse statement. Someone in the Kennedy entourage remarked that Nixon himself should have appeared, at least to thank his tens of thousands of campaign workers. Jack agreed and sneered, "He went out the way he came in—no class."[113]

The largest number of Americans ever—68,838,979—had gone to the polls. When the final tally was in, Kennedy had won 49.7 percent of the vote and Nixon had taken 49.6 percent. A mere 112,803 votes separated the two candidates—the smallest margin of the century. If only

4,500 voters in Illinois and 24,000 voters in Texas had changed their minds, Nixon would have been president. In eleven states a shift of less than 1 percent of the vote would have switched the state's electoral votes. Democrats captured twenty-three states with 303 electoral votes to the Republicans' twenty-six states and 220 electoral votes. But the Kennedy-Johnson ticket lost almost the entire West, the farm belt, and several Southern states.

Analysts later noted several important turning points in the election, including the first television debate, the big-city vote, and the religious issue. (The great majority of Catholics voted for Kennedy.) Most striking, perhaps, was the black vote: a greater proportion of blacks went to the polls in 1960 than in 1956, and a high percentage—an estimated 70 percent—voted Democratic. Blacks tipped the scales for Kennedy in several states. Had only whites gone to the polls, Nixon would have captured 52 percent of the vote. Eisenhower later blamed the GOP loss on "a couple of phone calls" by John and Robert Kennedy.[114]

One powerful explanation for Kennedy's success was the personal image he was able to communicate throughout the campaign. JFK, in person, in the media, in campaign literature, and even on millions of campaign signs and buttons, appeared to have extraordinary intelligence and sterling character. In *Kennedy or Nixon: Does It Make Any Difference?* by Arthur Schlesinger, Jr., for example, the Democrat was seen to be a man of principle, consistency, and self-confidence. He was "an exceptionally cerebral figure," "a committed liberal" who admired intellectuals and would turn to them for advice. Nixon was in the presidential race for private gratification, the author charged. "But Kennedy is ambitious because the Presidency alone would give him the power to fulfill purposes which have long lain in his mind and heart."[115]

Only a handful of people knew the other side of the story—the reality that involved the cynical manipulation of issues, unrestrained spending, vote fraud, the Mafia, ceaseless adultery, and dishonesty about Kennedy's intellectual achievements and physical condition. What mattered to the Kennedys was victory, and they had always been willing to pay any price for it. In 1960 as before, that approach proved successful.

On November 9, the morning after the election, family members struck up a touch football game on the ambassador's lawn. When the returns appeared conclusive, the president-elect was photographed lifting Caroline onto his back, which he did, according to one reporter, "with difficulty." Cars soon assembled to take Jack and his family to the National Guard Armory in Hyannis Port for the nationally televised victory statement. The ambassador, having been kept out of the spotlight for months, seemed reluctant to attend. His daughter Pat later remembered him "back a little in the shadows, looking very happy." Jack insisted that he come along, and he agreed, participating in the formal photographs taken after the speech.[116]

　　　Soon the ambassador was often seen in public with his son. When asked about his sudden reemergence, the father of the youngest man ever elected president said that it was no accident. "There are no accidents in politics." He had thought it discreet, he said, to let Jack run on his own. But with the election over, "I can appear with him any time I want to now."[117]

CHAPTER 11

Looking More Like
a President

→》》　《《←

THE KENNEDYS were deeply disappointed by their slim margin
of victory; the final tally represented the equivalent of about two votes per
precinct. It was the closest presidential election in seventy-six years. An
English journalist found Jack quite uneasy immediately after the election.
"I think it hurt his self-confidence and pride that he won with such a
narrow majority," he said later.[1] The ambassador soon told a reporter, "I
didn't think it would be that close. I was wrong on two things. First, I
thought he would get a bigger Catholic vote than he did. Second, I did not
think so many would vote against him because of his religion."[2]

Moreover, numerous stories of vote fraud cast doubt on the legitimacy of the returns. (Charges were made against both parties, and Nixon
soon decided not to contest the election.) Understandably, Kennedy was
eager to pursue what Schlesinger later called a "strategy of reassurance."[3]

On November 10, at his first formal news conference, the president-
elect announced the reappointment of J. Edgar Hoover as FBI Director
and Allen W. Dulles as head of the Central Intelligence Agency. The
night before, two close friends had urged Kennedy to fire both officials.
They did not know, of course, that Hoover had the tapes of Jack's
wartime escapade with Inga Arvad. Indeed, Kennedy could not be sure
about other information Hoover and Dulles might possess that could

seriously damage if not destroy his well-crafted image as a man of integrity and seriousness. (We now know that during the late 1950s, the FBI kept extensive files on Jack's extramarital affairs. An anonymous FBI informant referred to the senator's suite at Washington's Mayflower Hotel as "Kennedy's personal playpen.")[4]

Making his position even stronger, Hoover soon learned that the ambassador had recently sent Bobby on a secret mission: to take five hundred thousand dollars to a former fiancée of Jack's to quash a breach-of-promise suit. An FBI investigation indicated that Jack had made the woman pregnant. Hoover quietly let Bobby know that he was privy to the financial transaction. While the Kennedys would privately fuss and fume about Hoover throughout the Thousand Days, the director's tenure was unassailable. (That summer, the woman, Mrs. Alicia Darr Purdom, filed for divorce against her husband, actor Edmund Purdom. When Purdom filed a countersuit naming the president as a correspondent, a friend of the Kennedys quietly contacted Mrs. Purdom. She dropped her lawsuit and got a Mexican divorce. The entire matter was kept out of the press.)[5]

Shortly after the election Jack traveled with Powers and O'Donnell to the ambassador's home in Palm Beach for some badly needed rest and for consultations concerning the formation of the administration. Jackie and Caroline were left in Washington. The elder Kennedy was delighted to have his son on hand, and at Christmas he would place him at the head of the family table for the first time. The ambassador continued to tell reporters that the president-elect disagreed with him on many things and rarely asked for or heeded his advice—an assertation that is impossible to accept.[6]

On his first morning in Palm Beach, Jack became annoyed at the sight of Secret Service agents lurking near the swimming pool and decided to elude them. To the horror of the agents, the president-elect ran down to the beach and swam out beyond the breakers. For the rest of the visit, a Coast Guard cutter patrolled the water in front of the ambassador's home, partly to guard against intruders and partly to prevent any more recklessness. Jack complained, "Are they expecting Castro to invade Palm Beach?"[7] The Secret Service would soon learn bitter lessons about the new chief executive's unorthodox habits.

Through former President Hoover, the ambassador arranged for a meeting at Key Biscayne between Jack and Richard Nixon. Nixon later reported that Kennedy expressed nervous uncertainty about the election results. Assured that the election would not be contested, Jack offered the Republican a temporary assignment abroad in a few months. The invitation was graciously declined, and Jack seemed relieved. Kenny O'Donnell later reported that when Kennedy climbed back into his helicopter to return to Palm Beach, he said of his former opponent, "It was just as well for all of us that he didn't quite make it."[8]

Jack soon traveled to Texas with O'Donnell and Congressman Torbert Macdonald for a visit with the Lyndon Johnsons at their ranch. To the extreme displeasure of his guests, Johnson got everyone up the next morning before dawn for a deer hunt. After some effort, Jack bagged a deer. Macdonald managed merely to injure his shoulder when his rifle kicked back at him. O'Donnell made his kill with one shot while Kennedy and Johnson were helping Macdonald. When Jack learned of his special assistant's success, he flew into a rage and refused to speak to him for two hours. Kennedys did not like to place second; even close friends violated this dictum at their peril.

As repelled as Kennedy was by Johnson (who greeted the president-elect's plane dressed in a cream-colored leather jacket, cowboy boots, and a ten-gallon hat), he nevertheless sent an aide to buy a fine gift on learning that the Johnsons were celebrating their twenty-sixth wedding anniversary. He presented it to Lady Bird at dinner and made a speech that, according to O'Donnell, surprised and touched the couple.[9]

On November 18 CIA Director Dulles traveled to Palm Beach to brief Kennedy. At the top of the agenda was the Eisenhower administration's planned invasion of Cuba. The same issue of the *New York Times* that reported Dulles's visit carried a State Department bulletin describing massive Soviet military aid to Castro. In an adjoining column, Jacobo Arbenz, the president of Guatemala, whose country secretly bristled with CIA agents and contained a training camp for Cuban refugees, called publicly for a police action against Cuba similar to that taken by the United Nations in Korea.[10]

Less than a week later, President José Jiminez of Cuba declared that the election of Kennedy was unlikely to alter Washington's hostility toward the Castro regime. He also said that his government continued to worry that the United States might feel compelled to demonstrate its "big power" status by sending in the Marines.[11]

On November 23 Jack flew to Washington to spend Thanksgiving Day with his wife and daughter at their Georgetown home. Jackie was planning a delivery by cesarean section at Georgetown University Hospital in about three weeks.[12]

Soon after dinner Jack dismissed his wife's plea to stay in Washington until after the birth and headed back to Palm Beach aboard his private plane. There was much work to do, including the selection of cabinet members. Two hours later Jackie went into labor and was rushed to the hospital, accompanied by a priest; Jack received word aboard the *Caroline*.

According to O'Donnell, Jack exclaimed, "I'm never there when she needs me." If true, it was an extremely rare expression of personal guilt. Jack surely remembered the similar absence in 1956 that nearly cost him his marriage and realized that such indifference was now out of the question. Landing in Palm Beach, he immediately boarded a faster, four-engine plane carrying reporters and sped back toward Washington. In the pilot's cabin Jack heard by radio that John F. Kennedy, Jr. had been born by cesarean. The president-elect waved and bowed before applauding and cheering reporters.[13]

Jack soon learned that the birth had not been as routine as press reporters declared. Stephen Birmingham, Jackie's authorized biographer, wrote later, "For long hours the baby's life hung in the balance but, in the end, he survived." Young John spent his first five days in an incubator. His father visited the hospital three times a day during the next two weeks. When Jackie was released, the president-elect posed for photographs as he pushed her wheelchair. "Oh, Jack, please keep going," she said quietly, continuing to smile at reporters.[14]

Later that same day Mamie Eisenhower invited Jackie to the White House for a brief formal visit. The incoming first lady, despite her physical weakness, was soon on her way and spent an hour touring the private quarters. Jackie was privately horrified by what she considered the Eisenhowers' bad taste. Asked by reporters at the airport afterward if she would see the White House again before the inauguration, she replied, "No, this was it."[15]

Jackie already resented the loss of her privacy. Secret Service agents were everywhere. Crowds continuously surrounded the house in Georgetown. (Jack would appear at the front doorstep for a few minutes to greet the people. Jackie could not bring herself to look out the window.) Even in the hospital, an Associated Press photographer suddenly appeared, snapping pictures of her as she was wheeled from the delivery room.[16]

On December 6 Kennedy and Eisenhower had their first formal meeting at the White House. Privately the president held the Kennedys in contempt. He referred to Jack as "Little Boy Blue," dismissed Bobby as "that little shit," and called Teddy the "Bonus Baby." He did not respect Jack's Senate record and was convinced that the ambassador's money was the chief factor in his success.

The two men, twenty-seven years apart in age, conferred privately for seventy-five minutes. Ike lectured Jack on the White House bureaucracy; Cuba and the Defense Department came up, as did the balance-of-payments problem. ("I pray that he understands it," Eisenhower wrote in his diary.) The president soon expressed a more favorable impression of his successor to his diary, writing that his attitude "was that of a serious, earnest seeker for information." Jack privately thought his host as shallow and unprepared as he had anticipated. New Frontiersmen would joke that Ike couldn't read if his lips were chapped.[17]

The ambassador sat silently while watching Jack on television with Eisenhower. Then, with obvious satisfaction, he turned to a friend and said of his son, "He really looks more like a president every day."[18]

→>> <<←

Eisenhower was correct in thinking Kennedy eager for information. Earlier in the year Jack had sought advice from the executive branch and the postelection transitional period from Clark Clifford, a veteran Washington insider (once hired to defend Jack's claim that he wrote *Profiles in Courage*), and Richard Neustadt, a Columbia University political scientist with experience in government. "If I am elected," Jack said privately, "I don't want to wake up on the morning of November 9 and have to ask myself, 'What in the world do I do now?' "

After the election Clifford was named Kennedy's liaison with the outgoing administration. For further information Jack relied on a series of task forces assigned to study domestic and foreign policy. The president-elect soon confided to John Kenneth Galbraith that his only major new idea was the Peace Corps, adding that if James Reston of the *New York Times* "finds out that this is all there is on the New Frontier, he will write quite a story."[19]

The immediate problem facing Kennedy was the appointment of a personal staff, a cabinet, and the filling of some twelve hundred additional positions. In late November Neustadt heard Jack exclaim, "People, people, people! I don't know any people. I only know voters. How am I going to fill these 1,200 jobs?" He told Galbraith, "I must make the appointments now; a year hence I will know who I really want to appoint."[20]

Many of Jack's close friends were invited to accompany him to the White House. Sorensen donned the title special counsel; O'Donnell, O'Brien, Goodwin, and two other chums became special assistants: Salinger was named press secretary. Dave Powers was asked to serve in the executive mansion in several minor capacities and was soon nicknamed Court Jester.

"The Kennedy staff was *viciously* loyal," said Ed Walsh, an admirer. "They treated Kennedy as an extraordinary product." According to Myer Feldman, head of Kennedy's research team, "Our loyalty to Kennedy transcended everything." Ted Sorensen later said of the White House staff, "none of us ever questioned his decision once it was final. . . . We were appointed for our ability to fulfill the President's needs and talk the President's language." In victory the Kennedy people took themselves very seriously. Veteran observer Jim Rowe declared, "I've seen nobody as arrogant in Washington since we grew up."[21]

Jack was especially close to his longtime Irish cronies, O'Donnell, O'Brien, Powers, Ted Reardon, and "Muggsy" O'Leary, who were soon dubbed the Irish Mafia. They knew most of his secrets, of course, and could be counted on to keep tight-lipped. Their livelihoods, indeed virtually their identities, had long been intertwined with Kennedy. (Lewis Lapham later wrote of the similar devotees around Edward Kennedy that they "imagine that their own lives acquire meaning only insofar as they fall within the sphere of a magical object. The same kind of adulation attaches itself to rock stars, to celebrated criminals and to large denominations of money.")[22] O'Donnell, the lean, tough, blunt, and totally devoted appointments secretary, was especially formidable. He fussed endlessly about Kennedy's public image and used his authority as keeper of the keys to reward the faithful. He boasted privately, "The chain of command is from Jack to me to Bobby." A Washington reporter wrote in 1961, "Nobody who knows Kenny doubts that he would die for the President if need be."[23]

For advice on selecting a cabinet, Jack sought counsel from a wide variety of people, but he paid special attention to his father and former secretary of defense Robert A. Lovett. Lovett was a pillar in the conservative New York financial and legal establishments who had played a major role in both the Truman and Eisenhower administrations. Jack's youth, his ties to liberals, and his narrow victory had raised eyebrows within this elite eastern circle, and the president-elect was eager to demonstrate his reliability and lack of ideology. Soon Kennedy was prepared to offer Lovett his choice of State, Defense, or the Treasury, the top cabinet portfolios. Pleading ill health, the elder Republican chose to confine his activities to recommendation.

Jack also created a committee headed by Sargent Shriver to search for talent. Shriver later recalled Jack using the phrase "the brightest and best" when describing the sort of people he wanted. Clark Clifford later voiced the opinion that he thought the Kennedy men arrogant and overconfident, certain that appointees with the right combinations of brains, training, guts, and energy could right the world's wrongs. An important item in their minds as they screened credentials was "toughness." When word of this got out, some candidates actually telephoned to say, "I'm tough."[24]

The Shriver committee did much of its work by telephone and also developed a job application form. Harris Wofford, a committee member, later recalled, " 'Devotion to Kennedy's programs'—or his 'principles,' as one version of our form sheet had it—was a difficult category because the programs and principles were not always so clear."[25] Conservative Senator Richard Russell of Georgia, watching the selection process yield nominees, confided to a friend that while he was "not enamored of Kennedy," he could not see any reason to prefer Nixon to the president-elect. "On matters of vital concern to us, their thinking is almost identical."[26]

Both Lovett and the Shriver committee recommended Robert S. McNamara for a leading post in the cabinet. McNamara was young, just a year older than Kennedy, a graduate of the University of California and the Harvard Business School, and the newly named president of the Ford Motor Company. During the war he had worked for Lovett in the Pentagon, which Lovett and Eisenhower were now warning had grown out of hand.

McNamara was known to be aggressive, efficient, disciplined, hard-working, unemotional, and analytical. David Halberstam would later describe him as:

> taut, controlled, driving—climbing mountains harnessing generals—the hair slicked down in a way that made him look like a Grand Wood subject. The look was part of the drive: a fat McNamara was as hard to imagine as an uncertain one. The glasses straight and rimless, imposing; you looked at the glasses and kept your distance. He was a man of force, moving, pushing, getting things done, *Bob got things done,* the can-do man in the can-do society in the can-do era.[27]

McNamara was also thought to have modest liberal tendencies and broad intellectual interests. Although a Republican, he had voted for Kennedy in 1960 and made a financial contribution to the campaign.

Kennedy offered McNamara his choice of Treasury or Defense, and the auto executive selected the latter. But McNamara did not jump at the new opportunity; he was at first reluctant and raised a number of questions. At their first meeting McNamara asked the president-elect if he was the sole author of *Profiles in Courage.* Jack assured him that he was.[28]

Kennedy selected investment banker Douglas Dillon to be his secretary of the treasury. A Harvard man with experience in the Treasury Department, Dillon was currently an under secretary of state. He was a conservative Republican who had contributed more than twenty-six thousand dollars to the Nixon campaign. Bobby had initial misgivings and liberals protested, but the president-elect wanted a man he knew and liked and a man the financial community trusted. To satisfy liberal Democrats, Jack named Truman Special Assistant David Bell director of the Bureau of the Budget and Hubert Humphrey's favorite economist, Walter Heller, chairman of the Council of Economic Advisers.[29]

Kennedy and his advisers carefully considered and eventually rejected several people for secretary of state. Harvard College Dean McGeorge Bundy was brilliant, ambitious, and impressive, but at forty-one was thought to be too young. He became special assistant to the president for National Security Affairs.[30] Liberals wanted Adlai Stevenson, but the Kennedys could not forgive him for his unwillingness to put Jack on the ticket with him in 1956. (Bobby said later that the Illinois politician had acted like "an old woman.") After much indecision Stevenson accepted the ambassadorship to the United Nations, a post he thought beneath his dignity. Chester Bowles and G. Mennan Williams also had support, but both were considered too liberal.[31]

Jack was strongly inclined to name Arkansas Democrat J. William Fulbright, chairman of the Senate Foreign Relations Committee, as his secretary of state. ("He was the only person who was mentioned as Secretary of State whom he knew," Bobby said later. "And so he thought it was worthwhile doing.") But there was stiff opposition to the segregationist from civil rights groups, Jewish organizations, and Bobby. After a private discussion with Joseph P. Kennedy, who outlined the political drawbacks a Fulbright nomination would bring the new administration, the senator asked that his name be withdrawn from consideration.[32]

Bowles and former Secretary of State Acheson backed Dean Rusk, fifty-one, president of the Rockefeller Foundation. Jack telephoned Senator Richard Russell to ask if the former Rhodes scholar was sufficiently "tough-fibered." Though he was little known to the Kennedy people, Rusk's Establishment credentials were good, he had worked hard in the State Department under Acheson, and he had written a recent article in *Foreign Affairs* that Jack admired. When Lovett gave his support, Jack selected Rusk over career diplomat David Bruce, the choice of columnist Joseph Alsop and others.

Kennedy and Rusk would never be close; the extremely reserved and methodical secretary was the only cabinet officer Jack did not call by his first name. The president would soon have many complaints about the State Department, asking Soviet expert Charles Bohlen at one point,

"What's wrong with that goddamn department of yours, Chip?" Bobby would later condemn Rusk for lacking organizational skills, for failing to have strong points of view, and for being consistently wrong. "Jack was his own Secretary of State."[33]

→>> <<<

Bobby was named attorney general at the ambassador's insistence. At first Jack was privately uneasy about the mandate; the Justice Department had thirty-thousand employees and a $30 million budget, and his thirty-four-year-old brother had not even practiced law. Jack considered naming Bobby under secretary of defense or assistant secretary of state for Latin America. He even suggested at one point that his brother learn Russian and become ambassador to the Soviet Union. (Bobby said later, "In the first place, I couldn't possibly learn Russian, because I spent ten years learning second-year French.") Bobby himself was reluctant to head the Justice Department and thought about returning to Massachusetts and running for governor. "We just vacillated back and forth," Bobby later recalled, "almost like we did on the Vice President." Early in the deliberations, Connecticut Governor Abraham Ribicoff was asked if he would be interested in the post. The moderate Democrat, who had Supreme Court aspirations, declined, preferring a less controversial post.

Jack sent Clark Clifford to urge the elder Kennedy to drop his demand about Bobby, but the decision stood. As early as 1957 the Founding Father had told the *Saturday Evening Post* of his desire to see Jack in the White House, Bobby serving as attorney general, and Teddy sitting in the Senate. Things were on schedule.[34]

When Ben Bradlee learned about the appointment, he asked Jack how he intended to announce it. "Well," Kennedy replied, "I think I'll open the front door of the Georgetown house some morning about 2:00 A.M., look up and down the street, and if there's no one there, I'll whisper 'It's Bobby.' " Just before Jack faced reporters on his front steps a short time later, he said softly, "Damn it, Bobby, comb your hair," and added, "Don't smile too much or they'll think we are happy about this appointment."[35]

Many observers were less than pleased by the selection, including several legal experts, the *New York Times,* and a few senators. Lyndon Johnson told Bobby Baker that Richard Russell was "absolutely shittin' a squealin' worm. He thinks it's a disgrace for a kid who's never practiced law to be appointed. . . . I agree with him. . . . But I don't think Jack Kennedy's gonna let a little fart like Bobby lead him around by the nose."[36]

J. Edgar Hoover officially approved the appointment, but privately he seethed at the thought of having Kennedy as his superior. There was the age factor, of course: Hoover was sixty-six; he had become FBI director a year before Bobby was born. Politics was also a consideration. Hoover was an ultra-conservative who had quietly worked for his long-time friend Richard Nixon during the recent campaign.[37] Moreover, Hoover had personally disliked Bobby since the Joe McCarthy days, considering him an arrogant upstart. Nixon later recalled Hoover condemning "that sneaky little son of a bitch."[38]

Now the imperious director would be forced to serve an attorney general and, even worse, a president, he neither liked nor respected. And he knew it would be futile to appeal a decision of the attorney general to the Oval Office—a practice he had employed for decades. Tensions increased immediately when Bobby forced the FBI, for the first time, to clear its press releases and speeches with his office. He also required the press releases to be issued in the name of the Department of Justice rather than the FBI. Subtle warfare between Hoover and the Kennedys would continue throughout the Thousand Days.[39]

Other cabinet appointments were less controversial and were based largely on a conventional balance of politics, geography, and religion. Jack's view of women prohibited any feminine representation. No black had ever served in the cabinet, and Kennedy lacked the inclination to set a precedent.

To please black supporters, however, word was leaked to the press that veteran black Congressman William Dawson was being considered. Jack then announced that he had named the seventy-four-year-old Dawson postmaster general and that Dawson had declined to serve. In fact, the appointment was not made seriously and was designed merely to give the impression that Kennedy was concerned about blacks. Chicago's Mayor Daley played a role in this deception. Months later a writer reported : "The Kennedy high command is tight-lipped about the offer to Dawson."[40]

Former North Carolina Governor Luther Hodges, a successful businessman and Marshall Plan executive, became secretary of commerce. At sixty-two, he was the oldest man in the new cabinet. Stewart Udall of Arizona, a former congressional colleague of Jack's and an early Kennedy supporter, was named secretary of the interior. Governor Ribicoff, who had publicly favored the Kennedy candidacy since 1956, agreed to be secretary of health, education and welfare. Outgoing Minnesota Governor Orville Freeman, who had placed Kennedy's name in nomination at

Los Angeles, became secretary of agriculture. Veteran union attorney Arthur Goldberg was appointed secretary of labor. Goldberg had worked with the Kennedy brothers during the investigation of labor racketeering.

The last post to be filled was the postmaster generalship. It was mid-December and Jack was in a hurry to complete his cabinet. It had been quietly understood for some time that this relatively unimportant job would go to a Southern Californian. When someone suggested California attorney and insurance executive J. Edward Day, whom Jack had only met in passing, the president-elect impetuously picked up the telephone and offered Day the job. Day, who had not been active in the campaign, promptly accepted. Ben Bradlee later remembered Jack wondering privately ''why, in heaven's name, the Postmaster General should be in the Cabinet at all.''[41]

-»» ««-

Kennedy selected the youngest cabinet of the century; at an average age of forty-seven, it was a decade younger than Eisenhower's. When the ages of others close to the president were also considered—Sorensen (thirty-two), Salinger (thirty-five), O'Brien (forty-three), O'Donnell (thirty-six), Bundy (forty-one), Bundy deputy Walt Rostow (forty-four), Special Counsel Myer Feldman (forty-four), and Budget Director Bell (forty-one)—the Kennedy preoccupation with youth and vigor became even more evident.[42]

Cabinet members were, on the whole, politically inexperienced. Only four had ever sought political office; not one had held elective office as long as Kennedy; not one had a national following of his own. This was surely by design, and perhaps reflected the elder Kennedy's viewpoint. By surrounding himself with satellites rather than political equals or competitors, Jack could keep the spotlight on himself. Moreover, he could be sure of having his way—a Kennedy must. When a Washington hostess complained to Clark Clifford that the cabinet lacked glamour, Clifford replied, ''I don't want any mercurial, flashy, brilliant men in there. I want men who can make things run right, men who can carry out the orders of the boss.''[43]

Political considerations were obvious in the cabinet appointments. Liberal commentator David S. Broder later observed: ''The original Cabinet, like Noah's Ark, had two of every animal: two Catholics; two Jews; two Southerners; two Westerners; two Midwesterners.''[44]

Kennedy's selections also revealed his desire to be among men with highly respected intellectual credentials. One magazine counted sixteen

Phi Beta Kappas, four Rhodes scholars, and a Nobel Prizewinner. This emphasis was no doubt in part a response to the elder Kennedy's long-established policy of having his sons identified with people of "class." It helped win favorable attention from liberal reporters and commentators in the nation's major media. And it fit the Kennedy image: many thought that the appointments reflected the president's own brilliance, energy, and idealism. David Halberstam later said of the cabinet nominees: "They carried with them an exciting sense of American elitism, a sense that the best men had been summoned forth from the country," eager to give Americans a new sense of purpose and spread the American dream abroad.[45]

Several observers complained about the incoming president's penchant for East Coast diplomas; Lyndon Johnson grumbled for years about "the Harvards." And not everyone, of course, welcomed intellectuals to positions of power. "Eggheads," much to their irritation, were not greatly appreciated at the time. Truman had been highly critical; Eisenhower shunned them. In 1959 even the distinguished historian Jacques Barzun had warned against giving political authority to men of his bent and training, on the ground that those enamored of ideas and principles had historically caused great tragedy. "Thus the greatest danger to a democratic state," he wrote, "is probably the contamination of its politics by Intellect."[46]

A much simpler and more crafty man, House Speaker Rayburn, looked over the credentials of those named to the cabinet and told his protégé, the vice president–elect, "Well, Lyndon, you may be right and they may be every bit as intelligent as you say, but I'd feel a whole lot better about them if just one of them had run for sheriff once."[47]

Kennedy tended to fill top administration positions with men known to be practical and nonideological. NBC newsman David Brinkley soon wrote of "the careful unemotional mood that now fills Washington as smoke fills a room," and observed that in the nation's capital, "a good idea is one that works. And the best idea is the one that works fastest with the least fuss while irritating the fewest people."[48] This approach to values, dominating the highest levels of the new administration, was clearly a reflection of Jack's pragmatic character.

Prominent liberals active in the campaign had to be satisfied with secondary roles. Chester Bowles was named under secretary of state. G. Mennen Williams was appointed assistant secretary of state for Africa. ("I'm glad they sent Soapy Williams to Africa," said ultra-conservative Senator Barry Goldwater. "If we'd been elected, that's exactly where we'd have sent him.")[49] John Kenneth Galbraith became ambassador to India. (Victor Lasky later said that the famed economist was "exiled to New Dehli.")[50] Arthur Schlesinger, Jr., was named a special assistant to the president.

Galbraith, supremely self-confident, soon began writing regularly to the president, offering advice on a wide range of topics. Kennedy said that he enjoyed the letters, but Galbraith later conceded that the president's written responses were "few and sparing."[51]

Schlesinger was not assigned specific duties. Kenny O'Donnell, who thought less of liberals, perhaps, than even his boss, later wrote that the historian was "to be a liaison man in charge of keeping Adlai Stevenson happy, to receive complaints from the liberals, and to act as a sort of household devil's advocate who would complain about anything in the administration that bothered him."[52]

Jack liked Schlesinger and admired his excellent mind and remarkable writing ability. He also knew that Schlesinger's inevitable works on the administration could be influenced favorably if their author believed he was part of what C. S. Lewis, in a memorable essay on the lust for power, called the "Inner Ring." (In 1960 Schlesinger had dismissed the 1950s as "our decade of inertia" and declared proudly that "our intellectuals are beginning to draw the new portrait of America out of which new political initiatives will in due course come, and . . . people are responding to their portrayal.")[53] Ben Bradlee later remembered Kennedy having a deep concern for his historical image and saying of historians, "Those bastards, they are always there with their pencils out."[54] He was comfortable only with partisans. When Jackie's cousin John H. Davis suggested that he might write a book on the Kennedys, Kenny O'Donnell told him to "cool it, or else."[55]

Kennedy had no intention of giving Schlesinger any serious authority in the administration. Bradlee recalled that the president assigned his special assistant the task of seeing what could be done to prevent Kennedy imitators like comedian Vaughn Meader from being broadcast on the radio. "That was Arthur's assignment for the week," Jack said.[56] Bobby later recalled that his brother "liked Arthur Schlesinger, but he thought he was a little bit of a nut sometimes. He thought he was sort of a gadfly and that he was having a helluva good time in Washington. He didn't do a helluva lot, but he was good to have around."[57]

Torbert Macdonald asked to be appointed to the president-elect's Senate seat, and Jack agreed to arrange things for his old friend. But the ambassador preferred another candidate, and the position went to malleable Benjamin Smith, Jack's Harvard roommate. Smith understood that he was merely holding the seat for Teddy, who would satisfy the constitutional age requirement of thirty when the term expired in 1962. At a dinner party on Inauguration Day, Jack apologized to Mrs. Macdonald. "I'm sorry about the Senate seat." Obviously referring to a scene with his father, Jack said, "It was painful."[58]

→≫ ≪←

A lavish and memorable inauguration was planned. Reflecting Jackie's good taste and the Kennedy desire to project an image of high culture, brains, and art, some of the nation's leading literary figures were invited, including poets Robert Frost and Carl Sandburg. Frost would recite a poem at the swearing-in ceremony. Black contralto Marian Anderson was to sing the "Star Spangled Banner." There were to be five balls and an inaugural concert.

More to Jack's liking, a host of parties and receptions were planned, along with a gigantic parade. He pleaded with his mistress Judith Campbell to attend. Jack was no more sensitive about this sort of thing than his father had been. The young woman declined, saying, "I just wouldn't feel comfortable with your wife and family being there." Campbell later put photographs of her personal invitation and tickets to the inauguration and the largest of the balls in her book, *My Story.*[59]

In early December, while she was still in the Georgetown Hospital, Jackie began preparing her inaugural wardrobe. By this time she had been described as first lady of fashion and was on the list of best-dressed women of the world. Jackie was determined to set new standards in fashion. She also had plans to turn the White House into a showpiece and make it a center of world-class culture.

The new first lady selected aristocratic Oleg Cassini to be her exclusive fashion designer. Cassini had known Jack and his father since the late 1940s—he was married to actress Gene Tierney when she began her affair with Jack—and had designed clothes for Rose, Pat, Eunice, and Jean. A notorious womanizer himself, Cassini had provided the ambassador with "dates" for several years, a favor the elder Kennedy had returned. (In the mid-1950s, Cassini called Joe to mediate a tiff he was having with a current flame, Grace Kelly. Joe used the occasion to make a play for the actress. Jack later enjoyed calling on Cassini to tell friends "how Dad screwed you up with Grace Kelly.") The couturier first met Jackie several weeks before her marriage and was impressed by her wit and intelligence.

In an early letter to Cassini, Jackie instructed, "Just make sure no one has exactly the same dress I do. . . . I want all mine to be original & no fat little women hopping around in the same dress." Soon Cassini designed a wool coat and a pillbox hat for the inauguration that quickly swept the nation as the "Jackie look."[60]

However interested she was in her appearance, Jackie dreaded the inaugural celebrations. She had recovered from her cesarean operation and could withstand the physical demands. Her problem was an old one: She hated the crowds, the hot lights, and the endless handshaking of political life. She was also nervous about the presence of scores of relatives, who did not get along with each other and who remembered Jackie's troubled childhood and her father's shabby conduct behind the scenes at her wedding. Her biographer Stephen Birmingham later observed that as first lady, "Feeding the egos of her many relatives was not high on her list of duties."[61]

Moreover, Jackie had no desire to see the numerous actresses scheduled to attend pawing her husband while she was ignored. Unlike Jack she declined several invitations. She had Pierre Salinger issue a press release stating, "On the advice of her doctors, Mrs. Kennedy will restrict her participation to the main inaugural ceremonies and festivities."[62]

An almost eight-inch snowstorm hit Washington on the eve of the inauguration, snarling traffic all over the city. But it did not ruin the plans of the president-elect and thousands of other celebrants. After a reception, a party, and a concert at Constitution Hall, the Kennedys attended a star-studded gala at the National Guard Armory planned by Frank Sinatra.

By this time Sinatra and his pals Peter Lawford, Sammy Davis, Jr., Dean Martin, and Joey Bishop were good friends of Jack's. Labeled by the media "the Clan" or the "Rat Pack" (they called themselves "the Summit"), the entertainers had worked for Kennedy's election and publicly cheered his victory.[63] Lawford, of course, was important to this alliance. Their friendships were cemented by a love of show business and a sybaritic outlook on life that featured an endless pursuit of sexual pleasure. JFK and "the Clan" were, in the parlance of the day, serious "swingers."

Sinatra, moreover, was convinced that his mobilization of mob support in November had put Kennedy in the White House. One mob intimate, Skinny D'Amato, said years later, "Frank won Kennedy the election. All the guys knew it."[64] Right after the election, Sinatra had hurriedly added a heliport and a new guesthouse to his Palm Springs compound, convinced that it would become the Western White House. The president would have a home away from home where there would be plenty of "booze and broads."[65]

The by-invitation-only preinaugural gala was designed to raise a million dollars for the Democratic party. Boxes cost ten thousand dollars apiece, while individual seats went for one hundred dollars. By all accounts the entertainment was splendid. In an onstage speech afterward, Jack thanked Sinatra effusively, saying in part, "I know we're all indebted to a great friend—Frank Sinatra. Long before he could sing, he used to poll a Democratic precinct back in New Jersey. That precinct has grown to cover a country."

Sinatra later made much of the recorded tribute. "Frank would stand by the mantel and play it over and over," said a friend, "and we had to sit there for hours on end listening to every word." Sinatra also enjoyed boasting that Nevada was one of the two Western states that had gone for Kennedy, and he proudly showed friends personal notes from the candidate. One read: "Frank—How much can I count on the boys from Vegas for? JFK."[66]

Jackie and Rose left the gala at midnight, while Jack and his father stayed for the rest of the show and then went to a party hosted by the ambassador. The president-elect got to bed about 4:00 A.M.

A few hours later Jack attended mass alone, fulfilling the family requirement. In her memoirs Rose said that she was in the church when her son arrived and kept her presence secret until after the service. She wrote, "I realized that he was there of his own volition: that he wanted to start his presidency by offering his mind and heart, and expressing his hopes and fears to Almighty God, and asking his blessing as he began his great duties."[67]

Later that morning Jack and Jackie were escorted to the White House, and they were soon on their way to the Capitol and the inaugural ceremonies. Waiting in the bitter cold for dignitaries to take their places, Nancy Hanschman struck up a conversation with the nervous president-elect, who (although clad in thermal underwear) appeared without a hat or overcoat—to impress the world with the Kennedy image of toughness. "When did you think this would finally come to pass?" the reporter asked. Jack replied with a lie, saying that he had anticipated the event since his youth and was not half as surprised to be president as a lot of people were to see him in that office. Of more immediate interest to Kennedy was "when the hell" things would get under way.[68]

The inaugural address had gone through many hands, and its construction followed a review by Ted Sorensen of all previous such speeches. Kennedy undoubtedly made contributions, but Sorensen was clearly the principal architect. (As always, he loyally denied it.) The terse final product—at 1,355 words the shortest since 1944—contained many things that Kennedy had said before, but the eloquence of its language was superior to anything that had ostensibly come from his pen. Allen J. Matusow later called it "the best campaign speech Kennedy ever gave." Sorensen was later so proud that he published the speech in full in his Kennedy biography. Jack told Pierre Salinger that the address was "a smash." He confided to Jackie, however, that he thought Jefferson's was better.[69]

Jack became the nation's thirty-fifth president at 12:51 P.M. on January 20, 1961, when he was sworn in by Chief Justice Earl Warren. On his mind at the very moment he placed his left hand on the family Bible and raised his right hand to take the oath, he told Tip O'Neill that evening, was "how the hell" an influential and mysterious Boston businessman named George Kara managed to wrangle a seat next to O'Neill and behind the Kennedy family.[70]

Jack read the well-rehearsed inaugural address with a forcefulness that enhanced its brilliant rhetoric and thrilled millions all over the world. Greatness was now in command of the nation's government, he announced, and the future was bright.

> Let the world go forth from this time and place, to friend and foe alike, that the torch has been passed to a new generation of Americans born in this century, tempered by war, disciplined by a hard and bitter peace, proud of our ancient heritage, and unwilling to witness or permit the slow undoing of those human rights to which this nation has always been committed, and to which we are committed today at home and around the world.

Dwelling almost exclusively on foreign affairs, he declared, "Let every nation know, whether it wishes us well or ill, that we shall pay any price, bear any burden, meet any hardship, support any friend, oppose any foe to assure the survival and the success of liberty."

Hard-line anti-communism and the buildup of American military strength were the dominant themes of the address. (By contrast, Eisenhower, in his farewell address delivered a few days earlier, had warned of the dangers of the huge and growing "military-industrial complex.") Jack said exultantly, "In the long history of the world, only a few generations have been granted the role of defending freedom in its hour of maximum danger. I do not shrink from his responsibility; I welcome it." Still, he expressed the willingness to work for peace, "before the dark powers of destruction unleashed by science engulf all humanity in planned or accidental self-destruction."

Near the conclusion of the speech, the young president called for support in "a struggle against the common enemies of man: tyranny, poverty, disease and war itself." Kennedy seemed to demand of his country a new era of social activism. Standing in the freezing weather hatless and coatless, erect and seemingly fearless, JFK personified for many their hopes and dreams for future national greatness. Millions responded enthusiastically to the summons: "And so, my fellow Americans, ask not what your country can do for you; ask what you can do for your country."[71]

The address won praise from foreign diplomats, politicians of both parties, editorialists, and the public at large. Former President Truman called it "marvelous" and "wonderful." Adlai Stevenson said it was "eloquent, inspiring—a great speech." Hubert Humphrey described it as "The American message to the world—a true picture of our country." Only Richard Nixon chose not to comment.[72]

Ted Sorensen later wrote, "It seemed to me, as I watched the faces of the crowd, that they had forgotten the cold, forgotten party lines and forgotten all the old divisions of race, religion, and nation."[73]

Rose later asserted that as she watched her son, "I said to myself, drawing on Cardinal Newman's words, 'He will do good, he will do God's work.' " She continued, "I felt that Joe and I had given our country a young President whose words, manner, ideas, character, everything about him bespoke future greatness."

No one knew what went through the ambassador's mind at the time. Rose said later that several reported seeing tears glistening in his eyes. "Perhaps so," she wrote.[74]

After the ceremonies the new president and his wife, the Lyndon Johnsons, and members of the cabinet went into the Capitol for a luncheon given by the joint congressional inaugural committee. Joe and Rose headed for the Mayflower Hotel and a lavish luncheon for the Kennedys, Fitzgeralds, Bouviers, Lees, and Auchinclosses.

John H. Davis, one of the sixty or more in attendance at the Mayflower, observed that the Kennedys kept apart from the others. The Kennedys knew that Jackie's three families were all Republicans and that several members disliked the ambassador. Then too, the Kennedys had long been trained to distrust all outsiders. A cousin said to Davis, "Don't you understand? We're the enemy . . . that 's all there is to it." Someone else exclaimed, "Listen, they think we are Henry Cabot Lodge . . . in other words, anathema."[75]

The ambassador, the luncheon's host, seemed particularly aloof. "Who are all these people?" he asked Letitia Baldrige, who had handled the details of the event. "Your family, Mr. Ambassador," she replied. "They are *not*," he said. "Just who are all these freeloaders? I want to know exactly why you asked them." Baldrige explained that the guests were relatives by marriage. The ambassador confirmed the fact by asking several their names. He then returned to the future White House social secretary and declared, "This is going to cost me a lot of money, Tish. But you're right. They *are* all family. And it's the last time we get 'em all together, too, if I have anything to say about it."[76]

Administration officials and their families then went to the White House to observe the inaugural parade, which had as its theme "World Peace Through New Frontiers." Even before the president reached the reviewing stand, numerous Kennedys swarmed into the White House to investigate Jack's new home. When Eunice and Lem Billings reached the Lincoln bedroom, they took turns bouncing on the bed, giggling, and photographing each other stretched out on the counterpane. At one point, Eunice told Jack's closest friend, "You know what this reminds me of? That scene in *Gone With the Wind* where Scarlett's colored servants move into Tara after the war. I felt like the old mammy who takes a look around and then says, 'Man, we's rich now.' "[77]

Jack clearly enjoyed the parade, which featured more than forty bands, thousands of troops, and scores of floats. He was particularly taken with the Navy PT boat mounted on a truck and renumbered *PT 109*. A reporter noted, "As the ship passed, Mr. Kennedy waved to each of the crewmen with obvious excitement and followed its progress long after it had passed the reviewing stand."[78]

While the parade continued, some two hundred Kennedy relatives and friends gathered on the ground floor of the White House for the administration's first party. Jackie stayed upstairs, resisting all personal appeals, including one from her husband, to make an appearance. John Davis later learned from a cousin that Jackie could not bring herself to face all her relatives. "I just can't. I can't," she exclaimed. It was fear and shyness, Davis concluded, not snobbery. Guests were told that the first lady was resting. More than a few Bouviers, Lees, and Auchin-closses, and no doubt some Kennedys, were offended.[79]

During the party Davis approached the ambassador, introduced himself, shook hands, and attempted to make conversation. The elder Kennedy was quiet and even seemed blasé. When Davis asked him if he personally had some great national vision that the new president could help realize, the ambassador "laughed at me as if I were naive." The elder Kennedy had never confused the image and the reality. A cousin soon heard Joe mutter, "Jesus Christ, I didn't know Jackie had so many goddamned relatives."[80]

Jack was soon on his way to a private dinner party given by friends and campaign workers. Actress Angie Dickinson, a current flame, was on hand, escorted by Red Fay—her "beard" (official escort) for the evening.[81]

Jackie looked radiant when she and Jack met to begin the round of inaugural balls. Her Cassini gown was of white chiffon, covered by a floor-length white silk cape. Her diamonds had been borrowed from Tiffany's. The first ball was in the Mayflower Hotel, where former President and Mrs. Truman were among the guests. The Statler-Hilton was the scene of the second.[82]

At the Statler-Hilton, Jack slipped out of the presidential box and went upstairs to a private party given by Frank Sinatra. Angie Dickenson was there along with actresses Janet Leigh and Kim Novak. When he returned to Jackie, he looked rather sheepish and carried a copy of the *Washington Post* under his arm, as if he had just stepped outside to buy a newspaper. Kenny O'Donnell later recalled, "His knowing wife gave him a rather chilly look."[83]

The largest ball of the evening was at the Armory. Under the scrutiny of television cameras and a huge crowd, the president and first lady gave the impression of being close and happy. The ambassador and Rose, who had barely spoken to each other all day, appeared loving and extremely jovial; John Davis thought them "utterly transformed" from the reception four hours earlier. Davis, who well understood the difference between the Kennedy image and reality, later wrote that "the Kennedys were the greatest masters of myth and illusion American politics had ever known, and one pricked their balloons at some personal risk."[84]

After the Armory ball, Jackie returned to the White House. Jack carried on alone, attending two more balls and a party at the Georgetown home of columnist Joe Alsop. There Kennedy enjoyed a brief sexual encounter with a beautiful young woman who wept as he left, fearful that her relationship with the president was finished forever. In this way, more like an irresponsible playboy than a mature and idealistic chief executive, Jack concluded his first day in office.[85]

→» «←

Jackie began what she called the restoration ("not redecoration") of the White House the next day. On the whole she wanted the executive mansion to recall the time of President Monroe, when a French style was fashionable. This was a large and highly expensive project that would take more than a year to complete. "I want to make this into a grand house," she told J. Bernard West, the chief usher.[86]

Carpenters, painters, plumbers, and electricians started first on the seven family rooms on the second floor, transforming them according to the first lady's carefully detailed plans. Jackie appointed advisers and worked intensively to find appropriate antique furniture, artwork, rugs, drapes, and wallpaper. By the end of just two weeks, a fifty-thousand-dollar appropriation was exhausted. With the assistance of Parisian decorator Stephane Boudin, she soon turned her attentions to the downstairs rooms, often completely redoing them. The changes were such that in mid-February the president led the prime minister of Denmark and several other guests into the pantry instead of the Blue Room.

Chief Usher West, a White House employee since 1941, was astounded at the thirty-one-year-old first lady's grasp of detail and by her ability to get things done her own way. "She had a will of iron," he wrote later, "with more determination than anyone I have ever met. Yet she was so soft-spoken, so deft and subtle, that she could impose that will upon people without their ever knowing it." Jackie's masterful application of charm and pressure on wealthy friends and others brought numerous valuable additions to the White House collection of art and furniture.[87]

Jackie had no confidantes, West noted, with the possible exception of her sister. She refused to hold news conferences and sometimes chose not to participate in official functions. "Jackie lived a strangely remote life in the White House," Mary Gallagher later recalled, "busying herself with official entertainment, her own little family, and the projects of her own choice." At one point she boasted to a secretary, "People told me ninety-nine things that I had to do as first lady, and I haven't done one of them."[88]

West observed that Jackie did not enjoy the company of other women and would largely ignore them at both private and official functions. Her relations with Rose, the Kennedy sisters, and even her mother were strained. She seemed to like being around older men above all, and her favorite was the ambassador.[89]

There was undoubtedly an affection between the two, but another motive may well have entered into Jackie's extraordinarily warm approach toward the family patriarch. The personal financial affairs of the president and his wife were handled by the ambassador's office, and the elder Kennedy took an extreme interest in how the money was spent. Jack quickly became alarmed by the first lady's expenses, not only because they were high but also because he knew that his father had access to the books. Jackie's personal secretary, who wrote her employer's checks and kept her accounts, later observed that all the Kennedy sons and daughters "made it a point to show that they could handle their money properly." A happy ambassador, Jackie may have concluded, would decrease the tensions caused by her lavish spending.[90]

Kennedy was the wealthiest president in American history. His private income, before taxes, was estimated at about five hundred thousand a year. On his forty-fifth birthday, in 1962, his personal fortune went up an estimated $2.5 million when he received another fourth of his share in three trust funds established by the ambassador for his children. Still, from the start, Jack complained profusely about food and entertainment expenses. The Kennedy grocery account was transferred from a posh French market in Georgetown to a local wholesaler. After a dinner dance at the White House, Pierre Salinger saw the president chiding Chief Usher West about a number of half-full champagne bottles. In the future, Jack ordered, no waiter was to be permitted to open a full bottle until he turned in an empty one. "He seemed to get relaxation and a little respite," Salinger wrote, "by quarreling over food prices rather than atom bombs."[91]

Jackie's clothing expenditures deeply concerned the president. At one point he showed a congressman who happened to be in the Oval Office bills amounting to forty thousand dollars and asked angrily, "What would you do if your wife did that?" Ben Bradlee described the president as "boiling" over Jackie's spending.[92]

The first lady's dress scouts prowled Europe in search of new items. Storage closets on the third floor of the White House soon bulged with the latest fashions. Jackie's dressing room overflowed with clothes, and one closet, Gallagher recalled, "was almost like walking into a little shoe store." Gallagher observed, "If Jackie liked something, she ordered it and coped with the bills later. Then, when she saw the totals, she'd get economy-minded again." But not for long.

In July 1961 Jackie's personal expenses for the second quarter of the year totaled about $35,000, almost half going for clothes. By the late following year, the Kennedys were battling mightily. During one encounter, Gallagher recalled, the president was extremely distraught. But he was unable to reform his wife's compulsive spending. Family expenses for the year swelled from $105,446 in 1961 to $121,462 in 1962. Jack's wrath was compounded by the fact that he publicly donated his $100,000 annual salary to charity.[93]

Ben Bradlee heard the president express bewilderment about the high cost of living in the White House: "This is a place where a fellow should at least break even, with all the services provided." As it was, he had his personal valet and Jackie's maid both put on civil service.[94]

Jack paid careful attention to the changes in and around the executive mansion during his first months in office and, even though taxpayers and private donors were footing most of the bill, he fumed continuously about costs. He also fretted about departures from tradition, such as the height of fences and the color of walls. West recalled: "Unfortunately, we were never treated to samples of his famous humor. He was always entirely serious about the White House."[95]

Initial landscaping costs amounted to nearly two hundred thousand dollars, and the National Park Service was forced to contribute funds. Jack personally bawled out the Park Service director for saying that District of Columbia park projects were being neglected because "we have to spend all our money at the White House." Salinger later reported seeing the president and the head gardener in "a wild argument" over maintenance expenses. The Kennedy whom White House underlings knew in person was quite different from the smiling, witty, humane, and inspiring leader they saw on television.[96]

→≫   ≪←

From his first day in office, Jack enjoyed being president. He impressed friends by pushing buttons on his desk and getting instant reactions. He boasted that his switchboard operators could reach virtually anyone anywhere in the world with only the barest of instructions. He took obvious pleasure in showing the executive wing to relatives and friends. After one such tour for Teddy and Red Fay early in the administration, he spun around in his chair and asked, "Paul, do you think it is adequate?" Fay, soon to become assistant secretary of the Navy, could only sputter, "I feel any minute now that some guy is going to stick his head through one of those doors and say, 'All right, you three guys—out of here.' "[97]

Jack's daily schedule in Washington permitted ample relaxation and entertainment. Indeed, despite the rhetoric about energy, the pace was more like Eisenhower's than Truman's. Kennedy got up about 8:00 A.M., and each day he enjoyed a hot bath, a midday swim in the White House pool that sometimes lasted an hour (the ambassador commissioned artist Barnard Lamotte to paint a ninety-seven-foot mural around the pool), directed exercises in the gymnasium, and a nap or private time with Jackie that lasted at least an hour. West later recalled, "The Kennedys' early afternoons, while the children were napping, were spent in absolute privacy. Quite often, music was heard floating in the passageway between her bedroom and her husband's."[98]

Evenings were usually private and very often featured small dinners with friends that might be followed by a film. The movie theater was equipped with a chair that enabled the president virtually to lie down to view the screen, thus resting his back.

The Kennedys usually left the White House on weekends for rest and relaxation at Hyannis Port, Palm Beach, or elsewhere. Jackie especially enjoyed horseback riding, while her husband liked golf—a sport in which he showed talent—and swimming.[99]

In 1962 the Kennedys rented Glen Ora, a French villa in Virginia, as a winter retreat. (Jackie spent ten thousand dollars of family money redecorating it. ''When she was finished,'' West wrote, ''the president raised hell.'') Jack and the owner had a falling out, and the Kennedys left when the lease expired (after spending more money to restore the house to its pre-Jackie condition). They then built an expensive country home nearby that Jackie named Wexford, after the Irish county from which the first Kennedy emigrated. Jack did not care for it, perhaps because of the cost, and Camp David, Roosevelt's Shangri-la in Maryland's Caroctin Hills, thereafter became a favorite vacation spot.[100]

Ben Bradlee later remembered a spring day on which he and the president and several others were flying in the presidential helicopter to Camp David after a late-night party that left ''all of us a touch hung over.'' Jack turned to him and said, ''Do you think you could get used to this kind of life? Pretty hard to take, isn't it?''[101]

Also contributing to Jack's generally high spirits was the fact that he continued to enjoy extramarital relationships during Jackie's absences. Judith Campbell made the first of some twenty visits to the White House on May 4, 1961, and later described the experience in detail. She visited five times that summer and continued to see the president during the fall, winter, and following spring. She also traveled to Palm Springs to be with him. He once visited her at the Plaza Hotel in New York.

Jack wanted Judith to attend White House functions regularly. ''That way we could see each other a lot more often.'' Campbell declined. Several times the president suggested that she join him on Air Force One.

> He had no qualms about asking me. It wasn't maybe it could be done this way or that way—he had it all worked out. But I knew I wouldn't be walking out with him. I would be hiding back there in the plane until the excitement of his exit had died down. That was so far out of character for me that instead of being flattered by the offer, I was insulted and told him so in no uncertain terms. But Jack could laugh at me at times like that. I think he just loved intrigue.[102]

Mary Pinchot Meyer, Bobby's next-door neighbor, secretly visited the White House about thirty times between January 1962 and November 1963. In public she regularly attended White House soirées in the company of her sister and brother-in-law, the Ben Bradlees. The most careful observer of the affair later called Meyer "the secret Lady Ottoline of Camelot."[103]

When the Kennedy-Meyer story surfaced in 1976, Bradlee denied knowing of it. But he also admitted having read of it in 1964 in Meyer's personal diary, destroyed by a CIA official soon after the woman's murder.[104] Timothy Reardon, Jr., who along with Dave Powers was identified as a presidential aide involved in Meyer's clandestine visits, told the *Washington Post* "not so" and contended that "nothing like that every happened at the White House, with her or anyone else."[105]

In fact, a steady stream of young women was quietly admitted into the executive mansion. Veteran White House employee Traphes Bryant, who kept a diary, later revealed how the president arranged matters with aides and staff members. He described Jack's penchant for nude swimming with his female guests (a sport long enjoyed by the ambassador), and he outlined the efforts made by employees to scour rooms in the family quarters for hairpins and other incriminating evidence once the lady—or ladies—left:

> There was a conspiracy of silence to protect his secrets from Jacqueline and to keep her from finding out. The newspapers would tell how First Lady Jacqueline was off on another trip, but what they didn't report was how anxious the President sometimes was to see her go. And what consternation there sometimes was when she returned unexpectedly.

Jackie was often aware, of course, of what was going on behind her back. She once discovered a woman's undergarment tucked in a pillowcase and coldly presented it to Jack. Bryant recalled, "She delicately held it out to her husband between thumb and forefinger—about the way you hold a worm—saying, 'Would you please shop around and see who these belong to? They're not my size.' "

Bryant was amazed at the discrepancy between the public and private JFK. While, on formal occasions, the president could be eloquent, at home he would refer to an enemy as "that prick" and would tell off a friend with, "Oh, go screw yourself." While in public Jack treated his wife with enviable courtesy and attention, in private he cheated on her shamelessly. "Despite all the stories I've heard about other past Presidents," Bryant wrote, "I doubt we will ever have another one like Kennedy. I even heard him say to one of his buddies, 'I'm not through with a girl till I've had her three ways.' "[106]

George Smathers later recalled, "There's no question about the fact that Jack had the most active libido of any man I've ever known. He was really unbelievable—absolutely incredible in that regard, and he got more so the longer he was married.'' Smathers remembered that on one occasion Jackie caught her husband making love to a famous movie star. On a birthday cruise with Jackie (five months pregnant) and friends, Jack disappeared with actor David Niven's wife for ten minutes of sex. Smathers said, "It was like a rooster getting on top of a chicken real fast and then the poor little hen ruffles her feathers and wonders what the hell happened to her. Jack was something, almost like a Roto-Rooter."[107]

Insiders knew that Kennedy also enjoyed sex with several staff members. A twenty-one-year-old and a twenty-three-year-old were named "Fiddle" and "Faddle" by the Secret Service. One ostensibly worked for Evelyn Lincoln; the other for Pierre Salinger. Both of the attractive college graduates traveled with the president and often got calls at unusual hours to report for duty. Herbert Parmet later termed the roommates "office amusements."

At one point Peter Lawford brought some amyl nitrate to the White House. Knowing that the drug, called "poppers," was supposed to increase the sexual experience, Jack wanted to try some. Lawford refused, citing the extreme danger involved and warning the president not to take the risk. So Jack gave the drug to Fiddle or Faddle, and both men watched with interest as the young woman fell under the drug's powerful influence, appearing for a time to be hyperventilating. Neither Kennedy nor Lawford worried about the health of the recipient; the experiment satisfied their curiosity.[108]

Pamela Turnure, a twenty-three-year-old beauty who strongly resembled the first lady, was hired by Jackie as a press secretary even though she lacked newspaper experience. The action was taken at Jack's recommendation. "Of course he suggested her," George Smathers said later. "That way she'd be right there in the White House close at hand when he wanted her." Turnure had been Jack's receptionist and frequent bed partner for three years. When asked why Jackie would agree to such an arrangement, Smathers replied, "She figured, 'I'm going to make this so obvious and easy for you that you are going to be bored.' She knew what was going on." Betty Spalding later recalled, "The only indication I ever had that Jackie knew about all of Jack's women was when she asked me if I knew he was having an affair with Pamela Turnure."[109]

Turnure's former landlady, Mrs. Leonard Kater, had known of the relationship from its beginning and possessed a photograph that she claimed showed Kennedy leaving her house early one morning and trying to hide his face. (It could have been of anyone.) She alerted the media and religious and patriotic organizations, and in October 1961 wrote to the attorney general, attempting to expose the ''debaucher of a girl young enough to be his daughter.'' At one point she paraded in front of 1600 Pennsylvania Avenue with a sign asking, ''Do you want an adulterer in the White House?'' She also distributed copies of the purported photograph of the president. The accuser was dismissed as a crank, and her allegation failed to produce any discernible public reaction.[110]

Within the first few months of the administration, however, Jack's clandestine activities had become a source of gossip in Washington. Judith Campbell later reported that by that fall ''countless people'' knew of her affair with the president, including complete strangers who would ask, ''Are *you* the Judy that's going with Jack Kennedy?''[111]

The FBI learned of Campbell in early 1961 by way of a wiretap on John Roselli, one of the Mafia leaders she had met through Frank Sinatra. That fall agents discovered records of the first two of Campbell's seventy telephone calls to Evelyn Lincoln, who arranged the young woman's White House visits. (When asked in 1988 if guests could have entered the Oval Office without their names appearing on the visitors' log, Ron Whealan of the Kennedy Library said, ''There was an unofficial back door to the Oval Office that was supervised by Kenny O'Donnell, and we have no logs on any of those visits.'')[112]

Secret Service agents undoubtedly fretted about admitting numerous playmates into the White House under special presidential orders. But they, of course, kept their worries to themselves. They required several of the frequent visitors, including a number of airline stewardesses, to undergo full Secret Service investigations.

Outside the White House the Secret Service often had to take special precautions to conceal the president's lechery. Since reporters covered the lobby of New York's Carlyle Hotel, agents accompanied Kennedy through a series of tunnels beneath the Carlyle to nearby apartment houses and hotels for additional entertainment. Charles Spalding later recalled, ''It was kind of a weird sight. Jack and I and two Secret Service men walking in these huge tunnels underneath the city streets alongside those enormous pipes, each of us carrying a flashlight. One of the Secret Service men also had this underground map and every once in a while he would say, 'We turn this way, Mr. President.' ''[113]

At one point, according to consultant Langdon Marvin, Jack eluded his agents in New York to reach a party undetected. In doing so, he became separated from the Army officer who followed him with the nation's nuclear codes handcuffed to his wrist. (This separation surely happened more than once during Kennedy's private escapades.) Marvin recalled, "The Russians could have bombed us to hell and back, and there would have been nothing we could have done about it."[114]

Jack's sexual frolics often took little time out of his schedule. Traphes Bryant recalled a young woman saying that Kennedy was the only man she knew who could make love with one eye on his watch. Marilyn Monroe confided to a columnist that Jack would not indulge in foreplay because he lacked the time. When two foreign service advisers bearing a batch of secret cables knocked on the door of the Lincoln Bedroom one summer afternoon, Jack angrily flung the door wide open, revealing a woman in bed. The president quickly cooled down, read the dispatches, made his decisions, and returned to his guest.[115]

When circumstances and the woman warranted it, however, Jack would devote many hours to his romancing. Judith Campbell recalled several largely uninterrupted evenings with the president. "I was always the one who decided it was time to leave. I'd say, 'It's getting late and I really think I should go,' and he'd say, 'Stay a little longer.' " Unlike many other female visitors, Campbell did not stay overnight at the White House. Jack wished otherwise, saying at one point, "If only I could keep you right here, and have you waiting for me when I came back. Then in the morning we could make love before breakfast, and after lunch, of course."

As months passed, Campbell began noticing that the weight of Jack's office grew heavier on his shoulders. "He wasn't as happy-go-lucky, not as relaxed and cheerful. He was somber, sometimes downright solemn. He would drift off into his own private world, and I could feel him a million miles away. He had more important things on his mind."[116]

CHAPTER 12

The First Major Decision

→>> «←

IN HIS SPEECHES and publications, Kennedy often made references to the great American presidents—Lincoln, Washington, the Roosevelts, Wilson, and Jefferson—and identified himself with them. These chief executives, while compelled at times by politics and circumstances to be expedient (even Wilson), were nevertheless men of considerable rectitude.[1] Jack celebrated their integrity, repeatedly proclaiming a connection between sterling character and political greatness. Character, he declared correctly, was a major wellspring of behavior.

But unlike the nation's most admired presidents, Jack in fact lacked a moral code embracing the virtues cherished for centuries by those who linked character and leadership; his sense of right and wrong had been largely shaped by his father and was grounded primarily in a power- and pleasure-seeking ethic. Now in the Oval Office and faced with major questions that would effect the nation and the world, Jack, in order to move closer to the glowing images that had thrilled millions during his campaign, would need to grow in wisdom and virtue. Evidence of such growth might soon be at hand, for Jack had promised to make enormous progress in such areas as poverty and civil rights within his first few months in office. America, he had said repeatedly, was going to come alive. And in order for this renaissance

245

to occur, moral idealism and commitment must come from the White House.

→» «←

Kennedy had never taken much interest in administration, and his style of leadership contrasted sharply with his predecessor's. Eisenhower, a career military man, had created a detailed chain of command, appointed numerous committees, encouraged staff and cabinet meetings, and frequently delegated authority. Assistant to the President Sherman Adams, from 1953 until his resignation in 1958, was widely thought to be the second most important man in the executive branch. His influence was such that Eisenhower reportedly refused to approve policy papers that were not initialed "S. A., O.K."[2]

Jack disliked meetings, group decisions, and organizational charts. Even cabinet meetings, he thought, were a waste of time. The new president abolished numerous committees and positions, including the post once held by Adams. His approach was informal and personal, and he took a direct interest in a wide variety of issues; more than ever, he was eager to learn. Jack used the telephone frequently, confronted people on several levels of government in person, and read countless memos and documents. Kennedy stressed teamwork rather than intramural competition and made it clear to all that he was the coach. Above all he stressed action.

Veteran Washington insider George Ball, Kennedy's under secretary for economic affairs, later observed that the young president seemed present oriented and unconcerned with long-range national issues. "Let's not worry about five years from now," Jack would say. "What do we do tomorrow?" He tended to postpone unpleasant decisions in situations where results were not immediately apparent. Ball found Kennedy "intellectually alert and quick to understand a given problem," but not "profound in either his analysis or his judgement." As for character, Ball did not consider Jack much interested in the right and wrong of things, labeling him "the pragmatist *par excellence*."[3] It was an accurate impression.

Administration officials were excited about the prospects of policymaking power and were convinced that the nation's most difficult problems were no match for their enlightened leadership. Arthur Schlesinger, Jr., later boasted of his colleagues' educational attainments, publication records, and openness to ideas. The New Frontiersmen, he recalled, "swarmed in from state governments, the universities, the foundations, the newspapers, determined to complete the unfinished business of American society. Like [FDR adviser] Rexford G. Tugwell in another age, they proposed to roll up their sleeves and make America over."[4]

Jack knew from the start, however, that the New Frontier would face formidable opposition on Capitol Hill, even though Democrats controlled both houses of Congress. For one thing, his paper-thin margin of victory sharply limited his leverage. For another, the young president did not command the respect of congressional leaders, many of whom continued to think of him as the millionaire playboy they had known as a colleague. Moreover, in 1960, for the first time in this century, the party taking over the White House had lost seats in the House—twenty-two of them. While Democrats still held a commanding majority of 263 to 172, many of them were Southerners or conservatives or both and were opposed to expanding governmental authority and spending. The House Rules Committee, controlled by conservatives, could be counted on to block or slow down House consideration of Kennedy's legislative program.[5]

On the eve of the opening of the 87th Congress, Speaker Sam Rayburn announced that he would try to purge a Mississippi Democrat from the Rules Committee in order to expedite legislative proposals. When that effort failed, Rayburn reverted to an earlier plan, enlarging the size of the committee from twelve to fifteen, hoping to trim the authority of conservative chairman Howard W. Smith of Virginia. The president, who had earlier huddled with Rayburn in Palm Beach, publicly backed the proposal "as an interested citizen." In a move his more cautious predecessor would not have made, he privately telephoned key congressmen and ordered aides to apply pressure. James Reston observed that this was the first real test of Kennedy's effectiveness on Capitol Hill.

Rayburn and the administration won 217 to 212. The Speaker and the president expressed approval, but both knew that the narrow victory, achieved only after an embarrassing postponement to twist more arms, revealed strong resistance to the New Frontier.[6]

In the Senate, meanwhile, liberals tried to make it easier to terminate filibusters. Following six days of debate, Senate leaders sent the proposed reform to the Rules Committee, where it languished for months. Further efforts along this line were unsuccessful.[7]

Kennedy's legislative program was advanced by a congressional liaison team headed by Larry O'Brien. While O'Brien was personally charming and knowledgeable, he and his coworkers had numerous critics, including Congressman Tip O'Neill.[8] Lyndon Johnson provided little or no assistance. Congress rejected his bid, in the first days of the administration, to be the presiding officer of the Senate Democrats, and he withdrew into a shell of self-pity and inactivity. (He said later of his stint as vice president, "I detested every minute of it.")[9]

Kennedy acknowledged privately that much of his campaign rhetoric would not become reality. He knew, despite a flurry of well-publicized presidential activity, that his pledges about "100 days of action" to "get America moving again" would yield little. He told Chalmers Roberts of the *Washington Post* that the public was historically complacent and unlikely to accept self-sacrifice. He also commented on the disproportionate strength Southerners and conservatives enjoyed within the party. (Unwilling to cross swords with some of the most powerful figures in Congress, Kennedy would never become interested in party reform. Liberals were consistently disappointed with the president's cautious approach.)

Then, too, Jack had little personal interest in such domestic issues as agriculture and urban policy. When Anthony Celebrezze—named secretary of health, education, and welfare in 1962—once tried to speak to the president about new legislation, Kennedy dismissed him with, "You were the mayor of a large city. You know how to handle these problems. Now handle them." Historian David Burner later wrote of the President, "He put domestic issues aside whenever he could." Journalist Tom Wicker observed correctly that Kennedy's five priority bills in early 1961 were leftovers from the 1950s, "as familiar in Congress as Sam Rayburn's bald head."[10]

Despite pledges about civil rights initiatives, Jack put new proposals on hold, including a promise to abolish discrimination in federally financed housing by "a stroke of the presidential pen." He told Roy Wilkins, executive director of the NAACP, that while he did not choose to alienate Southern congressmen with a civil rights bill, he would issue executive orders to help blacks. He rejected proposals by Wilkins and Martin Luther King, Jr., for a sweeping executive order banning discrimination in the federal civil service, requiring federal contractors to provide equal employment opportunity, and making nondiscrimination a condition of federally-aided programs.

The only civil rights order issued in 1961 created the President's Committee on Equal Employment Opportunity, headed by Vice President Johnson. It devised a toothless volunteer program to encourage private corporations to reduce job discrimination, a program civil rights groups labeled a hoax. Kennedy, the pragmatic politician, had yet to experience the moral indignation that fueled the civil rights movement. George Ball recalled the president referring to that "goddamn civil rights mess," considering it, in Ball's judgment, "more an embarrassing problem than a serious cause that had gained many proponents."

Still, the president took some steps the black leaders applauded. Robert C. Weaver, president of the NAACP, was named administrator of the Housing and Home Finance Agency, and forty more blacks were selected for important government posts. Sorensen later boasted, "More Negroes were appointed to top Federal jobs than at any time in history—including a Deputy Assistant Secretary of State, an Assistant Secretary of Labor and members of several boards and commissions." The president would also name blacks to five federal judgeships, including the first two within the continental United States. Thurgood Marshall, the NAACP's leading lawyer, would be named to the Court of Appeals.

When federal district judges were appointed in the South, however, Senators from that region usually had their way. Four of the eight named for the Deep South would deliberately obstruct Justice Department efforts to enforce the law. Kennedy's first judicial appointment, William Harold Cox, once referred to blacks in his courtroom as "niggers" and compared them to "chimpanzees."[11]

Early in the administration, Jack admitted privately that one of his prominent campaign issues had been deceptive. When studies revealed that the "missile gap" was a fiction and that the United States in fact enjoyed a marked advantage over the Soviet Union in ballistic missiles, Jack smiled and asked, "Who ever believed in the missile gap anyway?" Journalist Joseph Kraft admitted years later that while he wrote campaign speeches for Kennedy about the "gap," he did not personally believe at any time that it existed. Bobby Kennedy said the same thing when asked.[12]

→>> <<←

From the beginning Kennedy paid close and careful attention to his public image. His initial executive order, for example, issued on his first day in office, directed the secretary of agriculture to double the rations of surplus foods provided by the federal government to some four million needy across the nation. The directive produced headlines portraying the new chief executive as a man of action and compassion. This was also a substantive decision, implementing a promise made during the West Virginia primary.[13]

Kennedy quickly grasped the value of televised press conferences. His first, held in the ampitheater of the new State Department Building on January 25, 1961, was carried live over the nation's television networks. This innovation had been Pierre Salinger's idea, and while some advisers and newsmen had raised objections (James Reston called it "the goofiest idea since the hula hoop"), Jack was confident that the publicity was worth the risk of a slip of the tongue. He was right. The initial conference vaulted him into the living rooms of millions, where his good looks, apparent warmth and self-confidence, and a grasp of much carefully memorized data won many admirers. During his first three months in office, Jack held ten such press conferences.

The president left little to chance and was thoroughly prepared by advisers. Opening statements were worked on at length. Questions were occasionally leaked to Kennedy in advance, and at times he planted questions with friendly reporters. Witty remarks were sometimes the well-timed products of professional comedy writers. Still, Jack undeniably put on a good show. After the Eisenhower years, it all seemed especially refreshing to the press.

Herbert Parmet later observed that "Kennedy brought presidential press conferences into the realm of effective public relations. He sold himself even more than his views." Salinger later commented, "Except for Franklin D. Roosevelt, no President of the modern era has been more expert in public relations than JFK." Sorensen later recalled that after each press conference Jack "always returned pleased with his own performance . . . occasionally resentful of a nasty question, but eager to tune in to watch its rebroadcast, chuckling appreciatively at some of his own answers." After watching one such program, Jack remarked, "We couldn't survive without TV."[14]

More than ever, Jack fussed about his personal appearance, which he knew was a vital part of his public image. He became irritable when cortisone made him appear a bit jowly at press conferences. "Few things interest him more than a discussion of his weight," Ben Bradlee wearily confided to his diary. McGeorge Bundy later recalled seeing "one of his pretty girls" rubbing a lotion of some kind into his hair as he sat in the Oval Office. "He was just terrible about his hair," Bundy added. "He had that damn comb in his pocket and went through that hair at least fifty times a day." (Jackie regularly clipped amusing cartoons of her husband, noting especially how his hair was sketched. She would show them to Jack, no doubt to taunt him about his vanity.) In 1963 Mary Gallagher noticed "that the President's hair had taken on reddish highlights, which gave him a new youthfulness."[15]

The Kennedys and their staff members shrewdly manipulated the media. They wined, dined, flattered, pressured, and bullied reporters and photographers. The president regularly read numerous newspapers and magazines, paying special attention to the coverage he received. Little escaped him, and editors and reporters were often contacted directly by the president to complain about an unflattering story or photograph. "He could find and fret over one paragraph of criticism deep in ten paragraphs of praise,'' Sorensen recalled.[16] One prominent member of a major publication complained, ''We support the President 90 percent of the time. Yet few weeks go by without a call from the White House to call attention to some point to which objection is made. Nothing less than 100 percent support seems to be appreciated.''[17]

Bobby said later that the president found the *New York Times* especially irritating. Every four days Jack would call him and exclaim, ''Did you read what those pricks said today?'' (Bobby then quickly added, ''Not that the President of the United States used that kind of language.'')[18]

Friends were often rewarded with private interviews and inside information. Jack shamelessly manipulated Ben Bradlee of *Newsweek,* giving him stories, classified documents, private correspondence, and even FBI materials in exchange for favorable coverage. When Bradlee played a role in a *Look* magazine article that critically examined the relationship between the president and the press, Jack banished him from the White House and refused to speak to him for five months.[19] Columnist Rowland Evans said later, ''I always had the feeling when I was writing about President Kennedy that he was standing right behind me, watching the words come and waiting to bore in. No question about it, friendship with a president can be a burden on a reporter's professionalism.''[20]

Several reporters resented Jack's heavy-handed tactics. In early 1963, veteran journalist Arthur Krock, who had fallen out with the Kennedys after many years of close personal friendship, declared, ''A news management policy not only exists but, in the form of *direct and deliberate* action, has been enforced more cynically and boldly than by any previous Administration in the period when the U.S. was not in a war or without visible means of regression from the verge of war.''[21]

Kennedy would surpass all other presidents in the number of private and sometimes off-the-record briefings extended to reporters. He would hold twenty-five White House luncheons with the nation's leading publishers on a state-by-state basis, giving a short speech and opening the meeting to questions. (Similar luncheons were held for foreign correspondents.) He could and often did call scores of reporters by name. At one point he told an aide that Hearst reporter Marianne Means wanted to be a columnist, ''so give her some stories. Give her all the help you can.'' One reporter complained, ''He wants us as a cheering squad.'' Sorensen later observed, ''Indeed he did.''[22]

Much to his wife's irritation, Jack encouraged Caroline to talk to reporters, and he permitted numerous photographs to be taken of both children. Charming pictures of little John hiding in the kneehole under the president's desk and of Carolyn on her pony Macaroni helped Kennedy's national popularity to soar. One unfriendly senator, wincing at the opinion polls, exclaimed, "The difference is Caroline, and there's nothing we can do about it."[23]

On several occasions the family was photographed together in an informal setting. The imagery was indelible. In March 1988 a PBS television program on lyricist Alan Jay Lerner and composer Frederick Loewe featured a movie clip showing a warm and relaxed president and first lady playing with their children. The music from *Camelot* could be heard, and a solemn announcer spoke of Kennedy's high ideals.

As early as April 1961 *Life* magazine called Kennedy "the most accessible American President in memory" and ran a series of photographs documenting "the President's expressions and moods during a working day in the White House." Jack seemed solemn, intense, and thoughtful. The text declared: "In his own way Kennedy is emulating the qualities of two predecessors whom he admires most: Theodore Roosevelt's zest and vitality and Franklin D. Roosevelt's complete immersion in the duties of the presidency."[24]

On at least two occasions Kennedy permitted television cameras to follow him around in his daily work. He granted exclusive interviews to television newsmen Walter Cronkite, David Schoenbrun, and others. One network program entitled *Crisis* showed the president and the attorney general in their offices allegedly discussing an actual civil rights matter. In late 1962 *A Conversation with the President* was seen and heard on all television and radio networks, giving Kennedy access to an audience of tens of millions. "Never before," Salinger later wrote, "had the American people had such an intimate glimpse of a President: his personality, his mind at work, his sense of history—and his sense of humor." It was good theater and excellent politics.[25]

→》》　《《←

On January 30, 1961, Jack telephoned his father to remind him to watch his first State of the Union address on television. Then he and Jackie rode to the Capitol. Evelyn Lincoln thought her employer to be in a particularly good mood.[26]

The president's formal tone, however, was somber, and his address presented a bleak picture, both at home and abroad. After some preliminary remarks, he began, "I speak today in an hour of national peril and national opportunity." The next two sentences later drew considerable negative reaction from Republicans: "Before my term has ended, we shall have to test anew whether a nation organized and governed such as ours can endure. The outcome is by no means certain.''

Kennedy expressed deep concern about the economy, which had not fully recovered from the recession of 1958, and he cited several areas, such as the cities and schools, in need of greater federal assistance. Overshadowing his domestic considerations, however, were his fears about national defense and the worldwide spread of communism. ''Each day the crises multiply. Each day we draw nearer the hour of maximum danger, as weapons spread and hostile forces grow stronger. . . . The tide of events has been running out and time has not been our friend.''

In language that Bruce Miroff later said ''verged on the apocalyptic,'' Kennedy called for a massive military buildup, including steps to increase the nation's missile, nuclear submarine, and airlift capacity. He made special mention of Fidel Castro's Cuba, with which the Eisenhower administration had recently broken diplomatic relations. Communists had secured a base only ninety miles from our shores, he said, a development that was intolerable. ''Communist domination in this hemisphere can never be negotiated. We are pledged to work with our sister Republics to free the Americas of all such foreign domination and all tyranny.'' In case Soviet Premier Nikita Khrushchev missed the hostile tone of the address, Kennedy announced new programs to promote ''the ultimate freedom and welfare of the Eastern European peoples.''

The president softened his remarks at times, calling for a new Alliance for Progress in Latin America, an expanded food-for-peace program, and a national Peace Corps, ''enlisting the services of all those with the desire and capacity to help foreign lands meet their urgent needs for trained personnel.''

His closing comments, however, were grim: ''Our problems are critical. The tide is unfavorable. The news will be worse before it is better. And while hoping and working for the best, we should prepare ourselves now for the worst.''[27]

Several observers were puzzled by the president's grave posture. Some particularly questioned his harsh stance toward the Soviet Union so early in the administration. James Reston expressed surprise that Kennedy would raise the ''delicate question'' of Eastern Europe, for Khrushchev had complained bitterly to Richard Nixon about the congressional resolution on the ''liberation'' of the ''captive nations'' in 1959.[28]

Any explanation, of course, must take into account Kennedy's virulent anti-communism, largely an ideological commitment. Also part of the equation, however, was Jack's macho outlook, drummed into the Kennedy males almost from birth and an integral part of their value system. It was vital for Jack to demonstrate that though he was young, he was tough. *(New York Times* headline: A TOUGHER KENNEDY.)

Of special importance at this point was the president's reaction to a speech delivered by Khrushchev on January 6 announcing that the world was moving inexorably toward socialism and endorsing "wars of national liberation" to push history along. Jack had his entire staff read the speech, convinced that Khrushchev was determined to bring the free world to its knees—and soon.[29]

Indeed, Kennedy was faced from the start of his administration with Communist activity in Laos, South Vietnam, and the Congo. Each trouble spot, in Sorensen's words, held "dire predictions of catastrophe before the year was out." As he warned Congress and the world of future challenge and turmoil, Jack may well also have had in mind the secret CIA operations against Castro.[30]

→》》　《《←

In the weeks and months that followed, the president's lack of a coherent and deeply committed legislative agenda became clear as he submitted numerous domestic proposals to Congress. Liberal journalist Tom Wicker expressed the views of many when he judged them stale and timid. The public, largely self-satisfied and content, showed little interest. Congress was largely unresponsive. And the president failed to be aggressive. Walter Heller said later that Kennedy lacked confidence in his ability to move things through Congress.

There was also the question of commitment. Chester Bowles, who had accompanied Jack on numerous meetings with labor and civil rights groups during the campaign, later recalled, "On almost every occasion he was uneasy and occasionally contentious, as though uncomfortable with the demands put upon him to demonstrate his liberal credentials by a show of emotional commitment to liberalism, a commitment he did not possess." Bowles, one of the nation's most prominent liberals, complained repeatedly in his autobiography of the Kennedy administration's lack of "a consistent framework of firm moral principle." During the campaign Jack had made hundreds of promises in order to win votes; almost everyone was promised something. Now, in the White House, his lack of an authentic sense of moral concern was obvious, at least to many insiders.[31]

Still the administration could boast of several achievements early in 1961. Kennedy's second executive order created the Food-for-Peace office. Designed to combat world hunger, the program was not new, but under the initial leadership of George McGovern it became effective.

Arthur Schlesinger would call it "the great unseen weapon of Kennedy's third world policy." Shipments averaged nearly $1.5 billion annually during the Kennedy years. National self-interest was also involved: The program helped reduce American agricultural surpluses and, since American ships were exclusively employed, to stimulate the nation's maritime industry.[32]

On March 1 the president issued an executive order creating the Peace Corps on a temporary basis. Congress passed enabling legislation six months later. In 1957 Wisconsin Congressman Henry S. Reuss had first proposed sending trained volunteers overseas to assist developing nations with their economic and social problems. Hubert Humphrey had introduced a Peace Corps bill in the Senate in mid-1960. (Eisenhower labeled the proposal a "juvenile experiment"; Richard Nixon warned that the corps could create "a haven for draft dodgers.") Jack adopted the proposal "a little tentatively" (to use Schlesinger's words) that fall, after discovering that college students greeted it warmly. He did not broach it in a formal campaign speech until six days before the election.

All Americans were now eligible to apply. Those accepted would be volunteers who lived in primitive conditions among the people they served. The Peace Corps, Sorensen later boasted, "represented the highest response to [Kennedy's] Inaugural injunction to 'ask not.' " R. Sargent Shriver became the first director on March 4. Jack said ("only half facetiously" according to Chester Bowles) that he appointed his brother-in-law so that when the Peace Corps failed it would be easier to fire its director. In fact, although it was a tiny effort in relation to other federal programs, the corps would turn out to be one of the administration's most successful—and newsworthy—projects. By the end of 1961, nearly one thousand volunteers were serving, and the president called them "a cross-section of the finest men and women that this nation has to offer."[33]

On March 13, at a White House reception for Latin American diplomats, Kennedy repeated a campaign proposal calling for an Alliance for Progress, a cooperative effort "unparalleled in magnitude and nobility of purpose, to satisfy the basic needs of the American people for homes, work and land, health and schools." The president then described ten steps he was taking to bolster Latin American economic development, education, inter-American cooperation, and democracy, including a request to Congress for half a billion dollars. "Let us once again awaken our American revolution," he concluded, "until it guides the struggles of people everywhere—not with an imperialism of force or fear—but the rule of courage and freedom and hope for the future of man."

While the idealism in his proposal was undeniable, Kennedy's anti-communism was also apparent. Few in the audience could fail to see the specter of Fidel Castro in much of what was said. New Dealer Adolf Berle, who headed a Kennedy task force on Latin America, was drawing a parallel between the Alliance and the Marshall Plan. Kennedy would later refer to the Alliance as a program "I believe can successfully counter the Communist onslaught in this hemisphere."[34]

⇢⟫ ⟪⟵

Castro had taken over the government of Cuba in January 1959. The charismatic attorney who called himself "the Maximum Leader" had led a small, middle-class guerrilla band to victory over a corrupt and brutal regime headed by Fulgencio Batista. Though Castro was known to be a left-wing intellectual, an ardent nationalist, and a political opportunist, he did not appear to be a Communist. (He later boasted that he had secretly been a "Marxist-Leninist" from his earliest guerrilla warfare days.) The Eisenhower administration, which had dissociated itself from Batista the previous March, quickly extended diplomatic recognition.

Within a few months, however, Communists were firmly entrenched in the Cuban government. By the end of the year, it was clear that a Marxist dictatorship ruled the nation, and Eisenhower approved a State Department recommendation to begin a secret war against Castro.

In February 1960 the president embargoed all arms shipments from the United States to Cuba. In March he secretly approved a CIA program called Operation Pluto that recommended, among other things, the creation of a Cuban government in exile and "a paramilitary force outside . . . Cuba for future guerrilla action." Guatemala, which the CIA had helped liberate from a leftist regime in 1954, was soon selected as the training site for the troops.

In April, fully aware of the plot, Castro publicly denounced the planned attack on his government. By this time the CIA was openly recruiting volunteers in Miami and New York. In July Nikita Khrushchev offered Soviet military support in the event of an invasion. Eisenhower soon signed legislation that reduced the Cuban sugar quota and eliminated it altogether for 1961. The president admitted that this amounted to economic sanctions.

Meanwhile the CIA quietly designed plans to destroy Castro's popular image. Schemes included dusting his shoes with a powder that would cause his beard to fall out and impregnating his cigars with a chemical that would produce temporary disorientation. The CIA also initiated the first of at least eight attempts on Castro's life.

In August Mafia leaders John Roselli, Sam Giancana, and Santos

Trafficante were recruited to assassinate Castro. The mobsters signed up with the CIA not only for the $150,000 bounty but also for the possibility of restoring the extremely lucrative gambling, drug, and prostitution operations they had enjoyed under Batista. The initial plan involved poison pills.

Mindful of the economic as well as the political mischief Castro might export, and smarting over the expropriation of American properties, Eisenhower quietly approved an expanded budget for the envisioned military action. He also authorized the use of Defense Department personnel and equipment to train anti-Castro Cubans. He drew the line, however, at the use of American combat troops. This reservation disappointed Richard Nixon, strongly anti-Castro and eager for some sort of spectacular event before the election.[35]

Kennedy had met several exile leaders just before the Democratic Convention. Afterward Allen Dulles briefed him on the military operation being planned by the CIA. During the campaign Jack used harsh language against Castro, implied that the Eisenhower administration was soft on the Reds, and then, after the last television debate, declared publicly, "I have never advocated and I do not advocate intervention in Cuba in violation of our treaty obligations."[36]

On November 18 Allen Dulles and Richard Bissell, the CIA's deputy for planning, called on the president-elect at Palm Beach. By this time the guerrilla action had been transformed into an amphibious invasion complete with a tiny rebel air force and naval task force. Bissell, the author of Operation Pluto and the man in charge of recruiting Mafia assassins, did most of the talking.

Richard Mervin Bissell, Jr. was exactly the sort of person capable of winning Kennedy's trust. He had gone to Groton and Yale and had been a college classmate of columnist Joe Alsop. He held a doctorate in economics from Yale, and there and at MIT his students included Walt Rostow and McGeorge and William Bundy. Brilliant, imperious, daring, aggressive, articulate, charming, and pragmatic, Bissell clearly had the credentials to be ranked among the "brightest and best."

Bissell had joined the CIA in 1954 and became a central figure in the successful Guatemalan putsch and in the U-2 spy plane project. He was just the man to present the CIA's plan for Castro to the young president-elect. Alsop later called him "a terrific dominator," and Rusk said he was "a persuasive briefer." Alsop had introduced Bissell to Kennedy before the election, and not long afterward Jack was talking about Bissell as Dulles's eventual successor.[37]

Jack was not trapped by events, as some later claimed. He could have discouraged the CIA at this time and curtailed the operation after taking office. Instead, he expressed approval, and Dulles left Florida prepared to step up the CIA's efforts.[38]

According to Sorensen, who got his information later from Kennedy, the CIA, then and in the next few months, made a persuasive case. For one thing, officials wanted to know in effect if Kennedy was going to be as strongly anti-Communist as the Republicans and help freedom-loving exiles rid the hemisphere of Reds. Jack's virulent anti-communism, his penchant for "toughness," his love of intrigue, and his commitment to victory at any cost virtually dictated his approval. Character, ideology, and policy almost automatically converged. Moreover, Jack still reveled in the euphoria of his election victory. The liberation of Cuba by a small band of freedom fighters would surely be but another chapter in the Kennedy success story.[39]

The CIA argued that the invasion had to be undertaken soon, while military conditions were right and before Castro could build up his armed forces with Soviet aid. Kennedy was assured that Castro could be toppled quietly, swiftly, with no risk of direct American involvement, and with little risk of failure. As in Guatemala, the United States could get away with it.[40]

As early as October 30, 1960, word of the training of Cuban exiles in Guatemala leaked into the Latin American press. In its November 19 issue, the *Nation* carried an editorial on the subject. By this time the State Department was reporting Soviet bloc arms pouring into Cuba. Cuban President Osvaldo Dorticos Torrado told reporters that Cuba intended to draw closer to the Communist nations, as "We are not optimistic about the United States. And we have no choice." He specifically expressed fear of an American invasion.[41]

On January 2, following a huge display of Soviet-bloc weaponry, Castro told a cheering, chanting crowd of 100,000 in Havana that "all the people of the world" would be involved in war if the United States attacked Cuba. The premier predicted that invasion was "imminent," and hundreds of thousands of militia were put on alert. The Eisenhower administration soon responded to the demand that it drastically reduce its embassy staff by breaking diplomatic relations.[42]

On January 5 the *New York Times* reported preparations by anti-Castro Cubans to invade from "some place in the Western Hemisphere—definitely not in the United States." Said one exile leader, "I expect to be in Cuba beginning in February." Cuban foreign minister Raul Roa soon told the United Nations Security Council that the Eisenhower administration had "approved the sinister plan of the Central Intelligence

Agency to create conditions for military aggression against the Government and people of Cuba." The Fair Play for Cuba Committee, an American organization, quickly called for a Congressional investigation of a possible CIA role in setting up "mysterious training camps" in Guatemala and in the "training of invasion forces in Florida and Nicaragua."[43]

All over Cuba thousands of troops and civilian militia awaited an invasion. Massive American naval maneuvers nearby fed tensions. Hundreds of suspected "counterrevolutionists" were reportedly arrested. Children played "Cubans and Yankee invaders" instead of "cowboys and Indians." A Cuban army plane was accidentally shot down amid the hysteria.[44]

On January 10 the *New York Times* ran a front-page story describing the military preparations in Guatemala and containing such details as the length of the airstrip used by unmarked planes. American officials refused comment, and the State Department press officer told reporters that he knew "absolutely nothing" about a base in Guatemala.[45]

When Eisenhower and Kennedy met at the White House on January 19 for a final briefing, the second question raised by the president-elect concerned United States support of anti-Castro guerrillas. Eisenhower endorsed the activities in Guatemala and said of Cuba, "we cannot let the present government there go on." (Jack soon expressed this same view in his State of the Union address.) He urged Kennedy to continue the current search for a leader "who was both anti-Batista and anti-Castro" to head a government-in-exile. Then, when the invasion of Cuba occurred at some-as-yet unspecified date, "it would have the appearance of a more legitimate operation." Clark Clifford, who took notes, saw no "reluctance or hesitation" on Eisenhower's part to pursue the overthrow of Castro.[46]

We do not know if Eisenhower was aware of the CIA's agreement with Mafia leaders to assassinate the Cuban premier. Allen Dulles knew, and he presumably briefed the president. But such matters were handled with great care so that they could not be directly tied to the chief of state. The phrase "plausibly deniable" dates from the Eisenhower administration. Stephen Ambrose, Eisenhower's most impressive biographer, doubts that the president was involved. An order to Dulles to proceed along that line, Ambrose states, would have been "out of character."[47]

It was not out of character for Eisenhower's successor to proceed. Kennedy, it is now all but certain, both knew and approved of the conspiracy to murder Castro.

Arthur Schlesinger, Jr., in his *Robert Kennedy and His Times,* makes an elaborate defense of both Jack and Bobby, contending that they knew nothing of the matter before the Bay of Pigs invasion. On May 7, 1962, the attorney general learned formally of the CIA-Giancana effort and was informed, incorrectly, that it had ended. That, Schlesinger states, was the full extent of things. The historian's zeal is such that he argues in his conclusion that the Kennedys were far too moral—and Catholic— to have countenanced such behavior.

Schlesinger's predictable partisanship aside, he does build an appealing case. He cites the fact, for example, that we lack proof of any CIA discussion with the president of Castro's assassination. He notes that Rusk, McNamara, Bundy, Rostow, and several other administration leaders later testified under oath of their ignorance of the CIA plot. He described an interesting interview between the president and Tad Szulc, the *New York Times* Latin American correspondent, in November 1961, in which Jack brought up the subject of Castro's assassination, noted that he was "under terrific pressure from advisers . . . to okay a Castro murder," and then expressed the view that he and his brother thought it morally wrong. Schlesinger also quotes the recollection of a CIA official that Bobby seemed upset upon hearing in May 1962 that the CIA had used Giancana.[48]

Part of Schlesinger's case is based on argument from silence, which of course is inconclusive when applied to presidents of this period, especially Jack, whose love of intrigue was a basic part of his character. One would not expect to find memoranda between the CIA and the president on plans to murder another chief of state. But who were the "advisers" trying, according to Kennedy, to persuade him to approve a Castro assassination? Szulc's notes reported, "(think he said intelligence people, but not positive)."

It seems clear, understandably, that the CIA plot was a carefully guarded secret. That surely explains much of the testimony cited by Schlesinger from leading administration officials who said they knew nothing about it. Secrecy was common in the Kennedy White House. Ted Sorensen did not know about the Bay of Pigs invasion until after it was over. Even Bobby later stated that he was brought in on the invasion planning only four or five days before the launching. Jack's closest aides were stunned in February 1982 to learn that the president had taped 325 White House conversations; he had not told them. Arthur Schlesinger, Jr. initially denied that the tapes existed, calling the idea "absolutely inconceivable" and adding: "It was not the sort of thing Kennedy would have done." (Most of the tapes are carefully kept from historians by the Kennedy Library.)[49]

Then, too, Schlesinger's account ignores the Kennedys' acting ability. Tad Szulc was hardly a man with whom to be frank; his stories in the *New York Times* prior to the invasion of Cuba were far too revealing for the president's comfort. Surely Jack knew that he was speaking for the record while declaring his high sense of morality. Bobby would have been foolish not to seem surprised when told officially of the link between the CIA and a mob leader he was trying to put behind bars. He played the same role, apparently, when talking of the matter with J. Edgar Hoover.

The attorney general was no stranger to his brother's relationship with Giancana and Roselli. As Jack's campaign manager in 1960, he was surely aware of the Mafia's contributions to the Kennedy victory. Moreover, Hoover had already informed Bobby in writing of the triangle between the president's mistress, Judith Campbell, and the two mobsters. The FBI director had already called on the president, apparently to warn him about the dangerous dalliance with Campbell. Extremely close as Jack and Bobby were, it is hard to believe that Hoover's visit went unmentioned.

Even in Schlesinger's account there is evidence that Bobby knew more about the CIA plots against Castro than he let on. Kennedy aide Frank Mankiewicz is quoted as saying, "He told me that there was some crazy CIA plan at one time for sending some Cubans in to get Castro which he called off." This and two similar statements by Kennedy loyalists imply knowledge and activity that exceeded the simple reaction on May 1962.

John H. Davis has called the assassination of Castro "the very linchpin" of the plan to invade Cuba; Schlesinger (sensing that Richard Nixon was somehow to blame) labeled it "an integral part." Bissell later admitted that he was hopeful "that Castro would be dead before the landing." Precisely: The premier was supposed to be in his grave when the invaders hit the beach. Two attempts on Castro's life were made just before the landing. Afterward the effort was suspended. It is difficult to accept the contention that the president was unaware of this part of the project.

It is also exceedingly difficult to suppose that Dulles acted entirely on his own authority in ordering the murder of a foreign chief of state. Bissell and his successor Richard Helms later testified that they believed Dulles had informed Kennedy. Three senators who studied the matter in 1975 held similar views. Thomas Powers's impressive *The Man Who Kept the Secrets: Richard Helms and the CIA* concluded that Kennedy knew exactly what the agency was doing.

George Smathers was with the president on the White House lawn when Jack asked him what he thought the public reaction would be should Castro be assassinated. Smathers later reported, "He was certain it could be accomplished—I remember that—it would be no problem." (Smathers added that Kennedy said he was against it.) After the invasion Jack met secretly with the Cuban national who had been assigned by the Mafia leaders to kill Castro—no doubt to ask what had gone wrong. How did the president know whom to contact if he was unaware of the plot?[50]

Moreover, we now know that Jack was engaged in a clandestine association with Sam Giancana, a relationship that began during the 1960 campaign and continued after the Bay of Pigs invasion. By the time Kennedy installed his desk in the Oval Office, Judith Campbell, at Jack's request, had already arranged several secret meetings between the two men. A few days after the Cuban invasion, she became a courier of messages between them. Several months later, the CIA–Mafia efforts to kill Castro formally resumed. (Schlesinger hurriedly passes over Campbell and her important revelations in *My Story,* preferring to quote her first husband, "B" actor William Campbell, to the effect that the woman was not very bright.)

What could the President and the Mafia leader have been so eager to discuss beyond the assassination of Castro? Campbell, who did not open the envelopes she carried, later feared that she was at the heart of the plot. She may well have been correct.[51]

→>>   <<←

Two days after the inauguration, top Kennedy administration officials were engaged in planning Castro's downfall. At a National Security Council meeting on January 28, Kennedy ordered the Joint Chiefs of Staff to review the military aspects of an American-supported invasion. He also authorized continued U-2 flights over Cuba and the continuation of the CIA operations already underway. The State Department was told to prepare the isolation and containment of Cuba through the normally pliable Organization of American States. The president may have been "wary and reserved," as Schlesinger later contended, but his commitment seemed clear.[52]

Castro now had a good idea what to expect. The day after the State of the Union address, Havana radio declared, "President Kennedy has taken off the mask. This is a new attack on Cuba by the United States." Soon the entire mass media in Cuba began a campaign to warn the nation and other Latin American countries of an impending armed attack by "Yankee imperialism." Castro dared the Cuban exiles to invade, boasting of the huge arsenal obtained from Communist nations. The State

Department rejected a tentative offer by Argentina to mediate the dispute between the United States and Cuba.[53]

Planning continued in Washington throughout February. Several factors appeared to warrant haste. The rainy season was imminent in the Caribbean, and the mud would plague troops. Dulles and Bissell warned of the impending arrival of Soviet MIG fighter planes accompanied by Czech-trained Cuban pilots. The president of Guatemala, embarrassed by publicity, informed Kennedy that he would like the exiles out of his country by the end of April. The exiles themselves were clamoring for action. Bissell told Kennedy repeatedly, "You can't mañana this thing."[54]

On March 11 Bissell and Dulles met with the president, the National Security Council, and several others, including Schlesinger. Both CIA officials argued strongly for prompt action against Cuba. Bissell advocated a landing at the South Central coastal town of Trinidad, a target favored by the Joint Chiefs. He contended that if the invasion failed to produce an expected anti-Castro revolt, the assault troops could become guerrillas in nearby mountains. Dulles said that if the proposed invasion was not carried out, the administration would be faced with frustrated and angry troops roaming around the country embarrassing it and the CIA. Did the administration, he asked, want anti-Communists here and abroad to think it had lost its nerve? Dulles, a longtime friend of the Kennedy family, knew exactly how to appeal to the new president.[55]

Kennedy agreed with the overall concept of invasion, but he requested new planning that would envision something less spectacular—a quiet landing, preferably at night. The CIA officials realized that this stealthy approach would greatly decrease the chances for the armed uprisings they predicted would break out all over Cuba at the news of a dramatic landing. But they said nothing, intent on obtaining presidential consent for the venture.

Kennedy also insisted that the plans stipulate that there be no American military intervention. No one in the room objected. Schlesinger later thought that the advocates simply could not believe that if events turned sour, Kennedy would refuse to come to the aid of the freedom fighters. Dulles later confirmed the accuracy of this view in his private papers: "We felt when the chips were down—when the crisis arose in reality, any action required for success would be authorized rather than permit the enterprise to fail."[56]

Working in haste, CIA planners took three days to come up with a new landing site: the Bay of Pigs, one hundred miles west of Trinidad. It was a thinly inhabited, swampy area that would, it was thought, require less air cover to invade. On March 15 the Joint Chiefs of Staff accepted the proposal. The following day Bissell presented it to the president, arguing that the new plan offered less risk. Kennedy authorized the CIA to proceed. However, he repeated his unwillingness to involve American troops and retained the right to cancel the operation up to twenty-four hours before it was scheduled to take place.[57]

Jack was wary of the CIA's continued hope of civilian uprisings, but neither he nor his advisers realized that the Bay of Pigs plan virtually ruled it out. "We all in the White House," Schlesinger wrote later, "considered uprisings behind the lines essential to the success of the operation; so too did the Joint Chiefs of Staff; and so, we thought, did the CIA." Kennedy also did not know that the Joint Chiefs had reservations about the site and continued to prefer Trinidad. This view was transmitted to Secretary of Defense McNamara, but he failed for some reason to tell the president. Thereafter, faced with the determination of Kennedy and the CIA to rid Cuba of Communists, the military leaders chose the path of the least resistance: compliance and silence.

Bissell and Dulles did not tell the president and his advisers—nor, incredibly, the exile leaders—that under the new plan the invaders would be unable to escape to the mountains in case of disaster; nearly eighty miles of roadless swamps and a hostile city lay between the Bay of Pigs and the foothills of the Escambrays. "I don't think we fully realized that," Schlesinger later admitted.[58]

News of the impending invasion began to appear regularly in American newspapers and magazines. Reporters sought out Cuban refugees wherever they could be found and published whatever could be learned. On March 15 Cuba's foreign minister told the United Nations that the United States was guilty of "illegal, perfidious and premeditated" aggressions. He accused Kennedy by name of encouraging "preparations for the invasion of Cuba," an invasion, he said a few days later, that was "imminent."[59]

Not everyone around Kennedy was oblivious to the disaster that was looming. Schlesinger sent a memorandum to the president in February arguing that an invasion would harm the administration's image. On March 30 Senator William Fulbright of Arkansas, chairman of the Foreign Relations Committee, personally delivered a memorandum to the president minimizing Castro's significance and contending that the invasion would violate the charter of the Organization of American States, signed in 1948, some hemisphere treaties, and our own federal laws:

To give this activity even covert support is of a piece with the hypocrisy and cynicism for which the United States is constantly denouncing the Soviet Union in the United Nations and elsewhere. This point will not be lost on the rest of the world—nor on our own consciences.

The entire project had been poorly thought out, Fulbright stated, and was hardly a secret. Even if successful, the invasion "would be denounced from the Rio Grande to Patagonia as an example of imperialism."[60]

Chester Bowles was appalled to learn of what he called "the Cuban adventure" while serving as acting secretary of state in Dean Rusk's absence overseas. On March 31 he gave Rusk a lengthy memorandum outlining his vigorous objections. His concern, he wrote, stemmed in considerable degree "from a deep personal conviction that our national interests are poorly served by a covert operation of this kind at a time when our new President is effectively appealing to world opinion on the basis of high principle." He was especially disturbed by the fact that an invasion would violate the OAS charter. "We cannot expect the benefits of treaties if we are unwilling to accept the limitations they impose on our freedom to act." Rusk seemed unmoved, and he discouraged Bowles from making his case directly to the president. Kennedy did not see the memo.[61]

The decisive meeting on the Bay of Pigs project was scheduled for April 4. In the meantime Jack flew to Palm Beach for Easter. On his return, according to Schlesinger, he seemed "more militant than when he left." This new aggressiveness might well have been attributable to the ambassador, never one to avoid a fight or pay heed to the idealistic whimperings of eggheads and liberals.[62]

Kennedy invited Fulbright to attend the climactic meeting. After presentations by Bissell and Dulles on combat preparations, in which they gave highly favorable odds for success, the president began asking everyone whether they approved of the invasion. Rank and experience were ignored; each person had an equal vote. Fulbright denounced the entire idea on the ground that it was inherently immoral. Everyone else in the room, including Rusk; McNamara, who had devoted much time and study to the matter; Adolf Berle, the State Department specialist on Latin America; and once-skeptical Thomas Mann, recently named ambassador to Mexico, appeared to approve the CIA proposal. Berle, in fact, was highly enthusiastic: "I say, 'let 'er rip!' "

Schlesinger, much to his later regret, remained silent during the meeting. He later thought a great deal of the acquiescence involved the unwillingness of participants to appear "soft." "To oppose the plan, one had to invoke intangibles—the moral position of the United States, the reputation of the President, the response of the United Nations, 'world public opinion' and other such odious concepts.'' Several said later that they simply wanted to close ranks with the president. McNamara would later testify that the administration was "hysterical" about Castro at the time.[63]

A few days later Kennedy decided to go ahead with the Bay of Pigs operation. Bobby told Schlesinger, who had recently submitted two memoranda to the president opposing the plan, to forget his opposition. It was now time to back the chief executive. Jack soon voiced his impatience with doubters by equating them with cowards. Just before the invasion he told Sorensen, "I know everybody is grabbing their nuts on this."[64]

In early April the *New York Times* ran lengthy front-page stories describing in detail the proposed military strategies and policy discussions within the administration. One quoted from the OAS charter, making the point that the document ruled out direct or indirect intervention. It also cited State Department estimates that in the past nine months, Cuba had accepted thirty thousand tons of arms, valued at more than fifty million dollars, from Communist countries. Nine days before the scheduled landing, Dr. Jose Miro Cardona, leader of the Cuban Revolutionary Council in exile, told newsmen in Miami that an uprising against Castro was "imminent." The next day he appealed to all Cubans still in the homeland to take up arms against the premier.[65]

Pierre Salinger later wrote of "the least covert military operation in history" and complained, "The only information Castro didn't have . . . was the exact time and place of the invasion." Jack was furious about the leaks, telling Salinger at one point, "I can't believe what I'm reading! Castro doesn't need agents over here. All he has to do is read our papers. It's all laid out for him." Kennedy managed to suppress one revealing article written for the *New Republic*. Schlesinger, to whom the article had first been sent, gave it to the president after having been "defeated by the moral issue" of censorship. Jack had no qualms.[66]

The administration also pressured the *New York Times* to water down some of its articles, seeking, among other things, elimination of references to the CIA. It planted false information in several stories. Multiple guerrilla landings were said to be the choice over an attempted large-scale invasion. Cardona told reporters that a major invasion would be a "tremendous mistake."[67]

On April 11, during a nationwide television interview, Jack made a revealing slip. While responding to a question about Schlesinger's recent tour of Latin America, he said, "I think Latin America is in a most crucial period in its relation with us. Therefore if we don't move now, Mr. Castro may become a greater danger than he is today." Salinger later told reporters that the president had referred to a move to aid Latin American nations and had not spoken of a direct move against the Castro regime.[68]

At his news conference the next day, Kennedy gave a firm pledge that United States armed forces would not intervene in Cuba "under any circumstances":

> The basic issue in Cuba is not one between the United States and Cuba. It is between the Cubans themselves. I intend to see that we adhere to that principle and as I understand it this administration's attitude is so understood by the anti-Castro exiles from Cuba in this country.

When asked if the United States was barred by its neutrality acts or by the OAS treaty from giving aid or arms to anti-Castro elements within its borders, Jack evaded the question.[69]

A Cuban exile leader soon told reporters, "We have repeatedly said that we are not thinking of invading Cuba from any point, and least of all from the United States. The fight will be produced inside Cuba by Cubans themselves."[70] In fact, the earliest stages of the assault on the Bay of Pigs had already begun.

On April 14 the president addressed the Council of the Organization of American States, declaring piously that the body "represents a great dream of those who believe that the people of this hemisphere must be bound more closely together."[71]

That same day, after reading a report from a veteran Marine colonel expressing total confidence in some fourteen hundred troops waiting in Guatemala, Kennedy dispelled whatever doubts he may have retained about the Cuban invasion. "The Brigade officers do not expect help from U.S. Armed Forces," the report concluded. "They ask only for continued delivery of supplies. This can be done covertly. [The] Cuban Air Force is motivated, strong, well-trained, armed to the teeth, and ready." Jack gave the order for the air stage of the attack to begin the next day.[72]

The sea and air invasion was to be launched from Nicaragua, with the blessing of the friendly dictator Luis Somoza. Two air strikes were planned: the first two days before the invasion while the six small troop ships were under way, and the second over the beachhead on the day of the invasion. Jack told Bissell that he wanted the initial air strike to be on a "minimal" scale, and the number of planes involved was reduced from sixteen to six. To conceal American participation, the pilots in the first raids were to pretend to be defectors from Castro's air force. Their planes were painted accordingly. One pilot was to fly directly from Nicaragua to Miami in a bullet-pierced plane to give the CIA cover story to the press.

On the morning of April 15 six elderly B-26 bombers supplied by the United States attacked three Cuban air bases. Only five planes, less than half of Castro's air force, were destroyed. The pilot in Miami said that he and three other defectors had planned the raid and stolen the planes. Complicating matters, a B-26 hit by ground fire made an emergency landing in Key West. Immigration officials immediately threw a cloak of secrecy over the pilots from both planes.

The White House denied any knowledge of the events beyond what appeared in screaming headlines. (Rusk had told Bowles he doubted that the entire operation would make the front page of the *New York Times*.) The Pentagon and State Department would not comment. Rebel leaders in Miami boasted publicly that the raids were part of an overall plan to bring about the downfall of Castro.

The Cuban premier guessed immediately that the attack was a prelude to an invasion and that the United States was behind it. He put the nation on full military alert and declared angrily, "Our country has been the victim of a criminal imperialistic attack which violates all the norms of international law." The entire foreign diplomatic corps in Havana was summoned and shown fragments of what a Cuban official described as rockets bearing the inscription "U.S.A."[73]

Castro now had forty-eight hours to prepare for the tiny flotilla of semitrained recruits. (Only about 135 of the 1,400 men were soldiers. Some recent volunteers had not even fired a gun.) With about 240,000 regulars and militia available, vast stores of weapons on hand, and three T-33 jet trainers, among other planes that survived the raids, he appeared easily capable of defending himself—unless the United States became directly involved. He also began rounding up some 100,000 suspects, thus eliminating any hope of an uprising. The first air strikes, as Trumbull Higgins later observed, had given the United States many of the disadvantages of a new Pearl Harbor without gaining the strategic advantages of that surprise attack.[74]

Cuban Foreign Minister Raúl Roa quickly charged in the United Nations that the United States was responsible for the bombing raids and was planning a large-scale invasion. Adlai Stevenson rejected Roa's charges "categorically" as "without foundation" and repeated the CIA cover story, even reading the statement issued by the pilot in Miami and holding up a photograph of one of the planes. "It has the markings of Castro's air force on the tail, which everyone can see for himself."

Stevenson had been briefed in general terms on Cuba by Schlesinger and a CIA agent. He strongly opposed an invasion but was led to believe, "inadvertently" according to Schlesinger, that the operation would not begin until after the General Assembly adjourned. His reaction to Roa was entirely sincere.

Kennedy had not consulted with Stevenson about Cuba despite earlier assurances from Rusk that the U.N. ambassador would "play a key role" in the formulation of foreign policy. Jack well knew that the liberal leader would object, fussing and fuming a lot about morality and justice. Schlesinger, despite his liberal credentials, had demonstrated a willingness to get on the team, and thus he could be trusted. Stevenson would surely play the preacher. To the Kennedys a daring and patriotic object like Operation Pluto was for men, not bleeding hearts.[75]

On Saturday afternoon, April 15, the president flew to his Virginia retreat at Glen Ora, pretending that this was just another weekend. Dulles went on a speaking engagement to Puerto Rico to feign noninvolvement. On Sunday at 1:45 P.M., after a bout of indecision on the local golf course, Kennedy gave his final authorization for the landing at the Bay of Pigs. It was his first major presidential decision.

Meanwhile reporters were beginning to poke holes in the CIA cover story. They wondered especially why American authorities continued to withhold the identities of the rebel pilots in Florida. In a speech at services for soldiers killed in the raid, Castro thundered, "If President Kennedy has one atom of decency, he will present the planes and pilots before the United Nations. If not, then the world has a right to call him a liar."[76]

Sensing trouble, Dean Rusk persuaded Kennedy to cancel the second air strike, which was supposed to appear to be coming from Cuban defectors on the beach airstrip. The secretary of state feared that the planes would betray American participation. He also worried about the uproar the first raid produced in the United Nations. CIA officials, certain that the entire project was now doomed, argued and pleaded in vain to reverse the decision. Several military leaders were badly shaken. One colonel shouted at a general, "This is criminally negligent!" General Lyman L. Lemnitzer, chairman of the Joint Chiefs, later called the president's action "absolutely reprehensible, almost criminal." Also vetoed was a proposal to provide air cover from the United States carrier *Essex*, in nearby international waters ostensibly participating in routine maneuvers. Jack, by this time, was becoming seriously worried about being found out.[77]

He was somehow blind to the obvious: Direct American military involvement was both necessary and transparent. American Navy jets escorted B-26s from bases six hundred miles away to within five miles of the scene of action. Seven U.S. destroyers escorted the seven small vessels of the invasion fleet. The destroyers were semidisguised, as was the *Essex*, but as one Navy captain put it, "Everyone knew who these ships belonged to." (Late in the struggle, two destroyers would come so close to shore that they were easily recognized by Cuban troops.) An American ship delivered the landing craft, turned over to the invaders by CIA agents. American frogmen, disguised as Cubans, were the first ashore and fired the first shots. The radio messages announcing to the Cuban people "the battle to liberate our homeland from the despotic rule of Fidel Castro" came from a CIA radio station located on Swan island, a U.S. possession. And then there were those rebel pilots in Florida.

Could United States involvement in all this be kept secret? Could Castro, or anyone else, possibly be persuaded that the long-predicted invasion was the exclusive work of fourteen hundred exiles? Did Kennedy think that people would fail to believe the *New York Times* accounts of the CIA's training of exiles in Guatemala?

The invasion, begun in the early hours of Monday, April 17, went badly from the start. A radio station on the beach, overlooked by the CIA, quickly alerted Cuban officials. Unexpected coral reefs obstructed and sank landing craft. One of the parachute drops failed to land men close enough to cut off a main road to the area. Castro's rocket-equipped T-33s and Sea Furies wreaked havoc on ships, landing craft, and the old B-26s flying defensive missions over the site. The ships carrying ammunition and all the broadcasting equipment were early casualties. Castro's fifty-four Soviet-made tanks, which could have been destroyed by an effective American air effort, were on the scene within twenty-four hours. Thousands of well-armed Cuban troops were soon on their way to surround the invaders. Castro himself went to the battlefield, a favorite fishing spot where the peasants were especially loyal, and personally directed the counterattack.[78]

Cuban Foreign Minister Roa charged in the United Nations that the attack had been orchestrated by the CIA, which he called the "Gestapo." The Soviet Union labeled the invaders "American hirelings," and Premier Khrushchev sent a strong note to Kennedy blaming the United States for everything and warning, "We shall render to Cuban people and their Government all necessary assistance in beating back the armed attack on Cuba."[79]

Ambassador Stevenson, now fully apprised of what had been planned for months, responded with a stinging attack on Castro. He loyally asserted, "The United States had committed no aggression against

Cuba and no offensive has been launched from Florida or from any other part of the United States." In a prepared statement Secretary Rusk expressed sympathy for those fighting communism in Cuba, but he emphasized, "The present struggle in Cuba . . . is a struggle by Cubans for their own freedom. There is not and will not be any intervention there by United States forces."[80]

Kennedy answered Khrushchev in kind, stating that he planned no direct American military intervention, but should the Soviet Union choose to do so, the United States would honor its "obligations" to protect the Western hemisphere against "external aggression." He expressed the hope that Khrushchev would not use Cuba as a pretext "to inflame other areas of the world." Kennedy also claimed that the military struggle underway in Cuba stemmed wholly from freedom-loving Cuban refugees. "The United States government can take no action to stifle the spirit of liberty."[81]

As the situation at the Bay of Pigs grew worse, pressure mounted on the president to come to the rescue. Members of Dr. Cardona's exile government were furious with the CIA for its bungling and with the administration for refusing to use its full military might. (The CIA had kept leaders of the Revolutionary Council under virtual house arrest in Miami, fearing their public statements at a crucial time.) American military men on the scene and in Washington were enraged over the orders prohibiting them from saving the lives of brave men on the beaches—men who had gone into battle counting on an American air strike. Some sixteen thousand wives, mothers, and friends of the invaders, meeting in Miami's Bayfront Park for a scheduled "Thank Kennedy" rally, began to cry anxiously and tearfully, "Kennedy! Help!"

In the early hours of the nineteenth, Kennedy and several advisers discussed the matter in the Oval Office. Bissell again pleaded for American air support from the *Essex*, now less than ten miles offshore. Several favored taking action; Rusk and McNamara were opposed. Jack agreed to a compromise. He authorized a one-hour flight of six unmarked jets from the *Essex* over the Bay of Pigs. They were to cover an attack of B-26s from Nicaragua. The pilots were forbidden to fire unless attacked.

The compromise proved worse than useless. Several Cuban pilots in Nicaragua refused to fly the dangerous mission, and their places were taken, without the president's knowledge, by American civilian pilots employed by the CIA. A mix-up in Nicaraguan and Cuban time zones caused the B-26s to arrive over the beachhead an hour ahead of their cover. They ran into heavy fire, and four Americans were killed.[82]

The invaders lost 114 men; Castro captured 1,189, along with a large cache of American weapons. American destroyers and landing craft helped rescue several exiles. At the White House Kennedy privately consoled leaders of the exile government, noting that he too had suffered in war and shared their grief. Schlesinger, who was present, later recalled, "the President concealed anguish under a mask of courtesy and composure." The vision of men shot down on the beaches or hauled off to Castro's prisons, Schlesinger wrote, "haunted him that week and many weeks and months to come."[83]

Of course, the president was also upset by the personal defeat and the blow to his personal image. As the full extent of American involvement in the debacle started to appear, condemnation and ridicule began to explode in the press and in diplomatic circles, both here and in Western Europe. Kennedy no longer seemed totally wise, virtuous, and brave. His three-month-old administration appeared to be in ruins. Schlesinger recalled, "The gay expectations of the Hundred Days were irrevocably over, the hour of euphoria past." The New Frontier, he wrote, suddenly "looked like a collection not only of imperialists but of ineffectual imperialists—and, what was worst of all, of stupid, ineffectual imperialists."[84]

As always, when in trouble, Jack turned to his father. The ambassador spent much of the nineteenth on the telephone to Washington and told his wife that he felt he was "dying" trying to raise Jack's morale. At one point he said disgustedly, "Oh hell, if that's the way you feel, give the job to Lyndon!" Bobby said later of his brother, "You know, we'd been through a lot of things together. And he was just more upset this time than he was any other." (Bobby, who also telephoned his father, became, in Bowles's words, "emotional and militant," irritating more than a few Kennedy advisers.) That night Jackie told Rose that Jack had practically been in tears all day, and said she had not seen him so depressed since his near-fatal back operation. Richard Cardinal Cushing, a longtime friend of the Kennedy family, later said, "It was the first time in my life that I ever saw tears come into his eyes."[85]

On April 20, in the hastily written, emotional and saber-rattling speech before the American Society of Newspaper editors, broadcast nationally on television and radio, Jack continued to lie about American participation in the Bay of Pigs fiasco. The United States, he claimed, had not involved its armed forces "in any way." (Bobby, Stevenson, Rusk, and Dr. Cardona followed the same public line.) He also warned that American restraint was "not inexhaustible" and solemnly declared that he did not intend to abandon Cuba to Communism.[86]

At the same time, Castro was publicly gloating about his victory over "imperialist invaders" and "mercenaries," and noisy celebrations

The regal couple leave the White House to attend a series of inaugural balls. The elegant and vibrant Kennedy style would soon create the Camelot mystique. *(Bettmann)*

The President's rapport with the press was exceptional. He was extremely sensitive about his public image and handled reporters with great skill. *(JFK Library)*

The brilliant young speech writer and adviser, Ted Sorensen, contributed invaluably to the making of the Kennedy image. *(JFK Library)*

The President and First Lady
arrive for a state dinner in
Paris with President Charles
de Gaulle. Jackie's personal
attractiveness and knowledge
of the French language and
history reportedly awed de
Gaulle, and left the press and
public ecstatic. *(Bettmann)*

Kennedy and Khrushchev
meet in Washington in June,
1961. After the Bay of Pigs
fiasco and their first meeting
in Vienna, the Soviet leader
was convinced that Kennedy
was a lightweight who could
be intimidated. *(JFK
Library)*

Judith Campbell (later Exner) in 1960, a Kennedy mistress who served as a link between the President and mobster Sam Giancana. Her book *My Story,* published in 1977, made damaging revelations about the President. *(AP/World Wide)*

Mafia chief Sam Giancana, who helped Kennedy win elections and played a major role in secret attempts to assassinate Fidel Castro. His murder remains unsolved. *(Bettmann)*

ExCom, with Robert McNamara seated on the President's left. During the Cuban Missile Crisis, the fate of the world rested in large part in the hands of this small group. *(JFK Library)*

The Kennedys at the Orange Bowl in December, 1962. The President promised victory in Cuba. Operation Mongoose was secretly underway. *(JFK Library)*

Jack and his children in the Oval Office. Such photographs won the hearts of millions. The President's feelings for his children had an impact on his decision-making late in the Administration. *(AP)*

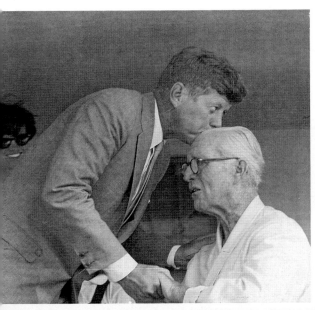

Jack with his stricken father. The elder Kennedy's influence on his son was profound all of his life. *(JFK Library)*

The movie star looks of the President and First Lady contributed greatly to their incredible appeal. Americans link physical attractiveness to good character, high intelligence, competence, and other positive qualities. *(JFK Library)*

The President's tragic assassination was captured on film, and his moving funeral service was seen worldwide on television. This scene, photographed as the casket was removed from St. Matthew's Cathedral in Washington, D.C., was one of many that contributed greatly to the love countless millions would have for the 35th President and his family. *(Bettmann)*

were underway all over Cuba. The *New York Times*, again describing in detail CIA-exile efforts in Guatemala and the debate within the administration over American intervention, declared that the United States had suffered "a disastrous loss of prestige and respect."[87]

That same day Kennedy met privately with Richard Nixon for almost an hour. Nixon later recalled that the president paced furiously in front of his desk with his fists clenched tightly. "His anger and frustration poured out in a profane barrage." Jack "cursed everyone who had advised him" and saw himself as an innocent victim of men in the CIA, the military, and the White House staff whom he had trusted. When asked what he would do, Nixon said he would find a proper legal cover and invade Cuba. Jack thought Khrushchev too dangerous at this point to make such a move. Soon Kennedy was talking about politics, and expressed the doubt that he would have a second term. He also reflected briefly on the responsibilities of his office: "It really is true that foreign affairs is the only important issue for a President to handle, isn't it? I mean, who gives a shit if the minimum wage is $1.15 or $1.25 in comparison to something like this?"[88]

Kennedy soon made appointments with GOP Senator Barry Goldwater, former Presidents Eisenhower and Hoover, and New York Republican Governor Nelson Rockefeller. The Vice President was dispatched to Kansas City to talk with former President Truman. The administration was obviously attempting to create a nonpartisan national front to back the president in a time of crisis. The effort also, of course, tacitly admitted the charge of American participation.

When Eisenhower visited Camp David, Jack described the military action as he understood it, including his disastrous decision to cancel the second air strike in order to conceal American involvement. Eisenhower was aghast and asked Kennedy how he ever expected the world to think that the United States had not been part of the invasion. Ike considered Jack "very frank but also very subdued and more than a little bewildered." The former president thought that Kennedy "looked upon the Presidency as not only a very personal thing, but as an institution that one man could handle with an assistant here and another there. He had no idea of the complexity of the job." A few weeks later, when fully informed of the details of the invasion, Eisenhower wrote privately that the operation "could be called a 'Profile in Timidity and Indecision.' "[89]

Kennedy met with the National Security Council three times in the days immediately following the defeat of the exiles. Bowles later described the president at the first meeting as "suffering from acute shock." Emotions ran high, and several advisers proposed a direct invasion of

Cuba. Kennedy soon elected merely to live with the humiliation, compounded daily by press accounts bearing further evidence of CIA and administration complicity. Bowles gave the president credit for keeping his head and not making a bad situation worse.[90]

Republican restraint undoubtedly contributed to the president's decision. Several GOP moderates realized that the price for calling Kennedy "soft" might well be further and greater disaster. It was clear that Jack had no moral or legal qualms about drastic action against Cuba. In his address to the newspaper editors, he "sent a shock wave through the Latin American community" in Washington, according to federal officials quoted by the *New York Times,* by declaring that if necessary the United States would bypass the Organization of American States and act unilaterally to stop Communism in this hemisphere.[91]

Continued warnings by Khrushchev also played a role. The Soviet premier blamed the United States completely for what he called "a crime that revolted the entire world," and he told Kennedy that by arming the invaders he had taken "a slippery and dangerous road which could lead the world to a new global war." Castro crowed openly that his Soviet allies kept the United States from a direct attack.[92]

Kennedy apologists have made much of the fact that the president shouldered the blame for the Bay of Pigs fiasco. Actually he had little choice; the press quickly discovered that he had known about and approved the invasion. But Jack was determined not to bear the shame alone. In the immediate aftermath of the defeat, White House officials quietly gave reporters background information that directly implicated the Joint Chiefs, the CIA, and even the Eisenhower administration. Some statements were so extreme that Salinger had to call reporters personally and plead that they be rescinded.[93]

Kennedy had good reasons, of course, to condemn the Joint Chiefs and the CIA. They had not served him well. Neither had Jack's closest advisers. When the *New York Times* reported that Rusk was claiming to have opposed the invasion, Jack confronted him directly, angrily reminding him of his earlier support. When members of the Joint Chiefs began saying that they had been bypassed, Jack told McNamara to crack down on them. When some CIA officials contended that they had been against the operation, Kennedy ordered Dulles to get them in line. As early as April 21, while still lying about American involvement, Jack asked retired Army General Maxwell Taylor to review United States intelligence, paramilitary, and guerrilla warfare capabilities. Bobby would serve on Taylor's committee. Heads were to roll, starting with Dulles's.[94]

Kennedy also sought to share the blame with the press. Eleven days after the invasion, he scolded reporters in a speech for jeopardizing national security with their revealing coverage of anti-Castro activities. "The reaction was violent," Salinger later reported. Editorials appeared all over the country accusing the president of encouraging censorship.

In early May, at a White House meeting with newspaper editors, Kennedy tried again, presenting clippings that he charged violated national security. The Cold War, he said, was a continuing emergency that required greater journalistic restraint. The editors were unimpressed. Privately Jack said to *New York Times* Managing Editor Turner Catledge: "Maybe if you had printed more about the operation you would have saved us from a colossal mistake." Catledge later questioned Kennedy's logic. "On the one hand, he condemned us for printing too much and in the next breath he condemned us for printing too little. He wanted it both ways."[95]

Among friends, Jack could also be highly self-critical. "How could I have done it?" Charles Spalding remembered him saying repeatedly.[96] Jack usually complained about his willingness to accept bad advice. But according to Sorensen he also realized that he should have studied the CIA proposal personally. (In Sorensen's apologia, there was no time for full consideration.) That now seems obvious. A careful look at a decent map of the Bay of Pigs would have revealed the impossibility of an escape route to the Escambray Mountains. An arched eyebrow in the direction of a general might have led to the discovery of the military's uneasiness about the landing site. A single shrewd question of Bissell might have thrown a cloud over the expectations of massive civilian uprisings in Cuba. A frank remark to Dulles might have brought to light the fact that the CIA was counting on American military might.

Richard Goodwin, who opposed the attack, later wondered why the president did not at least sense the absurdity of sending a force of some fourteen hundred men against a well-equipped army of more than two hundred thousand. "That fatal, decisive reality could have been exposed had Kennedy more forcefully probed, questioned, analyzed the expositions of his advisers; had he talked to those outside the operation who were not blinded by emotional commitment or professional hubris. Yet he did not do so."[97]

We know that Jack read, if nothing else, the *New York Times* accounts that revealed the level of Castro's military preparedness and the extent to which CIA plans for the exiles were public knowledge. But somehow that vital data made an insufficient impact.

Of course, Kennedy had rarely been given to serious study. Moreover, the ambassador's children had been taught to respect authority and not think things through for themselves. It seems that Jack, although he was commander in chief of the armed forces, simply did not feel qualified to question seriously a military action approved by the Joint Chiefs of Staff and experts of the caliber of Dulles and Bissell. After all, he had only commanded a PT boat—and rather badly.[98]

And yet Kennedy intervened in the Cuban operation just enough to ensure disaster. The president and his apologists would soon take the position that the invasion was doomed from the outset. Bobby would declare, "Victory was never close." Critics, however, have argued that if the invaders had enjoyed sufficient air cover they might have had a chance to hold the beach long enough for a provisional government to land and make an appeal to the Cuban people. The outcome then might have been very different. In any case, Kennedy's decisions to limit sharply the first bombing raid and cancel the second destroyed any chance for success.[99]

Ben Bradlee later remembered Jack saying, "Presumably I was going to learn these lessons some time, and maybe better sooner than later." But whatever else he learned, Kennedy did not come to grips with the moral dimensions of the entire action against Castro. The objections by Fulbright to the breaching of a nation's autonomy and the violation of international agreements failed to register as valid concerns. As always, Jack was determined to be manly ("Well, if he hadn't gone ahead with it," Bobby said later, "everybody would have said it showed that he had no courage"), to be stealthy, and to prove himself a winner. Kennedy emerged from the Bay of Pigs disaster unrepentant. Indeed, he and Bobby, now almost a team in the White House, were more eager than ever to use clandestine, illegal, and immoral activity to bring down the Cuban premier.[100]

In public the Kennedy brothers won applause for their no-doubt-genuine compassion toward the Bay of Pigs prisoners. In May Jack accepted an offer from Castro to release the men in exchange for five hundred bulldozers or $28 million. Kenny O'Donnell later called this "one of the most ill-advised moves in [Kennedy's] career," for Republicans balked at the idea of bartering with Castro for lives. Barry Goldwater raged against "surrender to blackmail." A distinguished committee created to raise the necessary funds soon dissolved.

Nine months later, when the prisoners were brought to trial and were in danger of being shot, Bobby led a drive to exchange food for prisoners. Shortly before Christmas 1962, Castro accepted $53 million worth of goods and medicine and $2.9 million in cash. Jack welcomed the effusive gratitude of the prisoners and their families and invited brigade leaders to visit him at Palm Beach.[101]

On December 29 Jack and Jackie appeared in Miami's Orange Bowl before a crowd of forty thousand to view rebel troops. Jackie drew great applause with a little speech in Spanish praising the courage of the exiles. Jack greeted brigade leaders on the field. He told one pilot, "You didn't get any help from us." The man replied, "No, Mr. President, but I expect it the next time." Jack responded, "You better believe that there's going to be a next time." Overwhelmed by the cheers accompanying the presentation of a rebel flag from the Bay of Pigs, Jack departed from his prepared speech and shouted, "I can assure you that this flag will be returned to this brigade on Cuban soil." A reporter observed, "The President moved from emotional appeal to fervent pledge, his voice ringing across the stadium as if it were that of a revolutionary orator." Chants of "Guerra! Guerra!" (War! War!) roared through the stadium. The Voice of America beamed Jack's address, promising freedom to Cuba, over much of the world.[102]

Behind the scenes the Kennedys took steps to even the score. Two days after the Bay of Pigs disaster, during a gloomy meeting of administration insiders, Bobby began to emerge as the president's principal adviser. The debacle had reinforced the ambassador's dictum that ultimately Kennedys could only trust each other. With Bobby providing the spark, the consensus was that it was time to get tough with Castro.[103]

Bobby turned to the CIA, which was eager to make amends with the Kennedys, to devise a secret plan for overthrowing the Cuban government. By November, the President approved Operation Mongoose, an effort that would cost $50 million a year. The attorney general told planners in early 1962, according to notes taken by a CIA aide, that "a solution to the Cuban problem today carried top priority in U.S. Govt. No time, money, effort—or manpower is to be spared. Yesterday . . . the President had indicated to him that the final chapter had not been written— it's got to be done and will be done."[104]

Mongoose, which was called the "Kennedy vendetta," involved four hundred American employees, two thousand Cuban agents, a small navy and air force, and more than fifty business fronts. Its headquarters in Miami became for a time the world's largest CIA station. Activities included intelligence gathering, propaganda, and minor sabotage. The CIA also reactivated the Mafia efforts to kill Castro. Richard Helms, Bissell's successor, later told Senate investigators that the Kennedys had told him flatly "to get rid of Castro," and he assumed that meant by any means. General Edward G. Landsdale, in charge of Mongoose operations, reportedly told a newsman in 1975 that "acting on orders from President John F. Kennedy, delivered through an intermediary, he developed plans for removing Cuban Premier Fidel Castro by any means, including assassination.'' (In a 1964 interview intended for historians, Bobby attempted to conceal Operation Mongoose and specifically denied that direct assassination attempts on Castro were either attempted or even contemplated.)[105] Jack continued his secret meetings with Giancana and continued to correspond with the Mafia chief through Judith Campbell—until mid-1962 a fairly frequent visitor to the White House.

Operation Mongoose was abandoned in the fall of 1962 in the wake of the Cuban Missile Crisis. The attorney general had repeatedly demanded more action from its leaders, but the sporadic efforts merely alerted Castro to the possibility of a new invasion and probably drove him further into the arms of the Soviet Union. Schlesinger later called Mongoose ''Robert Kennedy's most conspicuous folly.''[106]

In the spring of 1963 the administration took steps to stop minor exile raids on Cuba, and there was discussion about meaningful conversations with Castro. The president terminated CIA financial support of Dr. Cardona and the Cuban Revolutionary Council. But in June, at Bobby's insistence, a new sabotage program directed at the Cuban economy was approved. An anti-Castro base was soon set up in Nicaragua, probably managed either by the CIA or the attorney general himself. The CIA revived efforts to assassinate Castro, and a top CIA man, claiming to be Bobby's ''personal representative,'' met twice with a designated assassin, Cuban agent Rolando Cubela Secades. On the second visit the CIA man promised Cubela everything he needed and gave him a poison ballpoint pen as a down payment. A secret war of sorts was again under way.[107]

In early September the Cuban premier talked with an American reporter at a party in Havana and warned against assassination attempts. He stated, ''We are prepared to . . . answer in kind. United States leaders should think that if they assist in terrorist plans to eliminate Cuban leaders, they themselves will not be safe.''[108]

Kennedy's character clearly influenced his Cuban policy, from the decision to ignore the moral and legal objections to an invasion, through the blunder and panic, the cover-up, the eagerness to blame others, and the creation of Operation Mongoose. The ambassador had trained his sons to do what was necessary to win. And if an open invasion of Cuba would not get rid of its jeering Communist dictator, then clandestine efforts, however immoral, were resorted to. Jack emerged from the Bay of Pigs fiasco more determined to seek information and study it personally. But he was in no way more conscientious.

The public, of course, knew only of the firm, courageous, self-critical, and compassionate chief executive. (As often in a crisis, the nation rallied behind its president, and Kennedy's poll ratings soared after the Bay of Pigs.) The Camelot School would perpetuate this image. Not a single book on JFK mentioned, for example, Operation Mongoose before the Church Committee brought it to light in 1975. Only in the 1980s were the full dimensions of Kennedy's role in the Bay of Pigs story understood by scholars. And these findings were almost entirely unheard in the din of public praise and celebration of Kennedy's vision and virtue.

CHAPTER 13

A Militant Approach
→≫ ≪←

THE PRESIDENT had managed to turn the Bay of Pigs fiasco to his advantage, and he emerged with his image intact if not somewhat enhanced. But behind the scenes the real Jack Kennedy had revealed himself throughout the affair, as was inevitable. When confusion and dilemma reign and decisions are required, the inner resources of a man— his will, values, and beliefs—are called into play along with ideological, political, economic, and military considerations. The moral excellence that Kennedy promised early in his administration was far from evident in his first major foreign policy adventure.

The Kennedy administration inherited crises in Laos and Vietnam, where Communists were active and aggressive. The president responded in ways that reflected the nation's well-established commitment to anti-Communism, but he went a step beyond the actions of his predecessors. Here again there is evidence of the inner man in the president's decision making.

Laos, a tiny, landlocked country of two million, strategically located between Vietnam and Thailand, had warranted considerable attention from the Eisenhower administration. Like Truman, Ike believed strongly in America's global containment policy and was a firm believer in the "falling dominoes" theory of Communist expansion. Eisenhower saw Laos, after the departure of the French, as the principle bulwark of freedom in Southeast Asia.

Soon after the Geneva Accords of 1954 temporarily partitioned Vietnam along the seventeenth parallel and called for a cease-fire in Laos, Secretary of State Dulles introduced the Southeast Asia Treaty Organization (SEATO), which included a special protocol aimed at protecting South Vietnam, Cambodia, and Laos. To ensure the friendliness of the latter, the administration let the CIA secretly spend nearly $300 million on the underdeveloped "land of the million elephants," largely to build up the Royal Laotian Army.

In 1957 warring Laotian leaders agreed to create a neutral nation under a coalition government. A year later, fearful that neutralism would result in a Communist takeover, the Eisenhower administration backed an officer named Phoumi Nosavan. By early 1960 this inept, corrupt, but compliant strong man had become the leader of non-Communist Laos. The Communist Pathet Lao, long supported by North Vietnamese President Ho Chi Minh, resumed its civil war. When a young captain seized the government in August, Prince Souvanna Phouma, a prominent neutralist, tried to reconstruct a coalition government. He had the support of the British and French, who were unwilling to commit SEATO to a war on behalf of Phoumi. But the administration stuck by its Laotian client, prompting Souvanna to strike a bargain with the Soviets.

By December Laos was in turmoil. Getting nowhere and losing international backing, the State Department took a new line, declaring publicly that the United States "had no desire to establish a western military position in Laos" and would agree to talks proposed by the British if the Laotians desired them.[1]

Eisenhower, however, had not lost his strong desire to keep Laos from the Communists. When he met with Kennedy on January 19, the president stressed the strategic importance of Laos and said that he would even be willing "as a last desperate hope, to intervene unilaterally." He assured his inquisitive successor that a political solution would not work because it would involve a coalition government containing Communists. Jack told Ted Sorensen privately, "Whatever's going to happen in Laos, an American invasion, a Communist victory or whatever, I wish it would happen before we take over and get blamed for it."[2]

It was obvious to Kennedy and his advisers from the start that a neutral Laos was the best America could hope for. Massive military assistance had failed to construct an effective pro-Western army. The Pathet Lao, with aid from Hanoi and Moscow, was increasingly popular and successful. And America's allies seemed indifferent toward Eisenhower's goal of a free Laos. In his first news conference, Kennedy declared his hope for "a peaceful country—an independent country not dominated by either side but concerned with the life of the people within the country."[3] Jack established a task force on the issue and, according to Schlesinger, probably spent more time on the matter during the first two months of his administration than on any other.[4]

During February and March, the military situation in Laos grew worse. Hundreds of Soviet airlifts into the battle area were effective, and the Communists seemed on the brink of victory. State and Defense Department officials began to talk seriously about unilateral military intervention. Chester Bowles later reported that the Joint Chiefs were contemplating the use of nuclear weapons in case China entered the fray and threatened to overrun American troops.[5] At a meeting of the National Security Council on March 20, Walt Rostow "argued persuasively," in Schlesinger's words, for a limited American intervention.[6]

Three days later Jack brought three giant maps of Laos to a news conference to illustrate the progress of Communist forces. He implied that the United States had always supported Laotian neutrality and proceeded to claim that the Communists were solely responsible for frustrating that ideal. He made no mention of America's massive efforts to secure a pro-Western regime, claiming simply that the United States supported the "duly constituted government" and was in harmony with "the will of the Laotian people." Kennedy expressed the wish that the Soviet Union would support a British proposal for a cease-fire and prompt negotiations. If it did not, he said sternly, "those who support a truly neutral Laos will have to consider their response."[7]

The statement was widely thought to reflect the president's desire to prepare the American people for an invasion of Laos. Ted Sorensen and Kenny O'Donnell, however, later claimed that Jack was bluffing and had no intention of sending troops.[8] This claim is unconvincing. Jack, after all, also believed in the "falling dominoes" and was fiercely determined not to be blamed at election time for being "soft" and losing real estate to the Communists. (British Prime Minister Harold Macmillan told Eisenhower that Kennedy was under "considerable pressure about 'appeasement' in Laos.")[9] He told Schlesinger on March 20 that it was indispensible to prevent "an immediate Communist takeover" and said, "We cannot and will not accept any visible humiliation over Laos."[10]

Soon after his news conference, Kennedy began to take steps designed to prove that his threat should be taken seriously. The Seventh Fleet moved into the China Sea, combat troops were alerted, and five hundred Marines with helicopters moved toward the area. The president persuaded Prime Minister Macmillan to back a limited intervention. He also met with Soviet Foreign Minister Andrei Gromyko at the White House and made it clear that war was an active option. Secretary Rusk secured troop pledges from SEATO members Thailand, Pakistan, and the Philippines. Roving ambassador Averell Harriman delivered presidential notes to both Indian Prime Minister Nehru and a representative of the People's Republic of China, warning that Laos would not be abandoned even if the United States had to intervene militarily.[11]

On April 1 Soviet Premier Khrushchev agreed to consider international peace talks, but he stalled on a cease-fire. Kennedy told Chalmers Roberts of the *Washington Post* off the record that if he had to go into Laos he would, and the country would back him.[12] Schlesinger wrote later, "The problem now, in Kennedy's judgment, was to make Moscow understand the choice it confronted: cease-fire and neutralization on the one hand; American intervention on the other."[13]

The Bay of Pigs fiasco persuaded Kennedy to stay out of Laos. On April 20, in agony over Castro's victory, Jack told Richard Nixon, "I don't see how we can make any move in Laos, which is thousands of miles away, if we don't make a move in Cuba, which is only ninety miles away." Besides, he said, in Laos "we might find ourselves fighting millions of Chinese troops in the jungles."[14] In September he told Ted Sorensen, "Thank God the Bay of Pigs happened when it did. Otherwise we'd be in Laos by now—and that would be a hundred times worse."[15] Bobby Kennedy said later, "I think we would have sent troops into Laos—large numbers of American troops in Laos—if it hadn't been for Cuba."[16]

In late April military leaders and several Kennedy aides argued strongly in favor of intervention in Laos. United States Ambassador Winthrop Brown formally requested air strikes. But the president, now skeptical of assurances by the Joint Chiefs and noting conflicting answers to his questions, held off. Congressional leaders were of the same mind; when consulted, they unanimously opposed the dispatch of American troops to Laos.[17]

In early May the North Vietnamese agreed to a cease-fire, perhaps fearful that an American response in Laos would interfere with their designs on South Vietnam. A fourteen-nation conference soon convened in Geneva to negotiate a political settlement.

In the spring of 1962 North Vietnamese and Pathet Lao forces violated the cease-fire agreement and seized important territory in northern Laos. Kennedy sent the Seventh Fleet to the Gulf of Siam and air and ground forces to Thailand. This show of force was apparently effective, for a month later Laotian factions agreed to form a neutralist government under Souvanna Phouma. The Geneva Accords, signed in July with the approval of both the Unites States and the Soviet Union, required the withdrawal of all non-Laotian military forces and the cessation of all paramilitary assistance.[18]

Although Kennedy publicly endorsed a neutralist government, like Eisenhower, he privately distrusted it, fearing Communist representation.[19] Moreover, North Vietnam, not part of the bargain, quickly proved unwilling to alter its activities. Some seven thousand North Vietnamese troops remained in Laos and were soon aiding the expansion of their Pathet Lao allies. Hanoi also continued to send troops into South Vietnam through the jungles of southeastern Laos.

Two could play such games. Jack approved a secret CIA counter-insurgency program in Laos that involved the recruitment of 36,000 opium-growing Meo and other tribal warriors and thousands of Thai "volunteers" paid by the agency. Air America, the CIA-owned airline, became active in bombing operations as well as transportation. The agency also organized guerrilla raids into North Vietnam and China. The Soviet Union, apparently unable to control the North Vietnamese, and unwilling to risk a confrontation with the United States in Laos, chose to look the other way.

This "secret war" would go on for years before Congress became aware of it. In 1975 the Church Committee reported that the operation "eventually became the largest paramilitary effort in post-war history."[20] The CIA was privately pleased that its Laotian activities cost it "only" $20 to $30 million a year. When the expenditures of other agencies were added, however, the full cost of the war was close to a half billion dollars annually.[21]

Kennedy was responding to the threat of a Communist takeover in Laos in a way that was in step with similar efforts there and elsewhere by his predecessors. His action was based largely on his ideological commitment to halt the spread of communism, a view shared by almost all Americans at the time and vital to politicians who feared being called "soft" at election time. Still, the vast program operated by the CIA, promoting mayhem and death in a surreptitious war, was illegal, immoral, dangerous, and a far cry from the idealism so often expressed in the president's formal speeches. At least in part, this policy expressed the Kennedy willingness to use power illegally and showed Jack's macho aggressiveness, his eagerness for deception and risk, and his moral indifference.

→≫ ≪←

Vietnam had begun to be of major concern to the United States in early 1950. American leaders were interested in the country's strategic location and raw materials, but above all they saw Vietnam in the contest of global anti-Communism. Should Southeast Asia be lost, the National Security Council warned, "We shall have suffered a major political rout the repercussions of which will be felt throughout the world." With China recently taken over by Communists and the second Red scare underway in America, few in this country were willing to surrender another inch anywhere to the Communists. By 1952 the United States was bearing more than 40 percent of the cost of the war between the French and the Communist nationalists led by Ho Chi Minh. Two years later Americans were paying for 78 percent of the French war burden.[22]

In 1954 Eisenhower seriously considered American intervention to save the French, instructing Secretary Dulles in May to prepare a resolution he could take before a joint meeting of Congress. Nothing came of the proposal, however, and the French were defeated at Dien Bien Phu. The administration was unhappy about the subsequent Geneva Accords. The National Security Council called them a "disaster" that "completed a major forward stride of Communism which may lead to the loss of Southeast Asia." Eisenhower and Dulles proceeded to ignore the international agreement, forge SEATO, and create a non-Communist nation in the South under the control of the staunchly anti-French nationalist Ngo Dinh Diem.

From 1955 to 1961 the United States poured more than a billion dollars into South Vietnam, most of it in military aid. As early as mid-1954 a small CIA team was secretly engaged in sabotage, propaganda, and paramilitary operations on behalf of the government. Diem became a haughty and rigid authoritarian, exhibiting little or no interest in the democratic institutions formally espoused by his sponsors. Still, as historian George C. Herring has observed, "In the eyes of most Americans . . . the President's vigorous anti-Communism more than compensated for whatever shortcomings he might have."[23]

Diem, perhaps with American encouragement, refused to hold the national elections scheduled for 1956 by the Geneva Accords. The following year, resistance to the government began to develop in the South. North Vietnam endorsed the resistance in early 1959 and that summer began to send arms and advisers. The war, however, was to remain in large part a civil war—a struggle waged by South Vietnamese against each other.

Diem responded to the rebellion ineptly, and by late 1960 his government was in deep trouble. American advisers quarreled bitterly over how to save the situation, some advocating reforms and others insisting on increased military strength. The Eisenhower administration, occupied elsewhere and exaggerating the importance of Laos, did not resolve the debate. Herring noted, "The quirks of the electoral calendar spared Eisenhower from facing the ultimate failure of his policies in Vietnam."[24]

Jack was no stranger to turmoil in Vietnam. He had visited the country in 1951 and had made several speeches on the subject during the next several years as he attempted to become a candidate of national stature. He, like Eisenhower, was critical of French colonialism, and he warned that local Communists could exploit foreign resistance to national independence. However, he opposed sending American ground troops into French Indochina.

But Kennedy revealed a strong commitment to the "domino" principle in Southeast Asia and a deep concern for Vietnam. In 1956 he said, "Vietnam represents the cornerstone of the Free World in Southeast Asia, the keystone in the arch, the finger in the dike," and should the "red tide of Communism" wash in, much of Asia would be threatened. "It is our offspring, we cannot abandon it, we cannot ignore its needs." In addition Jack was one of several prominent American Catholics who were especially supportive of Diem, himself a devout Catholic.[25]

In its first hundred days, the Kennedy administration did not regard Vietnam as a serious trouble spot. After the Bay of Pigs and the start of the Laos negotiations, however, Jack decided that the place to take a firm stand against the Communists was Vietnam. In May he sent Vice President Johnson to Saigon with a personal letter to Diem pledging America's readiness "to join with you in an intensified endeavor to win the struggle against communism." Johnson, at the recommendation of the Joint Chiefs, raised the possibility of sending American combat troops. Diem, while eager for aid, did not want Western troops in his country; they would compromise his reputation as a nationalist and give the impression that he was an American puppet.

Johnson publicly hailed Diem as the Winston Churchill of South Asia. Privately, in a lengthy memorandum, he urged Kennedy to exert "a major effort in support of the forces of freedom in the area":

> We must decide whether to help these countries to the best of our ability or throw in the towel in the area and pull back our defenses to San Franciso and a 'Fortress America' concept. More important, we could say to the world in this case that we don't live up to our treaties and don't stand by our friends. This is not my concept.[26]

While Vice President Johnson toured Asia, Kennedy secretly ordered four hundred Special Forces troops and one hundred military advisers sent to Vietnam. The president's action violated the Geneva agreement, which had put a limit on the size of the American military mission in Saigon. Jack secretly ordered the start of a campaign of clandestine warfare against North Vietnam conducted by South Vietnamese agents trained by the CIA and American troops. Principal targets were to include railroads, highways, bridges, train depots, and trucks. American civilians were given permission to serve on air crews in North Vietnam operations "as appropriate." Moreover Kennedy instructed the Pentagon to determine "the size and composition of forces which would be desirable in the case of a possible commitment of U.S. forces to Vietnam."[27]

After the stormy Kennedy-Khrushchev talks in Vienna in early June and the provocative construction of the Berlin Wall in August, pressure mounted on the president for some sort of effective anti-Communist activity. Right-wing Republicans were especially restless and began to condemn the administration for being "soft." The GOP National Committee chairman charged worldwide appeasement. Again Vietnam seemed a good place to draw the line. This thinking was reinforced by the increased operations of the Viet Cong and urgent requests by Diem for more aid and advisers along with a bilateral defense treaty. By mid-October Diem was seeking American combat troops.[28]

That fall Kennedy was faced with two sharply divergent recommendations about South Vietnam. Deputy Under Secretary of State U. Alexis Johnson, for example, sought the introduction of American combat troops and an American commitment to defeat the Vietcong. The Joint Chiefs urged a strong military step-up and estimated that "40,000 U.S. troops will be needed to clean up the Vietcong threat." General Maxwell D. Taylor, after a trip to Saigon, urged the significant expansion of American aid, the employment of American advisers at every level of Diem's government, and the dispatch of a task force of some eight thousand American soldiers that would provide technical and combat assistance.[29]

On the other hand portions of the intelligence community, Secretary Rusk, Chester Bowles, W. Averell Harriman, and John Kenneth Galbraith were among those extremely wary of Diem. Rusk privately expressed reluctance to commit the United States too deeply for the sake of backing a "losing horse." (Rusk would soon change his mind and get in step with the president.) Galbraith favored abandoning Diem. Bowles and Harriman urged Kennedy to limit his commitments and work for a negotiated settlement.[30]

Kennedy chose a military approach. (Liberal Under Secretary of

State Bowles lost his job in what became known as the "Thanksgiving Day Massacre," and hawkish Walt Rostow was brought into the State Department. Bobby later referred scornfully to Bowles as "rather a weeper.")[31] Partly in response to reality and also because a Kennedy could think in no other way, Jack was convinced that the Communists only respected toughness. A memorandum written in November by Rusk and McNamara, and embraced almost in full by the president, began with a lengthy exposition of the domino principle. Kennedy was highly sensitive to the political consequences it might reap; he and his supporters could be hurt badly at the polls for any perceived weakness toward the Communists. McNamara and Rusk warned, "Further, loss of South Vietnam would stimulate bitter domestic controversies in the United States and would be seized upon by extreme elements to divide the country and harass the Administration." Jack told John Kenneth Galbraith, "There are limits to the number of defeats I can defend in one twelve-month period. I've had the Bay of Pigs and pulling out of Laos, and I can't accept a third."[32]

Despite his militant stance Kennedy declined to send combat troops. He reportedly told Schlesinger that, once granted, requests for soldiers would become addictive. General Taylor later recalled, "The last thing he wanted was to put in our ground forces." One reason for Jack's reluctance was the fact that he was "receiving static" from Congress, strongly opposed to the dispatch of troops to distant shores. He may also, as partisans later claimed, have been persuaded by General Douglas MacArthur in late April 1961 that it was a mistake to fight in Southeast Asia. Following a thirty-five-minute chat with the famed military leader, Jack wrote in a memorandum, "He thinks our line [of defense] should be Japan, Formosa, and the Philippines." Moreover, Kennedy was eager to avoid damaging a possible settlement in nearby Laos with an action certain to be disruptive and provocative.[33]

Subject to conflicting pressures, the president took the middle road, agreeing to a massive buildup of American aid and the dispatch of military "advisers," but no combat troops. The United States would continue to help Diem defend himself. At the time Kennedy and his advisers had little idea about the dimensions of their commitment. When Under Secretary of State George Ball warned that acceptance of General Taylor's recommendations would lead to sending hundreds of thousands of American soldiers in Vietnam, Jack snapped, "George, you're crazier than hell. That just isn't going to happen."[34] Long-range planning was not Kennedy's strength; throughout his life, Jack had rarely taken sufficient time to immerse himself in materials, reflect on them, and come up with a deeply considered and thought-through decision. The plan to expand America's commitment in South Vietnam was typically superficial. As he rose from the cabinet table after choosing to create a limited partnership with Diem, Jack remarked, "If this doesn't work perhaps we'll have to try Walt's Plan Six." This was a reference to Walt Rostow's call for a direct U.S. attack on North Vietnam.[35]

The administration knew that the boost in advisers would expose its violation of the Geneva Accords. On December 15 it released a "white paper" charging that Hanoi's aggression in South Vietnam justified the American response. Jack soon confided to Ben Bradlee, "The trouble is, we are violating the Geneva agreement. Not as much as the North Vietnamese are, but we're violating it. Whatever we have to do, we have to do in some kind of secrecy, and there's a lot of danger in that." But he made it clear that his primary consideration was political rather than moral, for he then spoke of the trouble Republicans were giving him and how eager they would be to blame Democrats for war.[36]

At first the administration informed Diem that the new counterinsurgency program would be contingent on specific government reforms, including greater participation by Americans in decision making. When Diem balked, declaring angrily that South Vietnam "did not want to be a protectorate," Kennedy and his advisers backed down. "Diem is Diem and the best we've got," Jack told Bradlee.[37] By surrendering to the South Vietnam strongman, the administration gave the military effort a higher priority than the political, permitted Diem to control the future course of the war, and further tied the United States to an increasingly unpopular regime.[38]

The American military buildup in Vietnam soon began to be orchestrated by Defense Secretary McNamara. Like Maxwell Taylor, he represented Kennedy's choice of adviser and administrator: cool, correct, intense, loyal, rational, dispassionate. Indeed, the secretary had built his reputation in large part on his mastery of data. When a CIA man later warned him about the dubious relevance of quantifying the Vietnam War, "It was as if I had been talking to a devout Catholic and had questioned the Virgin Birth." David Halberstam would later describe the Secretary as "intelligent, forceful, courageous, decent, everything, in fact, but wise." At a meeting with top military commanders in late 1961, McNamara called South Vietnam the administration's "number one priority" and left no doubt about his commitment "to win this battle."[39]

In early 1962 American arms and men poured into South Vietnam. Military assistance more than doubled during the year, and the number of advisers increased from 948 in November 1961 to 11,000 by the end of

1962. The advisers were sent without public announcement. In July 1962 the Pentagon admitted for the first time that "several thousand" American military men were in South Vietnam. The first figures would be released early the next year.[40] These advisers not only trained South Vietnam troops but increasingly played combat roles. According to Pentagon figures released later, the number of Americans killed and wounded in combat increased from 14 in 1961 to 109 in 1962. The figure would quadruple the following year.

In February 1962 Kennedy admitted at a news conference that American troops were "firing back" to protect themselves. In March McNamara acknowledged that American training of the South Vietnamese "occasionally takes place under combat conditions." That same month the president authorized the deployment of American jet interceptors to the area. Should American pilots shoot down a Communist plane, the administration planned to report that the plane had simply crashed. U.S. officials, according to a State Department policy directive, were "confident the Communists will in any event receive [the] message loud and clear." That spring newsmen told of American pilots flying in the action seats of "training" aircraft during combat while South Vietnamese trainees rode behind.[41]

In April the president was asked at a news conference what he intended to do about the deaths of two American soldiers at the hands of the Vietcong. Jack retorted: "We are attempting to help Vietnam maintain its independence and not fall under the domination of Communists. . . . We cannot desist in Vietnam."[42] About this same time, Jack put the Special Forces in distinctive green berets. Intensely interested in counterinsurgency, he and Bobby adulated these supermacho soldiers. Bobby kept a green beret on his desk, and even the ambassador wore one on occasion.

The president monitored developments in Vietnam with some care and took a special interest in the clandestine activities. In January 1962 he quietly created a committee, initially chaired by General Taylor, to oversee, among other things, the CIA paramilitary operations in Southeast Asia. Kennedy charged members with ensuring U.S. government recognition of subversive insurgency as "a major form of politico-military conflict equal in importance to conventional warfare." The attorney general represented his brother on the committee. Fiercely determined to prevent covert action failures of the sort that had plagued the Bay of Pigs invasion, Bobby questioned, prodded and browbeat bureaucrats throughout the government. A CIA official later told a Senate committee, "If you have seen Mr. Kennedy's eyes get steely and his jaw set and his voice get low and precise, you get a definite feeling of unhappiness.''[43] The Kennedys were in Vietnam to win.

In March 1962 the Diem regime announced the strategic hamlet program, a concept endorsed by Kennedy and assisted by U.S. forces in South Vietnam. The plan involved the regrouping of portions of the nation's population into fortified hamlets. The government could weed out Vietcong from the new structures and win popular support by providing security and improved local services.

The hamlet program, along with the overall military effort, produced such optimism that in July Secretary McNamara ordered the start of planning for an American withdrawal. (Kennedy's role in this order is unclear. While the planning went on, however, the number of American advisers continued to escalate.) The secretary, who had said in May, "Every quantitative measurement we have shows we're winning this war," expressed satisfaction over what he called "tremendous progress." He expressed privately a major administration concern about the negative swing in American public opinion and political pressure that might occur as U.S. losses mounted.[44]

By the end of the year the struggle in South Vietnam had taken a sharp turn for the worse. The hamlet program was largely unsuccessful. Diem and his domineering brother Ngo Dinh Nhu mistakenly applied the program nationwide, and peasants objected strenuously to being unrooted from their fields and ancestral lands. The increasingly repressive government used the program to control the population. Many hamlets proved vulnerable to the Vietcong.

On the military front the enemy recaptured the initiative. In February 1963 the number of Vietcong-initiated incidents would rise to more than a thousand. Both sides in the struggle were increasingly guilty of indiscriminate killing and wanton destruction. South Vietnamese and American military leaders were promoting the use of napalm and defoliants. Napalm was already a standard-issue item for Diem's air force. It "really puts the fear of God into the Vietcong," American General Paul D. Harkins declared. "And that is what counts."[45]

Kennedy did not like napalm and hated photographs of what it did to people. He was equally hostile toward defoliants. Still, he approved a limited use of both. General Harkins argued for free-fire zones, places in the unfriendly Iron Triangle to drop used bombs. Kennedy resisted but eventually gave the military very limited zones. The president was learning, as David Halberstam later put it, that once a military policy is initiated, it takes on a life of its own: "There is always the drive for more, more force, more tactics, wider latitudes of force."[46]

Despite the realities, official reports from the scene continued to be optimistic. The administration saw little reason to reappraise its overall effort. A fact-finding team reported to Kennedy in early 1963, "Our overall judgment, in sum, is that we are probably winning, but certainly more slowly than we hoped."[47]

American reporters in South Vietnam, however, grew increasingly critical of the war. David Halberstam of the *New York Times* and UPI's Neil Sheehan, in particular, called Diem a corrupt and unpopular dictator, criticized his army's lack of courage and efficiency, denounced the strategic hamlet program as counterproductive, and excoriated American military leaders for giving false and misleading information to Washington and the public.

Diem retaliated by making life difficult for the newsmen, even to the point of expelling them from the country. High American officers, eager to conceal the extent to American Air Force participation in the war and angry over the factual accounts of battles appearing in the press, were almost as hostile. They expected American reporters to "get on the team," as the Navy commander in chief, Pacific, told Malcolm Browne of the AP, and they treated critical reporting as unmanly and subversive.[48]

Administration leaders boiled over press accounts of the war. Kennedy, intent on victory and preferring to hear the rosy optimism of Taylor and McNamara, tried unsuccessfully to get the *New York Times* to recall Halberstam. When Senate Majority Leader Mike Mansfield returned from Saigon and presented the president with a highly realistic and pessimistic account of what he had seen and heard, in part from reporters, his effort was unappreciated. Jack was aboard his yacht, the *Honey Fitz*, and a party was going on when Mansfield, one of Kennedy's closest friends during his years in the Senate, handed in his report. Jack became angry as he read it and snapped, "Do you expect me to take this at face value?" Mansfield replied, "You asked me to go out there." Kennedy gave him an icy stare and said, "Well, I'll read it again." Halberstam later considered the incident revealing. "It showed that if this policy [of deliberate optimism] had not fooled anyone else, it had deceived the deceivers."[49] Jack's desire to win in Vietnam was so strong that he could not learn from or even hear a voice to the contrary.

>>> <<<

While American military involvement escalated in Southeast Asia under Kennedy's stewardship, another foreign crisis confronted the new president and tested his mettle as statesman and cold warrior. Locked in conflict over a crisis in Berlin with a skilled, crafty, and volatile opponent, Soviet Premier Nikita S. Khrushchev, Kennedy's inner strengths and weaknesses played a role in the tense developments that almost erupted into World War III. And in this case his actions proved popular and effective.

Berlin had been an international problem since 1945 when it was split into eastern and western sectors and left an island inside Communist East Germany. In 1949 Truman's dramatic airlift forced Stalin to abandon a 328-day blockade of the city of West Berlin. A decade later Khrushchev resumed the effort to drive out the occupying allies, demanding that West Berlin be made a demilitarized "free city" and threatening to sign a peace treaty with the Communist Democratic Republic of East Germany. Eisenhower had planned to discuss the issue with Khrushchev in the spring of 1960, but the cancellation of a proposed summit meeting left the Berlin crisis unresolved when Kennedy assumed office.

Jack had often discussed Berlin while campaigning, consistently taking a hard line. "We should make it very clear," he said in July 1960, "that we are not going to concede our position in Berlin, that we are going to meet our commitment to defend the liberty of the people of West Berlin, and that if Mr. Khrushchev pushes it to the ultimate, we are prepared to meet our obligations."[50]

By the spring of 1961 Khrushchev was again deeply concerned about Germany. West Germany appeared to be on the verge of acquiring nuclear weapons. Moreover, some four thousand people a week were fleeing the East for the West, making a mockery of Soviet propaganda and draining East Germany of the professional and skilled labor vital to its economic recovery.

The Soviet leader may also have been disturbed by the new American president's calls for large increases in military spending. In March, in a special message to Congress, Kennedy outlined numerous proposals and declared, "Our arms must be adequate to meet our commitments and ensure our security, without being bound by arbitrary budget ceilings." Two months later, smarting over his embarrassment at the Bay of Pigs, Kennedy had called for a large hike in conventional warfare capabilities, including twelve thousand new Marines, a civil defense appropriation more than three times larger than Eisenhower's, and a boost in foreign military assistance. He also sought a long-term commitment to the space program ("I believe we should go to the moon"), which the Soviets knew had military objectives. The president asked for a half billion dollars just for the space race in 1962, and he requested an estimated seven to nine billion more for the following five years. While expressing his nation's desire for peace, he fervently spoke of winning "the battle that is now going on around the world between freedom and tyranny."[51]

Khrushchev expressed the desire for a meeting with Kennedy, and the two leaders agreed that it should take place in Vienna in early June. The Russian was curious about the youthful president, after the Bay of Pigs no doubt thinking that he was irresolute and could be bullied. Jack too was eager to size up the sixty-seven-year-old Soviet premier and to impress him with Kennedy toughness. Kenny O'Donnell later wrote, "He came into office realizing that Khrushchev was certain that the United States would never take the risk of atomic war to defend its position of world leadership, and he decided that one of his first hard duties as President was to convince Khrushchev and the other Communists that their confident assumption was wrong. 'I have to show him that we can be just as tough as he is,' Kennedy said when he first discussed the possibility of a meeting with Khrushchev."[52]

Several observers understood that Jack was eager to don the mantle of the leader of the free world and force the image he had earned in Cuba—a portrait that haunted him—into the background. In a televised message before a joint session of Congress, Kennedy declared, "No formal agenda is planned and no negotiations will be undertaken; but we will make clear [that] America's enduring concern is for both peace *and* freedom."[53]

Before leaving for Vienna the president traveled to Ottawa, where he met with Canadian Prime Minister John Diefenbaker and addressed Parliament. At a tree-planting ceremony on May 16 in front of Government House, Jack shoveled several spadesful of dirt and felt a sudden sharp pain in his back. A camera caught him trying to conceal his agony by shielding his face with a hand as he left the scene. The pain grew more severe, and White House physician Janet Travell administered hot packs and injected the area with Novocaine.

The press ran the usual stories about Jack's congenitally weak back. "The President's . . . back trouble dates from a college football injury in 1937,"*Life* reported.[54] The White House was eager to minimize the matter. "According to Dr. Travell," *Time* stated, "the President's backache was of a common type that periodically afflicts one person out of every four over 40."[55] When reporters asked Pierre Salinger why the president was sometimes seen at the White House using a cane, the press secretary replied that that had occurred only two or three times, and "Lots of people go for a walk with a cane—it's kind of fashionable."[56]

Jack was in such misery that he needed crutches. But he would not use them on his European travels; Khrushchev and others might think him weak. He chose to endure what Kenny O'Donnell called "constant excruciating pain," described publicly as something like a steady toothache. Only after his tour would Jack give in and be photographed on crutches. Some reporters then noticed a slight limp and saw that he had difficulty with stairs. One photograph carried by *Time* showed him leaving his helicopter in obvious pain.[57]

Later research revealed that during the fall of 1961, Dr. Travell was giving the president two or three injections of procaine, a local anesthetic, daily. (Jack had been enduring these painful injections for several years. At one point, he sent his pal Red Fay to Dr. Travell for the same shot and telephoned the physician to see if Fay cried or screamed.)[58] Other physicians near Kennedy became alarmed, and in October an orthopedic surgeon who used physical therapy extensively was brought to the White House. He found Kennedy "completely unrehabilitated" and in pain. Daily therapy followed, and the president's condition improved somewhat. Kennedy had the treatments take place in the gymnasium in order to appear to be regular workouts. Dr. Travell was quietly taken off the case. She retained her title, however; Jack would not fire her for fear of what she might tell reporters about his true medical history.[59]

To buoy him up on his European journey, Jack secretly recruited Dr. Max Jacobson to join his entourage. The New York–based Jacobson was known among numerous celebrities as "Dr. Feelgood" for his willingness to inject amphetamines (laced with such things as steroids and animal cells) into wealthy clients. "Speed" was then thought to be harmless and was frequently used by entertainers. Singer Eddie Fisher, a regular customer, said of Jacobson after he lost his medical license, "He's still my God."

Jack had first been introduced to Jacobson by his friend Chuck Spalding in the fall of 1960, a week after the speech in Houston on church and state. After his first shot much of Jack's weariness and pain seemed to vanish. Soon he and Jackie were using the physician's services on a regular basis. The Kennedys took injections not only throughout the European trip but for the balance of the Thousand Days, using Jacobson's services at least once a week and sometimes as often as three and four times weekly. At one point Jack tried unsuccessfully to persuade Jacobson to move into the White House. According to evidence amassed by C. David Heymann, including Jacobson's unpublished autobiography, the president and first lady "had developed a strong dependence on amphetamines" by the summer of 1961.[60]

Ruth Mosse, a nurse who worked for the European-born Jacobson during part of the Kennedy administration, later described her employer as "absolutely a quack" and told of the unscientific way he concocted the ingredients added to "speed":

> Max was totally off the wall. When he gave an injection he would just spill the contents of his medical bag on the table and rummage around amid a jumble of unmarked bottles and nameless chemicals until he found what he was looking for. . . . Max was out of his mind. He would see 30 patients or more a day. He worked 24 hours a day, sometimes for days on end. He was a butcher. Blood was splattered all over his whites. That's why when they came to pick him up for Jackie, we would make him change. And because he was injecting himself with the stuff, his speech often became slurred. It was difficult to understand him at times. My father, who was a psychiatrist, made me quit the job because he feared that Max might begin to inject me.[61]

Bobby was suspicious of Jacobson and tried to discourage his brother from taking the injections. Chuck Spalding (who had broken with Jacobson) and several others in Kennedy's inner circle were of the same mind. At Bobby's urging Jack agreed to submit all of his medications to the Food and Drug Administration (FDA) for analysis. When the FDA reported that Jacobson's medications contained amphetamines and steroids, Jack declared, "I don't care if it's horse piss. It works." When Jacobson wrote a letter of resignation and presented it to the president, Jack laughed, tore it up, and exclaimed, "That's out of the question." During every major crisis he faced, including the Soviet missiles in Cuba, Jack summoned Dr. Jacobson to administer shots.[62]

Writer Truman Capote, another Jacobson client, later described the amphetamine treatment as one of "instant euphoria":

> You feel like Superman. You're flying. Ideas come at the speed of light. You go 72 hours straight without so much as a coffee break. You don't need sleep, you don't need nourishment. If it's sex you're after, you go all night. Then you crash—it's like falling down a well, like parachuting without a parachute.

It was reckless, if understandable, of Kennedy to become dependent on Jacobson's shots. The amphetamines, while alleviating pain, might have modified his decision-making faculties, endangering the nation and the world. Even first-time users, experts said later, are often restless, confused, and aggressive. Many individuals experience an exaggerated sense of personal power. Although we may never know the effects of Jacobson's chemicals on Kennedy's decision making, it is clear that the president placed his constituents at risk by taking them.

Then, too, the president was gambling with his personal health. Kennedy photographer Mark Shaw, who saw Jacobson regularly, later died at forty-seven. An autopsy showed his body to be filled with amphetamine residue. Jacobson blamed the death on a faulty heart, later on a blow to the head. The medical examiner ruled out both explanations. Other Jacobson patients also suffered from the doctor's treatments. Amphetamines, used over a long period in medium-to-large doses, have produced paranoia, schizophrenia, memory loss, hallucinations, and similar reactions, to say nothing of dependency.

Jack might have examined Jacobson's credentials—he was not a member of the American Medical Association or linked with any conventional hospital. He might have listened to Bobby or Chuck Spalding, or paid attention to the FDA's findings. Instead he opted for pain relief and "instant euphoria." It is sad, in retrospect, to realize that some of the "vigor" Jack so proudly possessed was chemically induced.[63]

Kennedy consulted with several Soviet experts prior to his departure for Vienna. Superhawkish advice from former Secretary of State Dean Acheson startled several administration liberals. No one was sure of the president's exact views. During a session with British Prime Minister Harold Macmillan in early April, he had let Acheson dominate the proceedings and seemed, in Schlesinger's words, "excessively diffident." In a birthday speech before the Democratic National Committee, he stuck to generalities.[64]

Kennedy was moody and apparently under stress just before embarking on an unprecedented presidential exercise in personal diplomacy. Encountering headlines about the Freedom Riders, civil rights activists who were being jailed for defying Southern segregation laws, Jack telephoned his adviser on such matters, Harris Wofford, and said sternly, "Stop them! Get your friends off those buses!" He thought that Martin Luther King, Jr., James Farmer, and the others were embarrassing him and the United States on the eve of his meetings with world leaders.[65]

Kennedy's first stop was Paris, where he met with French President Charles de Gaulle for nearly eight hours. According to Kenny O'Donnell, who spoke with Jack after each session, the two leaders, through their interpreters, talked about wartime personalities and agreements, nuclear weapons, the defense of Western Europe ("Kennedy promised him that if the Soviets prepared an attack on France and its neighbors, the United States would not hesitate to hit the first blow in the war"), and Khrushchev.[66] They also discussed Laos and Vietnam. In his memoirs de Gaulle claimed that Kennedy "made no secret of the fact that the United States were planning to intervene" in Indochina. "John Kennedy gave me to understand that the American aim was to establish a bulwark against the Soviets in the Indo-Chinese peninsula.'' De Gaulle also thought that Kennedy ignored his prediction that ''you will sink step by step into a bottomless military and political quagmire, however much you spend in men and money.''[67]

Publicly Kennedy and the imperious seventy-year-old president of the Fifth Republic expressed agreement on several matters, including the defense of Berlin. At a press conference, Kennedy said, ''I think that neither General de Gaulle nor I would feel it appropriate to have our rights, statutory rights, in West Berlin changed by force or the threat of force.'' Soviet officials in Vienna, awaiting the president's arrival, denounced the Paris talks, one member of Khrushchev's delegation telling reporters: ''It was a militaristic exercise and poor preparation for the meeting here.''[68]

The Kennedy image was as powerful overseas as it was at home. During the three days the Kennedys were in France, the couple's handsomeness deeply impressed the French. The adulation of the first lady began at the airport when a huge crowd began chanting, ''Vive Jackie! Vive Jackie!'' Along the route to Paris, some five hundred thousand people clapped enthusiastically when the first limousine, carrying Kennedy and de Gaulle, passed by. They burst into a deafening roar at the sight of the second car bearing Jackie and Mme. de Gaulle.

Jackie wore an eye-catching navy blue silk suit and a black velvet pillbox hat designed by Cassini. At an elaborate dinner in the Palace of Versailles' Hall of Mirrors, she was dressed in a stunning white silk evening gown, studded with rhinestones and made for her by Frenchman Hubert de Givenchy. Parisian hairdresser Alexandre created a seventeenth-century-style coiffure, bedecked with diamonds, designed to make Jackie look like ''a Gothic Madonna.'' The Parisian press was ecstatic. *Time* soon commented, ''From the moment of her smiling arrival at Orly Airport, the radiant young First Lady was the Kennedy who really mattered.''

De Gaulle was reportedly awed by Jackie's beauty and her knowledge of French language and history. Jack, plunging in and out of hot baths between sessions with the general to ease his back pain, told O'Donnell, ''De Gaulle and I are hitting it off all right, probably because I have such a charming wife.'' In a prepared speech before a press luncheon, he said, ''I am the man who accompanied Jacqueline Kennedy to Paris, and I have enjoyed it.''[69]

Jack also drew plaudits for his youthful good looks. Charles Bohlen said that the Kennedys ''made a very thrilling sight when they were all dressed up for this party at Versailles.'' Another State Department official recalled, ''I was there at the airport when they left for Vienna, and they looked great. My God, they looked beautiful.''[70]

In Vienna Jackie again stirred public enthusiasm. Wherever she went cheering crowds quickly gathered. One woman called her ''the American princess.'' Photographs showing her standing next to Khrushchev (who was shorter) and his wife (elderly, plain, and heavy set), seemed to intensify her stylish loveliness. The Soviet premier made a point of lavishing attention on Jackie at a state dinner, regaling her with humorous anecdotes which she appeared to enjoy.[71]

The two days of discussion with Jack, however, were without much levity. Khrushchev was stern, aggressive, and unyielding. Jack later told Lem Billings that dealing with the premier was like ''dealing with Dad— all give and no take.''[72] It was clear that the Soviet leader's respect for the president was minimal. Schlesinger later observed that Khrushchev ''hoped to unnerve Kennedy and force him into concessions.''[73]

Jack damaged his credentials as a statesman by getting into what Charles Bohlen later called ''a sort of ideological discussion'' of Marxist theory and colonialism with Khrushchev. In recent speeches, Kennedy had spoken about the tide of history flowing in the direction of freedom and democracy. That was fine banquet rhetoric, but it was not the sort of argumentation that would impress a committed, experienced, and informed Marxist. State Department adviser and Soviet expert Bohlen, who sat in on some of the conversations, admitted later that Jack was unprepared to discuss political theory with Khrushchev; he got ''a little bit out of his depth.'' An ardent Kennedy admirer, Bohlen said later: ''I never had the impression that President Kennedy had seriously read Marx or Lenin, or any of the Soviet theoretical writers very much.''[74]

At one point during the first day of talks, Kennedy referred to the danger that a Russian miscalculation might trigger a war. Suddenly, no doubt to rattle the younger man, Khrushchev appeared to become angry at the use of ''miscalculation'' and, as Jack said privately, ''went berserk,'' shouting, ''All I ever hear from you people and your news correspondents and your friends in Europe and every place else is that damned word miscalculation! You ought to take that word and bury it in cold storage and never use it again! I'm sick of it.'' At day's end Jack asked U.S. Ambassador to Moscow Llewellyn Thompson, ''Is it always like this?'' Thompson replied, ''Par for the course.''[75]

A full range of international topics came up, including Laos, nuclear testing, disarmament, and Germany. Both leaders agreed on a neutral and independent Laos, but that was as far as they went. Khrushchev refused to budge on Berlin and rejected a nuclear test ban proposal. The official statement issued by both parties was, in James Reston's words, "vaguely incomplete." Kennedy told Reston that on the larger disputes between Washington and Moscow "he had found absolutely no new grounds for encouragement."[76]

It soon became known that in their final talk Khrushchev threatened Kennedy with war. He had decided, he said, to sign a separate peace treaty with East Germany in six months, a move that in his judgment made all of Berlin East German territory. If the Allies refused to withdraw their troops by that time, force would settle the matter. His decision to sign, Khrushchev shouted, was "firm" and "irrevocable." He added, "You can tell that to Macmillan, de Gaulle, and Adenauer, and if that means war, the Soviet Union will accept the challenge."[77]

Khrushchev publicly called his talks with Kennedy "a very good beginning." The Soviet Foreign Ministry spokesman said that the premier was "very satisfied." A *New York Times* reporter observed that Khrushchev "left the impression with Austria that he was quite confident he had achieved what he had come here to obtain."[78]

The Soviet leader's elation may well have been over his belief that his earlier estimation of Kennedy was correct: he was a lightweight. (In his memoirs Khrushchev recalled thinking at the time that the young president "was a reasonable man" who "knew he wouldn't be justified in starting a war over Berlin.")[79] Scholar-diplomat George Kennan said later that he was sure Kennedy had given the premier that impression. After reading the transcript of the Vienna conclave himself, he was "very disappointed" and thought Kennedy "strangely tongue-tied." Kennan ascribed this failing to the President's youth, inexperience, and lack of a well-thought-out policy on communism.[80]

Shaken by the talks, Jack left Vienna, in Chester Bowles's words, "in a high state of alarm."[81] Khrushchev's brusqueness and militance had shocked him. He sensed that the premier had returned home thinking that the United States could be pushed around. Moreover, the agreement over Laos prompted Kennedy's fear that critics would start writing about Munich and branding him soft on the Communists.[82]

James Reston described Kennedy as "in a solemn, although confident mood."[83] On the way to London Jack told reporter Peter Lisagor that he could describe his mood as "somber."Lisagor thought the president and his aides "a pretty innocent and green bunch" who had been "chastened" by the cunning and incisive Soviet premier.[84] Schlesinger later called the trip "silent and gloomy" and said that the president was "filled with foreboding." Adviser Bohlen and Ambassador Thompson, experienced in such international meetings, thought that Kennedy had overreacted.[85]

In London the Kennedys were again greeted by huge, worshipful crowds. "Ooh, he's a handsome one, he is!" a breathless young woman cried. "I think he looks wonderful," a Dublin woman cooed. Jackie soon joined the queen for a striking photograph. A London cartoonist portrayed the first lady as a fashionable Statue of Liberty.[86]

Prime Minister Macmillan found Kennedy "rather stunned" and "baffled" by his encounter with Khrushchev. (Bobby later recalled, "I think Macmillan mistrusted the idea of Jack being President. It rather appalled him because he was so young.") At the London home of Jackie's brother-in-law and sister, Prince and Princess Radziwill, Jack went up to his hard-line journalist friend Joe Alsop and, in "an agonizing way," said, "Joe, I want you to know that I won't give in to the Russians no matter what happens. I won't give in."[87]

Only hours after returning to Washington, Kennedy delivered a well-crafted radio and television report to the nation. He heaped praise on de Gaulle, paying tribute to his "individual strength of character." In sharp contrast, he said of Khrushchev, "We have wholly different views of right and wrong, of what is an internal affair and what is aggression, and, above all, we have wholly different concepts of where the world is and where it is going." He described the Vienna talks as "sober," "very sober," and "somber," using the latter word three times.

The speech was harshly anti-Communist and contained appeals for further overseas military and economic aid. Kennedy tied American access rights to West Berlin to the security of the entire free world, and he declared that those rights would be defended "at any risk." He concluded, "We must be patient. We must be determined. We must be courageous. We must accept both risks and burdens, but with the will and the work freedom will prevail." A *New York Times* reporter wrote, "He has rarely spoken with such unbroken earnestness." Jack's determination and strength had been challenged by Khrushchev, and the only way a Kennedy could react was with militance.[88]

The Soviets countered by releasing the full texts of two memorandums Khrushchev had given to Kennedy at Vienna. The documents contained an assortment of serious charges against the West and a threat to seal off the access route to West Berlin "through appropriate agreements with the German Democratic Republic." Reprinted in the American press, the memorandums made Soviet-American differences seem even more extreme than Kennedy had described them.[89]

On June 15 Khrushchev went on Moscow television to report on his meeting with Kennedy, which he said was worthwhile, and to emphasize his intention to sign a peace treaty with East Germany within the year. The premier warned that if the West used force to maintain access to West Berlin, "It would mean war, and a thermonuclear war at that." That same day East German leader Walter Ulbricht threatened to interfere with Western air traffic to and from Berlin after a treaty was signed with the Soviet Union.[90]

Kennedy sought advice from several quarters. Dean Acheson opposed negotiations, called for a buildup of conventional and nuclear forces, and recommended an airlift and a dispatch of troops along the Berlin corridor in the event that access was blocked. The former secretary of state was convinced that the Soviet Union was interested primarily in the worldwide political humiliation of the United States. Others, such as Ambassadors Thompson and Harriman, stressed the need for more aggressive diplomatic efforts. Thompson argued that Khrushchev was merely trying to bolster Soviet influence in Eastern Europe with his threats. A Kennedy task force on Berlin dawdled for weeks and contributed little to the debate. No one seemed to know what Secretary of State Rusk thought.[91]

As always Jack was sensitive to the voices on the Right eager to challenge his manhood and his anti-Communism. Richard Nixon said in a speech that never in American history had a man talked so big and acted so little. Jack smiled at the attack during a June 28 press conference and declined comment. But he made it clear that he was taking a hard line on Berlin and that his critics need never think him soft. In prepared remarks he declared: "There is peace in Germany and in Berlin. If it is disturbed, it will be a direct Soviet responsibility. There is danger that totalitarian governments not subject to vigorous popular debate will underestimate the will and unity of democratic societies where vital interests are concerned." He did not categorically rule out negotiations, but he limited the parameters of discussion to "proposals which would give increased protection to the right of the people of Berlin to exercise their independent choice as free men."[92]

In early July Khrushchev increased tensions by announcing a one-third increase in the budget of the Soviet armed forces and repeating the threat to seal off West Berlin, "an island where the capitalist order has been preserved." He warned, "We shall sign the peace treaty and order our armed forces to administer a worthy rebuff to any aggressor if he dares to raise a hand against the Soviet Union or against our friends."

The debate within the administration intensified. Schlesinger, worried about macho posturing that might produce nuclear disaster, wrote a lengthy memorandum to the president urging caution and study. Acheson, backed by the vice president, called for a proclamation of national emergency, including an expansion of the armed forces, a huge increase in the defense budget, stand-by wage and price controls, and new taxation. The Russians would back down, Acheson said, only when they were faced with determination and strength—an argument that had been a foundation stone of postwar American foreign policy.

Several insiders were alarmed by Acheson's proposal. White House consultant Henry Kissinger warned against a single dramatic gesture that would make the United States appear "unnecessarily bellicose, perhaps even hysterical." Sorensen feared that a declaration of national emergency might well lead to a showdown with the Soviet premier and step up the arms race. [93]

The president gave the issue a great deal of attention. Stewart Udall remarked, "He's imprisoned by Berlin." Schlesinger later recalled, "he thought about little else that summer." Jack was pondering, of course, the risk of World War III and the nuclear annihilation of millions.

In an interview with journalist James Wechsler, Kennedy expressed his desire for peace. But he also told of his worry that Khrushchev might see his reluctance to wage nuclear war as a symbol of national cowardice. The president might have to run the supreme risk, Jack said, in order to convince the Soviet premier that the United States would not be humiliated. "If Khrushchev wants to rub my nose in the dirt, it's all over." [94] It was a natural reaction for a lifelong cold warrior. A politician of national stature in the United States had virtually no other choice. Moreover a Kennedy, brought up to react vigorously to aggressive challenges, could respond in no other way.

In a radio and television speech on July 25, Kennedy again revealed that his view of the world closely paralleled Acheson's. The Berlin crisis, he said, was the most recent effort by Communists to drive the United States out of Europe and Asia. With the aid of a map, he briefly explained the rights of the Allies to their presence in West Berlin. He then declared that the city was "the great testing place of Western courage and will, a focal point where our solemn commitments stretching back over the years since 1945, and Soviet ambitions now meet in basic confrontation."

Kennedy contended that he was seeking a path between "humiliation" and "all-out nuclear action." But the Communists must realize, he said, that the United States was prepared "to defend our rights at all costs." "We do not want to fight—but we have fought before. And others in earlier times have made the same dangerous mistake of assuming that the West was too selfish and too soft and too divided to resist invasions of freedom in other lands.''

Among other things, the president called for more than $3.2 billion in additional appropriations for the armed forces, sought an increase in the Army's total strength from 875,000 to approximately a million men, and favored a massive increase in non-nuclear weapons, ammunition, and equipment. He also announced that he would be doubling and tripling draft calls, ordering numerous reserve and National Guard units to active duty, and requesting new funds for civil defense that would bring the total for the year up to an unprecedented $47.5 billion. Jack spoke of air-raid warning and fallout detention systems and advocated clearly marked and fully stocked fallout shelters. "In the event of an attack, the lives of those families which are not hit in a nuclear blast and fire can still be saved—*if* they can be warned to take shelter and *if* that shelter is available.''

Kennedy left the door open for exploratory talks, and he offered to submit the legality of Western rights in Berlin to international adjudication. However, he said sternly, "The freedom of the city is not negotiable.'' Now it was largely up to the Russians to make war or peace. Moscow, not Berlin, was "the source of world trouble and tension.'' In summary, Jack said: "we seek peace—but shall not surrender. That is the central meaning of this crisis, and the meaning of your government's policy.''[95]

The American people responded warmly to Kennedy's tough talk about war and sacrifice. A Gallup poll showed that 71 percent agreed that Americans should fight their way into Berlin. Mail to the White House ran one hundred to one in favor of the president. Congress quickly approved the chief executive's requests. Harry Truman sent his congratulations. Thousands of young men volunteered for military duty. The bomb-shelter business suddenly flourished; one Chicago company sold 137 units in two days. Nobel Prizewinning chemist Willard Libby dug his own shelter in the side of a hill and fortified it with sandbags and railroad ties. People soon began debating whether one had the right to shoot a neighbor who tried to enter a crowded family shelter at the outbreak of war.[96]

A few observers, however, were critical of the president's stern tone and apparent willingness to risk the survival of the human race. Were the prospects for international peace, they asked, enhanced by an intensification of the arms race and the creation of a national mood that took nuclear war for granted? In light of the weaponry now available to the superpowers, wasn't it irresponsible and immoral to be rattling sabers like Teddy Roosevelt? Wasn't the world too dangerous for leaders to be issuing ultimatums and boasting of their unwillingness to be "chicken''?[97]

But this line of thought was limited to a handful. At stake in the minds of most Americans, according to every indicator, was the future of the free world: The Soviets were apparently prepared to challenge the entire postwar foreign policy of the United States, and most citizens were prepared to defend it at all cost. People in all walks of life applauded their brave, uncompromising chief executive.

Those few who knew Jack's background might have predicted his response to Khrushchev. During his formative years he had been taught to respond to challenge with as much energy, cunning, and force as possible. It had been the leitmotiv of the Kennedy clan. There was no pleasure or honor outside of victory. Thus Kennedy's instinctive reaction to Khrushchev's challenge was to confront him with militance, displaying his family's will to win at any cost.[98]

In the summer of 1961 Jack thought privately that the chance of war with the Soviet Union was good. Bobby said later that the odds were about one in five. The president was now concluding that the United States might strike first in such a conflict. In a later interview with Stewart Alsop, published in the *Saturday Evening Post,* he said that Khrushchev must not be permitted to think his opponents would never be the first to use nuclear weapons. As he put it, "In some circumstances we might have to take the initiative."[99]

Khrushchev was upset by Kennedy's pugnacious address of July 25, telling an American diplomat that the United States had declared preliminary war on his country. In a televised broadcast on August 7, the Soviet premier vowed to stand firm against warmongering capitalists. But he also spoke of the perils of a world war and called on Kennedy to use the conference table to settle their differences, to "rely on reason and not on the power of thermonuclear weapons." The administration did make a minor effort to set up a four-power conference. But de Gaulle was opposed, and there was actually little to discuss, since Kennedy had ruled out compromise on West Berlin.[100]

On August 13 East German troops and police began putting up roadblocks and barbed wire around East Berlin. The construction of a concrete wall began a few days later. It was soon clear that the Soviets were shutting off the embarrassing and debilitating flow of refugees to the West—perhaps the major source of Khrushchev's frustration all along. During the first twelve days of July 8, 231 East Germans had fled to the West. For the first six months of 1961 officials reported a total of 103,159 refugees. Several observers, including Kennedy, had wondered for some time why the Soviets had permitted the exodus.[101]

The erection of the Berlin Wall, however, caught the administration by surprise. Jack, who received word of the first border activities while in his golf cart at Hyannisport, was furious. He quickly huddled with advisers and set his Berlin task force to work on an appropriate response. This often inept body, after much discussion, concluded merely that the United States should increase its military buildup. It drafted a formal protest—and then took four days to deliver it to Moscow.[102]

At first the president did not know what to do. Some critics later declared that U.S. troops should have been sent in to knock down the wall. But no one in the State or Defense Departments made such a recommendation at the time. The wall was constructed on East German soil. The Allies would certainly have disapproved of a unilateral military effort. Moreover, of course, such an action would undoubtedly have triggered a war. So, for a time, Jack did nothing. The Allies took the official position that the Soviet Union had suffered a loss of prestige by sealing off the border.[103]

On August 16 West Berlin Mayor Willy Brandt wrote Kennedy a letter, made available to the press, saying that he expected "not merely words but political action." He compared the sealing off of East Berlin to Hitler's occupation of the Rhineland in 1936, and warned that Berlin might become "a new Munich." Angry West German newspapers and crowds condemned the Allies for what they perceived to be cowardice. A group of Bonn students sent Kennedy an umbrella, the symbol of Neville Chamberlain's appeasement.[104]

Three days later, implementing a proposal made originally by the CIA's Robert Amory and reinforced by a plea from Brandt, Jack sent a fifteen-hundred-man battle group to West Berlin. He also dispatched the vice president and retired General Lucius D. Clay, hero of the 1948–49 Berlin airlift, to Bonn. Johnson and Clay were to raise West German morale by giving assurances of American determination. Johnson pledged "our lives, our fortunes, our sacred honor" in defense of the city. The troops were to test Communist intentions along the access route to West Berlin.

The fully armed troops soon drove along the Autobahn to West Berlin in armored trucks, daring the East Germans to block their way. Tension was extreme in the White House. Talking to the President, an aide said later, "was like talking to a statue. There was the feeling that this mission could very well escalate into shooting before morning." Hugh Sidey later described Jack as "filled with unrelieved worry." A Kennedy military aide kept in constant touch with the convoy's commander.[105]

The troops completed their 110-mile journey without incident, and were greeted by the vice president. West German crowds cheered, and people all over the world sighed in relief. Khrushchev's goals, as Ambassador Thompson had advised earlier, were limited. In retrospect Schlesinger later admitted, the Berlin Wall was a defensive action that successfully stanched the blood flow from East Germany. Ironically its presence led to an improvement in Soviet-American relations and decreased, for a time, the likelihood of a showdown between the premier and his young adversary in Washington.[106]

→≫   ≪←

During the summer and fall tensions between the United States and the Soviet Union remained high. On August 30 the Soviets, citing the buildup of Allied forces, announced the resumption of atmospheric nuclear testing. Kennedy was furious, as Khrushchev had told him in Vienna that he would not test until America did. The move doomed disarmament talks then under way. The White House issued a blistering statement, asserting that the decision was "in utter disregard of the desire of mankind for a decrease in the arms race." A statement issued the next day called the Russian announcement "a form of atomic blackmail."[107]

Some congressmen charged incorrectly that the Soviets had broken "an agreement." The vice president and a number of senators clamored for the resumption of American tests. Numerous leading scientists agreed. Conservatives began blasting the administration for appeasement. When an aide suggested to the president that he deliver a speech declaring that the United States would not reply to the Russians in kind, Jack, alluding to his domestic critics, exclaimed, "They'd kick me in the nuts. I couldn't get away with it."[108]

Hugh Sidey reported that Kennedy decided to resume testing "instantly" after receiving the news of Soviet intentions. Sorensen later revealed that Kennedy had authorized preparations for underground testing in mid-August, delaying the order to test until it was clear that a treaty could not be negotiated. On September 5, following three Russian blasts, the president announced the start of underground nuclear testing in Nevada. He would not permit the Soviets to gain an advantage in nuclear strength. Nor would he allow his administration to appear soft on the Communists.[109]

In late October the Soviets earned worldwide condemnation by detonating a thirty-megaton blast, the largest ever. They soon followed this with a fifty-megaton explosion. When Kennedy declared the resumption of atmospheric testing the following March, placing restrictions on the explosions because of the fallout problem, two-thirds of the American people expressed approval. Bobby said later that Jack was reluctant to resume the tests, but was moved in large part by the possibility that scientists would use them to perfect an antimissile missile.[110]

Still, the crisis in Berlin faded during the fall of 1961. There were incidents of East German harassment along the access route to West Berlin, and in late October Soviet and American tanks lined up in two rows across the East-West border in Berlin and confronted one another, less that one hundred yards apart, for sixteen hours. Allied troops throughout West Berlin were placed on alert. Tempers subsided, however, and both sides on the whole seemed more conciliatory and cordial.[111]

Kennedy gave an eloquent speech before the United Nations that some saw as especially hopeful. While predictably belligerent toward the Soviet Union and unyielding about West Berlin, the address called for more discussion and less provocation. "I pledge you," the president said, "that we shall neither commit nor provoke aggression, that we shall neither flee nor invoke the threat of force, that we shall never negotiate out of fear, [but that] we shall never fear to negotiate." Kennedy also made a strong appeal for international disarmament and challenged the Soviets to a "peace race" to replace the arms race. "Together we shall save our planet, or together we shall perish in its flames. Save it we can—and save it we must— and then shall we earn the eternal thanks of mankind and, as peacemakers, the eternal blessing of God."[112]

Formal talks about Berlin got underway between diplomats. Khrushchev initiated an exchange of personal letters with Kennedy that would last until the latter's death. Both leaders agreed to a proposal by Pierre Salinger for a series of global television exchanges. (The deal fell through when Kennedy chose to resume atmospheric nuclear tests.) The premier gave interviews to American journalists and invited Salinger and Bobby Kennedy to Moscow. The president granted an exclusive and unprecedented interview to Khrushchev's son-in-law, Aleksei Adzhubei, the editor of the Soviet government newspaper *Izvestia,* an interview carried in full in the paper's Moscow edition. The Russians abandoned a provocative demand for a three-man secretary-generalship of the United Nations. Khrushchev did not sign a treaty with East Germany, and the access route to West Berlin remained open.[113]

There were several lessons to be learned from the Berlin crisis. The administration made the point that it would go all out to protect West Berlin. It maintained its legal right to enter the city. Kennedy showed Khrushchev, moreover, that he, like Harry Truman, could be daring and firm when directly challenged. Jack's handling of the crisis won the Russian's respect, and this led to constructive efforts by both sides to work together to ease tensions.[114] There were times, and the Berlin crisis was one of them, when the aggressive side of the Kennedy character proved to be both politically advantageous and in the best interests of the nation and the world.

Khrushchev revealed that for all of his menacing bluster and cold scheming, he could be responsible. He showed restraint when the American troops rolled down the Autobahn. When the Soviet and American tanks faced each other "eyeball to eyeball," the Soviet troops were the first to yield, thus preventing violence. Khrushchev later took direct responsibility for this action.[115] The premier also began a private correspondence with Kennedy, and Salinger later revealed, "Krushchev would always initiate the exchange of letters." After interviewing the premier at length, C. L. Sulzberger of the *New York Times* reported with some astonishment, "I consider him entirely normal and human."[116]

The Berlin crisis showed Kennedy beginning to confront the horrors of nuclear war and pondering the gravity of his responsibilities and actions. Journalist Hugh Sidey portrayed him one evening in the White House saying to his brother: "It really doesn't matter as far as you and I are concerned. What really matters are all the children."[117] The president's pledge before the United Nations not to fear to negotiate and his appeal for a "peace race" deserved the warm reception they received throughout the world.

The crisis also illustrated the fact that Congress and the American people were willing to applaud Kennedy's pugnacity and go to virtually any length to contain direct Soviet aggression.[118] Should the two superpowers again cross swords publicly, Jack would almost certainly have a blank check with which to attack the Communists. Such a confrontation, even more frightening than Berlin, would soon confront the young president, and both his intelligence and character were to be severely tested.

CHAPTER 14

Seemingly Invulnerable

➜➤➤ ⫷⫷⫷

DURING his first year in the White House, Jack remained closely tied to the values and many of the ideas his father had instilled in all the Kennedy children. The president's selection of pragmatic advisers, his overall lack of interest in domestic reform, his conservative economic views, his hard-nosed posture in foreign affairs, his often reckless and consistently libertine life-style, and his intense interest in public relations and his image were in general harmony with views long expressed by the elder Kennedy.

Although administration officials consistently denied that the ambassador had any influence on his son, the two kept in close contact. They exchanged telephone calls regularly, up to a half dozen a day at times, and saw each other periodically on weekends and vacations. The elder Kennedy said of the president, "You know, when he visits me, he still borrows my socks, if I have some clean ones."[1]

After celebrating his forty-fourth birthday at Hyannis Port, just before leaving for Europe, Jack stood in front of the family home waiting for the helicopter that would take him to the airport. Suddenly he felt in his pockets and then turned sheepishly toward his father. "Oh, Dad, I don't have a cent of money." The ambassador sent his secretary to get a packet of large bills. Jack accepted the cash with a grin and said, "I'll get this back to you, Dad." As he watched his son depart, the ambassador muttered, "That'll be the day."[2]

Jack was not his father's puppet. Still, it is impossible to accept the contention of family partisans that the ambassador rarely if ever gave Jack advice. (Schlesinger wrote, "The proud old man practiced self-abnegation with sensitivity and grace.")[3] Bobby later recalled that after his father's debilitating illness, Jack "often said how much he wished my father was well. On the tax bill and other matters that he would ordinarily talk to my father about, he could not do that any longer."[4] During the Cuban Missile Crisis, Rose burst into tears and said, "My son, my poor, poor son, so much to bear, and there is no way now for his father to help him."[5] George Smathers said later, "What nobody should ever forget was that Jack had a tremendous respect for his father, just a *tremendous* respect. He was really quite in awe of his father all the time; he had the greatest admiration for him of anyone, and I mean *anyone*!"[6]

We now know that Jack turned to his father for counsel in selecting a cabinet and for solace during the Bay of Pigs. The ambassador played a similar role in family public relations. He made arrangements for the production of *PT-109*, a highly flattering movie about Jack's alleged heroics in the South Pacific. (Jack personally approved the script and chose actor Cliff Robertson for the principal role. *Look* described the finished product as "just this side of *The Bobbsey Twins*," and it turned out to be a box-office dud.) He also took part in negotiating the movie rights for Bobby's book *The Enemy Within*. After Bobby and Twentieth Century–Fox had agreed on a contract, the ambassador raised an objection. "But your son, the Attorney General, said he was satisfied with the way that clause was drawn," said an exasperated studio executive. "What the hell does he know about it!" Joe snapped. The clause was revised.[7] A more complete view of the extent of the ambassador's role early in the administration awaits the release of his papers, currently in the exclusive control of the Kennedy family at the Kennedy Library.

It was widely known in Washington at the time that the elder Kennedy was the major force behind Teddy Kennedy's fledgling Senate campaign in Massachusetts. Teddy, at twenty-nine, was not yet old enough to serve and was only three years out of law school. Earlier he had been expelled from Harvard for cheating, and he was not considered to be one of the brighter or more mature members of the family. The Cambridge intellectual establishment was aghast at his candidacy. Local politicians were no happier, as Teddy had never held an elective office. The young man's experience in world affairs consisted merely of recent trips to Europe (eleven countries in twenty-five days), Latin America (nine countries in twenty-seven days), and Africa (nine countries in fifteen days). If those obstacles were insufficient, his older brothers were known to be less than enthusiastic about the race.

But the ambassador was determined. "You boys have what you want now," he told Jack and Bobby, "and everyone else helped you work to get it. Now it's Ted's turn. Whatever he wants, I'm going to see he gets it." So, with the aid of unlimited funds, control of federal patronage, and family participation in the campaign (Steve Smith ran things; Rose attracted eight hundred to a Brookline country club), Teddy worked tirelessly to continue the Kennedy success story. Campaigning for a seat once held by JFK, he used his brother's 1952 slogan, "He Can Do More for Massachusetts."

The president tried to steer clear of any direct involvement in the campaign, but he kept a careful eye on developments. When a journalist uncovered the story of Teddy's college expulsion, Jack twice summoned the reporter to the White House, attempting to apply pressure that would at least put the item on a back page. The reporter would not budge, and Jack wearily remarked, "We're having more fucking trouble with this than we did with the Bay of Pigs." McGeorge Bundy, a participant in the talks, replied, "Yes, and with just about the same results." Teddy soon issued a formal statement on the matter that said in its second sentence, "I made a mistake."[8]

Jack also provided counsel to his brother on occasion and loaned him Sorensen to stock his intellectual portfolio. Bobby became involved in minor ways. As always, the Kennedys played rough. At one point a frustrated opponent asked Bobby Kennedy's assistant John Riley, "You are going to win anyhow, so why use all of this muscle on me?" Riley reportedly replied, "Because we've got it."[9]

When an interviewer asked the ambassador in 1961 what problems his youngest son might encounter in his bid for the Senate, Joe paused thoughtfully for effect and then replied, "None."[10] His prediction proved correct. Teddy easily defeated Attorney General Eddie McCormack, House Speaker McCormack's nephew, at the party convention, won 69 percent of the primary vote, and breezed past Republican George Lodge, Henry Cabot Lodge's son, in the fall of 1962. Though the ambassador was delighted by the victory, his family had to read that elation in his eyes.[11]

On December 19, 1961, while playing golf in Palm Beach with his devoted niece Ann Gargan, the seventy-three-year-old Kennedy suffered a severe stroke. Gargan did not know what was wrong and put her uncle to bed. Extremely worried, she alerted Rose, saying that something serious might have happened. Rose looked in on her husband, said he simply needed rest, and went about her business. It was some four hours before the ambassador was hospitalized. (Even then, Rose played golf and went swimming before visiting the hospital.) By that time the damage was considerable: The right side of his body was paralyzed, and he was unable to speak. He was at first thought near death, and a priest at the hospital administered last rites. Lem Billings later recalled, "It was an opportunity to pull the plug. But Bobby said no, let him fight for his life."[12]

Jack had been in Palm Beach overnight, returning from a brief visit to Venezuela, and had flown to Washington that morning. He returned to Palm Beach as quickly as possible and joined Jackie and other family members at the hospital. The ambassador's condition was listed as "serious," and he was soon stricken by pneumonia and given a tracheotomy. But he survived, probably, as his private nurse later asserted, by sheer force of will.[13]

Joe's mind was reasonably intact. Frank Saunders, his chauffeur, later wrote, "That blue fire still flickered in his eyes, but not as brightly." (Jack once said, "Even if my Dad had only ten percent of his brain working, I'd still feel he had more sense than anyone else I know.") His body, however, would not respond adequately to constant therapy. The ambassador was confined to a wheelchair and could only say "Noooooo!" and "Yaaaaaa!" "Yaaaaaa!" His face was twisted out of shape and he drooled out of the right side of his mouth as he ate. His right hand was badly deformed and useless. At times he became visibly angry over his condition and would scream and lash out with his good left hand at Bobby, his doctors, or anyone else in sight. When Rose entered his room he frequently became violent. Saunders recalled, "He tried to write with his left hand, to give us instructions, and tell us what he wanted, but it frustrated him. I would see this look of fear creep into his eyes too—the look you can get from a wild caged animal."[14]

Jack, Jackie, Eunice, Bobby, and other family members were extremely kind to the family patriarch, reading to him, telling him stories, and trying everything in their power to brighten his spirits. The president visited Hyannis Port regularly on weekends. Bobby said later that Jack "was almost the best with my father because he really made him laugh and said outrageous things to him."[15] Privately, Jack grieved over his father's condition. (He also tried to keep his cane out of sight for fear that the elder Kennedy would think him weak.)[16] Saunders later recalled that the Kennedy children were frustrated and angered by the ambassador's fate. "He had been so independent, so in control, always able to do just what he wanted to do. Seeing him in that wheelchair tore them apart."[17]

Rose, on the other hand, expressed a minimum of emotion. The important things in her busy daily life—like playing golf (she would sneak on and off the local course to escape paying fees), attending mass, scolding servants, and planning her wardrobe—rarely included the invalid upstairs. She placed Ann Gargan in charge of the ambassador, and the young woman, through her domineering, inconsistent, and often indulgent approach to the patient, unintentionally impeded his recovery. When asked for advice about her husband, Rose would invariably say, "Ask Ann. Ask Ann."[18]

Rose purchased a black mourning dress for Joe's future funeral, which she took with her as the family moved between Hyannis Port and Palm Beach. The elder Kennedy's private nurse shuddered when Rose used the world *die* freely in conversations about her husband. Later, when Bobby was assassinated, Rose was heard exclaiming, "Oh, why did it have to be Bobby? Why couldn't it have been Joe?"[19]

At times Joe would reach out for one of his grandchildren, trying to talk, to be friendly. They would cry and run away; then Joe would weep. Actress Marlene Dietrich, an old friend, said later after a visit, "It is a cruel penance God has given him." The ambassador would live to see both Jack and Bobby murdered and Teddy disgraced at Chappaquiddick.[20]

The ambassador's debilitation meant that Jack, for the first time, was freed from the paternal grasp. There would no longer be orders and commands from the family head. All of his life Jack had emulated, at least in general terms, what the elder Kennedy had preached and taught by example. He still loved his father, of course, and would do what he could to please him. But the opportunity now arose for Jack to reach beyond the ambassador's vision and ambition and find his own way and agenda as president. He would have less than two years to do so.[21]

>>> <<<

Robert Frost's participation in the inaugural ceremony was emblematic of the Kennedy administration's official embrace of high culture. Metropolitan Opera stars, a troupe of Shakespearean actors, and legendary cellist Pablo Casals were among those invited to perform at the White House. Private and official guests at the executive mansion included such cultural luminaries as Carl Sandburg, Leonard Bernstein, Igor Stravinsky, André Malraux, George Balanchine, Elia Kazan, and Ralph Richardson. At a dinner honoring Western Hemisphere Nobel Prizewinners, Kennedy called the group before him "the most extraordinary collection of talent, of human knowledge, that has ever been gathered together at the White House, with the possible exception of when Thomas Jefferson dined alone."[22]

The president and his wife attended opening performances of the Opera Society and the National Symphony Orchestra. Kennedy gave his public support to the proposed National Cultural Center in Washington. He initiated the Medal of Freedom Awards to honor those "whose talent enlarges the public vision of the dignity with which life can be graced and the fullness with which it can be lived," and personally nominated Edmund Wilson. He also went out of his way to commend publicly such groups as the Theatre Guild American Repertory Company, which toured Europe, the Near East, and Latin America under the auspices of the State Department.

All this marked a sharp departure from recent tradition. The Trumans and Eisenhowers had displayed more middle-of-the-road tastes. The nation's capital had long been described as a cultural backwater. And Congress had been notoriously apathetic toward the arts. One Virginia congressman observed that poker playing was "an artful occupation" and argued that it was as logical to subsidize poker players as artists.

Now the handsome, highly educated, and sophisticated young couple in the gorgeously renovated executive mansion had changed things, elevating local and national taste to new heights. John Steinbeck, invited to the inauguration, wrote, "What a joy that literacy is no longer prima facie evidence of treason." An article in the *New York Times* bubbled in early 1962: "Not since Thomas Jefferson occupied what was then known as the President's Palace has culture had such good friends in the White House." The chairman of the Fine Arts Commission said of the Kennedys, they were "susceptible to the comfort of the arts. They couldn't live without them—it is woven into the pattern of their lives." Schlesinger, echoing Frost, later wrote of "a new Augustan age of poetry and power" and declared, "The President's curiosity and natural taste had been stimulated by Jacqueline's informed and exquisite responses: art had become a normal dimension of existence." Still, Schlesinger continued, "the character of his personal interest was less important than his conviction that the health of the arts was vitally related to the health of society. He saw the arts not as a distraction in the life of a nation but as something close to the heart of the nation's purpose."[23]

It was true that serious artists, writers, and architects had not received such attention in the White House since, perhaps, the Progressive Era. In 1964 Lewis Mumford described Kennedy as "the first American President to give art, literature and music a place of dignity and honor in our national life."[24] Still, his emphasis on the value of the arts and humanities tends to conceal Kennedy's personal dislike and distrust of intellectuals, an attitude instilled by his father. The president's personal musical tastes were actually inclined toward country and western, show tunes, and rock and roll. Jack could not read music and could barely carry a tune. Charles Spalding said that music to him was "just like the rustling of the wind in the trees." Sorensen admitted: "He had no interest in opera, dozed off at symphony concerts and was bored by ballet." (After suffering through a performance by the Bolshoi Ballet, Jack told his deputy press secretary, "I don't want my picture taken shaking hands with all those Russian fairies.") Jackie once cracked that the only music her husband really appreciated was "Hail to the Chief."[25]

Jack enjoyed popular movies and had an amateurish love of Anglo-American history and biography. He could recognize the works of certain major artists, knew the names of many famous authors, and read some contemporary best-sellers. But Jack was really a current events man, a New York Times junkie, a sports enthusiast, and a politician. (Charles Bartlett later said of Jack's absorption with politics: "That's basically all he talked about.") The Kennedys had never become involved with fine arts—the ambassador lacked any such inclination—and Jack was no exception. It is not difficult to accept White House reporter Peter Lisagor's belief that the president simply endured most of the cultural goings-on at the executive mansion, knowing that they produced glowing stories in the elitist media.[26]

One day, when the president was pointing out paintings by Renoir and Cézanne during a private White House tour, Red Fay asked, "Who are they?" The first lady and members of her White House Historical Association were standing nearby, and Jack was aghast. He whispered to his longtime pal, "My God, if you have to ask a question like that, do it in a whisper or wait till we get outside. We're trying to give this administration a semblance of class."[27]

Jack once told a friend: "Pablo Casals? I didn't know what the hell he played—someone had to tell me." At the White House dinner on the evening of the eighty-four-year-old musician's performance, however, Kennedy's prepared remarks sounded like the ruminations of a veteran connoisseur of the arts. "We believe that an artist, to be true to himself and his work, must be a free man."[28]

The impetus for classical culture in the White House came from Jackie. She had long been a serious student of the arts and humanities and genuinely enjoyed the poetry readings, chamber music, and operatic arias that echoed through the East Room during scores of gala evenings. Jack deserves credit for recognizing the importance of high culture to his administration and the nation and for giving it his official support.

The Kennedy administration's image of elegance, taste, and beauty became famous throughout the world. During the Thousand Days, the president met with seventy-four foreign leaders (a dozen more than Franklin D. Roosevelt received in his twelve years in office), and he and the first lady held sixty-six state receptions. "Each of these was an exquisite creation," John H. Davis later observed, "the product, almost exclusively, of Jacqueline's taste and imagination with only a few touches provided by her assistants." The press was filled with accounts of superb French cuisine, stunning flower arrangements, first-class entertainment, and Jackie's sleek Cassini evening gowns and bouffant hairdos. British Prime Minister Macmillan said, "They certainly have acquired something we have lost, a casual sort of grandeur about their evenings, pretty women, music and beautiful clothes and champagne and all that."[29]

The most memorable of the first lady's dinners took place on July 11, 1961, at Mt. Vernon, held in honor of President Mohammed Ayub Khan of Pakistan. It was the first state dinner ever held outside the White House. Inspired by the luxury she had seen at Versailles, Jackie was determined to spare no expense. An army of 150 workers was recruited to carry out her plans.

The presidential yacht *Honey Fitz* and three other ships borrowed from the Navy ferried 132 guests down the Potomac from Washington to George Washington's plantation. An orchestra aboard each boat played during cocktails. On arrival guests stood in the shade of a decorated tent pavilion and drank mint juleps from silver cups. Music was provided by the Continental Fife and Drum Corps (complete with powdered wigs and tricorn hats), the Air Force "Strolling Strings," a string trio donated by society bandleader Lester Lanin, and the National Symphony Orchestra, performing on a specially constructed bandstand. Jackie made a dramatic entrance flanked by Marine Honor Guard in full dress. She wore a long, white ruffled organza gown with a chartreuse sash. Tiffany's and Bonwit Teller created the table decor. Guests sat on gilded ballroom chairs and ate French cuisine by candlelight on White House china.[30] The Kennedys were the nation's "royal" family, and the public seemed to love the grandeur, elegance, and wealth displayed for all to see.

Perhaps more to Jack's taste was his forty-fifth birthday party in New York's Madison Square Garden on May 19, 1962. The televised celebration–Democratic fund-raiser attracted fifteen thousand people who paid one thousand dollars apiece. The entertainers included Maria Callas, Jack Benny, Peggy Lee, Jimmy Durante, and Ella Fitzgerald. Much of the excitement, however, surrounded the appearance of Marilyn Monroe.

Jackie did not attend. She undoubtedly knew about Monroe and her husband, and wanted nothing to do with the display of the actress's pulchritude. That spring, exhausted by social events and wearied by quarrels with her husband over money and infidelity, Jackie had begun to travel overseas alone. A two-month journey to Asia was soon followed by a trip to Italy (where she petitioned the pope for an annulment of her sister's first marriage). On the night of the birthday party, she was "a surprise participant" in a Virginia horse show.[31]

Monroe, thirty-six, had long had severe psychiatric problems and was often on drugs. Her film career was collapsing and a producer privately called her "one very ill, very paranoid lady." She had earlier been confined briefly in a New York mental hospital. She saw her psychiatrist daily. Men so regularly took advantage of her almost perpetual stupor and virtual amorality (thirteen abortions before she was thirty) that she sometimes complained of being treated "only as a plaything" and spoke regularly of suicide.[32]

On the night of her Madison Square Garden appearance, the actress was terrified of the huge crowd and she was drunk. Her psychiatrist's daughter, on learning of her fear, had encouraged the actress by telling her about the children's story of "The Little Engine That Could" ("I think I can, I think I can. . . ."). Sewn, literally, into her dress, Marilyn could barely move. Adlai Stevenson said later that she called the dress "skin and beads" and added, "I didn't see the beads." Pushed on stage by Peter Lawford's agent, Monroe managed to get through a brief happy birthday song. The crowd leered, roared, and whistled at her every movement and greeted her tottering exit with thunderous applause.

Jack then took the stage and said, "Thank you. I can now retire from politics after having had, ah, 'Happy Birthday' sung to me in such a sweet, wholesome way." At a party afterward Ambassador Stevenson succeeded in reaching the actress "only after breaking through the strong defenses established by Robert Kennedy, who was dodging around her like a moth around a flame."[33] It was unusual for Bobby, widely thought to be a somewhat prudish Kennedy, to be so demonstrably attentive to a woman in public.

In fact both Jack and Bobby enjoyed young women at Peter Lawford's ocean-front home in Santa Monica, an established retreat for the Rat Pack and other "swingers." Jeanne Martin, singer Dean Martin's former wife, later recalled, "Ethel could be in one room and Bobby could be in another with this or that woman. Yes, Bobby was a grabber, but not in the terms that Jack was. Jack was really instinctive, you know, straight

for the jugular—'Come upstairs, come in the bathroom, anything.' "
Martin had a friend who was alone with Bobby in the library, "and before
she knew it the door was locked and he threw her on the couch—amazing!
It was so blatant. Here was the President of the United States and the
Attorney General."[34]

→>> <<<

Jack had first had an affair with Marilyn Monroe some time in the
1950s. Senior Kennedy aide Peter Summers later revealed that the relationship was so obvious by the 1960s that advisers seriously cautioned
both Jack and Marilyn about its possible political implications. (Summers
personally saw the two emerge from the same shower.) But the warnings
went unheeded. The president and the actress saw each other on several
occasions during the Thousand Days in different parts of the country
(never, apparently, at the White House, where the risk was too great),
and the actress shared the news of her visits with friends. One confidant,
Henry Rosenfeld, later recalled, "Her opinion was that this was the most
important person in the world, and she was seeing him. She was so
excited, you'd have thought she was a teenager."[35]

Bobby first met Monroe in early February 1962 and was soon sharing her favors. (The attorney general played a role in securing Monroe's
presence at his brother's birthday party. When Twentieth Century–Fox
executive Milton Gould balked at the proposal, Bobby called him a
"no-good Jew bastard.")[36] The affair was a badly kept secret. George
Smathers remembered hearing about it directly from Jack, who expressed
"some concern." Baseball legend Joe DiMaggio, the most loyal of Monroe's ex-husbands, knew what was going on and, a friend reported, was
extremely angry about it. (DiMaggio would bar all Kennedys from Monroe's funeral service.) Actress Terry Moore later revealed that Monroe
told her of affairs with both Kennedys. "She even imagined herself as a
future First Lady with one or the other of them." Singer Phyllis McGuire
told Anthony Summers, "The initial relationship was with John. And
there definitely was a relationship with Bob. . . . They were seen together
in their little hideaways. And, you know, that's very like the Kennedys,
just to pass it down from one to the other—Joe Kennedy to John, Jack to
Bobby, Bobby to Ted. That's just the way they did things."[37]

Jeanne Carmen, a neighbor and friend of Monroe's, was present
during the preliminaries of one amorous visit by Bobby to the actress's
home. "Marilyn came flying out of the bathroom, and jumped into his
arms . . . she kissed him openly, which was out of character for her."
Later, Carmen went along when Bobby, on a dare, traveled with Marilyn

to a local nudist beach in disguise. She also recalled a time when Jack and Bobby arrived together at Monroe's door with a couple of male companions.[38]

Natalie Jacobs, the widow of a prominent Hollywood producer, said of Monroe, "Everyone that knew her knew about her and the Kennedys." Milo Speriglio, a detective who investigated Monroe for more than a decade, wrote in 1986, "Through the years, friends and associates of Bobby have stopped denying it, giving the excuse that Marilyn was Robert Kennedy's 'one serious extramarital romance.' "[39]

Mafioso Sam Giancana, Phyllis McGuire's lover, was among those who knew about the Kennedys and Monroe. He also, of course, had firsthand knowledge of Judith Campbell's relationship with the president, as well as the plots to kill Fidel Castro. The potential for blackmail was enormous. Hassled by the FBI at O'Hare Airport, Giancana angrily told agents that he knew who was giving them orders, and he blurted out, "I know all about the Kennedys, and Phyllis knows a lot more about the Kennedys, and one of these days we are going to tell all. . . . You lit a fire tonight that will never go out. You'll rue the day."[40]

Frank Sinatra was close to Monroe (they had had an affair in 1960), Giancana, and Peter Lawford, and he and his cronies were fully informed about the Kennedys and the actress. "Skinny" D'Amato later told Anthony Summers, "I knew—we knew—about Monroe and the Kennedys, and about Robert especially, but I'm not going to be quoted on it. Imagine it, a friend of Frank Sinatra being quoted as saying what we knew about Marilyn."[41]

In late 1961 the FBI began to be aware of the president's reckless behavior. J. Edgar Hoover privately warned the attorney general in December that mobsters intended to use Sinatra to intercede on their behalf to call off federal investigations. Three contacts had already been made between the singer and the ambassador. In February 1962 the FBI director informed the attorney general and Kenny O'Donnell that Judith Campbell was also seeing mobsters Giancana and Johnny Roselli. On March 22 Hoover lunched with the president and presumably discussed the matter.[42]

Hoover was a force the Kennedys did not wish to arouse. Jack quickly cancelled a weekend stay at Sinatra's house and soon severed all ties with the singer.[43] Campbell's visits to the White House ended shortly thereafter, and the FBI stepped up its surveillance of the young woman and Giancana. The wiretapping, break-ins, and round-the-clock personal harassment soon became so severe that Campbell attempted suicide. She later wrote, "Hoover was God and the special agents were his avenging angels."[44]

Both Sinatra and Giancana realized that they had been double-crossed by the Kennedys. They and their friends had poured a lot of money and effort into the presidential campaign. Assurances had been given; the victors, being pros, understood that they had obligations. Giancana was overheard by a federal wiretap bitterly telling a lieutenant, "After all, if I'm taking somebody's money, I'm gonna make sure that this money is gonna do something, like, do you want it or don't you want it. If the money is accepted, maybe one of these days the guy will do me a favor."[45] Giancana, moreover, had been plugged into the Castro assassination effort, and he and the president exchanged messages regularly. Now the administration was his enemy. Where was the gratitude?

It was probably the entrance of Hoover into the picture that changed things entirely. The FBI director already knew enough about Jack to jeopardize his political future. (He regularly dispatched files full of inside information and gossip to the president, letting him know that little that was lurid in Washington escaped him.) He was not a man to be crossed, and if he wanted to purge the administration of the mobsters and molls Jack and Bobby had foolishly become entangled with, then it would be done.

Judith Campbell called the president several times to complain of the tactics FBI agents were using on her. Jack was reassuring at first. "They won't do anything to you. And don't worry about Sam. You know he works for us." Jack explained that the harassment was "just part of Hoover's vendetta against me." Kennedy hated Hoover, Campbell later recalled, "and called him a queer son of a bitch." As the FBI agents became more aggressive, Jack lost patience with their young victim. " 'You've got to learn to handle this,' he'd say. 'I've got more important things to deal with.' " Mary Pinchot Meyer was now the presidential favorite.[46]

Then, too, Bobby was extremely proud of his highly publicized war on organized crime. It was a benchmark of Kennedy toughness and zeal. In 1960 there had been only 19 indictments of mobsters; by the end of 1961, 121 had been indicted. The Justice Department convicted 96 racketeers in 1961 and 101 in 1962. Perhaps the Kennedys had never thought at all of giving Giancana and his pals a break, despite the generous help in the campaign and in Cuba. They were not above such cynicism, of course. Liberal activist John P. Roche, who knew Bobby well, wrote later that the attorney general was "a clone" of the ambassador: "He couldn't distinguish a principle from a fireplug."[47]

Hoover apparently did not warn Jack about Marilyn Monroe. Two days after the March 22 conversation between the president and the director, Jack was with the actress at the Bing Crosby home near Palm Springs, California. A witness later recalled seeing the two together at a cottage. "The President was wearing a turtleneck sweater, and she was dressed in a kind of robe thing. She had obviously had a lot to drink. It was obvious that they were intimate, that they were staying there together for the night." During the weekend, Monroe called her masseur and said that she and the president were arguing about anatomy. She put Jack on the telephone to explain the issue.[48]

By this time Marilyn had told numerous people of her relationship with the Kennedys. Several mobsters and Teamster boss Jimmy Hoffa, Bobby's personal enemy and premier target in his war on crime, sought concrete evidence, hoping to blackmail the Kennedys. Wiretaps were placed in strategic locations, including the actress's home and the Peter Lawford residence. Hoffa's personal wiretapper, Bernard Spindel, acquired revealing tapes of Monroe with both Jack and Bobby. The fate of these tapes is unknown. In 1966 New York state police raided Spindel's home and seized the tapes and other confidential Monroe materials. (Copies of the tapes were probably made; one was offered to conservative writer Ralph de Toledano just before RFK's death in 1968.) A lawsuit by Spindel's widow requesting their return failed. The FBI contended that its New York investigative file on Spindel had been routinely destroyed. Hoffa disappeared, presumed murdered, in 1975, the same year that Sam Giancana and Johnny Roselli were murdered.[49]

Monroe suspected that her telephone was being tapped, and she began using pay phones. Robert Slatzer, a confidant of the actress, recalled, "She seemed very paranoid." Spindel's widow later told an investigator, "Marilyn was a very frightened woman. . . . There was so much going on then. The assassination attempts against Castro—all that stuff with Giancana and Sinatra, the Kennedys' affairs . . . the Hoffa feud . . . I think Marilyn was afraid for her life."[50]

By the early summer of 1962, the actress was telling friends that Bobby would marry her. Perhaps Kennedy had used that well-worn family ploy on her, or perhaps Monroe merely hoped or fantasized that he would take that step. She and the attorney general were together at the Lawford home in late June and at her home the next evening. Then, suddenly, the Kennedys cut her off, and she was told not to contact either Bobby or Jack again.

Bobby no doubt realized that the actress was serious about marriage and that things had gotten out of hand. But other factors may also have been involved. Perhaps Hoover had gotten wind of what was going on.

Perhaps Bobby knew that too many rumors were circulating about the relationship. Bobby may even have learned of the tapes; private detective Fred Otash, involved in wiretapping Monroe, later told Anthony Summers that government agents forced him to hand over files on both Jack and Bobby midway through the Thousand Days.[51]

Monroe began trying, without success, to reach Bobby by telephone. She slumped into a deep depression, survived a drug overdose, and told friends she had had an abortion. A close friend later recalled that "she looked like death." The actress saw her psychiatrist on twenty-seven of thirty-five days. Sinatra and Lawford brought her to Lake Tahoe for some "orgies" that she bitterly resented but seemed powerless to resist.[52]

Marilyn was now a problem not only to herself but to the Kennedy administration. She possessed handwritten notes from Bobby and had kept a diary of sorts, reportedly containing references to things Bobby told her. She was privy to numerous secrets about the Kennedys and their underworld connections. Moreover, she was highly unstable and might talk at any time. A world-famous celebrity, the actress had the power to do incalculable damage to the Kennedy image.[53]

On August 3 Bobby, Ethel, and four of their children arrived for the weekend at the ranch of a friend in Gilroy, California, about three hundred miles north of Los Angeles. In the early hours of August 5 police found Marilyn Monroe dead in her Los Angeles home, the apparent victim of a drug overdose.

The events surrounding and including the actress's death have been painstakingly probed on several occasions, and most of the details need not be repeated here. Some of the evidence remains controversial. The story contains examples of lying, theft, official incompetence, and cover-up, along with allegations of murder.

Bobby's name entered the picture immediately. Joe DiMaggio privately blamed him for the death. So many insiders were soon linking the attorney general's name with Monroe that Los Angeles Police Chief William Parker treated the case from the start as a top-secret national security matter. His successor, then Deputy Chief Tom Reddin, said later, "The Kennedy connection was a matter of common knowledge at the Police Department level I was at. The Kennedy—I should say Kennedys'—relationship with Marilyn Monroe was pretty generally accepted." As early as 1964 an article in *Photoplay* magazine and a book entitled *The Strange Death of Marilyn Monroe* placed Bobby at Monroe's home on the day of her death.[54]

As the story may now be reconstructed with a somewhat reasonable measure of confidence, on August 4 Bobby secretly traveled by helicopter to Lawford's home in Santa Monica. During the afternoon, he had a stormy meeting with Monroe at her home. Bobby had tried earlier to sever the ties and now felt obligated to tell the actress to her face that the affair was over and that marriage was out of the question.

After Bobby left Monroe called her psychiatrist, Dr. Ralph Greenson, sounding drugged and severely depressed. She made other calls that evening, including one to the White House. Jack was away at Hyannis Port, and she failed to reach him. At about 10:00 P.M., she telephoned Lawford, expressing fear that she had taken too many sleeping pills. Someone called an ambulance, and the actress was alive when it arrived. Monroe died soon afterward, either at her home or en route to the hospital.

On someone's orders the body was placed on the bed, nude, lying facedown. A telephone was placed in Marilyn's hand, making it appear that she had died in midconversation. Lawford went through the house, destroying a note—or half-written letter—that mentioned the Kennedys, and proceeded to tidy up the place. One or perhaps two other friends were also on hand. Lawford placed a call to Washington. He also contacted Hollywood private detective Fred Otash, telling him that Marilyn was dead, that Bobby had been in her house earlier, and that they had gotten him out of the city and back to Northern California. Lawford told Otash that he had destroyed what he could find at Monroe's but would feel better if a professional looked around for anything incriminating the Kennedys. (Before an Otash agent reached the scene at 9:00 A.M., someone had broken open a file cabinet. Monroe's diary and personal notes were never found.)

At about 3:30 A.M., Monroe's housekeeper, Mrs. Eunice Murray, telephoned Dr. Greenson. He broke into the locked room and found the body. Another physician who had treated the actress arrived fifteen minutes later. He and Greenson spent some time discussing the sources of the pill bottles littering Marilyn's bedroom, no doubt worrying that they might be implicated in the death. At 4:25 A.M. Mrs. Murray called the police. By this time the body was in an advanced state of rigor mortis.

Having narrowly escaped his own Chappaquiddick, Bobby appeared at mass with his family at 9:30 A.M. in Gilroy. An elaborate cover-up quickly got under way.

Within hours after police found Monroe's body, either FBI agents or the Los Angeles police impounded records of the actress's recent long-distant telephone calls. If it was the FBI, as Anthony Summers contends, then the order came from the president or the attorney general. Either way the action was obviously designed to protect the Kennedys. And either way J. Edgar Hoover was undoubtedly privy to the latest Kennedy mess and had even more juicy material to hold over his superiors whenever he needed to.[56]

Three days after the incident, Peter Lawford fled to the Bobby Kennedy home in Hyannis Port to avoid questioning. It would take thirteen years to obtain an interview with the actor on the matter, and then he would tell several conflicting stories. He consistently claimed, however, to be the last person to speak to Marilyn Monroe. In 1975 he told police that the actress's last words to him over the telephone were, "Say goodbye to Jack, and say goodbye to yourself, because you're a nice guy."[57]

Lawford was joined at Bobby's home by Pat Newcomb, a close friend and press adviser of Marilyn's. Newcomb had been with Monroe on the last day of her life, and the two had quarreled, probably over their mutual infatuation with Bobby. Newcomb's employer was Arthur Jacobs, one of the men in the Monroe home before Dr. Greenson was called. The young woman obviously knew a great deal. She declined to be interviewed before leaving California, and she continues her silence to this day.[58]

The investigation by Los Angeles officials was completed hastily. A week after Monroe's death a veteran police reporter observed that "strong pressures" were being put on police. "They apparently are coming from persons who had been closely in touch with Marilyn the past few weeks." Five days later, the county coroner closed the case, announcing the verdict of "probable suicide" by an overdose of barbituates. Failure by the coroner's office to conduct necessary tests, the result of apparent bungling, later fed murder theories.[59]

Later investigators would discover that virtually all the relevant documents and photographs were missing. (Two weeks after Monroe's death, FBI agents visited New York's Globe Photos, which had covered the birthday party, and made off with photographs showing the president and the actress together at the event. Today not a single photo exists containing Monroe with the Kennedy brothers.) The former senior desk man in Police Intelligence told Anthony Summers that he did not know what had happened to the file. In 1962 he had been informed that Chief Parker "had taken the file to show someone in Washington. That was the last we heard of it." Parker's widow revealed that her husband had been "very fond" of Bobby Kennedy.[60]

James Hamilton, who personally directed the Monroe investigation for Parker, was well known to the attorney general and was mentioned several times in *The Enemy Within*. Hamilton's son later implied that they had been personal friends. Hamilton kept the facts of the investigation under tight security, and even leading police officials such as Tom Reddin remained in the dark. "Hamilton talked to only two people," Reddin said, "God and Chief Parker." A year after Monroe's death, Bobby wrote Hamilton a letter of recommendation that helped him become chief security officer for the National Football League.[61]

Bobby, of course, contended that he had had only a slight acquaintance with the late actress. Right after Monroe's death, FBI Assistant Director Courtney Evans had a talk with the attorney general about reports of his womanizing. Evans reported in an internal document: "He said he had at least met Marilyn Monroe since she was a good friend of his sister, Pat Lawford," but Kennedy contended that allegations of anything beyond that "just had a way of growing beyond any semblance of the truth."[62]

On the very day Evans signed his report, FBI surveillance microphones picked up a conversation between three mobsters discussing how pressure might be applied to the Kennedys. The weapon was the Marilyn Monroe matter. "They will go for every name," one syndicate figure said. "Unless the brother—it's big enough to cause a scandal against them. Would he like to see a headline about Marilyn Monroe come out? And him? How would he like it? Don't you know? . . . he has been in there plenty of times. It's been a hard affair—and this [female associate of Marilyn's] used to be in all the time with him—do you think it's a secret?"[63]

The heavily censored documents obtained from the FBI and CIA under the Freedom of Information Act do not yet reveal whether mobsters actually attempted to blackmail the attorney general. We do know that it was on their mind and that for a time they possessed the necessary means, including, perhaps, tapes of conversations in Marilyn's home on the day she died. This changed, however, with the rapid disappearance of documents in the Monroe case and the police raid on Bernard Spindel's home. Although he revealed some delicacy at times toward Giancana, Bobby continued the warfare on Hoffa and the Mafia as long as he remained in office.[64]

Controversy swirled around Monroe's death, and several official and private investigations were made. Dr. Ralph Greenson, the actress's psychiatrist, died without shedding much light on the subject. He made it clear to Deputy District Attorney John Miner, however, that he did not believe the actress committed suicide. He told inquirers repeatedly that professional ethics prohibited him from discussing his late client in depth.

To one persistent questioner, he said somewhat irritably that he simply could not tell everything he knew: "Listen . . . talk to Bobby Kennedy."[65]

Jack's relationship with the actress (and his toleration of Bobby's exploits) was reckless in the extreme. His behavior made him seriously vulnerable to blackmail. It also demeaned the nation's highest office; such irresponsibility was an affront to the people who had elected Kennedy in the belief that the power and prestige of the presidency were precious and would come before all self-indulgence. While his conduct did not apparently interfere directly with the broader issues of peace and prosperity facing the chief executive, the potential for disaster was real should organized crime or foreign powers have decided to expose Kennedy's foibles.

The Camelot School, obsessed with protecting the Kennedy image, chose not to discuss this reality. Schlesinger admitted privately to Anthony Summers, "Bobby was human. He liked to drink and he liked young women. He indulged that liking when he traveled—and he had to travel a great deal." In the historian's publications, however, any suggestion of an intimate relationship between the Kennedys and Monroe was briskly dismissed. To Schlesinger—in print—Jack was "urbane, objective, analytical, controlled, contained, masterful, a man of perspective;" he was "witty and meditative" a "man of cerebration," "a life enhancer," so giant a figure that he "seemed invulnerable." And Bobby, "the Puritan," was "his conscience."[66]

CHAPTER 15

Cold and Deliberate

⇉≫ ⇇≪

AN ENORMOUS GAP existed between the image of JFK—dignified public servant, faithful husband, cultivated, judicious, reflective, well-mannered—and the real man, often insensitive, lascivious, and irresponsible. But what about Kennedy as a public official? How did his official actions converge with the good intentions and ideals of his rhetoric? Was the image of youth, energy, intelligence, and concern only skin deep? Or was there more to the president?

By mid-1962, the record of Kennedy's relations with Congress was fairly unimpressive. Some administration proposals had been welcomed on Capitol Hill, including the Peace Corps, the Alliance for Progress, the United States Arms Control and Disarmament Agency, a speedup in the space program, a minimum-wage increase and extension, and increases in Social Security benefits. On the whole, however, the 87th Congress, despite its Democratic control, was unresponsive to the president. Kennedy got just 44.3 percent of his legislative requests in 1962.[1]

This was a conservative Congress; a coalition of Republicans and Southern Democrats made the passage of bills favoring increased spending and the expansion of federal authority difficult at best. Moreover, few leaders on Capitol Hill were captivated by the Kennedy image. Jack had never impressed congressional insiders, and his youth was a handicap.

The average House member was a decade older than the chief executive, and the average senator was even older. The House Appropriations Committee Chairman was eighty-three; his counterpart in the Senate was eighty-four. Many Congressmen found it difficult to take the young president and his often-even-younger aides seriously.[2]

At the same time, Jack continued to be largely inattentive to legislative matters. He often seemed remote and lacked patience and the will to build a record that would match the idealistic rhetoric of his speeches. Kennedy's detachment undoubtedly stemmed from his lack of deep personal conviction about many of the causes he championed on the stump. Also, Jack's life-style often dictated his priorities. One member of Larry O'Brien's staff later complained that the president devoted too much time to personal pleasure. Powerful Congressman Wilbur Mills labeled Kennedy's approach "timid." Senator Allan Ellender of Louisiana said that he could not recall a president who had been "less aggressive." The friendly Hugh Sidey reported, "Kennedy refused to get tough with Congress. . . . There was the faint sensation that Kennedy did not really have his heart in his congressional relations."[3]

Still, Jack was not inactive. He met weekly with Senate and House leaders, always being polite and respectful, flattering his elders with praise and patronage. Kennedy once flew to Oklahoma to woo arrogant Robert Kerr, the "uncrowned king of the Senate." (Bobby later called Kerr a "bandit," but added that his brother liked him for his toughness.) He often courted Senate Finance Committee Chairman Harry Byrd, once dropping in by helicopter to help celebrate the Virginian's annual birthday picnic. Right-wing Republican leader Everett Dirksen of Illinois was consistently given compliments and favors. Jack delivered pep talks at White House receptions and was often on the telephone with congressmen. He expended considerable energy on behalf of a Medicare bill that narrowly failed in the Senate, and he was involved annually in battles over foreign aid.[4] There were causes Jack was willing to work for.

To increase his leverage with Congress and to fulfill his role as party leader, Jack took an active role in the elections of 1962. In a July 23 press conference, he announced that he would go all out to defeat Republicans and said that the elections would give people the "clear" choice either to "anchor down" with the GOP or to "sail" by voting Democratic. Starting in midsummer, the president made numerous campaign trips. Democrats did well in November, gaining four Senate seats and losing only two in the House. Jack's record of success with Congress, however, soon became worse than ever, dropping to 27.2 percent of his legislative requests, the lowest score for a president in ten years.[5]

➔➔➔   ⟵⟵⟵

The president's determination and energy were tested in early 1962 by the steel industry. The confrontation attracted national and international attention, and at the time and afterward it was commonly misunderstood.

In January 1962 the Council of Economic Advisers expressed concern about America's balance of international payments and inflation, and it recommended that industry, in the national interest, grant only minimal wage increases. This proposal had been prominent from the beginning in the administration's plan for economic recovery. The steel industry required special attention; "as goes steel, so goes inflation" was an accurate epigram. On March 31, after meetings with the president and Secretary of Labor Arthur Goldberg, the steel industry and the United Steelworkers agreed to terms that froze wages for a year and granted an increase in fringe benefits of only 2.5 percent. The new contract was hailed throughout the nation.

On April 10, however, the giant United States Steel Corporation suddenly announced an immediate increase of six dollars a ton in the price of steel, four times the cost of the new labor agreement. Five other steel companies quickly fell into step. Labor leaders expressed outrage, claiming they had been betrayed. Roger Blough, chairman of U.S. Steel, said that he had made no commitment about prices during the talks on wages.[6]

Kennedy was furious, believing that there had been an implicit agreement by industry leaders to hold prices steady if the workers made concessions. The administration had convinced union leaders to drop their seventeen-cent-an-hour proposal on the understanding that all parties concerned were helping to contain inflation and improve the nation's competitive position abroad. Jack thought he had been double-crossed and knew that if he failed to resist the price increase he would be in deep trouble with labor, a vital backer of the Democratic Party. (Goldberg, a former counsel to the steelworkers union, threatened to resign.) He called union leader David McDonald and said bluntly: "Dave, you've been screwed, and I've been screwed." He even thought the steel industry's move an attack on the presidency. Sorensen wrote later, "His trust had been abused, his office had been used." Jack quickly contacted Bobby, and they were soon huddling with advisers. The Kennedys, predictably if one understood their character, were determined to fight back with no holds barred. Bobby said later: "We were trying to play hardball with this effort."[7]

A *New York Times* reporter quoted the president as saying, "My father always told me that all businessmen were sons of bitches, but I never really believed him until now." Jack later claimed he was misquoted. (He told Ben Bradlee, "I said sons of bitches or bastards, or pricks. I don't know which. But I never said anything about *all* businessmen."[8]) However, he did not try to conceal his anger. In a press conference statement, he labeled the price hike "a wholly unjustifiable and irresponsible defiance of the public interest" and condemned "a tiny handful of steel executives, whose pursuit of power and profit exceeds their sense of public responsibility." Alluding to crises in Berlin and Vietnam, he even implied that the steel executives were un-American. Hugh Sidey said later: "It was Kennedy's most withering public fire."[9]

Responding to a request by his brother to check out a newspaper interview with the president of Bethlehem Steel in which the executive was quoted as opposing a price rise, Bobby ordered FBI agents to question reporters and steel executives. Director Hoover, apparently acting on his own to embarrass the administration, dispatched the agents late that night and into the next morning. Several people were pulled from their beds in a fashion that reminded many of Gestapo tactics. Bobby also convened a grand jury and had FBI agents begin combing corporate records for evidence of price-fixing and issuing subpoenas for personal files. "I agree it was a tough way to operate," he said later. "But under the circumstances, we couldn't afford to lose."[10]

The president created an informal task force on the issue. Clark Clifford, Robert McNamara, John McCone, and Arthur Goldberg were among several Kennedy insiders recruited to apply pressure on business leaders to force the steel companies to roll back their price increase. The White House released data charging that U.S. Steel did not need the hike. The Defense Department announced that a $5.5 million order for steel plates would go entirely to a smaller company that had not raised prices, instead of being divided between the smaller firm and U.S. Steel. Cabinet officers McNamara, Hodges, and Dillon were told to hold press conferences to make their case. The Federal Trade Commission promised a price-fixing probe. Senator Estes Kefauver announced that his Anti-trust and Monopoly Subcommittee would investigate the steel industry. The president directed the battle personally and carefully monitored public opinion.[11]

Jack told Ben Bradlee that the steel companies "kicked us right in the balls. And we kicked back. The question really is: are we supposed to sit there and take a cold, deliberate fucking." He was going to battle it out, feeling an emotional need to lash out against those who did not play with the team. "They fucked us, and we've got to try to fuck them." Later that same day Jack read a telegram to Bradlee from the general counsel of U.S. Steel claiming that he was too busy to talk to FBI agents. "Who the fuck do they think they are?" the president asked.[12]

The resolve of the steel magnates broke when Inland Steel of Chicago, the eighth largest company in the industry, refused to raise its prices. Before long, Bethlehem Steel, the nation's second largest producer, capitulated, and then U.S. Steel caved in. Steel prices returned to the level they had been at the start of the week, and the seventy-two-hour struggle was over.[13]

Jack relished the victory. Bobby said later, "You know, he liked fights. And he liked to *win*. And *he* won it."[14] The Kennedy determination to win and to use all means to do so had proved effective in the service of labor relations.

Although public opinion rallied behind the president during the crisis, there was much criticism of the administration for its heavy-handed, if legal, tactics. The *New York Herald Tribune* ran an editorial depicting Pierre Salinger telling the president: "Mr. Khrushchev said he liked your style in the steel crisis." (Jack promptly cancelled all twenty-two White House subscriptions to the newspaper.) The *Wall Street Journal* complained of "naked power." Republicans spoke bitterly about what they called the administration's assault on free enterprise; the GOP congressional leadership warned, "We have passed within the shadow of police-state methods." Bumper stickers appeared reading "I miss Ike— Hell, I even miss Harry." Businessmen wore buttons displaying "SOB: Sons of Business." A popular cartoon had one tycoon saying to another within the plush confines of a private club, "My father always told me that all Presidents were sons-of-bitches." A *Business Week* survey of executives found the general mood to be that "the damage [was] irreparable." Some of the executives were so fearful of reprisals on government contracts that they refused to talk, even anonymously.[15]

Kennedy was also blamed for the May 28 stock market crash, the worst since 1929. Conservatives claimed that the president's assault on Roger Blough had undermined business confidence. Jack was keenly aware of his critics, telling aides, "They are starting to call me the Democratic Hoover."[16]

Liberals were delighted by Kennedy's victory over the steel men and were convinced that he had freed the presidency from the domination of Big Business. Schlesinger later wrote of "a bravura public performance" and compared Kennedy to Jackson, Wilson, Roosevelt, and Truman—the "activist" chief executives.[17]

In fact Kennedy well appreciated the vast power of the corporations and banks and understood, as most "practical" politicians had for more than a century, that it was futile and self-destructive to alienate them. Kennedy was the first chief executive since McKinley to address an annual convention of the conservative National Association of Manufacturers, and he made repeated efforts early in the administration to convince businessmen of his support. The Kennedy administration's policies on taxes, trade, and antitrust were in harmony with corporate tastes. From his conservative State of the Union message through the steel crisis, the president largely resisted the Keynesian appeals of Walter Heller and other liberal advisers. Jack knew little about economics and, like his father, continued to see balanced budgets as the ultimate badge of economic wisdom.[18]

Soon after the steel crisis, Jack began courting business leaders, hoping to regain their confidence. At a news conference he emphatically declared that the administration harbored "no ill will against any individual, any industry, corporation, or segment of the American economy." Treasury Secretary Douglas Dillon, a prominent Wall Street banker before his appointment, was among several presidential ambassadors dispatched all over the country to assure business groups of the administration's favor. Dillon decried the "misconception that the Kennedy Administration is pursuing overall anti-business policies." Ted Sorensen sent memoranda to the heads of twenty-four departments and agencies requesting input for a list he was making of actions proposed or undertaken by the administration that were "pro-business" or "pro-free enterprise." The president sent a congratulatory telegram to U.S. Steel's Roger Blough when Yale University honored the executive, and he said repeatedly: "The steel action won't happen again. That was a personal thing."[19] Precisely: The steel crisis had revealed more about Jack's character than about his identification with the American working man. The steel companies had abused his trust and flaunted their power at his expense. They were chastised and taught that they would have to play along with the president to get what they wanted.

When the probusiness campaign faltered and the stock market panic threatened to trigger a recession, Kennedy became slightly more receptive to Heller and other administration liberals. In mid-June he delivered a much-discussed speech at Yale, written in part by Schlesinger and John Kenneth Galbraith, that explored "myths and clichés" about business and government. The president criticized the idea that the federal government had grown excessively large, the belief that the national debt was growing at a dangerous rate, and the argument that federal deficits created inflation. Kennedy seemed to be endorsing Keynes, preferring "the practical management of a modern economy" to free-market principles. Numerous business leaders were displeased. They had not expected this of Ambassador Kennedy's son.[20]

That summer Heller persuaded Dillon to embrace a permanent tax cut of some $10 billion. The president announced the general idea in August in what Sorensen later called "the worst speech he ever gave from the White House on television."[21] Jack was unconvincing in part because he continued to be uncomfortable with the prospect of large federal deficits. In December Heller noted: "As of the moment, the President is shaken on the question of a tax cut. . . . I have never seen the President so anguished and uncertain about the correctness of his course on a domestic matter in the two years that I have served with him."[22]

Above all Jack was afraid of further alienating the corporate powers. To test their reaction to a tax cut, which some business leaders already favored, he decided to broach the idea to the Economic Club of New York. The speech, filled with rhetoric extolling free enterprise and balanced budgets, stunned many liberals. John Kenneth Galbraith called it the most "Republican speech since McKinley." *Time* magazine thought that Kennedy sounded like an officer of the National Association of Manufacturers. The response from business was highly positive, and from then on Jack expressed enthusiasm for a tax cut.[23]

Kennedy's proposal favored the wealthy. Liberal economist Leon Keyserling estimated that the richest 12 percent of the taxpayers would obtain 45 percent of the cut. Socialist Michael Harrington called the proposal "reactionary Keynesianism." The corporate community unswervingly supported Kennedy's plan.[24]

Business learned at last that Kennedy was an ally, and that the steel crisis had been an aberration. Eugene V. Debs was not in the White House; all was well. Bobby would soon boast that "more was done for business in the United States during the last three years than has ever been done."[25] Allen J. Matusow, in his persuasive study of the issue, called Jack the "quintessential corporate liberal," declaring that his economic policies were "framed above all to create a stable environment for corporate prosperity and corporate expansion. What was good for the corporate system would be good for the country."[26]

Throughout the remainder of the Kennedy administration, business reaped the benefits of liberal depreciation allowances, new tax credits, lower margin requirements for buying stocks, and a new trade bill. The president supported a drug bill endorsed by drug manufacturers, and he backed satellite legislation favored by the private communications industry. In April 1963, a year to the month after the steel crisis, Kennedy gave his tacit approval to selective price increases by steel companies.[27]

→>> <<←

The civil rights movement attracted much attention during the Thousand Days. An increasing momentum was building throughout the early 1960s, and many wondered how far the president would move on behalf of racial justice. Kennedy had often lauded efforts to end segregation and put the federal government solidly behind the pursuit of equality. The chief executive had an unparalleled authority to sow harmony among blacks and whites, by executive action, through legislative proposals, and above all by his powers of public persuasion.

Pressures to end racial discrimination in America had been mounting for decades. With the decline of the cotton industry during the Great Depression, millions of blacks began migrating northward. Eager for their votes, northern Democrats promised to work for integration throughout the country. Ideals of racial integration and equality began to be voiced by Democrats and Republicans alike. After World War II, with its struggles against fascism and racism, the Jim Crow laws and customs that had segregated blacks since the late nineteenth century seemed more than ever to clash with the highest principles embodied in the Declaration of Independence and the Constitution.

In 1948, an election year, President Truman called for an assortment of bold civil rights laws and ordered the integration of the armed forces. In 1954 the United States Supreme Court ruled against segregation in the nation's public schools. Two years later, Martin Luther King, Jr., led an inspired and successful attempt to integrate the buses of Montgomery, Alabama. In 1957 President Eisenhower used the Army in Little Rock, Arkansas, to enforce a court order integrating Central High School. The same year Congress passed the first civil rights law since Reconstruction. Among other things, it strengthened the authority of the attorney general to intervene when blacks were denied the right to vote. In 1960 black students led sit-ins that recruited fifty thousand people and desegregated public facilities in 140 cities and towns.

Both Nixon and Kennedy embraced civil rights in 1960, but the Democrats, led by the party's liberal wing, portrayed themselves as champions of the movement. The party adopted the boldest civil rights plank in its history, calling for federal action to end discrimination in housing and education, endorsing passage of fair employment practices legislation, and pledging bold enforcement of the voting laws. Throughout the campaign Jack declared that a president should use his executive authority to wipe out racial discrimination "in every field of Federal activity" and lead the fight for even stronger civil rights legislation. He publicly regarded the civil rights issue as a moral question. After the election black leaders had every reason to believe that, on the basis of Kennedy's rhetoric and his public sympathy for Martin Luther King, the new chief executive would be a fiery advocate of equality.[28]

Once in office, however, Kennedy showed great restraint on the civil rights issue. The opportunity to lead the country in a historic movement of reunion and justice was bypassed in favor of political expediency. Instead of keeping his eye on the protests and rage of his black citizens, he feared alienating Southern Democrats, whose support in Congress was needed to pass legislation higher on the administration's agenda.

Jack had never had a deep moral commitment to racial equality. Bobby later acknowledged that the Kennedys had not given much consideration to the issue. "I don't think that it was a matter that we were extra-concerned about as we were growing up. There wasn't any great problem." Civil rights legislation "was never an issue in Massachusetts."[29] (Arthur Krock said later, "I never saw a Negro on level social terms with the Kennedys in all my years of acquaintance with them. And I never heard the subject mentioned." During the late stages of the 1960 campaign, the ambassador privately berated Krock for claiming that Jack favored "total racial integration" in the United States.)[30] Sorensen wrote of Jack in the 1950s, "When he talked privately about Negroes at all . . . it was usually about winning Negro votes."[31]

Along with the great majority of Northern Democrats and Republicans, however, the Kennedys clearly understood that racial discrimination was wrong. Their numerous efforts to pressure the federal government into hiring more blacks contained at least some ethical as well as political considerations. (Nonetheless, Jack had only a single black on his staff, Assistant White House Press Secretary Andrew Hatcher, and his influence was minimal at best.)[32] The same should be said about public statements and actions favoring school desegregation. The Kennedys expressed concern privately as well as publicly that racial segregation damaged the nation's image abroad. And the Justice Department's initial emphasis on black voting rights involved more than the desire to recruit Democrats.[33]

But the Kennedys failed to initiate or achieve any significant or lasting progress in this critical area of American life for the basic reason that, being pragmatic politicians primarily interested in winning and maintaining political power, they put votes ahead of principles. Moreover, the president and his brother, as attorney general, treated those consumed by these principles as objects of scorn. Bobby later called activist Harris Wofford "in some areas a slight madman." (Wofford was moved from the Justice Department to the Peace Corps in 1962 and sent to Africa.) He labeled the Stevenson liberals "sons of bitches," adding, "I thought that an awful lot of them, as I said at the time, were in love with death."[34]

The president took modest steps early in the administration to implement some of the civil rights promises made by Democrats during the campaign. But his actions were sharply limited. He refused to honor his pledge to end discrimination in federally assisted housing with a stroke of the pen because it was politically disadvantageous. (Jack was privately peeved with Harris Wofford for putting the "stroke of the pen" phrase in his campaign speech, and when people flooded the White House with pens to remind the president of his moral duty, he sent the pens to Wofford.) In early 1962 Kennedy continued to delay, as he sought authority to create a new Department of Urban Affairs headed by Robert Weaver, a black housing expert who had been chairman of the board of the NAACP. His caution proved futile when both houses of Congress soundly defeated the proposed department. Moreover, several liberals privately asked the president to delay the housing order because they thought it could damage their fall campaigns. Bobby said later: "There's no question that we waited until after the election because of the political implications."[35]

The president opposed sending new civil rights legislation to Capitol Hill for equally pragmatic reasons. Bobby said later that such proposals could not have passed and would have alienated key Southern Democrats in Congress. "I don't think we really seriously considered sending any legislation up. There was so much unfinished business that needed to be done." He listed economic problems, housing, education, and Medicare and noted the foreign crises that were also claiming administration attentions.[36]

The President's Committee on Equal Employment Opportunity, chaired by the vice president, soon earned the wrath of the Kennedys, in part because of its practice of publicizing unsettling data about racial discrimination. When the president got a look at some of the statistics compiled by the committee staff, Bobby later recalled, "Oh, he almost had a fit." One questionnaire showed that few of the approximately 35,000 U.S. companies with government contracts employed blacks.

Bobby said later: "I could just see going into the elections of 1964, and eventually these statistics or figures would get out. There would just be a public scandal."[37]

The Kennedys were also privately upset by the Civil Rights Commission, a body established in 1957 to investigate the oppression of minorities and issue recommendations. Dominated by liberals, the commission saw itself as "the duly appointed conscience of the government in regard to civil rights" and prodded the president and the Justice Department to make greater efforts. Bobby later unintentionally revealed that the commission's idealism and moralistic tone turned off the Kennedys. And veteran commission member Father Theodore M. Hesburgh recalled that both Jack and Bobby pressured the commission to postpone public hearings in Mississippi because of political considerations. "I had the impression all along that . . . political expediency was a very strong force in [Kennedy's] whole Administration. He did what was the politically expedient thing to do."[38]

The initial civil rights strategy of the Kennedy administration, then, had its positive side. The federal government was encouraged to hire blacks. Quiet efforts were made to integrate public schools. The Justice Department worked to ensure voting rights, an activity that, as one scholar has noted, "risked the least political capital." On the other hand, executive orders were not issued as promised, and legislation was placed on the back burner. The attorney general concurred with the view of J. Edgar Hoover (himself violently opposed to the civil rights movement) that the federal government lacked the legal authority to protect civil rights workers. All over the South activists were beaten at will while FBI agents looked the other way.

The Kennedys thought that with a modest effort they could appease both blacks and Southern Democrats. They hoped that the racial issue would gradually take care of itself while they devoted their attention to other matters. Theirs was a rational policy that might have worked a few years earlier. But the Kennedys underestimated the passion for justice within the civil rights movement—because they did not share it. They failed to realize that their eloquent campaign rhetoric about equality and democracy would be taken seriously by people who had suffered long enough.

The administration was unprepared for the jarring and bloody developments in civil rights that began in the spring of 1961 and grew more intense during the Thousand Days. What Victor Navasky wrote later of the attorney general also applied to the president: They "became deeply involved in civil rights through events rather than planning, through necessity rather than philosophy, through emergency rather than deliberation."[39]

On May 4, 1961, two busloads of blacks and whites left Washington, D.C., for the Deep South to challenge segregation in interstate bus terminals and facilities. Activist James Farmer, head of the nonviolent Congress of Racial Equality (CORE), who led the movement personally, was confident that he had an ally in the White House who would sooner or later come to the rescue of the Freedom Riders with the full authority of the federal government. A sympathizer said later, "The feeling was: After Ike, at least we'll have an activist Administration. We were all unsophisticated about power. We thought it was there to be used. This was exciting."[40]

The riders encountered fights and arrests en route, and in Anniston, Alabama, a mob of whites burned one of the buses and beat its passengers. There were more beatings in Birmingham. Local hospitals closed their doors, and local police and FBI agents turned their backs. (Of the five black agents then on the FBI's 5,500-man roster, three functioned as servants.) Alabama Governor John Patterson urged demonstrators to leave the state immediately. However, more activists from Nashville soon joined the effort and headed for Montgomery, the state capital. They were soon at the mercy of an angry mob of a thousand people armed with clubs and pipes. John Seigenthaler, a representative of the president, was beaten and left unconscious in the street for twenty-five minutes.

The president was extremely unhappy about the Freedom Riders. "Undoubtedly," Schlesinger later wrote, "he wanted to keep control over the demand for civil rights." Now this disruptive activity was taking place on its own, threatening the peace Jack enjoyed with Southern voters and politicians and embarrassing him on the eve of his trip to meet Khrushchev.[41]

Bobby stayed on top of developments, quietly trying to prevent violence, get the Riders out of Alabama, and minimize the political harm. He made telephone calls to Anniston and Birmingham, and he attempted unsuccessfully to reach Governor Patterson, a personal friend and political ally. Jack also tried to contact Patterson, hoping to persuade him to keep order and spare the administration the necessity of using federal force. Patterson finally agreed to see Seigenthaler, expressing his willingness and ability to protect everyone in Alabama. The assurance proved worthless, however, and the violence in Montgomery on May 20, including the attack on Seigenthaler, persuaded the Kennedys that federal action was required. The legal theory focused on the right of Americans to engage freely in interstate travel.[42]

A sympathetic federal judge was found to issue a restraining order against the Montgomery police and the Ku Klux Klan, and the attorney general dispatched six hundred marshals to restore peace. During the election campaign Jack had told Southerners of his unwillingness to use the Army in such circumstances if at all possible. Bobby said later: "The reason we sent marshals was to avoid the idea of sending troops. We thought that marshals would be much more accepted in the South and that you could get away from the idea of military occupation. We had to do something."[43] The Kennedys were trying to placate Southern Democrats, of course, as well as retain crucial black support. Also present was the urgent need to quash violence, which had the potential of doing great damage to the image of the party, the administration, and the nation.

The next day the marshals protected Martin Luther King, Jr., James Farmer, and fifteen hundred other blacks gathered in a Montgomery church from a howling mob. When King called Bobby to complain about the violence, Bobby replied that the clergyman and his associates would be "as dead as Kelsey's nuts" (an Irish expression that Bobby could not explain) if it had not been for his efforts.[44]

Patterson soon felt compelled to dispatch the Alabama National Guard to the capitol to restore order. He was soon blaming Bobby publicly for the entire series of incidents, and the charge was widely believed. The Louisiana legislature, expressing sympathy for its white neighbors, passed a resolution accusing the Kennedys of mounting a "hate-the-South" campaign. The attorney general's efforts to avoid political damage had failed. Referring to his personal reputation in the South, Bobby said later, "I never recovered from it. That was damaging."[45]

On May 20, as the mob ran out of control in Montgomery, the president issued a terse, six-sentence statement expressing his "deepest concern," requesting local officials to keep order, and asking all sides of refrain from provocative actions. No mention was made of the moral or constitutional issues involved.[46]

When Jack met informally at the White House with members of the Peace Corps National Advisory Council, actor Harry Belafonte and Yale Law School Dean Eugene Rostow suggested politely that the president should say more on behalf of the Freedom Riders and provide some moral leadership in civil rights. Afterward Jack flew into a rage, saying of Rostow, "Doesn't he know I've done more for civil rights than any President in American history? How could any man have done more than I've done?"[47] The argument placing morality above politics simply did not register.

Despite a public appeal by Bobby for a "cooling-off period," the

Freedom Ride campaign continued. As activists headed toward Jackson, Mississippi, the attorney general made scores of telephone calls to Senator James Eastland of Mississippi, an ardent segregationist and the powerful chairman of the Judiciary Committee. The Kennedys courted Eastland because of his ability to obstruct legislation. He could also delay judicial appointments. Bobby made a quiet deal with Eastland in which the senator agreed to have highway patrolmen arrest all of the riders for violating a variety of local ordinances, thus avoiding further violence and federal intervention. (Bobby said later, "I found it much more pleasant to deal with [Eastland] than many of the so-called liberals in the House Judiciary Committee or in other parts of Congress or the Senate.") The buses traveled under police escort from Montgomery to Jackson.[48]

That evening Martin Luther King telephoned Bobby, and the two had a sometimes heated conversation about the future of those under arrest. Rejecting the idea of bail, King exclaimed, "It's a matter of conscience and morality," and added, "They must use their lives and their bodies to right a wrong." Bobby responded coldly. When King suggested that the jails of Jackson might be filled with thousands of other students to make their point, Bobby warned him not to "make statements that sound like a threat. That's not the way to deal with us." After an hour on the phone with the attorney general and Assistant Attorney General Burke Marshall, King said to friends: "You know, they don't understand the social revolution going on in the world, and therefore they don't understand what we're doing."[49]

In a telephone conversation with Wofford, Bobby expressed extreme displeasure with King and his allies. "The President is going abroad and this is all embarrassing him," he said.[50]

King and his fellow activists had other reasons for disillusionment with the Kennedys. The president ignored an appeal to issue a "second Emancipation Proclamation." He refused requests to personally welcome the Freedom Riders back to Washington. And when he returned from Europe, he rejected the suggestion that his report to the nation contain references to the racial crisis.[51]

Despite the suspicions of civil rights leaders and the enmity of diehard segregationists, however, the Kennedys had good cause to be optimistic about the restrained, politically expedient approach to civil rights. Many Southerners, like Eastland and Senate patriarch John McClellan of Arkansas, were pleased. Governor Patterson said that he still considered the president a friend. The Gallup poll revealed that 50 percent of those polled in the South agreed with the President's decision to send marshals into Montgomery. (Eisenhower had won only 36 percent approval for the intervention in Little Rock.) Nationally, 70 percent approved Kennedy's action, while only 13 percent disapproved.[52]

In June the attorney general met with civil rights activists and attempted to persuade them to direct their energies away from militant confrontation and into voter registration. (Bobby said later, "I felt strongly about the fact that voting was at the heart of the problem. If enough Negroes registered, they could obtain redress of their grievances internally, without the federal government being involved in it at all.") In 1960 only 28 percent of Southern blacks were registered to vote, while close to 70 percent of whites were registered. The proposal became a reality the following year with the Voter Education Project, funded principally by private philanthropy. White opposition to the effort often erupted into violence, however, and the peace desired by the Kennedys proved elusive. Several civil rights leaders expressed unhappiness with the federal government's failure to intervene on their behalf. King and others said that Bobby had promised them full protection.[53]

Activists were pleased when the revitalized Civil Rights Division of the Justice Department made extensive investigations into the tactics used to deny blacks the vote. Lawsuits were filed throughout the South. Still, the results were negligible. A leading Justice Department official lamented after two years, "We have moved from no registration to token registration." The President's Southern judicial appointees were instrumental in blocking and delaying much progress.[54]

Bobby achieved more by asking the Interstate Commerce Commission (ICC) to issue regulations ending segregation in all interstate travel. Secretary of State Rusk backed the request with evidence showing how segregation damaged America's image abroad. Under heavy administration pressure, the ICC responded in September 1961. Thereafter the Justice Department worked quietly throughout the South to bring down the segregation signs in all bus, railroad, and airport terminals. By the end of 1962 CORE officials were satisfied that this particular issue was settled.[55]

In July 1961 the president personally welcomed a large number of delegates from the NAACP's annual convention to the White House. He set up chairs for the women, listened attentively, and was generally so charming that the visitors barely realized the he had rejected their appeals for new civil rights legislation.[56]

The following month civil rights leader Roy Wilkins presented the White House with a sixty-page paper entitled *Federally Supported Discrimination*. The study, compiled on behalf of thirty-five liberal organizations, cited substantial evidence documenting Dr. King's belief that the federal government was "the nation's highest investor in segregation." Minor moves by the administration followed. The Office of Education, for example, declared that federally aided libraries must be open to all citizens, but the agency did not penalize the defiant. Civil rights activists remained dissatisfied.[57]

In early 1962 the administration submitted two voting rights measures to Congress. A fairly uncontroversial constitutional amendment outlawing poll taxes in federal elections was soon approved. (Only five states still used poll taxes.) A bill exempting those with at least a sixth-grade education from literacy tests in federal elections irritated liberals because, among other things, it failed to include state elections. Wilkins called it "a token offering on the full civil rights program pledged by the administration's party platform of 1960."[58]

The attorney general testified on behalf of the voter-literacy bill, but the president did little on its behalf. According to Assistant Attorney General Burke Marshall, Jack was merely "tolerant of letting the Attorney General try this." A Southern filibuster killed the proposal. Liberal Senator Joseph Clark said that the bill's principal difficulty had been the "lack of any deep conviction behind it." Neither congressional leaders nor the White House had been enthusiastic about the politically divisive legislation.[59]

Bobby later defended the administration by claiming that no one paid any attention to civil rights at the time. (Senate Majority Leader Mansfield predicted privately after the defeat of the voter literacy proposal that Congress would never again pass a civil rights bill.) As for his brother: "There wasn't anything he could do then. He didn't believe in just going through the motions about things. If giving some leadership would have accomplished something, then even if it was going to fail, he might have done it."[60]

The president was deeply disturbed by violence that erupted in Albany, Georgia, during the summer of 1962. Members of the Student Nonviolent Coordinating Committee (SNCC) and others had faced intense resistance in late 1961 to efforts to integrate a bus terminal. Mass protests and marches followed, and 550 blacks, including Martin Luther King, were arrested. Integration and voting registration efforts intensified during the spring, and in July whites reacted with extreme violence. One SNCC activist, who dodged bullets as he prepared for bed, said later, "We were working together on Voter Registration. We had been shot at. Some were hit. There was blood. We were afraid. Where was the Federal Government?"[61]

Although the Justice Department carefully monitored developments in Albany, the administration's principal concern was the restoration of civic tranquillity. Responding to criticism by a black leader, Jack told a news conference that he could not understand why the City Council of Albany refused to sit down with demonstrators "and attempt to secure them, in a peaceful way, their rights."[62] But little else was done, and civil rights leaders were furious.

Several activists condemned the president for failing to use the moral influence of his office. In a telegram to the White House, one said: "Ignoring the acts of demagogs and tyrants perpetuating segregation and discrimination is tantamount to aiding and abetting. You cannot continue to ignore the cries of these oppressed people." Dr. King told a reporter that "if the President would counsel the people, it would mean a great deal." There was also the question of direct federal action. Although restrained by law and the Constitution from entering certain situations, the chief executive possessed broad authority to suppress domestic violence. Kennedy chose not to use it, hoping to placate white Southerners and their powerful representatives in Congress.[63]

From the beginning Jack had left civil rights largely to his brother. During 1962 he continued to remain aloof. At a May 17 news conference, a reporter reminded him that it was the eighth anniversary of the Brown decision and asked if he thought that progress in this area had been adequate. Jack's two-sentence reply concluded: "There is a good deal left undone, and while progress has been made I think we can always improve equality of opportunity in the United States." In violent July he responded to criticism from King with a single sentence: "I made it very clear that I'm for every American citizen having his Constitutional rights, and the United States Government under this Administration has taken a variety of very effective steps to improve the equal opportunities for all Americans, and will continue to do so."[64]

This attitude was politically profitable. In September the Gallup poll found the president almost as popular below the Mason-Dixon line (65 percent approval) as above it (68 percent). Southerners were helpful in securing four administration victories in the House during the year.[65]

The administration sought to avoid civil rights measures that smacked of retribution against the South. It did not want federal funds, for example, withheld from segregated school districts. Increasingly it sought to emphasize black economic improvement, which Southerners found less controversial than civil rights proposals. Bobby encouraged a black business association to help black school dropouts who might otherwise become "malcontents, criminals, and persons who have little faith in freedom and democratic ways" to return to school or enter vocational programs. The Attorney General also called racial progress through voluntary action a "far more important" alternative to violence.[66]

The administration's approach was severely tested in September when James Meredith, a twenty-nine-year-old native of Mississippi whose grandfather had been a slave, attempted to enroll in the all-white University of Mississippi at Oxford. (The effort had begun in early 1961 when Meredith became inspired by the new President's civil rights rhetoric.) Sixty-four-year-old Governor Ross Barnett, who had been elected in 1959 with strong segregationist support, defied a federal court decree ordering Meredith's admission and vowed to uphold segregation in all Mississippi schools. After Supreme Court Justice Hugo Black ruled in favor of the court order, the governor declared on statewide television: "We will not surrender to the evil and illegal forces of tyranny."[67]

Bobby, fearing an explosive confrontation at "Ole Miss," began a series of telephone calls to the Governor, urging him to yield to the court ruling, keep the peace, and avoid federal intervention. When Barnett, whom Bobby privately thought "loony," proved intransigent, however, federal marshalls were dispatched to escort Meredith on campus. On September 20, in a dramatic and tension-filled move, Barnett personally turned Meredith away. During the next week, the Governor again defied federal courts (and was found guilty of contempt), blocked Meredith's enrollment, and appeared ready to lead a civil war of sorts.[68]

On September 29 the president entered the picture by telephoning Barnett. (The two would converse six times during the next twenty-four hours.) "I am concerned about, un, this situation," Jack said. "This, un, listen, I didn't, uh, put [Meredith] in the university, but on the other hand, under the Constitution I have to carry that order out and I don't, I get, uh, I don't want to do it in any way that causes, uh, difficulty to you or to anyone else."

When Jack asked for the governor's help, Barnett described the intense political pressure he was under in his state. Jack said that he understood, but emphasized, "Well, we don't have to have a, we don't want to have a lot of people getting hurt or killed down there."[69]

In a second conversation with the Governor, the President said again, "This is not my order, I just have to carry it out. So I want to get together and try to do it with you in a way which is the most satisfactory and causes the least chance of, uh, damage to, uh, people in, uh, Mississippi. That's my interest." Kennedy was doing his best to restore peace and minimize the political damage. By emphasizing his obligation as president, he was assuring the governor and his followers that he was not a civil rights zealot.[70]

The Kennedys agreed to a Barnett proposal to let Meredith be registered secretly in Jackson, the state capitol, while the governor diverted attention to Oxford. As a precaution Jack signed a proclamation similar to Eisenhower's in 1957, federalizing portions of the Mississippi National Guard and ordering all persons obstructing justice in the state to desist and disperse.

When Barnett cancelled the deal with the Kennedys, Bobby threatened him with blackmail: His brother would go on television and tell the world of the governor's plan to register Meredith if he failed to let the young man on campus. Whining and pleading, Barnett capitulated, saying that the registration could proceed at Oxford and that state police would keep order.

Thinking all was well, the president gave a televised address in which he announced that Meredith was in residence at Oxford and expressed his hope that all Mississippians would now consider the matter closed. He lavished praise on Southerners and declared: "I deeply regret the fact that any action by the executive branch was necessary in this case, but all other avenues and alternatives including persuasion and conciliation, had been tried and exhausted."[71]

As Kennedy spoke, however, a wild riot was underway in Oxford. A mob armed with guns, clubs, pipes, rocks, fire bombs, bricks, and bottles attacked Meredith and the three hundred marshals escorting him. Jack had forbidden the federal officials to fire their pistols unless it was necessary to save Meredith's life, so they were forced to defend themselves with tear gas. Appeals to Washington to rescind the virtual ban on bullets were apparently successful. Tape recordings reveal Bobby telling Deputy Attorney General Nicholas Katzenbach, who was on the scene, "Stay right by Meredith and shoot anybody that puts a hand on him." The president, "terribly disheartened," in Sorensen's words, by the violence, was forced to send in troops standing by in Memphis.[72]

After numerous foul-ups by the military that took four and one-half hours and rattled and infuriated the president, some twenty-three thousand soldiers—three times Oxford's population—reached the scene and restored order. (So as not to enflame Southerners further, the Kennedys made sure that all the troops were white.) Bobby said later: "The idea that we got through the evening without the marshals being killed and without Meredith being killed was a miracle." For hours he and his brother had been in anguish over the possibility of another Bay of Pigs. Two people died in the melee, and hundreds, including 166 marshals, were wounded. But the federal court orders were enforced, and Meredith became a student at Ole Miss.[73]

Although the Mississippi State Senate passed a resolution conveying its "complete, entire and utter contempt for the Kennedy Administration and its puppet courts," the president emerged from the struggle with his national and even regional popularity largely intact. He had appeared to be a moderate, reluctantly drawn into the fray by extremists eager to defend a rigid racial segregation that most Americans no longer found justifiable. Even in the South, school desegregation was thought inevitable by most educated citizens.

Jack was not entirely pleased with the course of events. He was annoyed with himself for believing that a deal with Barnett was possible. He wished he had ordered troops sent in earlier, and he remained angry with Pentagon officials over their inability to dispatch soldiers efficiently. The administration's politically oriented approach toward the civil rights movement, however, was largely unaltered by the Oxford crisis. Reflecting the president's desire not to make more of a political martyr out of Barnett than he already was, the Justice Department failed to recommend a criminal contempt charge or a prison term for the governor. Kennedy's position upset some liberals and was ignored by the Fifth Circuit Court of Appeals, which directed the attorney general to prepare criminal contempt charges against Barnett and his lieutenant governor.[74]

Despite Meredith's success Martin Luther King and other civil rights leaders were again critical of the president for his lack of moral leadership. In his speech to the nation stressing law and order, Kennedy had said nothing about Meredith's personal courage and only casually mentioned the justice of his cause. Moreover, the clandestine dealings with Governor Barnett, King thought, "made Negroes feel like pawns in a white man's political game."[75] It was a shrewd analysis.

In late November, with the elections over, Congress adjourned, and the public concerned with Thanksgiving and football, the president issued his much-delayed housing order prohibiting racial discrimination in federally assisted housing. In order to minimize adverse reactions, he deliberately sandwiched the announcement between statements on Soviet bombers leaving Cuba and developments in the Indian border conflict with China. Heeding the advice of conservative politicians and cautious Justice Department lawyers (split over the legal range of presidential authority in the matter), Kennedy signed the narrowest order possible. It covered only 20 percent of newly built houses and less than 3 percent of existing housing. The order did not effect financial institutions, and depended for enforcement on complaints made by victims of discrimination, an approach that had failed on the state and local levels. It was soon apparent that the order would have little impact on racial patterns in housing.[76]

After a meeting with the president in mid-December, several civil rights leaders expressed bitterness toward the administration. One declared to a reporter: "We've gotten the best snow job in history. We've lost two years because we admired him [the president] for what should have been done years ago." Another said: "We're not going about this right. We shouldn't have been here. We've got to quit begging the Kennedys for this and that. We've got to start demanding our rights."[77]

In January 1963, still unwilling to upset Southern congressmen, Jack rejected pleas from liberals to back new civil rights legislation. His State of the Union message virtually ignored civil rights, containing a mere two sentences expressing the belief that all Americans should have the right to vote.[78] Soon the president chose to remain aloof from a Senate struggle to amend Rule 22, and so-called filibuster rule. Martin Luther King lamented, "Had he entered the fray, the amendment would probably have passed and the greatest obstacle to the passage of civil-rights legislation would have been smashed." Bobby later admitted that his brother "didn't feel strongly about it [Rule 22]. I think he thought it was a matter for the Senate. He wasn't going to get involved in it."[79]

Jack, however, did not dismiss the issue of civil rights. He remained mildly sympathetic to the cause, especially toward school integration. Moreover, he could in no way afford to lose black political support. In January he hosted a White House dinner and reception commemorating the centennial of the Emancipation Proclamation. As many as fourteen hundred civil rights enthusiasts were on hand, including the largest contingent of blacks ever welcomed at the executive mansion. (Jack learned that black entertainer Sammy Davis, Jr., was bringing his wife, Swedish actress Mai Britt. Fearing a politically damaging reaction from racists, he had news photographers barred from the reception. The White House later released its own pictures of the event. Davis and Britt were not in them.)[80]

In late February the president sent a special message on civil rights to Congress. It renewed his request that completion of six grades of school should qualify applicants for registration. It sought legislation to provide technical assistance to schools voluntarily desegregating. And it asked that the life of the Civil Rights Commission be extended. In an unusual move Kennedy described the issue in moral terms: "Let it be clear, in our own hearts and minds, that it is not merely because of the

Cold War, and not merely because of the economic waste of discrimination, that we are committed to achieving true equality of opportunity. The basic reason is because it is right.'' These words were included at the request of the top-ranking black member of the Democratic National Committee.[81]

Still, it was clear that the cautious presidential proposals were designed principally to deflect criticism by black leaders. Liberal activist Joseph Rauh, Jr., later described the recommendations as ''such an inane package of legislation as to make the civil rights movement feel that it wasn't worth going for.'' Kennedy knew that his proposals had little chance for passage, and he did not work actively for them. The Justice Department dallied for more than a month before it submitted draft legislation to the House. Jack continued to hope that the civil rights movement would remain quiet and peaceful, permitting him to continue to woo Southern legislators.[82]

Both the president and the attorney general soon applied pressure on the Civil Rights Commission to cancel planned hearings in Mississippi on segregationist terror. The commission gave in, one liberal member saying, ''One hates to go directly against something that a President thinks you shouldn't do.'' Jack also attempted unsuccessfully to persuade commission members not to publish a report describing violence in Mississippi and recommending that the president explore his authority to cut off all federal funds to the state. Soon after the report appeared, Jack publicly rejected its recommendation. *Time* commented, ''The Administration, painfully conscious of the 81 electoral votes that Southern states contributed to John Kennedy's narrow win in 1960, surprised no one with its lack of enthusiasm for the Commission's ideas.''[83]

By the end of March Martin Luther King was expressing fear that the civil rights movement was running out of steam. Much of the blame, he wrote in the *Nation*, could be laid to the administration. ''The demand for progress was somehow drained of its moral imperative, and the issue no longer commanded the conscience of the nation as it had in previous years.'' Citing numerous examples of federal timidity (''While merely 7 percent of Negro children in the South attend integrated schools, the major battle of the year was over one Negro in a Mississippi university''), King complained that the government seemed satisfied with ''tokenism,'' a policy that did more harm, in his judgment, than good. ''It is a palliative which relieves emotional distress but leaves the disease and its ravages unaffected. It tends to demobilize and relax the militant spirit which alone drives us forward to real change.'' The administration should reassess its goals, King urged, and treat civil rights as seriously as trade, tax, and military matters. "The time has come when the government must commit its resources squarely on the side of the quest for freedom." Throughout American history, he wrote, "the moral decision has always been the correct decision."

Still, King was not as harsh toward the Kennedys as some activists were. "I am not ready to make a judgment condemning the motives of the Administration as hypocritical. I believe that it sincerely wishes to achieve change, but that it has misunderstood the forces at play."[84]

King's next target was Birmingham, Alabama, which he labeled "the most thoroughly segregated big city in the U.S." Bobby persuaded him to delay demonstrations until after a local election on April 2. Even though moderates won and Bobby continued to plead for restraint, parades, sit-ins, boycotts, picketing, and petitions got under way, initially to integrate department store lunch counters. Police Commissioner T. Eugene ("Bull") Conner fought back during the next few weeks with often excessive zeal, eventually arresting more than 3,300 demonstrators, including King. Newspapers and television photographers stunned the nation with pictures of savage beatings, police dog attacks, and the use of high-pressure fire hoses against largely nonviolent demonstrators. Many of those involved were young people who stood their ground singing "We Shall Overcome."

The *New York Times* declared, "No American schooled in respect for human dignity can read without shame of the barbarities committed by Alabama police authorities against Negro and white demonstrators for civil rights." It joined a chorus of voices calling on the president to take action. "We cannot stand mute against this degradation." Governor George C. Wallace soon told the Alabama legislature that he would resist "outside meddling, whether it is from high Government sources or otherwise."[85]

On May 4 Jack told a delegation of liberals at the White House that the photograph in morning newspapers of a police dog lunging at a black woman made him "sick." But he also observed that he lacked constitutional authority to intervene directly, and he expressed regret that demonstrators had not waited (as Bobby advised) until the newly elected, more moderate city administration had taken office.[86]

At a news conference four days later, the president said that the administration had been monitoring the crisis looking for violations of federal law. "We have committed all the power of the Federal Government to insure respect and obedience of court decisions and the law of the land." (By this time much of the nation was in an uproar over the indefensible violence.) Jack spoke of "the very real abuses too long inflicted on the Negro citizens of that community" and added that the solution to the problem, "in time," was to "take steps to provide equal treatment of all our citizens."[87]

The administration's principal concern was the restoration of order. Jack was especially concerned about the negative impact of the crisis on America's image abroad. Bobby dispatched Assistant Attorney General Burke Marshall to Birmingham during the height of the violence to mediate between local leaders and demonstrators. Jack had cabinet members contact business associates with ties to Birmingham, urging them to exert pressure for peace. Both Jack and Bobby made personal telephone calls to leading corporate executives with the same message. The attorney general held private meetings in New York and Washington with concerned businessmen.[88]

On May 10 a truce was announced. Blacks were to call off demonstrations and end boycotts; department store owners agreed to desegregate lunch counters and to hire and promote blacks. The following evening, however, the agreement nearly collapsed when bombs destroyed a black home and motel. Rejecting King's nonviolent principle, blacks took to the streets of Birmingham and, in the riot that followed, destroyed nine blocks of the ghetto.

In a brief radio and television speech to the nation, Jack announced that he was putting the Alabama National Guard on alert and dispatching federal troops to bases near Birmingham. "It is my hope," he said, "that the citizens of Birmingham themselves will maintain standards of responsible conduct that will make outside intervention unnecessary."[89]

By this time civil rights leaders were angry with the administration. They wanted the president to denounce Birmingham's ruling elite for its racism. They sought an endorsement of nonviolent demonstrations. They wanted a ringing speech from Kennedy embracing the morality of their cause. Some even suggested that the president personally appear in Birmingham and take a black child by the hand into a segregated school or lunch counter. From his Birmingham jail cell, Martin Luther King wrote of his grave disappointment with the white moderate "who prefers a negative peace which is the absence of tension to a positive peace which is the presence of justice," one who "paternalistically feels that he can set the timetable for another man's freedom."[90]

Jack was aware of his hostility and understood its negative political implications. Bobby experienced black rage firsthand during a private meeting in New York with a group of blacks that included novelist James Baldwin, entertainers Harry Belafonte and Lena Horne, social psychologist Kenneth Clark, playwright Lorraine Hansberry, and young CORE activist Jerome Smith. The attorney general was seeking "new ideas" for dealing with segregation.

After an initial attack by Smith, who seemed to say that he was nauseated by being in the same room with Kennedy, the discussion grew increasingly heated. For three hours the blacks vented their rage at Bobby, his brother, the FBI, the Justice Department, and the system of government in general. Smith said he did not know how much longer he could remain nonviolent, and declared that he would never fight for his country. Baldwin wanted Bobby to escort two black students George Wallace was threatening to bar from the University of Alabama. Hansberry talked about giving guns to blacks so that they could start killing whites. The group criticized the president for failing to use "the great prestige of his office as the moral forum it can be."

Bobby burned with anger, prompting Baldwin to say later that he "didn't understand what we were trying to tell him . . . didn't understand our urgency." Clark said: "There was no chance that Bobby heard anything we said. . . . Kennedy was not unimpressive. He didn't minimize or condescend. But he just didn't seem to get it." The blacks made much of the encounter in the press, compounding the administration's uneasiness. Baldwin said publicly of the attorney general: "We were a little shocked at the extent of his naïveté."[91]

Bobby was so angered by Baldwin and his friends that he had the FBI check them out, hoping to find something he might use against them in the future. (He shared the findings with Jack.) Schlesinger later called the clash an educational experience for the attorney general, who began for the first time to grasp the nature of black anguish, and that seems to be the case. In an oral interview for the Kennedy Library, Bobby made it clear that he was shaken by the anger and radicalism of Baldwin and his colleagues.[92]

The Kennedys were jolted by the series of black riots, disturbances, and demonstrations that began to break out in nearly a thousand cities across the nation. Journalists doted on the violence, filling front pages and television screens with often-frightening scenes of bloodshed and property damage. A Chicago Urban League official warned: "My messages from the beer gardens and the barbershops all indicate the fact that the Negro is at war." In response to increasing mayhem in that city, the mayor ordered a hog-wire enclosure, able to handle ten thousand prisoners, erected on the state fairgrounds. *Newsweek* declared, "Everywhere plain signs arose that Birmingham had thrust the whole U.S. racial problem into a new phase—more intense, more flammable, more urgent. . . .

Among whites, North and South, the crisis not only spurred conscience but touched a nerve of fear."[93]

On the horizon was Black Muslim leader Malcolm X, whose gospel of racial hatred and violence attracted thousands. Even moderate black leaders now seemed eager to endorse the new militance. Herbert Hill, national labor secretary of the NAACP, warned, "The arena of combat for the NAACP has shifted from the courtroom to direct mass action." Martin Luther King brought an audience of 5,500 to its feet in Chicago by declaring: "We're through with tokenism and gradualism and see-how-far-you've-comism. We're through with we've-done-more-for-your-people-than-anyone-elseism. We can't wait any longer. Now is the time."[94]

Politicians knew that something had to be done to restore peace. Some of them understood that they must deal more directly with the causes of racial outbursts. The Army could not be dispatched every-where, and even if it could the result would be political disaster. Bobby said later, "From our own experience, we could see that these demon-strations were going to continue. They were going to spread. There was going to be more violence. There were going to be more people involved, because students were getting out of school for the summer."[95]

The Kennedys decided to submit civil rights legislation to Congress, and they began a series of meetings with congressional leaders to see what might have a chance of passing. There was controversy about whether to anchor the proposals on the Fourteenth Amendment or the commerce clause of the Constitution. There was resistance at various stages of planning from the vice president, Sorensen, O'Donnell, and O'Brien. Southern Congressmen were certain to be upset and might re-taliate by blocking other Administration measures. Republicans were unlikely to be cooperative. But the Kennedys were determined to persist. Burke Marshall, closely involved in these matters, later explained that after Birmingham he and the attorney general realized that the "terrible problem" was "going to get worse and worse and worse and had to be dealt with."[96]

While the legislative discussions continued, a crisis developed in Alabama, the only state in the union without a desegregated state uni-versity. The previous September, when James Meredith was being in-stalled at the University of Mississippi, Alabama Governor George Wallace had vowed to defy the federal government and "stand in the doorway" of any school under court order to integrate. Anticipating trouble, Bobby, cabinet members, and Justice Department officials met for months with leading Alabama educators, politicians, and business-men, trying to avoid violence and federal intervention. Bobby even called personally on the governor, a demagogue with considerable political ambitions, whom university trustees privately thought mad.

On June 11 Wallace made his publicity-inspired stand at the University of Alabama campus in Tuscaloosa—a city known to be the head-quarters of the Ku Klux Klan. Under the threat by a federal judge of a substantial jail sentence, and feeling intense pressure from local business leaders, the governor stepped aside and permitted two black students to register. There was no violence. The president, who had reluctantly fed-eralized some Alabama National Guard units, followed developments carefully.[97]

In recent speeches Jack had made several references to civil rights. At Vanderbilt University, he declared that an educated citizen had a special obligation to uphold the law and to treat fellow Americans with decency and dignity. At Muscle Shoals, Alabama, with Governor Wal-lace in attendance, he spoke of the wisdom of all Americans working together for progress and praised the beneficence of the federal govern-ment. On June 8 in Honolulu, the president was more forthright, an-nouncing to the U.S. Conference of Mayors the impending introduction of federal civil rights legislation and calling for local action to quell expected urban turmoil over the summer. Although Kennedy identified a "moral" as well as "constitutional" crisis, his language remained cau-tious:

> I do not say that all men are equal in their ability, their character, or their motivation, but I say they should be equal in their chance to develop their character, their motivation, and their ability. They should be given a fair chance to develop all the talents that they have, which is a basic assump-tion and presumption of this democracy of ours.[98]

On the afternoon of June 11, immediately following the conclusion of the scare in Tuscaloosa, Jack suddenly asked Sorensen to prepare a civil rights speech. It was to be delivered at 7:00 P.M. over national radio and television. Bobby, deeply concerned about urban violence, had been pushing for such an address since Birmingham, but the political timing had never seemed quite right. Now, with a major crisis overcome, Jack impulsively decided to go all-out for his civil rights legislation.

Jack was also undoubtedly responding to a harsh public attack by Martin Luther King, who said that Kennedy had been as ineffective in civil rights as Eisenhower. Above all, King declared, the president should start talking about integration in moral terms, showing himself capable of rising above politics.[99]

As Sorensen wrote frantically, Jack and Bobby huddled, preparing notes that the president could use in case he was forced to extemporize. Sorensen was able to complete only a first draft, which was handed to the president three minutes before he went on the air. Even Bobby, Burke Marshall later revealed, was shaken by his brother's lack of preparation. As it turned out, Jack used his notes to add a conclusion of his own (echoing the Honolulu address) to Sorensen's manuscript.[100]

The speech made clear that the president was responding to the turmoil in the headlines. "The fires of frustration are burning in every city, North and South, where legal remedies are not at hand. Redress is sought in the streets, in demonstrations, parades, and protests which create tensions and threaten violence and threaten lives." (Sorensen later wrote, "The Kennedy commitment was designed to preserve the fabric of our social order—to prevent the unsatisfied grievances of an entire race from rending that fabric in two.")[101] Echoing King, Jack said: "Now the time has come for this Nation to fulfill its promise," adding that the crisis "cannot be quieted by token moves or talk." Jack announced that he would soon be submitting far-reaching legislation to Congress that would integrate public accommodations, hasten school desegregation, and add protection for the right to vote.

The most striking component of the speech was the president's repeated emphasis on morality: "We are confronted primarily with a moral issue. It is as old as the scriptures and is as clear as the American Constitution." Appeals were made to the Golden Rule. "In short, every American ought to have the right to be treated as he would wish to be treated, as one would wish his children to be treated." And justice demanded action, Jack exclaimed: "Those who do nothing are inviting shame as well as violence. Those who act boldly are recognizing right as well as reality."[102]

Pro-Kennedy polemicists would later describe this speech as a golden moment in the administration, a time when the president, mature and wise as never before, publicly embraced civilization's highest principles. Schlesinger called it "a great speech, its power deriving from a passionate declaration on racial justice never before uttered by an American President."[103] No doubt a bit of the idealism of the long-suffering activists had indeed rubbed off on the Kennedys by this time. But it seems in retrospect highly likely that the moralistic rhetoric of the June 11 speech was designed in large part for a pragmatic purpose: Jack was wrapping the proposed legislation in the loftiest possible language in the hope of securing its passage. The tactic was familiar to students of American history.

Jack and Bobby were undoubtedly sincere in seeking to better the educational and economic opportunities for blacks. But this was by no means a distinctive attitude in Washington at the time. The ultraconservative pragmatist Everett Dirksen of Illinois had similar sentiments; the violence had shaken even the least sensitive observers of the nation's social problems. The Kennedys were unquestionably eager to see more blacks registered to vote. But anyone with the dimmest knowledge of contemporary affairs understood that virtually every new black voter helped the Democrats. Above all Jack and Bobby wanted to quell the turmoil that threatened to disrupt the entire nation and thus destroy their administration. As always, the Kennedys were thinking primarily about politics and their own political futures.

The decision to back civil rights legislation was a bit risky. Many powerful Southern congressmen would be angered, further burying hopes for legislation in other fields. Some Republicans might well side with their conservative allies. In the months ahead, Jack would often ask Bobby privately if they had made a wise move. "He always felt that maybe that was going to be his political swan song," Bobby said later. Still, there was considerable support for new legislation throughout the nation, especially in the wake of black violence. Syndicated columnist William S. White observed, "Because all recognized both the national and political dangers inherent in the situation, there is a curious tendency to treat it with far less overt partisanship than used to be the case." Bobby said later: "We thought the feeling of the country was behind the steps that were being taken." And then there was the entirely probably alternative to taking action: continued violence and politically destructive armed intervention.[104]

In a private meeting with senators, a participant reported, Bobby "painted a terrible picture of the situation which could become uncontrollable" without new civil rights legislation. James Reston declared in the *New York Times* that the president was "apprehensive that the demonstrations will get beyond police control and is trying to get the issue out of the streets and back into the courts."[105]

The ugliness of the racial climate was underscored on the very evening of the president's speech. Medgar Evers, a thirty-seven-year-old NAACP field representative, was murdered outside his home in Jackson, Mississippi. (Both Jack and Bobby showed personal kindness to the victim's widow and brother.) A few days later, following an emotional funeral service, blacks rioted in downtown Jackson. A brawl followed, with local police and firemen using guns, clubs, hoses, and dogs. Jack and Bobby monitored the violence in detail.[106]

During the following week blacks rioted, marched, sat in, or picketed in Savannah, Georgia; Danville, Virginia; Cambridge, Maryland; New York City; Providence, Rhode Island; and dozens of other cities. In Washington Bobby personally faced a crowd of three thousand blacks marching on the Justice Department. Using a bullhorn, he responded angrily to a charge of employment discrimination. "Individuals will be hired according to their ability, not their color," he shouted. A radical reporter on the scene thought it "exactly the sort of impersonal, legalistic response, blind to the larger moral implications of our protest, that we felt made Kennedy such an inadequate attorney general."[107]

On June 19, in a special message to Congress, Jack again spoke of the moral dimension of the struggle for civil rights and stressed the need to prevent further violence. If the federal government failed to take legislative action, he declared, there would be "continued, if not increased, racial strife—causing the leadership on both sides to pass from the hands of reasonable and responsible men to the purveyors of hate and violence, endangering domestic tranquillity, retarding our Nation's economic and social progress and weakening the respect with which the rest of the world regards us." Kennedy's Civil Rights Act of 1963 called for federal authority to guarantee blacks the right to be served in public places, to attend an integrated school, to receive federally financed training and education, and to look for a job without fear of racial discrimination. "In short, the time has come for the Congress of the United States to join with the Executive and Judicial Branches in making it clear to all that race has no place in American life or law."[108]

As expected, Southern Democrats denounced the president's proposals and vowed to resist. Northern Democrats were largely supportive. Republicans decided to devise their own bill. The *New York Times* predicted that the struggle on Capitol Hill would be "long and often bitter." Lyndon Johnson privately expressed pessimism about the success of any civil rights legislation. Several black leaders said they would ignore Kennedy's appeal for restraint during the congressional debates and continue demonstrations. To Jack's horror, there was talk of a "massive march" on the Senate and House galleries.[109]

The president and other administration leaders worked hard to ensure passage of the bill. Its fate would play a major role in both determining the president's reputation for leadership and setting the stage for the election of 1964. An unprecedented series of private meetings at the

White House, involving more than sixteen hundred national leaders from a variety of professions and organizations, proved helpful. Bobby and Burke Marshall met regularly with members of Congress. Jack held sessions with Congressional leaders and kept former President Eisenhower informed. In late June the president talked privately with civil rights activists, explaining the difficulties his legislation faced in Congress, and urging their cooperation and support. Marshall later remembered him saying: "You have to remember that I'm in this too, right up to my neck now."[110]

The summer of 1963 proved to be as strife-ridden as many had feared: Justice Department records showed 978 demonstrations in 209 cities in the period from May 20 to August 8. No doubt responding to the turbulence, Congress seemed more favorable toward civil rights legislation than many had thought. Indeed, a bipartisan coalition was at work strengthening the Kennedy bill across the board.

Eager to avoid more unrest, the president opposed a decision by civil rights leaders to march on Washington in late August to mobilize support for legislation. Jack called Americans for Democratic Action chairman John P. Roche and complained bitterly that a bunch of "crusaders" organizing the march, including the ADA, were going to bring about a bloodbath. Roche later observed: "It is clear that he looked on the civil rights movement as an obstruction to a nice, tidy deal with Southern politicians."[111]

Kennedy dropped his opposition to the march on Washington when it became clear that he could not prevent it. Under his influence, march leaders soon called for a peaceful gathering at the Lincoln Memorial. At a July 17 news conference, Jack endorsed the "peaceful assembly calling for a redress of grievances," saying, "I think that's in the great tradition." He added that he looked forward to attending the event, and declared, "This is not a march on the Capitol."[112]

Bobby Kennedy supervised every detail of the march so carefully that Burke Marshall later boasted, "the person who organized it, as a matter of fact, was the Attorney General." Assistant Attorney General John Douglas worked almost full-time for a month on the project, seeing that a sufficient quantity of food, soft drinks (in paper cups, so that there would not be bottles to throw), and portable toilets would be on hand. Justice Department officials worked closely with Roy Wilkins, head of the NAACP, to prevent Communists from participating in—and thus tainting—the march. The Kennedys recruited whites from labor and the churches to participate in the demonstration, thinking that an all-black march would cost votes on Capitol Hill.

Spurred by Bobby and his lieutenants, civil rights leaders persuaded

SNCC head John Lewis to agree to modifications of a proposed speech criticizing the administration's bill and calling for further demonstrations. Bobby was particularly disturbed by such statements as: "We are now involved in a serious revolution. This nation is still a place of cheap political leaders who build their careers on immoral compromises and ally themselves with open forms of political, economic, and social exploitation." As amended, the sentence "We will march through the South, through the Heart of Dixie, the way Sherman did" became "But we will march with the spirit of love and the spirit of dignity that we have shown here today." The question "I want to know, which side is the federal government on?" was dropped. The Justice Department's control of the situation was such that Burke Marshall personally presented the edited speech to Lewis just before its delivery. Two Kennedy aides stood ready to disconnect the public-address system in case anything went wrong. Malcolm X later commented: "There wasn't a simple logistics aspect uncontrolled," and he labeled the march the "Farce on Washington."[113]

As a precaution the administration had thousands of extra police and 4,000 troops on hand. The careful behind-the-scenes preparations paid off, and the huge event of August 28, involving a crowd of 230,000, remained peaceful. The *New York Times* compared the activities to a church picnic. Without a word about his brother, the president declared in a formal statement: "The leaders of the organizations sponsoring the march and all who have participated in it deserve our appreciation for the detailed preparations that made it possible and for the orderly manner in which it has been conducted."[114]

Fearing violence and controversy, Jack chose not to attend the March. He watched Martin Luther King's dramatic and inspiring "I Have a Dream" speech on television. Afterward he met with march leaders for an hour at the White House, discussing with them the politics of passing a civil rights bill. (At one point in the meeting, secretly taped by the president, Jack urged blacks to emulate the Jewish emphasis on education. Jews, too, he said, had been persecuted.) At a news conference, Dr. King, whom Roy Wilkins introduced as "the moral leader of the nation," said that the president had "made it very clear that he would need very strong bipartisan support to get civil rights legislation this year."[115]

Privately Jack and Bobby worried about King. In early January 1962 the FBI had told the attorney general that King aide Stanley Levison, a New York lawyer, was a Communist. (The FBI had begun wiretapping and following Levison in 1954.) Bobby quietly had Burke Marshall and Harris Wofford alert King to the problem and urge him to sever relations with his friend. King rejected the advice, telling Wofford that he had more reason to trust Levison, a close friend and adviser since 1956, than he had to trust the FBI. Soon a bureau report noted that another King aide, Hunter Pitts (''Jack'') O'Dell, hired by Levison, had a long record of Communist party ties.

With Bobby's approval the FBI tapped Levison's office telephone. A few days later bureau agents broke into the office and planted a microphone. Summaries of telephone conversations between Levison and King were sent to the attorney general, vice president Johnson, and to Kenny O'Donnell at the White House. In November Bobby approved a wiretap on Levison's home phone as well. None of the surveillance devices uncovered anything subversive.[116]

In mid-1963, with the new civil rights bill a top administration priority, Jack sent Burke Marshall to Hoover to see what sort of hard evidence the FBI had on Levison. Segregationists were clamoring about ties between civil rights and Communists, and every precaution had to be taken to avoid the charge. The director told Marshall that Levison was a key figure in the Soviet intelligence apparatus. The Kennedys accepted the director's allegation at face value.[117]

On June 22 King met privately with Jack, Bobby, and Marshall, receiving stern warnings about Levison and O'Dell. During a stroll in the Rose Garden, Jack told King bluntly that his two aides were Communists and must be dismissed. ''If they [the opponents of civil rights] shoot *you* down, they'll shoot *us* down too—so we're asking you to be careful.'' Jack also advised the civil rights leader that he was under ''very close surveillance.''

When King asked for evidence against his friends, Jack said that he would have Marshall turn over proof to King aide Andrew Young. In fact Marshall could not produce any documentation; he was only able to cite Hoover. Young said later: ''They were all scared to death of the Bureau; they really were.''[118]

On the weight of administration appeals, and no doubt prodded by newspaper articles (planted by the FBI) linking him with Communists, King formally broke with O'Dell. He proved unable, however, to sever all ties with Levison. Bobby approved an FBI request to tap the home and office telephones of Clarence B. Jones, a young attorney who served as a channel of communications between Levison and Young.[119]

That summer, while Congress held hearings on the administration's civil rights bill, Hoover flooded the attorney general's office with materials alleging Communist domination of King. (Bobby forwarded a report on King's extramarital sexual activities to Jack, stating: ''I thought you would be interested in the attached memorandum.'') A major purpose of the campaign was to persuade Bobby to approve a wiretap on King's telephone, a proposal Bobby had rejected when it was first made.[120]

To protect the civil rights bill from critics, the president told a news conference on July 17: "We have no evidence that any of the leaders of the civil rights movements in the United States are Communists. We have no evidence that the demonstrations are Communist-inspired." A few days later the attorney general released a public letter denying that civil rights leaders, and specifically Dr. King, were "Communists, or Communist-controlled." Bobby carefully avoided mentioning Communist *influence,* however, undoubtedly mindful of Hoover's wrath.[121]

Yielding to pressure from the director, and perhaps fearful that, unless mollified, Hoover would go public with his charges, Bobby agreed in early October to authorize wiretaps on King's Atlanta residence and New York office. His only reservation, he told an FBI official, was that the tap in Atlanta might be discovered and bring embarrassment to the administration. A short time later Bobby authorized a wiretap on the Atlanta office of King's Southern Christian Leadership Conference. (Although some of them were scheduled for reevaluation in thirty days, all the wiretaps remained active during the remainder of Bobby's term in office.)[122]

The wiretaps would prove to be ineffective. Two attorneys general would later admit that the surveillance yielded nothing detrimental to King or Levison. No charges would ever be brought against the latter, who swore under oath before the Senate Internal Security Subcommittee that he was not and had never been a member of the Communist party. A careful investigation by historian David Garrow, published in 1981, concluded that Levison had been involved in Communist party financial activities between 1952 and 1955 and that he had abandoned that relationship before he met Dr. King. The FBI had no evidence linking Levison to Communist party activity during the years he was associated with King. Arthur Schlesinger, Jr., who interviewed Levison, called him "a goodhearted and undiscriminating liberal of the type for whom there was no enemy to the left."[123]

The campaign against King was almost exclusively a product of Hoover's irrational hatred of the civil rights leader. In part this stemmed from the director's racism; he privately referred to King as "the burr-head." Hoover was also deeply upset by the evidence uncovered by eavesdropping devices concerning the minister's sexual promiscuity. He condemned King in private as a " 'tom cat' with degenerate sexual urges." On top of this Hoover believed that King was a Communist—or at the very least a pro-Communist. He was furious about King's public criticism of the Bureau. "One of the great problems we face with the FBI in the South," King told a reporter in late 1962, "is that the agents are white Southerners who have been influenced by the mores of the community. To maintain their status, they have to be friendly with the local police and people, who are promoting segregation."[124]

In late October Hoover's passions were at such a pitch that he sent a lengthy memorandum blasting King and his alleged Communist connections to the White House, the State Department, the Defense Department, the CIA, and Navy and Army Intelligence. Burke Marshall later recalled, "it was a very explosive document in the sense that it was at the time the bill was before Congress" and might easily be leaked. This was too much for Bobby, who demanded, in a face-to-face confrontation with the director, recall of all copies of the document. Hoover complied promptly, and the threat of a leak was averted.[125]

But Bobby did not often challenge Hoover. He agreed to the wiretap of King, he said later, because he and his brother were convinced that Levison was a top official of the Communist party and had influence over the civil rights leader. "We never wanted to get very close to [King] just because of these contacts and connections that he had, which we felt were damaging to the civil rights movement. And because we were so intimately involved in the struggle for civil rights, it also damaged us."[126]

Bobby chose not to discuss, however, another important reason he constantly acceded to the director's wishes: the data Hoover kept in his private files on the Kennedy family foibles. And as Hoover grew older, more petulant, more reactionary, and more jealous of his authority, there was no telling what he might do if crossed. Harris Wofford later observed: "In retrospect I recognize that the fear of Hoover, distrust of what the FBI would do, and a desire to get Hoover and the FBI on their side pervaded John and Robert Kennedy's approach to civil rights at some of the most critical moments."[127]

(After Jack's death the director and the attorney general refused to speak to each other. Without resistance from Bobby, Hoover and his assistant William Sullivan launched a vicious vendetta against King designed to destroy the minister's public credibility. The campaign included the transmission of a tape to the attorney general featuring a private joke told by King about the late president's flamboyant sexual activities. After Bobby's death Hoover claimed publicly that the telephone surveillance of King had been Bobby's idea.)[128]

By the fall of 1963 numerous battles had been fought over the administration's civil rights bill. When a House subcommittee, with the enthusiastic support of liberals, strengthened it, the Kennedys worked to get a more modest piece of legislation, one that could pass with bipartisan support. (King warned the president privately: "The Negro community is about to reach the breaking point," and said that he feared "the worst race riot that we've ever seen in this country.") In late October the House Judiciary Committee reported out a compromise version. In the Senate, where Bobby spent nine days sparring verbally with arch-opponent Senator Sam Ervin of North Carolina, the bill's future looked bleak.[129]

Although polls showed that a majority of white Americans favored the civil rights bill, there was strong resistance throughout the nation. According to Sorensen, Jack privately confided to a black leader: "This issue could cost me the election, but we're not turning back."[130] This statement, even if true, sounded more heroic than it was. The Kennedys could not think of abandoning what had become one of the administration's principal and most loudly proclaimed objectives.

By late November considerable doubt remained among political observers whether or not the compromise bill would win approval on Capitol Hill. Bobby later admitted that the Senate was a major hurdle and that Jack kept asking him where they were going to get the necessary votes.[131] Senator Allen J. Ellender of Louisiana, a personal friend of Jack's, said later that the bill would not have passed if the president had lived. In part this was because of the president's consistently ineffective approach toward Congress. Though Ellender attributed the eventual passage of the Civil Rights Act of 1964 to the worldwide wave of emotionalism following the assassination, others have seen passage of the legislation as inevitable by the fall of 1963. In any case, amid the grief after Kennedy's death, favorable comparisons between him and Abraham Lincoln were commonplace.[132]

CHAPTER 16

Blinking First

➜➤➤ ⫷⫷⫷

WHILE the civil rights movement challenged the president's domestic policies, Kennedy faced a crisis in foreign affairs that threatened to unleash a nuclear holocaust. The immediate problem centered on developments in Cuba, but the larger issues involved the Cold War, the arms race, and the very future of the earth's people.

By the spring of 1962 Fidel Castro was convinced that the United States was preparing to invade Cuba. Operation Mongoose, the secret "Kennedy vendetta" created to disrupt the Cuban economy and government and to assassinate its leader, was in full swing. An exile leader returned from a visit to the White House telling friends that the Cuban premier would soon be overthrown. American Marines held maneuvers in the Caribbean. (Several weeks later American reporters were invited to a huge military exercise off the southeast coast of Puerto Rico designed to liberate a mythical republic controlled by a dictator named Ortsac—Castro spelled backward.)[1]

In early July, fearing imminent invasion, Castro's brother Raul went to Moscow and frantically requested military aid. Khrushchev said he would send intermediate-range nuclear missiles, a move he had apparently decided to make a few months earlier. Evidence suggests that Castro, hardly eager to provoke Washington, initially resisted the idea. He went along with the Soviet plan when he was persuaded that the United States would not be intimidated by conventional weapons, and perhaps when he discovered that he had no choice in the matter.[2]

Khrushchev would always claim that he had been solely concerned about the defense of Cuba. He said later that the island's loss would have been a "terrible" blow to the Soviet Union's international prestige.[3] In 1987 Soviet participants in a panel on the Cuban Missile Crisis contended that Khrushchev's installation of missiles was, at least in part, designed to prevent an impending invasion of Cuba. The Soviet panel members added, however, that Khrushchev was also using the weapons to enhance his nation's position in the Cold War. Fyodor M. Burlatsky, a former Khrushchev speech writer, declared: "I think the installation of missiles was a first step toward nuclear parity."[4]

In 1961 the Kennedy administration had announced that the "missile gap" was nonexistent and that the United States enjoyed a vast superiority in this area of weaponry. A year later American experts thought that Washington's nuclear superiority was on a ratio of about 16 to 1. (The United States had some five thousand warheads against the Soviets' three hundred, plus a 3-to-1 advantage in long-range bombers and a 6-to-1 lead in long-range missiles.) The president had proceeded, however, to accelerate the nation's missile programs, to emphasize the need for fallout shelters, and to move missile targets in a way that suggested a first-strike readiness. Khrushchev apparently believed he had cause for alarm. Unable politically and financially to match the U.S. military buildup, he thought that missiles in Cuba, pointed directly at America's vulnerable underbelly (the Soviets knew that the nation's radar network did not face south), would double Russia's first-strike capability and perhaps give his country time to develop a more advanced missile program. In secret tape recordings, first released in 1990, Khrushchev said "We picked targets in the U.S. to inflict the maximum damage. We saw that our weapons could inspire terror."[5]

Khrushchev may also have sought to install missiles in Cuba in the hope of gaining leverage to have his way in Berlin. In addition he may have thought that this coup would strengthen his shaky hand in Kremlin politics. Yugoslavian leaders later told Soviet expert George Kennan that Khrushchev was being challenged within his top ranks by hard-liners who sought an aggressive stance toward the United States. In any case, the Soviet leader was gambling that he could make his unprecedented move without substantial opposition. Sergei A. Mikoyan, whose father had been Khrushchev's special emissary to Castro, said in 1987: "I agree that to install missiles on that island was adventurous because it did not take into consideration what would be the American response."[6]

Khrushchev continued to consider Kennedy immature and weak. He may have thought as well that the 1962 political campaigns would tie the president's hands. Statements by Senator J. William Fulbright in mid-1961 and by the State Department in early 1962, predicting the siting of Soviet missiles in Cuba, may have led the Kremlin to believe that Washington would not react aggressively. The president himself had not expressed opposition to strategic weapons in Cuba. Historian David Detzer later concluded: "Had he taken an absolutely firm stance on the matter before the spring of 1962, the missile crisis probably could have been avoided."[7]

During July and August Soviet construction workers, troops, and supplies began pouring into Cuba. Washington was aware of the activity and thought at first that it meant merely a strengthening of coastal and air defense systems. In early August CIA Director John A. McCone became convinced that the Russians intended to install long-range missiles. He sent a memo to the president on August 10 and soon raised the matter with cabinet members. Getting nowhere, McCone went directly to the president. Daily intelligence reports on Cuba soon began. On August 29 a U-2 photographed SAM (surface-to-air-missile) installations under construction. McCone concluded that the SAMs, designed to knock out high-flying spy planes, were there to protect long-range missile installations. The Kennedys, who did not entirely trust McCone, thinking him self-serving and extraordinarily hawkish, were inclined to dismiss the warnings. So was Defense Secretary McNamara. (Bobby later claimed that McCone failed to communicate his fears to the president.)[8]

In his August 29 news conference, the president was stunned to learn that unnamed State Department officials had leaked information to reporters about Soviet troops and missiles in Cuba. Jack denied having any such information. (According to Sorensen Kennedy did not have "hard intelligence" about these matters until two days later.) He became slightly flustered when asked about the suggestion that Cuba be invaded:

> I'm not for invading Cuba at this time. No, I don't—the words do not have some secondary meaning. I think it would be a mistake to invade Cuba, because I think it would lead to—that it should be very—an action like that, which could be very casually suggested, could lead to very serious consequences for many people.[9]

On August 31 Republican Senator Kenneth Keating of New York began a series of twenty-five attacks on the administration's Cuban policy. His sources of information were unidentified. (The Kennedys suspected McCone.) This became part of a growing GOP effort to influence the fall congressional elections by painting the president as soft on the Reds. Right-wing Senator Homer Capehart, up for reelection in Indiana, called for an all-out military attack. The Republican high command announced that Cuba would be the "dominant issue of the 1962 campaign." Public opinion polls showed an increasing frustration over the presence of Soviet troops and weapons ninety miles from Florida.[10]

On September 2 the Soviets publicly acknowledged for the first time that they were sending "armaments" and technical advisers to Cuba. The action, the Kremlin declared, was in response to threats from "aggressive imperialist quarters with regard to Cuba." (This was lost on the public, of course, for it knew nothing of Operation Mongoose.) The White House responded two days later, announcing that the United States had spotted SAM installations and technicians in Cuba but had "no evidence of any organized combat force . . . of offensive ground-to-ground missiles, or of other significant offensive capability." Should Castro obtain offensive weapons and attempt to use them to export communism to elsewhere in Latin America, the United States would use "whatever means may be necessary" to halt the move.[11]

That same day Soviet Ambassador Anatoly Dobrynin assured Bobby that Khrushchev would not export offensive weapons or do anything to embarrass the administration during the congressional election campaigns. On September 6 Dobrynin read Ted Sorensen a message from Khrushchev to the president, making the same assurances and contending that the movements in Cuba were strictly defensive. Georgi Bolshakov, a Soviet official in Washington who often relayed private messages between the Kremlin and the White House, soon let it be known that no missile capable of reaching the United States would be placed in Cuba. On September 11 the Soviet government stated that it had no need to locate its most powerful missiles in other countries, specifically mentioning Cuba. The "armaments and military equipment sent to Cuba are designed exclusively for defensive purposes" and were unable to threaten the United States.

The Russians were lying, for at that same time, unknown to Washington, forty-two Soviet medium- and intermediate-range ballistic missiles were on their way to Cuba. Each was capable of striking deep into the heart of the United States and, if armed with a nuclear warhead, could land a blow twenty to thirty times more powerful than the explosion at Hiroshima.[12]

Bobby now began to share John McCone's suspicions about Soviet intentions. As always, he was particularly concerned about the political ramifications. On September 11 he wrote privately, "Cuba obtaining [nuclear] missiles from the Soviet Union would create a major political problem here."[13]

At a news conference two days later, Jack attacked the Republicans who were rattling sabers:

> While I recognize that rash talk is cheap, particularly on the part of those who do not have the responsibility, I would hope that the future record will show that the only people talking about a war or an invasion at this time are the Communist spokesmen in Moscow and Havana, and that the American people defending as we do so much of the free world, will in this nuclear age, as they have in the past, keep both their nerve and their head.

When asked specifically, however, if Republicans were trying to take advantage of the tensions surrounding Cuba, Jack denied that politics had anything to do with the issue.

To show his toughness the president spelled out several circumstances that, in his judgment, would warrant American military intervention in Cuba. The brief list included the extension of Cuban communism and the possibility that the island might become "an offensive military base of significant capacity for the Soviet Union." When a reporter sought to probe the latter statement further, Jack said bluntly, "Well, I have indicated that if Cuba should possess a capacity to carry out offensive actions against the United States, that the United States would act." He also made it clear that he had full authority to order such an invasion and, should it come to that, "all of Castro's Communist-supplied weapons and technicians would not change the result or significantly extend the time required to achieve that result." To underscore his militance, the president asked Congress for a mobilization bill that would empower him to muster 150,000 military reservists for one year and extend present active service tours for one year.[14]

To the Far Right, all this continued to smack of appeasement. Republican Senator Barry Goldwater of Arizona, often mentioned as a candidate for his party's presidential nomination in 1964, contended publicly that the administration had a "do-nothing" policy toward Cuba. Kennedy's statement, said Goldwater, "virtually promised the Communist world that the United States will take no action to remove the threat of Soviet armed might in the Western Hemisphere."[15]

The Democratic-controlled Congress swiftly gave the president his mobilization bill. It also passed a joint resolution declaring that "the United States is determined by whatever means may be necessary, including the use of arms . . . to prevent in Cuba the creation or use of an externally supported military capability endangering the security of the United States.''[16]

The Soviets, on the other hand, contended that Kennedy was preparing for an invasion. In a formal statement on Cuba, they warned that attacks on Cuba or Soviet ships bound for the island could lead to nuclear war.[17]

By early October, there were thousands of Soviet soldiers and technicians in Cuba. The Russian arsenal on the island soon included 42 high-performance jet fighter planes, 42 unassembled jet bombers (capable of delivering nuclear or nonnuclear destruction to a range of 600 nautical miles and returning), about 350 medium and heavy tanks, 40 ships, 1,300 pieces of field artillery, and 700 antiaircraft guns. Although conclusive evidence was lacking, American intelligence agencies began to suspect that the Soviets might be preparing long-range missile sites. In the State Department, Roger Hilsman urged the administration to draft a contingency plan. But nothing was done. On October 5 ultra-conservative Clare Boothe Luce wrote in *Life*, ''What is now at stake in the decision for intervention or nonintervention in Cuba is the question not only of American prestige but of American survival.''[18]

On October 10 Senator Keating charged that construction was under way in Cuba of at least a half-dozen launching sites for intermediate-range tactical missiles with the power ''to hurl rockets into the American heartland and as far as the Panama Canal Zone.'' The next day the American Legion adopted a resolution demanding action against Cuba, including ''unilateral'' military force if necessary. Republican National Committee Chairman William Miller soon taunted the administration for cowardice, saying that if GOP candidates made the most of the ''irresolution'' on Cuba, ''they will make sure that no author will ever write a book about the present era entitled 'Why America Slept' '' (a reference to Jack's first book.)[19]

During a campaign trip in Indiana, the president ripped into Senator Capehart for demanding that the United States invade Cuba. ''Those self-appointed generals and admirals who want to send someone else's sons to war, and who consistently voted against the instruments of peace, ought to be kept at home by the voters and replaced by someone who has some understanding of what the twentieth century is all about.''[20]

On October 15 a U-2 plane photographed long-range missile-launching sites under construction in Cuba. Jack received the shocking news early the next morning, realizing that the Soviets had been lying and were intent on more than the defense of Cuba. His first thoughts were about the politics of the situation. "We've just elected Capehart in Indiana," he told Kenny O'Donnell, "and Ken Keating will probably be the next President of the United States."[21] The Cuban Missile Crisis was under way, the first direct nuclear confrontation in history.

Jack quickly created an advisory committee consisting of his brother, Sorensen, three cabinet members (Rusk, McNamara, Dillon), John McCone, national security aide McGeorge Bundy, three Defense Department representatives (General Maxwell Taylor, Roswell Gilpatric, Paul Nitze), and four State Department officials (George Ball, U. Alexis Johnson, Edwin Martin, Llewellyn Thompson). Vice President Johnson and Kenny O'Donnell sat in on several meetings. Adlai Stevenson, former Secretary of State Dean Acheson, Robert Lovett, and Donald M. Wilson, acting head of the United States Information Agency, would also attend from time to time.[22]

The composition of this ad hoc committee, later dubbed by reporters the Executive Committee of the National Security Council, or "ExCom," revealed the president's reliance upon trusted confidantes and hard-liners who were determined not to give an inch to Khrushchev or Castro. Indeed, eight members of ExCom were also part of the secret committee overseeing Operation Mongoose.[23]

Even before ExCom assembled on the first day of the crisis, Jack sent Bobby to the Mongoose overseers to express his dissatisfaction with the effort. Bobby promised to meet daily with the advisers until they turned up the heat. The Kennedys no doubt wanted Castro dead.[24]

At their first meeting on October 16, ExCom members were briefed on the details of what the Soviets had in Cuba. They learned, among other things, that several missiles were already on the island and that at least some of them probably had a range of eleven hundred nautical miles— meaning that they could hit Washington, Dallas, Cape Canaveral, St. Louis, and all the Strategic Air Command bases and cities in between.[25]

From the start it was apparent that the president wanted action. According to Roswell Gilpatric, he was "very clipped, very tense," by no means as calm and cool as partisans would later portray him. "He seemed to me to believe that the Soviets meant business in the most real sense, and this was the biggest national crisis he'd faced."[26]

According to Sorensen, Jack was convinced that Khrushchev was testing his toughness. In Kennedy's view the Soviet leader was betting that the United States would merely lodge a protest when confronted with the missiles, thereby appearing weak and irresolute. This impression would cause allies to lose confidence in the nation's leadership. It would also increase Communist prestige and power throughout the world, especially in Latin America. Moreover, direct pressure might be applied elsewhere, notably Berlin.[27]

Unspoken, but understood by many insiders, was the president's additional concern about the elections. If he did nothing, or merely complained, or attempted prolonged negotiations, Republicans would condemn him for cowardice and use that label against Democratic candidates.

From the beginning Jack felt compelled to be forceful. Something had to be done before the missiles became operational. And there was not much time—perhaps less than two weeks. General Taylor and the majority of ExCom members favored surprise air attacks against the missile sites. Tape recordings of the meeting, secretly made by the president and released in 1983, reveal Jack tending to agree: "I think we ought to, beginning right now, be preparing. . . . We're certainly going to . . . take out these, uh missiles." (McNamara said later: "I don't believe that the President or I *ever* thought that we would launch a first strike under *any* circumstances.")[28]

Jack ordered more U-2 flights and, at the close of the session, demanded strict secrecy. As he walked back to the executive mansion with Bobby, he agreed to avoid future ExCom meetings for a time so that participants would feel able to speak more freely. Soon he decided to continue his political campaigning (while receiving regular reports of the ExCom sessions) to give the impression that all was well.[29]

On the evening of the sixteenth, McNamara attempted to lower ExCom's emotional thermostat by reminding members that the new missiles would not alter the nuclear balance of power: "This is a domestic, political problem." McNamara was far from "soft," however; he suggested a quarantine or blockade of Cuba and soon became its strongest advocate.

Bobby, also leery about an air strike, suggested the invention of an incident to involve the United States directly in Cuba, perhaps involving Guantanamo or shipping, "sink the *Maine* again or something."

George Ball was more bold about his opposition to air strikes. He raised the specter of Pearl Harbor, and said that an American attack on Cuba "just frightens the hell out of me." This apparently had an effect on Bobby, who said later that he passed a note to his brother reading: "I now know how Tojo felt when he was planning Pearl Harbor."[30]

During the rest of the week ExCom met daily, its members debating forcefully an assortment of possible responses that soon boiled down to either an air strike or a blockade. A sudden, swift, "surgical" air strike continued to appeal to many, including the president. It would knock out the missiles and serve as an unequivocal warning to the Reds that the United States would not tolerate such activity.

In the course of the discussion, however, it became clear that the bombing would inevitably kill Russians and Cubans. (ExCom thought that the Soviets had about 10,000 men on the island and that Cubans had approximately 100,000 under arms. In 1989 Cuban and Soviet officials revealed that there had been more than 40,000 Russian troops and 270,000 armed Cubans on the island.) That meant, of course, that Khrushchev might be forced into a counterattack on the United States. He might even use the missiles on the island, for there was no guarantee that air strikes could eliminate all of them. Moreover, the military leaders who favored the attacks admitted that many no-doubt costly and dangerous air raids would be necessary. "The more we looked at the air strike," Sorensen wrote later, "the clearer it became that the resultant chaos and political collapse would ultimately necessitate a U.S. invasion." And that was a move that Jack, after the Bay of Pigs fiasco, was reluctant to attempt.[31]

Bobby's allusion to Pearl Harbor also carried weight when he shared it with ExCom members. This sort of first strike on a small neighbor could blacken the reputation of the United States permanently, especially in Latin America. And no one on ExCom could figure out a method of advance warning to the Soviets that would not do more harm than good.

Bobby later claimed that moral questions dominated ExCom discussions during the first five days of the crisis. Much more likely, ExCom members were primarily concerned about the bad publicity or unpredictable results the *open* raids would bring the administration.[32]

By Thursday the consensus was moving toward the notion of blockade. There were several reasons for favoring this approach. It was a limited action that gave the administration time to ponder further strategy. (There might even be enough time for Mongoose to eliminate Castro.) It offered Khrushchev the opportunity to avoid a direct military clash by turning his ships around. Then, too, America's allies might find this nonviolent step more prudent and appealing than air strikes.

The proposal, however, faced many objections. By the time a blockade could be established, the Soviet missiles would be operational. A blockade around Cuba might invite the Russians to do the same in Berlin. A blockade was a dubious legality: Since it was clear that Havana had requested assistance from Moscow, and the Soviets had not committed a belligerent act, on what legal grounds could America stop their ships? And what about Cuba's other allies, such as Great Britain? According to international law, stopping third-party shipping was an act of war. Moreover, a blockade could not actually work. Enough missiles were already in Cuba to give the Soviets the military advantage they sought.

New U-2 photographs revealed more medium-range missile sites, now totaling six, along with excavations for three intercontinental (2,200 nautical-mile-range) ballistic missile sites. The larger missiles, when in place, could reach every corner of the United States except the Pacific Northwest. Their range would include southeastern Canada, all of Mexico and Central America, and much of South America. Work to complete these installations appeared to be going at a feverish pace. Sorensen recalled: "The knowledge that time was running out dominated our discussions and kept us meeting late into the night." Jack told Kenny O'Donnell that the Soviets were building enough launching sites to fire a single volley of missiles capable of killing eighty million Americans.[33]

Complicating matters somewhat, however, was the fact that the CIA had not spotted nuclear warheads on the island. Storage facilities were ready, and there were indications that the Russians might be prepared to send warheads. But at no time during the crisis was there hard evidence of their presence. Historically Russian leaders had been extremely cautious with their nuclear warheads, even forbidding their own military custody of them within the Soviet Union.[34]

The Kennedys and ExCom knew well what the CIA had and had not discovered. But they were taking no chances. The Soviets had lied repeatedly about their intentions. (During the week, Soviet Foreign Minister Gromyko visited the President and continued to contend that the weapons sent to Cuba were strictly defensive. Khrushchev said the same thing to Foy Kohler, the new American ambassador to Moscow.) The Americans chose to proceed as though the nuclear warheads were fully part of the Soviet plot. CIA man Robert Amory said later that the warheads were "something that we couldn't tell; we couldn't see. They could be in the [ships'] hold. After all, they're not very big. . . . And we just assumed they wouldn't send the missiles without the warheads."[35] Secretary McNamara said later that while the White House lacked evidence that warheads were in Cuba, it was "prudent for us to act as if they were." (In 1989 Soviet officials revealed that warheads had indeed been in Cuba but had not been placed on the missiles. Sergei Khrushchev, a son of the Soviet leader, said that the missiles could have been made operational in a couple of hours if his father had given the order.)[36]

Douglas Dillon later recalled the intense emotions of the time. "I felt—and so did the Joint Chiefs of Staff—that there *was* a change in the strategic balance. We felt a tremendous shock that the Soviets were putting these things so near to us."[37] Early in the crisis, while still keeping the activities in Cuba a secret, Jack told a group of newsmen: "I don't think it is unfair to say that the United States, and the world, is now passing through one of its most critical periods. Our major problem, after all, is the survival of our country, the protection of its vital interests, without the beginning of the third and perhaps the last war."[38]

On Thursday evening ExCom voted 11–6 for a blockade over an air strike. Jack now preferred a blockade and ordered the start of work on details. Still, the arguing continued and no firm decision was made. Hawkish Dean Acheson, highly critical of the president throughout the crisis, later called the sessions "repetitive, leaderless, and a waste of time."[39]

On Friday, October 19, military leaders again argued for air strikes, and several ExCom members reversed themselves. Bundy now favored taking no action at all. Exhaustion was beginning to take a toll, and tempers flared. Bobby wrote later: "Each one of us was being asked to make a recommendation which, if wrong and if accepted, could mean the destruction of the human race."[40] No small responsibility for an un-elected body.

Jack was impatient and discouraged by the inability of his advisers to make up their minds. He worried, too, that the secret of the missiles would soon get out. By the end of the work week, probably a hundred people at the Pentagon and the State Department were aware of the crisis. The *Miami News* reported that plans were underway for a quarantine on Cuban shipping. Two newspaper columnists, Paul Scott and Robert S. Allen, referred in print to missiles in Cuba.[41]

ExCom, with the president presiding, met on Saturday afternoon. Advocates of air strikes and a blockade again made their cases. (The sides would later be misleadingly labeled "hawks" and "doves.") Agreeing with Bobby, Sorensen, McNamara, Rusk, and a majority of ExCom, Jack finally opted for a blockade. He wanted to begin with limited action, he said, preserving his options and leaving some for Khrushchev. This approach, he added, "seems the least objectionable." Sorensen carefully noted another of the president's statements for later inclusion in a speech: "The worst course of all would be to do nothing."

Still, Jack wavered. Until he could personally consult with the head of the Air Force Tactical Bombing Command and be assured that a pinpoint "surgical strike" was impossible, he said, his position would remain provisional. He chose to adopt the term "quarantine" instead of "blockade," which in international law is an act of war.[42]

When the subject turned to diplomacy, Adlai Stevenson took the floor. Earlier in the week, the UN ambassador had attended an ExCom meeting and submitted a note to the President stating in part: "I feel you should have made it clear that the existence of nuclear missile bases anywhere is negotiable before we start anything. . . . I confess I have many misgivings about the proposed course of action." The specter of nuclear war haunted Stevenson, and he urged restraint and caution. He felt obliged to warn Kennedy that "the judgments of history seldom coincide with the tempers of the moment." Sorensen later reported that Jack was "annoyed" by the note.[43]

Now, on Saturday, Stevenson declared that the crisis demanded careful, rational diplomacy. Since it was certain that the Soviets would make counterdemands in return for the removal of the missiles, he suggested that the United States be willing to give up something in return. The ambassador recommended that the president propose the demilitarization and neutralization of Cuba and offer a pledge not to invade the island. This approach would mean the dismantling of the American base at Guantanamo, which Stevenson thought of little use anyway. He also suggested that Washington consider taking its Jupiter missiles out of Turkey and Italy if the Soviets would comply with American demands.

The Jupiters were part of a missile system set up in Britain, Italy, and Turkey under arrangements made initially in 1957 by the Eisenhower administration. It was the Kennedy administration, however, that put fifteen Jupiters on Turkish soil. Following a presidentially ordered review of the matter, the missiles became operational in about July 1962. Evidence suggests that Kennedy chose to proceed with the project because, after his poor showing with Khrushchev in Vienna, he did not want the Soviets to think him weak. He also wanted to avoid offending Turkey, an important NATO ally, which resisted the idea of removing the Jupiters.

The missiles were aimed, of course, directly at the Soviet Union across the Black Sea. Widely considered in Washington to be obsolete, they were useful militarily only for a first strike. Historian David Detzer later observed that "the Soviet missiles in Cuba which the Kennedy Administration called 'threatening,' 'aggressive' and 'offensive,' were quite comparable to the 'obsolete' Jupiters."[44]

In late August, concerned that the Jupiters might be used to justify the massive Soviet military buildup in Cuba, the president ordered a study of the feasibility of withdrawing the newly positioned missiles. Nothing conclusive had been done by the time the Jupiters became an issue in the missile crisis. (Kennedy partisans would later claim that Jack *ordered* the missiles out of Turkey on numerous occasions, and that the command was ignored by bureaucrats. In fact, as McGeorge Bundy later acknowledged, the president did not order the missiles out of Turkey until after the crisis had ended).[45]

Stevenson spoke as well of a summit meeting, and of vigorous actions by the UN to prevent war. One plan envisioned a standstill of military activities on both sides—thus leaving the missiles in Cuba without a blockade. Another idea involved UN inspection teams that would scrutinize not only Cuba but possible U.S. bases for attacking Cuba—a proposal that would undoubtedly bring Operation Mongoose to light.[46]

As Sorensen later admitted, nothing in Stevenson's remarks suggested appeasement. Earlier in the week, advocates of air strikes had themselves proposed a summit and a pledge by the United States to withdraw all of its nuclear forces based in Turkey—aircraft as well as missiles. But now the ambassador was bitterly attacked by emotional and weary ExCom members for being "soft." A *Saturday Evening Post* article written by Kennedy's personal friends Stewart Alsop and Charles Bartlett soon condemned Stevenson for proposing a "Munich" settlement with Khrushchev.[47]

Jack may have admired Stevenson's courage, as partisans later claimed, but he was having nothing to do with the ambassador's proposal. Concessions, he said, would prompt the nation's European allies to lose confidence in the United States. As Sorensen paraphrased the president's remarks: "Instead of being on the diplomatic defensive, we should be indicting the Soviet Union for its duplicity and its threat to world peace."[48]

After the meeting Bobby was furious with Stevenson for suggesting compromise with Khrushchev. "He's not strong enough or tough enough," he told his brother, "to be representing us at the UN at a time like this. Why not get him out of there, and put someone like John McCloy in his place?" Robert Lovett, a leader in the Cold War establishment, soon made a similar recommendation. The president quickly called McCloy, a "tough-minded" Republican and veteran Washington insider, home from Europe and sent him to the United Nations to help "stiffen" the ambassador.[49]

Even Kenny O'Donnell later admitted that the president was rattled after Saturday's ExCom meeting. Jack telephoned Jackie, away for the weekend, and asked her to return to the White House with the children. He wanted them to join him and a few friends (including Powers, O'Donnell, Sorensen, Rusk, and McNamara) in an underground shelter should Khrushchev, learning about the quarantine, decide to launch a nuclear attack on Washington.[50]

To quash leaks in the press, Jack personally telephoned the *New York Times* and *Washington Post*, convincing editors to withhold stories for a day or two until the blockade was ready. By this time, U.S. missile crews were placed on maximum alert, the B-52 bomber force went into the air loaded with atomic weapons, 180 ships began moving into the Caribbean, and troops were sent to Florida, preparing to invade Cuba if the blockade failed. That evening, newspaper columnist Walter Lippmann, who had good sources inside the administration, told a friend that the United States was on the brink of war.[51]

On Sunday, October 21, Jack again flirted with an air strike. He decided to proceed with the blockade when Air Force leaders still were unable to assure him that all missile sites could be knocked out with a single blow. Letters were written and representatives were dispatched to brief allies. Congressional leaders were hastily summoned from around the country. Guantanamo was strengthened, and preparations were made to evacuate American civilians from the base. Ted Sorensen worked frantically on the presidential address.

That afternoon ExCom met to go over the speech draft and review military strategy. Jack questioned and then accepted an assertion by the Navy chief of staff that if a Soviet ship refused to honor the blockade, a shot could be fired into its rudder, stopping the ship without sinking it.[52]

The following day the president met with ExCom, the National Security Council, and the cabinet. He spoke by telephone to several prominent people, including former Presidents Hoover, Truman, and Eisenhower. At five-thirty he joined McNamara, Rusk, and McCone in briefing seventeen congressional leaders about the crisis. Two weeks from the elections, several of the politicians squirmed in their seats. Several thought that a blockade was too weak a response. Powerful Democratic Senators Richard Russell and J. William Fulbright favored a direct invasion of Cuba. Republican leaders Everett Dirksen and Charles Halleck agreed to back the administration, but Halleck wanted it on the record that Kennedy had told him what he was preparing to do and had not asked his advice.

Jack was furious about the criticism, the first he had encountered in the crisis. He told the group that a military attack might be the second step, but in any case the Armed Forces were not yet prepared to stage an invasion. After the meeting Jack privately mocked Halleck and told Sorensen angrily: "If they want this job, they can have it—it's no great joy to me."[53]

At 7:00 P.M., the president went on radio and television to deliver a seventeen-minute address heard, seen, and later read throughout most of the world. He announced the discovery of "a series of offensive missile sites" being constructed by the Soviets in Cuba, the purpose being "none other than to provide a nuclear strike capability against the Western Hemisphere." The United States, he said, had an "unswerving objective" to rid the hemisphere of these missiles and would not shrink from the risk of "world-wide nuclear war" to achieve that end.

Jack announced several "initial" steps to be taken, including the quarantine ("All ships of any kind bound for Cuba from whatever nation or port will, if found to contain cargoes of offensive weapons, be turned back"), an American military buildup, and appeals to the UN and the Organization of American States. He called on Khrushchev "to halt and eliminate this clandestine, reckless and provocative threat to world peace and to stable relations between our two nations."

Kennedy stated unequivocally that if any of the Cuban missiles were fired at anyone in the hemisphere, the United States would react with "a fully retaliatory response upon the Soviet Union." He also promised American action if the Russians moved against allies anywhere in the world, "including in particular the brave people of West Berlin." He continued:

> The path we have chosen for the present is full of hazards, as all paths are—but it is the one most consistent with our character and courage as a nation and our commitments around the world. The cost of freedom is always high—but Americans have always paid it. And one path we shall never choose, and that is the path of surrender or submission.[54]

Prior to the broadcast Foy Kohler delivered a copy of the address to Khrushchev's office. (Rusk went through the speech in Washington with Soviet Ambassador Dobrynin and, he said later, watched the Russian "age ten years right in front of my eyes.") Kohler also carried a personal letter from Kennedy to the Soviet premier, emphasizing his nation's determination. Jack thought it vital for Khrushchev to understand at last that he was truly tough. Still, the letter stressed the basic insanity of nuclear war, "which it is crystal clear no country could win and which could only result in catastrophic consequences to the whole world, including the aggressor."[55]

Leaders of both political parties rallied behind Kennedy, and the public joined in. Gallup pollsters found that 84 percent of those aware of the Cuban situation favored the blockade, while only 4 percent opposed it. Few Americans expressed fear of nuclear war erupting. Telegrams received at the White House favored the president's action by a ratio of 10 to 1. The strongest negative reactions came from the Far Left. The Far Right backed the president grudgingly, with some grumbling about the loss of a good campaign issue.

Britain and France pledged firm support, a British Foreign Office statement declaring that the Soviet Union had been "guilty of deception" in Cuba and of opening "a new era of instability." There was surprisingly strong backing in the United Nations, due in part, as Sorensen later put it, "to world-wide recognition that this was an East-West nuclear confrontation, not a U.S. quarrel with Cuba."[56]

Jack and his advisers had feared an immediate Soviet military reaction to the quarantine speech. When Tuesday, October 23, dawned with the world still at peace, there were sighs of relief in the White House. Bobby wrote later: "We had taken the first step, it wasn't so bad, and we were still alive."[57]

Later that day, following a personal visit from Secretary Rusk, the Organization of American States voted unanimously to back the quarantine. It also called for the immediate dismantling and withdrawal of all missiles and other offensive weapons from Cuba. (Four of the twenty governments failed to support a clause recommending the use of military force if the quarantine failed.) This gave the administration the authority under international law to do what it intended to do in any case. A jubilant Adlai Stevenson quickly read the OAS resolution into the record of the UN Security Council. One observer commented: "There is reason to think that Moscow was staggered by the show of inter-American solidarity." The Soviets soon charged that the OAS was merely a puppet of the United States, an allegation that in retrospect appears false.[58]

ExCom met twice on Tuesday, discussing details of the blockade and the military responses to Soviet aggression anywhere in the world. Jack, eager to avoid another Bay of Pigs, demanded personal direction of the quarantine's operation and asked detailed questions about military preparedness. Still, such crucial issues as the exact location of the quarantine line and the procedures for dealing with ships not carrying military equipment remained hazy. To avoid a major military confrontation, the Navy was ordered to shoot at a vessel's rudders and propellers if it refused to stop.[59]

Jack knew well how perilous the situation was. There were already reports of at least twenty-five Soviet ships and a few Russian submarines, perhaps nuclear armed, on their way to Cuba. In a chat with Bobby, Sorensen, and O'Donnell after the last ExCom meeting, he talked about the blunders and miscalculations that had triggered major tragedies twice in the century. He mentioned Barbara Tuchman's best-selling *The Guns of August*, a study of the origins of World War I, and expressed the wish that a copy of the book could be sent "to every Navy officer on every Navy ship right now." Then he said: "But they probably wouldn't read it."[60]

The Kennedys were convinced that they alone were sufficiently tough and shrewd to shoulder the burdens that lay ahead. Bobby later wrote: "We were not going to misjudge, or miscalculate, or challenge the other side needlessly, or precipitously push our adversaries into a course of action that was not intended or anticipated." Neither, of course, were the Kennedys prepared to accept anything short of victory. At 7:06 P.M., the grim-faced president signed the quarantine proclamation that was to go into effect at 10:00 A.M. the next morning.[61]

The Soviets issued a public statement on Tuesday calling the quarantine "piracy." Khrushchev sent two private letters to Kennedy and soon answered public appeals from pacifist philosopher Bertrand Russell and UN Acting Secretary-General U Thant. The Soviet premier took inconsistent positions, appearing to be a hard-liner one day and a dove the next. ExCom members began wondering if he was involved in an internal power struggle.[62]

On Wednesday afternoon Khrushchev requested an interview with Westinghouse Electric president William Knox, in Moscow by invitation on business. According to Knox, the premier, "calm, friendly and frank," declared that the blockade was a very dangerous matter, and warned that if the United States stopped and searched unarmed Soviet commercial vessels, he would instruct his submarines to sink the American ships. Khrushchev stressed the importance of negotiations and expressed the thought (shared by Arthur Krock and Barry Goldwater) that Kennedy might be posturing to influence the coming elections. At the root of much of the current difficulty, he said, was Kennedy's immaturity. His eldest son, he remarked, was older than the president.

Khrushchev contended that all Soviet weapons in Cuba were defensive. If the United States wanted to learn more about the weapons, he stated, it had only to attack Cuba. "He then said," Knox wrote, "he was not interested in the destruction of the world, but if we all wanted to meet in hell, it was up to us."[63]

On Wednesday morning, 63 ships, including several from Latin American nations, were in place to enforce the quarantine. If one adds the vessels preparing for a Cuban invasion, the United States had 183 ships poised for action. Some 33,000 American military men were directly involved in the quarantine, while hundreds of thousands of others were awaiting orders to invade. The missile crisis, the most dangerous moment in history, was coming to a head.[64]

ExCom saw photographs taken by U-2s and low-flying jets that made it clear, despite Soviet camouflage, that work on the missile sites was progressing rapidly. Within a few days, experts thought, the missiles would be ready to fire (assuming, of course, they had nuclear warheads).

Then, at 10:00 A.M., McNamara announced that two Russian ships were approaching the quarantine barrier, five hundred miles from Cuba. Word followed that a Soviet submarine had moved into position between the two ships.

As he thought of the horrific holocaust he might quickly have to initiate, Jack revealed extreme emotional distress. One can only imagine the true extent of the terror that shook him by reading what Bobby later admitted: "His hand went up to his face and covered his mouth. He opened and closed his fist. His face seemed drawn, his eyes pained, almost gray." As he looked across the table at his brother, Bobby lapsed into what one psychologist later called "momentary disassociation":

> Inexplicably, I thought of when he was ill and almost died; when he lost his child; when we learned that our oldest brother had been killed; of personal times of strain and hurt. The voices droned on, but I didn't seem to hear anything.

Seeking a way out, Jack asked McNamara if there was no alternative to attacking the submarine with depth charges, which seemed likely to be the first confrontation. McNamara said no. The president then ordered final preparations for the defense of Berlin. Perhaps the world had only a few minutes left to exist. Bobby later wrote: "I felt we were on the edge of a precipice with no way off."[65]

Jack and his advisers had issued an ultimatum, drawn a line, and left the rest to Khrushchev. As Bobby later admitted: "President Kennedy had initiated the course of events, but he no longer had control over them." The United States had placed the future in the hands of the Soviet premier. Jack could only wait and see what he would do.[66]

At 10:25 A.M. word arrived that some Soviet ships had stopped dead in the water on the edge of the quarantine line. A few minutes later a second message confirmed the news and added that other ships were turning back toward the Soviet Union. Khrushchev had proved to be rational. Jack issued orders to the Navy not to interfere with the retreat. Bobby later reported that every member of ExCom "looked like a different person." Dean Rusk nudged McGeorge Bundy and quietly crowed: "We're eyeball to eyeball and I think the other fellow just blinked." The Kennedys had been tougher.[67]

Tensions surrounding the quarantine continued for three days. Jack decided to permit the Soviet tanker *Bucharest* to pass through the blockade; he knew that its cargo was merely oil, and he was unwilling to push Khrushchev too far on the matter. When a Republican congressional candidate leaked the news and implied that the president was "soft,"

Jack became furious. (He reportedly became angry on a dozen different occasions during the crisis.)[68] To make the point that the United States was serious about the blockade, Jack permitted the Navy to stop inside the zone and inspect the harmless old freighter *Marcula*, manned by Greeks and flying a neutral flag. (The skipper offered his interrogators coffee.) The destroyer *Joseph P. Kennedy, Jr.*, was chosen to be one of the two ships intercepting the freighter.[69]

The blockade, of course, could do nothing about the missiles already on Cuba, and at this late stage in the crisis Jack still lacked a plan, short of invasion, to deal with them. He was hoping that world opinion might force Khrushchev to dismantle the weapons. On Tuesday Adlai Stevenson gave a forceful performance before the United Nations, arguing that the crucial issue at stake was the Soviet placement of offensive weapons in the Western Hemisphere. (NATO missiles near the Soviet Union were entirely defensive, he claimed, and had been installed openly.) He submitted a draft resolution to the Security Council calling for the immediate withdrawal of the Soviet missiles and the dispatch of a UN observer corps to Cuba to report on compliance. On Thursday Stevenson dramatically presented photographs to the UN documenting American charges of Soviet activity in Cuba.[70]

The Kennedys might well also have hoped that Operation Mongoose would pay a long-awaited dividend. (Soviet UN Ambassador Valerian Zorin proposed that UN observers be sent to the U.S. bases "from which invaders and pirates emerge to punish and harass a small state."[71]) Were Castro in his grave, the entire situation would be altered.

But what would happen if Khrushchev decided to ignore OAS and UN resolutions? Construction of missile launch sites inside Cuba was continuing. Late Wednesday afternoon Jack asked *Time* and *Life* owner Henry Luce, a longtime family friend (and perhaps a substitute for the elder Kennedy), several times what he thought about an American invasion.[72]

That evening veteran diplomat Averell Harriman telephoned Schlesinger and said that he believed events indicated that Khrushchev was desperately seeking a peaceful way out of the crisis. "If we do nothing but get tougher and tougher," Harriman said, "we will force him into countermeasures." Harriman believed that a struggle was going on inside the Kremlin in which Khrushchev was trying to please both sides. "We must give him an out. If we do this shrewdly, we can downgrade the tough group in the Soviet Union which persuaded him to do this. But if we deny him an out, then we will escalate this business into a nuclear war." Schlesinger took the message to the president.[73]

On Thursday Khrushchev seemed to substantiate Harriman's judgment by accepting U Thant's plan calling for a two-week voluntary suspension of all arms shipments to Cuba, cancellation of the quarantine, and immediate negotiations. Jack rejected the proposal because it said nothing about the missiles already in Cuba. The crisis, he said, had been "created by the secret introduction of offensive weapons into Cuba, and the answer lies in the removal of such weapons." He was not backing down.[74]

By Friday, October 26, the administration was back where it started. Missile sites were still being constructed, missiles were being assembled, and the United States would apparently have to invade Cuba to remove them—a step that seemed almost certain to trigger a nuclear war. Expecting the invasion to be "a very bloody fight," the president requested that a list be drawn up of the names of all Cuban physicians living in the Miami area, in case their services were needed. He also approved the preparation of six million propaganda leaflets to be dropped over the island during the invasion.[75]

Jack was nervous and irritable. He lost his temper when newspaper headlines predicted an imminent invasion or air strike. He telephoned the secretary of state, the assistant secretary, and then State Department Press Secretary Lincoln White, "his voice," Sorensen later wrote, "rising and his language intensifying with each call." He was especially angry with White for having responded to newsmen's questions with a quotation from the president's Monday-night speech, pledging further action if the quarantine failed to halt Cuban military preparations. Jack did not want the Russians to think that he was personally threatening them.[76]

The gloom in Washington lifted somewhat when ExCom received a memorandum from ABC-TV's State Department correspondent John Scali. That afternoon Scali had been urgently summoned to a private luncheon meeting by Aleksandr S. Fomin, a counselor at the Soviet Embassy, known by insiders to be a top KGB agent and a personal friend of Khrushchev's. Looking haggard, Fomin said: "The situation is very serious." When the waiter had gone, he whispered: "Perhaps a way can be found to solve this crisis."

The proposal was simple and sensible. (It had been made several weeks earlier by Cuban President Osvaldo Dorticos.) In return for an American pledge never to invade Cuba, the Soviets would dismantle, remove, and promise never to reintroduce the missiles to the island. The United Nations could inspect the missile sites to insure Soviet compliance.

This plan would benefit and save face on both sides. The Russians could retain their principal ally in the Western Hemisphere while claiming that their recent actions had successfully prevented American aggression. Kennedy could take credit for driving out the missiles and defending tens of millions from nuclear blackmail. Each side could contend that it had prevented World War III.

On the other hand, Khrushchev's bid for instant nuclear parity, as well as whatever other advantages he envisioned from the introduction of missiles, would have to be abandoned. And Jack would be forced to shut down Operation Mongoose and concede Castro a permanent place in the hemisphere—which could be politically damaging.

Fomin pleaded with Scali to submit the proposal quickly to top State Department officials and get back to him. Rusk liked the proposal, and he took Scali to meet the president. Jack, too, thought the plan acceptable. "But don't use my name," he told Scali. "That's against the rules. Give them the impression that you talked to me, but don't say so. Tell them you've gotten a favorable response from the highest authority in the government."[77]

Scali and Fomin met again that evening, and the newsman communicated, as instructed, the positive reactions to the Soviet proposal. Fomin then raised another issue: How about a UN inspection of American bases in Florida and the Caribbean to make sure that the United States disbanded its invasion forces? He dropped the idea when Scali angrily observed that this new matter might be politically difficult for the president. Fomin assured Scali that he would convey what he had heard "to the highest levels."

When Scali again met with Rusk to tell him of his second meeting with the Russian, the secretary was complimentary: "John, you have served your country well." Then the secretary repeated his macho metaphor: "Remember, when you report this—that, eyeball to eyeball, they blinked first."[78]

That same evening the president received a lengthy, obviously personal letter from Khrushchev. The Soviet leader pleaded with Kennedy not to lose his "self-control" or be influenced by elections. The missiles in Cuba, he said, were there strictly to prevent the United States from overthrowing the Cuban government, "as the U.S. had actively attempted to overthrow the Communist government in the Soviet Union after their revolution." The Soviet leadership, he stressed, was rational enough to understand that an attack on the United States would be met in kind. "Only lunatics or suicides, who themselves want to perish and to destroy the whole world before they die" would start such a conflict. It was time, he said, for peace. And he repeated Fomin's proposal.[79]

State Department official Roger Hilsman later recalled that the president and ExCom saw Fomin's approach and the Khrushchev cable as "a single package." The Soviet leader seemed sincerely desirous of avoiding a holocaust. O'Donnell later reported that Jack and his advisers went to bed that night "to enjoy the first relaxed sleep [they had had] all week." Perhaps the crisis was over.[80]

The next morning, Saturday, October 27, J. Edgar Hoover informed the attorney general that certain Soviet officials in New York were apparently preparing, in the event of armed conflict, to destroy secret documents. Bobby suddenly feared that the Russians were planning for something other than peace.[81]

ExCom soon received a new message from Khrushchev—an impersonal, official document that obviously came from the Kremlin's Foreign Office. The public letter added a new element to the negotiations: Before the missiles would be removed from Cuba, the United States had to promise not only to leave Cuba alone but also to remove its own missiles from Turkey. (Khrushchev said later that the Jupiters had important symbolic value for the Soviets.)

How could the two strikingly different communications from the Soviet premier be explained? Perhaps the Russians were confused. Perhaps militarists had overruled or even overthrown Khrushchev during the night. Maybe the Soviets were stalling for time. Secretary McNamara said that they were working night and day on all the missile sites. This was hardly the conduct of people prepared to pack up and go home.

Jack immediately realized that the offer to swap missiles was reasonable and would appeal to a great many people. Columnist Walter Lippmann (in an article Jack had not read) had publicly suggested such an exchange, and the State Department and several members of ExCom were pondering the idea. In an ExCom session Jack and Bobby cautiously indicated their approval. Still, such a deal involved many complications. The Turks would be especially sensitive about losing the newly installed weapons. Perhaps all the NATO allies would have to be consulted and convinced that America was not trading European security for Cuba. And what about the United Nations? And the Republicans? During the long, tense, and often-confusing ExCom meetings, Jack repeatedly expressed his concern about a possible Soviet attack on Berlin. He also emphasized his desire to have the Soviets halt their construction efforts in Cuba as a prelude to negotiations.[82]

To make matters worse, a Soviet vessel, carrying ammonia and bound for a nickel factory in Cuba was moving directly toward the quarantine line. Khrushchev had said that such incidents would be avoided.

Perhaps the Russians were now determined to prove their toughness.[83]

The situation became even more critical when word arrived that an American U-2 had been shot down over Cuba by a Soviet SAM missile, and that the American pilot, Major Rudolf Anderson, Jr., was killed. (Four surveillance planes had been fired on that day.) Some ExCom members thought that war was imminent. Members had decided earlier that if a U-2 were shot down, the SAM site responsible would be attacked. Should a second U-2 be downed, all the SAM sites on the island would be knocked out. "It was the blackest hour of the crisis," Roger Hilsman later recalled.[84]

Bobby wrote later: "There was the feeling that the noose was tightening on all of us, on Americans, on mankind, and the bridges to escape were crumbling." The president approved plans for air strikes on Soviet missile sites, air bases, and antiaircraft installations in Cuba. America's conventional and nuclear forces were alerted all over the world.[85]

Compounding the crisis, a U-2 plane on a routine air-testing flight over the North Pole accidentally strayed into Russian territory. Soviet fighter planes responded quickly, and American fighters took off from Alaska. When Secretary McNamara learned of the incident, he reportedly turned white and yelled, "This means war with the Soviet Union!" Shortly the U-2 pilot returned to his flight path and got back to his base without further incident. The president chose not to make an issue of the matter unless the Soviets raised it in public. Still, the tension in ExCom remained almost unbearable. Sorensen later wrote: "Our little group seated around the Cabinet table in continuous session that Saturday felt nuclear war to be closer on that day than at any time in the nuclear age."[86]

Transcripts of the tape recordings made at the October 27 ExCom meetings show the president taking an active part in the discussions. At times, however, he seemed poorly informed (at the conclusion of three meetings, he was still asking about the basic offer in Khrushchev's second letter) and confused. He did not encourage the militants and appeared intent on solving the crisis peacefully. Jack sought details of the U-2 incident over Cuba, to make sure that the plane had not crashed accidentally. He ordered preparations made to diffuse the Turkish missiles so that they could not be used without his personal permission. "We must remind ourselves," he reportedly told ExCom, "we are embarking on a very hazardous course."[87]

During ExCom discussions about a reply to Khrushchev's letters, Bobby advocated a diplomatic maneuver (later dubbed the "Trollope Ploy," after the familiar scene in Anthony Trollope's novels in which the girl interprets a squeeze of her hand as a marriage proposal) that won considerable support.[88] Why not, he asked, respond to Friday's personal letter, and the approach through Scali, and ignore the more formal demand made in Saturday's? This tactic, he contended, was far preferable to the negative State Department reply that simply rejected the Soviets' proposed missile trade. After heated argument among committee members, Jack asked Bobby and Ted Sorensen to go into his office and prepare a draft.[89]

About the same time, Secretary Rusk sent John Scali to meet again with Aleksandr Fomin and to ask what was going on in the Kremlin. Scali, reflecting the State Department line, was angry and threatening during the discussion with the KGB leader, accusing the Soviets of a "stinking double cross." He said that the idea of swapping missiles in Cuba for missiles in Turkey was totally and forever unacceptable. Fomin was unhappy and apologetic. The second letter from the Soviet Union, he said, was sent before he had been able to report on his earlier meeting with Scali. The problem was simply bad communications. Scali's account of the conversation went directly to ExCom.[90]

Bobby and Sorensen took forty-five minutes to write a draft reply to Khrushchev. The Russians were to remove their missiles from Cuba, under United Nations supervision, and agree not to reintroduce them. In return the United States would drop its quarantine and give assurances there would be no invasion of Cuba. If the Soviets agreed to these terms, the letter declared, the agreement could be made public in a couple of days. "The effect of such a settlement on easing world tensions would enable us to work toward a more general arrangement regarding 'other armaments,' as proposed in your second letter, which you made public." The first step, however, to be taken as a sign of Soviet willingness to bargain, must be the cessation of work on the Cuban missile sites. Measures must also be taken to render the missiles inoperable. Jack soon signed the letter, and it was transmitted to the Kremlin and made public.[91]

According to Bobby, Jack spoke at length to him that evening about his desire for peace. He was convinced that the Soviets wanted to avoid nuclear war as much as he did. He fretted once again about the miscalculations that could lead to the death of millions.[92]

At some point during the evening, it appears, Jack and Bobby privately agreed to go all the way to assure world peace. They would secretly assure the Russians that the Jupiter missiles would be taken out of Turkey and Italy. The concession could not be made public, for any hint of a trade with the Soviets would prompt Republicans to scream appeasement, rattle NATO allies, and cause fury in the Pentagon and among militant ExCom members.

Bobby summoned Ambassador Dobrynin to his office, where, in circuitous but understandable language, he stated that within a short time after the crisis ended, the Jupiter missiles would be dismantled. He also talked tough, giving the Russians only until the following day to agree to terms. (In later Soviet versions of the conversation, the weary and emotional attorney general warned the ambassador that the military was bringing strong pressure to bear on the president, and that the situation might get out of control if Khrushchev failed to act swiftly.) If they refused or stalled, the United States would remove the missiles in Cuba by force.

The Kennedys had again drawn a line and left the future in the hands of Soviet leaders. Bobby later wrote: "What hope there was now rested with Khrushchev's revising his course within the next few hours." Preparations for an invasion accelerated, another signal to the Russians about the alternative to compliance.[93]

The president, however, had a secret fallback plan in case the Soviets proved intransigent—a scheme even Bobby may not have known about. Through an intermediary, former UN official Andrew Cordier, UN Secretary General Thant was to be given a statement, dictated by the administration, proposing the exchange of American missiles in Turkey for Soviet missiles in Cuba. Thant would offer in public what Bobby offered in private. Jack, in short, was prepared to pay the political price rather than go to war.[94]

Only the president and a few people close to him were aware of these machinations. (Bobby first described his talk with Dobrynin a half dozen years later in *Thirteen Days*, his account of the crisis. Dean Rusk brought the fallback plan to light in 1987.) ExCom, Congress, the American people, the nation's allies, the United Nations—as far as they knew, the Kennedys were in no mood to bargain with the Communists about the Jupiter missiles. They were too tough. The Camelot School, led by Schlesinger and Sorensen, would perpetuate that interpretation.[95]

On Sunday morning, October 28, the White House learned that Khrushchev had agreed to dismantle and withdraw the Cuban missiles under adequate supervision and inspection. The crisis was over.

→≫≫ ≪≪←

Jack and Bobby met in the Oval Office and savored their triumph at length. Jack telephoned former Presidents Truman and Eisenhower. Almost all insiders were ecstatic at the conclusion of their ordeal. The exceptions were a few military leaders who still yearned to invade. (Jack soon told Schlesinger: "The military are mad. They wanted to do this. It's lucky for us that we have McNamara over there.")[96] Donald Wilson, a sometime ExCom member, said in 1964, "All of a sudden this huge burden was lifted and I felt like laughing or yelling or dancing. . . . I'll never forget it as long as I live."[97]

At ExCom's Sunday meeting the president halted all U-2 flights, stopped military operations by Cuban exiles, told the Navy to let ships through the quarantine line, and instructed his colleagues not to gloat in public. Khrushchev was no doubt under considerable pressure at home, and the United States did not want to weaken the political position of a Russian it could deal with. In a formal message to the premier, the president congratulated him for his "statesmanlike decision."[98]

Although Castro balked at the agreement (he said contemptuously that Khrushchev lacked *cojones*—balls), and U.N. observers were never permitted to enter Cuba, the Soviets removed their offensive weapons from the island. In April 1963, the Administration quietly removed 105 missiles, including the Jupiters, located in England, Italy, and Turkey. They were replaced with submarine-launched Polaris missiles.

The world appeared to be a safer place. And the prestige of the United States seemed to be at the highest level since the end of World War Two. The applause for the President was overwhelming. Congratulations poured into the White House from all over the world, and Kennedy's popularity at home soared. (In mid-November, he received a 74 percent overall approval rating in the Gallup poll.) *Newsweek* exclaimed, "his total victory in the head-on clash with Khrushchev marked his greatest political triumph."[99] The accolades, at first, were bipartisan. Richard Nixon declared, "it demonstrates again that when you stand up to Communist aggressors, they back down."[100]

In extensive newspaper and magazine accounts of the missile crisis, Jack was portrayed as a man of cool courage and iron strength, a sort of warrior-king who stood up to the Russians, scoffed at their Cuba-Turkey rocket proposal, and got his way. Liberal Washington observer Richard Rovere wrote: "No one who watched developments here failed to be impressed by the forethought, precision, subtlety, and steady nerves of the President and those around him in preparing our bold and ultimately successful initiative." *Time* bubbled: "Once again a foreign dictator had seemingly misread the character of the U.S. and of a U.S. President."[101]

ExCom assumed equally glowing features in the press. One participant told *Life* that the group had experienced almost total harmony. "At the start there was a lot of discussion about what particular course to take, but there was never any real disagreement."[102]

Much of this media praise was generated by Kennedy insiders and friends. In a valuable *Saturday Evening Post* piece, for example, Stewart Alsop and Charles Bartlett described the president as a paragon of wisdom and strength. Bobby and ExCom were said to be astute, compassionate, and realistic. Several references were made to Khrushchev's "blink."[103]

Jack handled the media with considerable skill. After a highly praised television interview at year's end (edited to enhance the president's effectiveness), liberal journalist Max Ascoli wrote, "It was nearly incredible to think that this was the same John F. Kennedy who appeared in the campaign debates as nearly identical or interchangeable with his opponent, mercilessly repeating the same few phrases in basic English." Another reporter observed, "The final product—disjointed syntax and all—brought the President closer to the people last week than any program since FDR's 'fireside chats.' "[104]

Of course, the Cuban missile crisis had its critics. From the Left came cries that the President had recklessly and needlessly endangered mankind. I. F. Stone asked: "Mr. Kennedy's gamble paid off. But what if it had failed? Unless we can achieve a fundamental change of behavior among nations, the Cuban confrontation is only a pre-view."[105]

Many on the Right, observing that Castro now had a guaranteed grip on Cuba, claimed that Kennedy had been too lenient with the Reds. Changing his earlier tune, Richard Nixon wrote in 1964 that White House doves "enabled the United States to pull defeat out of the jaws of victory."[106]

A few weeks after the crisis concluded, Khrushchev began portraying himself as the victor. In a speech to the Soviet people, he claimed that Russian missiles and other weapons were sent to Cuba strictly to protect the island from an invasion by the United States. The decision to remove the missiles, he said, was made to prevent Americans from setting off a nuclear war. "In what way have we retreated, one may ask. Socialist Cuba exists. Cuba remains a beacon of Marxist-Leninist ideas in the Western Hemisphere. The impact of her revolutionary example will grow."[107]

Few objective students of the missile crisis, however, have described Khrushchev as the hero. True, he was sufficiently rational and responsible to concede, thus preventing an American invasion of Cuba and the probable beginning of nuclear war. But he had started the crisis and was clearly attempting far more than the defense of Cuba. He had escalated the danger by accelerating construction of the missile sites when detected. And he withdrew, apparently, only realizing, at last, that

Kennedy meant what he said publicly on October 22: He would not, at any cost, permit his nation and the Western Hemisphere to be conned and blackmailed by Communists.

Even at the time Khrushchev had difficulty persuading many that he was triumphant in retreat. Castro was outraged by the Russian pullout. His top aide, Ernesto ("Che") Guevera, told a reporter defiantly, "If the rockets had remained, we would have used them all and directed them against the very heart of the United States, including New York." The Red Chinese were appalled by Moscow's backdown, some officials in Peking calling Cuba "a Soviet Munich."[108]

Defense Department official Roswell Gilpatric later called Khrushchev "an opportunist, an adventurer, who was taking a big gamble." True, and he lost. On October 15, 1964, the Soviets announced that Khrushchev had been removed from the government. The complaints against him included "harebrained scheming, hasty conclusions, rash decisions and actions based on wishful thinking."[109]

Almost thirty years after the event, and in light of many revelations of the intervening years, Kennedy's conduct in the Cuban Missile Crisis can now be properly assessed. It must be acknowledged that Operation Mongoose bears some responsibility for the turmoil since it apparently drove Castro to Khrushchev seeking protection from the United States. Still, Georgi Shaknazarov, senior staff member of the Central Committee of the Communist Party of the Soviet Union, declared in 1987 that Khrushchev's major purpose "was to publicly attain military parity. . . . He was trying for cheap parity. The crisis between the United States and the Soviet Union on parity was inevitable. If not here, there; if not now, then—but inevitable."[110]

During the crisis Kennedy at times seemed unduly militant, and his aggressive and competitive instincts led him to grant the initiative to the Soviets at critical points where more skilled diplomacy might have avoided it. Moreover, politics entered into ExCom's deliberations: Fears about Republicans and the fall elections were on the minds of at least some participants, including the president.[111] And Kennedy and his advisers were certainly not as unflappable and omniscient as they later wanted others to believe. (Dean Rusk later told an interviewer that the president was "as calm as an iceberg throughout this situation.") The highly critical Dean Acheson later wrote that the president had been "phenomenally lucky," his success being helped by "Khrushchev's befuddlement and loss of nerve."[112]

Lucky or not, the president's success is ultimately attributable to his leadership and conduct during the crisis. Jack's personal agony over the conflict, his several efforts to avoid bloodshed, and his willingness to make a trade of Turkish for Cuban missiles, revealed a deeper concern for the nation and the world than many who knew him well might have suspected. There was more to Kennedy's character by this time than the pursuit of power and pleasure that had shaped his career. Jack's political and behavioral instincts were contained by a larger moral purpose, and that revealed a growing maturity.

A large number of powerful men in Washington, including ExCom members, Pentagon officials, and congressional leaders, would have speedily invaded Cuba and dared the Soviets to engage in nuclear war in an effort to establish our predominance in global power. No doubt because of lessons learned about the military in the Bay of Pigs fiasco (Bobby said later that "we didn't have an exercise with the Army in which they didn't screw up"), and surely for deeper reasons concerning the fate of the human race, Jack chose to resist this course of action. During what Dean Rusk called "the most dangerous crisis the world has ever seen," Kennedy was not reckless. Indeed, he demonstrated the ability to seek counsel, make decisions, and maintain reasonable control of an enormously complex crisis to the benefit of all.[113]

What is clear is that the administration's overall conduct was highly popular at home and abroad. The domestic unity was based not only on a concern for personal safety, but also on a consensus about the nature of communism and a principle expressed in the president's October 22 address: "The 1930s taught us a clear lesson: aggressive conduct, if allowed to go unchecked and unchallenged, ultimately leads to war." Kennedy's general response to the missile crisis was in harmony with presidential decisions made since World War II to contain Communist aggression. Henry Kissinger observed: "No President could have avoided taking action in the face of such a challenge, and the public would not have tolerated acquiescence." Columnist David Lawrence wrote, "President Kennedy has interpreted correctly the wishes of the American people. The nation has demanded that the United States protest vigorously the Soviet invasion of Cuba and use force if necessary to assure the safety of the countries of this hemisphere."[114]

John H. Davis has asked if Khrushchev's surrender was worth the risk of nuclear holocaust. "Is *anything* worth taking such a risk?" The free world thought so in 1962, and its peoples cheered the Kennedys when the Cuban missiles were dismantled. Most American historians have continued the applause.[115]

Still, it galled the president to see Cuba in Soviet hands. He knew that the Russians intended to use the island as a base for spreading communism in Latin America. (Cubans were soon engaged in a secret war in Venezuela.) And his personal hatred of Castro remained extreme. In late December 1962, following the release of the Bay of Pigs prisoners, Jack made his impromptu promise in the Orange Bowl that the rebel flag would be returned to ''a free Havana.'' The following March, he sent his brother a memorandum urging a revival of efforts to foment an ''internal breakup in Cuba,'' specifically mentioning the CIA and the United States Information Agency.

In mid-June 1963 the administration renewed the secret campaign, shut down after the missile crisis, to sabotage the Cuban economy and assassinate Castro. Inasmuch as a Cuban invasion was now prohibited, and Castro seemed willing, at last, to get along with the United States, Schlesinger later called the new terrorism ''perplexing'' and without logic. ''Robert Kennedy understood so lucidly the enormity of a Pearl Harbor air strike on a small country. It is odd that he did not see that the same principle applied to the secret war.'' The historian believed that Bobby was unaware of the more sordid details of the war.[116]

It now seems highly likely that the new program was simply a continuation of the old; Jack and Bobby were renewing the well-established efforts, led by the CIA, to get rid of an old foe and drive the Reds out of the hemisphere. After the agreement reached during the missile crisis, this was the only avenue open to them. The morality of Operation Mongoose had not bothered them earlier, and their consciences did not appear to cry out in mid-1963.

CHAPTER 17

A New Prince of Peace and Freedom

➸➺ ⤚⤙

DURING the Cuban Missile Crisis, the president, more than many of his advisers, revealed a deep concern about the dangers of nuclear war. Part of this attitude may well have reflected a growing sensitivity Kennedy was experiencing toward his own family. From all accounts, Jack had reached out to his children and had become emotionally engaged in their lives. He enjoyed them, fretted about their well-being, and worried about their future. Dave Powers later remembered Kennedy saying during the missile crisis: "I keep thinking about the children whose lives would be wiped out."[1]

But Kennedy was no stranger to the issues of the nuclear arms race. In Los Angeles in late 1959, for example, he had opposed the resumption of nuclear testing, arguing that, among other things, it might threaten "the very existence of human life." A month later in Washington, he warned that the United States and USSR together were "in a position to exterminate all human life seven times over." He urged that the United States "press forward now for any practical disarmament agreement within reach. . . . Our job is to bring the peaceful processes of history into play quickly, even though the ultimate resolution may take generations—or even centuries. . . . We should not let our fears hold us back from pursuing our hopes." In 1960 Senator Kennedy sponsored legislation to create an arms control research institute.[2]

Much of this was campaign rhetoric, expected of all liberal and moderate candidates. While Kennedy appealed to the Left with talk of peace, he attracted the votes of others by calling for increased American military expenditures and warning that America was falling behind in the arms race. Still, after his election, Jack followed through on his disarmament proposals. He devoted ten paragraphs of his inaugural address to arms control and urged the United States and the Soviet Union to "begin anew the quest for peace, before the dark powers of destruction unleashed by science engulf all humanity in planned or accidental self-destruction."[3] Two weeks later, the president met with Glenn T. Seaborg, the noted scientist and former chancellor of the University of California at Berkeley who was his choice as chairman of the Atomic Energy Committee. Kennedy stressed the need for disarmament and criticized efforts by the Eisenhower administration. A few days later he visited AEC headquarters and asked detailed questions about the weapons program.[4]

The president named John H. McCloy his special adviser on disarmament, and early in the administration the Republican attorney was seriously at work on the issue. Jerome Weisner became Kennedy's special assistant on science and technology. Weisner, an electrical engineer from MIT, was an outspoken proponent of a nuclear test ban. Weisner later recalled Kennedy's deep concern about nuclear fallout:

> I remember one day when he asked me what happens to the radioactive fallout, and I told him it was washed out of the clouds by the rain and would be brought to earth by the rain. And he said, looking out the window, 'You mean, it's in the rain out there?' and I said, 'Yes.' He looked out the window, very sad, and didn't say a word for a few minutes.[5]

Early in his administration, then, Kennedy seems genuinely to have realized the dangers of nuclear war. Of course, there was nothing novel about such an acknowledgment. In the 1956 campaign, Adlai Stevenson had called for a test ban and bold action to end the arms race. George Kennan, the philosopher of America's containment policy, proposed "disengagement," a de-escalation of the nuclear arms race coupled with a pullback of Soviet and American forces in Central Europe. Numerous voices on the Left had long been crying for weapons control.

Eisenhower, especially in his second term, became deeply interested in reducing military expenditures and thwarting nuclear proliferation. As Stephen Ambrose has noted: "By early 1960, Eisenhower had made a test-ban treaty, to be followed by some actual disarmament, the major goal of his Presidency, indeed of his entire career." In February 1960 the president declared that he would agree to a ban that would end testing in the atmosphere, the oceans, outer space, and underground. At one point he was on the verge of accepting an unsupervised test ban; Khrushchev seemed willing to permit inspection teams to enter the Soviet Union. Both sides abstained from testing for nearly three years while talks went on in Geneva.

Still, by the time Eisenhower left office, he had failed to hammer out an agreement. Verification was a persistent stumbling block; the collapse of the Paris summit conference, following the shooting down over Sverdlovsk of U-2 pilot Francis Gary Powers, seriously damaged American-Soviet relations. Gloomy about his inability to curb the Cold War, Eisenhower urged the president-elect to resume nuclear testing immediately.[6]

During the first months of the new administration, tensions between the two superpowers remained extremely high, intensified by the Bay of Pigs, the Berlin crisis, developments in Southeast Asia and the Congo (where the United States was supporting UN efforts to calm a bloody civil war), Kennedy's commitment to an arms buildup, and Soviet achievements in space. In March the Soviets presented demands at the Geneva test-ban talks that made nuclear disarmament unlikely. On September 1, in a clear attempt at intimidation, they resumed nuclear testing.

The administration responded with an offer to accept any form of test ban without inspection. After three Russian explosions (the United States monitored fifty atmospheric tests within sixty days), Kennedy angrily ordered the resumption of U.S. underground testing. On March 1, 1962, following months of vacillation, the president announced the resumption of atmospheric tests. "What Kennedy seemed to hope for," Glenn Seaborg later recalled, "was some eleventh hour agreement with the Russians that would make testing unnecessary."[7]

At first, according to Sorensen, Kennedy was skeptical about the possibilities of disarmament. Gradually, however, he came to believe that it was achievable. Sorensen observed: "He increasingly recognized that there was no ultimate security in armaments, that tensions and danger were rising even as our nuclear stockpiles rose."[8]

On September 25, 1961, in an address to the United Nations, Kennedy made an eloquent plea for disarmament. The following day, he signed a bill establishing the United States Arms Control and Disarmament Agency, commenting: "The new agency brings renewed hope for

agreement and progress in the critical battle for the survival of mankind."
In press conferences, White House statements, and speeches, Kennedy
repeatedly emphasized his concern about the arms race.[9]

At the same time, however, Kennedy presided over the largest and
most rapid military expansion in America's peacetime history. At the
heart of the buildup, which cost $17 billion in additional appropriations,
was a nuclear "deterrent" that featured the production and development
of nuclear-armed bombers, Polaris submarines, and underground Min-
uteman missiles. Kennedy increased America's arsenal of nuclear weapons by 150 percent. Tactical nuclear weapons were increased by 60
percent in Western Europe alone. The administration was committed to
being number one in arms. Sorensen later observed: "Because our safety
as a second-strike nation required a great enough force to survive a first
strike and still retaliate effectively, and because our strategy required
enough weapons to destroy all important enemy targets, there was no
absolute level of sufficiency." Historian Thomas G. Paterson has looked
at this matter in a different way: "Given his Cold War past and personality, one cannot think of Kennedy ever accepting nuclear parity."[10]

Kennedy continued to pursue disarmament—perhaps as only a distant goal but nevertheless a real one. He was particularly concerned about
the Chinese obtaining nuclear weapons.[11] When the United States resumed atmospheric testing in April 1962, in large part out of fear that the
Russians were developing an antimissile missile, Kennedy limited the
total yield of the series to approximately twenty megatons. The Soviet
tests in the fall of 1961 had yielded some ten times as much. A high
altitude explosion in July, which drew widespread criticism for its adverse affect on the Van Allen radiation belt and three space satellites, was
approved by the president only after scientists had erroneously predicted
that the shot would be harmless. While the full schedule of tests took
more than six months to complete, Kennedy had sought to limit the
undertaking to two and a half months.[12]

At the conclusion of the Cuban Missile Crisis, both Kennedy and
Khrushchev expressed willingness to talk further about nuclear disarmament. Now, more than ever, it seemed imperative to limit the possibilities
of mutual destruction. For months, however, both sides continued to
wrangle about the number and location of unmanned monitoring stations
and the U.S. demand (required by suspicious Senate leaders) for numerous on-site inspections.

In early May 1963 Kennedy authorized a new series of atmospheric
tests, scheduled for the following year. Khrushchev continued to be belligerent, and Jack soon told a news conference that he was "not hopeful"

about a test ban. Later that month, however, after the Soviets agreed to host a delegation of American scientists and permit them to see nuclear reactors, Jack told the reporters that the administration was going to "push very hard" and use "every forum" to reach an agreement.[13]

On June 8 Khrushchev agreed to receive Western emissaries in Moscow for high-level talks on a test ban. Two days later, in a commencement address at American University, Kennedy delivered what the *Manchester Guardian* called "one of the great state papers of American history." The speech was a bold effort to change the entire mood of the Cold War and promote disarmament and world peace.

Kennedy defined peace, "the most important topic on earth," as "the necessary rational end of rational men." He said that he was not seeking "a Pax Americana enforced on the world by American weapons of war" or "the peace of the grave or the security of the slave."

> I am talking about genuine peace, the kind of peace that makes life on earth worth living, the kind that enables men and nations to grow and to hope and to build a better life for their children—not merely peace for Americans but peace for all men and women—not merely peace in our time but peace for all time.

Jack spoke of the insanity of total war, and he decried the expenditure of billions of dollars annually on weapons. As a prelude to peace, he proposed that both the United States and the Soviet Union reexamine their basic attitudes about each other. Russian blasts against U.S. "imperialists" were baseless, he said. And Americans should not fall into the same trap:

> No government or social system is so evil that its people must be considered as lacking in virtue. As Americans, we find communism profoundly repugnant as a negation of personal freedom and dignity. But we can still hail the Russian people for their many achievements—in science and space, in economic and industrial growth, in culture and in acts of courage.

If the two superpowers could not resolve their differences, Kennedy stated, at least they could "help make the world safe for diversity":

> For, in the final analysis, our most basic common link is that we all inhabit this small planet. We all breathe the same air. We all cherish our children's future. And we are all mortal.

Jack asserted that the United States was peace loving and that the Soviet Union was not: "The Communist drive to impose their political and economic system on others is the primary cause of world tension today." (A memorandum issued by the White House the following day assured bureaucrats that the president was not soft on the Communists.) Still, he thought world peace possible and called for new efforts to achieve it. At the top of Kennedy's agenda was a treaty to outlaw nuclear tests. He announced that new talks would soon be underway and that his country would suspend atmospheric tests as long as others did.

The United States would never start a war, the president declared. "This generation of Americans has already had enough—more than enough—of war and hate and oppression," he said, continuing:

> We shall be prepared if others wish it. We shall be alert to try to stop it. But we shall also do our part to build a world of peace where the weak are safe and the strong are just. We are not helpless before that task or hopeless of its success. Confident and unafraid, we labor on—not toward a strategy of annihilation but toward a strategy of peace.[14]

Khrushchev's response was immediate and highly favorable. The full text of the speech was published in the Soviet press and heard on the Voice of America. Soon the Soviets stopped all jamming of Western broadcasts. On June 20 a memorandum was signed establishing a direct telephone link, a "hot line," between Washington and Moscow. (According to Peter Lawford, the first time the red telephone rang, Jack refused to answer it, terrified of what it might mean. The call turned out to have been a technical fluke.)[15] The next day Kennedy learned that the Soviet Union had made a crucial concession about international inspections of nuclear facilities, a sign that the Russians were at last serious about a test ban. His efforts had reaped the rewards of increased cooperation.[16]

On June 22 Kennedy flew to West Germany to begin a ten-day European tour that would include stops in Ireland, England, and Italy. Rusk, Bundy, Sorensen, Salinger, O'Donnell, and Powers, among others, accompanied him. Huge cheering throngs greeted Jack wherever he went. In West Berlin, during a thirty-five-mile tour of the city, it seemed that most of the embattled area's 2,200,000 people were on hand. A reporter observed, "For them the only matter of importance was to give a heartfelt and spectacular welcome to the United States President and to see a youthful-looking, smiling man obviously respond to their warmth." Herbert Parmet later said of Jack: "It was as though he was a new prince of peace and freedom."[17]

Kennedy's famous *"Ich bin ein Berliner"* speech was given at the city hall in West Berlin before a crowd of 150,000. According to O'Donnell, the speech was largely spontaneous. (The German phrase came from conservative journalist and Kennedy assistant James P. O'Donnell.)[18]

Moved by the masses of people and shocked by the sight of the Berlin Wall, Jack gave an emotional, harshly anti-Communist talk that threatened to undo much of what had been achieved by the American University address.

> There are many people in the world who really don't understand, or say they don't, what is the great issue between the free world and the Communist world. Let them come to Berlin. There are some who say that communism is the wave of the future. Let them come to Berlin. And there are some who say in Europe and elsewhere we can work with the Communists. Let them come to Berlin.[19]

Kenny O'Donnell later acknowledged that the speech was a "grave political risk," and that Jack knew it. Tass, the official Soviet press agency, charged that the remarks "further whipped up anti-Communist hysteria, fanned these days by the West Berlin advocates of the cold war." Later that day, in an address delivered at the Free University of Berlin, Kennedy returned to the theme of peace, attempting to repair whatever damage he had done. "But I do believe in the necessity of great powers working together to preserve the human race, or otherwise we can be destroyed."[20]

→→→ ←←←

Jackie, seven months pregnant, stayed in Washington during her husband's trip. In early August, a little more than a month after her husband's return, the first lady underwent emergency cesarean surgery and gave birth to a boy. Immediately baptized Patrick Bouvier Kennedy, the underweight infant, five and a half weeks premature, quickly developed a serious respiratory problem.

Although at first Jackie did not want her husband to be alerted to her condition, the president was quickly on the scene. He soon accompanied Patrick to a Boston hospital, where special assistance was available. The next day, he visited the hospital four times. When the baby died, Jack wept bitterly. Cardinal Cushing later recalled: "It was an agonizing moment for a man never known to have had an emotional outburst." Jackie said later that Jack had wanted another boy. "He felt the loss of the baby in the house as much as I did."[21]

Jack and Jackie were brought closer together by Patrick's death. Their friend Bill Walton spent the weekend with them, and said later: "She hung onto him and he held her in his arms—something nobody ever saw at any other time because they were very private people." Deputy Defense Secretary Roswell Gilpatric recalled: "There was a growing tenderness between them. . . . I think their marriage was really beginning to work at the end."[22] Once more it appeared that Jack's ability to empathize, to care as well as think about others, was growing beyond his earlier, more self-absorbed detachment.

>>> <<<

On July 15 test-ban talks between the United States, Great Britain, and the Soviet Union opened in Moscow. The American delegation was headed by Under Secretary of State W. Averell Harriman, who had helped engineer the settlement in Laos. In daily White House meetings, the president paid careful attention to the progress of the negotiations. Benjamin Read, executive secretary of the State Department, later recalled, "He'd delve into the subject with gusto and in considerable detail. And I remember many occasions in which he set the tone of the outgoing instruction very personally and directly in his own words."[23]

From the beginning it was clear that Khrushchev would accept only a limited treaty, prohibiting testing in those environments—outer space, the atmosphere, and the oceans—where on-site inspections would be unnecessary. Thus, a comprehensive test ban was removed from the agenda three days after the talks commenced. In any case the U.S. Joint Chiefs of Staff, and probably the Senate, would have opposed the more sweeping agreement. Glenn Seaborg wrote later: "To put the matter in its baldest form, the Soviets were persuaded that the United States wanted to inspect in order to spy; many on our side were convinced that without adequate inspection the Soviets would cheat."[24]

It took only twelve days for Harriman and his counterparts to agree to a limited test-ban treaty. Article One pledged the parties not to carry out nuclear explosions in the prohibited environments and to refrain from abetting such explosions by others. Underground testing was permitted to continue.[25]

In a July 26 radio and television speech to the nation, Kennedy warmly and eloquently endorsed the agreement. "Yesterday a shaft of light cut into the darkness," he said, calling the treaty "an important first step—a step towards peace—a step towards reason—a step away from war." The president acknowledged that the treaty would soon face the Senate, and he urged the public to make its support known.

> Now, for the first time in many years, the path of peace may be open. No one can be certain what the future will bring. No one can say whether the time has come for an easing of the struggle. But history and our conscience will judge us harsher if we do not now make every effort to test our hopes by action, and this is the place to begin.[26]

    Editorial commentary about the treaty was highly favorable, and an assortment of major organizations, including the National Council of Churches and the AFL-CIO, expressed support. Soon some one hundred nations assented to the treaty. Still, debate in the Senate was intense. Two committees conducted hearings and issued conflicting reports. The most formidable treaty opponent was hawkish nuclear scientist Edward Teller. Several military leaders, including General Thomas Power, commander of the Strategic Air Command, expressed strong opposition. (General Curtis LeMay fell in line with General Maxwell Taylor and the Joint Chiefs in approving the treaty.) Ultra-conservatives, such as activist Phyllis Schlafly, referred to the agreement as "the Moscow Treaty."[27]

    The president worked hard for the treaty, privately wooing the military, nuclear laboratory directors, and key senators. (Tape recordings of some of his telephone calls are now available.)[28] He coordinated the parade of administration officials before Senate committees and urged approval at press conferences. In a lengthy letter of September 10, Kennedy pledged his unyielding toughness on communism and his firm commitment to continue underground testing. That document, read to the Senate by Senator Dirksen, appeared to win over many conservatives.

    On September 24 the treaty was approved by a vote of 80 to 19— fourteen more than the required two-thirds majority. The opposition consisted of 11 Democrats (all but one from the South) and 8 Republicans.[29]

    On October 7, at the formal signing of the test-ban treaty, Kennedy made a brief speech expressing optimism about the future of disarmament. "This small step toward safety can be followed by others longer and less limited, if also harder in the taking. With our courage and understanding enlarged by this achievement, let us press onward in quest of man's essential desire for peace." Sorensen wrote later of Kennedy and the treaty, "No other single accomplishment in the White House ever gave him greater satisfaction."[30]

    Jack quickly took a further step to demonstrate his desire for improved relations with the Kremlin. At an October 9 news conference, he endorsed the sale of several million tons of surplus wheat to the Soviet Union. He argued principally that the deal benefited the American economy: "We have got 1 billion bushels of this in surplus, and American taxpayers are paying to keep it, and I think we can use the $200 million or $250 million of gold which will help our balance of payments." He also made the point that the nation's allies had long been making similar sales to the Russians.

    But Jack did not fail to hint at a larger reason for the proposed transaction: "It shows that peaceful agreements with the United States which serve the interests of both sides are a far more worthwhile course than a course of isolation and hostility.'' After a successful campaign by the president that resembled his efforts on behalf of the test-ban treaty, the wheat was sold. For the brief remainder of his life, Kennedy spoke repeatedly of his hope to reduce the tensions and dangers of the Cold War.[31]

➨➤➤ ◄◄◄

But war as well as peace was on JFK's mind during the last months of his life, prompted by the increasing danger in Southeast Asia. By the spring of 1963, despite official optimism from the Pentagon and the intelligence community, the American effort in South Vietnam was marred by tension and uncertainty. The rapid growth in the number of Americans in the country (twenty-five thousand by September) and U.S. demands for efficiency and reform had made Diem and his highly controversial brother and sister-in-law, the Nhus, resentful and uncooperative. Moreover, the government, which the United States had backed for nine years, was proving to be increasingly unpopular at home.

In May South Vietnamese Buddhists began to suffer persecution at the hands of the largely Catholic government. (Of the nation's fourteen million people, only about a million and a half were Catholics.) Demonstrations and violence followed, and the government responded with force. Soon, even protesting grade-schoolers were hauled off by the hundreds to jail. Madame Nhu charged that the Buddhists had been infiltrated by Communist agents. (In fact, the uprising involved class and radical ideology as well as religion; Schlesinger later described participants as "angry young men massing to throw out the mandarins.")[32]

In June a monk immolated himself in front of a crowd in Saigon. Several other monks and nuns would meet fiery deaths. Photos of these incidents horrified millions across the world, including Kennedy. "How could this have happened?" the president asked National Security Council staff man Michael Forrestal, who had been to Saigon earlier in the year. "Who are these people? Why didn't we know about them before?"[33]

Diem resisted U.S. efforts at reconciliation. Madam Nhu made things worse by referring to the immolations as "barbecues" and offering matches and fuel for more. On August 21 the government carried out a mass raid against Buddhists in several cities, ransacking pagodas and arresting more than fourteen thousand monks and nuns. The action took place just days after Diem had assured outgoing U.S. Ambassador Frederick Nolting that, as a personal favor, he would take no further repressive steps against the Buddhists. If that was insufficient to enrage his U.S. supporters, American intelligence soon reported that Diem was secretly trying to reach an agreement with Hanoi.[34]

Shortly two South Vietnamese Army generals made a quiet overture to American officials. They reported that Diem's brother Ngo Dinh Nhu had been responsible for the pagoda raids, not the Army, and that he might be trying to make a deal with Hanoi to sell out the entire nation. The officers wanted to know how the United States would respond if they moved against the government.

Three State Department officials—Averell Harriman, Roger Hilsman, and Michael Forrestal—were at work on Saturday, August 24, when the message arrived in Washington. They decided to take immediate action. In a cable cleared with the president (vacationing at Hyannis Port) and every interested agency except the Joint Chiefs, they instructed the new ambassador, Henry Cabot Lodge, to demand that Diem get rid of the Nhus and redress Buddhist grievances. If Diem proved obdurate, Lodge was to extend encouragement to the generals. The United States, the cable continued, would provide the officers with "direct support in any interim period of breakdown [of the] central government mechanism." The U.S. mission was to "make detailed plans as to how we might bring about Diem's replacement if this should become necessary."[35]

Ambassador Lodge, staunchly anti-Diem, soon contacted the generals through CIA operatives, making it clear that they would receive American support should they topple Diem. They were warned, however, that the United States would not assist the coup in a direct way or bail out the generals if things went wrong.

Several senior Kennedy advisers, who had not been consulted personally before the cable was sent, soon expressed reservations about the course of action. The issue was discussed at length; Jack asked a great many questions. There was no retreat, however. The president and his advisers had no moral qualms about quietly plotting the overthrow of the government of South Vietnam. Indeed Lodge (appointed in large part to make the Vietnam effort appear bipartisan) was soon given the authority to announce publicly, at his discretion, the suspension of economic aid to Diem, the signal the dissident generals had requested as a sign of American support.[36] The administration even contemplated direct military assistance. A U.S. attack carrier task group cruised off the coast of Vietnam, and some three thousand Marines in Okinawa were put on twenty-four-hour alert.

Nothing came of the proposed coup. The generals did not fully trust their American allies, and they failed to recruit the necessary military backing. What, if anything, Kennedy and his advisers learned from the incident is uncertain. Lodge was convinced, as he cabled to Rusk on August 29: "We are launched on a course from which there is no respectable turning back: the overthrow of the Diem government."[37]

In an off-the-record press briefing on August 30, and in television interviews on September 2 and 9, the president expressed his firm commitment to defend South Vietnam from communism. Of course, he preferred that the South Vietnamese carry most of the burden: "In the final analysis, it is their war. They are the ones who have to win it or lose it." But he made it clear that the United States would not withdraw and let the Communists take over. On September 9 Jack expressed his unequivocal commitment to the "domino theory":

> I believe it. I think that the struggle is close enough. China is so large, looms so high just beyond the frontiers, that if South Viet-Nam went, it would not only give them an improved geographic position for a guerrilla assault on Malaya, but would also give the impression that the wave of the future in southeast Asia was China and the Communists. So I believe it.[38]

The next day the president and his advisers met at the White House and heard reports from two recent travelers to Vietnam and two officials in the American mission there. Kennedy was upset by receiving conflicting data and advice. A week later Ambassador Lodge urged U.S. officials to apply selective economic sanctions and to try again to spark a coup. A CIA analysis, however, recommended there be no economic cuts, fearing that such a move would push Diem and Nhu into the arms of Hanoi.

By mid-September, Sorensen later admitted: "Kennedy's advisers were more deeply divided on the internal situation in Saigon than on any previous issue." Jack told a news conference simply: "What helps to win the war, we support; what interferes with the war effort, we oppose." Historian George C. Herring later observed: "The administration drifted along, divided against itself, with no clear idea where it was going." The president could not even be certain if the war was being won or lost. (It would later be revealed that much of the data provided by the South Vietnamese military were false.) The press and Congress were also restive. Meanwhile the Buddhist demonstrations continued to grow, and the Diem government seemed more intractable than ever. The Nhus' *Times of Vietnam* regularly attacked the United States, at one point accusing the CIA of spending $24 million, in cooperation with the Viet Cong, to organize a coup.[39]

To obtain better information Jack soon sent a mission to South Vietnam headed by Defense Secretary McNamara, allegedly a master of statistics, and General Taylor, chairman of the Joint Chiefs of Staff. McNamara and Taylor traveled exensively for ten days and met with Diem—who appeared hostile and obtuse. Their report on October 2 expressed optimism about the military progress of the war but recommended economic and military cuts that might improve the political situation. These cuts, it was thought, would lead either to reconciliation with Diem or a coup. The American commitment to the struggle in Vietnam was unequivocal: "The security of South Vietnam remains vital to United States security. For this reason, we adhere to the overriding objective of denying this country to Communism and of suppressing the Viet Cong insurgency as promptly as possible."[40]

Jack embraced the report and urged unity among his advisers. "Reports of disagreements," he told the National Security Council, "do not help the war effort in Vietnam and do no good to the government as a whole. We must all sign on."[41]

On the very day McNamara and Taylor made their report, South Vietnamese generals informed the American embassy, through CIA agent Lou Conein, that they were planning another coup attempt. Lodge soon informed the State Department in detail of proposals by General Duong Van Minh (known as "Big Minh"), including the assassination of Diem and his youngest brother Ngo Dinh Can, who ruled central Vietnam. Minh requested only assurances that the United States would not thwart the coup.

Kennedy's initial response was vague: He discouraged active encouragement of a coup but said that there should be an "urgent covert effort with closest security, under broad guidance of [the] Ambassador to identify and build contacts with possible alternative leadership as and when it appears." Above all, the president was afraid of leaks. Plotting was all right as long as you were not caught at it. Jack wanted the anti-Diem efforts "totally secure and fully deniable."[42] Information about the proposed coup was to be transmitted exclusively on the CIA channel, considered safer than State Department communications. Lodge's orders were to be issued orally. Conein later recalled: "Ambassador Lodge made it very clear to me that if something went wrong . . . he would have to be able to have deniability that I even existed."[43]

The next day, October 6, the White House warmed a bit more to the idea of a coup. Lodge was informed that while the president and his advisers still did not wish to stimulate a coup, "we also do not wish to leave [the] impression that [the] U.S. would thwart a change of government or deny economic and military assistance to a new regime if it appeared capable of increasing [the] effectiveness of [the] military effort.'' More information was sought about the ''character of any alternate leadership.''[44]

The administration thus appeared to be giving the conspiring generals a green light. Selective economic and military cuts were in store for Diem; a new regime was promised U.S. assistance; Lodge, who was not speaking to Diem, was encouraged. Moreover, Saigon CIA Station Chief John Richardson, thought to be a Nhu supporter, was recalled. Roger Hilsman wrote later that this move helped ''signal our determination not to cooperate with a government that continued to leave Nhu in a position of predominance.''[45]

In fact, Jack's approach to the subject was highly pragmatic. As Bobby put it later, ''He would have liked to have gotten rid of Diem if he could get rid of him and get somebody proper to replace him. He was against getting rid of him until you knew what was going to come along, whether the government that was going to replace it had any stability, whether it would, in fact, be a successful coup.[46] A good coup, in short, was one that worked.

Considerable confusion stemmed from this unclear and unprincipled position. In Saigon, for example, Ambassador Lodge, who favored a coup, feuded with General Harkins, commander of U.S. Military Assistance Command–Vietnam, who did not. (Harkins argued that the Nhus, not Diem, were the problem. He told General Taylor: ''To me it seems incongruous now to get [Diem] down, kick him around and get rid of him. The U.S. has been his mother superior and father confessor since he's been in office and he has leaned on us heavily.'')[47] Both men interpreted Washington's instructions differently and sent sharply conflicting advice. Dissident South Vietnamese military leaders were thus uncertain about whom they could trust. When a coup planned for October 26 had to be scrubbed, one of the generals accused Harkins of leaking the plan to Diem.[48]

The administration, meanwhile, tried to learn more about the generals who sought to overthrow Diem. Their dossiers were often less than encouraging: One officer was alleged to be a Communist, while another seemed at times to be in all camps. The fear even existed that a coup might be merely another of Nhu's machinations. (It turned out that Nhu had indeed planned a fake coup.)

The White House also wanted to know more about the details of a new plan designed to be carried out no later than November 2. McGeorge Bundy, handling much of the work on this topic for Jack, cabled Lodge, ''while sharing your view that we should not be in [the] position of thwarting [a] coup, we would like to have [the] option of judging and warning on any plan with poor prospects of success. We recognize that this is a large order, but [the] President wants you to know of our concern." In another cable, Bundy emphasized, "We reiterate [that the] burden of proof must be on [the] coup group to show a substantial possibility of quick success."[49]

Lodge, fully endorsing the planned coup, replied that it was "essentially a Vietnamese affair," and contended that the United States could not delay or discourage it. Bundy disagreed, and instructed Lodge to stop or delay any coup that appeared to lack a high prospect of success.

Bundy also gave Lodge "standing instructions" for the American posture in the event of a coup. The guidelines included a rejection of appeals from either side for direct intervention, a willingness to mediate an indecisive struggle, and an offer of asylum to certain coup leaders ("those to whom there is any express or implied obligation") if their attempt should fail. The instructions concluded: "But once a coup under responsible leadership has begun, and within these restrictions, it is in the interest of the U.S. Government that it should succeed."[50]

With the active support of the CIA's Lou Conein, and the tacit approval of Lodge, the coup began in the early afternoon of November 1. (Schlesinger would later contend: "It is important to state clearly that the coup of November 1, 1963, was entirely planned and carried out by the Vietnamese. Neither the American Embassy nor the CIA were involved in instigation or execution.")[51] The rebels outnumbered Diem's troops, and within a few hours they had made significant gains. Soon all the nation's top military commanders had declared their loyalty to the junta. Diem, refusing to surrender, appealed to Lodge. "After all, I am a chief of state. I have tried to do my duty." The ambassador replied that he was "not acquainted with all of the facts" of the coup and contended that Washington had no view on the matter. Lodge offered to help insure Diem's physical safety. In fact, however, he made no arrangements to fly Diem and his brother out of the country; to do so would have admitted U.S. involvement in the conspiracy. As instructed, the ambassador left matters in the hands of the dissident generals.[52]

That evening Diem and Nhu managed to escape from the besieged Gia Long Palace. Early the next morning, however, realizing that continued resistance was futile, they surrendered to the rebels and were picked up in a Catholic church, where they had gone to pray. Soon both men were murdered by the personal bodyguard of "Big Minh." The complicity of other rebel generals remains unresolved.

At the White House Jack monitored coup developments throughout the day. By all accounts he was shocked and depressed by the news of the assassination. Michael Forrestal called Kennedy's reaction "both personal and religious," observing that Jack was especially sensitive to the implication that a Catholic president had been involved in a plot to assassinate a coreligionist.[53]

We now know that Jack, lacking confidence in the CIA and Lodge, sent his close friend Torby Macdonald on a secret mission to Vietnam to contact Diem personally and warn him that Minh and his cohorts were contemplating assassination. Macdonald told Diem, "They're going to kill you. You've got to get out of there temporarily to seek sanctuary in the American embassy and you must get rid of your sister-in-law and your brother." But the haughty South Vietnamese ruler refused.[54]

At one point during the fighting, Jack ordered the CIA to find Diem. Kennedy later told Cardinal Spellman he had known in advance that Diem would probably be killed in the uprising, but in the end he could not control the situation. It is likely that no American official desired Diem's death. But Jack had failed to make his acquiescence in the coup plot contingent on sparing the lives of Diem or his brothers. Schlesinger recalled, "I had not seen him so depressed since the Bay of Pigs. No doubt he realized that Vietnam was his great failure in foreign policy, and that he had never really given it his full attention."[55]

When Bobby was later asked about the coup, he stressed administration confusion and dissension among the president's advisers. The secretary of state "was for a coup and then he was against it. He was all over the lot." McGeorge Bundy "wasn't particularly helpful." The president had lost confidence in Roger Hilsman, and, "We were going to try to get rid of Henry Cabot Lodge." Bobby admitted that the entire situation was poorly handled by his brother, but he remained unsure what approach might have been successful.[56]

We cannot know for certain what path Kennedy would have followed in Vietnam had he not died three weeks later than Diem. Kenny O'Donnell has argued that the President was determined to avoid further involvement, and would have steadily decreased the number of American military advisers and technicians after the 1964 elections, when a pullout was politically possible. Arthur Schlesinger, Jr., has likewise contended that Kennedy was committed to disengagement, pointing especially to the president's insistence that a clause regarding the recall of one thousand advisers be retained in the McNamara-Taylor report. "He was a prudent executive, not inclined to heavy investments in lost causes. His whole

Presidency was marked precisely by his capacity to *refuse* escalation—as in Laos, the Bay of Pigs, the Berlin Wall, the missile crisis."[57]

There is evidence to the contrary. Dean Rusk has reported, for example, that at no time did JFK ever speak to him of pulling out of Vietnam. Bobby Kennedy, in an oral history for the Kennedy Library, asserted that there was no talk of a withdrawal. Indeed, he said, his brother had reached the conclusion that "probably it was worthwhile for psychological, political reasons" to stay in Vietnam. "The President felt that he had a strong, overwhelming reason for being in Vietnam and that we should win the war in Vietnam." The reason was "The loss of all of Southeast Asia if you lost Vietnam. I think everybody was quite clear that the rest of Southeast Asia would fall."[58]

Jack's final speeches in Texas bristled with military data, anticommunism, and appeals for courage to maintain freedom throughout the world. In Dallas he was supposed to trumpet the importance of military and economic aid to nations on the periphery of the Communist world. "Our assistance to these nations can be painful, risky and costly, as is true in Southeast Asia today. But we dare not weary of the task."[59]

Kennedy critics have also noted the escalation figures. In early 1961 there were 685 American military advisers in Vietnam; in October 1963, there were 16,732. Aid to the Diem regime increased to $400 million per year under Kennedy.[60] Then, too, of course, it was Kennedy's advisers who later encouraged Lyndon Johnson to escalate the war in Vietnam to unprecedented heights. Reporter David Halberstam, whose frank and gloomy dispatches from South Vietnam enraged Diem and Kennedy, wrote later of "the best and the brightest" that they had "for all their brilliance and hubris and sense of themselves, been unwilling to look to and learn from the past and they had been swept forward by their belief in the importance of anti-Communism (and the dangers of not paying sufficient homage to it) and by the sense of power and glory, omnipotence and omniscience of America in this century."[61]

It now seems highly likely that in November 1963 Jack had not reached a firm conclusion about the nation's future conduct in Vietnam. He did not think in long-range terms; he had not developed any sort of sophisticated intellectual or moral framework around his pragmatic and reflexive anti-communism. He told two insiders that after the next presidential election, he was going to order a complete review of American policy toward Vietnam. But politics came first. (By November Jack was absorbed with his reelection bid. Following an extensive partisan junket in the West, he summoned his first formal organization meeting for the 1964 campaign. His trip to Dallas was politically motivated.)[62]

On the other hand, Kennedy was clearly getting restless about the growing number of American troops in Vietnam. According to his military aide Ted Clifton, he agreed to a request from the Joint Chiefs to raise the number to seventeen thousand but warned that no more would be approved. Reporter Henry Brandon thought that by the autumn of 1963 the president "seemed sick of [the war] and frequently asked how to be rid of the commitment." He hoped, as he said repeatedly, that the South Vietnamese could win their own battles.[63]

In mid-November Kennedy announced the convening in Honolulu of a top-level conference on Vietnam to consider, as he told reporters, "what our aid policy should be, how we can intensify the struggle, how we can bring Americans out of there." At the same press conference, he was asked about possible cuts in foreign aid. Jack bristled at the suggestion, noting that the chief executive is the one who bears the full brunt of failures overseas. "No, I can't believe that the Congress of the United States is going to be so unwise unless we are going to retreat from the world. Are we going to give up in South Viet-Nam?"[64] Kennedys had been conditioned never to concede.

The Kennedy desire for victory appeared in a later interview with Bobby. When asked if the President was convinced that the United States had to stay in Vietnam, Bobby said simply, "Yes."

> MARTIN: And we couldn't lose it?
> KENNEDY: Yes.
> MARTIN: And if the Vietnamese were about to lose it, would he propose to go in on land if he had to?
> KENNEDY: We'd face that when we came to it.[65]

Given his belief in the global struggle between east and west, his acceptance of the domino theory, his conviction that Vietnam was the testing ground for combatting "wars of liberation," his often zealous commitment to counterinsurgency (the Green Berets, covert sabotage, strategic hamlets, napalm, defoliation), and his determination never to appear soft on Communism, Jack might well have been compelled, as conditions worsened, to commit more American troops to Vietnam. It is clear that his harsh public rhetoric made disengagement more difficult. And his clumsy and unprincipled acquiescence in the coup tied the United States closely to the eight military governments that briefly succeeded Diem. Foreign affairs expert Francis X. Winters has observed, "Instability was Kennedy's legacy to South Vietnam. Instability in Saigon bred inflexibility in Washington."[66]

At the time he left for Dallas, the president had apparently not made up his mind about Vietnam. William J. Rust has noted the "absence of a clear direction to Kennedy's policy."[67] Still, Jack had significantly expanded America's role and commitment in Vietnam. Most of the tragedy that followed under Lyndon Johnson can be traced to assumptions and actions pursued during the Kennedy administration. George C. Herring has concluded of Jack, "Whatever his fears or his ultimate intentions, he bequeathed to his successor a problem eminently more dangerous than the one he had inherited from Eisenhower."[68]

CHAPTER 18

The Man, the President

⇉⇉ ⇇⇇

THE MAJOR FIGURE in an account of the life of John F. Kennedy must be Jack's father. The elder Kennedy, that autocratic and exacting patriarch, largely formed the minds and hearts of his children, and his teachings and example were assimilated by all the youngsters, forming their essential core values. Rose Kennedy's principal contribution seems to have been a ritualistic and demanding brand of Christianity she passed on to her children, in which form mattered more than substance, public performance more than private conviction. Rose's personal detachment from domestic life, however understandable given the nature of her marriage, and her frequent absences from the home also played a role in creating an emotionally confusing environment in which intense claims of family solidarity and unswerving loyalty covered up underlying anxieties and tensions.[1]

Instilled in the Kennedys, above all, was an intense selfcenteredness, aggressiveness, and a passionate desire to win at any cost. The principal aim of life for the Kennedy youngsters—as defined by their father—was to achieve public success and prestige. For the male members of the family, the primary goal was the acquisition of political power and influence, and the eldest son was expected to reach the the highest level of such power in America and perhaps the world—the White House.

413

At the death of Joe Junior, this responsibility fell on Jack—less aggressive, less obviously bright, clearly less healthy, and much less ambitious than his older brother. Until coerced into politics by his father, Jack had dreamed mostly about becoming a great athlete. Much of his energy was spent in sports and the pursuit of women. After the war, he was commanded to be the family's torchbearer. The quest for political office—essentially the desire to fulfill his father's mandate—would consume his life.

Joseph P. Kennedy saw himself as the founding father of a dynasty, an American form of royalty based on wealth, power, and influence. As such, he was determined to raise his children to recognize their obligations to the family and to sustain the ambition, self-aggrandizement, and power which had led to his own success and which he did everything to ensure would lead to theirs.

It was the elder Kennedy who financed and directed Jack's political campaigns for House and Senate seats and for the presidency. It was he who originally created the image of JFK the hero; the intellectual, visionary leader; and the ideal family man. It was Joe Kennedy's iron will that compelled Jack to overcome continuous exhaustion, sickness, and pain in the pursuit of votes. Along the way, substantive political and moral issues were secondary; for the most part, one did and said what appealed at the ballot box. Jack was expected to win, and he obediently worked hard to do so.

Unable throughout his early life to live up to the intellectual and physical endowments of his older brother, Joe Junior, Jack compensated with an easy charm and ironic wit that attracted people to him in both private and public life. Jack's appealing personality was an important component of his phenomenal political success, as was his determination and energy. However, it was his father's imperatives, and the resources to support them, which were the relentless engine driving this success story.

What kind of man was John F. Kennedy when he entered the White House? He was indeed, as his official biographers claimed, intelligent, politically experienced, eager for information, respectful of first-class minds, and willing to link the presidency with good taste and high culture. He communicated exceptionally well with the press and public. He was capable of inspiring vast audiences with his rhetoric. He had at times in his life shown considerable courage. Ideologically, Kennedy was at best a sort of centrist Democrat, interested in using the federal government to right a number of wrongs. He was militantly anti-Communist and committed to an aggressive foreign policy.

Beneath the surface, however, Jack was pragmatic to the point of amorality; his sole standard seemed to be political expediency. Gifted with good looks, youth, and wealth, he was often, in his personal life, reckless, vain, selfish, petty, and lecherous. Jack's character, so much a reflection of his father's single-minded pursuit of political power and personal indulgence, lacked a moral center, a reference point that went beyond self-aggrandizement.

It is precisely on that question of character that the gap between the Kennedy image, perpetuated by the Camelot School of modern American history, and reality is most profound. Chief executives may draw upon their intelligence, experience, and ideology; they may seek advice from experts in every field; they may master the political arts. But ultimately the character of the individual, his essential values and priorities, his sense of right and wrong, will determine the ends to which these resources will be used.

A person of good character may lack some qualities essential for a strong leader. One thinks of Jimmy Carter—a man of integrity, self-discipline, industriousness, and deep religious faith.[2] Clearly, more is required of a first-rate president than good character. The reverse may also be true: Lyndon Johnson, we now know, was in some ways a man of deplorable morals, and yet in 1965 he presided over more morally significant domestic legislative innovations than any president in any single session of Congress in this century.

A president must play several roles, including administrative director, legislative leader, party head, commander in chief, number-one diplomat, spokesman for social justice, friend of business and labor, and molder of the federal judicial system. He is also a moral exemplar to his people, one whose office commands and enables him to set the standard of ethics and excellence for all. As James David Barber put it, "The President is expected to personify our betterness in an inspiring way, to express in what he does and is (not just in what he says) a moral idealism which, in much of the public mind, is the very opposite of 'politics.' "[3] Michael Novak has observed: "Every four years Americans elect a king— but not only a king, also a high priest and prophet."[4] Harry Truman reflected late in life: "I've said before, the President is the only person in the government who represents the whole people . . . and when there's a moral issue involved, the President has to be the moral leader of the country."[5]

The media largely shapes the public's perceptions of a President, and, during the Thousand Days and after his assassination, JFK was portrayed in large part as a saint and superman. However, we may now confidently conclude that Jack was not the man projected in the image. His attractiveness, easy confidence, wit, and charm were persuasive and seductive. He and his family were every reporter's dream and a nation's fantasy of what all families should look like and be. Jack's seeming energy, sincerity, and fidelity were congruent with America's self-image in the world. It all seemed glorious at the time and long after. But the sober truth, which readers of history seek when time has passed, was more complex and often much less flattering than the media of the moment would have had us believe.

As an administrator Kennedy was competent if unorthodox. He was more friendly to business than to labor. His judicial appointments, especially outside the South, seemed to reflect good judgment. Kennedy made little impact as a party leader; having usually worked outside the normal channels, he was not highly regarded within them.

As a legislative leader, Kennedy was relatively ineffective. Weak support in Congress was part of the problem. The president's lack of conviction and personal fervor for what he was advocating was partly responsible. His reluctant approach to civil rights, until quite late in his Thousand Days, is a case in point.

Jack was primarily interested in foreign affairs, and it was in his roles as commander in chief and diplomatic leader that he made his principal contributions. It is also in this area of presidential activity that Kennedy's character may be seen most vividly in the decision-making process.

In the Bay of Pigs fiasco, Jack rejected moral and legal objections to an invasion; he lied, exhibited an almost adolescent macho temperament, became involved with military operations just enough to make them worse, and then blamed others for the failure. He soon approved Operation Mongoose, the clandestine exercise in terrorism and murder. Determined to win in Cuba at any cost, Jack had secret dealings with one of the top mobsters involved in the assassination attempts. This reveals an irresponsibility and lack of judgment bordering on dereliction.

The administration's response to the crisis in Southeast Asia involved complex ideological, military, and political considerations. In Laos Jack approved a "secret war" that for years spread mayhem and death throughout the strife-torn nation. In Vietnam the president revealed an almost reckless posture and an intense determination to win. He approved the CIA's most aggressive operations, greatly increased the American presence in the conflict, and became involved in the overthrow of the government of South Vietnam. Moral and legal objections had little or no impact on Kennedy or his advisers as they assumed, by reason of American strength and power, the right to manipulate that country's affairs.

In the Berlin crisis, on the other hand, Kennedy's pugnacity in defense of free world rights was morally defensible, effective, and highly popular. The administration's diplomatic posture—drawing a line and daring the Soviets to cross it—was risky but, given the nature of Khrushchev's temperament and ambitions, probably inevitable. In retrospect the president's firm stand seems to merit the widespread praise it received at the time. And so does his postcrisis appeal to the United Nations for increased negotiations and a "peace race." Courage was an aspect of character which in Jack was almost always sufficient.

Similarly, in the Cuban Missile Crisis, Kennedy's courage in defending the nation and hemisphere from Khrushchev's appalling aggression continues to earn applause, and rightly so. One might well question ExCom's diplomatic moves, which left far too much in the hands of the Soviets. At times Jack seemed overly bellicose, and yet he showed prudence and restraint at key moments in the struggle and quietly agreed even to risk his political career—sacred to a Kennedy—in the interest of peace.

The renewal of the CIA's "secret war" against Cuba after the missile crisis again reveals an overreaching of power and influence which marked Jack's administration and revealed a lack of moral constraint in the pursuit of political ends. Not even Arthur Schlesinger, Jr., chose to defend this conduct when others brought it to light.

In assessing Kennedy's record as top diplomat and commander in chief, it is important to acknowledge his caution as well as courage. Against the recommendations of top advisers, he sharply limited America's role in the Bay of Pigs invasion and refused to send American troops into Laos and Vietnam. He elected not to attack East Germany when the Berlin Wall was constructed. During the missile crisis, he did what he reasonably could to avoid an invasion of Cuba, revealing a sensitivity about nuclear war that many others in Washington and elsewhere did not share.

Kennedy deserves credit for his efforts in 1963 to deintensify the Cold War and achieve meaningful disarmament. The American University speech and the test-ban treaty were significant achievements that signaled a measure of growth in such qualities as compassion and responsibility.

Due in part to a preoccupation with his own political agenda and an intense hostility toward reformers, Kennedy was a reluctant spokesman for social justice. As David Burner and Thomas R. West have concluded, "The most loyal and affectionate liberal partisan of John Kennedy cannot make him into a dedicated, consistent, and impassioned champion of a leftward movement in American politics."[6] Still, he could boast of several achievements, including the Area Redevelopment Act of 1961, which promoted public works in such economically crippled areas as West Virginia, and the civil rights legislation that occupied much of his attention in 1963. He also worked persistently, if unsuccessfully, on behalf of legislation to aid education.[7] If Kennedy lacked a grand vision of what America might be, there were nonetheless a few programs he did feel strongly about.

In fairness it must also be observed that the electorate was not crying out for social justice legislation in the early 1960s. Bobby later said repeatedly that this was a major reason for the administration's late entry into the field of civil rights. Moreover, no chief executive has ever been the kind of social zealot who would have pleased, say, Joseph Rauh or James Baldwin; the political system precludes it. As Louis W. Koenig has observed: "To win election, [the president] must cast the net of his promises wide; the more he can offer to more people of diverse economic interests, geographic sections, and national and racial groups, the most likely he is to triumph. The balancing effect of promise upon promise keeps the President from extremes." Like all politicians, the chief executive "can at most push his ideas only a little beyond the tolerance of his constituents."[8] However, the president can and must protect the political and moral rights of all the nation's citizens. Great presidents not only encourage the public to strive for the noblest ideals and the highest principles but pursue the goals in practice.

If Kennedy was far from a moral crusader, what may be said in summary about his personal misconduct as it related to the presidency? Given the facts now available, it is clear that Kennedy abused his high position for personal self-gratification. His reckless liaisons with women and mobsters were irresponsible, dangerous, and demeaning to the office of the chief executive. They were irresponsible because of the enormous potential for scandal and blackmail they posed. Any number of women, gangsters, intelligence agents, and journalists might have used their knowledge of Kennedy's sexual meandering to force concessions from the office of the president. The Kennedys had purchased silence in the past, but the stakes were far higher now that Jack was in the White House, and money might well have been inadequate. Had Kennedy lived to see a second term, the realities of his lechery and his dealings with Sam Giancana might have leaked out while he was still in office, gravely damaging the presidency, debilitating his administration, and severely disillusioning a populace which, no matter how jaded it seems, looks to a president with hope for reassurance and leadership. Impeachment might well have followed such public disclosure.[9]

Kennedy's personal foibles were also dangerous to the welfare of this country and the free world. While we know of only one specific case in which the president was separated from the official who carries the secret information vital to the nation's nuclear defense, and is supposed to be near the chief executive at all times, such incidents surely happened often in the course of Jack's clandestine prowlings. When the president, for example, was roaming through the tunnels beneath New York's Carlyle Hotel to evade reporters and reach intimate friends, was he prepared to handle national security matters?[10]

Kennedy's adultery also demeaned the presidency. Many people in Washington, Hollywood, and elsewhere made the man the butt of jokes and gossip which surely lowered their, and others', respect for the nation's highest office. Subsequent revelations have no doubt contributed further to the widespread public cynicism about the ability of politicians to sacrifice their personal indulgences in the service of national purpose and priorities.[11]

It is true that one must pay heed to the realities of American presidential politics: they are rough, often dirty, and at best require numerous compromises of principle. A Saint Francis is highly unlikely to reach the White House. There is truth in Michael Novak's observation that the "higher persons advance in any social organization, the greater their complicity in the injustices of which that institution is the inevitable carrier."[12] Still, this nation has had numerous chief executives who achieved greatness. And they were great, in part, because they were men of exceptional character. Good character is an essential framework for the complex mixture of qualities that make an outstanding President and a model leader for a democratic people. Character is a question of values, inclinations, and judgment, all of which are brought to bear in the day-to-day work of leadership.

The real Kennedy—as opposed to the celebrated hero espoused by the Kennedy family, the media, and the Camelot School—lacked greatness in large part because he lacked the qualities inherent in good character. While he had ample courage and at times showed considerable prudence, he was deficient in integrity, compassion, and temperance. He was not a crusading reformer, especially early in his administration, because such idealism was low on his agenda of personal priorities. He backed unwise and clandestine activities in Cuba, Laos, and Vietnam largely because he was oblivious to the moral content of arguments against them. He failed to be a true moral leader of the American people because he lacked the conviction and commitment that create such exemplars of character for all to emulate.

True, Kennedy was showing signs of a new awareness in 1963, and one could argue, as Ted Sorensen has, that personal and political greatness lay ahead. But it should be noted that Jack was still incapable of monogamy at the time of his assassination. And it is just as likely that news of the dark side of the president's personal and official activities might have ruined Kennedy's second term and brought the nation another kind of grief and mourning than that which tragically did ensue.

America needs great presidents, which means that this country must find and elect people of high moral character, as well as intelligence and experience. Character and conduct are clearly linked, and the personal weaknesses of a chief executive can often turn out to be public liabilities. It is wise to encourage the careful scrutiny of presidential aspirants that has become the practice in recent years. It is neither priggish nor unrealistic to seek to determine, to the best of our ability, which presidential aspirants live by values that we hope they will uphold in public, values such as honesty, responsibility, fairness, loyalty, and respect for others. Indeed, the pursuit seems simply sensible.

At the same time, the American people must resist the temptation to be won over by a handsome face, expensive campaign efforts, and thrilling rhetoric. In the early 1960s, we became involved in a sort of mindless worship of celebrity; it was a love affair largely with images. That could happen again, despite the media's experience with Vietnam, Watergate, and the Iran-Contra affair. In our longing to find heroes in a greedy, anonymous, and insensitive age, we might once more be swayed by someone who is wonderfully attractive, has a glib tongue, a bottomless wallet, and a conscience that asks little and demands even less. And the target of our affections might be much worse than Jack Kennedy.

In retrospect the real Kennedy seems similar to two other flawed political giants of his era, Lyndon Johnson and Richard Nixon. All three were pragmatic, bellicose, secretive, deceptive, and insensitive toward others. All three used the FBI to their personal advantage and promoted major CIA machinations overseas. Their anticommunism was intense, and they were determined to stop the Communists in Vietnam. Nixon, like Kennedy, largely determined his stand on social issues by public opinion polls and the positions taken by political opponents.[13]

All three presidents knew achievement and failure, of course. But Johnson and Nixon left the White House in disgrace. Kennedy died a hero. This has less to do with the facts about Jack than with the image erected during and after his life by romantic, misguided, and sometimes cynical partisans. In 1983 Arthur Schlesinger, Jr., wrote of JFK: "Did he fool us? I think not. The public man was no different from the private man."[14] The elder Kennedy would have gratefully agreed with that.

A major lesson that emerges from a careful look at Jack Kennedy's life concerns the moral responsibility of our presidents. From the nation's beginnings, in the exemplary George Washington, who thought about such things, there has been an implicit contract between the chief executive and the American people, an understanding that the nation's highest public official should exhibit such virtues as dignity, moderation, disinterestedness, self-mastery, resoluteness, strength of will, and personal integrity. Washington indeed was regarded as an "exemplification of moral values," a president widely perceived to be great because he was good. The public later attributed the same virtues to Abraham Lincoln.[15]

Studies show that expectations remain high. The presidency is venerated by Americans in all walks of life; the inhabitant of the Oval Office is supposed, at best, to reflect our highest virtues and at the very least be trustworthy. (In one survey of public opinion on the president's character, 79 percent favored a man whose private and public life is exemplary. Sixty-two percent agreed that "a president should give a perfect example for all Americans, at all times.")[16] That some presidents have failed to live up to the minimal standard has not changed the ideal.

During the Thousand Days, Kennedy arrogantly and irresponsibly violated his covenant with the people. While saying and doing the appropriate things in the public light, he acted covertly in ways that seriously demeaned himself and his office. He got away with it at the time, and the cover-up that followed kept the truth hidden for decades. That this could happen again makes it imperative that we search for presidential candidates who can, by example, elevate and inspire the American people, restoring confidence in their institutions and in themselves. Kennedy's political skills are desirable, to be sure: the charisma, the inspiring oratory, the wit, the intelligence, the courage. But all of these qualities must be connected to an effort to live and lead by those values, known and declared for centuries, that link good character with effective leadership.[17] The United States—and now the world—cannot settle for less.

Notes

CHAPTER 1. The Vital Framework

1. *New York Times*, January 21, 1961.

2. Allen J. Matusow, *The Unraveling of America: A History of Liberalism in the 1960s* (New York, 1984), pp. 30–31.

3. See George Gallup, *The Gallup Poll: Public Opinion 1935–1971*, vol. 3 (New York, 1972), 1707, 1712, 1717, 1722, 1727, 1732, 1742, 1751, 1755, 1759, 1772, 1786, 1793, 1800, 1807, 1810, 1811, 1827, 1835, 1840, 1850.

4. See, for example, Karen Dion, Ellen Berscheid, and Elaine Walster, "What Is Beautiful Is Good," *Journal of Personality and Social Psychology* 24 (1972): 285–90; David Landy and Harold Sigall, "Beauty Is Talent: Task Evaluation as a Function of the Performer's Physical Attractiveness," *Journal of Personality and Social Psychology* 29 (1974): 299–304; Janet S. Moore, William G. Graziano, and Murray G. Millar, "Physical Attractiveness, Sex Role Orientation, and the Evaluation of Adults and Children," *Personality and Social Psychology Bulletin* 13 (March 1987): 95–102; Jane Brody, "Effects of Beauty Found to Run Surprisingly Deep," *New York Times*, September 11, 1981; "Bias Against Ugly People—How They Can Fight It," *U.S. News & World Report*, November 28, 1983, pp. 53–54.

5. Fletcher Knebel, "What You Don't Know About Kennedy," *Look*, January 7, 1961, p. 82.

6. "Man or Myth?" *Newsweek*, September 23, 1963, p. 27; Victor Lasky, *JFK: The Man and the Myth* (New York, 1977), esp. pp. 1–7, 277–92.

7. Arthur Schlesinger, Jr., *A Thousand Days: John F. Kennedy in the White House* (Boston, 1965), p. 1029.

8. Laura Bergquist and Stanley Tretick, *A Very Special President* (New York, 1965), p. 2. For a similar tribute by leading British and American poets, see Erwin A. Glikes and Paul Schwaber, eds., *Of Poetry and Power: Poems Occasioned by the Presidency and by the Death of John F. Kennedy* (New York, 1964).

9. Doris Kearns, *Lyndon Johnson and the American Dream* (New York, 1976), p. 171.

10. Evelyn Lincoln, *My Twelve Years with John F. Kennedy* (New York, 1965), p. 370.

11. Theodore Sorensen, *Kennedy* (New York, 1965), esp. pp. 11–49, 366–92, 751–57.

12. Schlesinger, *A Thousand Days*, esp. pp. 86–87, 95–117, 665–91, 714–58.

13. Ibid., pp. ix–xi; Sorensen, *Kennedy*, pp. 5, 763; the acknowledgments in Paul B. Fay, Jr., *The Pleasure of His Company* (New York, 1966); the relevant articles in *Publishers Weekly*, September 26, 1966, and January 2, 1967; *New York Times*, December 7, 1966; and "William Manchester's Own Story," *Look*, April 4, 1967, pp. 62–77; "Salinger vs. Manchester," *Look*, May 16, 1967, p. 8; John Corry, *The Manchester Affair* (New York, 1967). On Kennedy "treason," see Peter Collier and David Horowitz, *The Kennedys: An American Drama* (New York, 1984), pp. 455–58.

14. See Scott Jaschik, "Scholarship," *Chronicle of Higher Education*, September 12, 1990, pp. A4, A8, A10; and the vehement and unconvincing reply by the library's chief archivist, William Johnson, *ibid.*, September 26, 1990, pp. B3–4.

15. Richard J. Whalen, *The Founding Father: The Story of Joseph P. Kennedy* (New York, 1966), p. 427.

16. "Kennedy Remembered," *Newsweek*, November 28, 1983, pp. 76, 78.

17. Benjamin C. Bradlee, *Conversations with Kennedy* (New York, 1975), esp. pp. 27, 29, 52, 54, 68–70, 76–78, 100, 115–17, 135, 139, 144, 146–47, 151, 154, 166, 182–83, 198–99, 201–202, 204–206, 209, 215, 227–30.

18. When I interviewed Powers on December 8, 1983, at the Kennedy Library, where he is a top official, he categorically denied ever having met Exner. I found him unconvincing. When asked how the young woman obtained tickets to the Democratic National Convention, an invitation to the Inaugural Ball, and private Kennedy telephone numbers, as described and documented in her book, Powers blushed and reluctantly suggested that Mrs. Lincoln might somehow have been responsible. Materials from J. Edgar Hoover's private files, obtained in late 1977, confirmed much of Exner's story. *New York Times*, December 15, 1977.

19. Judith Exner, *My Story* (New York, 1977). Book reviewers in the major media, however, largely ignored or discounted *My Story*. It quickly went out of print and today is a rare book. Note the hostile review in Ben Bradlee's *Washington Post*, June 26, 1977. See also Robert San Anson, "Jack, Judy, Sam and Johnny . . . ," *New Times Magazine*, January 23, 1976, pp. 20–23, 27–30, 32–33; *Washington Post*, November 16, 1975; *New York Times*, December 15, 16, 18, 22, 1975; January 5, 26, 29; March 4; April 12, 13, 14, 1976; June 13, 1977.

20. "J.F.K. and the Mobsters' Moll," *Time*, December 29, 1975, pp. 10–12; "A Shadow Over Camelot," *Newsweek*, December 29, 1975, pp. 14–16. See also, for example, Maitland Zane, "Joan Hitchcock's Evenings with JFK," *OUI*, July 15, 1976, pp. 77, 116; Gene Tierney, *Self-Portrait* (New York, 1978), pp. 124, 126, 131–34; Earl Wilson, *Sinatra: An Unauthorized Biography* (New York, 1976), pp. 152–74; Nancy Dickerson, *Among Those Present: A Reporter's View of 25 Years in Washington* (New York, 1976), p. 67; Hervé Alphand, *L'éttonement d'être: Journal (1939–1973)* (Paris, 1977), p. 382; Bobby Baker, *Wheeling and Dealing: Confessions of a Capitol Hill Operator* (New York, 1978), pp. 45, 76–80.

21. Traphes Bryant, *Dog Days at the White House: The Outrageous Memoirs of the*

Presidential Kennel Keeper (New York, 1975), esp. pp. 4, 12, 17, 22–25, 35, 40, 62, 66. Cf. J. B. West, *Upstairs at the White House: My Life with the First Ladies* (New York, 1973), pp. 214–15, 279–82.

22. *Washington Post*, February 23, 1976; "More Pillow Talk," *Newsweek*, March 1, 1976, p. 32; Philip Nobile and Ron Rosenblum, "The Curious Aftermath of JFK's Best and Brightest Affair," *New Times Magazine*, July 9, 1976, pp. 22–25, 29–33; C. David Heymann, *A Woman Named Jackie* (New York, 1989), pp. 375–76. See the correspondence between David Berg and authors Peter Collier and David Horowitz, in *New York Times Book Review*, October 21, 1984.

23. Joan and Clay Blair, Jr., *The Search for JFK* (New York, 1976), p. 616, passim.

24. Herbert S. Parmet, *Jack: The Struggles of John F. Kennedy* (New York, 1980).

25. Herbert S. Parmet, *JFK: The Presidency of John F. Kennedy* (New York, 1983). See also Garry Wills, *The Kennedy Imprisonment: A Meditation on Power* (Boston, 1981). pp. 32–35, 242–85.

26. See Collier and Horowitz, *The Kennedys*, esp. pp. 64–66, 90–91, 175–76, 194, 196–97; John H. Davis, *The Kennedys: Dynasty and Disaster, 1848–1983* (New York, 1984), esp. pp. 319–20, 386. See my detailed review of both volumes in the *Wisconsin Magazine of History* 69 (Spring 1986): 228–31.

27. Midge Decter, "Dissolute Dynasty," *New Republic*, August 28, 1984, p. 31; Midge Decter, "Kennedyism," *Commentary*, January 1970, p. 22; "Kennedy Remembered," *Newsweek*, November 28, 1983, pp. 61, 64–65.

28. Arthur Schlesinger, Jr., "What the Thousand Days Wrought," *New Republic*, November 21, 1983, p. 20.

29. E.g., Robert Kelley, *The Shaping of the American Past*, vol. 2, 4th ed., (Englewood Cliffs, N. J., 1986), 702. In the fifth edition, published in 1990, Kelley omitted a reference to a resemblance between Theodore Roosevelt's "personal characteristics" and JFK's.

30. Arledge denied that his friendship with Ethel Kennedy influenced his decision. He referred to the program as "gossip" and "a sleazy story." According to San Francisco television reporter Sylvia Chase, in a telephone interview with me, Jeff Ruhe, an Arledge assistant, was married to the fifth of Bobby Kennedy's eleven children. David Burke, vice president of ABC News, was a former Ted Kennedy aide. See *Los Angeles Times*, September 29, and October 7, 26, 1985; *New York Times*, October 5, 29, and November 23, 1985; Milo Speriglio, *The Marilyn Conspiracy* (New York, 1986), pp. 58–59; William Plummer, "The Monroe Report," *People*, October 21, 1985, pp. 36–38; C. D. B. Bryan, "Say Goodbye to Camelot: Marilyn Monroe and the Kennedys," *Rolling Stone*, December 5, 1985, pp. 36, 39, 41, 74–76, 80; and the paperback edition of Anthony Summers, *Goddess: The Secret Lives of Marilyn Monroe* (New York, 1986)— hereafter cited as *Goddess* (1986)—pp. 419–23. The British Broadcasting Corporation (BBC) and American independent producers soon ran a highly similar documentary called *The Last Days of Marilyn Monroe*. It was seen in the United States on American independent television channels. The film was nominated for three British Academy of Film and Television Arts awards. On the CBS program, see Harry F. Waters, "RFK: Once Over Lightly," *Newsweek*, January 28, 1985, p. 79.

31. "Beyond the Generations," *U.S. News & World Report*, October 24, 1988, p. 33. See also Carl M. Brauer, "John F. Kennedy: The Endurance of Inspirational Leadership," in Fred I. Greenstein, ed., *Leadership in the Modern Presidency* (Cambridge, Mass., 1988), pp. 108–133.

32. *Racine Journal Times*, July 3, 1988; *Milwaukee Journal*, July 18, 1988.

33. See, for example, Nancy Gager Clinch, *The Kennedy Neurosis* (New York, 1973). Historian William E. Leuchtenburg commented, "Throughout her volume she employs psychological jargon with an abandon that would make Joyce Brothers blush." William E. Leuchtenburg, "John F. Kennedy, Twenty Years Later," *American Heritage* 35 (December 1983): 56.

34. Edmund Fuller, ed., *Plutarch: Lives of the Noble Romans* (New York, 1959), p. 116.

35. H. Mattingly, ed., *Tacitus on Britain and Germany* (Baltimore, 1948), p. 59.

36. The Venerable Bede, *The Ecclesiastical History of the English Nation* (New York, 1910), pp. 104–12.

37. Einhard, *The Life of Charlemagne* (Ann Arbor, 1960), pp. 42–54.

38. *Memoirs of the Crusades by Villehardouin and De Joinville* (New York, 1958), pp. 135–52. See a similar description of Louis XI of France by Philippe de Commynes in Philippe de Commynes, *Memoirs: The Reign of Louis XI, 1461–83* (Baltimore, 1972), p. 400. See also the similar standards for rulers set down by the great medieval Jewish scholar Moses Maimonides in *The Wisdom of Moses Maimonides* (Mount Vernon, N. Y., 1963), pp. 45–46.

39. Vespasiano, *Renaissance Princes, Popes, and Prelates* (New York, 1963), pp. 213–34, 247. See also pp. 277 and 285.

40. Desiderius Erasmus, *The Education of a Christian Prince* (New York, 1968), see esp. pp. 151, 189.

41. See John Addington Symonds, *The Age of the Despots* (New York, 1960), pp. 263–90.

42. Bernard Mayo, ed., *Jefferson Himself: The Personal Narrative of a Many-Sided American* (Charlottesville, Va., 1970), pp. 161–62. Jefferson also said: "The whole art of government consists in the art of being honest"(ibid., p. 52).

43. James David Barber, *The Presidential Character: Predicting Performance in the White House* 2nd ed., (Englewood Cliffs, N. J., 1977), pp. x–xi, 3–14.

44. See Edwin C. Hargrove, "Presidential Personality and Revisionist Views of the Presidency," *American Journal of Political Science* 17 (November 1973): 826, 833. See also Thomas E. Cronin, *The State of the Presidency* (Boston 1975), pp. 31–49, 316, 319–20; Alexander L. George, "Assessing Presidential Character," *World Politics* 27 (January 1974): 236–38, 249.

45. Barber, *The Presidential Character*, pp. 293–343. See also Edwin C. Hargrove, *Presidential Leadership, Personality and Political Style* (New York, 1966); and Louis W. Koenig, *The Chief Executive* 4th ed. (New York, 1981), esp. p. 326.

46. David Knowles, *The Historian and Character, and Other Essays* (Cambridge, 1963), p. 11.

47. James Stenson, "Peer Pressure," *National Catholic Register* 65 (August 20, 1989): 8. See William Damon, *The Moral Child: Nurturing Children's Natural Moral Growth* (New York, 1988), esp. pp. 51-72, 115–30; Carol Gilligan and Grant Wiggins, "The Origins of Morality in Early Childhood Relationships," in Carol Gilligan et al., eds., *Mapping the Moral Domain: A Contribution of Women's Thinking to Psychological Theory and Education* (Cambridge, Mass., 1988), pp. 111–37; and Henry C. Johnson, Jr., "Society, Culture, and Character Development," in Kevin Ryan and George F. McLean, *Character Development in Schools and Beyond* (New York, 1987), pp. 59–93. Child expert Karl S. Bernhardt defined character as "the quality of the total make-up of

the individual." See Karl S. Bernhardt, "Where Does 'Character' Come From?" *New York Times Magazine*, August 25, 1963, p. 50. On the growing understanding of the influence of heredity, see Stanley N. Wellborn, "How Genes Shape Personality," *U.S. News & World Report*, April 13, 1987, pp. 58–62.

48. Jacques Barzun, *Clio and the Doctors: Psycho-History, Quanto-History, and History* (Chicago, 1974), p. 69. See Knowles, *The Historian and Character*, pp 7–8.

49. E.g., Theodore C. Sorensen, *The Kennedy Legacy: A Peaceful Revolution for the Seventies* (New York, 1969), pp. 15, 27. James David Barber said in 1983, "He was a learning President and was developing morally," *New York Times*, November 21, 1983. On the alleged relationship between higher education and good character, see Herbert I. London, "The Traditional Curriculum as Fable," *Academic Questions* 2 (Summer 1989): 5–9; Milton Mayer, "To Know and to Do," in Arthur A. Cohen ed., *Humanistic Education and Western Civilization: Essays for Robert M. Hutchins* (New York, 1964), pp. 206–30; Theodore S. Hamerow, *Reflections on History and Historians* (Madison, Wis., 1987), pp. 28–32, 103, 111.

CHAPTER 2. The Founding Family

1. Whalen, *The Founding Father*, p. 24.
2. See Davis, *The Kennedys*, pp. 3–23.
3. Whalen, *The Founding Father*, p. 29.
4. Ibid.; Davis, *The Kennedys*, pp. 27–30.
5. William J. Duncliffe, *The Life and Times of Joseph P. Kennedy* (New York, 1965), p. 34.
6. David E. Koskoff, *Joseph P. Kennedy: A Life and Times* (Englewood Cliffs, N. J., 1974), p. 15.
7. Collier and Horowitz, *The Kennedys*, p. 462 n. 34; Whalen, *The Founding Father*, p. 33.
8. Ibid., p. 37.
9. Koskoff, *Joseph P. Kennedy*, p. 33.
10. Davis, *The Kennedys*, p. 37; Collier and Horowitz, *The Kennedys*, p. 37; Rose Fitzgerald Kennedy, *Times to Remember* (New York, 1974), p. 66.
11. Ibid., pp. 6–26, 53; Davis, *The Kennedys*, pp. 37–38, 41–43; Doris Kearns Goodwin, *The Fitzgeralds and the Kennedys* (New York, 1987), pp. 58–197.
12. Kennedy, *Times to Remember*, pp. 27–45.
13. Ibid., pp. 49–52.
14. Ibid., pp. 13–15.
15. Ibid., p. 14.
16. Ibid., pp. 13, 53–55.
17. See John Henry Cutler, *"Honey Fitz": Three Steps to the White House* (Indianapolis, 1962), pp. 37–60, 177–79, 215–18, 220–29.
18. Kennedy, *Times to Remember*, pp. 17, 57.
19. Ibid., p. 67.
20. Koskoff, *Joseph P. Kennedy*, p. 22.
21. See Kennedy, *Times to Remember*, pp. 57–72, 75.
22. Whalen, *The Founding Father*, p. 50. Cf. Koskoff, *Joseph P. Kennedy*, pp. 22–23.

23. Ibid., p. 23.

24. Whalen, *The Founding Father*, pp. 56–59, 62. On Kennedy and the draft, see Goodwin, *The Fitzgeralds and the Kennedys*, pp. 280–83.

25. Whalen, *The Founding Father*, pp. 59, 68–71.

26. Ibid., pp. 72–73; Michael R. Beschloss, *Kennedy and Roosevelt: The Uneasy Alliance* (New York, 1980), p. 60.

27. Whalen, *The Founding Father*, p. 66.

28. *New York Times*, July 27, 1973.

29. Dennis Eisenberg et al., *Meyer Lansky, Mogul of the Mob* (New York, 1979), pp. 108–9. According to Judith Exner, Mafia boss Sam Giancana often said in the early 1960s, "Joe Kennedy was one of the biggest crooks that ever lived." Moreover, she recalled, "He often intimated that he knew a great deal of derogatory information about Joe Kennedy's background." Exner, *My Story*, pp. 189–90. Two of Honey Fitz's brothers were in the illicit liquor trade, and Joe may have been involved with them. See Goodwin, *The Fitzgeralds and the Kennedys*, pp. 441–43.

30. Collier and Horowitz, *The Kennedys*, pp. 44–45.

31. Koskoff, *Joseph P. Kennedy*, p. 30.

32. Ibid., p. 34; see Whalen, *The Founding Father*, pp. 80–103.

33. Frank Saunders, *Torn Lace Curtain* (New York, 1982), pp. 80–81.

34. Collier and Horowitz, *The Kennedys*, p. 51.

35. Gloria Swanson, *Swanson on Swanson* (New York, 1980), pp. 306–411, 427, 445–46, 457. Kennedy contacted the actress later on several occasions, usually to boast about a new honor or position.

36. Saunders, *Torn Lace Curtain*, pp. 43, 48–51, passim. See Kennedy, *Times to Remember*, p. 75.

37. See ibid., pp. 81–84, 99–169. See also Gail Cameron, *Rose: A Biography of Rose Fitzgerald Kennedy* (New York, 1971), pp. 80–90, 98–103.

38. See Saunders, *Torn Lace Curtain*, esp. pp. 89–92, 108–13, 123, 182–83, 254–57, 276–77, 283, 288–89, 306, 322, 331; Blair, *The Search for J.F.K.*, p. 11; Collier and Horowitz, *The Kennedys*, pp. 57–58; Ralph G. Martin, *A Hero for Our Time: An Intimate Story of the Kennedy Years* (New York, 1983), p. 28; Goodwin, *The Fitzgeralds and the Kennedys*, p. 353. See Gallagher, *My Life with Jacqueline Kennedy*, p. 173.

39. Hank Searls, *The Lost Prince: Young Joe, The Forgotten Kennedy, The Story of the Oldest Brother* (New York, 1969), p. 45; James MacGregor Burns, *John Kennedy: A Political Profile* (New York, 1959), p. 23; Kennedy, *Times to Remember*, pp. 332–34; Blair, *The Search for J.F.K.*, p. 479.

40. Kennedy, *Times to Remember*, p. 57.

41. Goodwin, *The Fitzgeralds and the Kennedys*, p. 351; Kennedy, *Times to Remember*, p. 80. Cf. Saunders, *Torn Lace Curtain*, pp. 34, 36–37.

42. Kennedy, *Times to Remember*, pp. 138–41.

43. Ibid., p. 139; Goodwin, *The Fitzgeralds and the Kennedys*, p. 351.

44. Saunders, *Torn Lace Curtain*, p. 192.

CHAPTER 3.   Getting into Shape

1. Whalen, *The Founding Father*, p. 79.

2. Collier and Horowitz, *The Kennedys*, p. 58.

3. Martin, *A Hero for Our Time*, p. 31.

4. Cameron, *Rose*, p. 89.

5. Kennedy, *Times to Remember*, p. 101.

6. Blair, *The Search for J.F.K.*, p. 149.

7. Davis, *The Kennedys*, p. 71. Joe would cut off outsiders when they attempted to enter the question-and-answer session. A guest said later, "He was only concerned about educating his own children." Ralph Horton Oral History, JFK Library. See the account of Lemoyne Billings in Blair, *The Search for J.F.K.*, p. 27.

8. Whalen, *The Founding Father*, p. 95; Searls, *The Lost Prince*, pp. 58–60.

9. Parmet, *Jack*, p. 16.

10. Cameron, *Rose*, pp. 105–6.

11. Collier and Horowitz, *The Kennedys*, p. 59.

12. Cameron, *Rose*, p. 106. See also the account by Jewel Reed in Blair, *The Search for J.F.K.*, p. 356.

13. Goodwin, *The Fitzgeralds and the Kennedys*, pp. 639–44; Cameron, *Rose*, pp. 90–91; Kennedy, *Times to Remember*, pp. 151–59, 285–86; Blair, *The Search for J.F.K.*, pp. 13–14; Swanson, *Swanson on Swanson*, pp. 379–80. See also Joan Zyda, "The Kennedy No One Knows," *Chicago Tribune*, January 7, 1976; and *Milwaukee Journal*, October 3, 1983.

14. See Joseph Dinneen, *The Kennedy Family* (Boston, 1959), pp. 37–38.

15. See Searls, *The Lost Prince*, pp. 38–81; Felix Frankfurter Oral History, JFK Library; Kennedy, *Times to Remember*, pp. 170–74.

16. Collier and Horowitz, *The Kennedys*, p. 60; Searls, *The Lost Prince*, pp. 55–61, 65–67, 72.

17. Ibid., pp. 40, 60; Kennedy, *Times to Remember*, p. 120; Collier and Horowitz, *The Kennedys*, p. 62. Jack said later of his brother, "He had a pugnacious personality. Later on it smoothed out but it was a problem in my boyhood." Burns, *John Kennedy*, p. 28.

18. Quoted in Kennedy, *Times to Remember*, p. 121.

19. Collier and Horowitz, *The Kennedys*, p. 62; Payson Wild and Arthur Krock Oral Histories, JFK Library.

20. Meyers, ed., *John Fitzgerald Kennedy*, p. vi.

21. Kennedy, *Times to Remember*, p. 85.

22. See Blair, *The Search for J.F.K.*, pp. 17–18. Cf. Schlesinger, *A Thousand Days*, p. 95.

23. Blair, *The Search for J.F.K.*, pp. 15–16.

24. Kennedy, *Times to Remember*, p. 94.

25. Ibid., pp. 110–13, 126; Kay Halle Oral History, JFK Library. Cf. Schlesinger, *A Thousand Days*, p. 80.

26. Kennedy, *Times to Remember*, pp. 102, 108; Meyers, ed., *John Fitzgerald Kennedy*, p. vi.

27. Blair, *The Search for J.F.K.*, p. 328.

28. See Collier and Horowitz, *The Kennedys*, pp. 194, 341.

29. Blair, *The Search for J.F.K.*, p. 540. For an update of the authorized version, see Arthur Schlesinger, Jr., *Robert Kennedy and His Times* (New York, 1979), pp. 17–19.

30. Collier and Horowitz, *The Kennedys*, p. 174.

31. Burns, *John Kennedy*, p. 21.

32. Sorensen, *Kennedy*, p. 37.

33. Kennedy, *Times to Remember*, pp. 93–94, 153.

34. Collier and Horowitz, *The Kennedys*, pp. 59, 466. See Blair, *The Search for J.F.K.*, p. 363.

35. Collier and Horowitz, *The Kennedys*, p. 466.

36. Ibid., p. 63.

37. Martin, *A Hero for Our Time*, p. 49.

38. Collier and Horowitz, *The Kennedys*, pp. 61, 174; Kay Halle Oral History, JFK Library.

39. Burns, *John Kennedy*, p. 23.

40. Parmet, *Jack*, p. 22.

41. Martin, *A Hero for Our Time*, p. 29.

42. E.g., Blair, *The Search for J.F.K.*, pp. 350–51. His terrible penmanship is a curse for Kennedy scholars.

43. Kennedy, *Times to Remember*, pp. 174–75; Burns, *John Kennedy*, pp. 24–25. See Parmet, *Jack*, pp. 27–29.

44. Ibid., pp. 31–32, 40; Ralph Horton Oral History, JFK Library. A complete school biography is on page 76 of the Choate yearbook for 1935. See box 1, JFK Personal Papers, JFK Library. Approximately one hundred Kennedy letters, grades, and reports from Choate (now Choate Rosemary Hall) are unavailable to scholars. The campus archivist reports that "the Kennedy family lawyer agrees with our policy." Lee Sylvester to the author, January 4, 1990.

45. Blair, *The Search for J.F.K.*, p. 24.

46. Kennedy, *Times to Remember*, pp. 175–76; Parmet, *Jack*, pp. 38–40; Burns, *John Kennedy*, p. 27; Meyers, ed., *John Fitzgerald Kennedy*, p. 13. On Jack's health, see the correspondence in box 1, JFK personal papers, JFK Library.

47. Parmet, *Jack*, p. 33.

48. Blair, *The Search for J.F.K.*, pp. 24–25.

49. Kennedy, *Times to Remember*, pp. 177–80.

50. Ibid., pp. 180–83; Parmet, *Jack*, pp. 34–37; Goodwin, *The Fitzgeralds and the Kennedys*, pp. 487–48. See Joseph P. Kennedy to George St. John, September 1, 1943, box 1, JFK Personal Papers, JFK Library.

51. In Schlesinger, *Robert Kennedy and His Times*, p. 16.

52. Blair, *The Search for J.F.K.*, pp. 26–27; Collier and Horowitz, *The Kennedys*, p. 65.

53. Ibid., pp. 75, 470; Koskoff, *Joseph P. Kennedy*, p. 53.

54. See Beschloss, *Kennedy and Roosevelt*, pp. 83–113; Whalen, *The Founding Father*, pp. 175–76.

55. Blair, *The Search for J.F.K.*, pp. 31–33; Kennedy, *Times to Remember*, p. 201.

56. Blair, *The Search for J.F.K.*, pp. 33–35. See Jack's lewd letters to Billings from his hospital bed in Collier and Horowitz, *The Kennedys*, pp. 66–67.

57. Blair, *The Search for J.F.K.*, pp. 35–37; Collier and Horowitz, *The Kennedys*, p. 67.

58. Parmet, *Jack*, pp. 41, 43.

59. Martin, *A Hero for Our Time*, p. 32.

60. Blair, *The Search for J.F.K.*, pp. 38–39.

61. Parmet, *Jack*, p. 47.

62. Ibid.

63. Blair, *The Search for J.F.K.*, pp. 46, 52.

64. Burns, *John Kennedy*, p. 31.

65. Blair, *The Search for J.F.K.*, pp. 45–46.

66. Parmet, *Jack*, p. 44.

67. Collier and Horowitz, *The Kennedys*, pp. 90–91.

68. Ibid., p. 91.

69. Parmet, *Jack*, pp. 50–54; Blair, *The Search for J.F.K.*, pp. 49–52.

70. Whalen, *The Founding Father*, pp. 181–201.

71. Arthur Krock, *Memoirs: Sixty Years on the Firing Line* (New York, 1968), p. 318.

72. Burns, *John Kennedy*, p. 38.

73. George F. Kennan, *Memoirs, 1925–1950* (Boston, 1967), pp. 91–92.

74. Collier and Horowitz, *The Kennedys*, p. 100.

75. Blair, *The Search for J.F.K.*, pp. 58–59.

76. Parmet, *Jack*, pp. 57–59.

77. Koskoff, *Joseph P. Kennedy*, pp. 140–41. See Walter Trohan, *Political Animals: Memoirs of a Sentimental Cynic* (New York, 1975), pp. 113–15.

78. Parmet, *Jack*, pp. 48–50. Cf. Payson Wild Oral History, JFK Library. Wild, a Harvard tutor, later thought Jack had the ability "to think deeply and in theoretical terms." Parmet (p. 44) concluded that while Joe Junior was more athletic and a better bet for success than his younger brother, "Jack remained more introspective, giving the aura of a philosopher, dreamer, and idealist, not as one prepared for worldly enterprises."

79. Ibid., p. 61; Burns, *John Kennedy*, p. 39; Blair, *The Search for J.F.K.*, pp. 69–71.

80. Ibid., pp. 71–75; Searls, *The Lost Prince*, pp. 156–57; Payson Wild Oral History, JFK Library.

81. Krock, *Memoirs*, pp. 306–10.

82. Justus D. Doenecke, ed., *In Danger Undaunted: The Anti-Interventionist Movement of 1940–1941 as Revealed in the Papers of the America First Committee* (Stanford, Calif. 1990), p. 17. As Doenecke reveals, the contribution may well have come from the ambassador through Jack.

83. Blair, *The Search for J.F.K.*, pp. 75–79; Arthur Krock Oral History, JFK Library; Krock, *Memoirs*, pp. 325–26; Jack to Dad, n.d., box 1, JFK Personal Papers, JFK Library; Collier and Horowitz, *The Kennedys*, pp. 477–78.

84. Kennedy, *Times to Remember*, p. 262; Henry Luce Oral History, JFK Library.

85. Parmet, *Jack*, pp. 74–78; Heymann, *A Woman Named Jackie*, p. 174. See "Guns v. Butter," *Time*, August 12, 1940, pp. 64, 66. Jack made $40,000 on the book and donated his British royalties to the bombed-out city of Coventry.

86. Max Freedman, ed., *Roosevelt and Frankfurter: Their Correspondence, 1928–1945* (Boston, 1967), p. 590.

87. Freda Laski Oral History, JFK Library.

88. Schlesinger, *A Thousand Days*, p. 84.

89. Martin, *A Hero for Our Time*, pp. 36, 128.

CHAPTER 4.   Some Kind of Hero

1. See Whalen, *The Founding Father*, pp. 264–339.

2. Searls, *The Lost Prince*, pp. 148–49.

3. Ibid., pp. 150–53.

4. Ibid., pp. 156, 168–69, 172–73; Krock, *Memoirs*, p. 317.

5. Blair, *The Search for J.F.K.*, pp. 86–87; Kennedy, *Times to Remember*, p. 277.

6. Blair, *The Search for J.F.K.*, pp. 86–87; Kennedy, *Times to Remember*, p. 277.

7. Jack also attended an Institute of World Affairs and wrote a few reports on the proceedings, but he had his picture taken at Universal Studios in Hollywood one day before the conference adjourned. Blair, *The Search for J.F.K.*, pp. 103–7.

8. Burns, *John Kennedy*, p. 47; Kennedy, *Times to Remember*, p. 277.

9. Ibid., p. 278; Blair, *The Search for J.F.K.*, pp. 103–7.

10. Searls, *The Lost Prince*, pp. 174, 177–78.

11. Burns, *John Kennedy*, p. 47; Kennedy, *Times to Remember*, p. 284.

12. Blair, *The Search for J.F.K.*, pp. 108–11.

13. Ibid., p. 110. See also pp. 93, 147, 181–83 in ibid.; Searls, *The Lost Prince*, p. 181.

14. Blair, *The Search for J.F.K.*, pp. 118, 124.

15. Ibid., pp. 116, 121–46; Parmet, *Jack*, pp. 88–92; William C. Sullivan, *The Bureau: My Thirty Years in Hoover's FBI* (New York, 1979), p. 48; Robert J. Donovan, *PT 109: John F. Kennedy in World War II* (New York, 1967), p. 24. See "The Secret Files of J. Edgar Hoover," *U.S. News & World Report*, December 19, 1983, 45–50; Heymann, *A Woman Named Jackie*, pp. 153–57.

16. Collier and Horowitz, *The Kennedys*, pp. 122–23; Goodwin, *The Fitzgeralds and the Kennedys*, p. 631

17. Collier and Horowitz, *The Kennedys*, p. 92. See Goodwin, *The Fitzgeralds and the Kennedys*, p. 635; Blair, *The Search for J.F.K.*, pp. 124, 184; Kay Halle Oral history, JFK Library.

18. Blair, *The Search for J.F.K.*, pp. 143, 151–52. See Goodwin, *The Fitzgeralds and the Kennedys*, pp. 630–33.

19. Blair, *The Search for J.F.K.*, p. 142.

20. Collier and Horowitz, *The Kennedys*, p. 122. See Goodwin, *The Fitzgeralds and the Kennedys*, pp. 628–30.

21. Burns later reported that Jack had sought sea duty after Pearl Harbor, and when it did not come asked his father to get it for him. Letters recently brought to light by Doris Kearns Goodwin tend to confirm the view that the elder Kennedy acted at his son's request. Collier and Horowitz, *The Kennedys*, p. 124; Blair, *The Search for J.F.K.*, pp. 147–54, 161; Burns, *John Kennedy*, p. 48; Goodwin, *The Fitzgeralds and the Kennedys*, pp. 628–30.

22. Searls, *The Lost Prince*, pp. 179–89.

23. Blair, *The Search for J.F.K.*, pp. 156–57, 175–76, 185, 214.

24. Ibid., pp. 157–58.

25. Ibid., pp. 156, 160; Collier and Horowitz, *The Kennedys*, p. 126.

26. Koskoff, *Joseph P. Kennedy*, pp. 315–33.

27. Blair, *The Search for J.F.K.*, pp. 160–62. See ibid., pp. 504, 564, 575–76. See also Kennedy, *Times to Remember*, p. 116; Burns, *John Kennedy*, p. 20.

28. Blair, *The Search for J.F.K.*, pp. 165–67.

29. Ibid., pp. 168–71.

30. Ibid., p. 169; Donovan, *PT 109*, p. 27.

31. Searls, *The Lost Prince*, pp. 190–97; Kennedy, *Times to Remember*, p. 285.

32. Blair, *The Search for J.F.K.*, pp. 176–77.

33. Donovan, *PT 109*, p. 31.

34. Ibid.

35. Blair, *The Search for J.F.K.*, p. 185.

36. Ibid., pp. 180–82, 204; Donovan, *PT 109*, pp. 38–39.

37. Ibid., pp. 45–47.

38. Ibid., pp. 61–63.

39. Blair, *The Search for J.F.K.*, pp. 212–34.

40. Ibid., p. 245. The historian of PT boats in World War II wrote of the entire skirmish with the Express, "This was perhaps the most confused and least effectively executed action the PT's had been in. Eight PT's fired 30 torpedoes. The only confirmed results are the loss of PT 109 and damage to the Japanese destroyer *Amagiri*." Robert J. Bulkley, Jr., *At Close Quarters: PT Boats in the United States Navy* (Washington, 1962), p. 123.

41. Donovan, *PT 109*, p. 86.

42. Blair, *The Search for J.F.K.*, pp. 238, 243–44.

43. Ibid., pp. 240, 244–45, 321.

44. Ibid., pp. 270, 280, 291. There are numerous Kennedy letters from this period, including the one cited, in box 5, JFK Personal Papers, JFK Library. See also box 11, which contains a compilation, made in 1975, of Kennedy's official naval duty stations and the dates he served.

45. Ibid., pp. 216, 247–70, 342. I supplemented the Blairs' meticulous account with several details from Donovan. See also Bulkley, *At Close Quarters*, pp. 120–28.

46. Blair, *The Search for J.F.K.*, pp. 271–76.

47. Ibid., pp. 281–83, 343; Collier and Horowitz, *The Kennedys*, p. 483.

48. Donovan, *PT 109*, p. 135; Blair, *The Search for J.F.K.*, p. 342; Collier and Horowitz, *The Kennedys*, p. 483.

49. Blair, *The Search for J.F.K.*, pp. 342, 345.

50. Ibid., pp. 336–37; Donovan, *PT 109*, p. 155.

51. Blair, *The Search for J.F.K.*, p. 320.

52. Parmet, *Jack*, pp. 111–12.

CHAPTER 5.   In His Brother's Shoes

1. Blair, *The Search for J.F.K.*, pp. 285–310.

2. Ibid.p. 333. Donovan (*PT 109*, p. 151), Burns (*John Kennedy*, p. 53), and Rose Kennedy (*Times to Remember*, p. 298) blamed the *PT 109* incident for Jack's departure from the South Pacific. The Navy awarded Jack the Purple Heart. However, in a late-October letter to his father, and in a November 14 letter to Bobby, Jack had reported that his health was good and that he had passed a routine physical examination. See ibid., pp. 311–13, 325–26.

3. Ibid., pp. 314–21, 334.

4. Ibid., p. 324.

5. Kennedy, *Times to Remember*, pp. 287–98; Blair, *The Search for J.F.K.*, pp. 339–40; Goodwin, *The Fitzgeralds and the Kennedys*, pp. 668–82. According to one insider, Rose was "burning up the cables with dire warnings of hell fire to come" because of her daughter's marriage. Marie Brenner, *House of Dreams: The Bingham Family of Louisville* (New York, 1988), p. 181.

6. Kennedy, *Times to Remember*, p. 292. See Collier and Horowitz, *The Kennedys*, p. 133.

7. Blair, *The Search for J.F.K.*, pp. 336–41.

8. Ibid., pp. 347–51.

9. Krock, *Memoirs*, pp. 324–25.

10. Goodwin, *The Fitzgeralds and the Kennedys*, p. 687; Searls, *The Lost Prince*, pp. 201–3, 227, 236–92.

11. Whalen, *The Founding Father*, pp. 362–64; Krock, *Memoirs*, p. 324; Merle Miller, *Plain Speaking: An Oral Biography of Harry S. Truman* (New York, 1973), p. 186. Truman told Miller, "Old Joe Kennedy is as big a crook as we've got anywhere in this country."

12. Blair, *The Search for J.F.K.*, pp. 124, 357–58; Cameron, *Rose*, p. 152; Collier and Horowitz, *The Kennedys*, p. 144.

13. Parmet, *Jack*, p. 122; Blair, *The Search for J.F.K.*, pp. 360–61.

14. Blair, *The Search for J.F.K.*, p. 365.

15. Charles Spalding Oral History, JFK Library.

16. Blair, *The Search for J.F.K.*, pp. 368–72; Fay, *The Pleasure of His Company*, p. 152. See also the Charles Spalding, Frank More O'Farrall, and John J. Droney Oral Histories, JFK Library, and Krock, *Memoirs*, p. 306–7.

17. Sorensen, *Kennedy*, p. 15; Schlesinger, *A Thousand Days*, p. 89. See also Kenneth P. O'Donnell and David F. Powers, *"Johnny, We Hardly Knew Ye": Memories of John Fitzgerald Kennedy* (Boston, 1970), pp. 50–51; Parmet, *Jack*, p. 125.

18. Blair, *The Search for J.F.K.*, pp. 373–74.

19. Ibid., pp. 375–81. According to his friend, Jack read all the volumes.

20. Ibid., pp. 382–83.

21. Ibid., pp. 384–92; Parmet, *Jack*, p. 133. See also Krock, *Memoirs*, pp. 326–27.

22. Blair, *The Search for J.F.K.*, pp. 395, 397, 400.

23. Ibid., pp. 398–99.

24. Ibid., pp. 401–2, 590.

25. James A. Reed Oral History, JFK Library.

26. Collier and Horowitz, *The Kennedys*, p. 150; Parmet, *Jack*, pp. 144–45; Searls, *The Lost Prince*, p. 302.

27. Blair, *The Search for J.F.K.*, pp. 413–14, 482; Mark Dalton Oral History, JFK Library. Jack had to clear his selection for campaign treasurer with his father. John J. Droney Oral History, JFK Library.

28. Burns, *John Kennedy*, pp. 68–69; O'Donnell and Powers, *"Johnny, We Hardly Knew Ye,"* pp. 61–62; Parmet, *Jack*, p. 138.

29. Leo Damore, *The Cape Cod Years of John Fitzgerald Kennedy* (Englewood Cliffs, N. J., 1967), p. 87.

30. Blair, *The Search for J.F.K.*, pp. 446–47; Goodwin, *The Fitzgeralds and the Kennedys*, pp. 708–10.

31. Blair, *The Search for J.F.K.*, pp. 414–15, 443–44; Kennedy, *Times to Remember*, p. 309; Patrick J. Mulkern Oral History, JFK Library.

32. Blair, *The Search for J.F.K.*, pp. 412–13, 449–58.

33. Ibid., pp. 457, 463; John J. Droney and Thomas Broderick Oral Histories, JFK Library.

34. Blair, *The Search for J.F.K.*, pp. 460, 468.

35. Ibid., p. 469; Thomas P. O'Neill, *Man of the House: The Life and Political Memories of Speaker Tip O'Neill* (New York, 1987), p. 85.

36. Blair, *The Search for J.F.K.*, pp. 425, 462, 466; Goodwin, *The Fitzgeralds and the Kennedys*, p. 707.

37. John J. Droney Oral History, JFK Library; Blair, *The Search for J.F.K.*, pp. 461–62.

38. Ibid., pp. 459, 479, 482, 489; Patrick J. Mulkern, John J. Droney, and Robert L. Lee Oral Histories, JFK Library; Damore, *The Cape Cod Years*, p. 91; Burton Hersh, *The Education of Edward Kennedy: A Family Biography* (New York, 1972), p. 48.

39. *New York Times*, April 10, 23, 1946.

40. Mark Dalton, George Taylor, Patrick J. Mulkern, and John J. Droney Oral Histories, JFK Library; O'Donnell and Powers, *"Johnny, We Hardly Knew Ye,"* p. 78.

41. Kennedy, *Times to Remember*, pp. 319–20; Blair, *The Search for J.F.K.*, pp. 489–97; Collier and Horowitz, *The Kennedys*, p. 159; Schlesinger, *Robert Kennedy*, pp. 68–69; Mark Dalton Oral History, JFK Library.

42. Ibid.; Koskoff, *Joseph P. Kennedy*, p. 407; Ralph F. Martin and Ed Plaut, *Front Runner, Dark Horse* (New York, 1960), pp. 133–34, 140; O'Neill, *Man of the House*, pp. 77–78; Burns, *John Kennedy*, pp. 65, 67; Blair, *The Search for J.F.K.*, p. 517; Goodwin, *The Fitzgeralds and the Kennedys*, pp. 713, 720; David Halberstam, *The Powers That Be* (New York, 1980), p. 78. O'Neill (*Man of the House*, p. 81) recalled, "Every time a Democrat ran for governor, he would go down to see Joe, who would always send him home with a briefcase full of cash. The word was that if Joe Kennedy liked you, he'd give you fifty thousand dollars. If he *really* liked you, he'd give you a hundred thousand."

43. Cutler, *Honey Fitz*, p. 308; O'Neill, *Man of the House*, p. 76.

44. "Promise Kept," *Time*, July 1, 1946, p. 23; O'Donnell and Powers, *"Johnny, We Hardly Knew Ye,"* p. 73; National League of Women Voters questionnaire, box 74, Pre-Presidential Papers, JFK Library.

45. Blair, *The Search for J.F.K.*, pp. 484, 486; "A Kennedy Runs for Congress," *Look*, June 11, 1946, pp. 32–36; O'Neill, *Man of the House*, p. 76. Examples from the *Look* article: "His family described him as Van Johnson, Jr., but he looks more like a young Lindbergh. He has his father's gift for making you feel you're the greatest guy in the world. . . . In the Pacific, he constantly urged his men to hurry 'so we can save America and the things we are fighting for.' "

46. Blair, *The Search for J.F.K.*, pp. 485–47.

47. Ibid., pp. 499–500; *New York Times*, June 17, 19, 1946; "Promise Kept," *Time*, July 1, 1946, p. 23. See Thomas Broderick Oral History, JFK Library. Only about 30 percent of the registered voters went to the polls on that rainy Tuesday.

48. Tierney, *Self-Portrait*, p. 126.

49. Blair, *The Search for J.F.K.*, pp. 503–4. During the primary race Jack had taken a special interest in the placement of his billboards. See ibid., pp. 486–87, 504–5.

50. Ibid., pp. 512–17; *New York Times*, November 6, 1946.

51. Blair, *The Search for J.F.K.*, pp. 547–48, The ambassador wrote to an acquaintance, "I find myself with a new occupation—that is, furthering young Jack's political career." Goodwin, *The Fitzgeralds and the Kennedys*, p. 721.

CHAPTER 6.   His New Career

1. Blair, *The Search for J.F.K.*, pp. 519–24.

2. Ibid., pp. 507–8, 518, 537; Krock, *Memoirs*, p. 331; O'Neill, *Man of the House*, p. 82.

3. Blair, *The Search for J.F.K.*, pp. 536–37; *New York Times*, January 20, 1947.

4. Blair, *The Search for J.F.K.*, pp. 530–32.

5. Ibid., pp. 534–35, 564.

6. Ibid., pp. 533, 540, 547; Richard Bolling Oral History, JFK Library.

7. Burns, *John Kennedy*, pp. 71–72; Blair, *The Search for J.F.K.*, pp. 541, 548; William O. Douglas Oral History, JFK Library.

8. Blair, *The Search for J.F.K.*, p. 540. See Burns, *John Kennedy*, pp. 72–73.

9. Blair, *The Search for J.F.K.*, pp. 541, 543, 546.

10. Ibid., pp. 540, 544; O'Neill, *Man of the House*, p. 87.

11. Collier and Horowitz, *The Kennedys*, p. 162.

12. Blair, *The Search for J.F.K.*, pp. 533–34; Collier and Horowitz, *The Kennedys*, p. 174.

13. Blair, *The Search for J.F.K.*, pp. 533–34; Patrick J. Mulkern and George Smathers Oral Histories, JFK Library; Parmet, *Jack*, p. 169.

14. George Smathers Oral History, JFK Library; Collier and Horowitz, *The Kennedys*, pp. 494–95. Judith Campbell Exner recalled, "Oh, but he loved gossip. He adored it. . . . 'I don't want the phony stuff. I want the real inside dope.' I think he wanted to know a little dirt about everybody." Exner, *My Story*, p. 148.

15. Blair, *The Search for J.F.K.*, pp. 535, 538, 564; Fay, *The Pleasure of His Company*, pp. 82–85; Salinger, *With Kennedy*, p. 181; Patrick Mulkern Oral History, JFK Library; Saunders, *Torn Lace Curtain*, pp. 58–60. Cf. Sorensen, *Kennedy*, p. 36.

16. Parmet, *Jack*, p. 171.

17. George Smathers, James A. Reed Oral Histories, JFK Library; Thomas C. Reeves, *The Life and Times of Joe McCarthy; A Biography* (New York, 1982), pp. 56, 100, 129, 247, 262, 267.

18. *Milwaukee Journal*, March 14, 15, 16, 17, 18, 19, 20, 24, 1947; *New York Times*, March 14, June 1, 1947; Parmet, *Jack*, pp. 179–82; Blair, *The Search for J.F.K.*, pp. 554–55. The committee report advocated the right of any employer or union to discharge Communists. Allis-Chalmers fired Christoffel, Buce, and one hundred others. The union ended the strike on March 23 without a contract.

19. Burns, *John Kennedy*, pp. 73–95. In a *Cosmopolitan* poll, Jack listed housing as the most urgent problem facing the nation. *New York Post*, July 7, 1947. Cf. Parmet's misreading of the *Post* article, in *Jack*, p. 182.

20. Ibid., pp. 188–89. On Jack's unhappiness in the House, see John Sharon Oral History, JFK Library; O'Donnell and Powers, *"Johnny, We Hardly Knew Ye,"* pp. 85–86.

21. Parmet, *Jack*, pp. 183–84, 187, 192–95; Mark Dalton Oral History, JFK Library. Cf. O'Donnell and Powers, *"Johnny, We Hardly Knew Ye,"* pp. 81–82, which calls the Curley decision "a startling display of political courage."

22. Parmet, *Jack*, pp. 206–14, 220; John P. Mallan, "Massachusetts: Liberal and Corrupt," *New Republic*, October 13, 1952, pp. 10–12; Koskoff, *Joseph P. Kennedy*, p. 599; George Smathers Oral History, JFK Library; Richard Nixon, *RN: The Memoirs of*

Richard Nixon (New York, 1978), p. 75; Burns, *John Kennedy*, p. 83; O'Neill, *Man of the House*, p. 81.

23. Damore, *The Cape Cod Years of John Fitzgerald Kennedy*, p. 103; Burns, *John Kennedy*, p. 91.

24. Blair, *The Search for J.F.K.*, p. 607.

25. Burns, *John Kennedy*, p. 159.

26. Blair, *The Search for J.F.K.*, pp. 587–89, 603–5.

27. In 1967 the subject reappeared when Dr. John Nichols, a University of Kansas pathologist, declared in the *Journal of the American Medical Association* that as a result of his research, "it can be strongly presumed that President John F. Kennedy had Addison's Disease." In 1972 a physician who examined Kennedy's autopsy photographs concluded, "It is the author's firm belief that the President suffered from bilateral adrenal atrophy," which meant Addison's disease. The Blairs were the first to tell the story in full. See Blair, *The Search for J.F.K.*, pp. 583–608; *New York Times*, July 5, 1960; Bradlee, *Conversations with Kennedy*, pp. 68–69; Sorensen, *Kennedy*, pp. 38–39; Schlesinger, *A Thousand Days*, pp. 95–96; "Pathologist-sleuth Reopens Kennedy Controversy," *Science News*, July 22, 1967, pp. 79–80; Janet Travell, *Office Hours: Day and Night, the Autobiography of Janet Travell, M.D.* (New York, 1968), pp. 3–7, 305–427, 457.

28. Lynn McTaggart, *Kathleen Kennedy, Her Life and Times* (Garden City, N. Y., 1983), esp. pp. 15–21, 96–104, 220–48; Collier and Horowitz, *The Kennedys*, pp. 167–71; Koskoff, *Joseph P. Kennedy*, p. 375; Goodwin, *The Fitzgeralds and the Kennedys*, pp. 737–39; *New York Times*, May 14, 1948.

29. Collier and Horowitz, *The Kennedys*, pp. 171–72; "Kennedy Remembered," *Newsweek*, November 28, 1983, 83. Charles Spalding recalled, "I think he hated the thought of death. I remember one time Caroline had a little pet bird, and the bird died, and she took it down to his office to show it to him before she buried it. And he really was upset. . . . He insisted that she get it out of his sight." Charles Spalding Oral History, JFK Library.

30. Collier and Horowitz, *The Kennedys*, p. 175.

31. Ibid., pp. 175–76.

32. Ibid., p. 176.

33. Ibid., p. 175.

34. Ibid., p. 172.

35. Lasky, *JFK: The Man and the Myth*, p. 141.

36. Ibid., p. 179.

37. Burns, *John Kennedy*, p. 96.

38. Blair, *The Search for J.F.K.*, p. 534.

39. Krock, *Memoirs*, p. 357. See also Mark Dalton Oral History, JFK Library. In retrospect, many of Jack's friends thought he had his eye on the Senate right after reaching the House. Blair, *The Search for J.F.K.*, pp. 572–73. Jack dated his push for the Senate "four and a half years ahead of time," no doubt to disguise his ill health and early ambivalence about politics. See Lasky, *JFK: The Man and the Myth*, pp. 180–81.

40. Ibid., p. 93. See John Sharon Oral History, JFK Library.

41. Burns, *John Kennedy*, p. 100

42. Collier and Horowitz, *The Kennedys*, p. 178.

43. Parmet, *Jack*, pp. 217–20.

44. Ibid., pp. 225–26; Burns, *Jack*, p. 101; O'Donnell and Powers, *"Johnny, We Hardly Knew Ye,"* pp. 86–89.

45. Parmet, *Jack*, pp. 226–30; Blair, *The Search for J.F.K.*, pp. 609–10; Schlesinger, *Robert Kennedy and his Times*, pp. 97–101.

46. Ibid., p. 100.

47. Ralph M. Blagden, "Cabot Lodge's Toughest Fight," *Reporter*, September 30, 1952, p. 11. See Krock, *Memoirs*, p. 357.

48. Martin and Plaut, *Front Runner*, p. 168.

49. Lincoln, *My Twelve Years with John F. Kennedy*, p. 13.

50. "The Campaign," *Time*, July 11, 1960, p. 22.

51. Whalen, *The Founding Father*, p. 408; Blagden, "Cabot Lodge's Toughest Fight," *Reporter*, September 30, 1952, p. 10; Koskoff, *Joseph P. Kennedy*, p. 413.

52. Parmet, *Jack*, p. 233.

53. Lawrence O'Brien, *No Final Victories* (New York, 1974), p. 26.

54. Martin and Plaut, *Front Runner*, p. 158. See Burns, *John Kennedy*, p. 102; Patrick J. Mulkern Oral History, JFK Library.

55. Parmet, *Jack*, p. 234.

56. Martin and Plaut, *Front Runner*, p. 161.

57. Kennedy, *Times to Remember*, p. 321.

58. Collier and Horowitz, *The Kennedys*, p. 184.

59. Lasky, *JFK: The Man and the Myth*, p. 183. "Sometimes you couldn't get anybody to make a decision," a worker later recalled. "You'd have to call the old man. Then you'd get a decision." Martin and Plaut, *Front Runner*, p. 185.

60. Lasky, *JFK: The Man and the Myth*, p. 181; Burns, *John Kennedy*, p. 105.

61. Whalen, *The Founding Father*, pp. 412–14, 416–17. The ultra-conservative *Chicago Tribune* and the Far Right Constitution party both endorsed Jack. Blagden, "Cabot Lodge's Toughest Fight," *Reporter*, September 30, 1952, p. 13.

62. Burns, *John Kennedy*, pp. 107, 115; Whalen, *The Founding Father*, p. 423; Lasky, *JFK: The Man and the Myth*, p. 182; Paul F. Healy, "The Senate's Gay Young Bachelor," *Saturday Evening Post*, June 13, 1953, p. 129.

63. Whalen, *The Founding Father*, pp. 412–13. A few weeks before the election, Kennedy headquarters released a letter to the press from the commander of the Japanese destroyer that hit *PT 109*. Kennedy's election, it stated, "would no doubt contribute not only to the promotion of genuine friendship between Japan and the United States but also the establishment of the universal peace." Dinneen, *The Kennedy Family*, pp. 148–50.

64. Whalen, *The Founding Father*, pp. 419–20; Parmet, *Jack*, pp. 242–43, 511. Fox approached other candidates for loans in return for newspaper support. See Lasky, *JFK: The Man and the Myth*, p. 192; *New York Times*, June 17, 18, 28, 1958. In 1967, Bobby admitted that "there was a connection" between the ambassador's loan and Fox's endorsement. He said of Fox, "I know he was an unsavory figure." Edwin O. Guthman and Jeffrey Shulman, eds., *Robert Kennedy in His Own Words: The Unpublished Recollections of The Kennedy Years* (New York, 1988), p. 444. This fine, reedited collection of three RFK interviews I studied at the JFK Library will hereafter be cited as *Robert Kennedy in His Own Words*.

65. Lasky, *JFK: The Man and the Myth*, p. 189; Parmet, *Jack*, p. 252.

66. See Reeves, *The Life and Times of Joe McCarthy*, pp. 442–43.

67. Ibid., pp. 442–44; Whalen, *The Founding Father*, pp. 416–17; Parmet, *Jack*, p. 249. Cf. Burns, *John Kennedy*, pp. 108–9. Bobby later admitted that Lodge invited McCarthy into the campaign, but he claimed that the Wisconsinite failed to appear solely

because "he just didn't like Henry Cabot Lodge." *Robert Kennedy in His Own Words*, p. 444. On Jack's personal fondness for McCarthy, see Kenneth Birkhead, William O. Douglas, and George Smathers Oral Histories, JFK Library.

68. Krock, *Memoirs*, p. 319.

69. Whalen, *The Founding Father*, p. 418; Martin and Plaut, *Front Runner*, pp. 174–75. The ambassador later denied that the incident occurred. Cf. a slightly sanitized version in Burns, *John Kennedy*, pp. 109–10. For an interesting example of Jack's straddling on McCarthy, see Richard M. Fried, *Men Against McCarthy* (New York, 1976), p. 246. On JFK's difficulties winning the Jewish vote due to his father's anti-Semitism, see Parmet, *Jack*, pp. 246–49, and O'Neill, *Man of the House*, p. 119.

70. Whalen, *The Founding Father*, p. 410; John J. Droney Oral History, JFK Library. Rose, in *Times to Remember* (p. 322), claimed that her husband and Jack selected Bobby. Burns, in *John Kennedy* (p. 107), had Jack appointing him. Kenny O'Donnell, always eager to minimize the ambassador's influence on his son, took personal credit in *"Johnny, We Hardly Knew Ye,"* (pp. 90–96) for Bobby's entrance into the race. Cf. Schlesinger, *Robert Kennedy and His Times*, pp. 101–2.

71. Jean Stein and George Plimpton, eds., *American Journey: The Times of Robert Kennedy* (New York, 1970), p. 41.

72. Ibid., p. 42; O'Neill, *Man of the House*, p. 83; Collier and Horowitz, *The Kennedys*, pp. 185–86; Patrick J. Mulkern Oral History, JFK Library.

73. Schlesinger, *Robert Kennedy and His Times*, pp. 104–5; O'Neill, *Man of the House*, p. 83.

74. Schlesinger, *Robert Kennedy and His Times*, p. 104.

75. O'Brien, *No Final Victories* p. 30.

76. O'Donnell and Powers, *"Johnny, We Hardly Knew Ye,"* p. 96.

77. Collier and Horowitz, *The Kennedys*, p. 186.

78. Kennedy, *Times to Remember*, pp. 322–27; Healy, "The Senate's Gay Young Bachelor," *Saturday Evening Post*, June 13, 1953, pp. 28, 126–27; John J. Droney and Jean McGonigle Mannix Oral Histories, JFK Library.

79. Whalen, *The Founding Father*, p. 421; "The Campaign," *Time*, July 11, 1960, p. 22.

80. Parmet, *Jack*, pp. 239, 253; O'Donnell and Powers, *"Johnny, We Hardly Knew Ye,"* p. 88.

81. Ibid.; Patrick J. Mulkern Oral History, JFK Library; O'Brien, *No Final Victories*, p. 31; Hersh, *The Education of Edward Kennedy*, p. 73.

82. Healy, "The Senate's Gay Young Bachelor," *Saturday Evening Post*, June 13, 1953, p. 129.

83. Damore, *The Cape Cod Years of John Fitzgerald Kennedy*, p. 115.

84. Patrick J. Mulkern Oral History, JFK Library.

85. Healy, "The Senate's Gay Young Bachelor," *Saturday Evening Post*, June 13, 1953, pp. 28, 126. "When he spoke before women's groups, he often began by telling the ladies that there were more women than men in Massachusetts. 'Ladies,' he'd say, 'I need you.' And then he'd tell them about the race between his grandfather and Henry Cabot Lodge, Sr., and complain that the election had been lost because women did not yet have the right to vote." Cameron, *Rose*, p. 165.

86. Ibid., p. 164; Healy, "The Senate's Gay Young Bachelor," *Saturday Evening Post*, June 13, 1953, p. 126.

87. Blagden, "Cabot Lodge's Toughest Fight," *Reporter*, September 30, 1952, pp. 10–11; Burns, *John Kennedy*, pp. 111–12.

88. O'Brien, *No Final Victories*, p. 37.

89. Whalen, *The Founding Father*, p. 423.

90. John J. Droney Oral History, JFK Library.

91. Parmet, *Jack*, p. 351.

CHAPTER 7. Full of Ideals

1. Stephen Birmingham, *Jacqueline Bouvier Kennedy Onassis* (New York, 1978), pp. 60–64; Davis, *The Kennedys*, pp. 150–51.

2. Ibid., pp. 157, 163–72.

3. Ibid., p. 180.

4. Ibid., p. 186.

5. Ibid., pp. 187–210.

6. Ibid., p. 205; Gallagher, *My Life with Jacqueline Kennedy*, p. 167; Birmingham, *Jacqueline Bouvier Kennedy Onassis*, pp. 61–63.

7. Davis, *The Kennedys*, pp. 159, 207–8.

8. Blair, *The Search for J.F.K.*, p. 329.

9. Stanley Tretick Oral History, JFK Library. See also Gallagher, *My Life with Jacqueline Kennedy*, pp. 26, 46, 52.

10. See Davis, *The Kennedys*, pp. 148–211; Dickerson, *Among Those Present*, p. 64. See also Kitty Kelley, *Jackie Oh!* (Secaucus, N.J., 1978), pp. 13–16. Kelley's publications, designed for maximum sales, must be approached cautiously. Still, they contain many interviews that require the historian's attention.

11. See Martin, *A Hero for Our Time*, pp. 73–74; Kelley, *Jackie Oh!* p. 30; Bradlee, *Conversations with Kennedy*, p. 170. See also Charles Spalding Oral History, JFK Library. The ambassador picked a marriage partner for Eunice, who was wed to R. Sargent Shriver in May 1953. Koskoff, *Joseph P. Kennedy*, p. 388.

12. Bradlee, *Conversations with Kennedy*, p. 135. Arthur Schlesinger, Jr. would later contend, "[Joe] McCarthy's vulgarity was hardly to John Kennedy's Brahmin taste." Schlesinger, *Robert Kennedy and His Times*, p. 107.

13. Dickerson, *Among Those Present*, p. 65; Fay, *The Pleasure of His Company*, pp. 181–82; Collier and Horowitz, *The Kennedys*, pp. 194, 197; Charles Spalding Oral History, JFK Library; Gallagher, *My Life with Jacqueline Kennedy*, p. 167; Davis, *The Kennedys*, p. 158.

14. Collier and Horowitz, *The Kennedys*, pp. 193–94.

15. Gallagher, *My Life with Jacqueline Kennedy*, p. 176.

16. Martin, *A Hero for Our Time*, p. 74.

17. Kelley, *Jackie Oh!* p. 20; Birmingham, *Jacqueline Bouvier Kennedy Onassis*, pp. 71–72; Davis, *The Kennedys*, pp. 210–12.

18. Martin, *A Hero for Our Time*, pp. 74, 77; Kelley, *Jackie Oh!* pp. 38–39, 41–42, 84.

19. Martin, *A Hero for Our Time*, pp. 75–76; Cameron, *Rose*, pp. 191–92.

20. Kelley, *Jackie Oh!* p. 37.

21. Ibid. p. 75; see Martin, *A Hero for Our Time*, pp. 75–76; *New York Times*, November 18, 19, 1955.

22. Collier and Horowitz, *The Kennedys*, p. 195.

23. Healy, "The Senate's Gay Young Bachelor," *Saturday Evening Post*, June 13, 1953, pp. 28, 126–27.

24. Martin, *A Hero for Our Time*, p. 75.

25. See Davis, *The Kennedys*, pp. 215–22; Martin, *A Hero for Our Time*, pp. 81–82; Gallagher, *My Life with Jacqueline Kennedy*, pp. 27–29; Eleanor Harris, "The Senator Is in a Hurry," *McCalls*, August 1957, p. 123; *New York Times*, September 13, 1953.

26. Martin, *A Hero for Our Time*, p. 82.

27. Fay, *The Pleasure of His Company*, p. 163.

28. Martin, *A Hero for Our Time*, pp. 92–94; Parmet, *Jack*, p. 298.

29. Martin, *A Hero for Our Time*, p. 95.

30. Gallagher, *My Life with Jacqueline Kennedy*, pp. 40–41, passim.

31. Collier and Horowitz, *The Kennedys*, p. 197.

32. Ibid.; Parmet, *Jack*, pp. 299–300.

33. Gallagher, *My Life with Jacqueline Kennedy*, pp. 163–64.

34. Collier and Horowitz, *The Kennedys*, p. 197. See Blair, *The Search for J.F.K.*, p. 329.

35. Sorensen, *The Kennedy Legacy*, p. 27.

36. Collier and Horowitz, *The Kennedys*, pp. 196–97.

37. Parmet, *Jack*, pp. 296–99.

38. Sorensen, *Kennedy*, pp. 11–13; Lincoln, *My Twelve Years with John F. Kennedy*, p. 18; Jean McGonigle Mannix Oral History, JFK Library; Parmet, *Jack*, p. 263; Bergquist and Tretick, *A Very Special President*, p. 6; Lasky, *JFK: The Man and the Myth*, p. 212–14.

39. The ambassador revised a piece in *New York Times Magazine* entitled "What's the Matter in New England?" He also had Dean James Landis and two other personal attorneys assist Jack with his senatorial duties. Landis helped write speeches and articles for the ambassador, Jack, Bobby, and Eunice. Parmet, *Jack*, pp. 265, 269–70; Koskoff, *Joseph P. Kennedy*, pp. 383–84.

40. Sorensen, *Kennedy*, pp. 23–27.

41. Ibid., pp. 60–61. Cf. John Kelso Oral History, JFK Library. Kelso was a Boston journalist, close to the Kennedys, who saw no substantial change in JFK at all as he grew older.

42. Gallagher, *My Life with Jacqueline Kennedy*, pp. 16–21; Jean McGonigle Mannix Oral History, JFK Library. See Sorensen, *Kennedy*, pp. 55–57.

43. Healy, "The Senate's Gay Young Bachelor," *Saturday Evening Post*, June 13, 1953, p. 127. Jack later told an AVC Chapter secretary that he could not remember making such a remark about the veterans' group.

44. Sorensen, *Kennedy*, pp. 58–59. See Parmet, *Jack*, pp. 266–72; Burns, *John Kennedy*, pp. 120–21, 125–26.

45. Parmet, *Jack*, pp. 276–91.

46. See Reeves, *The Life and Times of Joe McCarthy*, pp. 203, 462–63; Koskoff, *Joseph P. Kennedy*, pp. 363–65; Ruth Watt Young, and William O. Douglas Oral Histories, JFK Library. Robert Amory, Jr., in his oral history at the Kennedy Library, told how JFK defended McCarthy in February 1954 at Harvard University's Spee Club. According to Amory, a speaker at a dinner commemorating the one hundredth anniversary of the club attacked both Alger Hiss and Joe McCarthy in similar terms. This brought Kennedy to his feet with an angry interruption: "How dare you couple the name of a great

American patriot with that of a traitor!'' If the incident occurred, it took place two years earlier, as described in Parmet, *Jack*, pp. 245–46. The Spee Club was founded in 1852.

47. Martin and Plaut, *Front Runner*, pp. 206–7; Parmet, *Jack*, pp. 289, 301–3; Burns, *John Kennedy*, p. 142.

48. Parmet, *Jack*, p. 300.

49. Martin and Plaut, *Front Runner*, pp. 203–4.

50. See Reeves, *The Life and Times of Joe McCarthy*, pp. 644–47.

51. See Martin and Plaut, *Front Runner*, pp. 204–5.

52. Ibid.; Parmet, *Jack*, pp. 305–6; Burns, *John Kennedy*, pp. 145–46. The document, dated July 31, 1954, is in box 12 of the Theodore Sorensen Papers, JFK Library.

53. Parmet, *Jack*, pp. 302, 307.

54. David Caute, *The Great Fear: The Anti-Communist Purge Under Truman and Eisenhower* (New York, 1978), p. 51.

55. Lincoln, *My Twelve Years with John F. Kennedy*, pp. 53–55.

56. Birmingham, *Jacqueline Bouvier Kennedy Onassis*, p. 78; O'Donnell and Powers, *"Johnny, We Hardly Knew Ye,"* p. 108.

57. Parmet, *Jack*, pp. 291–95. Cf. Burns, *John Kennedy*, pp. 147–48. O'Donnell and Powers, *"Johnny, We Hardly Knew Ye,"* pp. 95–96, declared: "It was probably the only wrong political move Jack Kennedy ever made, but he was in intense pain at the time."

58. Ibid., p. 112; Blair, *The Search for J.F.K.*, pp. 597–99.

59. Ernest Warren Oral History, JFK Library.

60. Collier and Horowitz, *The Kennedys*, pp. 309, 313; Arthur Krock Oral History, JFK Library. There were rumors on Capitol Hill after the operation that Jack had died. Jean McGonigle Mannix Oral History, JFK Library.

61. O'Donnell and Powers, *"Johnny, We Hardly Knew Ye,"* p. 111. See Blair, *The Search for J.F.K.*, p. 599.

62. Parmet, *Jack*, p. 310. Earlier Sorensen told a different story. See his *Kennedy*, pp. 48–49, and Martin and Plaut, *Front Runner*, p. 205.

63. Charles Spalding Oral History, JFK Library.

64. Martin and Plaut, *Front Runner*, p. 206.

65. Burns, *John Kennedy*, pp. 149–52.

66. Collier and Horowitz, *The Kennedys*, p. 204; Martin, *A Hero for Our Time*, p. 89.

67. Ibid.

68. Collier and Horowitz, *The Kennedys*, p. 204.

69. Kelley, *Jackie Oh!*, p. 47.

70. Martin, *A Hero for Our Time*, p. 90.

71. Collier and Horowitz, *The Kennedys*, p. 204. Cf. Schlesinger, *A Thousand Days*, p. 97: "Kennedy endured all this with total stoicism."

72. O'Donnell and Powers, *"Johnny, We Hardly Knew Ye,"* p. 113.

73. Ibid., p. 115.

74. Parmet, *Jack*, pp. 313–14; Lincoln, *My Twelve Years with John F. Kennedy*, p. 69.

75. Charles Spalding Oral History, JFK Library.

76. Parmet, *Jack*, pp. 315–16; *New York Times*, May 24, 25, 1955.

77. Travell, *Office Hours*, pp. 5–7.

78. Ibid.; Parmet, *Jack*, p. 317; Blair, *The Search for J.F.K.*, p. 600.

79. Travell, *Office Hours*, pp. 5–7.

80. Parmet, *Jack*, pp. 320–33. See also the Jean McGonigle Mannix and Charles

Spalding Oral Histories and the *Profiles in Courage* papers, boxes 27–35, JFK Personal Papers, JFK Library.

81. Parmet, *Jack*, pp. 330–31; Tyler Abell, ed., *Drew Pearson: Diaries, 1949–1959* (New York, 1974), pp. 407, 420–21.

82. Sorensen, *Kennedy*, pp. 66–70; Schlesinger, *A Thousand Days*, pp. 97, 100–101, 112; Burns, *John Kennedy*, pp. 161–63. See Krock, *Memoirs*, pp. 354–55.

83. Cabell Phillips, "Men Who Dared to Stand Alone," *New York Times Book Review*, January 1, 1956, pp. 1, 21.

84. Parmet, *Jack*, p. 329; Abell, *Drew Pearson*, p. 420.

CHAPTER 8.   The Upstart

1. Lasky, *JFK: The Man and the Myth*, p. 226.

2. Schlesinger, *A Thousand Days*, p. 99; Parmet, *Jack*, pp. 334–35, John Barlow Martin, *Adlai Stevenson and the World*, vol. 2 of *The Life of Adlai E. Stevenson* (Garden City, N.Y., 1977), p. 235; Koskoff, *Joseph P. Kennedy*, pp. 368, 417–18.

3. Parmet, *Jack*, pp. 340–44; *New York Times*, February 8, 1956; Hugh Sidey Oral History, JFK Library.

4. Parmet, *Jack*, pp. 338, 345; *New York Times*, March 9, 1956.

5. Ibid., April 25, 1956.

6. Burns, *John Kennedy*, pp. 177–80; *New York Times*, May 13, 1956; Parmet, *Jack*, pp. 346–55; O'Donnell and Powers, *"Johnny, We Hardly Knew Ye,"* pp. 117–32; Lasky, *JFK: The Man and the Myth*, p. 230. See Sorensen, *Kennedy*, pp. 78–80.

7. See Burns, *John Kennedy*, p. 180; Sorensen, *Kennedy*, p. 83; O'Donnell and Powers, *"Johnny, We Hardly Knew Ye,"* pp. 119–20, 124, 129, 138; Schlesinger, *Robert Kennedy and His Times*, pp. 140–42.

8. O'Donnell and Powers, *"Johnny, We Hardly Knew Ye,"* p. 138; Goodwin, *The Fitzgeralds and the Kennedys*, p. 785.

9. Koskoff, *Joseph P. Kennedy*, p. 418.

10. Martin, *A Hero for Our Time*, p. 103; Koskoff, *Joseph P. Kennedy*, pp. 369–70, 418–19; Collier and Horowitz, *The Kennedys*, p. 208; Martin and Plaut, *Dark Horse*, pp. 68, 106; Parmet, *Jack*, pp. 363–64; Lasky, *JFK: The Man and the Myth*, p. 238; *New York Times*, August 14, 1956; Lincoln, *My Twelve Years with John F. Kennedy*, p. 79.

11. Lasky, *JFK: The Man and the Myth*, p. 230.

12. *New York Times*, May 31, June 9, 1956.

13. Parmet, *Jack*, pp. 358–61; Lasky, *JFK: The Man and the Myth*, pp. 231–3, 753–67. The ambassador's friend Arthur Krock used the memo in his *New York Times* column to lend support to Jack's vice presidential bid. *New York Times*, July 5, 1956.

14. Ibid., June 26, 1956.

15. Parmet, *Jack*, p. 363.

16. Ibid., pp. 356–57; Lasky, *JFK: The Man and the Myth*, p. 230.

17. Martin, *Adlai Stevenson and the World*, p. 344; *New York Times*, July 25, August 7, 1956.

18. Ibid., August 10, 1956; Lincoln, *My Twelve Years with John F. Kennedy*, pp. 75–77; O'Donnell and Powers, *"Johnny, We Hardly Knew Ye,"* p. 135; Harris, "The Senator Is in a Hurry," *McCalls*, August 1957, p. 125.

19. Lincoln, *My Twelve Years with John F. Kennedy*, p. 76; *New York Times*, August 11, 12, 13, 1956.

20. Ibid., August 14, 16, 1956; Parmet, *Jack*, pp. 356–57; Martin, *A Hero for Our Time*, p. 100.

21. O'Donnell and Powers, *"Johnny, We Hardly Knew Ye,"* p. 136; Parmet, *Jack*, p. 369. See Martin, *A Hero for Our Time*, pp. 99–100.

22. *New York Times*, August 17, 1956; Parmet, *Jack*, pp. 369–72.

23. See Martin, *Adlai Stevenson and the World*, p. 350. Stevenson's later avowal that he had wanted JFK all along does not ring true.

24. *New York Times*, August 18, 1956; Goodwin, *The Fitzgeralds and the Kennedys*, p. 783; Parmet, *Jack*, p. 375.

25. Ibid.p. 377; Martin, *A Hero for Our Time*, p. 104; Lincoln, *My Twelve Years with John F. Kennedy*, pp. 80–81; Lasky, *JFK: The Man and the Myth*, p. 240; Goodwin, *The Fitzgeralds and the Kennedys*, p. 780.

26. Parmet, *Jack*, pp. 378–82.

27. Kelley, *Jackie Oh!* p. 57; O'Donnell and Powers, *"Johnny, We Hardly Knew Ye,"* pp. 140–41.

28. *New York Times*, August 18, 1956.

29. Burns, *John Kennedy*, p. 190.

30. See Martin, *A Hero for Our Time*, p. 113; Kelley, *Jackie Oh!* p. 57.

31. Collier and Horowitz, *The Kennedys*, p. 209.

32. Ibid.

33. Ibid.; Kelley, *Jackie Oh!* p. 58.

34. Ibid., pp. 128–29. For the official line, see Burns, *John Kennedy*, p. 192 and Goodwin, *The Fitzgeralds and the Kennedys*, p. 785.

35. Martin, *A Hero for Our Time*, p. 119.

36. Kelley, *Jackie Oh!* p. 61.

37. Davis, *The Kennedys*, p. 227; Kelley, *Jackie Oh!* pp. 60–62, 68; Bradlee, *Conversations with Kennedy*, pp. 28–29, 201–2.

38. Lasky, *JFK: The Man and the Myth*, pp. 251–52.

39. Ibid., pp. 252–53; Martin, *Adlai Stevenson and the World*, p. 389; Parmet, *Jack*, p. 386.

40. Schlesinger, *Robert Kennedy and His Times*, pp. 143–47; O'Donnell and Powers, *"Johnny, We Hardly Knew Ye,"* pp. 142–43.

41. Burns, *John Kennedy*, p. 193; *New York Times*, November 11, 1956.

42. O'Donnell and Powers, *"Johnny, We Hardly Knew Ye,"* p. 144; Harris, "The Senator Is in a Hurry," *McCalls*, August 1957, p. 125.

43. Sorensen, *Kennedy*, pp. 99–105, 113–15; Lasky, *JFK: The Man and the Myth*, pp. 255–58.

44. Goodwin, *The Fitzgeralds and the Kennedys*, p. 790.

45. Parmet, *Jack*, p. 409.

46. Ibid., pp. 387–93, 408–14; Burns, *John Kennedy*, pp. 200–206; Lasky, *JFK: The Man and the Myth*, pp. 258–62, 267; *New York Times*, August 5, 1957; "Democrats: Through the Roadblock," *Time*, October 28, 1957, p. 23.

47. Lasky, *JFK: The Man and the Myth*, pp. 271–76.

48. "Democrats: Man Out Front," *Time*, December 2, 1957, p. 18; Russell Turner, "Senator Kennedy: The Perfect Politician," *American Mercury*, March 1957, p. 33. Cf. Sorensen, *Kennedy*, pp. 102–3.

49. Parmet, *Jack*, p. 394.

50. *New York Times*, May 7, 1957; Harold H. Martin, "The Amazing Kennedys,"

Saturday Evening Post, September 7, 1957, p. 48; Sorensen, *Kennedy*, p. 68. Jack soon won further media attention by donating his $500 Pulitzer check to the United Negro College Fund. *New York Times*, May 12, 1957.

51. It is possible, however, that the predominently liberal journalists on the board were simply carried away by their bias and the force of current events. Joseph P. Pulitzer, Jr., a board member, said later of *Profiles*: "It was not history as much as it was a journalistic achievement at that time—and a political achievement. I think that's the point." See Parmet, *Jack*, pp. 395–97. On Krock, see Manchester, *Portrait of a President*, p. 112.

52. Collier and Horowitz, *The Kennedys*, p. 229. See "The Kennedy Brothers: Off to a Fast Start," *U.S. News & World Report*, April 12, 1957, pp. 77–79; "The Rise of the Brothers Kennedy," *Look*, August 6, 1957, pp. 18–24, 27.

53. "Democrats: Man Out Front," *Time*, December 2, 1957, p. 18; Collier and Horowitz, *The Kennedys*, p. 232; *New York Times*, August 24, December 3, 6, 8, 1957.

54. Lasky, *JFK: The Man and the Myth*, p. 257.

55. Whalen, *The Founding Father*, p. 434; "Democrats: Man Out Front," *Time*, December 2, 1957, p. 18; O'Donnell and Powers, *"Johnny, We Hardly Knew Ye,"* pp. 147–48.

56. Whalen, *The Founding Father*, pp. 433–34; Parmet, *Jack*, pp. 435–37. One Observer reported: "All the children, a closely knit clan, now hold the 'conservative' elder Kennedy in great awe and affection, and consult him frequently." "Most Talked About Candidate for 1960," *U.S. News & World Report*, November 8, 1957, p. 64.

57. Collier and Horowitz, *The Kennedys*, p. 228.

58. See Kelley, *Jackie Oh!* pp. 75–78. Kelley claimed that Jackie received electroshock therapy at a private psychiatric facility in Carlisle, Massachusetts. That seems unlikely. See Heymann, *A Woman Named Jackie*, pp. 196–97.

59. Kelley, *Jackie Oh!* pp. 82, 85; "Democrats: Man Out Front," *Time*, December 2, 1957, pp. 18, 20.

60. Goodwin, *The Fitzgeralds and the Kennedys*, p. 793; Burns, *John Kennedy*, p. 217.

61. Gallagher, *My Life with Jacqueline Kennedy*, pp. 43–47.

62. Ibid., p. 44; Martin, *A Hero for Our Time*, pp. 119–20. Jack complained to Dave Powers at one point that the Georgetown house cost $82,000 plus $18,000 for remodeling. O'Donnell and Powers, *"Johnny, We Hardly Knew Ye,"* p. 146. Cf. Burns, *John Kennedy*, p. 216.

63. Martin, *A Hero for Our Time*, p. 120.

64. Gallagher, *My Life with Jacqueline Kennedy*, p. 54; "This is John Fitzgerald Kennedy," *Newsweek*, June 23, 1958, p. 30. See *New York Times*, May 18 and June 28, 1958, for accounts of speeches.

65. Sorensen, *Kennedy*, pp. 63–5. Cf. *New York Times*, May 11, 1958.

66. See "This is John Fitzgerald Kennedy," *Newsweek*, June 23, 1958, p. 30; Cabell Phillips, "How to be a Presidential Candidate," *New York Times Magazine*, July 13, 1958, p. 54.

67. "This is John Fitzgerald Kennedy," *Newsweek*, June 23, 1958, pp. 29–30.

68. Phillips, "How to Be a Presidential Candidate," *New York Times Magazine*, July 13, 1958, p. 11; Eleanor Roosevelt, "On My Own: Of Stevenson, Truman and Kennedy," *Saturday Evening Post*, March 8, 1958, pp. 72–73; *New York Times*, March 31, 1958; "Behind the Scenes," *Time*, May 5, 1958, 18; Whalen, *The Founding Father*, p. 435.

69. Burns, *John Kennedy*, p. 220; Whalen, *The Founding Father*, p. 436.

70. "This Is John Fitzgerald Kennedy," *Newsweek*, June 23, 1958, p. 33; Burns, *John Kennedy*, pp. 220–21; *New York Times*, October 19, 1958.

71. Hersh, *The Education of Edward Kennedy*, p. 152.

72. Whalen, *The Founding Father*, p. 436; O'Donnell and Powers, *"Johnny, We Hardly Knew Ye,"* p. 157.

73. O'Brien, *No Final Victories*, p. 53; Parmet, *Jack*, pp. 456–57; O'Donnell and Powers, *"Johnny, We Hardly Knew Ye,"* pp. 158–60.

74. Ibid., pp. 157–64; Birmingham, *Jacqueline Bouvier Kennedy Onassis*, pp. 87–88.

75. O'Donnell and Powers, *"Johnny, We Hardly Knew Ye,"* p. 161.

76. Ibid., pp. 161–62.

77. Ibid., p. 164. See *New York Times*, November 5, 6, 1958.

78. Goodwin, *The Fitzgeralds and the Kennedys*, p. 59.

79. Parmet, *Jack*, p. 458; O'Donnell and Powers, *"Johnny, We Hardly Knew Ye,"* p. 164.

80. Parmet, *Jack*, p. 459; *New York Times*, November 10, 1958.

CHAPTER 9.   The Center of Moral Leadership

1. *New York Times*, November 10, 16, 1958.

2. Ibid., December 8, 1958, February 17, 23, 1959. Prodded by Jack, Mrs. Roosevelt admitted privately that she lacked evidence about the ambassador's activities. Parmet, *Jack*, pp. 462–64. See Lawrence Fuchs Oral History, JFK Library.

3. Martin, *A Hero for Our Time*, pp. 130–31.

4. Peter Lisagor Oral History, JFK Library.

5. Ibid.; *New York Times*, October 26, 1957; Parmet, *Jack*, pp. 406–7.

6. For a summary of key Kennedy votes in the House and Senate, see Congressional Quarterly, *Almanac, 86th Cong., 2d Sess., 1960*, (Washington, D.C., 1960), vol. 16, pp. 835–39. See also Phillips, "How to Be a Presidential Candidate," *New York Times Magazine*, July 13, 1958, pp. 52, 54; Martin, "The Amazing Kennedys," *Saturday Evening Post*, September 7, 1957, p. 48; "This is John Fitzgerald Kennedy," *Newsweek*, June 23, 1958, pp. 33–34; "Most-Talked-About Candidate for 1960," *U.S. News & World Report*, November 8, 1957, p. 64.

7. Parmet, *Jack*, pp. 465–67, 477–78; "Kennedy on McCarthy," *Newsweek*, July 6, 1959, pp. 25–26; Douglass Cater, "The Cool Eye of John F. Kennedy," *Reporter*, December 10, 1959, p. 30.

8. *New York Times*, February 17, 23, 1959; Cater, "The Cool Eye of John F. Kennedy," *Reporter*, December 10, 1959, p. 31; Parmet, *Jack*, pp. 501–2.

9. Peter Lisagor Oral History, JFK Library; Parmet, *Jack*, p. 476. See Lawrence Fuchs Oral History, JFK Library.

10. Sorensen, *Kennedy*, pp. 117–18; Abram Chayes Oral History, JFK Library; Parmet, *Jack*, pp. 461–62; Martin and Plaut, *Front Runner*, p. 251.

11. Sorensen, *Kennedy*, pp. 116–21.

12. Parmet, *Jack*, p. 512; Sorensen, *Kennedy*, p. 121; Martin and Plaut, *Front Runner*, pp. 256, 258–62, 463.

13. Collier and Horowitz, *The Kennedys*, p. 238.

14. Cater, "The Cool Eye of John F. Kennedy," *Reporter*, December 10, 1959, p.

31; Parmet, *Jack*, pp. 508–12; Collier and Horowitz, *The Kennedys*, pp. 238–39; O'Neill, *Man of the House*, p. 91; Whalen, *The Founding Father*, pp. 438–41. Cf. Sorensen, *Kennedy*, p. 119.

15. Bradlee, *Conversations with Kennedy*, p. 69; Exner, *My Story*, p. 146.

16. Joe McCarthy, "Jack Kennedy: His Religion May Elect Him," *Look*, November 10, 1959, p. 110.

17. Cabell Phillips, "Two Candidates on the Road," *New York Times Magazine*, October 25, 1959, p. 24.

18. Benjamin Bradlee, "Keeping Up with Kennedy," *Newsweek*, November 23, 1959, p. 33.

19. Martin and Plaut, *Front Runner*, p. 256.

20. Phillips, "Two Candidates on the Road," *New York Times Magazine*, October 25, 1959, pp. 24, 50; Martin, *A Hero for Our Time*, p. 140; Martin and Plaut, *Front Runner*, p. 256.

21. Bradlee, "Keeping Up with Kennedy," *Newsweek*, November 23, 1959, p. 33.

22. Martin and Plaut, *Front Runner*, p. 461.

23. Cf. Martin, *A Hero for Our Time*, pp. 135–39, and Sorensen, *Kennedy*, p. 120.

24. Phillips, "Two Candidates on the Road," *New York Times Magazine*, October 25, 1959, p. 24.

25. McCarthy, "Jack Kennedy: His Religion May Election Him," *Look*, November 10, 1959, p. 105.

26. Joe McCarthy, "Jack Kennedy: Heir to Power," *Look*, October 27, 1959, p. 91.

27. Joe McCarthy, "Jack Kennedy: Front Man for a Dynasty," *Look*, October 13, 1959, p. 32. See Joe McCarthy, *The Remarkable Kennedys* (New York, 1960).

28. Jack was very sensitive about photographs that showed him without a shirt, wanting to conceal what he scornfully called his (slightly large) "Fitzgerald breasts." Bradlee, *Conversations with Kennedy*, p. 29.

29. Parmet, *Jack*, pp. 482–85.

30. Ibid., p. 481.

31. Ibid., pp. 479–81, 485–88; Burns, *John Kennedy*, p. 212. See Sorensen, *Kennedy*, pp. 113, 118.

32. *New York Times*, January 3, 1960.

33. Ibid., January 15, 1960.

34. Stewart Alsop, "Kennedy vs. Humphrey," *Saturday Evening Post*, April 2, 1960, p. 93; Sorensen, *Kennedy*, p. 134; Richard N. Goodwin, *Remembering America: A Voice from the Sixties* (Boston, 1988), p. 76. On Harris, see Halberstam, *The Powers That Be*, pp. 451–54.

35. Sorensen, *Kennedy*, pp. 134–36; Goodwin, *The Fitzgeralds and the Kennedys*, p. 797; O'Donnell and Powers, *"Johnny, We Hardly Knew Ye,"* p. 177; Theodore H. White, *The Making of the President, 1960* (New York, 1961), p. 93; *Milwaukee Journal*, March 31, 1960; Hubert H. Humphrey, *The Education of a Public Man* (Garden City, N.Y., 1976), p. 208. On Bobby as a tireless and tough campaign manager, see Schlesinger, *Robert Kennedy and His Times*, pp. 207–8.

36. Peter Lisagor Oral History, JFK Library; *Milwaukee Journal*, April 2, 3, 1960.

37. Alsop, "Kennedy vs. Humphrey," *Saturday Evening Post*, April 2, 1960, p. 20.

38. See O'Donnell and Powers, *"Johnny, We Hardly Knew Ye,"* pp. 172–74.

39. *Milwaukee Journal*, April 2, 1960; Alsop, "Kennedy vs. Humphrey," *Saturday Evening Post*, April 2, 1960, p. 20.

40. Alsop, "Kennedy vs. Humphrey," *Saturday Evening Post*, p. 20; Martin, *A Hero for Our Time*, p. 142.

41. *Milwaukee Journal*, March 21, April 3, 1960; O'Donnell and Powers, *"Johnny, We Hardly Knew Ye,"* pp. 175–76; Martin, *A Hero for Our Time*, p. 142. See White, *The Making of the President*, pp. 83–86.

42. *Milwaukee Journal*, April 6, 1960; White, *The Making of the President*, pp. 94–95.

43. Goodwin, *Remembering America*, pp. 82–83; Humphrey, *The Education of a Public Man*, p. 208.

44. O'Donnell and Powers, *"Johnny, We Hardly Knew Ye,"* pp. 181–85; Kennedy, *Times to Remember*, p. 368; White, *The Making of the President*, pp. 103–4; *New York Times*, May 1, 2, 8, 1960.

45. O'Donnell and Powers, *"Johnny, We Hardly Knew Ye,"* pp. 185–86. See Kennedy, *Times to Remember*, pp. 369–70; *New York Times*, May 2, 1960.

46. Lasky, *JFK: The Man and the Myth*, p. 436; O'Donnell and Powers, *"Johnny, We Hardly Knew Ye,"* p. 186; *Milwaukee Journal*, April 3, 1960; Sorensen, *Kennedy*, p. 141.

47. O'Donnell and Powers, *"Johnny, We Hardly Knew Ye,"* pp. 187–88; *New York Times*, April 19, 25, 1960.

48. Ibid., May 9, 1960; White, *The Making of the President*, pp. 107–8. See Goodwin, *Remembering America*, pp. 85–88, 91.

49. White, *The Making of the President*, pp. 109–10.

50. *New York Times*, May 3, 1960; "The Campaign," *Time*, May 9, 1960, p. 21; O'Brien, *No Final Victories*, pp. 72–73; Lasky, *JFK: The Man and the Myth*, pp. 437–39; Goodwin, *The Fitzgeralds and the Kennedys*, p. 799. Cf. Goodwin, *Remembering America*, p. 88. For Jack's disparaging private comment on the "draft-dodger" issue, see *Washington Post*, May 29, 1987. Roosevelt later apologized to Humphrey.

51. *New York Times*, April 15, 1960; White, *The Making of the President*, p. 108.

52. Lasky, *JFK: The Man and the Myth*, pp. 432–33; Sorensen, *Kennedy*, pp. 143–44; White, *The Making of the President*, p. 109.

53. Ibid., p. 106; Martin, *A Hero for Our Time*, pp. 144–45; Lasky, *JFK: The Man and the Myth*, p. 431; *New York Times*, April 26, May 5, 1960.

54. Ibid., May 3, 4, 9, 1960; Harold Lavine, "How Up Is 'Uphill' ?" *Newsweek*, May 2, 1960, p. 33; White, *The Making of the President*, pp. 97, 110–13; O'Brien, *No Final Victories*, pp. 68–70; Humphrey, *The Education of a Public Man*, pp. 322–23. In Missouri, Tip O'Neill later revealed, wealthy brewer August Busch raised $29,000 for Kennedy from local businessmen: $17,000 in cash and $12,000 in checks. Jack asked for the cash and told Busch to give the checks, which were, of course, traceable, to O'Donnell. "Jeez," O'Neill commented, "This business is no different if you're running for ward leader or president of the United States." O'Neill, *Man of the House*, p. 98.

55. Kitty Kelley, "The Dark Side of Camelot," *People*, February 29, 1988, pp. 109–11. In this article, Exner, terminally ill with cancer, added several important pieces of information to *My Story* "so that I can die peacefully." Her earlier silence about the Kennedy-Giancana relationship, she said, was out of fear for her life. "With the exception of Sinatra, all the key figures involved in my story have been murdered." To buttress her account, she turned over plane tickets, hotel bills, her appointment books from 1960–61 and 1962 to *People*. In a photograph for the article, Exner wore the expensive brooch given to her by JFK and described in *My Story*.

56. Antoinette Giancana and Thomas C. Renner, *Mafia Princess, Growing Up in Sam Giancana's Family* (New York, 1985), pp. 278–81, 309–11.

57. *Washington Post*, May 29, 1987; *New York Times*, May 5, 1960; Sorensen, *Kennedy*, pp. 140–41.

58. Bradlee, *Conversations with Kennedy*, p. 27.

59. *New York Times*, May 11, 12, 1960; Humphrey, *The Education of a Public Man*, p. 221; "The Night That Glowed," *Newsweek*, May 23, 1960, pp. 56–57; White, *The Making of the President*, p. 114.

60. Martin, *A Hero for Our Time*, pp. 147–48.

61. White, *The Making of the President*, pp. 118–35; Martin, *A Hero for Our Time*, p. 149; Sorensen, *Kennedy*, p. 151.

62. O'Neill, *Man of the House*, p. 181; Peter Lisagor Oral History, JFK Library.

63. Lasky, *JFK: The Man and the Myth*, pp. 452–53.

64. Ibid., p. 470.

65. Sorensen, *Kennedy*, p. 156; Schlesinger, *Robert Kennedy and His Times*, pp. 218–19.

66. *New York Times*, May 13, 1960.

67. Ibid., June 24, 1960; Lasky, *JFK: The Man and the Myth*, pp. 466–68.

68. *New York Times*, May 13, 14, 1960; Lasky, *JFK: The Man and the Myth*, pp. 450–51.

69. Schlesinger, *Robert Kennedy and His Times*, p. 219.

70. White, *The Making of the President*, pp. 144–49.

71. *New York Times*, July 3, 1960.

72. O'Donnell and Powers, *"Johnny, We Hardly Knew Ye,"* p. 203; White, *The Making of the President*, pp. 178–79; Lasky, *JFK: The Man and the Myth*, pp. 445–47, 473–74; Martin, *A Hero for Our Time*, pp. 150–51; Koskoff, *Joseph P. Kennedy*, p. 422; *New York Times*, July 3, 5, 11, 1960.

73. Sorensen, *Kennedy*, p. 151; *New York Times*, July 5, 6, 1960; Lasky, *JFK: The Man and the Myth*, pp. 474–75.

74. Sorensen, *Kennedy*, p. 153.

75. *New York Times*, July 5, 1960; Lasky, *JFK: The Man and the Myth*, pp. 476–78. See the interviews in Parmet, *JFK*, p. 18. In June Jack had asked liberal Joseph Rauh to block a *New York Post* story linking him with an adrenal problem and medication. Jack denied taking drugs and said that his adrenal condition was a thing of the past. Joseph Rauh Oral History, JFK Library.

76. Baker, *Wheeling and Dealing*, p. 121.

77. *New York Times*, July 6, 1960; Dickerson, *Among Those Present*, p. 44.

78. *New York Times*, July 8, 9, 1960.

79. At the close of the Wisconsin primary, Humphrey had imported black baseball star Jackie Robinson, who told of the secret breakfast meeting in a campaign address. *Milwaukee Journal*, April 4, 1960. Patterson, a Kennedy admirer, had actually sought out the candidate. See John Patterson Oral History, JFK Library. Adam Clayton Powell, Jr., as was his custom, requested cash in return for his support. *Robert Kennedy in His Own Words*, pp. 72–73.

80. *New York Times*, July 7, 8, 10, 11, 13, 1960; Carl M. Brauer, *John F. Kennedy and the Second Reconstruction* (New York, 1977), pp. 33–34; *Robert Kennedy in His Own Words*, pp. 90–91.

81. Goodwin, *The Fitzgeralds and the Kennedys*, pp. 800–801.

82. *New York Times*, July 9, 10, 1960.

83. "JFK and the Mobster's Moll," *Time*, December 29, 1975, p. 12.

84. Zane, "Joan Hitchcock's Evenings with JFK," *OUI*, July 15, 1976, p. 11.

85. Exner, *My Story*, pp. 162–71.

86. Ibid., pp. 132, 147–48.

87. White, *The Making of the President*, p. 157.

88. Lasky, *JFK: The Man and the Myth*, pp. 485–87, 503; *New York Times*, July 7, 1960; Schlesinger, *Robert Kennedy and His Times*, p. 221; Dickerson, *Among Those Present*, p. 68.

89. *New York Times*, July 10, 11, 1960; O'Donnell and Powers, *"Johnny, We Hardly Knew Ye,"* p. 206; Martin, *Adlai Stevenson and The World*, p. 522; Martin, *A Hero for Our Time*, pp. 150, 156–57.

90. *New York Times*, July 12, 1960; "The Campaign," *Time*, May 9, 1960, pp. 19, 23.

91. *New York Times*, July 12, 1960.

92. Collier and Horowitz, *The Kennedys*, p. 242.

93. Lasky, *JFK: The Man and the Myth*, pp. 497–99; *New York Times*, July 13, 1960; Hedley Donovan, *Roosevelt to Reagan: A Reporter's Encounters with Nine Presidents* (New York, 1987), p. 73. Cf. O'Brien, *No Final Victories*, p. 82.

94. *New York Times*, July 14, 1960.

95. Ibid., July 14, 15, 1960.

96. O'Donnell and Powers, *"Johnny, We Hardly Knew Ye,"* p. 212; *New York Times*, July 14, 15, 1960.

97. Schlesinger, *A Thousand Days*, pp. 40–41. See "Kennedy's Veeps," *Time*, May 23, 1960, 15–16.

98. Dickerson, *Among Those Present*, p. 43. Cf. Clark Clifford Oral History, JFK Library.

99. Schlesinger, *A Thousand Days*, pp. 42–43, 51; Parmet, *JFK*, p.23; O'Neill, *Man of the House*, pp. 93–95; O'Donnell and Powers, *"Johnny, We Hardly Knew Ye,"* p. 213.

100. William W. Prochnau and Richard W. Larsen, *A Certain Democrat: Senator Henry M. Jackson, A Political Biography* (Englewood Cliffs, N.J., 1972), p. 191; Dickerson, *Among Those Present*, p. 43; Schlesinger, *A Thousand Days*, p. 45.

101. *New York Times*, July 15, 1960; Phillip Potter, "How LBJ Got the Nomination," *Reporter*, June 18, 1964, pp. 17, 20; Dickerson, *Among Those Present*, pp. 43–44; Prochnau and Larsen, *A Certain Democrat*, p. 60.

102. O'Donnell and Powers, *"Johnny, We Hardly Knew Ye,"* pp. 214–15; Schlesinger, *A Thousand Days*, pp. 45–49; Sorensen, *Kennedy*, p. 163. See also Potter, "How LBJ Got the Nomination," *Reporter*, June 18, 1964, p. 16; White, *The Making of the President*, p. 174.

103. Harris Wofford, *Of Kennedys and Kings: Making Sense of the Sixties* (New York, 1980), p. 53.

104. Baker, *Wheeling and Dealing*, pp. 124–5; Lincoln, *My Twelve Years with John F. Kennedy*, pp. 162–4; O'Brien, *No Final Victories*, p. 84; Schlesinger, *A Thousand Days*, pp. 45–48; Martin, *A Hero for Our Time*, pp. 169–70.

105. Baker, *Wheeling and Dealing*, p. 126; Parmet, *JFK*, p. 25; Potter, "How LBJ Got the Nomination," *Reporter*, June 18, 1964, p. 17.

106. Schlesinger, *A Thousand Days*, p. 48.

107. Lincoln, *My Twelve Years with John F. Kennedy*, pp. 164–65.

108. Potter, "How LBJ Got the Nomination," *Reporter*, June 18, 1964, p. 17; O'Donnell and Powers, *"Johnny, We Hardly Knew Ye,"* pp. 217–18.

109. Alfred Steinberg, *Sam Rayburn: A Biography* (New York, 1975), p. 330; O'Donnell and Powers, *"Johnny, We Hardly Knew Ye,"* pp. 215–20; *New York Times*, July 15, 1960. Cf. Parmet, *JFK*, p. 27.

110. Ibid., pp. 27–28.

111. Potter, "How LBJ Got the Nomination," *Reporter*, June 18, 1964, p. 20; Schlesinger, *Robert Kennedy and His Times*, pp. 222–27; Parmet, *JFK*, pp. 28–30; Dickerson, *Among Those Present*, pp. 45–47; Baker, *Wheeling and Dealing*, pp. 113, 128–30; George Reedy to the author, July 15, 1987; *Robert Kennedy in His Own Words*, pp. 19–25, 304, 417; *New York Times*, July 16, 1960; Hersh, *The Education of Edward Kennedy*, p. 183. Cf. Lyndon Baines Johnson, *The Vantage Point: Perspectives of the Presidency, 1963–1969* (New York, 1971), p. 1; O'Donnell and Powers, *"Johnny, We Hardly Knew Ye,"* pp. 219–24; Schlesinger, *A Thousand Days*, pp. 53–57. JFK told Pierre Salinger, "The whole story will never be known. And it's just as well that it won't be." Salinger, *With Kennedy*, p. 46.

112. *New York Times*, July 15, 1960; Lasky, *JFK: The Man and the Myth*, pp. 509–10, 513.

113. Baker, *Wheeling and Dealing*, p. 126; Dickerson, *Among Those Present*, p. 48.

114. O'Donnell and Powers, *"Johnny, We Hardly Knew Ye,"* pp. 222–23; *New York Times*, July 16, 1960; O'Brien, *No Final Victories*, pp. 85–6; Lasky, *JFK: The Man and the Myth*, pp. 518–19.

115. Collier and Horowitz, *The Kennedys*, p. 244; Schlesinger, *A Thousand Days*, pp. 57–8.

116. *New York Times*, July 16, 1960.

CHAPTER 10. Moving Ahead

1. *New York Times*, July 16, 1960; Sorensen, *Kennedy*, pp. 166–67; Walt Rostow Oral History, JFK Library. According to Rostow, Jack also took the theme, "This country is ready to start moving again and I am prepared to lead it" from him. Earlier Kennedy had toyed with the slogan "first frontier." *Washington Post*, May 29, 1987.

2. *New York Times*, July 16, 1960.

3. White, *The Making of the President*, p. 178.

4. Collier and Horowitz, *The Kennedys*, p. 244.

5. Lasky, *JFK: The Man and the Myth*, pp. 507, 521.

6. Martin, *Adlai Stevenson and the World*, pp. 531, 533; Parmet, *JFK*, pp. 36–37; Lasky, *JFK: The Man and the Myth*, p. 522.

7. White, *The Making of the President*, p. 240; *Robert Kennedy in His Own Words*, p. 451; Koskoff, *Joseph P. Kennedy*, p. 385; Parmet, *JFK*, pp. 37–38; Martin, *A Hero for Our Time*, p. 202.

8. Lasky, *JFK: The Man and the Myth*, p. 522.

9. *New York Times*, May 21, July 15, 1960.

10. Dickerson, *Among Those Present*, p. 59; Martin, *Adlai Stevenson and the World*, p. 532.

11. *New York Times*, July 17, 1960; Martin, *Adlai Stevenson and the World*, p. 532.

12. Ibid., pp. 530–31.

13. *New York Times*, July 23, 24, 31, 1960.

14. Ibid., August 2, 9, 11, 13, 24, 1960.

15. Dickerson, *Among Those Present*, pp. 50–51.

16. *New York Times*, August 13, 19, 22, 1960.

17. White, *The Making of the President*, pp. 250–51; *New York Times*, August 22, 31, 1960.

18. Parmet, *JFK*, p. 36; O'Donnell and Powers, *"Johnny, We Hardly Knew Ye,"* pp. 227–28.

19. Lasky, *JFK: The Man and the Myth*, p. 527.

20. Ibid.; Margaret Truman, *Bess W. Truman* (New York, 1987), p. 479; Exner, *My Story*, p. 176.

21. White, *The Making of the President*, p. 250.

22. O'Donnell and Powers, *"Johnny, We Hardly Knew Ye,"* p. 228; Sorensen, *Kennedy*, p. 179; White, *The Making of the President*, p. 252.

23. Martin, *A Hero for Our Time*, pp. 183–84; Salinger, *With Kennedy*, p. 41.

24. White, *The Making of the President*, pp. 251, 255–58, 319, 324–28; Sorensen, *Kennedy*, pp. 177–86; Goodwin, *Remembering America*, p. 105; Martin, *A Hero for Our Time*, pp. 191–92.

25. Ibid., p. 190; Goodwin, *Remembering America*, pp. 119–20. For a collection of the Kennedy campaign themes, see John F. Kennedy, " 'We Must Climb to the Hilltop,' " *Life*, August 22, 1960, pp. 70, 72, 75–77, clearly a Sorensen product.

26. Richard John Neuhaus, *The Catholic Moment: The Paradox of the Church in the Postmodern World* (San Francisco, 1987), pp. 233–50; *New York Times*, August 28, 1960.

27. Ibid., September 8, 1960.

28. Ibid., September 8, 9, 10, 12, 1960. See Douglass Cater, "The Protestant Issue," *Reporter*, October 13, 1960, pp. 30–32.

29. *New York Times*, September 13, 1960; Sorensen, *Kennedy*, pp. 189–93; John Cogley Oral History, JFK Library. Riding down Fifth Avenue shortly after his election, Kennedy leaned out of the car window and waved at St. Patrick's Cathedral. "Thanks," he said. "Thanks a lot." Goodwin, *Remembering America*, p. 111.

30. *New York Times*, September 14, 1960.

31. John W. Turnbull, "The Clergy Faces Mr. Kennedy," *Reporter*, October 13, 1960, pp. 33–34.

32. *New York Times*, September 13, 1960.

33. Ibid., September 15, 1960. On Jackson, see Prochnau and Larsen, *A Certain Democrat*, pp. 198–200.

34. White, *The Making of the President*, p. 262; *New York Times*, October 25, 1960.

35. Dickerson, *Among Those Present*, p. 54.

36. Lasky, *JFK: The Man and the Myth*, pp. 544–46. See Philip M. Kaiser Oral History, JFK Library.

37. Lasky, *JFK: The Man and the Myth*, p. 624; "Midwest: A Campaign Report," *U.S. News & World Report*, October 24, 1960, p. 46; *New York Times*, October 16, 17, 22, 23, 25, 26, November 2, 3, 6, 8, 9, 1960. See O'Brien, *No Final Victories*, p. 94. Cf. Sorensen, *Kennedy*, pp. 193–95. Just before the election, the Vatican declared its complete impartiality on the presidential race. *New York Times*, November 5, 1960.

38. White, *The Making of the President*, pp. 283, 293; *New York Times*, September 27, 1960. See Halberstam, *The Powers That Be*, pp. 461, 472–79.

39. White, *The Making of the President*, pp. 272–73, 283–86; Sorensen, *Kennedy*, p. 198; *New York Times*, September 27, 1960.

40. O'Brien, *No Final Victories*, p. 93.

41. See the verbatim transcript in Sidney Kraus, ed., *The Great Debates: Back ground-Perspective-Effects* (Bloomington, Ind., 1962), pp. 348–68; *New York Times*, September 27, 1960.

42. Martin, *A Hero for Our Time*, p. 208.

43. Dickerson, *Among Those Present*, p. 56.

44. White, *The Making of the President*, pp. 288–90; Lasky, *JFK: The Man and the Myth*, p. 603; "TV Debate Backstage: Did the Cameras Lie?" *Newsweek*, October 10, 1960, p. 25; Richard M. Nixon, *Six Crises* (Garden City, N.Y., 1962), pp. 340–42.

45. White, *The Making of the President*, p. 330. *Newsweek* observed, "A Nixon crowd is far more mannerly." "This is Kennedy," *Newsweek*, October 10, 1960, p. 26.

46. "Stormy K . . . and Television: How Much Influence on Voters?" ibid., p. 28.

47. O'Donnell and Powers, *"Johnny, We Hardly Knew Ye,"* p. 241; *New York Times*, October 22, 1960.

48. White, *The Making of the President*, p. 321; O'Donnell and Powers, *"Johnny, We Hardly Knew Ye,"* p. 243.

49. Kraus, *The Great Debates*, pp. 369–89; *New York Times*, October 8, 1960; Nixon, *Six Crises*, pp. 344–46. Judd told the GOP Convention that Roosevelt and Truman "got along famously with the Communists—as long as they gave in to them." See "The Convention," *Time*, August 1, 1960, p. 13.

50. Kraus, *The Great Debates*, pp. 390–410; *New York Times*, October 14, 1960; White, *The Making of the President*, p. 290; Nixon, *Six Crises*, pp. 346–48.

51. Kraus, *The Great Debates*, pp. 411–40.

52. *New York Times*, October 22, 1960; Martin, *A Hero for Our Time*, p. 209.

53. Nixon, *Six Crises*, pp. 353–54; Kraus, *The Great Debates*, p. 417.

54. Nixon, *Six Crises*, pp. 351–57. See Nixon, *RN*, vol. 1, pp. 272–73.

55. Parmet, *JFK*, pp. 46–9; Sorensen, *Kennedy*, pp. 205–6; Chester Bowles, *Promises to Keep: My Years in Public Life, 1941–1969* (New York, 1972), p. 297.

56. Goodwin, *Remembering America*, pp. 124–26.

57. Kraus, *The Great Debates*, pp. 417–18; Nixon, *Six Crises*, pp. 356–57; Lasky, *JFK: The Man and the Myth*, pp. 572–77.

58. Parmet, *JFK*, p. 49.

59. Nixon, *Six Crises*, p. 357.

60. *New York Times*, November 5, 1960. See Kurt Lang and Gladys Engel Lang, "Reactions of Viewers," in Kraus, *The Great Debates*, pp. 313–30; Saul Ben-Zeev and Irving S. White, "Effects and Implications," ibid., pp. 331–37.

61. "Interviews: How the Democrats Won," *U.S. News & World Report*, November 21, 1960, p. 74.

62. Samuel Lubell, "Personalities vs. Issues," in Kraus, *The Great Debates*, p. 155. Arthur Krock, in a not-so-subtle plug for Kennedy in the *New York Times*, argued that the better presidents had been elected for personality reasons. Arthur Krock, " 'The Man Who'—Not 'The Issue Which,' " *New York Times Magazine*, October 14, 1960, pp. 19, 107–8, 110–11.

63. *New York Times*, November 4, 1960.

64. Ibid., October 18, 1960.

65. Summers, *Goddess* , pp. 211–16, 220–21. See Trohan, *Political Animals*, p. 331.

66. Kitty Kelley, *His Way: The Unauthorized Biography of Frank Sinatra* (New York, 1987), p. 293. See Patricia Seaton Lawford, *The Peter Lawford Story: Life with the Kennedys, Monroe and the Rat Pack* (New York, 1988), pp. 115, 134–35, 142.

67. Exner, *My Story*, pp. 174–79, 181, 190–94; Martin, *A Hero for Our Time*, pp. 185–86; *Washington Post*, May 29, 1987; Lincoln, *My Twelve Years with John Kennedy*, p. 178. See the interview in Heymann, *A Woman Named Jackie*, pp. 229–30.

68. Ibid., p. 242.

69. *Washington Post*, May 29, 1987; author interview with George Reedy, April 17, 1986.

70. See Trohan, *Political Animals*, pp. 133–40. Trohan was a virulent FDR hater. See also Hugh Sidey, "Upstairs at the White House," *Time*, May 18, 1987, p. 20; Gloria Berger et al., "Private Lives, Public Figures," *U.S. News & World Report*, May 18, 1987, p. 23.

71. R. W. Apple, Jr., quoted in *Milwaukee Journal*, May 6, 1987.

72. Salinger, *With Kennedy*, p. 46. On the elder Kennedy and the press, see Goodwin, *The Fitzgeralds and the Kennedys*, p. 500.

73. White, *The Making of the President*, pp. 336–37. See Sorensen, *Kennedy*, pp. 169, 186–87; Peter Lisagor Oral History, JFK Library.

74. Hersh, *The Education of Edward Kennedy*, pp. 185–89; Marcia Cehllis, *The Joan Kennedy Story: Living with the Kennedys* (New York, 1985), pp. 27–28, 33; Exner, *My Story*, pp. 86–89.

75. Lasky, *JFK: The Man and the Myth*, p. 580; Martin, *A Hero for Our Time*, p. 183.

76. Collier and Horowitz, *The Kennedys*, p. 248; Martin, *A Hero for Our Time*, p. 183; Kennedy, *Times to Remember*, p. 371; *New York Times*, September 15, 19, 1960.

77. Martin, *A Hero for Our Time*, pp. 193–95; *New York Times*, September 14, 20, 1960; Birmingham, *Jacqueline Bouvier Kennedy Onassis*, pp. 88–89.

78. Gallagher, *My Life with Jacqueline Kennedy*, pp. 58–59.

79. *New York Times*, September 15, 1960; Gallagher, *My Life with Jacqueline Kennedy*, pp. 56–57. See the discussion of Oleg Cassini in chapter 11.

80. Kelley, *Jackie Oh!*, pp. 89–91.

81. Lasky, *JFK: The Man and the Myth*, pp. 548–49.

82. Schlesinger, *Robert Kennedy and His Times*, pp. 228–30.

83. "Kennedy Abroad," *Newsweek*, August 8, 1960, p. 23.

84. "A Talk with the Silent Kennedy," *U.S. News & World Report*, August 22, 1960, 58.

85. *New York Times*, November 5, 1960; Whalen, *The Founding Father*, p. 447; "The Mystery of Joe Kennedy. . . . Why All the Talk and Why All the Silence," *Newsweek*, September 12, 1960, pp. 26–28, 30; Whalen, *The Founding Father*, p. 444.

86. Fay, *The Pleasure of His Company*, pp. 31–35.

87. Whalen, *The Founding Father*, p. 446; Hugh Sidey, "Joe Kennedy's Feelings About His Son," *Life*, December 19, 1960, p. 32.

88. Collier and Horowitz, *The Kennedys*, pp. 245–46; Trohan, *Political Animals*, p. 331; Harris Wofford, *Of Kennedys and Kings*, pp. 38–39. Krock, *Memoirs*, p. 307.

89. Koskoff, *Joseph P. Kennedy*, p. 427. Jack told Ben Bradlee, "I spent thirteen million dollars in 1960." Bradlee, *Conversations with Kennedy*, p. 201.

90. Lasky, *JFK: The Man and the Myth*, pp. 551–54; Dickerson, *Among Those Present*, pp. 54–57. See Parmet, *JFK*, pp. 52–53.

91. See Sorensen, *Kennedy*, pp. 470–71; Schlesinger, *A Thousand Days*, pp. 930–31; Congressional Quarterly, *Almanac*, p. 838.

92. See Brauer, *John F. Kennedy and the Second Reconstruction*, pp. 40–46, 54–60; Lasky, *JFK: The Man and the Myth*, pp. 510–13, 530–36, 550–52.

93. Wofford, *Of Kennedys and Kings*, pp. 12–13.

94. Ibid., pp. 13–19.

95. Ibid., pp. 19–22, See *Robert Kennedy in His Own Words*, pp. 69–71; Schlesinger, *Robert Kennedy and His Times*, pp. 233–35.

96. Wofford, *Of Kennedy and Kings*, pp. 22–23.

97. Ibid., p. 28.

98. Ibid., p. 22.

99. Ibid., pp. 23–25.

100. Ibid., pp. 25–26; John Kenneth Galbraith, *Ambassador's Journal: A Personal Account of the Kennedy Years* (Boston, 1969), p. 6.

101. *New York Times*, November 3–8, 1960; White, *The Making of the President*, pp. 311–13.

102. See Lasky, *JFK: The Man and the Myth*, p. 599.

103. *New York Times*, November 3, 1960.

104. Lasky, *JFK: The Man and the Myth*, pp. 580–81, 598.

105. *New York Times*, November 3, 1960.

106. Ibid., November 4, 6, 10, 11, 1960. See Martin, *A Hero for Our Time*, p. 196.

107. *New York Times*, November 7, 8, 9, 1960.

108. Ibid., November 9, 1960.

109. White, *The Making of the President*, p. 404; Davis, *The Kennedys*, p. 250.

110. Goodwin, *The Fitzgeralds and the Kennedys*, pp. 805–6; O'Donnell and Powers, *"Johnny, We Hardly Knew Ye,"* pp. 251–52; Bradlee, *Conversations with Kennedy*, pp. 33, 151.

111. Davis, *The Kennedys*, p. 252.

112. Exner, *My Story*, pp. 194–96; Davis, *The Kennedys*, pp. 252–54; Kelley, "The Dark Side of Camelot," *People*, February 29, 1988, p. 111.

113. Salinger, *With Kennedy*, p. 51.

114. Congressional Quarterly, *Congress and the Nation, 1945–1964: A Review of Government and Politics in the Postwar Years* (Washington, D.C., 1965), p. 39; White, *The Making of the President*, pp. 350–65; Lubell, "Personalities Vs. Issues," in Kraus, *The Great Debates*, pp. 159–62; Schlesinger, *A Thousand Days*, p. 930; Wofford, *Of Kennedys and Kings*, p. 25.

115. Arthur Schlesinger, Jr., *Kennedy or Nixon; Does It Make Any Difference?* (New York, 1960), pp. 1–34. Schlesinger omitted this title in a list of his books published in *Thousand Days*.

116. *New York Times*, November 10, 1960; Kennedy, *Times to Remember*, p. 377.

117. *New York Times*, January 8, 1961.

CHAPTER 11. Looking More Like a President

1. *New York Times*, November 9, 11, December 16, 1960; Parmet, *JFK*, p. 60.
2. Sidey, "Joe Kennedy's Feelings About His Son," *Life*, December 19, 1960, p. 32. The University of Michigan Center for Political Studies, in an analysis challenged by Republicans, later claimed that Kennedy suffered a net loss of about 1.5 million votes because of his religion. David S. Broder, *The Party's Over* (New York, 1972), p. 30.
3. Lasky, *JFK: The Man and the Myth*, pp. 629–30; Schlesinger, *A Thousand Days*, p. 125.
4. *New York Times*, November 11, 1960; Damore, *The Cape Cod Years of John Fitzgerald Kennedy*, p. 230; Schlesinger, *A Thousand Days*, p. 125.
5. The story of the early 1961 hush money came to light in 1977 when *New York Times* columnist William Safire obtained portions of Hoover's private files through the Freedom of Information Act. Alicia Darr had been engaged to Jack in 1951; the ambassador terminated the relationship over the young woman's Polish-Jewish background. In 1977 the former Miss Darr reluctantly told reporters that she and Jack, though engaged, had not had a sexual relationship: "He used to say to me 'I love you' and I used to say to him 'I love you too' but what does it mean?" This, of course, is impossible to believe. Darr also denied having received any money from the Kennedys. However, Edmund Purdom told reporters that his former wife had had a habit of waving a check around with a Kennedy signature. See *New York Times*, December 17, 1977; "Walter Scott's Personality Parade," *Parade Magazine*, in *St. Louis Post-Dispatch*, April 2, 1978; Heymann, *A Woman Named Jackie*, pp. 160–61. An unconvincing denial on Bobby's behalf is in Schlesinger, *Robert Kennedy and His Times*, p. 279.
6. *New York Times*, December 26, 1960; Sidey, "Joe Kennedy's Feelings About His Son," *Life*, December 19, 1960, p. 32; Sidey, *John F. Kennedy, President*, pp. 17–20.
7. O'Donnell and Powers, *"Johnny, We Hardly Knew Ye,"* p. 257.
8. Nixon, *Six Crises*, pp. 406–10; O'Donnell and Powers, *"Johnny, We Hardly Knew Ye,"* p. 258; *New York Times*, November 15, 1960.
9. O'Donnell and Powers, *"Johnny, We Hardly Knew Ye,"* pp. 259–62.
10. Parmet, *JFK*, p. 70; *New York Times*, November 19, 1960.
11. Ibid., November 26, 1960.
12. Ibid., November 24, 1960.
13. Ibid., November 25, 26, 27, 1960; O'Donnell and Powers, *"Johnny, We Hardly Knew Ye,"* pp. 263–64.
14. Birmingham, *Jacqueline Bouvier Kennedy Onassis*, p. 89; Shaw, *White House Nannie*, p. 78; O'Donnell and Powers, *"Johnny, We Hardly Knew Ye,"* p. 264; *New York Times*, December 10, 1960.
15. Ibid.; West, *Upstairs at the White House*, pp. 192–94.
16. Gallagher, *My Life with Jacqueline Kennedy*, pp. 62–63, 78; *New York Times*, November 26, 1960.
17. Parmet, *JFK*, pp. 72–74; Stephen E. Ambrose, *Eisenhower the President* (New York, 1984), pp. 606–7; *New York Times*, December 7, 1960; Galbraith, *Ambassador's Journal*, p. 9.
18. Sidey, "Joe Kennedy's Feelings About His Son," *Life*, December 19, 1960; p. 32; Kennedy, *Times to Remember*, p. 378.
19. Schlesinger, *A Thousand Days*, pp. 121–24; Parmet, *JFK*, p. 61; Galbraith, *Ambassador's Journal*, pp. 8–9.

20. Schlesinger, *A Thousand Days*, p. 127; Galbraith, *Ambassador's Journal*, p. 7. See O'Donnell and Powers, *"Johnny, We Hardly Knew Ye,"* p. 265.

21. Martin, *A Hero for Our Time*, p. 239; Sorensen, *Kennedy*, p. 260.

22. Lapham, *Money and Class in America*, p. 105.

23. Martin, *A Hero for Our Time*, pp. 227–28, 239–40; Bradlee, *Conversations with Kennedy*, p. 148; Mary McGrory, "The Right-Hand Men," in Lester Tanzer, ed., *The Kennedy Circle* (Washington, D.C., 1961), pp. 76–77; Exner, *My Story*, pp. 164, 166–68. When O'Donnell became a candidate for governor of Massachusetts in 1966, his campaign literature quoted Bobby Kennedy as saying, "There wasn't a major decision that was made by President Kennedy during the period of 1961 to November 22, 1963, that Ken O'Donnell did not share in." Leo Damore, *Senatorial Privilege: The Chappaquiddick Coverup* (Washington, D.C., 1988), p. 274.

24. *Robert Kennedy in his Own Words*, pp. 34–35; David Halberstam, *The Best and the Brightest*, pp. 10–17; Schlesinger, *A Thousand Days*, p. 129; O'Donnell and Powers, *"Johnny, We Hardly Knew Ye,"* pp. 265–66; Wofford, *Of Kennedys and Kings*, pp. 68–69; Parmet, *JFK*, p. 63; *New York Times*, December 2, 1960.

25. Wofford, *Of Kennedys and Kings*, p. 76.

26. Parmet, *JFK*, p. 69.

27. *Robert Kennedy in his Own Words*, pp. 34–36; Halberstam, *The Best and the Brightest*, p. 265.

28. Schlesinger, *A Thousand Days*, pp. 131–33; Wofford, *Of Kennedys and Kings*, pp. 70–71; O'Donnell and Powers, *"Johnny, We Hardly Knew Ye,"* pp. 267–69.

29. Schlesinger, *A Thousand Days*, pp. 135–36; Parmet, *JFK*, pp. 65–66; Sorensen, *Kennedy*, p. 252; Dean Acheson Oral History, JFK Library. Bobby later claimed that his father opposed Dillon. It seems highly unlikely that Jack would oppose his father on an appointment vital to the financial community. *Robert Kennedy in his Own Words*, pp. 39–40. Wofford observed that Dillon soon "became the cabinet member who was probably closest to the President and his family." Bobby named a son after him. Wofford, *Of Kennedys and Kings*, p. 77.

30. See Halberstam, *The Best and the Brightest*, pp. 56–81.

31. Wofford, *Of Kennedys and Kings*, pp. 78–85; Parmet, *JFK*, p. 68; *Robert Kennedy in his Own Words*, pp. 38–39; Martin, *Adlai Stevenson and the World*, pp. 551–65.

32. Parmet, *JFK*, p. 68; Schlesinger, *A Thousand Days*, pp. 139–40; *Robert Kennedy in his Own Words*, pp. 37–38.

33. Parmet, *JFK*, p. 68; Wofford, *Of Kennedys and Kings*, p. 81; Schlesinger, *A Thousand Days*, pp. 140–41; Dean Acheson and Charles Bohlen Oral Histories, JFK Library; *Robert Kennedy in his Own Words*, pp. 5–11, 37–38, 44–45, 268–69, 287–88.

34. *Robert Kennedy in his Own Words*, pp. 42–43, 74–77; Martin, "The Amazing Kennedys," *Saturday Evening Post*, September 7, 1957, pp. 19–20, 40, 46–48.

35. Bradlee, *Conversations with Kennedy*, p. 38; Wofford, *Of Kennedys and Kings*, p. 92. See Schlesinger, *A Thousand Days*, pp. 129, 141–42; Schlesinger, *Robert Kennedy and His Times*, pp. 246–51; Dean Acheson Oral History, JFK Library; Parmet, *JFK*, p. 64; Ben H. Bagdikian, "Honest Abe—The Vote-Getter," in Tanzer, *The Kennedy Circle*, pp. 229–30; Dickerson, *Among Those Present*, p. 58; *New York Times*, November 12, 16, 19, 23, 29, December 2, 1960.

36. Schlesinger, *Robert Kennedy and His Times*, pp. 251–54; Baker, *Wheeling and Dealing*, pp. 120–21.

37. Sullivan, *The Bureau*, pp. 48–49.

38. Schlesinger, *Robert Kennedy and His Times*, p. 279.

39. Sullivan, *The Bureau*, pp. 48–55; Schlesinger, *Robert Kennedy and His Times*, pp. 263, 273–80; Richard Gid Powers, *Secrecy and Power: The Life of J. Edgar Hoover* (New York, 1987), pp. 358–59; *Robert Kennedy in His Own Words*, pp. 119–35.

40. Ibid., pp. 41–42; Schlesinger, *A Thousand Days*, p. 144; Sorensen, *Kennedy*, p. 252; Wofford, *Of Kennedys and Kings*, pp. 89–90, 95–96; Don Oberdorfer and Walter Pincus, "Businessmen in Politics—Luther Hodges and J. Edward Day," in Tanzer, *The Kennedy Circle*, pp. 261–62; *New York Times*, December 16, 1960.

41. Schlesinger, *Robert Kennedy and His Times*, pp. 242–45; Schlesinger, *A Thousand Days*, pp. 130–31, 143–45; Parmet, *JFK*, p. 66; Wofford, *Of Kennedys and Kings*, pp. 89–90; Sorensen, *Kennedy*, p. 253; Oberdorfer and Pincus, "Businessmen in Politics," in Tanzer, *The Kennedy Circle*, p. 261; Bradlee, *Conversations with Kennedy*, p. 159.

42. See Sidney Hyman, "Inside the Kennedy 'Kitchen Cabinet,' " *New York Times Magazine*, March 5, 1961, pp. 27, 86–89; editorial, *New York Times*, December 18, 1960.

43. See editorial, ibid., December 17, 1960; William G. Carleton, "The Cult of Personality Comes to the White House," *Harper's Magazine*, December 1961, pp. 63–64; Manchester, *Portrait of a President*, p. 185; Sidey, *John F. Kennedy, President*, p. 15.

44. Broder, *The Party's Over*, p. 32.

45. David Brinkley, "The New Man," in Tanzer, *The Kennedy Circle*, p. xvi; Sorensen, *Kennedy*, pp. 252–54; Halberstam, *The Best and the Brightest*, pp. 53–54. See Schlesinger, *A Thousand Days*, pp. 728–29.

46. Jacques Barzun, *The House of Intellect* (New York, 1961), pp. 145–46.

47. Halberstam, *The Best and the Brightest*, p. 53.

48. Brinkley, "The New Men," in Tanzer, *The Kennedy Circle*, pp. xiv–xv.

49. Ibid., p. xv.

50. Lasky, *JFK: The Man and the Myth*, p. 23.

51. Galbraith, *Ambassador's Journal*, p. xv.

52. O'Donnell and Powers, *"Johnny, We Hardly Knew Ye,"* p. 274.

53. Arthur Schlesinger, Jr., *The Politics of Hope* (Boston, 1962), pp. 82, 86. See Lasky, *JFK: The Man and the Myth*, pp. 381–89. The Lewis article is in C. S. Lewis, *The Weight of Glory and Other Addresses* (Grand Rapids, Mich., 1965), pp. 55–66. Garry Wills later commented, "Kennedy did not liberate the intellectuals who praised him; he subverted them. He played to all that was weakest and worst in them. . . . Camelot was the opium of the intellectuals." Wills, *The Kennedy Imprisonment*, pp. 148–49. See also Decter, "Kennedyism," *Commentary*, January 1970, pp. 21–22.

54. Bradlee, *Conversations with Kennedy*, pp. 70, 127–28.

55. Davis, *The Kennedys*, p. 278.

56. Bradlee, *Conversations with Kennedy*, p. 124. See Lincoln, *My Twelve Years with John F. Kennedy*, pp. 248–49. Meader's gentle comedy infuriated Jackie. Gallagher, *My Life with Jacqueline Kennedy*, p. 177.

57. *Robert Kennedy in his Own Words*, p. 419.

58. Sherill, *The Last Kennedy*, pp. 35–36; Hersh, *The Education of Edward Kennedy*, pp. 196–99; Collier and Horowitz, *The Kennedys*, p. 255.

59. Exner, *My Story*, p. 197. The photographs follow page 152. See Bradlee, *Conversations with Kennedy*, p. 39.

60. Oleg Cassini, *In My Own Fashion: An Autobiography* (New York, 1987), pp. 195, 197, 202, 264–65, 297–330. Cassini became close to the first family and often spent hours with the president gossiping about women. Ibid., pp. 302–3, 324–25.

61. Gallagher, *My Life with Jacqueline Kennedy*, pp. 105–6; Davis, *The Kennedys*, p. 270; Birmingham, *Jacqueline Bouvier Kennedy Onassis*, p. 93.

62. Kelley, *Jackie Oh!*, pp. 105–6.

63. *New York Times*, November 11, 1960.

64. Kelley, *His Way*, p. 307.

65. Ibid., pp. 306–7.

66. Ibid., pp. 308–11.

67. Kennedy, *Times to Remember*, pp. 384–85; O'Donnell and Powers, *"Johnny, We Hardly Knew Ye,"* p. 278.

68. Dickerson, *Among Those Present*, p. 60.

69. *New York Times*, January 13, 21, 1961; Sorensen, *Kennedy*, pp. 240–48; Allen J. Matusow, *The Unraveling of America: A History of Liberalism in the 1960s* (New York, 1984), p. 30; Salinger, *With Kennedy*, pp. 108–9; Parmet, *JFK*, p. 82. See Kennedy, *Times to Remember*, p. 388.

70. O'Neill, *Man of the House*, pp. 101–3.

71. *New York Times*, January 21, 1961. President Warren G. Harding had said in 1923, "Think more of what you can do for your government than what your government can do for you." Robert K. Murray, *The Harding Era: Warren G. Harding and His Administration* (Minneapolis, 1969), p. 536.

72. *New York Times*, January 21, 1961.

73. Sorensen, *Kennedy*, p. 248. For another Sorensen-Kennedy speech that attracted much attention, see *New York Times*, January 10, 1961. Before a joint session of the Massachusetts legislature, Jack pledged to be guided by courage, judgment, integrity, and dedication.

74. Kennedy, *Times to Remember*, p. 388.

75. Davis, *The Kennedys*, pp. 260–62.

76. Letitia Baldrige, *Of Diamonds and Diplomats* (Boston, 1968), p. 153.

77. Collier and Horowitz, *The Kennedys*, p. 260.

78. *New York Times*, January 21, 1961.

79. Davis, *The Kennedys*, pp. 268–70.

80. Ibid., pp. 265–66.

81. Ibid., p. 270; Cf. Fay, *The Pleasure Of His Company*, pp. 93–96.

82. Kelley, *Jackie Oh!*, pp. 108, 115; Gallagher, *My Life with Jacqueline Kennedy*, pp. 87–88.

83. O'Donnell and Powers, *"Johnny, We Hardly Knew Ye,"* pp. 280–81. See Hugh Sidey, "Upstairs at the White House," *Time*, May 18, 1987, p. 20.

84. Davis, *The Kennedys*, pp. 271–2.

85. Davis, *The Kennedys*, p. 272; Kelley, *Jackie Oh!*, p. 116; Edwin M. Yoder, Jr., "Remembering Joe Alsop," *National Review*, November 10, 1989, p. 49; *New York Times*, January 22, 1961. I distrust the alleged quotation by Peter Lawford in Heymann, *A Woman Named Jackie*, p. 261. Lawford was consistently far too secretive to have made such a statement.

86. *New York Times*, January 22, 1961; West, *Upstairs at the White House*, pp. 197, 242.

87. Ibid., p. 195. See ibid., pp. 197–200, 205–13, 216–19, 229–30, 254–55; Gal-

lagher, *My Life with Jacqueline Kennedy*, pp. 120–27, 145, 237–41; Hugh Sidey, "The First Lady Brings History and Beauty to the White House," *Life*, September 1, 1961, p. 62; *New York Times*, February 15, 16, 1962; "Mrs. Kennedy's White House," *New York Times Magazine*, January 28, 1962, pp. 10–11; Perry Wolff, *A Tour of the White House with Mrs. John F. Kennedy* (New York, 1962), passim.

88. West, *Upstairs at the White House*, p. 233; Gallagher, *My Life with Jacqueline Kennedy*, pp. 164–65. See Cassini, *In My Own Fashion*, p. 304.

89. West, *Upstairs at the White House*, pp. 233–5.

90. Gallagher, *My Life with Jacqueline Kennedy*, pp. 111–12. In order to conceal the costs from the public (and perhaps from the president), the ambassador personally paid for the clothes designed by Oleg Cassini. Cassini, *In My Own Fashion*, p. 308; Gallagher, *My Life with Jacqueline Kennedy*, p. 156.

91. West, *Upstairs at the White House*, pp. 211–12, 231–32, 266–67; Salinger, *With Kennedy*, pp. 87–88.

92. Parmet, *JFK*, p. 110; Bradlee, *Conversations with Kennedy*, pp. 118–19.

93. Gallagher, *My Life with Jacqueline Kennedy*, pp. 124–25, 153–58, 217–27, 259–60, 273–74.

94. Bradlee, *Conversations with Kennedy*, pp. 119, 186–87.

95. Gallagher, *My Life with Jacqueline Kennedy*, p. 121; West, *Upstairs at the White House*, pp. 215, 229, 238, 244, 266. To help finance the restoration, Jackie came up with the idea of a White House guidebook and supervised the production of the publication in detail. It appeared first on July 4, 1962. The initial printing of 250,000 was sold out in three months, and two more printings appeared that same year. Heymann, *A Woman Named Jackie*, pp. 324–28.

96. West, *Upstairs at the White House*, p. 266; Salinger, *With Kennedy*, p. 75.

97. Bradlee, *Conversations with Kennedy*, pp. 106–7; Fay, *The Pleasure of His Company*, pp. 100–101.

98. West, *Upstairs at the White House*, pp. 202–3, 238; Gallagher, *My Life with Jacqueline Kennedy*, p. 111; Bradlee, *Conversations with Kennedy*, p. 100.

99. See Salinger, *With Kennedy*, pp. 89–97; Baldrige, *Diamonds and Diplomats*, pp. 228–29; Bradlee, *Conversations with Kennedy*, pp. 99–100, 209–12, 235–36.

100. West, *Upstairs at the White House*, pp. 236–38; Bradlee, *Conversations with Kennedy*, p. 187.

101. Ibid., p. 199.

102. Exner, *My Story*, pp. 215–22, 230–34, 238–56.

103. Nobile and Rosenbaum, "The Curious Aftermath of JFK's Best and Brightest Affair," *New Times Magazine*, p. 25. Lady Ottoline Violet Anne Morrell (1873–1938) was an English bohemian around whom prominent intellectuals gathered.

104. Ibid., p. 33.

105. *Washington Post*, February 23, 1976.

106. Bryant, *Dog Days at the White House*, pp. 4, 12–13, 22–25, 35–40, 62.

107. Kelley, *Jackie Oh!*, pp. 125–26.

108. "JFK and the Mobsters' Moll," *Time*, December 29, 1975, p. 12; Sidey, "Upstairs at the White House," *Time*, May 18, 1987, p. 20; Bergquist and Tretick, *A Very Special President*, pp. 5–6; Kelley, *Jackie Oh!*, p. 130; Parmet, *JFK*, p. 111; Lawford, *The Peter Lawford Story*, pp. 137–38.

109. Kelley, *Jackie Oh!*, pp. 141–42; Martin, *A Hero for Our Time*, pp. 292–93. See Gallagher, *My Life with Jacqueline Kennedy*, pp. 113, 153, 272.

110. Parmet, *JFK*, p. 112.

111. Exner, *My Story*, p. 253.

112. *New York Times*, April 12, 1976; Kelley, "The Dark Side of Camelot," *People*, February 29, 1988 p. 113.

113. "JFK and the Mobsters' Moll," *Time*, December 29, 1975, p. 12; Martin, *A Hero for Our Time*, pp. 376–77. See Larry King, *Tell It to the King* (New York, 1988), pp. 91–92, for a similar story.

114. Heymann, *A Woman Named Jackie*, p. 291. Heymann's book must, however, be handled with care. Secret Service officials have informed me that agent Marty Venker, quoted extensively by Heymann on pages 245, 278–82, did not serve President Kennedy. He worked for the service from 1971–81. Telephone interviews with Public Affairs official Jane Vezeris, August 22, 1989, and Archivist Joseph F. Kohler, September 1, 1989. The Secret Service files for the Kennedy administration are in the possession of the Kennedy Library and are closed.

115. Bryant, *Dog Days at the White House*, p. 38: Summers, *Goddess* pp. 223–25; "JFK and the Mobsters' Moll," *Time*, December 29, 1975, p. 12. At one point several Kennedy friends put money in a pool, held by the president, the funds to go to the first man who could have sex in the Lincoln Bedroom with a woman other than his wife. Peter Lawford accidentally chose a lesbian, who spurned his advances, for the contest. The actor pretended to have been successful, however, and Jack paid off. Lawford, *The Peter Lawford Story*, pp. 136–37.

116. Exner, *My Story*, pp. 243–45.

CHAPTER 12.   The First Major Decision

1. FDR haters would do well to read Merlin Gustafson and Jerry Rosenberg, "The Faith of Franklin Roosevelt," *Presidential Studies Quarterly* 19 (Summer 1989): 559–66.

2. Cf. Fred I. Greenstein, *The Hidden-Hand Presidency: Eisenhower as Leader* (New York, 1982), pp. 138–51.

3. Salinger, *With Kennedy*, p. 74; Sorensen, *Kennedy*, pp. 281–85, 389–92; Wofford, *Of Kennedys and Kings*, p. 134; Charles Bohlen Oral History, JFK Library (which observes the influence of Richard Neustadt's book *Presidential Power* on Kennedy's informal and direct style of administration; cf. Sorensen, *Kennedy*, p. 389); George Ball, *The Past Has Another Pattern: Memoirs* (New York, 1982), pp. 167–68. For views similar to Ball's, see W. W. Rostow, *The Diffusion of Power: An Essay in Recent History* (New York, 1972), p. 126, and U. Alexis Johnson Oral History, JFK Library.

4. Schlesinger, *A Thousand Days*, pp. 210–11.

5. See Sorensen, *Kennedy*, pp. 345–53.

6. *New York Times*, January 3, 5, 7, 9, 12, 24, 26, 27, 31, February 1, 2, 3, 4, 6, 1961; O'Neill, *Man of the House*, pp. 165–66; Sorensen, *Kennedy*, pp. 340–42. On Eisenhower and Congress, see Emmet John Hughes, *The Ordeal of Power* (New York, 1964), p. 112.

7. *New York Times*, January 5, 6, 9, 10, 11, May 7, June 17, August 8, 24, September 15, 17, 20, 1961.

8. See O'Neill, *Man of the House*, p. 175. See also Charles Halleck Oral History, JFK Library. Cf. Sorensen, *Kennedy*, pp. 356–57; Schlesinger, *A Thousand Days*, pp. 711–12.

9. Walt Rostow Oral History, JFK Library; Schlesinger, *A Thousand Days*, pp. 706–7; Kearns, *Lyndon Johnson and the American Dream*, pp. 164–65, 225–26.

10. Parmet, *JFK*, pp. 90, 92, 96–98; Lasky, *JFK: The Man and the Myth*, p. 636; Miroff, *Pragmatic Illusions*, p. 31; Charles U. Daley Oral History, JFK Library; David Burner, *John F. Kennedy and a New Generation* (Glenview, Ill., 1988), p. 141: Tom Wicker, *JFK and LBJ: The Influence of Personality upon Politics* (Baltimore, 1969), p. 141.

11. Roy Wilkins Oral History, JFK Library; Matusow, *The Unraveling of America*, pp. 62–70; Brauer, *John F. Kennedy and the Second Reconstruction*, pp. 62–69; Sorensen, *Kennedy*, pp. 473–82; Ball, *The Past Has Another Pattern*, p. 165; Victor S. Navasky, *Kennedy Justice* (New York, 1971), p. 245.

12. *New York Times*, February 7, 1961; Lasky, *JFK: The Man and the Myth*, pp. 647–51; Maxwell Taylor, *Swords and Plowshares* (New York, 1972), p. 205; Collier and Horowitz, *The Kennedys*, p. 517; *Robert Kennedy in his Own Words*, p. 305. Roger Hilsman, State Department director of intelligence and research from 1961 to 1963, later claimed that the "gap" was leaked to Senator Kennedy and others by members of the intelligence community. These experts, wrote Hilsman, argued that a gap did not exist at the time, but would develop in 1963. During the summer of 1961, spy satellites learned that the United States was far ahead of the Soviet Union in deployed ICBMs. *New York Times*, September 26, 1987. See Roswell Gilpatric Oral History, JFK Library.

13. *New York Times*, January 22, 1961. On early White House visitors and photographs, see Lincoln, *My Twelve Years with Kennedy*, p. 231, and Salinger, *With Kennedy*, p. 124.

14. *New York Times*, January 22, 1961; Parmet, *JFK*, p. 86; Salinger, *With Kennedy*, pp. 73, 139–44; Sorensen, *Kennedy*, pp. 322–26.

15. Bradlee, *Conversations with Kennedy*, pp. 69, 151–52; Martin, *A Hero for Our Time*, p. 280; Luella R. Hennessey, "Bringing Up the Kennedys," *Good Housekeeping*, August 1961, p. 118; Gallagher, *My Life with Jacqueline Kennedy*, p. 271. The Hennessey article is an interesting example of how far historical truth was being stretched at this time by Kennedy insiders.

16. Sorensen, *Kennedy*, p. 311.

17. See "The Kennedy 'Image'—How It's Built," *U.S. News & World Report*, April 9, 1962, pp. 56–69.

18. *Robert Kennedy in His Own Words*, p. 149.

19. Bradlee, *Conversations with Kennedy*, pp. 50–51, 108–18, 182–83, 204–5.

20. Martin, *A Hero for Our Time*, p. 285.

21. Arthur Krock, "Mr. Kennedy's Management of the News," *Fortune*, March 1963, p. 82.

22. Salinger, *With Kennedy*, pp. 72–73, 119–21, 129–31; Martin, *A Hero for Our Time*, p. 285; Sorensen, *Kennedy*, pp. 311–22. Bobby also reproved reporters for articles he disliked. The FBI questioned six newspapermen in connection with stories on the administration. Sorensen, Salinger, Schlesinger, Ethel Kennedy, and Jean Smith also pressured the press. Fletcher Knebel, "Kennedy vs. the Press," *Look*, August 28, 1962, pp. 17–21.

23. Salinger, *With Kennedy*, p. 119; Kelley, *Jackie Oh!*, pp. 144–45.

24. "The Closest Look Yet at JFK," *Life*, April 28, 1961, pp. 35–38.

25. Salinger, *With Kennedy*, pp. 113–15.

26. Lincoln, *My Twelve Years with Kennedy*, p. 237.

27. *Public Papers of the Presidents of the United States, John F. Kennedy, Containing the Public Messages, Speeches, and Statements of the President, January 20 to December 31, 1961* (Washington, D.C., 1962), pp. 19–28, hereafter cited as *Public Papers*, followed by the year in the three-volume series; James Reston in *New York Times*, January 31, 1961; Miroff, *Pragmatic Illusions*, p. 42.

28. *New York Times*, January 31, 1961.

29. See Miroff, *Pragmatic Illusions*, p. 42.

30. Sorensen, *Kennedy*, p. 634.

31. Wicker, *JFK and LBJ*, pp. 86–89; Bowles, *Promises to Keep*, pp. 444–45.

32. *Public Papers, 1961*, p. 6; Schlesinger, *A Thousand Days*, pp. 604–5.

33. *Public Papers, 1961*, pp. 134–35; Schlesinger, *A Thousand Days*, pp. 605–9; Sorensen, *Kennedy*, pp. 347, 531–32; Bowles, *Promises to Keep*, p. 449; *New York Times*, January 8, 9, 12, 31, March 5, 1961. On Reuss, see *Milwaukee Journal*, November 3, 1985.

34. *Public Papers, 1961*, pp. 134–35; Schlesinger, *A Thousand Days*, p. 202; Parmet, *JFK*, p. 221.

35. See Trumbull Higgins, *The Perfect Failure; Kennedy, Eisenhower, and the CIA at the Bay of Pigs* (New York, 1987), pp. 39–57; John Prados, *Presidents' Secret Wars: CIA and Pentagon Covert Operations Since World War II* (New York, 1986), pp. 171–88; Ambrose, *Eisenhower the President*, pp. 554–57, 583–84; Warren Hinckle and William W. Turner, *The Fish Is Red: The Story of the Secret War Against Castro* (New York, 1981), pp. 23–38. On Castro's early Marxism, see *New York Times*, December 23, 1961.

36. Higgins, *The Perfect Failure*, pp. 59–60; Hinckle and Turner, *The Fish Is Red*, pp. 38–41; Schlesinger, *A Thousand Days*, pp. 224–25.

37. On Bissell, see Peter Wyden, *Bay of Pigs: The Untold Story* (New York, 1979), pp. 9–19.

38. Higgins, *The Perfect Failure*, pp. 67–68. Cf. O'Donnell and Powers, *"Johnny, We Hardly Knew Ye,"* p. 306. See *New York Times*, November 19, 1960.

39. See Parmet, *JFK*, pp. 158–61; Sorensen, *Kennedy*, pp. 306–7; Schlesinger, *A Thousand Days*, p. 259; Charles Spalding Oral History, JFK Library.

40. Sorensen, *Kennedy*, pp. 295–96, 302–4.

41. Prados, *Presidents' Secret Wars*, p. 188; *New York Times*, November 19, 25, 1960.

42. Ibid., January 3, 5, 6, 1961.

43. Ibid., January 5, 6, 1961.

44. Ibid., January 5, 6, 7, 9, 1961.

45. Ibid., January 10, 1961.

46. Ambrose, *Eisenhower the President*, pp. 615–16.

47. Ibid., p. 557; Hinckle and Turner, *The Fish Is Red*, pp. 14, 34; Wyden, *Bay of Pigs*, pp. 24, 30–31, 38–45.

48. Schlesinger, *Robert Kennedy and His Times*, pp. 517–37. McNamara, however, once told Richard Goodwin that he favored the murder of Castro. "I mean it, Dick, it's the only way." Goodwin, *Remembering America*, p. 189.

49. See Sorensen, *Kennedy*, p. 295; *Robert Kennedy in His Own Words*, p. 240; Schlesinger, *Robert Kennedy and His Times*, p. 477; *New York Times*, February 5, 1982; June 24, 1983.

50. See Davis, *The Kennedys*, p. 247. Davis is especially effective on this issue and

on the post-Kennedy assassination cover-up by the Kennedys, the FBI, the CIA, and the Defense Department, a cover-up designed in part to conceal the plot to kill Castro.

51. See Senate Select Committee to Study Governmental Operations with Respect to Intelligence Activities (hereafter cited as Church Committee), *Interim Report: Alleged Assassination Plots Involving Foreign Leaders*, 94th Cong., 1st Sess. (1975), pp. 116–39, 181–89, 263–70, 324–26, 330–31; Davis, *The Kennedys*, pp. 286–90, 297, 319–20, 329–31, 460–65, 614–17; Thomas C. Paterson, "Fixation with Cuba: The Bay of Pigs, Missile Crisis, and Covert War Against Castro," in Thomas G. Paterson, ed., *Kennedy's Quest for Victory: American Foreign Policy, 1961–1963* (New York, 1989), p. 133: George Smathers Oral History, JFK Library; Kelley, "The Dark Side of Camelot," *People*, February 29, 1988, pp. 110–11; Thomas Powers, *The Man Who Kept the Secrets: Richard Helms and the CIA* (New York, 1980), p. 218. For another example of Jack's acting ability at this time and Schlesinger's apparent gullibility, see Schlesinger, *A Thousand Days*, pp. 275–76.

52. Ibid., p. 238; Higgins, *The Perfect Failure*, pp. 80–82, 84.

53. *New York Times*, February 1, March 1, 5, 7, 1961.

54. Higgins, *The Perfect Failure*, pp. 90–91; Schlesinger, *A Thousand Days*, pp. 239–40.

55. Ibid. pp. 240–42.

56. Ibid., pp. 242–43; Schlesinger, *Robert Kennedy and His Times*, pp. 487–88; Wyden, *Bay of Pigs*, p. 102.

57. Schlesinger, *A Thousand Days*, p. 243.

58. Ibid., pp. 247–50.

59. Salinger, *With Kennedy*, pp. 146–47; *New York Times*, March 16, 19, April 6, 10, 11, 1961; Schlesinger, *A Thousand Days*, pp. 259–62.

60. Ibid., pp. 240, 251; Haynes Johnson and Bernard M. Gwertzman, *Fulbright: The Dissenter* (Garden City, N.Y., 1968), pp. 174–75.

61. Bowles, *Promises to Keep*, pp. 326–29.

62. Schlesinger, *A Thousand Days*, p. 251.

63. Ibid., pp. 251–56; Higgins, *The Perfect Failure*, pp. 110–13; Wyden, *Bay of Pigs*, pp. 146–50; Stewart Alsop, "The Lessons of the Cuban Disaster," *Saturday Evening Post*, June 24, 1961, p. 69.

64. *Robert Kennedy in His Own Words*, p. 242; Schlesinger, *A Thousand Days*, p. 259; Wyden, *Bay of Pigs*, p. 165.

65. *New York Times*, April 6, 10, 11, 1961.

66. Salinger, *With Kennedy*, pp. 146–47; Schlesinger, *A Thousand Days*, pp. 259–62.

67. *New York Times*, April 10, 1961. One administration official said that the FBI "had checked out some of the stories [about anti-Castro training camps] and they didn't check out." Ibid., April 12, 1961. See Wyden, *Bay of Pigs*, pp. 153–55; Turner Catledge, *My Life and the Times* (New York, 1971), pp. 259–65.

68. *New York Times*, April 12, 1961.

69. *Public Papers, 1961*, pp. 258–59, 264–65.

70. *New York Times*, April 13, 1961.

71. *Public Papers, 1961*, p. 276.

72. Higgins, *The Perfect Failure*, pp. 125–26; *Robert Kennedy in His Own Words*, p. 241.

73. Schlesinger, *A Thousand Days*, pp. 269–70; *New York Times*, April 16, 1961; Bowles, *Promises to Keep*, p. 329.

74. Higgins, *The Perfect Failure*, pp. 129–30; Schlesinger, *A Thousand Days*, p. 268. A diversionary landing east of Guantanamo planned by the CIA had to be aborted. Leaders of the 170 exiles refused to land because of what they said was too much enemy activity in the area. See Higgins, *The Perfect Failure*, p. 126; *New York Times*, April 17, 1961.

75. Martin, *Adlai Stevenson and the World*, pp. 565, 624–28; Wyden, *Bay of Pigs*, pp. 185–90; *New York Times*, April 16, 1961; Charles Spalding Oral History, JFK Library.

76. *New York Times*, April 17, 1961; Higgins, *The Perfect Failure*, pp. 131–32.

77. Ibid., pp. 132–35; Schlesinger, *A Thousand Days*, pp. 273–74; Wyden, *Bay of Pigs*, pp. 196–206. See Powers, *The Man Who Kept the Secrets*, pp. 114–17.

78. Schlesinger, *A Thousand Days*, pp. 274–75; Higgins, *The Perfect Failure*, pp. 138–43.

79. *New York Times*, April 18, 1961; Higgins, *The Perfect Failure*, p. 145.

80. Martin, *Adlai Stevenson and the World*, pp. 628–29; *New York Times*, April 18, 1961.

81. *Public Papers, 1961*, pp. 132–33; *New York Times*, April 19, 1961.

82. Higgins, *The Perfect Failure*, pp. 146–48; "Cuba," *Time*, April 28, 1961, p. 23; Schlesinger, *A Thousand Days*, pp. 278–82.

83. Ibid., p. 285.

84. Ibid., pp. 285, 291; Dean Acheson Oral History, JFK Library.

85. Kennedy, *Times to Remember*, p. 400; Whalen, *The Founding Father*, p. 460; *Robert Kennedy in His Own Words*, p. 245; Bowles, *Promises to Keep*, p. 332; Richard Cardinal Cushing Oral History, JFK Library. See the recollections of Lem Billings in Collier and Horowitz, *The Kennedys*, p. 271. See also Clark Clifford Oral History, JFK Library, and O'Donnell and Powers, *"Johnny, We Hardly Knew Ye,"* p. 311.

86. *Public Papers, 1961*, pp. 304–6; *New York Times*, April 21, 1961.

87. Ibid.

88. Nixon, *RN*, pp. 288–91. Nixon accused Kennedy of being "soft" on the Communists in Richard M. Nixon, "Cuba, Castro and John Kennedy," *The Reader's Digest*, November 1964, pp. 283–84, 286, 288–92, 295, 297–300.

89. Ambrose, *Eisenhower the President*, pp. 638–39; Parmet, *JFK*, pp. 175–77; *New York Times*, April 23, 26, 1961.

90. Bowles, *Promises to Keep*, pp. 329–32.

91. *New York Times*, April 26, 1961.

92. Ibid., April 22, 23, 1961; *Robert Kennedy in His Own Words*, p. 244. See Schlesinger, *Robert Kennedy and His Times*, pp. 508–9.

93. Sidey, *John F. Kennedy, President*, p. 118.

94. "Cuba: The Consequences," *Newsweek*, May 1, 1961, pp. 27–28; Dickerson, *Among Those Present*, pp. 72–73; *New York Times*, April 23, 1961; Taylor, *Swords and Plowshares*, pp. 179–94. See Schlesinger, *Robert Kennedy and His Times*, pp. 480–94. Chester Bowles showed diplomats and others his memorandum opposing the Bay of Pigs invasion. The story reached the press, further damaging the Kennedy-Bowles relationship. U. Alexis Johnson Oral History, JFK Library.

95. Salinger, *With Kennedy*, pp. 155–59; Catledge, *My Life and the Times*, p. 264. Cf. O'Donnell and Powers, *"Johnny, We Hardly Knew Ye,"* p. 313.

96. Charles Spalding Oral History, JFK Library. See also Fay, *The Pleasure of His Company*, p. 189.

97. Goodwin, *Remembering America*, p. 183.

98. Davis, *The Kennedys*, p. 291; Sorensen, *Kennedy*, pp. 304–7.

99. Sorensen, *Kennedy*, p. 301; Sidey, *John F. Kennedy, President*, p. 120; "Inside Story of Cuba 'Fiasco,' " *U.S. News & World Report*, May 15, 1961, p. 76. Cf. Higgins, *The Perfect Failure*, pp. 165–68; Schlesinger, *A Thousand Days*, pp. 293–95; Taylor, *Swords and Plowshares*, pp. 191, 193–94. Kenny O'Donnell made a virtue of Kennedy's air strike decision! See O'Donnell and Powers, *"Johnny, We Hardly Knew Ye,"* pp. 309–10. See also Rostow, *The Diffusion of Power*, pp. 210–15. John H. Davis speculated that Kennedy withheld air support after learning that the attempts on Castro's life had been unsuccessful and that therefore the invasion would fail. Davis, *The Kennedys*, p. 297.

100. *Robert Kennedy in His Own Words*, p. 247. When Jack heard that Schlesinger was taking credit for being the only insider to oppose the Bay of Pigs, he told Red Fay: "Artie thinks he's going to write a history of this administration, but if he doesn't watch it he'll wind up writing a history of the White House furniture and nothing more than that." See Bradlee, *Conversations with Kennedy*, pp. 42–43; Wyden, *Bay of Pigs*, p. 305; Collier and Horowitz, *The Kennedys*, p. 290.

101. Schlesinger, *Robert Kennedy and His Times*, pp. 503–6, 575–79; O'Donnell and Powers, *"Johnny, We Hardly Knew Ye,"* pp. 310–13.

102. Wyden, *Bay of Pigs*, pp. 303–4; *New York Times*, December 20, 1962. Since this event occurred after the Cuban Missile Crisis, and the United States had pledged not to invade Cuba, White House sources soon assured reporters that the President was "speaking in general terms of the ultimate liberation of Cuba, without committing the United States to use its military force to achieve it." Ibid.

103. *Robert Kennedy in His Own Words*, pp. 248–49; Schlesinger, *Robert Kennedy and His Times*, p. 507; Chester Bowles Oral History, JFK Library; O'Donnell and Powers, *"Johnny, We Hardly Knew Ye,"* pp. 314–15.

104. Davis, *The Kennedys*, pp. 329–30; Church Committee, pp. 149–52, 166–69. See Schlesinger, *Robert Kennedy and His Times*, pp. 514–17, 521–22.

105. Davis, *The Kennedys*, pp. 329–30; Church Committee, pp. 149–52, 166–69; *Robert Kennedy in His Own Words*, pp. 376–79. See Schlesinger, *Robert Kennedy and His Times*, pp. 514–17, 521–22.

106. Ibid., pp. 574–75; Davis, *The Kennedys*, pp. 326–31; Powers, *The Man Who Kept the Secrets*, pp. 132–43.

107. See Church Committee, pp. 86–90, 170–76; Schlesinger, *Robert Kennedy and His Times*, pp. 582–602.

108. Ibid., p. 589.

CHAPTER 13.   A Militant Approach

1. See Schlesinger, *A Thousand Days*, pp. 323–29; Charles A. Stevenson, *The End of Nowhere: American Policy Toward Laos Since 1954* (Boston, 1972), pp. 6–7, 16–128.

2. Parmet, *JFK*, p. 81; Ambrose, *Eisenhower the President*, pp. 614–15; Rostow, *The Diffusion of Power*, pp. 44–49, 108–10; Sorensen, *Kennedy*, p. 640.

3. *Public Papers, 1961*, pp. 213–15.

4. Schlesinger, *A Thousand Days*, pp. 329–30.

5. Bowles, *Promises to Keep*, pp. 336–37.

6. Schlesinger, *A Thousand Days*, p. 332. See Stevenson, *The End of Nowhere*, p. 133.

7. *Public Papers, 1961*, pp. 213–15.

8. Sorensen, *Kennedy*, p. 643; O'Donnell and Powers, *"Johnny, We Hardly Knew Ye,"* pp. 302–3. See also the misleading recollection by Dean Rusk in William J. Rust, *Kennedy in Vietnam* (New York, 1985), p. 30.

9. Parmet, *JFK*, p. 146.

10. Schlesinger, *A Thousand Days*, pp. 332–33.

11. Ibid., pp. 333–34.

12. Parmet, *JFK*, p. 144.

13. Schlesinger, *A Thousand Days*, p. 333.

14. Nixon, *RN*, p. 290. General Douglas MacArthur had warned Kennedy about the Chinese. See Collier and Horowitz, *The Kennedys*, p. 519; Schlesinger, *Robert Kennedy and His Times*, pp. 759–60.

15. Sorensen, *Kennedy*, p. 644. Cf. O'Donnell and Powers, *"Johnny, We Hardly Knew Ye,"* p. 302.

16. *Robert Kennedy in His Own Words*, p. 247. See Sidey, *John F. Kennedy, President*, p. 190.

17. Stevenson, *The End of Nowhere*, pp. 151–52; U. Alexis Johnson Oral History, JFK Library.

18. Rust, *Kennedy In Vietnam*, pp. 73–77.

19. Parmet, *JFK*, p. 147.

20. See Church Committee, pp. 147, 156. Cf. Stevenson, *The End of Nowhere*, pp. 181–87.

21. Victor Marchetti and John D. Marks, *The CIA and the Cult of Intelligence* (New York, rev. ed., 1980), pp. 29, 109–10, 213–14, 285–86; William Colby, *Honorable Men: My Life in the CIA* (New York, 1978), pp. 191–202. Cf. Rostow, *The Diffusion of Power*, pp. 288–90.

22. George C. Herring, *America's Longest War: The United States and Vietnam, 1950–1975* (New York, 1979), pp. 10–11, 22; Neil Sheehan et al., *The Pentagon Papers, as Published by the New York Times* (New York, 1971), p. 10, hereafter cited as *Pentagon Papers*.

23. Ibid., pp. 15–19, 70–72, 87–91; Herring, *America's Longest War*, p. 72.

24. *Pentagon Papers*, pp. 21–25, 67–78; Herring, *America's Longest War*, p. 72.

25. John F. Kennedy, "America's Stake in Vietnam," *Vital Speeches* 22 (August 1, 1956): 617–19; Herring, *America's Longest War*, pp. 48–49.

26. *Pentagon Papers*, pp. 128–30.

27. Rust, *Kennedy in Vietnam*, pp. 34–36; Schlesinger, *A Thousand Days*, pp. 540–47; *Pentagon Papers*, pp. 79–82, 91–93, 126–27; Sidey, *John F. Kennedy, President*, p. 205; Sorensen, *Kennedy*, pp. 631–33. Insider Roswell Gilpatric said later that Kennedy dispatched the Americans "with a great deal of impatience. He showed at the very outset an aversion to sending more people out there." Roswell Gilpatric Oral History, JFK Library.

28. Herring, *America's Longest War*, pp. 79–80, 82; *Pentagon Papers*, pp. 94–97, 99, 140–41.

29. Ibid., pp. 97–101, 141–48; U. Alexis Johnson Oral History, JFK Library; Schlesinger, *A Thousand Days*, pp. 544–47; Rostow, *The Diffusion of Power*, pp. 272–78; Halberstam, *The Best and the Brightest*, pp. 192–213.

30. Herring, *America's Longest War*, pp. 81–82; Rust, *Kennedy in Vietnam*, pp. 54–56, 70–71; *Pentagon Papers*, p. 102.

31. *Robert Kennedy in His Own Words*, p. 264.

32. Bowles, *Promises to Keep*, pp. 342–67; *Robert Kennedy in His Own Words*, pp. 264–65; Herring, *America's Longest War*, pp. 82–83; *Pentagon Papers*, pp. 106–9, 148–53; Rostow, *The Diffusion of Power*, pp. 270–72; Schlesinger, *Robert Kennedy and His Times*, p. 761.

33. Schlesinger, *A Thousand Days*, p. 547; Schlesinger, *Robert Kennedy and His Times*, pp. 759–60; *Pentagon Papers*, p. 108; Parmet, *JFK*, pp. 178–79; Sidey, *John F. Kennedy, President*, p. 188; U. Alexis Johnson Oral History, JFK Library.

34. Ball, *The Past Has Another Pattern*, p. 366.

35. Rostow, *The Diffusion of Power*, p. 278.

36. Herring, *America's Longest War*, p. 84; Bradlee, *Conversations with Kennedy*, p. 58.

37. Herring, *America's Longest War*, p. 84; *Pentagon Papers*, pp. 108–9; Bradlee, *Conversations With Kennedy*, p. 58.

38. *Pentagon Papers*, p. 109; Rust, *Kennedy in Vietnam*, p. 59.

39. Ibid., pp. 60–64; Halberstam, *The Best and the Brightest*, p. 263.

40. Wise, *The Politics of Lying*, p. 57. Cf. Schlesinger, *Robert Kennedy and His Times*, pp. 761–62.

41. *Pentagon Papers*, pp. 109–11; Rust, *Kennedy in Vietnam*, pp. 71–73; Herring, *America's Longest War*, pp. 86–87.

42. *Pentagon Papers*, p. 110.

43. Rust, *Kennedy in Vietnam*, pp. 64–65. See Hilsman, *To Move a Nation*, p. 415.

44. *Pentagon Papers*, pp. 111–13; Hilsman, *To Move a Nation*, pp. 429–39. Cf. Schlesinger, *Robert Kennedy and His Times*, p. 765.

45. Hilsman, *To Move a Nation*, pp. 440–67.

46. Halberstam, *The Best and the Brightest*, pp. 258–61.

47. Hilsman, *To Move a Nation*, pp. 449–53, 463–67.

48. Ibid., pp. 446–47, 456–59; Halberstam, *The Best and the Brightest*, pp. 221–23, 227–32, 247–56; Schlesinger, *A Thousand Days*, pp. 983–85; Herring, *America's Longest War*, pp. 91–92.

49. Ibid., pp. 92–93; Halberstam, *The Best and the Brightest*, pp. 253, 256–57.

50. Schlesinger, *A Thousand Days*, pp. 346–47.

51. *Public Papers, 1961*, pp. 229–40, 396–406.

52. O'Donnell and Powers, *"Johnny, We Hardly Knew Ye,"* p. 323.

53. *Public Papers, 1961*, p. 406.

54. "Backache," *Life*, June 23, 1961, p. 51.

55. "Backache," *Time*, June 16, 1961, p. 15.

56. "Kennedy's Backache—How Bad It Really Is," *U.S. News & World Report*, June 19, 1961, pp. 40–41.

57. O'Donnell and Powers, *"Johnny, We Hardly Knew Ye,"* p. 326; "Gritted Teeth," *Newsweek*, June 19, 1961, 25; "The Presidency," *Time*, June 16, 1961, p. 13.

58. Fay, *The Pleasure of His Company*, pp. 175–76.

59. Parmet, *JFK*, pp. 121–24. See *New York Times*, December 25, 28, 1961. In March 1963, Jack was still complaining to Ben Bradlee of his continual back pain. Bradlee, *Conversations with Kennedy*, p. 150. See Saunders, *Torn Lace Curtain*, p. 193.

60. Heymann, *A Woman Named Jackie*, p. 308.

61. Ibid., p. 311.

62. Ibid., pp. 312–14.

63. See ibid, pp. 296–320; *New York Times*, December 4, 1972; Exner, *My Story*, pp. 263–65; Parmet, *JFK*, pp. 121, 183; Saunders, *Torn Lace Curtain*, p. 194.

64. Schlesinger, *A Thousand Days*, pp. 375, 380–81; *Public Papers, 1961*, pp. 412–14.

65. Parmet, *JFK*, pp. 185–86; "The Presidency," *Time*, June 9, 1961, 9; Wofford, *Of Kennedys and Kings*, p. 125.

66. O'Donnell and Powers, *"Johnny, We Hardly Knew Ye,"* pp. 328–31.

67. Charles de Gaulle, *Memoirs of Hope: Renewal and Endeavor* (New York, 1971), pp. 255–56. See Bohlen, *Witness to History*, pp. 479–80. Cf. Schlesinger, *A Thousand Days*, pp. 349–58, and the footnote in Schlesinger, *Robert Kennedy and His Times*, p. 759.

68. See *New York Times*, June 1, 2, 3, 1961; *Public Papers, 1961*, p. 433.

69. *New York Times*, June 1, 2, 1961; Birmingham, *Jacqueline Bouvier Kennedy Onassis*, pp. 101–2; O'Donnell and Powers, *"Johnny, We Hardly Knew Ye,"* pp. 326–28; "La Presidente," *Time*, June 9, 1961, p. 13; *Public Papers, 1961*, p. 429.

70. Abram Chayes and Charles Bohlen Oral Histories, JFK Library. See Bohlen, *Witness to History*, p. 480. See also the front page photograph of the Kennedys in the *New York Times*, June 2, 1961.

71. Ibid., June 4, 1961.

72. Collier and Horowitz, *The Kennedys*, p. 277.

73. Schlesinger, *A Thousand Days*, p. 367. See Abram Chayes Oral History, JFK Library.

74. Bohlen, *Witness to History*, pp. 481–82; Charles Bohlen Oral History, JFK Library. See Harold Macmillan, *Pointing the Way, 1959–1961* (London, 1972), p. 358. Cf. Schlesinger, *A Thousand Days*, pp. 366–67.

75. O'Donnell and Powers, *"Johnny, We Hardly Knew Ye,"* pp. 334–35; Schlesinger, *A Thousand Days*, p. 365.

76. *New York Times*, June 5, 1961.

77. O'Donnell and Powers, *"Johnny, We Hardly Knew Ye,"* pp. 336–37; Schlesinger, *A Thousand Days*, pp. 372–74.

78. *New York Times*, June 5, 6, 1961.

79. Edward Crankshaw, ed., *Khrushchev Remembers* (Boston, 1970), p. 458. Khrushchev, however, also wrote that Kennedy "impressed me as a better statesman than Eisenhower. Unlike Eisenhower, Kennedy had a precisely formulated opinion on every subject." See Salinger, *With Kennedy*, p. 182.

80. George Kennan Oral History, JFK Library.

81. Bowles, *Promises to Keep*, p. 342.

82. Charles Spalding Oral History, JFK Library; James Reston in the *New York Times*, June 6, 1961; *Robert Kennedy in His Own Words*, pp. 262–63.

83. Ibid., June 5, 1961.

84. Peter Lisagor Oral History, JFK Library. Cf. O'Donnell and Powers, *"Johnny, We Hardly Knew Ye,"* pp. 337–41, one of the least believable accounts in the entire volume.

85. Schlesinger, *A Thousand Days*, pp. 374–75; Bohlen, *Witness to History*, pp. 482–83.

86. *New York Times*, June 5, 6, 7, 1961.

87. Macmillan, *Pointing the Way*, p. 357; *Robert Kennedy in His Own Words*, p. 262; Collier and Horowitz, *The Kennedys*, p. 278. Alsop had written columns warning

against appeasement by the administration. See Abram Chayes Oral History, JFK Library.

88. *Public Papers, 1961*, pp. 441–46; *New York Times*, June, 7, 8, 1961.

89. Ibid., June 8, 9, 12, 1961; Robert M. Slusser, *The Berlin Crisis of 1961: Soviet-American Relations and the Struggle for Power in the Kremlin, June–November 1961* (Baltimore, 1973), pp. 5–6.

90. *New York Times*, June 16, 1961.

91. Schlesinger, *A Thousand Days*, pp. 381–85; Abram Chayes Oral History, JFK Library. See *New York Times*, July 18, 1961.

92. *Public Papers, 1961*, pp. 476–84.

93. Slusser, *The Berlin Crisis of 1961*, pp. 51–61; Schlesinger, *A Thousand Days*, pp. 385–90.

94. Ibid., pp. 390–91.

95. *Public Papers, 1961*, pp. 533–40. See Sidey, *John F. Kennedy, President*, pp. 186–93. Sorensen described this address as "more somber than any previous Presidential speech in the age of mutual nuclear capabilities." Sorensen, *Kennedy*, p. 592. Cf. Schlesinger, *Robert Kennedy and His Times*, p. 460.

96. Sidey, *John F. Kennedy, President*, p. 193; Parmet, *JFK*, p. 198; Schlesinger, *Robert Kennedy and His Times*, p. 461. Kennedy's concern for a federal civil defense program was announced initially in a May 25 address to Congress. See Sorensen, *Kennedy*, pp. 613–14.

97. See James Reston in *New York Times*, July 26, 1961; editorial, "Berlin in Perspective," and Eugene Rabinowitch, "A Scientist Looks at the Berlin Crisis," *New Republic*, August 7, 1961, pp. 2, 7–8.

98. See Davis, *The Kennedys*, p. 358.

99. *Robert Kennedy in His Own Words*, p. 277; Parmet, *JFK*, pp. 196–97; Stewart Alsop, "Kennedy's Grand Strategy," *Saturday Evening Post*, March 31, 1962, p. 14.

100. Slusser, *The Berlin Crisis of 1961*, pp. 107–14; Schlesinger, *A Thousand Days*, pp. 392–94. A Soviet diplomat said later that Khrushchev considered the July 25 speech a "warlike ultimatum." Salinger, *With Kennedy*, p. 192.

101. Slusser, *The Berlin Crisis of 1961*, pp. 67, 94; Parmet, *JFK*, p. 199.

102. Schlesinger, *A Thousand Days*, p. 395.

103. See ibid., pp. 395, 402; Sidey, *John F. Kennedy, President*, p. 195; Sorensen, *Kennedy*, pp. 593–94; *New York Times*, August 17, 1961. On de Gaulle, see *Robert Kennedy in His Own Words*, pp. 281–83.

104. Ibid.

105. Ibid., August 19, 1961; Robert Amory Oral History, JFK Library; Sidey, *John F. Kennedy, President*, pp. 195–200; Sorensen, *Kennedy*, p. 594.

106. Schlesinger, *A Thousand Days*, p. 397; *Robert Kennedy in His Own Words*, p. 284. See Bohlen, *Witness to History*, pp. 483–86; Slusser, *The Berlin Crisis of 1961*, pp. 131–32.

107. Slusser, *The Berlin Crisis of 1961*, pp. 160–69; *Public Papers, 1961*, pp. 580–81, 584–85.

108. Parmet, *JFK*, p. 201.

109. Sidey, *John F. Kennedy, President*, pp. 201–4; Sorensen, *Kennedy*, pp. 618–19.

110. Parmet, *JFK*, pp. 200–202; *Public Papers, 1961*, pp. 589–90; Slusser, *The Berlin Crisis of 1961*, pp. 387–91; *Robert Kennedy in His Own Words*, pp. 278–81. Cf. Khrushchev's speech reported in *New York Times*, October 29, 1961.

111. See Slusser, *The Berlin Crisis of 1961*, pp. 372–76, 399, 419, 422–23, 440–43; *New York Times*, October 28, 29, 1961.

112. *Public Papers, 1961*, pp. 618–26. See Salinger, *With Kennedy*, pp. 192–96.

113. See ibid, pp. 191–220; "What Kennedy Told the Russian People," *U.S. News & World Report*, December 11, 1961, pp. 84–90; Slusser, *The Berlin Crisis of 1961*, pp. 207–10; Sorensen, *Kennedy*, pp. 552–53.

114. At times Kennedy's advisers were even more militant. See Sidey, *John F. Kennedy, President*, p. 193. Unknown to the administration, during the crisis Khrushchev survived what seems to have been a series of attacks on his authority by Soviet hardliners. See Slusser, *The Berlin Crisis of 1961*, pp. 51–61, 151–52, 179–83, 191–92, 202, 205, 209, 250, 254–55, 264–82, 286–334, 355–58, 377–80, 387–91, 396–404, 423–43, 461–71.

115. Crankshaw, *Khrushchev Remembers*, pp. 458–60. Bobby later gave his brother credit for the easing of tension, claiming that through Bobby and a Soviet agent, the president asked Khrushchev to remove the tanks within twenty-four hours. *Robert Kennedy in His Own Words*, pp. 259–60.

116. Salinger, *With Kennedy*, p. 200; C. L. Sulzberger, "The Need to Choose Words Precisely," *New York Times*, September 16, 1961.

117. Sidey, *John F. Kennedy, President*, pp. 203–4. See Kennedy's news conference comments on nuclear war and negotiations in *Public Papers, 1961*, pp. 573–74, 576–78. See also Sorensen, *Kennedy*, pp. 621–26.

118. See Kennedy's press conference summary of his Administration's massive military buildup in *Public Papers, 1961*, pp. 658–59.

CHAPTER 14.   Seemingly Invulnerable

1. Manchester, *Portrait of a President*, p. 186; Martin, *A Hero for Our Time*, p. 404. The ambassador apparently did not visit the White House until after his stroke. Even then his visits were kept secret for fear that the press would charge the elder Kennedy with directing his son's activities. Rita Dallas and Jeanira Ratcliffe, *The Kennedy Case* (New York, 1973), p. 214. Dallas was the ambassador's private nurse for the last eight and one half years of his life. Her book is unusually frank for its time and consistently fascinating.

2. Collier and Horowitz, *The Kennedys*, pp. 275–76.

3. Schlesinger, *Robert Kennedy and His Times*, p. 632.

4. *Robert Kennedy in His Own Words*, p. 309.

5. Dallas and Ratcliffe, *The Kennedy Case*, p. 147.

6. Martin, *A Hero for Our Time*, p. 300. See Exner, *My Story*, pp. 52, 92.

7. Parmet, *Jaek*, pp. 110–12; "Care and Feeding of the Kennedy Image," *U.S. News & World Report*, September 9, 1963, pp. 92–93; Whalen, *The Founding Father*, pp. 455–56; Salinger, *With Kennedy*, pp. 103–5.

8. Hersh, *The Education of Edward Kennedy*, p. 210.

9. Ibid., p. 232.

10. Ibid., p. 205.

11. See Whalen, *The Founding Father*, pp. 461–65; Hersh, *The Education of Edward Kennedy*, pp. 199–242; Saunders, *Torn Lace Curtain*, pp. 128–29, 161–62; Kennedy, *Times to Remember*, pp. 427–33. Bobby later admitted that his father was responsible for

Teddy's candidacy, "just as I would never have been Attorney General if it hadn't been for him." *Robert Kennedy in His Own Words*, p. 328.

12. Saunders, *Torn Lace Curtain*, pp. 108–15; Collier and Horowitz, *The Kennedys*, pp. 286–88. To conceal Rose's insensitivity, the story soon appeared that the ambassador had told his wife not to call a physician. See Schlesinger, *Robert Kennedy and His Times*, p. 632, and Cameron, *Rose*, p. 181. While carefully attempting to exonerate herself in *Times to Remember*, pp. 416–21, Rose chose not to repeat that tale.

13. Lincoln, *My Twelve Years with John F. Kennedy*, pp. 286–89; *New York Times*, December 20, 23, 24, 25, 1961.

14. Saunders, *Torn Lace Curtain*, pp. 123, 141–42, 170; Dallas and Ratcliffe, *The Kennedy Case*, pp. 109, 145.

15. *Robert Kennedy in His Own Words*, p. 309.

16. Dallas and Ratcliffe, *The Kennedy Case*, p. 144.

17. Saunders, *Torn Lace Curtain*, pp. 121–22.

18. Ibid., pp. 34–35, 49–50, 124, 182–86, 264; Dallas and Ratcliffe, *The Kennedy Case*, pp. 71, 219–20; Saunders, *Torn Lace Curtain*, 151–54.

19. Dallas and Ratcliffe, *The Kennedy Case*, pp. 73; Saunders, *Torn Lace Curtain*, pp. 151–54; Cameron, *Rose*, p. 181.

20. Saunders, *Torn Lace Curtain*, p. 131.

21. See Exner, *My Story*, pp. 248–49.

22. Schlesinger, *A Thousand Days*, pp. 732–33; *Public Papers, 1962*, p. 347. See *Robert Kennedy in His Own Words*, pp. 349–50.

23. See Arthur and Barbara Gelb, "Culture Makes a Hit at the White House," *New York Times Magazine*, January 28, 1962, pp. 9, 64; Schlesinger, *A Thousand Days*, pp. 729–38.

24. Ibid., p. 738.

25. O'Donnell and Powers, *"Johnny, We Hardly Knew Ye,"* p. 427; Bradlee, *Conversations with Kennedy*, pp. 52, 55, 137, 158, 198, 222; Charles Spalding Oral History, JFK Library; Sorensen, *Kennedy*, p. 387; Heymann, *A Woman Named Jackie*, pp. 370–71; Sidey, *John F. Kennedy, President*, p. 229.

26. Heymann, *A Woman Named Jackie*, p. 347; Peter Lisagor Oral History, JFK Library. See Lasky, *JFK: The Man and the Myth*, p. 209.

27. Fay, *The Pleasure of His Company*, pp. 101–2. The chief usher at the White House later wrote that Jackie tried to bring her husband "into her world of the arts." West, *Upstairs at the White House*, p. 239.

28. Martin, *A Hero for Our Time*, p. 364. Cf. Henry Luce's extravagant praise for Jack's "impromptu" remarks at a university graduation ceremony in 1961. "Anvil or Hammer?" *Time*, October 20, 1961, pp. 42–43.

29. Davis, *The Kennedys*, p. 392; West, *Upstairs at the White House*, pp. 254–60.

30. See ibid., pp. 259–60; Birmingham, *Jacqueline Bouvier Kennedy Onassis*, pp. 108–9; *New York Times*, July 12, 1961.

31. See Birmingham, *Jacqueline Bouvier Kennedy Onassis*, pp. 109–10; *New York Times*, May 20, 1962.

32. Summers, *Goddess*, pp. 147–48, 187–94, 198–204, 242–43, 268–70.

33. Ibid., pp. 270–72, 278, 296; Schlesinger, *Robert Kennedy and His Times*, p. 636. The psychiatrist's daughter was Joan Greenson. See her interview in the important documentary film *The Last Days of Marilyn Monroe*, hereafter cited as *TLD*.

34. Summers, *Goddess*, pp. 214–15.

35. Ibid., pp. 215–18, 220–28; Peter Summers interview in *TLD*.

36. Summers, *Goddess* (1986), pp. 429–30.

37. See ibid., pp. 425–29; Summers, *Goddess*, pp. 225, 239, 250. See also the Jeanne Carmen interview in *TLD*.

38. Summers, *Goddess*, pp. 226–27.

39. Ibid., p. 286; Speriglio, *The Marilyn Conspiracy*, p. 44. Anthony Summers revealed in 1986 that ABC and BBC producers, in the course of their research, learned that Bobby had had extramarital affairs with at least four women. One was the wife of a key Kennedy aide. Summers, *Goddess* (1986), p. 427.

40. Summers, *Goddess*, pp. 233–39.

41. Ibid., pp. 229–33, 262. See Kelley, *His Way*, pp. 266, 287–95, 312.

42. Summers, *Goddess*, pp. 257–58; Kelley, *His Way*, pp. 316–22; Davis, *The Kennedys*, p. 315. It was later revealed that a federal wiretap overheard Giancana lieutenant John Roselli telling mob associates openly about Campbell and her trysts with the president. "JFK and the Mobsters' Moll," *Time*, December 29, 1975, p. 10.

43. Summers, *Goddess*, pp. 327–30. Cf. O'Donnell and Powers, *"Johnny, We Hardly Knew Ye,"* pp. 432–33.

44. See Exner, *My Story*, pp. 244–52, 272–75, passim.

45. Kelley, *His Way*, pp. 320, 330.

46. Kelley, "The Dark Side of Camelot, " *People*, February 29, 1988, p. 113.

47. John P. Roche, "The Second Coming of RFK," *National Review*, July 22, 1988, pp. 32–33.

48. Summers, *Goddess*, pp. 258–60.

49. Ibid., pp. 260–65, 364–66; Summers, *Goddess* (1986), pp. 432–36, 446; Speriglio, *The Marilyn Conspiracy*, pp. 202–11; John Danoff and Ralph de Toledano interviews in *TLD*

50. Summers, *Goddess*, pp. 265–67; Speriglio, *The Marilyn Conspiracy*, pp. 202–3. Two Hoffa associates later claimed that Bobby was seeing Marilyn as early as 1957 and that Hoffa owned several tapes containing proof of their intimacy. Max Block and Chuck O'Brien interviews in *TLD*.

51. See Summers, *Goddess*, pp. 261, 286, 292; Summers, *Goddess* (1986), pp. 443–44; Arthur James interview in *TLD*.

52. Summers, *Goddess*, pp. 284–86, 293–97.

53. Ibid., pp. 281–97, 303; Speriglio, *The Marilyn Conspiracy*, pp. 33–34, 47–48, 78, 144–47, 206. According to Slatzer and Deborah Gould, who attributed her information to her husband Peter Lawford, Monroe had scheduled a press conference for August 6 and intended to reveal everything she knew about Jack and Bobby. Robert Slatzer and Deborah Gould interviews in *TLD*. I am inclined to doubt both Slatzer and Gould on this and certain other matters.

54. Summers, *Goddess*, pp. 314–16, 337, 364; Speriglio, *The Marilyn Conspiracy*, pp. 88, 175–77; Tom Reddin interview in *TLD*. See Saunders, *Torn Lace Curtain*, p. 130, for a description of the stunned reaction at Hyannis Port when news arrived of Monroe's death. In his *TLD* interview, Saunders said that the whole house was "like a morgue."

55. Summers, *Goddess*, pp. 303–56; Summers, *Goddess* (1986), pp. 438–45; Speriglio, *The Marilyn Conspiracy*, pp. 58–60, 203–7.

56. Summers, *Goddess*, pp. 334–36, 364; Speriglio, *The Marilyn Conspiracy*, pp. 104, 122–23. Hoover privately attempted to intimidate Bobby regularly by giving him

information about himself and his family and friends. He even had the attorney general check out at least one allegation involving the president and women. During the Johnson administration, Hoover sent material on Bobby to the Oval Office, and Johnson read it to McNamara. *Robert Kennedy in His Own Words*, pp. 128–32.

57. Summers, *Goddess*, p. 341.

58. Ibid., pp. 153–54, 307–9, 338–40.

59. Ibid., pp. 318–25, 331–32.

60. Ibid., pp. 317, 328–29. Summers, *Goddess* (1986), p. 441. Bobby later acknowledged that he and Parker "had a friendly relationship." *Robert Kennedy in His Own Words*, p. 257.

61. Summers, *Goddess*, p. 337.

62. Ibid., pp. 362–63.

63. Ibid., p. 362.

64. Ibid., pp. 362–66. In May 1962 Bobby agreed not to prosecute Giancana in a wiretapping case due to the mobster's involvement with the CIA. In 1963 the attorney general intervened to block government cross-examination of Giancana after the mobster, in an unprecedented action, sought a court injunction to stop intensive FBI harassment. Again, Bobby did not want the Mafia don's connections to Cuba made public. Under questioning, Giancana might also talk about Campbell and the 1960 campaign, of course. When an appeals court permitted the resumption of FBI surveillance without his testimony, Giancana exclaimed to his lawyer, "They can't do this to me, I'm working for the government." See ibid., p. 292; Davis, *The Kennedys*, pp. 335–39. For more on Bobby and Monroe, see Summers, *Goddess*, pp. 204–6, 242–44, 330–31, 350–53; Summers, *Goddess* (1986), p. 436; John Bates, William Woodfield, Sam Yorty, Jack Clemmons, Ward Wood, Eunice Murray interviews, *TLD*; Speriglio, *The Marilyn Conspiracy*, pp. 11–18, 25, 118–22, 196–97, 214. Cf. Lawford, *The Peter Lawford Story*, pp. 162–68. I strongly distrust the extraordinarily frank and detailed statements attributed to Lawford in Heymann, *A Woman Named Jackie*, pp. 368–70.

65. The taped remark by Greenson appears in *TLD*.

66. Summers, *Goddess*, p. 213; Schlesinger, *Robert Kennedy and His Times*, pp. 532–34, 636–38, 647–49. Cf. Parmet, *JFK*, p. 304.

CHAPTER 15.   Cold and Deliberate

1. Eisenhower had batted .647 in his first two years. See *Congress and the Nation*, pp. 21, 44–45; Parmet, *JFK*, p. 206.

2. Sorensen, *Kennedy*, p. 345. See *Robert Kennedy in His Own Words*, p. 51.

3. Parmet, *JFK*, pp. 207–8; Charles U. Daly and Allen J. Ellender Oral Histories, JFK Library; Sorensen, *Kennedy*, pp. 339–53, 356–57; Ralph A. Dungen in Emmet John Hughes, *The Living Presidency: The Resources and Dilemmas of the American Presidential Office* (New York, 1973), p. 328; Sidey, *John F. Kennedy, President*, p. 346–47; David Burner and Thomas R. West, *The Torch Is Passed: The Kennedy Brothers and American Liberalism* (New York, 1984), pp. 187–89.

4. Sorensen, *Kennedy*, pp. 341–52; Parmet, *JFK*, pp. 206–9; *Robert Kennedy in His Own Words*, pp. 51, 111; Mike Mansfield Oral History, JFK Library.

5. See *Congress and the Nation*, pp. 45–46; Parmet, *JFK*, p. 206. Cf. George C. Edwards III, *At the Margins: Presidential Leadership of Congress* (New Haven, 1989),

pp. 18–33, 40–43, 48–50, 71, 76, 129, 161, 169–78, 188. Through exhaustive and sometimes controversial recalculations of Congressional voting on issues favored by recent presidents (issues on which they "took a stand"), Edwards concluded that Kennedy enjoyed more success with Congress than virtually anyone—then or since—has believed. Edwards did not, however, attribute this success to Kennedy's legislative skills. Indeed, the author concluded (p. 211): "Presidential legislative skills are not closely related to presidential support in Congress. . . . In essence, a president's legislative skills operate in an environment largely beyond the president's control. In most instances presidents exercise them at the margins of coalition building, not at the core. . . ."

6. See *Congress and the Nation*, p. 378; Sorensen, *Kennedy*, pp. 443–48; *New York Times*, April 11, 1962.

7. Sorensen, *Kennedy*, p. 448; David McDonald Oral History, JFK Library; *Robert Kennedy in His Own Words*, pp. 332–33.

8. Bradlee, *Conversations with Kennedy*, pp. 81–82. The president had long conversations with Deputy Secretary of Defense Roswell L. Gilpatric, trying to understand businessmen, Roger Blough in particular. Gilpatric recalled, "He would ask about the banking community and different people in the business world, and many of his questions were very naive because, obviously, what he'd learned from his father was . . . only one slant on the thing." Roswell L. Gilpatric Oral History, JFK Library. See *Robert Kennedy in His Own Words*, pp. 204, 351.

9. See Sidey, *John F. Kennedy, President*, pp. 246–47.

10. See Schlesinger, *Robert Kennedy and His Times*, p. 434; *Robert Kennedy in His Own Words*, pp. 333–34. During the Thousand Days, the president also ordered wiretaps on at least one congressman, and the administration got the Internal Revenue Service to audit groups it wanted to harass. Burner, *John F. Kennedy*, p. 129.

11. Ibid., pp. 334–35; Sidey, *John F. Kennedy, President*, pp. 248–50.

12. Bradlee, *Conversations with Kennedy*, pp. 76–8.

13. See the summary in *New York Times*, April 23, 1962. A study published the following year suggested that the price rollback had to do more with market conditions and insufficient demand than pressure from the White House. See Grant McConnell, *Steel and the Presidency, 1962* (New York, 1963), pp. 104–15. This was the position taken by steel executives in 1962. Cf. Sorensen, *Kennedy*, pp. 456–58.

14. *Robert Kennedy in His Own Words*, p. 335.

15. Schlesinger, *A Thousand Days*, pp. 638–39; Parmet, *JFK*, p. 239; Schlesinger, *Robert Kennedy and His Times*, p. 437; Martin, *A Hero for Our Time*, p. 387; Sorensen, *Kennedy*, p. 461; Jim Heath, *John F. Kennedy and the Business Community* (Chicago, 1969), pp. 69–70.

16. Schlesinger, *A Thousand Days*, p. 641. See *Robert Kennedy in His Own Words*, pp. 337–38.

17. Schlesinger, *A Thousand Days*, p. 639.

18. *Public Papers, 1961*, pp. 86–87, 708, 773–75; Matusow, *The Unraveling of America*, pp. 42–47. Presidential scholar Louis W. Koenig has observed: "No President can be said to be antibusiness. . . . At the very least, Presidents desire to rouse business confidence in their administrations." Koenig, *The Chief Executive*, pp. 266–67.

19. *Public Papers, 1962*, pp. 331–33, 336; Parmet, *JFK*, pp. 242–43; Sidey, *John F. Kennedy, President*, pp. 254–57.

20. Schlesinger, *A Thousand Days*, pp. 645–47; Matusow, *The Unraveling of America*, p. 50; *Public Papers, 1962*, pp. 470–75.

21. Sorensen, *Kennedy*, pp. 426–27.

22. Matusow, *The Unraveling of America*, p. 50.

23. Ibid., pp. 50–51; Parmet, *JFK*, pp. 245–46. The president secured illegal access to secret tax returns. At one point he told friends about the sums paid by multimillionaires J. Paul Getty and H. L. Hunt. When Ben Bradlee mentioned what he and his wife had paid the previous year, Jack replied, "The tax laws really screw people in your bracket, buddy boy." Bradlee, *Conversations with Kennedy*, p. 218.

24. Matusow, *The Unraveling of America*, p. 51–55.

25. *Robert Kennedy in His Own Words*, p. 301.

26. Matusow, *The Unraveling of America*, p. 33. See Heath, *John F. Kennedy and the Business Community*, pp. 66–85, 124–29; Seymour E. Harris, *Economics of the Kennedy Years and a Look Ahead* (New York, 1964), esp. pp. 17–20, 23, 55–65. The tax cut, minus reforms urged by liberals, passed in 1964. Matusow (p. 59) notes, "Johnson reaped the political rewards of what Kennedy had sown." Wall Street and the major corporations strongly supported LBJ in the election of 1964.

27. See Heath, *John F. Kennedy and the Business Community*, pp. 75–76. Cf. Sorensen, *Kennedy*, p. 464: "John Kennedy was no more probusiness than he was prolabor." See also Schlesinger, *A Thousand Days*, p. 639, for a sympathetic appraisal of the 1963 price increases.

28. Brauer, *John F. Kennedy and the Second Reconstruction*, pp. 30–60.

29. *Robert Kennedy in His Own Words*, pp. 64–68. Bobby added (p. 64), however, that "as I was growing up, I suppose two out of my four best friends were Negroes."

30. Arthur Krock Oral History, JFK Library; Krock, *Memoirs*, p. 340.

31. Sorensen, *Kennedy*, p. 471. Schlesinger recalled that civil rights activists in the late 1950s considered Kennedy sympathetic but detached. Martin Luther King, Jr., had a similar impression after breakfasting with Jack a month before the 1960 Democratic National Convention. Schlesinger, *A Thousand Days*, p. 928.

32. Brauer, *John F. Kennedy and the Second Reconstruction*, pp. 46, 68, 84, 220; Schlesinger, *A Thousand Days*, pp. 932–33.

33. See Brauer, *John F. Kennedy and the Second Reconstruction*, pp. 77, 84–85; Wofford, *Of Kennedys and Kings*, p. 144; Schlesinger, *A Thousand Days*, pp. 933–35. "The Kennedys viewed voting litigation—a strategy of moderation, compromise, and confrontation avoidance—as the antithesis of direction action." Kenneth O'Reilly, *"Racial Matters": The FBI's Secret File on Black America, 1960–1972* (New York, 1989), p. 49.

34. *Robert Kennedy in His Own Words*, pp. 78–79, 204.

35. Ibid., pp. 154–56; Wofford, *Of Kennedys and Kings*, pp. 124, 126; Brauer, *John F. Kennedy and the Second Reconstruction*, pp. 207–11. Kennedy also listened to his economic advisers' worries that a presidential order might decrease housing starts and damage economic growth. Burke Marshall Oral History, JFK Library.

36. *Robert Kennedy in His Own Words*, pp. 148–49.

37. Ibid., pp. 150–52. See Brauer, *John F. Kennedy and the Second Reconstruction*, pp. 72–73, 79–83, 147–51.

38. See Schlesinger, *A Thousand Days*, pp. 938–39; *Robert Kennedy in His Own Words*, pp. 157–58; Theodore M. Hesburgh Oral History, JFK Library; Wofford, *Of Kennedys and Kings*, pp. 160–64; O'Reilly, *"Racial Matters"*, pp. 69–77.

39. O'Reilly, *"Racial Matters"*, pp. 50, 61–69, 79–81; Navasky, *Kennedy Justice*, pp. 98–99; *Robert Kennedy in His Own Words*, pp. 98–99, 102–7, 138–39, 149–50.

40. Navasky, *Kennedy Justice*, p. 118.

41. Schlesinger, *A Thousand Days*, p. 931; O'Reilly, *"Racial Matters"*, pp. 97–99; *Robert Kennedy in His Own Words*, pp. 82–84. According to Bobby, he and his brother first learned of the Freedom Riders from newspaper accounts.

42. Ibid., pp. 85–86.

43. Ibid., pp. 87–88.

44. Ibid., pp.88–89.

45. Ibid., pp. 92–93; Brauer, *John F. Kennedy and the Second Reconstruction*, p. 111. For a detailed account of the Freedom Riders' activities and the federal response, see Burke Marshall Oral History, JFK Library.

46. *Public Papers, 1961*, p. 391. See Miroff, *Pragmatic Illusions*, p. 235.

47. Wofford, *Of Kennedys and Kings*, pp. 125–26.

48. *New York Times*, May 25, 1961; *Robert Kennedy in His Own Words*, pp. 77–79, 97–101. Eastland and other Southern Congressional leaders had strongly supported Kennedy's nomination for attorney general. In part this stemmed from Bobby's investigations of labor unions.

49. Wofford, *Of Kennedys and Kings*, pp. 155–56.

50. Ibid., p. 156.

51. Parmet, *JFK*, p. 255; Wofford, *Of Kennedys and Kings*, p. 157.

52. Brauer, *John F. Kennedy and the Second Reconstruction*, pp. 111–12, 127.

53. See *Robert Kennedy in His Own Words*, pp. 98–99, 201. See also Brauer, *John F. Kennedy and the Second Reconstruction*, pp. 110–11, 152–53, 157–68; Miroff, *Pragmatic Illusions*, pp. 245–46.

54. See Brauer, *John F. Kennedy and the Second Reconstruction*, pp. 112–25; *Robert Kennedy in His Own Words*, pp. 107–19. Between April 1, 1962, and November 1, 1964, 688,800 blacks were registered. Parmet, *JFK*, p. 256.

55. Brauer, *John F. Kennedy and the Second Reconstruction*, pp. 108–9; Wofford, *Of Kennedys and Kings*, p. 157; *Robert Kennedy in His Own Words*, p. 98.

56. Roy Wilkins Oral History, JFK Library.

57. Matusow, *The Unraveling of America*, pp. 67–68.

58. Brauer, *John F. Kennedy and the Second Reconstruction*, pp. 131–32, 134.

59. Ibid., pp. 132–37; Burke Marshall Oral History, JFK Library.

60. *Robert Kennedy in His Own Words*, pp. 149–50, 202. In early 1962 Bobby privately recommended black Judge William H. Hastie to be the administration's first Supreme Court appointee. He changed his mind when faced with off-the-record objections from Court members Earl Warren and William O. Douglas, who opposed Hastie's conservatism. Moreover, Bobby said later, "I think a lot of people in the White House were opposed to having a Negro." Jack selected Byron White, who accepted the appointment. Ibid., pp. 115–16.

61. Matusow, *The Unraveling of America*, p. 76; Brauer, *John F. Kennedy and the Second Reconstruction*, pp. 154–56, 168–79.

62. *Public Papers, 1962*, pp. 592–93.

63. Matusow, *The Unraveling of America*, p. 76; Brauer, *John F. Kennedy and the Second Reconstruction*, pp. 154–56, 168–79.

64. *Public Papers, 1962*, pp. 404, 572.

65. Brauer, *John F. Kennedy and the Second Reconstruction*, pp. 138–39. See Charles U. Daley Oral History, JFK Library.

66. Brauer, *John F. Kennedy and the Second Reconstruction*, pp. 143–44.

67. Schlesinger, *Robert Kennedy and His Times*, p. 341.

68. Schlesinger, *Robert Kennedy and His Times*, pp. 340–44; *Robert Kennedy in His Own Words*, pp. 159–60.

69. "Presidential Recordings, Transcripts, Integration of the University of Mississippi," JFK Library.

70. Ibid.

71. Schlesinger, *Robert Kennedy and His Times*, pp. 345–47; Sorensen, *Kennedy*, pp. 484–86; *Public Papers, 1962*, pp. 726–28.

72. Sorensen, *Kennedy*, pp. 486–87.

73. Schlesinger, *Robert Kennedy and His Times*, pp. 347–50; *Robert Kennedy in His Own Words*, pp. 161–69; Burke Marshall Oral History, JFK Library; Edwin Guthman, *We Band of Brothers* (New York, 1971), pp. 198, 200–205.

74. Brauer, *John F. Kennedy and the Second Reconstruction*, pp. 196–204; Sorensen, *Kennedy*, p. 488; *Robert Kennedy in His Own Words*, pp. 167–69. Cf. Schlesinger, *Robert Kennedy and His Times*, pp. 350–51. Tapes of White House discussions during the crisis reveal the president requesting legal information about the possible arrest of Governor Barnett. Jack favored the arrest of right-wing extremist Major General Edwin A. Walker, who appeared at the university and incited the mob. He said at one point, "Imagine that son of a bitch having been commander of a division." "Presidential Recordings, Transcripts, Integration of the University of Mississippi," JFK Library.

75. Schlesinger, *Robert Kennedy and His Times*, pp. 351–52. See also Miroff, *Pragmatic Illusions*, pp. 248–49, and Brauer, *John F. Kennedy and the Second Reconstruction*, p. 202.

76. Burke Marshall Oral History, JFK Library; Brauer, *John F. Kennedy and the Second Reconstruction*, pp. 206–11; Sorensen, *Kennedy*, p. 482; Matusow, *The Unraveling of America*, pp. 68–69.

77. Brauer, *John F. Kennedy and the Second Reconstruction*, p. 212.

78. *Public Papers, 1963*, pp. 11–19.

79. Brauer, *John F. Kennedy and the Second Reconstruction*, pp. 213, 220; Martin Luther King, Jr., "Bold Design for a New South," *Nation*, March 30, 1963, p. 259; *Robert Kennedy in His Own Words*, p. 375.

80. Brauer, *John F. Kennedy and the Second Reconstruction*, pp. 219–20, 352. Davis, a member of the "Rat Pack," had been a prominent supporter of JFK in the 1960 campaign. He delayed his marriage to Britt until after the election in order to avoid embarrassing Kennedy. Later, for the same reason, Jack had Evelyn Lincoln cancel the Davises' invitation to the inauguration. Davis was bitter but remained loyal. Sammy Davis, Jr., *Why Me? The Sammy Davis, Jr. Story* (New York, 1989), pp. 116–20, 128–34.

81. *Public Papers, 1963*, pp. 221–30; Brauer, *John F. Kennedy and the Second Reconstruction*, p. 222. Eighty-nine House members submitted civil rights bills early in the year. Matusow, *The Unraveling of America*, pp. 85–86.

82. Joseph L. Rauh, Jr. Oral History, JFK Library; Miroff, *Pragmatic Illusions*, p. 251; Matusow, *The Unraveling of America*, pp. 85–86; Brauer, *John F. Kennedy and the Second Reconstruction*, pp. 222–24.

83. Miroff, *Pragmatic Illusions*, p. 251; Brauer, *John F. Kennedy and the Second Reconstruction*, pp. 224–28; *Public Papers, 1963*, pp. 333, 347–48; "Civil Rights," *Time*, April 26, 1963, p. 25.

84. King credited the administration with outstripping "all previous ones in the

breadth of its civil rights activities.'' King, ''Bold Design for a New South,'' *Nation*, March 30, 1963, pp. 260, 262.

85. Burke Marshall Oral History, JFK Library; Sorensen, *Kennedy*, p. 489; *New York Times*, May 3, 5, 9, 1963;

86. Schlesinger, *A Thousand Days*, p. 959. On the president's constitutional limitations, see Anthony Lewis, ''Birmingham—Impact of Racial Tensions on the Deep South,'' *New York Times*, May 12, 1963.

87. *Public Papers, 1963*, pp. 372–74.

88. Burke Marshall Oral History, JFK Library; *Robert Kennedy in His Own Words*, p. 170.

89. *New York Times*, May 12, 13, 1963; *Public Papers, 1963*, pp. 397–98.

90. Sorensen, *Kennedy*, p. 490; Martin Luther King, Jr., ''Letter from Birmingham Jail,'' in Alan F. Westin ed, *Freedom Now: The Civil Rights Struggle in America* (New York, 1964), p. 16.

91. *Robert Kennedy in His Own Words*, pp. 223–26; Schlesinger, *Robert Kennedy and His Times*, pp. 355–62; ''War in the North,'' *Time*, May 31, 1963, 17.

92. Brauer, *John F. Kennedy and the Second Reconstruction*, p. 245; Schlesinger, *Robert Kennedy and His Times*, p. 360; *Robert Kennedy in His Own Words*, pp. 198, 225.

93. ''The Jitters,'' *Newsweek*, May 27, 1963, p. 27.

94. ''War in the North,'' *Time*, May 31, 1963, p. 16; ''Races,'' *Time*, June 7, 1963, pp. 17–19.

95. Burke Marshall Oral History, JFK Library; *Robert Kennedy in His Own Words*, p. 182. Cf. *Public Papers, 1963*, pp. 454–55.

96. *Robert Kennedy in His Own Words*, pp. 177–80; Burke Marshall Oral History, JFK Library. See Sorensen, *Kennedy*, pp. 493–94. On the president's private fear about nationwide violence, see the transcription of his telephone conversation with James H. Davis, governor of Louisiana, on June 3, 1963, in ''Presidential Recordings, Logs and Transcripts, Civil Rights, 1963,'' JFK Library.

97. *Robert Kennedy in His Own Words*, pp. 185–95; Sorensen, *Kennedy*, pp. 491–93.

98. *Public Papers, 1963*, pp. 408, 411, 454–59.

99. *Robert Kennedy in His Own Words*, pp. 197–200; *Atlanta Constitution*, June 10, 1963.

100. *Robert Kennedy in His Own Words*, pp. 200–201; Sorensen, *Kennedy*, pp. 493–95; Burke Marshall Oral History, JFK Library.

101. Sorensen, *Kennedy*, p. 496. See James Reston in *New York Times*, June 13, 1962.

102. *Public Papers, 1963*, pp. 468–71.

103. Schlesinger, *Robert Kennedy and His Times*, p. 369. See also Sorensen, *The Kennedy Legacy*, pp. 169–70; Ralph McGill in *Atlanta Constitution*, June 13, 1963. Civil rights leader Roy Wilkins later called the speech ''a compassionate appeal, man-to-man, heart-to-heart. . . . That was his peak.'' Roy Wilkins Oral History, JFK Library.

104. *Robert Kennedy in His Own Words*, pp. 201–3; William S. White in *Atlanta Constitution*, June 11, 1963.

105. Arthur Krock in *New York Times*, June 11, 1963; James Reston in ibid., June 12, 1963. See ''The Two Genii,'' *Nation*, July 6, 1963, pp. 1–2.

106. ''Life and Death in Jackson,'' *Time*, June 21, 1963, pp. 17–18; Schlesinger, *Robert Kennedy and His Times*, p. 370. See transcripts of Jack's telephone conversations

with Jackson Mayor Allen C. Thompson, June 17, 18, 1963, in "Presidential Recordings, Logs and Transcripts, Civil Rights, 1963," JFK Library.

107. "Races," *Time*, June 7, 1963, p. 14; Schlesinger, *Robert Kennedy and His Times*, p. 371.

108. *Public Papers, 1963*, pp. 483–94.

109. *New York Times*, June 20, 23, 1963; Burke Marshall Oral History, JFK Library; Sorensen, *Kennedy*, p. 498. A few days before the special message, the House shocked the administration by defeating a bill to boost a program aimed at assisting distressed areas. Southerners, upset by the president's civil rights declarations, made the difference. *Atlanta Constitution*, June 13, 1963.

110. *Robert Kennedy in His Own Words*, pp. 205–10; Burke Marshall Oral History, JFK Library; Sorensen, *Kennedy*, p. 501. See transcripts of telephone conversations between the president and Senators Warren Magnuson, Russell Long, and Mike Mansfield; Congressmen Carl Albert and Charles Halleck; and Mayor Richard Daley, in "Presidential Recordings, Logs and Transcripts, Civil Rights, 1963," JFK Library. Jack complained to Daley that Illinois Congressman Roland V. Libonati was going to join "the extreme liberals who are gonna end up with no bill at all."

111. Brauer, *John F. Kennedy and the Second Reconstruction*, p. 288; *Robert Kennedy in His Own Words*, p. 226; Roche, "The Second Coming of RFK," *National Review*, July 22, 1988, p. 34. See O'Reilly, *"Racial Matters,"* p. 64.

112. *Public Papers, 1963*, p. 572.

113. *Robert Kennedy in His Own Words*, pp. 227–29; David J. Garrow, *Bearing the Cross: Martin Luther King, Jr., and the Southern Christian Leadership Conference* (New York, 1988), pp. 280–85; *New York Times*, August 29, 1963; Navasky, *Kennedy Justice*, pp. 226–27; Schlesinger, *Robert Kennedy and His Times*, pp. 376–78.

114. Sorensen, *Kennedy*, p. 504; *New York Times*, August 29, 1963.

115. Sorensen, *Kennedy*, p. 504; *Robert Kennedy in His Own Words*, p. 229; *New York Times*, August 29, 1963; audio tape 108, item 2, "Presidential Recordings, Civil Rights, 1963," JFK Library.

116. David J. Garrow, *The FBI and Martin Luther King, Jr.* (New York, 1983), pp. 22–57; Schlesinger, *Robert Kennedy and His Times*, pp. 379–82.

117. Ibid., pp. 382–84.

118. Ibid., pp. 384–85; *Robert Kennedy in His Own Words*, pp. 140–47.

119. Garrow, *The FBI and Martin Luther King, Jr.*, pp. 62–65.

120. Ibid., pp. 65–67.

121. Schlesinger, *Robert Kennedy and His Times*, p. 385; Garrow, *The FBI and Martin Luther King, Jr.*, p. 66.

122. Schlesinger, *Robert Kennedy and His Times*, pp. 386–88; Garrow, *The FBI and Martin Luther King, Jr.*, pp. 69–77.

123. Ibid., pp. 85–100; Schlesinger, *Robert Kennedy and His Times*, p. 382.

124. Garrow, *The FBI and Martin Luther King, Jr.*, pp. 54–55, 101–7; Wofford, *Of Kennedys and Kings*, pp. 214–18.

125. *Robert Kennedy in His Own Words*, p. 145; Schlesinger, *Robert Kennedy and His Times*, pp. 388–89.

126. *Robert Kennedy in His Own Words*, p. 143.

127. Wofford, *Of Kennedys and Kings*, pp. 223–24.

128. Ibid., p. 207; Schlesinger, *Robert Kennedy and His Times*, pp. 390–91; Garrow, *The FBI and Martin Luther King, Jr.*, pp. 151, 157–65. Also on this story, see O'Reilly,

"Racial Matters," pp. 126–55; Garrow, *Bearing the Cross*, pp. 310, 312, 323, 360–67, 373–78, 587; Taylor Branch, *Parting the Waters: America in the King Years, 1954–1963* (New York, 1988), pp. 833–42, 850–62. For the president's press conference statement, see *Public Papers, 1963*, p. 574. For a fascinating look at King, see C. Vann Woodward, "The Dreams of Martin Luther King," *New York Review of Books*, January 15, 1987, pp. 3, 6, 8–9.

129. Audio tape 11, item 7, "Presidential Recordings, Civil Rights, 1963," JFK Library; *Robert Kennedy in His Own Words*, pp. 206–10; Sorensen, *Kennedy*, pp. 499–501.

130. Ibid., p. 506.

131. *Robert Kennedy in His Own Words*, pp. 210, 212.

132. Allen J. Ellender Oral History, JFK Library; Michael Barone, *Our Country: The Shaping of America from Roosevelt to Reagan* (New York, 1990), p. 363.

CHAPTER 16. Blinking First

1. David Detzer, *The Brink: Cuban Missile Crisis, 1962* (New York, 1979), pp. 37–41.

2. Schlesinger, *Robert Kennedy and His Times*, pp. 541–42.

3. Crankshaw ed., *Khrushchev Remembers*, pp. 493–94.

4. *New York Times*, October 14, 1987. For a full account of this and another conference on the crisis, plus valuable interviews, see James C. Blight and David A. Welch, *On the Brink: Americans and Soviets Reexamine the Cuban Missile Crisis* (New York, 1989).

5. *New York Times*, August 30, 1987; Detzer, *The Brink*, pp. 48–50; "Khrushchev's Secret Tapes," *Time*, October 1, 1990, pp. 74–75. See Graham T. Allison, *Essence of Decision, Explaining the Cuban Missile Crisis* (Boston, 1971), pp. 40–56, 109–13; and Blight and Welch, *On the Brink*, pp. 30–31, 238–44. In 1989 Soviet officials revealed that their country had been even farther behind in nuclear weaponry than Americans supposed. They said also that at the time of the crisis, two-thirds of the Soviets' entire missile stock of about sixty launchers were deployed in Cuba. *Milwaukee Journal*, January 28, 1989.

6. Detzer, *The Brink*, pp. 50–53; George Kennan Oral History, JFK Library; *New York Times*, October 14, 1987. See the analyses by State Department expert Francis B. Stevens in "War of Words: Turning Point," *U.S. News & World Report*, November 5, 1962, p. 57; and by Henry Kissinger in "Reflections on Cuba," *Reporter*, November 22, 1962, pp. 21–27.

7. Blight and Welch, *On the Brink*, p. 236; *New York Times*, October 14, 1987; Detzer, *The Brink*, pp. 53–54.

8. Ibid., pp. 62–65; *Robert Kennedy in His Own Words*, pp. 14–15; Robert F. Kennedy, *Thirteen Days: A Memoir of the Cuban Missile Crisis* (New York, 1969), pp. 5–6: "No official within the government had even suggested to President Kennedy that the Russian buildup in Cuba would include missiles." Khrushchev later admitted: "We wanted to do the whole thing in secret. Our security organs assured us this was possible even though American planes overflew Cuban territory all the time. . . . It was our intention after installing the missiles to announce their presence in a loud voice." "Khrushchev's Secret Tapes," *Time*, October 1, 1990, p. 75.

9. *Public Papers, 1962*, pp. 652–54; Sorensen, *Kennedy*, p. 670.

10. *Robert Kennedy in His Own Words*, pp. 15–16; *New York Times*, September 3, 8, 10, October 17, 1962; Sorensen, *Kennedy*, pp. 669–70. See the post-crisis interview with Keating in "Inside Story on Cuba . . . Why the U.S. Almost Got Caught," *U.S. News & World Report*, November 19, 1962, pp. 86–89. On Capehart, see *New York Times*, October 9, 1962.

11. Detzer, *The Brink*, pp. 65–66.

12. Schlesinger, *Robert Kennedy and His Times*, pp. 540–41; Sorensen, *Kennedy*, pp. 667–68.

13. Schlesinger, *Robert Kennedy and His Times*, p. 544.

14. *Public Papers, 1962*, pp. 674–78.

15. *New York Times*, September 15, 1962. For a vivid example of the appeasement charge, see "Kennedy's Fateful Decision: The Night the Reds Clinched Cuba," *U.S. News & World Report*, September 17, 1962, 41–42, which points to allegedly weak positions taken on Laos and Berlin as well as the Bay of Pigs.

16. *New York Times*, September 15, 1962; Abram Chayes, *The Cuban Missile Crisis, International Crises and the Role of Law* (New York, 1974), pp. 10–11.

17. *New York Times*, September 15, 1962.

18. Detzer, *The Brink*, pp. 58, 68–77; Schlesinger, *Robert Kennedy and His Times*, p. 545; Allison, *Essence of Decision*, pp. 102–9.

19. *New York Times*, October 11, 12, 17, 1962.

20. Ibid., October 14, 1962.

21. O'Donnell and Powers, *"Johnny, We Hardly Knew Ye,"* p. 352.

22. Sorensen, *Kennedy*, pp. 674–75.

23. Detzer, *The Brink*, pp. 103, 114–15.

24. Ibid.

25. "Presidential Recordings, Transcripts, Cuban Missile Crisis Meetings, October 16, 1962," JFK Library (hereafter cited as *Crisis Transcripts*), pp. 1–7. Cf. Sorensen, *Kennedy*, p. 675.

26. Roswell Gilpatric Oral History, JFK Library.

27. Sorensen, *Kennedy*, pp. 676–78. See *Robert Kennedy in His Own Words*, pp. 28–29. Dean Rusk was deeply concerned about Berlin. See *Crisis Transcripts*, October 16, 1962, p. 15.

28. *Crisis Transcripts*, October 16, 1962, p. 27; Blight and Welch, *On the Brink*, pp. 29–30. See Detzer, *The Brink*, p. 104; Sorensen's remarks in J. Anthony Lukas, "Class Reunion: Kennedy's Men Relive the Cuban Missile Crisis," *New York Times Magazine*, August 30, 1987, p. 27; *Milwaukee Journal*, October 30, 1983.

29. *Crisis Transcripts*, October 16, 1962, pp. 27–28; Kennedy, *Thirteen Days*, p. 9; Detzer, *The Brink*, p. 111; Sorensen, *Kennedy*, p. 679.

30. *Crisis Transcripts*, October 16, 1962, evening session, pp. 12, 24–25, 27–28, 45–46, 49; Detzer, *The Brink*, p. 115; Kennedy, *Thirteen Days*, p. 12; Roswell Gilpatric Oral History, JFK Library. In 1987, McNamara continued to defend his view of the Cuban missiles and the balance of power. Blight and Welch, *On the Brink*, pp. 186–88.

31. Sorensen, *Kennedy*, pp. 682–85.

32. Kennedy, *Thirteen Days*, pp. 15, 17; Schlesinger, *Robert Kennedy and His Times*, p. 547; Detzer, *The Brink*, p. 140. On the 1989 troop figures, see *Milwaukee Journal*, January 30, 1989. Cf. Walt Rostow Oral History, JFK Library. Rostow commented, "There is a sense of *noblesse oblige* in Bobby." Rostow's interviewer, Richard Neustadt, added, "As nearly as I can tell, on the critical issues Bob brought a morality into play

which hasn't been attempted since Wilson's time.'' See also ''No Yearning to be Loved—Dean Acheson Talks to Kenneth Harris,'' *The Listener*, April 8, 1971, p. 444.

33. Detzer, *The Brink*, pp. 132–37; Sorensen, *Kennedy*, pp. 679–80, 682–89; Kennedy, *Thirteen Days*, pp. 12–13; O'Donnell and Powers, *''Johnny, We Hardly Knew Ye,''* p. 358. On the range of Soviet missiles, see ''When Reds Point Missiles at U.S.,'' *U.S. News & World Report*, November 5, 1962, p. 41. These CIA estimates have been challenged as exaggerations. Detzer, *The Brink*, pp. 72–73. None of the large missiles reached Cuban soil.

34. See Lukas, ''Class Reunion,'' *New York Times Magazine*, August 30, 1987, p. 51.

35. Robert Amory Oral History, JFK Library. See Sorensen, *Kennedy*, p. 691; ''Red Missiles in Cuba: Inside Story from Secretary McNamara,'' *U.S. News & World Report*, November 5, 1962, p. 45.

36. See Lukas, ''Class Reunion,'' *New York Times Magazine*, August 30, 1987, p. 51; *Milwaukee Journal*, January 29, 30, 1989.

37. Lukas, ''Class Reunion,'' *New York Times Magazine*, August 30, 1987, p. 27.

38. O'Donnell and Powers, *''Johnny, We Hardly Knew Ye,''* pp. 357–58.

39. Detzer, *The Brink*, pp. 131, 144; Dean Acheson, ''Dean Acheson's Version of Robert Kennedy's Version of the Cuban Missile Affair,'' *Esquire*, February 1969, p. 77. See Dean Rusk's criticism of Acheson in Blight and Welch, *On the Brink*, p. 185.

40. Kennedy, *Thirteen Days*, p. 22.

41. Sorensen, *Kennedy*, pp. 691–92; Detzer, *The Brink*, pp. 147–48.

42. Ibid., pp. 154–55; Sorensen, *Kennedy*, pp. 693–94; Martin, *Adlai Stevenson and the World*, p. 722.

43. Ibid., pp. 721–22; Sorensen, *Kennedy*, p. 695. In his account Sorensen attempted to conceal Stevenson's identity as the note's author.

44. Barton J. Bernstein, ''The Cuban Missile Crisis: Trading the Jupiters in Turkey?,'' *Political Science Quarterly* 95 (Spring 1980): 98–102; Detzer, *The Brink*, pp. 156–57.

45. Bernstein, ''The Cuban Missile Crisis: Trading the Jupiters in Turkey?'' *Political Science Quarterly*, pp. 102–4. Cf. Walt Rostow Oral History, JFK Library; O'Donnell and Powers, *''Johnny, We Hardly Knew Ye,''* p. 382 (which claims that Jack ordered the Jupiters removed at least five times); and Kennedy, *Thirteen Days*, pp. 71–73. Jack was uncertain about the Jupiters when they were first mentioned at the ExCom meetings. See *Crisis Transcripts*, October 16, 1962, pp. 14, (evening meeting) 26. See also Blight and Welch, *On the Brink*, pp. 261–62.

46. Sorensen, *Kennedy*, pp. 695–96; Martin, *Adlai Stevenson and the World*, pp. 723–24.

47. Sorensen, *Kennedy*, p. 696; O'Donnell and Powers, *''Johnny, We Hardly Knew Ye,''* pp. 366–67; Stewart Alsop and Charles Bartlett, ''In Time of Crisis,'' *Saturday Evening Post*, December 8, 1962, p. 20.

48. O'Donnell and Powers, *''Johnny, We Hardly Knew Ye,''* 366–67; Sorensen, *Kennedy*, p. 696.

49. O'Donnell and Powers, *''Johnny, We Hardly Knew Ye,''* p. 366; Martin, *Adlai Stevenson and the World*, p. 724. Cf. Kennedy, *Thirteen Days*, p. 28.

50. O'Donnell and Powers, *''Johnny, We Hardly Knew Ye,''* pp. 367–69; Detzer, *The Brink*, p. 163. See Blight and Welch, *On the Brink*, pp. 184, 262.

51. Ibid., pp. 163–65; Kennedy, *Thirteen Days*, p. 30.

52. Sorensen, *Kennedy*, pp. 697–701.

53. Ibid., pp. 702–3; O'Donnell and Powers, *"Johnny, We Hardly Knew Ye,"* pp. 371–73; Kennedy, *Thirteen Days*, pp. 31–33; Detzer, *The Brink*, pp. 179–82.

54. *Public Papers, 1962*, pp. 806–9.

55. Blight and Welch, *On the Brink*, p. 185; O'Donnell and Powers, *"Johnny, We Hardly Knew Ye,"* p. 374.

56. *New York Times*, October 23, 24, 1962; *St. Louis Post-Dispatch*, October 24, 1962; Sorensen, *Kennedy*, pp. 706–7.

57. Elie Abel, *The Missile Crisis* (Philadelphia, 1966), p. 127; Kennedy, *Thirteen Days*, p. 35.

58. Chayes, *The Cuban Missile Crisis*, pp. 14–17, 22–23, 44–53, 66–88; Sorensen, *Kennedy*, pp. 699, 706; Abel, *The Missile Crisis*, p. 131; Blight and Welch, *On the Brink*, pp. 266–68. Bobby later wrote that the OAS vote "had a major psychological and practical effect on the Russians and changed our position from that of an outlaw acting in violation of international law into a country acting in accordance with twenty allies legally protecting their position." Kennedy, *Thirteen Days*, p. 99.

59. Kennedy, *Thirteen Days*, pp. 38–39, 44–45.

60. O'Donnell and Powers, *"Johnny, We Hardly Knew Ye,"* p. 375.

61. Kennedy, *Thirteen Days*, pp. 40–41.

62. Sorensen, *Kennedy*, p. 709; O'Donnell and Powers, *"Johnny, We Hardly Knew Ye,"* p. 375. A meeting on Tuesday evening between Bobby and Soviet Ambassador Dobrynin raised the same question. Dobrynin seemed extremely concerned, embarrassed, and defensive. Kennedy, *Thirteen Days*, pp. 43–44.

63. William E. Knox, "Close-up of Khrushchev During a Crisis," *New York Times Magazine*, November 18, 1962, pp. 32, 128–29. On Krock and Goldwater, see *New York Times*, October 23, 24, 1962.

64. Detzer, *The Brink*, pp. 205–6.

65. Kennedy, *Thirteen Days*, pp. 46–49; Detzer, *The Brink*, p. 209.

66. Kennedy, *Thirteen Days*, p. 49.

67. Kennedy, *Thirteen Days*, pp. 49–50. Cf. O'Donnell and Powers, *"Johnny, We Hardly Knew Ye,"* pp. 376–77. On the possibility that Khrushchev was overruled in the decision to retreat, see Blight and Welch, *On the Brink*, p. 306.

68. Detzer, *The Brink*, p. 229. Cf. Salinger, *With Kennedy*, p. 267; Sorensen, *Kennedy*, p. 705.

69. Kennedy, *Thirteen Days*, pp. 51–52, 59–60; Detzer, *The Brink*, pp. 227–32. The selection of the *Joseph P. Kennedy, Jr.* was made by Admiral Wallace Morris Beakley and apparently surprised the president. Ibid., p. 230; Sorensen, *Kennedy*, p. 710.

70. Martin, *Adlai Stevenson and the World*, pp. 725–36. Watching Stevenson on television, Jack said privately, "I never knew Adlai had it in him. Too bad he didn't show some of this steam in the 1956 campaign." O'Donnell and Powers, *"Johnny, We Hardly Knew Ye,"* p. 379. Cf. Bradlee, *Conversations with Kennedy*, pp. 120–21.

71. Martin, *Adlai Stevenson and the World*, p. 728.

72. Henry Luce Oral History, JFK Library.

73. Schlesinger, *A Thousand Days*, pp. 821–22.

74. Ibid., pp. 820–23; Sorensen, *Kennedy*, pp. 709–10.

75. Kennedy, *Thirteen Days*, pp. 63–64. After the crisis the pamphlets were burned. Donald M. Wilson Oral History, JFK Library.

76. Detzer, *The Brink*, pp. 234–35; Sorensen, *Kennedy*, p. 712.

77. O'Donnell and Powers, *"Johnny, We Hardly Knew Ye,"* pp. 379–80.

78. See Detzer, *The Brink*, pp. 236–37; Hilsman, *To Move a Nation*, pp. 217–19.

79. Kennedy, *Thirteen Days*, pp. 64–68; "Chairman Khrushchev's Message of October 26, 1962," *Department of State Bulletin* 69 (November 19, 1972): 640–45.

80. Hilsman, *To Move a Nation*, pp. 219–20; O'Donnell and Powers, *"Johnny, We Hardly Knew Ye,"* p. 380.

81. Kennedy, *Thirteen Days*, p. 71; Detzer, *The Brink*, p. 243.

82. Kennedy, *Thirteen Days*, pp. 72–74; *Crisis Transcripts*, October 27, 1962, pp. 1–3, 9–10, 16, 18–19, 25, 27–31, 44, 50, 65. See also Bernstein, "The Cuban Missile Crisis: Trading the Jupiters in Turkey" *Political Science Quarterly*, pp. 106–12, 118–19; Blight and Welch, *On the Brink*, pp. 253–7.

83. *Crisis Transcripts*, October 27, 1962, pp. 40, 72, 80; Detzer, *The Brink*, pp. 242–44, 280; O'Donnell and Powers, *"Johnny, We Hardly Knew Ye,"* pp. 381–82; Kennedy, *Thirteen Days*, p. 74.

84. Hilsman, *To Move a Nation*, p. 220. See *Crisis Transcripts*, October 27, 1962, pp. 45–49, 57, 66. In 1987 Cuban General Rafael de Pino Diaz said that Soviet officers in Cuba were so outraged at Khrushchev's compliance with the American quarantine that they shot down the U-2 without authorization. The officers "wanted to provoke a confrontation." *Milwaukee Journal*, October 23, 1987. The Soviet officer responsible was soon named by Sergo Mikoyan, whose father was a close associate of Khrushchev's and special envoy to Cuba at the time. The circumstances of the incident, however, remain in doubt. Blight and Welch, *On the Brink*, p. 311. The Khrushchev tapes released in 1990 revealed that about this time in the crisis Castro was urging the Soviets to launch a pre-emptive strike against the U.S. "Khrushchev's Secret Tapes," *Time*, October 1, 1990, p. 75. Castro has since revealed a letter to Khrushchev in which he advocated a Soviet nuclear attack only if the U.S. invaded Cuba: see *New York Times*, December 20, 1990.

85. Kennedy, *Thirteen Days* pp. 75–76; Sorensen, *Kennedy*, p. 713; *Milwaukee Journal*, August 7, 1985, October 23, 1987. The censored and often sketchy *Crisis Transcripts* casts doubt on the traditional accounts of the sequence of events on October 27.

86. Detzer, *The Brink*, p. 246; Hilsman, *To Move a Nation*, p. 221; Sorensen, *Kennedy*, pp. 713–14. At one point a Soviet plane unexpectedly flew from Canada to Cuba. According to McNamara aide Roswell Gilpatric, near panic broke out among ExCom members. The Kennedy Library has censored the portion of Gilpatric's interview in which he discusses the president's reaction. Roswell L. Gilpatric Oral History, JFK Library.

87. *Crisis Transcripts*, October 27, 1962, pp. 12, 23, 26, 51, 53–54, 65, 66; Kennedy, *Thirteen Days*, pp. 74–79; Allison, *Essence of Decision*, p. 225; *Milwaukee Journal*, October 23, 1987.

88. The transcripts of the October 27 meetings indicate, however, that Bundy, JFK, and Sorensen expressed the basic idea before Bobby did. See *Crisis Transcripts*, October 27, 1962, pp. 2, 3, 12, 15, 28, 38, 65. Dean Rusk said later that the idea originated with Llewellyn Thompson, former American ambassador to the Soviet Union and a member of ExCom. Bobby, Rusk observed, first brought it before the body. Blight and Welch, *On the Brink*, p. 179.

89. Kennedy, *Thirteen Days*, pp. 79–80.

90. Hilsman, *To Move a Nation*, pp. 222–23. See Salinger, *With Kennedy*, pp. 274–80. In 1989 former Soviet Ambassador Anatoly Dobrynin revealed that during the Thousand Days the Soviet Embassy in Washington lacked a direct telephone or radio line of communication to Moscow. At the height of the missile crisis, the embassy spoke with Moscow via Western Union, which often sent messengers on bicycles to pick up coded and urgent messages! "That is . . . why in the decisive phase of the conflict, a couple of messages from Khrushchev to Kennedy were conveyed simultaneously through me and announced over Radio Moscow, to make sure they reached the White House as fast as possible." *Milwaukee Journal*, November 19, 1989.

91. *Public Papers, 1962*, pp. 813–14; Hilsman, *To Move a Nation*, pp. 223–24; Kennedy, *Thirteen Days*, pp. 81–82.

92. Ibid.pp. 83–84.

93. Ibid., pp. 85–87; Schlesinger, *Robert Kennedy and His Times*, pp. 561–66; Blight and Welch, *On the Brink*, pp. 264–65. In February 1963 the secretary of defense told the House Committee on Appropriations:

> We had a force of several hundred thousand men ready to invade Cuba. . . . Khrushchev knew without any question whatsoever that he faced the full military power of the United States, including its nuclear weapons. . . . We faced that night the possibility of launching nuclear weapons . . . and that is the reason, and the only reason, why he withdrew those weapons.

Quoted in Allison, *Essence of Decision*, p. 65. See Schlesinger, *Robert Kennedy and His Times*, p. 569.

94. *New York Times*, August 28, 1987; Blight and Welch, *On the Brink*, pp. 83–84, 108, 113–15, 162.

95. See Blight and Welch, *On the Brink*, pp. 333–34.

96. Schlesinger, *Robert Kennedy and His Times*, p. 565. Bobby later wrote that the president "regarded Secretary McNamara as the most valuable public servant in his Administration and in the government." Kennedy, *Thirteen Days*, p. 98. Roswell Gilpatric later reported that Jack hated superhawkish General Curtis LeMay, and once became extremely upset after a meeting with him. The president tried to avoid the general whenever possible. Roswell L. Gilpatric Oral History, JFK Library. In 1968 LeMay bitterly criticized JFK in print for removing U.S. missiles from Europe after the Cuban crisis. Curtis LeMay, *America Is in Danger* (New York, 1968), pp. 139–40, 290.

97. Kennedy, *Thirteen Days*, pp. 88, 97; Donald Wilson Oral History, JFK Library.

98. Detzer, *The Brink*, pp. 257–58; Kennedy, *Thirteen Days*, pp. 105–6; *Public Paper, 1962*, p. 815. In 1967 Castro said that he thought Kennedy "acted as he did partly to save Khrushchev, out of fear that any successor would be tougher." Schlesinger, *Robert Kennedy and His Times*, p. 573.

99. Detzer, *The Brink*, pp. 260–61; "Foreign Relations," *Time*, November 2, 1962, p. 16; *Gallup Poll*, III, 1793; "Political Fallout: Who Gains?" *Newsweek*, November 5, 1962, p. 35. For foreign reactions, see "The Big Showdown?" *U.S. News & World Report*, November 5, 1962, pp. 36–37. In early February 1963 Kennedy's handling of foreign affairs was given a 64 percent favorable rating. A year earlier the figure had been 67 percent. *Gallup Poll*, III, 1759, 1807.

100. *New York Times*, October 29, 1962. Cf. "From Washington Straight," *National*

Review, November 5, 1962, p. 347. Confidence in Kennedy grew when photographs of the Cuban missile sites were made public. Ironically, Jack had opposed the release of the photos, which became available only because of a leak in London. Donald M. Wilson Oral History, JFK Library.

101. Richard Rovere, "Letter from Washington," *The New Yorker*, November 3, 1962, pp. 120–21; "Foreign Relations," *Time*, November 2, 1962, p. 15.

102. "The Blockade: U.S. Puts It on the Line," *Life*, November 2, 1962, p. 47. See "Cuba: Almost a 'Pearl Harbor'?" *U.S. News & World Report*, November 12, 1962, p. 47.

103. Alsop and Bartlett, "In Time of Crisis," *Saturday Evening Post*, December 8, 1962, pp. 16–20. On the press and the missile crisis, see " 'Managed' News—A New 'Weapon' in U.S. Arsenal," *U.S. News & World Report*, November 12, 1962, p. 48; Salinger, *With Kennedy*, pp. 285–302. For a fascinating look at Kennedy's close relationship with Washington's three most influential columnists (Walter Lippmann, Joseph Alsop, and James Reston), see "The Columnists JFK Reads Every Morning," *Newsweek*, December 18, 1961, pp. 65–70.

104. Max Ascoli, "A Great Performance," *Reporter*, January 3, 1963, p. 12; "The Presidency: 'Rather Pleased,' " *Newsweek*, December 31, 1962, p. 14.

105. "The Reprieve and What Needs to Be Done with It," *I. F. Stone's Weekly*, November 5, 1962, p. 1.

106. Richard Nixon, "Cuba, Castro, and John F. Kennedy," *Reader's Digest*, November 1964, p. 297.

107. "Backdown on Cuba—How Khrushchev Explains It at Home," *U.S. News & World Report*, December 24, 1962, pp. 36, 38.

108. "What Castro Planned: Destroy U.S. Cities," ibid., p. 36; "Russia: The Adventurer," *Time*, November 9, 1962, pp. 26–29; Blight and Welch, *On the Brink*, pp. 234–35, 250–51, 268–69; "Khrushchev's Secret Tapes," *Time*, October 1, 1990, p. 77.

109. Roswell L. Gilpatric Oral History, JFK Library; Michel Tatu, *Power in The Kremlin: From Khrushchev to Kosygin* (New York, 1969), p. 422. See Blight and Welch, *On the Brink*, p. 251.

110. Ibid., pp. 257–58.

111. See Allison, *Essence of Decision*, pp. 187–90, 193–95, 232; Theodore Sorensen Oral History, JFK Library; *Crisis Transcripts*, October 16, 1962, p. 46.

112. Acheson, "Dean Acheson's Version of Robert Kennedy's Version of the Cuban Missile Affair," *Esquire*, February 1969, pp. 46, 76; Blight and Welch, *On the Brink*, pp. 180, 185.

113. Ibid., p. 179; *Robert Kennedy in His Own Words*, p. 167.

114. *Public Papers, 1962*, p. 807; Kissinger, "Reflections on Cuba," *Reporter*, November 22, 1962, p. 22; David Lawrence, "Advance," *U.S. News & World Report*, November 5, 1962, p. 120. George Kennan later called the president's handling of the crisis "masterful." George Kennan Oral History, JFK Library. The public agreed with Kennedy's resistance to an invasion of Cuba. In late September 1962, 63 percent opposed an invasion, 51 percent thinking it would lead to all-out war between the United States and the Soviet Union. In early February 1963, 64 percent continued to oppose an invasion. *Gallup Poll*, III, 1787, 1807.

115. Davis, *The Kennedys*, p. 364.

116. Schlesinger, *Robert Kennedy and His Times*, pp. 574–602.

CHAPTER 17.   A New Prince of Peace and Freedom

1. O'Donnell and Powers, *"Johnny, We Hardly Knew Ye,"* pp. 368–69, 385; Sorensen, *Kennedy*, pp. 367, 705; Blair, *The Search for J.F.K.*, p. 329; Bradlee, *Conversations with Kennedy*, pp. 159–61, 192.

2. Glenn T. Seaborg, *Kennedy, Khrushchev, and the Test Ban* (Berkeley and Los Angeles, 1981), pp. 32–33, 95.

3. *Public Papers, 1961*, p. 2.

4. Seaborg, *Kennedy, Khrushchev, and the Test Ban*, pp. 30–32.

5. Ibid., pp. 32, 36–45.

6. Ibid., pp. 3–25; Ambrose, *Eisenhower the President*, pp. 563–64, 580; Dwight D. Eisenhower, *Waging Peace, 1956–1961* (New York, 1965), p. 481.

7. Seaborg, *Kennedy, Khrushchev, and the Test Ban*, pp. 132–39.

8. Sorensen, *Kennedy*, pp. 517–19.

9. *Public Papers, 1961*, pp. 618–27; Seaborg, *Kennedy, Khrushchev, and the Test Ban*, pp. 92–99.

10. Sorensen, *Kennedy*, pp. 608–10, 625–26; Thomas G. Paterson, "John F. Kennedy and the World," in J. Richard Snyder ed., *John F. Kennedy: Person, Policy, Presidency* (Wilmington, Del., 1988), p. 135. See *Public Papers, 1963*, pp. 888–89.

11. In February 1963 Kennedy told advisers that his principal reason for supporting a test ban was its possible affect on China. Seaborg later observed, "It was never quite clear to me how he expected a test ban negotiated between ourselves and the Soviets to affect the Chinese unless it were through the force of world opinion, since the Chinese were quite certain to reject such a treaty." See Seaborg, *Kennedy, Khrushchev, and the Test Ban*, pp. 181, 188, 239.

12. Ibid., pp. 150–58.

13. Ibid., pp. 176–93, 202–4, 209–10; *Public Papers, 1963*, pp. 377, 424.

14. *Public Papers, 1963*, pp. 459–64; Sorensen, *Kennedy*, pp. 729–33; Seaborg, *Kennedy, Khrushchev, and the Test Ban*, pp. 216–17.

15. Lawford, *The Peter Lawford Story*, p. 141.

16. Seaborg, *Kennedy, Khrushchev, and the Test Ban*, pp. 206–7, 217–18; Sorensen, *Kennedy*, p. 733; *New York Times*, June 16, 1963; *Public Papers, 1963*, p. 495.

17. *New York Times*, June 27, 1963; Parmet, *JFK*, p. 321.

18. "James P. O'Donnell, RIP," *National Review*, May 28, 1990, pp. 17–18.

19. O'Donnell and Powers, *"Johnny, We Hardly Knew Ye,"* pp. 409–11; *Public Papers, 1963*, pp. 524–25; *New York Times*, June 27, 1963; Sorensen, *Kennedy*, pp. 600–601; "James P. O'Donnell, RIP," *National Review*, May 28, 1990, pp. 17–18.

20. O'Donnell and Powers, *"Johnny, We Hardly Knew Ye,"* pp. 410–11; *New York Times*, June 27, 1963; *Public Papers, 1963*, pp. 526–29.

21. O'Donnell and Powers, *"Johnny, We Hardly Knew Ye,"* pp. 427–31; Kelley, *Jackie Oh!, pp. 190–92;* Martin, *A Hero for Our Time*, pp. 491–93; Gallagher, *My Life with Jacqueline Kennedy*, pp. 284–92; Lincoln, *My Twelve Years with John F. Kennedy*, pp. 349–55. Evelyn Lincoln and Kenny O'Donnell attribute different saintlike activities to Jack during this period of acute stress. Both accounts are difficult to accept. See ibid., p. 353, and O'Donnell and Powers, *"Johnny, We Hardly Knew Ye,"* p. 429.

22. Martin, *A Hero for Our Time*, pp. 492–27; Bradlee, *Conversations with Kennedy*, pp. 206–9; Heymann, *A Woman Named Jackie*, pp. 417–18.

23. Benjamin Read Oral History, JFK Library.

24. Seaborg, *Kennedy, Khrushchev, and the Test Ban*, pp. 220, 227, 228, 238–42.

25. Ibid., pp. 302–5. Historian Robert A. Divine has reminded us that the ban on atmospheric testing simply drove nuclear tests underground: "Far more nuclear tests have been conducted since the signing of the limited test ban treaty than in the period from 1945 to 1963. The unresolvable problem of inspection, together with the continuing tension of the cold war, frustrated the best efforts of test ban advocates to bring the arms race under control." Robert A. Divine, *Blowing on the Wind: The Nuclear Test Ban Debate, 1954–1960* (New York, 1989), pp. 317–18.

26. *Public Papers, 1963*, pp. 599–606.

27. Seaborg, *Kennedy, Khrushchev, and the Test Ban*, pp. 276–77.

28. See "Presidential Records, Transcripts, Winning Senate Support for the Nuclear Test Ban Treaty, 1963," JFK Library. These heavily edited fragments of Jack's secret tape recordings reveal virtually nothing beyond interesting examples of Kennedy's off-the-record conversational tone and language.

29. Seaborg, *Kennedy, Khrushchev, and the Test Ban*, pp. 263–82; Sorensen, *Kennedy*, pp. 736–40. Dirksen's support may actually have been achieved through a complex deal that involved dropping a Justice Department indictment against top Eisenhower aide Sherman Adams. See Baker, *Wheeling and Dealing: Confessions of a Capitol Hill Operator*, pp. 82–84; Schlesinger, *Robert Kennedy and His Times*, pp. 414–16.

30. *Public Papers, 1963*, pp. 765–66; Sorensen, *Kennedy*, p. 740.

31. *Public Papers, 1963*, pp. 767–68; Sorensen, *Kennedy*, pp. 742–46.

32. Schlesinger, *A Thousand Days*, p. 987.

33. Rust, *Kennedy in Vietnam*, p. 102; Henry Cabot Lodge Oral History, JFK Library.

34. See Rust, *Kennedy in Vietnam*, pp. 90–107; Herring, *America's Longest War*, pp. 94–97; Hilsman, *To Move a Nation*, pp. 468–82.

35. Rust, *Kennedy in Vietnam*, pp. 108–16.

36. A secretly recorded White House conversation of August 15, 1963, between the president and Lodge, has been reported "lost" between the time it left Evelyn Lincoln (and the custody of the Kennedy family) and the deposit of similar materials at the Kennedy Library. Four other tapes, concerning the missile crisis and the test ban negotiations with the Soviet Union, are also reported missing. See Burner and West, *The Torch is Passed*, p. 285, f. 37.

37. Rust, *Kennedy in Vietnam*, pp. 116–27; Hilsman, *To Move a Nation*, 482–94; Herring, *America's Longest War*, pp. 97–100; *Pentagon Papers*, pp. 194–205; Roswell Gilpatric Oral History, JFK Library; *Robert Kennedy in His Own Words*, pp. 396–98.

38. Parmet, *JFK*, p. 328; *Public Papers, 1963*, pp. 652–53, 659.

39. Sorensen, *Kennedy*, p. 659; *Public Papers, 1963*, p. 673; Herring, *America's Longest War*, p. 102; Rust, *Kennedy in Vietnam*, pp. 134–39; *Pentagon Papers*, pp. 206–10; Hilsman, *To Move a Nation*, p. 498.

40. Rust, *Kennedy in Vietnam*, pp. 140–44; *Pentagon Papers*, pp. 210–13.

41. Rust, *Kennedy in Vietnam*, p. 145.

42. Ibid., p. 216.

43. Ibid., pp. 213–18; Rust, *Kennedy in Vietnam*, p. 148.

44. *Pentagon Papers*, pp. 216–17.

45. Hilsman, *To Move a Nation*, p. 515.

46. *Robert Kennedy in His Own Words*, p. 400.

47. *Pentagon Papers*, p. 221.

48. Rust, *Kennedy in Vietnam*, pp. 152–53. See *Pentagon Papers*, pp. 219–21, 227.

49. Rust, *Kennedy in Vietnam*, pp. 154–59; *Pentagon Papers*, pp. 217–19, 227.

50. Ibid., pp. 226–31.

51. Schlesinger, *A Thousand Days*, p. 997.

52. *Pentagon Papers*, p. 232.

53. *Robert Kennedy in His Own Words*, pp. 326, 400–404; Schlesinger, *A Thousand Days*, p. 998; Sorensen, *Kennedy*, p. 659; Parmet, *JFK*, p. 335. See also Taylor, *Swords and Plowshares*, p. 301; Hilsman, *To Move a Nation*, p. 521; and O'Donnell and Powers, *"Johnny, We Hardly Knew Ye,"* p. 436.

54. Parmet, *JFK*, pp. 334–35.

55. Ibid., p. 335; Rust, *Kennedy in Vietnam*, pp. 150–52, 162–76; Schlesinger, *A Thousand Days*, p. 997. Lodge succeeded in flying Nhu's children out of the country. Soon, however, he turned over Ngo Dinh Can, Diem's youngest brother, to the generals. Can was convicted of high crimes and, despite a plea for clemency by Lodge, was executed. Schlesinger, *Robert Kennedy and His Times*, p. 778; Rust, *Kennedy in Vietnam*, pp. 176–78.

56. *Robert Kennedy in His Own Words*, pp. 400–404.

57. O'Donnell and Powers, *"Johnny, We Hardly Knew Ye,"* pp. 16–18, 436; Schlesinger, *Robert Kennedy and His Times*, pp. 772–73, 780.

58. Parmet, *JFK*, p. 336; *Robert Kennedy in His Own Words*, pp. 394–95.

59. *Public Papers, 1963*, p. 892. See Halberstam, *The Best and the Brightest*, p. 366.

60. Only seventy-three American soldiers had been killed as a result of hostile action. See Schlesinger, *Robert Kennedy and His Times*, pp. 779–80.

61. Halberstam, *The Best and the Brightest*, p. 796. For more on the press and Vietnam, see Salinger, *With Kennedy*, pp. 319–29.

62. Schlesinger, *Robert Kennedy and His Times*, p. 779; Sidey, *John F. Kennedy, President*, pp. 349–52.

63. Parmet, *JFK*, p. 336; Schlesinger, *Robert Kennedy and His Times*, p. 772. On the president's wariness, see Roswell Gilpatric Oral History (especially the interview of August 12, 1970), JFK Library.

64. *Public Papers, 1963*, pp. 846–48.

65. *Robert Kennedy in His Own Words*, p. 395.

66. Francis X. Winter, "They Shoot Allies, Don't They?," *National Review*, November 25, 1988, p. 37.

67. Rust, *Kennedy in Vietnam*, p. 181.

68. Herring, *America's Longest War*, p. 107.

CHAPTER 18.   The Man, the President

1. Cf. Lance Morrow, "Rose Kennedy," *Life*, July, 1990, pp. 29–33, an uncritical eulogy, followed by glowing tributes and photos, that again reminds us of the vast support the Kennedys enjoy in the media.

2. See Leo P. Ribuffo, "Jimmy Carter and the Ironies of American Liberalism," *Gettysburg Review* 1 (Autumn 1988): 738–49; Leo P. Ribuffo, "God and Jimmy Carter," in M. L. Bradbury and James B. Gilbert, eds., *Transforming Faith: The Sacred and the Secular in Modern American History* (Westport, Conn., 1989), pp. 141–59.

3. Barber, *The Presidential Character*, p. 9.

4. Michael Novak, *Choosing Our King: Powerful Symbols in Presidential Politics*

(New York, 1974), p. 3. Novak continues on the following page: "The president, whoever he is, affects our internal images of authority, legitimacy, leadership, concerns. . . . the election of a president is an almost religious task; it intimately affects the life of the spirit, our identity."

5. Miller, *Plain Speaking*, p. 415. For the historian of character, the life of Truman is especially instructive. See, for example, Irwin Ross, *The Loneliest Campaign: The Truman Victory of 1948* (New York, 1968), pp. 33–35; Dean Acheson, *Present at the Creation: My Years in the State Department* (New York, 1969), pp. 151–52, 927–33; Cabell Phillips, *The Truman Presidency: The History of a Triumphant Succession* (Baltimore, 1969), pp. 11–12; Alonzo L. Hamby, *Beyond the New Deal; Harry S. Truman and American Liberalism* (New York, 1973), pp. 41–51, 459–60; Robert H. Ferrell, *Harry S. Truman and the Modern American Presidency* (Boston, 1983), pp. 179–85; Donald R. McCoy, *The Presidency of Harry S. Truman* (Lawrence, Kan., 1984), pp. 2, 15, 20, 143–45. Truman's character shines through the three volumes written and edited by his daughter, Margaret, in Robert H. Ferrell's *Off the Record: The Private Papers of Harry S. Truman* (New York, 1980), and in Miller's *Plain Speaking*.

6. Burner and West, *The Torch is Passed*, p. 191.

7. See Sorensen, *Kennedy*, pp. 357–62.

8. Koenig, *The Chief Executive*, p. 300.

9. See David J. Garrow, "The Myth of Camelot Lives On," *The Washington Post National Weekly Edition*, November 28–December 4, 1988, p. 36.

10. See Heymann, *A Woman Named Jackie*, pp. 245, 291; Martin, *A Hero for Our Time*, pp. 376–77. Cf. Exner, *My Story*, pp. 242, 248.

11. A public opinion poll taken by the Gallup Organization and published in September 1987, showed the strongest Kennedy support coming from the least informed sectors of the populace, groups known to be avid television watchers. See the Times Mirror Company's *The Press and Politics* (Washington D.C., 1987), pp. 13–17.

12. Novak, *Choosing Our King*, p. 284.

13. In a 1983 poll of historians, Johnson was rated the tenth most successful president, Kennedy thirteenth, and Nixon thirty-fourth. See Jack E. Holmes and Robert E. Elder, Jr., "Our Best and Worst Presidents: Some Possible Reasons for Perceived Performance," *Presidential Studies Quarterly* 19 (Summer 1989): 529–77. Recent biographies by Stephen Ambrose and Herbert Parmet should do much to make Nixon more respectable. Stanley Kutler's impressive study of the Watergate scandal, however, revives the Nixon many have long loved to hate. The scathing studies by Robert Caro of Lyndon Johnson will probably cause LBJ to drop in future polls. On the other hand, their strident tone may have a reverse effect. See Victor Gold's review of Caro's *The Years of Lyndon Johnson: Means of Ascent* in *The American Spectator*, July, 1990, pp. 37–38.

14. Schlesinger, "What the Thousand Days Wrought," *New Republic*, November 21, 1983, p. 30.

15. Barry Schwartz, *George Washington: The Making of an American Symbol* (New York, 1987), pp. 7–9, 147–48, 196–67, 201–3.

16. Roberta A. Sigel, "Image of the American Presidency—Part II of an Exploration into Popular Views of Presidential Power," *Midwest Journal of Political Science* 10 (February, 1966): 130–31, 134.

17. "In a democratic regime, morality cannot be a substitute for politics; in the best case, it helps to orient or contain it." Tzvetan Todorov, "Post-Totalitarian Depression," *New Republic*, June 25, 1990, p. 24.

Index